SIXTH EDITION

Educational Research

COMPETENCIES FOR ANALYSIS AND APPLICATION

L.R. Gay *Late of Florida University*

Peter Airasian *Boston College*

MERRILL
an imprint of Prentice Hall
Upper Saddle River, New Jersey   Columbus, Ohio

Research is a creative and scholarly endeavor . . .

LORRAINE RUMBEL GAY
1944 to 1997

In 1997, shortly after the publication of this text's fifth edition, L.R. Gay died at much too young an age.

Twenty-four years ago Merrill published the first edition of *Educational Research: Competencies for Analysis and Application.* It had a brown, unassuming cover with only the book's title and the author's name on it. The cover did not even have the author's full name, only the last name and the first and middle initials—L.R. Gay. It was intentional that the first name (Lorraine) was not spelled out. Though it might seem odd now, at that time a research book written by a woman would not have been taken as seriously as one written by a man. And so Lorraine Rumbel Gay agreed to simply use her initials. The book has gone on to be the most widely used educational research text ever published. Since its first edition, literally hundreds of thousands of education students have been introduced to research through Lorraine's text. And, because of the book's impeccable scholarship and clarity, its popularity continues to grow.

Lorraine was a gifted writer—one of the very best with whom I have worked. She also had an exceptionally deep understanding of research. This combination of traits gave her an uncanny ability to get to the essence of very complex ideas and then express them in such a way that they became lucid to those who had no previous experience with research. Hers is that rare text that does not just tell students what theory and research say; it tells students what theory and research mean. A market research firm recently estimated that one out of every two introductory educational research students uses Gay's *Educational Research.* In many ways, this text is a generation's introduction to what educational research is and to how one goes about doing it. Lorraine's work has touched many more lives than most of the rest of us can dream of touching. She was a rare educator.

Lorrie, as I and her other friends knew her, knew much more than just research though, and, as gifted a writer and educator as she was, she was an even more exceptional human being. Funny, intelligent, warm, honest, and incredibly generous, she was one of those rare friends who cannot be replaced and will always be missed.

Kevin M. Davis
Executive Editor

To GWEN, LYNN, AND GREG

Library of Congress Cataloging-in-Publication Data
Gay, L.R.
    Educational research : competencies for analysis and application /
L.R. Gay, Peter Airasian. —6th ed.
        p.   cm.
    Includes bibliographical references and indexes.
    ISBN 0-13-096103-5
    1. Education—Research.   I. Airasian, Peter W.   II. Title.
LB1028.G37   2000
370'.7'2—dc21   99-21766
                                                             CIP

Cover Photo: Superstock
Editor: Kevin M. Davis
Production Editor: Julie Peters
Photo Editor: Sherry Mitchell
Design Coordinator: Diane Lorenzo
Design and Project Management: Elm Street Publishing Services, Inc.
Cover Design: Thomas Mack
Production Manager: Laura M. Messerly
Illustrations: The Clarinda Company
Director of Marketing: Kevin Flanagan
Marketing Manager: Meghan McCauley
Marketing Coordinator: Krista Groshong

This book was set in Palatino by The Clarinda Company and was printed and bound by
Von Hoffmann Press, Inc. The cover was printed by Von Hoffmann Press, Inc.

© 2000 by Prentice-Hall, Inc.
Pearson Education
Upper Saddle River, New Jersey 07458

Printed in the United States of America

10 9 8 7 6 5 4 3 2

ISBN: 0-13-096103-5

Prentice-Hall International (UK) Limited, *London*
Prentice-Hall of Australia Pty. Limited, *Sydney*
Prentice-Hall of Canada, Inc., *Toronto*
Prentice-Hall Hispanoamericana, S. A., *Mexico*
Prentice-Hall of India Private Limited, *New Delhi*
Prentice-Hall of Japan, Inc., *Tokyo*
Prentice-Hall (Singapore) Pte. Ltd., *Singapore*
Editora Prentice-Hall do Brasil, Ltda., *Rio de Janeiro*

PREFACE

PHILOSOPHY AND PURPOSE

This text is designed primarily for use in the introductory course in educational research that is a basic requirement for many graduate programs. Since the topic coverage of the text is relatively comprehensive, it also may be easily adapted for use in either a senior-level undergraduate course or a more advanced graduate-level course.

The philosophy that guided the development of the current and previous editions of this text was the conviction that an introductory research course should be more skill and application oriented than theory oriented. Thus the purpose of this text is to have students become familiar with research mainly at a "how to" skill and application level. The text does not mystify students with theoretical and statistical jargon. It strives to provide a down-to-earth approach that aids students in the acquisition of the skills and knowledge required of a competent consumer and producer of educational research. The emphasis is not just on what the student knows but also on what the student can do with what he or she knows. It is recognized that being a "good" researcher involves more than the acquisition of skills and knowledge; in any field, significant research is usually produced by persons who through experience have acquired insights, intuitions, and strategies related to the research process. Research of any worth, however, is rarely conducted in the absence of basic research skills and knowledge. A basic assumption of this text is that there is considerable overlap in the competencies required of a competent consumer of research and a competent producer of research, and that a person is in a much better position to evaluate the work of others after she or he has performed the major tasks involved in the research process.

ORGANIZATION AND STRATEGY

The overall strategy of the text is to promote attainment of a degree of expertise in research through the acquisition of knowledge and by involvement in the research process.

ORGANIZATION

Part One discusses the scientific and disciplined inquiry approach and its application in education. It describes the main steps in the research process and the purpose and methods of the various approaches to research. In Part Two, each student selects and delineates a research problem of interest that has relevance to his or her professional area. In Part Two, and in succeeding parts, the student then simulates the procedures that would be followed in conducting a study designed to investigate the problem; each part develops a specific skill or set of skills required for the execution of a research study. Specifically, the student reviews and analyzes related literature and formulates hypotheses (Part Two), develops a research plan (Part Three), selects and defines samples (Part Four), evaluates and selects mea-

v

suring instruments (Part Five), selects a research design and delineates procedures to conduct it (Part Six), analyzes data (Part Seven), and prepares a research report (Part Eight). In Part Nine the student applies the skills and knowledge acquired in Parts One through Eight and evaluates a research report. Part Ten introduces the student to the rationale and conduct of action research.

STRATEGY

This text represents more than just a textbook to be incorporated into a course; it is actually a total instructional system that includes stated objectives, or competencies, instruction, and procedures for evaluating each competency. The instructional strategy of the system emphasizes demonstration of skills and individualization within structure. The format for each part is essentially the same. Following a brief introduction, each task to be performed is described. Tasks require students to demonstrate that they can perform particular research functions. Since each student works with a different problem, each student demonstrates the competency required by a task as it applies to her or his problem. With the exception of Part One, each part is directed toward the attainment of one task, and the text discussion of chapters within each part relates to that task. Each chapter begins with a list of chapter objectives that entail knowledge and skills that facilitate students' abilities to perform a related task. In many instances objectives may be assessed either as written exercises submitted by students or by tests, whichever the instructor prefers. For some objectives the first option is clearly preferable. Text discussion is intended to be as simple and straightforward as possible. Whenever feasible, procedures are presented as a series of steps and concepts are explained in terms of illustrative examples. In a number of cases, relatively complex topics or topics beyond the scope of the text are presented at a very elementary level, and students are directed to other sources for additional, in-depth discussion. There is also a degree of intentional repetition; a number of concepts are discussed in different contexts and from different perspectives. Also, at the risk of eliciting more than a few groans, an attempt has been made to sprinkle the text with touches of humor. Each chapter includes a detailed, often lengthy, summary with headings and subheadings directly paralleling those in the chapter. The summaries are designed to facilitate both review and location of related text discussion. Finally, each part concludes with suggested criteria for elevation of the task, and an example of the task produced by a former introductory educational research student.

MAJOR REVISIONS

Like the fifth edition, the sixth edition reflects a combination of both unsolicited and solicited input. Positive feedback suggested aspects of the text and supplementary materials that should not be changed, the writing style, for example. Every effort, however, was made to incorporate suggestions, even if made by only a few persons. For example, several users requested an increased focus on qualitative research and technology. We are indebted to everyone who took the time to send a letter or complete a feedback form.

Content changes reflect the inclusion of new topics, the expansion of existing topics, or the clarification of existing topics. While all parts have been revised to some degree, some of the highlights are described below.

1. Qualitative research methods have been increased in coverage and integrated throughout the text. Two new chapters on qualitative methods have been added: chapter 6, Qualitative Research: Data Collection, and chapter 7, Qualitative Research: Data Analysis. The introductory chapter as well as chapters on research problems (2), research plans (3), research participants (4), research critiques (16), and other chapters include aspects of qualitative research. While the text still focuses mainly on quantitative methods, this edition provides a more balanced view of qualitative and quantitative research methods.

2. A new chapter on action research (chapter 17) has been added. Classroom-level self-examination and self-evaluation to improve the educational process are growing trends. The new chapter describes the rationale and presents strategies for conducting action research in classrooms and schools.

3. The use of technology in educational research has been infused into this edition of the text. The function and use of technologies such as e-mail, word processing, brainstorming, bibliographic software, spreadsheets, and statistical software programs are described. The technologies, some including pertinent Web sites, are placed in the sections of the text where their use is most pertinent to the topic being described. Useful Web sites are also provided in chapter 2 to aid in finding and obtaining pertinent literature sources. A companion Web site also accompanies the text.

In addition, new tables and figures have been added. Each chapter has been edited and updated. References have been updated.

SUPPLEMENTARY MATERIALS

A number of ancillaries are available to complement the text, including a Student Guide and Instructor's Manual. For each part in the text there is a corresponding part in these two ancillaries. Other supplementary materials include Prentice Hall Custom Test computerized testbank software, STATPAK statistical software, a free companion Web site, an Educational Research CD-ROM tutorial, and a CD-ROM with interactive computer simulations of educational research concepts and scenarios.

STUDENT GUIDE

The Student Guide has been updated for this edition to include new and revised chapters. It contains examples, exercises, and suggested responses. Part One contains reprints of a number of journal articles representing each of the types of research discussed in the text (e.g., correlational research). In consonance with Part One in the text, students are asked to analyze each article in terms of study components (e.g., the problem) and types of research. In Parts Two through Eight, examples of tasks based on work submitted by previous students are presented, as well as a number of self-test exercises. Whenever feasible, exercises are application oriented; given independent and dependent variables, for example, the student is asked to write the corresponding hypotheses. Part Nine presents a journal article reprint and a detailed form for evaluating the research reported.

INSTRUCTOR'S MANUAL

The Instructor's Manual (ISBN 0-13-013944-0) contains suggestions and test items. General suggestions are given regarding evaluation of tasks and chapter objectives, and specific suggestions regarding instructional strategies are given for each part. Suggestions are based on personal experience teaching the course, feedback from text users, and research. In addition, more than 500 test items are presented representing a variety of item types, primarily multiple-choice. New test items have been added to this edition of the Instructor's Manual to reflect text additions and expansions—in particular, questions related to qualitative research.

PRENTICE HALL CUSTOM TEST COMPUTERIZED TESTBANK SOFTWARE

The computerized testbank software gives instructors electronic access to the test questions printed in the Instructor's Manual and allows them to create and customize exams. The computerized testbank is available in both Macintosh (0-13-013947-5) and PC/Windows (0-13-013645-9) versions.

STATPAK STATISTICAL SOFTWARE

STATPAK statistical software computes all of the statistics that are calculated in the text and shows students the intermediate stages as well as the final answers. The STATPAK software has been upgraded for this edition and is available in both Macintosh (ISBN 0-13-013949-1) and PC/Windows (0-13-013948-3) versions.

COMPANION WEB SITE

This site, located at **http://www.prenhall.com/gay,** allows students and professors using the text free access to a wealth of online resources. Here students can review chapter objectives and test their knowledge by taking chapter quizzes that provide immediate feedback with a percentage score and correct answers. In addition, students can do research on the Internet using suggested educational research-related Web sites. The companion Web site also contains Message Board and Live Chat areas to encourage student interaction. Additional resources include demonstrations of the educational research CD-ROM tutorial and computer simulation CD-ROM described below. For professors, the Syllabus Builder allows easy instructional planning and convenient online access for their course.

EDUCATIONAL RESEARCH CD-ROM TUTORIAL

This CD-ROM (ISBN 0-13-997719-8, Windows only) by John E. Bonfadini is an electronic study guide for the first course in educational research and follows the framework of the textbook. It defines the basic concepts of quantitative and qualitative research and provides interactive activities to help students understand

and apply these concepts. The tutorial also provides three different self-tests. It can be used to fulfill a computer lab component of the course or can provide out-of-class tutorials.

COMPUTER SIMULATION SOFTWARE

These simulations feature four psychological/educational experiments in which students can participate. Exercises and readings help students explore the research concepts and procedures connected to these experiments. Qualitative and quantitative designs are included.

SPECIAL ACKNOWLEDGMENTS

I sincerely thank everyone who provided input for the development of this edition. The following individuals reviewed the current edition: James H. Banning, Colorado State University; John O. Bolvin, University of Pittsburgh; John E. Bonfadini, George Mason University; Beverly Cabello, California State University, Northridge; William T. Coombs, Oklahoma State University; Kevin D. Crehan, University of Nevada, Las Vegas; Ayres D'Costa, The Ohio State University; Thomas P. Evans, Oregon State University; David J. Flinders, Indiana University; Dale R. Fuqua, Oklahoma State University; Jo D. Gallagher, Florida International University; Andrea Guillaume, California State University, Fullerton; Gretchen Guiton, University of Southern California; Geoffrey Mills, Southern Oregon University; Malina Monaco, Georgia State University; Alan D. Moore, University of Wyoming; Charles L. Thomas, George Mason University; Karen L. Westberg, University of Connecticut; and Paul H. Westmeyer, University of Texas, San Antonio. The following individuals reviewed the previous edition: John E. Bonfadini, George Mason University; J. Kent Davis, Purdue University; Ayres D'Costa, The Ohio State University; Jo D. Gallagher, Florida International University; Paul J. Staskey, Northern Arizona University; and Kenneth W. Wunderlich, University of Texas, San Antonio. These reviewers' thoughtful and detailed comments and suggestions contributed greatly to the sixth edition. Their efforts are very much appreciated.

My thanks to Kevin Davis for including me in the writing of this edition and for his support and encouragement throughout the process. Thanks also to Gianna Marsella and Holly Jennings for their timely and responsive help. Martha Beyerlein ably shepherded the manuscript through copyediting and production, kept me from falling behind, and made the process almost painless. Copyeditor Cheryl Ferguson also merits a thank you.

Two of my Boston College colleagues, Larry Ludlow and John Jensen, read and critiqued draft chapters. Larry also contributed in a number of other ways, including helping to clarify difficult research concepts in accurate and understandable ways. Susan Garcia, my graduate assistant, provided invaluable assistance as a keen proofreader, master of the library and Internet, and insightful critic. My thanks to them all.

Peter Airasian
Boston College

A VIRTUAL LEARNING ENVIRONMENT

Technology is a constantly growing and changing aspect of our field that is creating a need for content and resources. To address this emerging need, we have developed an online learning environment for students and professors alike—Companion Web Sites—to support our textbooks.

In creating a Companion Web Site, our goal is to build on and enhance what the textbook already offers. For this reason, the content for each user-friendly Web Site is organized by chapter and provides the professor and student with a variety of meaningful resources. Common features of a Companion Web Site include the following:

FOR THE PROFESSOR

Every Companion Web Site integrates **Syllabus Manager**™, an online syllabus creation and management utility.

- **Syllabus Manager**™ provides you, the instructor, with an easy, step-by-step process to create and revise syllabi, with direct links into the Companion Web Site and other online content without having to learn HTML.
- Students may log on to your syllabus during any study session. All they need to know is the Web address for the Companion Web Site, and the password you've assigned to your syllabus.
- After you have created a syllabus using **Syllabus Manager**™, students may enter the syllabus for their course section from any point in the Companion Web Site.
- Class dates are highlighted in white, and assignment due dates appear in blue. Clicking on a date, the student is shown the list of activities for the assignment. The activities for each assignment are linked directly to actual content, saving time for students.
- Adding assignments consists of clicking on the desired due date, then filling in the details of the assignment—name of the assignment, instructions, and whether or not it is a one-time or repeating assignment.
- In addition, links to other activities can be created easily. If the activity is online, a URL can be entered in the space provided, and it will be linked automatically in the final syllabus.
- Your completed syllabus is hosted on our servers, allowing convenient updates from any computer on the Internet. Changes you make to your syllabus are immediately available to your students at their next log on.

FOR THE STUDENT

- **Chapter Objectives** outline key concepts from the text.
- **Interactive Self-Quizzes,** complete with hints and automatic grading, provide immediate feedback for students.
- After students submit their answers for the interactive self-quizzes, the Companion Web Site **Results Reporter** computes a percentage grade, provides a graphic representation of how many questions were answered correctly and incorrectly, and gives a question by question analysis of the quiz. Students are given the option to send their quiz to four email addresses (professor, teaching assistant, study partner, etc.).
- The **Message Board** serves as a virtual bulletin board to post, or respond to, questions or comments for a national audience.
- **Net Searches** offer links by key terms from each chapter to related Internet content.
- **Web Destinations** offer links to World Wide Web sites that relate to chapter content.

To take advantage of these resources, please visit the *Educational Research* Companion Web Site at **http://www.prenhall.com/gay**

BRIEF CONTENTS

CONTENTS

TABLES AND FIGURES

TABLES

FIGURES

PART ONE

Introduction

If you are taking a research course because it is required in your program of studies, raise your right hand. If you are taking a research course because it seemed like it would be a real fun elective, raise your left hand. When you have stopped laughing, read on. No, you are not the innocent victim of one or more sadists. There are several legitimate reasons why your faculty believe this research course is an essential component of your education.

First, educational research findings significantly contribute to both educational theory and educational practice. The pros and cons of practices such as grouping, testing, and reinforcing students have been studied by educational researchers. Their findings provide a guide to understanding these and many other educational practices. It is important that you, as a professional, know how to access, understand, and evaluate such findings.

Second, whether or not you seek them out, you are constantly exposed to research findings in professional publications and, increasingly, in the media. For example, research results about low student achievement scores and how to improve them, the benefits of technology in the classroom, and the effects of whole language versus phonics on pupils are recurrent social and educational themes. As a professional, you have a responsibility to be able to distinguish between legitimate research claims and ill-founded ones.

And third, believe it or not, research courses provide a fruitful source of future researchers. Despite a popular stereotype that depicts researchers as spectacled, stoop-shouldered, elderly gentlemen who endlessly add chemicals to test tubes, every day thousands of men and women of all ages conduct educational research in a wide variety of settings. A number of the authors' students have become sufficiently intrigued by the research process that they have carried out their own research studies. Many continue to find that using the research process to examine and answer their own educational questions is both engaging and intellectually rewarding. A career in research opens the door to a wide variety of employment opportunities. Members of the American Educational Research Association work in such diverse settings as colleges and universities, research and development centers, federal and state agencies, public and private school systems, and business and industry.

We recognize that for many of you educational research is a relatively unfamiliar discipline. In order to meaningfully learn about and carry out the research process, it is first necessary to develop an overview into which succeeding information and experiences can be integrated. Therefore, the goal of Part One is to help you acquire a general understanding of research processes and strategies that will help you learn about specific research knowledge and skills. In succeeding parts, specific components of the research process will be systematically studied and executed.

After you have read Part One, you should be able to perform the following tasks.

TASK 1-A

Given a reprint of a research study, identify and briefly state:

1. The topic (purpose of the study)
2. The procedures
3. The method of analysis
4. The major conclusions

(See Performance Criteria, p. 27.)

TASK 1-B

Classify a given research study as historical, qualitative, descriptive, correlational, causal-comparative, or experimental, and list the characteristics of each study that support your classification (see Performance Criteria, p. 27).

"Despite a popular stereotype that depicts researchers as spectacled, stoop-shouldered, elderly gentlemen who endlessly add chemicals to test tubes, every day thousands of men and women of all ages conduct educational research in a wide variety of settings (p. 1)."

Introduction to Educational Research

![] OBJECTIVES

OBJECTIVES

After reading chapter 1, you should be able to:

1. List and briefly describe the major steps involved in conducting a research study.
2. Given a published article, identify and state:
   (a) the problem,
   (b) the procedures,
   (c) the method of analysis, and
   (d) the major conclusion.
3. Briefly define and state the major characteristics of the following six types of research: historical, qualitative, descriptive, correlational, causal-comparative, and experimental.
4. For each of these six types of research, briefly describe three possible research studies.

Example:
Experimental—A study to determine the effect of peer tutoring on the computational skill of third graders.

EDUCATIONAL RESEARCH: SCIENTIFIC AND DISCIPLINED INQUIRY

Research is the systematic application of a family of methods that are employed to provide trustworthy information about problems. Educational research is the systematic application of a family of methods that are employed to provide trustworthy information about educational problems. Most researchers, including educational researchers, undertake their inquiry to gain understanding about some issue or topic that they don't fully comprehend. Having a stake in the outcome of the research makes conducting research more interesting and useful for the researcher. Once research questions are explained or understood, many secondary purposes of research come into play, such as helping others understand the research results, using those results to predict or im-prove future research and practice, and raising new topics or questions to study. Rarely, however, does a single research study produce the certainty needed to assume that the same results will apply in all or most settings. Rather, research is usually an ongoing process, based on many accumulated understandings and explanations that, when taken together, lead to generalizations about educational issues and ultimately, to the development of theories.

We humans go about understanding or explaining something in a variety of ways. At times we rely on tradition: This is what we've always believed or the way we've always done things. At other times we rely on the opinions of people who are viewed as experts: a leading expert in the field says. . . . Our own personal experiences and our ability to generalize and make predictions based on these experiences provide us with much of our understanding. Often we use inductive and deductive reasoning to come to an understanding of something.

Inductive reasoning is based on developing generalizations from a limited number of specific observations or experiences.

> **Example:** You examine the tables of contents of four research books, all of which contain a chapter on sampling (limited observation).
> Therefore, all research methods books contain a chapter on sampling (generalization).

Deductive reasoning is based on developing specific predictions from general principles, observations, or experiences.

> **Example:** All research texts contain a chapter on sampling (generalization).
> This book is a research text.
> Therefore, this book contains a chapter on sampling (specific conclusion). (By the way, does it?)

Although commonly used, each of these approaches to understanding has limitations. Relying on tradition inhibits change in one's perspective, thus stifling exploration and eliminating potentially new and fruitful understandings. As for depending solely on experts, even experts are not infallible. Personal experience can be subject to idiosyncratic interpretations and even prejudices. Moreover, most of us have relatively limited experience on many of the issues we might seek to understand.

Some problems with relying on experts and personal experience are illustrated by a story told about Aristotle. According to the story, one day Aristotle caught a fly and carefully counted and recounted the legs. He then announced that flies have five legs. No one questioned the word of Aristotle. For years his finding was uncritically accepted. Of course, the fly that Aristotle caught just happened to be missing a leg! Whether you believe the story, it does illustrate the limitations of relying on personal experience and experts as sources of explanation and understanding. This story also says something about inductive reasoning. The quality of inductive reasoning (specifics to generalizations) is highly dependent on the number and representativeness of the specific observations used to make the generalization. Inductive reasoning provides no guide for the number and quality of the specific examples needed to make viable generalizations. Selecting too few or atypical examples undermines the logic of inductive reasoning. As for deductive reasoning (generalizations to specifics), it depends on the truth of the generalizations it uses as a basis for its logic. That is, if the generalization is not true, its extension to specific instances will not always be accurate. For example, if one accepts the generalization that all professors are boring, extending this generalization to specific professors will not be accurate for at least 10% of the professoriate. Although inductive and deductive reasoning are of limited value when used individually, when combined they are very important.

A scientific and disciplined inquiry approach to research is based on a systematic approach to examining educational issues and questions. It combines features of inductive and deductive reasoning with other characteristics to produce an approach to understanding that, though fallible, is generally more viable than tradition, experts, personal experience, or inductive or deductive reasoning alone. However, it is extremely difficult to totally remove the biases and beliefs of the researcher in any research study. We can lessen but never eliminate errors in research studies that arise from the complexity and variability of humans and the contexts in which they act. Even the most extensive study cannot examine all the human and contextual factors that might affect a researcher's findings. Although the scientific and disciplined inquiry approach cannot guarantee error-free research results, it does incorporate checks and balances to minimize the likelihood that the researcher's emotions or biases will influence the research conclusions.

One very important aspect distinguishes the scientific and disciplined inquiry approach from other ways of understanding. The researcher is expected to describe in detail the procedures used to conduct the research study, thus providing a basis for examination and verification of the results. These checks and balances allow research to be understood and critiqued in ways not available using tradition, experts, personal experience, or inductive or deductive reasoning alone.

At the heart of a scientific and disciplined inquiry approach is an orderly process that, at a minimum, involves four basic steps:

1. *Recognize and identify a topic to be studied.* A topic is a question, issue, or problem related to education that can be examined or answered through the collection and analysis of data.

2. *Describe and execute procedures to collect information about the topic being studied.* The procedures include identification of the research participants, the measures needed to collect data related to the topic, and the activities describing how, when, and from whom the data will be collected. The procedures dictate to a large extent the specific activities that will take place during data collection.

3. *Analyze the collected data.* The analysis of the collected data is related to the nature of the topic studied (step 1) and to the data collected (step 2). Some research topics are best analyzed using quantitative, numerical data and a variety of statistical approaches. Other research topics are more qualitative in form and rely upon data in the form of narratives, tape recordings, and field notes. Qualitative data are usually analyzed using interpretive rather than statistical analysis. Regardless of the kind of data collected, some form of analysis is necessary.

4. *State the results or implications based on analysis of the data.* Conclusions reached in the research study should relate back to the original research topic. What can be concluded about this topic based on the results of the study?

RESEARCH TOPICS: DEFINING PURPOSE AND METHODS

Consider the many questions about educational processes, activities, and theories that can be asked and systematically examined through research. Read the following research topics.

1. Do students learn more from our new social studies program than from the prior one?

2. What is the effect of positive versus negative reinforcement on elementary students' attitudes toward school?
3. How do teachers in our school district rate the quality of our teacher evaluation program?
4. What do high school principals consider to be the most pressing administrative problems they face?
5. Is there a relationship between middle school students' grades and their self-confidence in science and mathematics?
6. Do students' high scores on an anxiety test relate to the scores they get on the Scholastic Assessment Test?
7. What factors led to the development of standardized achievement tests from 1900 to 1930?
8. What were the effects of the GI Bill on state colleges in the Midwest in the 1950s?
9. How do special needs students adapt to the culture of junior high school when transitioning from a strongly child-centered elementary school?
10. How do the first 5 weeks of school in Ms. Foley's classroom influence activities and interactions in succeeding months?

Make a list of a few research questions or topics you might wish to study.

Consider the differences among these questions. For example, note the purpose of the topics posed. Questions 1 and 2 are concerned with *comparing* two things: the new versus the old social studies program and positive versus negative reinforcement. Questions 3 and 4 are concerned with *describing* teachers' ratings of their school district's teacher evaluation procedure and administrators' listing of their most pressing problems. Questions 5 and 6 are concerned with *relating* two things, grades to self-confidence and anxiety level to math and science performance. Questions 7 and 8 focus on events in the past, and are concerned with describing the *history* about each question. Questions 9 and 10 are concerned with using long-term, in-depth observation to obtain information about the adaptation of special needs students in a new culture (junior high school) and the impact of how one begins the school year on later classroom interactions. Approaches using in-depth description and analysis of cultures or social settings are called *qualitative* studies.

Logically, if there are differences in the purposes of research topics, there also should be differences in the strategies and methods for investigating these topics. Some questions require selection of a large sample of people to provide data (e.g., question 2). Others focus in-depth on the performance or activities of a small number of people to obtain data (e.g., question 9). Still others may not gather data from people at all, relying instead on artifacts, documents, pictures, and the like to provide needed data (questions 7 and 8). The way data are collected and analyzed also differs among research topics. Some methods rely heavily on formal tests and questionnaires to collect data (questions 1–6). Others rely heavily on in-depth personal observation, interviews, and tape recordings to collect data (questions 9–10). Methods that emphasize the use of tests typically are analyzed with statistical procedures (questions 1–6). Methods based on observation, interviews, and the like rarely employ statistical analysis, relying instead on the researcher's interpretive skills to analyze, integrate, and make sense of the data collected (questions 7–10).

Although there are a number of different questions, methods, and analyses related to conducting research, the threads that unite these differences are the four basic steps in the scientific and disciplined inquiry approach. Regardless of the nature of a research study, sections of it will be devoted to the purpose of the research, the methods used to carry out the research, the procedures used to analyze the collected data, and the interpretations or conclusions of the study.

This text focuses on a range of research methods exemplified by the 10 questions just discussed. Research methods can be classified by the degree of direct applicability of the research to educational settings (basic or applied research), or by the methods the researcher uses to conduct the study (quantitative or qualitative research). The intent of this book is to provide you with basic insights and understandings about a variety of research methods and strategies. It seeks to help you think about and critique your own and other people's research studies. To this end, it focuses on issues of finding research topics, selecting appropriate and ethical procedures for collecting data, and applying meaningful methods to analyze and present research outcomes and implications.

BASIC AND APPLIED RESEARCH

It is difficult to discuss basic and applied research separately because they are on a single continuum. Classification of a given study along the basic–applied continuum is made primarily on the degree to which the findings have direct applicability and the degree to which they are generalizable to other educational settings. Basic research involves the process of collecting and analyzing information to develop or enhance a theory. Theory development is a conceptual process that requires many research studies conducted over a period of time. Basic researchers may not be directly concerned with the social utility of their findings, and it might be years before basic research finds some educational application. The early work of Skinner on reinforcement with birds and Piaget on cognitive development with his two children were basic research efforts that subsequently led to educational applications.

Applied research is conducted for the purpose of applying or testing theory and evaluating its usefulness in solving educational problems. A teacher who asks, "Will application of multiple intelligence theory improve my students' learning?" is seeking an answer to a practical classroom question. The teacher is not interested in building a general theory or even generalizing beyond her classroom, but is seeking specific information about a theory for use in his or her own classroom. Letting teachers try out two methods of covering study hall and then having them decide which one results in greater student attentiveness is an example of applied research. Using portfolios in a classroom to see whether writing improves is also applied research.

There is disagreement among educators and researchers about which end of the basic–applied continuum research should be emphasized. In its purest form, basic research is conducted solely for the purpose of theory development; it most closely resembles the laboratory conditions and controls usually associated with scientific research. Applied educational research is conducted to solve current educational problems. Most educational research studies would be located on the applied end of the continuum; they are more focused on "what" works best than on finding out "why" it works best. Studies located in the middle of the basic–

applied continuum try to integrate both approaches. Both basic and applied research are necessary and, to a point, interdependent. Basic research provides the theory that produces the concepts for examining educational problems. Applied research provides data that can help support, guide, and revise the development of theory.

EVALUATION RESEARCH

At the far end of applied research is evaluation, an important, widely used, and explicitly practical form of research. Evaluation research is concerned with making decisions about the quality, effectiveness, or value of educational programs, products, or practices. Unlike other forms of research that seek new knowledge or understanding, evaluation focuses on decision making, a highly applied and practical purpose. Although the methods of evaluation research are not different from the methods of other forms of research, evaluation is distinguished by its decision-making purpose.

Typical evaluation research questions are: "Is this special science program worth its costs?" "Is the new reading curriculum better than the old one?" and "Did students reach the objectives of the diversity sensitivity program?"

Evaluations come in various forms and have different purposes.[1] Two of their main purposes are to monitor the ongoing progress of a program or product and to subsequently judge the overall impact of a program or product at its completion. Evaluators monitor an ongoing program or product in order to identify weaknesses that can be remedied during implementation. This evaluation purpose is called *formative evaluation* because its function is to form and improve what is being evaluated while it is being developed. Evaluators also make decisions about the program or product at its completion in order to make a decision about the overall quality or worth of the program or product. This approach is called *summative evaluation* because its function is to make a decision that sums up the overall quality or worth of the program or product.

QUANTITATIVE AND QUALITATIVE RESEARCH

We have noted that the fundamental purpose of educational research is to increase our understanding of educational processes, practices, and issues. For most of the history of educational research, the methods of science have been used to obtain these understandings. There were well-defined, widely accepted procedures for stating research topics, carrying out the research process, analyzing the resulting data, and verifying the quality of the study and its conclusions. For the most part, the accepted research procedures were based on a quantitative approach to conducting and obtaining educational understandings. Quantitative methods of research are based on the collection and analysis of numerical data, usually obtained from questionnaires, tests, checklists, and other formal paper-and-pencil instruments. But a quantitative approach entails more than just the use of numerical data. It also involves (1) stating both the hypotheses studied and

---

[1]Gredler, M. E. (1996). *Program evaluation.* Englewood Cliffs, NJ: Prentice-Hall. Madaus, G. F., Scriven, M., & Stufflebeam, D. L. (1983). *Evaluation models.* Hingham, MA: Kluwer Academic.

the research procedures that will be implemented prior to conducting the study, (2) maintaining control over contextual factors that might interfere with the data collected, (3) using large enough samples of participants to provide statistically meaningful data, and (4) employing data analyses that rely on statistical procedures. Quantitative researchers generally have little personal interaction with the people they study, since most data are gathered using paper and pencil, structured, noninteractive instruments.

Underlying quantitative research methods is the belief or assumption that we inhabit a relatively stable, uniform, and coherent world that can be measured, understood, and generalized about. This view, which the field of education adopted from the natural sciences, holds that the world and the laws that govern it are relatively stable and predictable, and they can be understood by scientific examination. In this quantitative—also called *positivist*—perspective of research, claims about the world are not considered meaningful unless they can be verified through direct observation. This approach to research has been and continues to be the dominant one in education.

However, in recent years, other, nonquantitative approaches to educational research have emerged and attracted many advocates. These methods of research are generally called *qualitative*. They are based on the collection and analysis of nonnumerical data such as observations, interviews, and other more discursive sources of information. Qualitative research methods are based on different beliefs and purposes than quantitative research methods. For example, qualitative research does not accept the view of a stable, coherent, uniform world. It argues that meaning is situated in a particular perspective or context, and, since different people and groups often have different perspectives and contexts, there are many different meanings in the world, none of which is necessarily more valid or true than another.

Some fundamental differences in how quantitative or qualitative research is often conducted reflect these different perspectives on meaning and how one can approach it. For example, qualitative research tends not to state hypotheses or research procedures before any data are collected; research problems and methods tend to evolve as understanding of the research context deepens. In qualitative research, context is not controlled. Additionally, in qualitative research the number of participants studied tends to be small, in part because of time-intensive methods like interviews and observations. Qualitative research analyzes data interpretively by organizing the data into categories, identifying patterns, and producing a descriptive narrative synthesis, whereas quantitative analysis involves statistical procedures. Finally, because of the data collection methods and the effort to understand the participants' own perspective, researchers using qualitative methods often interact extensively with the participants during the study. In quantitative research, researchers strive to control context, so they do not interact with the participants.

Despite the differences between them, quantitative and qualitative research should not be considered oppositional. Taken together, they represent the full range of educational research methods. The terms *quantitative* and *qualitative* are used to conveniently differentiate one research approach from the other. If you see yourself as a positivist, that does not mean you cannot use or learn from qualitative research methods. The same holds true for you non-positivists about quantitative research. Depending on the nature of the question or topic to be investigated, either a qualitative or quantitative approach will generally be more appropriate. In fact, both may be utilized in the same studies, as when the administration of a questionnaire (quantitative) is followed up by a small number of detailed interviews (qualitative) to obtain deeper explanations for the numerical data. Qualitative and quantitative approaches represent complementary components of the scientific and disciplined inquiry approach; qualitative approaches involve primarily inductive reasoning while quantitative approaches involve primarily deductive reasoning. If hypotheses are involved, a qualitative study is much more likely to generate them, whereas a quantitative study is much more likely to test them. At an operational level, qualitative approaches are more holistic and process-oriented, whereas quantitative approaches are more narrowly focused and outcome-oriented. Qualitative research typically studies many variables intensely over an extended period of time to capture the richness of the context and the personal perspectives of subjects. Conversely, quantitative research focuses on a small number of variables and tries to eliminate the influence of contextual factors (e.g., class size, teacher experience, student characteristics). While qualitative research might study in-depth the way two or three teachers were acclimating to the use of a new reading textbook over a 6-month period, quantitative research might gather evidence from 200 students to compare the self-esteem of two groups of students, equivalent to each other except that one group was mentored and the other was not.

At this point, you should have a basic sense of the essence of the two approaches. Table 1.1 summarizes differences in the conduct of quantitative and qualitative research. However, to help you broadly understand the field of educational research as a whole, we probably need to make one more level of distinction among types of educational research. So, let's look now at more specific types of research that fall under the broad categories of quantitative and qualitative research. In succeeding chapters we will examine the procedures and underlying beliefs associated with a number of specific quantitative and qualitative research approaches.

TABLE 1.1		
Comparison of Quantitative and Qualitative Research		
	QUANTITATIVE	**QUALITATIVE**
approach	deductive	inductive
purpose	theory testing, prediction, establishing facts, hypothesis testing	describing multiple realities, developing deep understanding, capturing everyday life and human perspectives
research focus	isolates variables, uses large samples, is often anonymous to participants, collects data using tests and formal instruments	examines full context, interacts with participants, collects data face-to-face from participants
research plan	developed before study is initiated, structured, proposal is formal	begins with an initial idea that evolves as researcher learns more about participants and setting, flexible, proposal is tentative
data analysis	mainly statistical, quantitative	mainly interpretive, descriptive

QUANTITATIVE APPROACHES

Quantitative approaches are used to describe current conditions, investigate relationships, and study cause–effect phenomena. Studies designed to describe current conditions are referred to as *descriptive* or *survey* research. Studies designed to investigate the relationship between two or more quantified variables are referred to as *correlational* research, and those designed to investigate cause–effect relationships are called *causal–comparative* or *experimental* research, depending on whether the relationship is studied after the fact or in a controlled environment.

Descriptive Research

Quantitative descriptive or survey research involves collecting data in order to answer questions about the current status of the subject or topic of study. Note that qualitative research also relies heavily on description, but qualitative description is usually in the form of verbal reports and narratives, not quantitative results. Quantitative descriptive studies are carried out to obtain information about the preferences, attitudes, practices, concerns, or interests of some group of people. For example, a pre-election political poll or a survey about the public's perception of the quality of its local schools are examples of descriptive research. A substantial portion of all the quantitative research conducted today is descriptive research.

Quantitative descriptive data are mainly collected through questionnaires that are self-administered by those chosen to provide data. Another common (but slightly more annoying) form of survey data is the telephone interview. At one time or another most of us have received a phone call from some organization or company that wants to obtain our opinions of their organization or product. Usually they read questions and ask us to choose from a limited number of categories: "Select your answer from these choices: highly favorable, favorable, neutral, unfavorable, or highly unfavorable." Usually they call in the middle of supper.

There is considerably more to conducting descriptive research than just asking questions and reporting answers. Since one is often asking questions that have not been asked before, instruments must be developed to suit each specific descriptive study. Instrument development is not easy. It requires clarity, consistency, and tact in constructing questions. Other major problems that face descriptive researchers are participants' failure to return questionnaires, to agree to be surveyed over the phone, and to attend scheduled data collection sessions. The descriptive researcher depends on the chosen individuals to care enough to make the time to provide the desired information. If the response rate is low, valid conclusions about the issues studied cannot be drawn. Suppose you were doing a study to determine attitudes of principals toward research in their schools. You send a questionnaire to 100 principals and ask the question, "Do you usually cooperate if your school is asked to participate in a research study?" Suppose 40 principals respond and they all answer yes. Could you then conclude that principals in general cooperate with researchers? No! Even though all those who responded said yes, 60 principals did not respond to your questionnaire. They may never cooperate with researchers. After all, they didn't cooperate with you! Without their responses it is not possible to make judgments about how all principals feel about research in their schools.

Here are some examples of questions investigated by quantitative descriptive research studies:

1. *How do second-grade teachers spend their teaching time?* Categories of teaching time would be identified (e.g., lecture, discussion, asking and answering questions, individual student help). Second-grade teachers would be asked to fill out a questionnaire and results would probably be presented as percentages (e.g., 50% of their time is spent lecturing, 20% asking or answering questions, 20% discussion, and 10% individual student help).

2. *How will citizens of Yourtown vote in the next presidential election?* A survey of Yourtown citizens would be taken (questionnaire or interview), and results would probably be presented as percentages (e.g., 70% indicated they will vote for Peter Pure, 20% for George Graft, and 10% are undecided).

3. *How do parents feel about a 12-month school year?* Parents would be surveyed and results would probably be presented in terms of the percentages for, against, or undecided.

Correlational Research

Correlational research attempts to determine whether, and to what degree, a relationship exists between two or more variables.[2] The purpose of a correlational study is either to establish a relationship (or lack of it) or to use relationships to make predictions. A correlation is a quantitative measure of the degree of correspondence between two or more variables. For example, a college admissions director might be interested in answering the question "How does the performance of high school seniors on the SAT correspond to their first semester college grades?" Is there a high correlation between the two variables, suggesting that SAT scores might be useful in predicting how students will perform in their freshman year of college? Or is there a low correlation between the two variables, suggesting that SAT scores likely will not be useful in predicting freshman performance? The degree of correspondence between variables is measured by a correlation coefficient, which is a number between −1.00 and +1.00. Two variables that are not related will have a correlation coefficient near .00, between −1.00 and +1.00. Two variables that are highly related will have a correlation coefficient near −1.00 or +1.00. A correlation that is positive means that as one variable increases, the other variable also increases. A coefficient that is negative means that when one variable increases the other variable decreases. Since very few pairs of variables are perfectly correlated, predictions based on them are also rarely perfect. Although correlations do not indicate a cause–effect relationship, for many decisions, predictions based on known relationships can be useful.

At a minimum, correlation research requires information about at least two variables obtained from a single group of people. In larger correlational studies, a number of variables believed to be related to a complex concept such as achievement may be examined. Variables found not to be highly correlated to achievement would be eliminated from further consideration, while vari-

---

[2] A variable can assume any one of a range of values. Examples of variables include height, weight, income, achievement, ability, gender, and motivation. Got the idea?

ables that were highly correlated to achievement might prompt further examination.

It is very important to note that correlational studies do not establish causal relations between variables. Other, more powerful methods (discussed later) are needed to establish cause–effect relationships. Thus, the fact that there is a high correlation between self-concept and achievement does not imply that self-concept "causes" achievement or that achievement "causes" self-concept. The correlation only indicates that students with higher self-concepts tend to have higher levels of achievement and that students with lower self-concepts tend to have lower levels of achievement. Without additional data, we cannot conclude that one variable is the cause of the other. There may be a third factor, such as the amount of encouragement and support parents give their children, that underlies both variables and influences high or low achievement and self-concept. The important point to remember is that correlational research never establishes cause–effect links between variables.

The following are examples of correlational studies:

1. *The correlation between intelligence and self-esteem.* Scores on an intelligence test and on a measure of self-esteem would be acquired from each member of a given group. The two sets of scores would be correlated and the resulting coefficient would indicate the degree of relationship.
2. *The relationship between anxiety and achievement.* Scores on an anxiety scale and on an achievement test would be acquired from each member of a group. The two sets of scores would be correlated and the resulting coefficient would indicate the degree of relationship.
3. *Use of an aptitude test to predict success in an algebra course.* Scores on an algebra aptitude test would be correlated with success in algebra measured by algebra final exam scores. If the resulting correlation were high, the aptitude test might be a good predictor of grades in algebra.

Causal–Comparative Research

Causal–comparative and experimental research are the final two forms of quantitative research we will examine. Both are aimed at making cause–effect statements about the performance of two or more groups, methods, or programs. The basic difference between the two is in the amount of control the researcher has over the comparisons studied. In experimental research, the alleged *cause* is under the control of the researcher and is manipulated by the researcher while in causal-comparative research it is not. The alleged cause, that is, the characteristic believed to make a difference, is often referred to as the *treatment*. The more formal name for the cause or treatment is the *independent variable*. It is the variable believed to cause a difference between groups. The difference, or *effect,* of the independent variable is called the *dependent variable* because it is dependent on what happens to the independent variable. For example, in the statement "giving students assertiveness training will improve their self-confidence," the causal factor or independent variable is assertiveness training and the effect or dependent variable is self-confidence. What happens to self-confidence will depend on the success of assertiveness training. Try to identify the independent and dependent variables in this statement: "Careful study of the Gay and Airasian textbook will make readers high quality researchers." What is the cause and what is the effect? Note that experimental and causal–comparative research produce stronger relationships among variables than descriptive and correlational research because they link a cause to an effect.

In a causal–comparative study (note, the word is *causal,* not *casual*) the independent variable, or cause, has already occurred or cannot be manipulated, so the researcher has no control over it. For this reason, causal–comparative research is also called *ex post facto* (after the fact) research. The independent variables in causal–comparative studies either cannot be manipulated (e.g., gender, height) or should not be manipulated (e.g., smoking, prenatal care). In causal–comparative research, at least two different groups are compared on some dependent variable or measurement of performance (the effect). For example, a causal–comparative study might involve the independent or causal variable "smoking," with a comparison between a group of long-time smokers and a group of nonsmokers. Causal–comparative and experimental research always involves the comparison of two or more groups or treatments. The dependent variable (the effect) might be the comparative frequency of lung cancer diagnoses in the two groups. In this example and in causal–comparative research in general, the researcher does not have control over the independent variable. That is, the smokers and nonsmokers had already formed themselves into groups *before* the researcher began the study. The researcher has to select research participants from two different, preexisting groups. This creates a problem. Suppose that unknown to the researcher, a large number of the long-time smokers selected had lived in a smoggy, urban environment and that only a few of the nonsmoking group did. Due to the lack of control over the selection of study participants, attempts to draw cause–effect conclusions in the study would be at best tenuous and tentative. Is it smoking that causes higher rates of lung cancer? Is it living in a smoggy, urban environment? Is it some unknown combination of smoking and environment? A clear cause–effect link cannot be obtained from this study because the researcher did not have complete control of the selection of the participants and their characteristics.

Although causal–comparative research produces limited cause–effect information, it is an important form of educational research because in many cases, seeking true cause–effect relationships would be inappropriate or unethical to research. Our smoking study is an example of the need for causal–comparative methods. To conduct the smoking study as an experiment so that causal statements about smoking and lung cancer could be obtained would require the researcher's control over the selection of the participants for the two groups. To attain this control, the researcher would have to select a large group of participants who had never smoked and divide them into two groups, one forced to become heavy smokers and one forbidden to smoke. Obviously such a study would be unethical because of the potential harm to those forced to become heavy smokers. Thus, the only reasonable option is to conduct a causal–comparative study that approximates cause–effect results without harming the participants. The results of causal–comparative studies sometimes lead to more rigorous experimental studies designed to confirm the causal-comparative findings. The following are examples of causal–comparative studies:

1. *The effect of preschool attendance on social maturity at the end of the first grade.*
   The independent variable, or cause, is preschool attendance (students attending preschool and students not attending); the dependent variable, or effect, is social maturity at the end of the first grade. Two groups of first graders would be identified—one group who had attended

preschool and one group who had not. The social maturity of the two groups would be compared at the end of grade one.

2. *The effect of having a working mother on school absenteeism.* The independent variable is the employment status of the mother (the mother works or does not work); the dependent variable is absenteeism, or number of days absent. Two groups of students would be identified—one group who had working mothers and one group who did not. The absenteeism of the two groups would be compared.

3. *The effect of gender on algebra achievement.* The independent variable is gender (male or female); the dependent variable is algebra achievement. The achievement of males would be compared to the achievement of females.

Experimental Research

The major difference between causal–comparative and experimental research is that in the experiment the researcher controls the alleged independent variable. In fact, the experiment is the quantitative approach that provides the greatest degree of control over the research procedures. The experimental researcher controls the selection of participants for the study and divides the selected participants into two or more groups having similar characteristics at the start of the experiment. The researcher then applies different programs or treatments to the groups. The researcher also controls conditions in the research setting, such as when the treatments are applied, by whom, and for how long. Finally, the researcher selects a test or measure to determine the effects of the treatments on the groups.

It is the selection of participants from a single pool and the ability to apply different treatments or programs to participants with similar characteristics that separates experimental from causal–comparative research. The essence of experimentation is control, although in many education settings it is not possible or feasible to meet the stringent control conditions required by experimental research.

The following are examples of experimental studies:

1. *The comparative effectiveness of personalized instruction from a teacher versus computer instruction on computational skills.* The independent variable is type of instruction (personalized teacher instruction versus computer instruction); the dependent variable is computational skills. A group of students who had never experienced either personalized teacher instruction or computer instruction would be selected and randomly divided into two groups, each taught by one of the methods. After a predetermined period of time, the students' computational skills would be measured and compared to determine which, if either, treatment produced the higher computational skills.

2. *The effect of self-paced instruction on self-concept.* The independent variable is pacing (self-pacing versus teacher pacing); the dependent is self-concept. Two groups would be randomly formed from a single group of students who had not previously been exposed to either of the two pacing methods. Each group would receive its respective treatment. After a predetermined time period, their scores on a self-concept test would be compared.

3. *The effect of positive reinforcement on attitude toward school.* The independent variable is type of reinforcement (e.g., positive, negative, and no

reinforcement); the dependent variable is attitude toward school. In this example three groups will be studied. The three groups would be randomly formed from a large group of students. One group would receive positive reinforcement, another negative reinforcement, and the third no reinforcement. After the treatments were applied for some period of time, student attitudes toward school would be measured and compared for each of the three groups.

QUALITATIVE APPROACHES

Qualitative research seeks to probe deeply into the research setting in order to obtain understandings about the way things are, *why* they are that way, and *how* the participants in the context perceive them. There are many approaches to qualitative research. For the most part, however, many qualitative research approaches use similar methodologies to examine different aspects of social contexts and their inhabitants. Also, the methods used to examine these areas are similar. Because of this and the large number of qualitative approaches, our discussion will not focus on every approach. Nor will we describe and provide examples of every qualitative approach. Rather, we provide generic descriptions and examples that we will term *qualitative approaches*. Thus, our use of the term *qualitative approach* encompasses a variety of particular qualitative approaches. In treating a variety of approaches in a generic, undifferentiated manner, we recognize that nuances associated with particular approaches are omitted. It is beyond the scope of this book to provide in-depth discussion on each particular approach, and we encourage readers interested in carrying out qualitative research studies to examine their chosen method in more depth than is provided here.

Historical Research Methods

Although it is commonly viewed as a qualitative approach, we discuss historical research separately because it is past-oriented rather than present-oriented and because it collects different kinds of data than that of most other qualitative approaches.

Historical research involves studying, understanding, and interpreting past events. The purpose of historical research is to reach insights or conclusions about past persons or occurrences. Often, the results of historical research provide insights into current events. Historical research, like all qualitative approaches, entails more than simply compiling and presenting factual information; it also requires interpretation of the information. It is this characteristic, along with the fact that historical research deals mainly with nonnumerical data, that places historical research in the domain of qualitative approaches.

Typically, histories focus on particular individuals (e.g., John Dewey, Malcolm X, Margaret Thatcher, Barbara Jordan), important social issues (e.g., school desegregation, the consequences of standardized testing), and links between the old and the new (e.g., comparing teaching methods across generations, examining and explaining reasons for textbook changes in the last six decades). Some historical research is aimed at reinterpreting prior historical work (e.g., why schools foster intolerance, how tracking diminishes incentives); this approach is often termed *revisionist history* because it attempts to revise existing understandings and replace them with new, often politically charged ones.

Historical researchers work with data that are already available, except in those instances when living reporters of past events can provide information. The potential range of data sources used by historical researchers is extensive, including newspapers, legislative documents, court testimony, diaries, committee meeting records, yearbooks, memoirs, relics, and photographs. Occasionally a historical researcher may collect quantitative information for a study, as when the researcher investigates a topic that includes information about the number of women graduated from medical school between 1990 and 1997. However, the main emphasis in historical research is on interpretation of documents, diaries, and the like.

Historical data are categorized into primary or secondary sources. *Primary sources* include first-hand information, such as eyewitness reports and original documents. *Secondary sources* include second-hand information, such as a description of an event by someone other than an eyewitness, or a textbook author's explanation of a researcher's theory. If you interview someone who witnessed an accident, that someone is a primary source; if you interview someone who heard about the accident from a friend, that person is a secondary source. Primary sources are admittedly harder to acquire (it would be quite a feat to find an eyewitness to the Boston Tea Party!) but are generally more accurate and preferred by historical researchers. A major problem with much historical research is excessive reliance upon secondary sources.

Researchers cannot accept historical data at face value, since many diaries, memoirs, reports, and testimonies are written to enhance the writer's position, stature, or importance. Because of this possibility, historical data have to be examined for their authenticity and truthfulness. Such examination is done through external and internal criticism. *External criticism* assesses the authenticity of the data: was this diary really written by Bonnie Parker; is this her handwriting; is the diary paper and ink of the right age for her time? Questions such as these help determine the authenticity of the data. *Internal criticism* evaluates the worth or truthfulness of the content of the data. Are the writer's statements biased for some reason? Are important pieces of information omitted? Is the writer's description of the event in line with descriptions written by others? Historical researchers care about the value of the data and the degree to which they are accurate and useful.

In his book *Chariots of the Gods?*[3] Erich Von Däniken hypothesizes that thousands of years ago our ancestors were visited by intelligent beings from other worlds who, among other things, presented early humanity with advanced technology. Von Däniken points to such remains as cave drawings, ancient maps, and relics of advanced, early civilizations as evidence in support of his theory. In general, authenticity of his evidence is without question; the drawings, maps, and relics are all thousands of years old. The evidence passes the external criticism test. However, his interpretation of what these remains mean is certainly debatable, as he has little additional evidence to support his theory. A cave drawing of a strange being, which is an ancient astronaut to Von Däniken, may be seen as simply an imaginary god to an archaeologist. Von Däniken's evidence fails the test of internal criticism.

---

[3]Von Däniken, E. (1972). *Chariots of the Gods?* New York: Bantam Books.

The following are examples of historical research studies:

1. *Factors leading to the development and growth of cooperative learning.* The researcher would probably fully define the issue or topic to be examined only after spending time reading and collecting preliminary information about the topic. The bulk of the work would be in identifying book and electronic sources pertinent to the topic. The researcher would seek primary sources, but probably would also rely on some secondary sources. Certainly the researcher would subject the data collected to internal and external criticism. Lengthy and in-depth notes, photocopied documents, and, if possible, interviews would be compiled, organized into categories, and examined for common and related themes. Ultimately the historical researcher will produce a work indicating his or her interpretation of the data collected and analyzed.

2. *Trends in elementary school reading instruction, 1940–1995.* The researcher narrowed the focus of the historical study to the period 1940–1995 and to the topic elementary school reading. The researcher would examine a number of potential sources: reading textbooks of the selected period, educational movements that affected reading methods (e.g., back to basics movement; whole language approach), students' reading achievement (quantitative data), professional development opportunities for reading teachers, and the articles in major reading publications. The researcher would keep copious and detailed notes related to these sources. External and internal criticism would be applied to the data. Finally, the researcher would apply interpretive and writing skills to present a coherent, logically presented report about the nature and reasons for elementary reading trends between 1940 and 1995.

Qualitative Research Methods

As noted, there are many different approaches to qualitative research, but although somewhat different in some respects, they are similar to each other in many ways. For this reason, we focus on common or generic aspects of qualitative research approaches.

Qualitative researchers are not concerned simply with describing the way things are, they also wish to provide insights into what people believe and feel about the way things are and how they got to be the way they are. In order to achieve the detailed understandings they seek, qualitative researchers must undertake in-depth, in-context research that allows them the opportunity to uncover more subtle, less overt understandings. Thus, qualitative researchers typically maintain a lengthy physical presence in the chosen setting. In these settings they can assume a range of involvement—from an observer, to an interviewer, to a participant observer who literally becomes a participant in the setting. These three levels of involvement lead to different levels of understanding. Being actively present in the setting of the study provides insights not available to "outsiders" who are peripherally present. It is recommended that novice qualitative researchers begin their studies as observers or interviewers. Only very experienced researchers should become active participants in the setting.

Most qualitative approaches manifest the six characteristics described in Table 1.2. Each emphasizes the need to understand context. Each is concerned with identifying and reporting the participants', not the researcher's, perspective.

Each involves researcher immersion into the context being studied. In each, the researcher collects large amounts of qualitative data. In each, the researcher analyzes data using interpretive and writing skills.

Qualitative researchers carry out in-depth examinations of a topic or problem over a sustained period of time. Although the amount of time qualitative researchers spend in the contexts they study varies, they typically spend months, not days, immersed in the context. The researcher often strives to enter the setting with no preconceived notions about the context, participants, or data desired, letting the purpose of the study emerge as more is observed and understood about the setting and participants. To tell the "story" of the participants and context requires both substantial time in the natural setting and the collection of a great deal of data. The qualitative researcher needs time to become accepted by the individuals who will provide the needed data. Inability to obtain the acceptance and trust of research participants can doom any study, but particularly a qualitative research study. Researchers hope to obtain some degree of acceptance to permit them to get close to participants and situations so that they can better understand those situations.

Data are gathered from *fieldwork,* that is, from spending sustained periods of time in the setting where participants normally spend their time. Types of data commonly collected include records of formal and informal conversations, observations, documents, audio and video tapes, and interviews. For the most part, though not exclusively, the data collected are open-ended and nonnumerical.

Data analysis of most qualitative approaches is ongoing; as initial observations, conversations, and interviews are collected, the researcher analyzes and codes them to discover the nuances of the context and the perspectives and beliefs of the participants. As more data are collected, the researcher refines prior analyses and understandings, trying to focus on the key aspects to be studied

TABLE	1.2

Common Features of Qualitative Research

1. Qualitative researchers tend to *spend a great deal of time in the settings they study.* That is, qualitative studies are field centered.

2. Qualitative researchers *rely on themselves as the main instrument of data collection.* It is the researcher who enters the setting, collects observational and other qualitative data, and provides his or her own interpretation of the data.

3. Qualitative researchers *use interpretation to analyze their data.* The researcher both describes and provides an explanation of what has been observed and what it means to the participants.

4. Qualitative researchers *employ expressive language and voice in their descriptions and explanations.* In addition to good interpretive skills, qualitative research requires good writing and expressive skills.

5. Qualitative researchers *seek depth of perspective in their studies* rather than breadth. Most qualitative studies include a small number of participants who are studied in depth over time.

6. Qualitative researchers *are judged in terms of the believability, trustworthiness, coherence, and logic of their interpretations.* Qualitative researchers persuade by the logic of their process and interpretations.

and described. Thus, data collection, analysis, and interpretation occur through-out the study rather than at the end of the study, as is common with quantitative research. We can think of qualitative research as collecting waves of data; each successive wave provides some information that further focuses the nature of the study until the researcher gradually zeros in on the important and recurring themes of the culture and its participants. The ongoing collection and analysis of data is important because the relationship between the researcher and partici-pants changes as they become more familiar with each other. As the fieldwork is collected, the researcher analyzes and interprets it in search of connections, un-derlying themes or processes, and participants' understanding.

The final product of the study is a rich description or narrative of the essen-tial aspects of the topic as viewed by the participants. Quotations commonly are used to illustrate the *voice* and understandings of the participants. Words and pic-tures, not numbers and statistical analyses, are used to convey meaning. The main focus of the qualitative study is to use language to paint a rich picture of the setting and its participants. Following are two examples of qualitative ap-proaches.

1. *The problems, successes, and understandings of Jack, during his first year of teaching.* The researcher would probably meet with Jack initially to obtain his formal agreement to participate, explain the nature of the study and the time involved, and discuss the planned final research product. The researcher might start by obtaining Jack's general educational history. The researcher would want to view Jack's classroom (his context), and would spend a great deal of time discussing, observing, and taking notes about Jack, both in and out of class. Jack's thoughts about his experiences and perceptions would be particularly important to obtain. Class materi-als and comments of colleagues and students would supplement the re-searcher's information. Over time, major themes related to Jack's first year would emerge. A literature search would be undertaken to help place the study in the context of existing research on the topic. The re-searcher might ask Jack to react to the conclusions that have been made about him. At the end of the year, a descriptive narrative would be pro-duced that described changes in Jack's teaching perspectives and prac-tices. The narrative might be supplemented with descriptions of the problems he encountered, his high and low points as a first-year teacher, and his own insights of his progress and feelings toward teaching. An ef-fort would be made to explain why he is the teacher he is.

2. *Study of the Hispanic student culture in an urban community college.* The study begins with a general research question that requires a site that is a community college with Hispanic students. The researcher must gain entry to the chosen community college and establish rapport with the participants of the study. This might be a lengthy process, depending on the characteristics of the researcher (e.g., non-Hispanic vs. Hispanic; Spanish speaking vs. non-Spanish speaking). As is common in qualitative approaches, the researcher would simultaneously collect and interpret data to help focus the general research question initially posed. Observa-tions and interviews would be common methods of data gathering, per-haps supplemented by actual participation in group activities (depend-ing on the researcher's experience). Throughout data collection the researcher would identify recurrent themes, integrate them into existing

categories, and add new categories as new themes or topics arise. The success of the study relies heavily on the researcher's skills in analyzing and synthesizing the qualitative data into coherent and meaningful descriptions. The research report would include a holistic description of the culture, the common understandings and beliefs shared by participants, how these relate to life in the culture, and how the findings compare to literature already published about similar groups. In a sense, the researcher seeks to provide guidelines that would enable someone not in the culture to know how to think and behave in the culture.

GUIDELINES FOR CLASSIFICATION

We have seen that there are many types of educational research. We have noted important features of the different approaches to educational research. Determining which type is appropriate for a given study depends on the way the research topic is defined. The same general topic area can often be investigated by several different types of research. For example, suppose you wanted to do a study in the general area of anxiety and achievement. The following, quite different, studies might be conducted.

1. A survey of teachers to determine how and to what degree they believe anxiety affects achievement (descriptive)
2. A study to determine the relationship between scores on an anxiety scale and scores on an achievement measure (correlational)
3. A study to compare the achievement of a group of students classified as high-anxious and a group classified as low-anxious (causal–comparative)
4. A study to compare the achievement of two groups—one group taught in an anxiety-producing environment and one group taught in an anxiety-reducing environment (experimental)
5. A study of the research on the effect of anxiety on achievement from 1900 to 1990 (historical)
6. A study of SAT preparation by three students, with particular emphasis on their anxiety (qualitative)

Note that it is the question or problem to be addressed that determines which research approach is appropriate. Method should follow, not precede, the topic or question to be studied. Note also that the general topic will have to be narrowed in order to plan the conduct of the study.

When analyzing a study in order to determine the specific type of research represented, one strategy is to ask yourself a series of questions. First, does the study represent a qualitative or a quantitative approach? If the answer is quantitative, was the researcher attempting to establish a cause–effect relationship? If yes, the research is either causal–comparative or experimental. The next question is, Was the alleged cause, or independent variable, manipulated by the researcher? Did the researcher control who got what and what they got? If yes, the research is experimental; if no, the research is causal–comparative. If the researcher was not attempting to establish a cause–effect relationship, the next question should be, Was the researcher attempting to establish a relationship or use a relationship for prediction? If yes, the research is correlational. If no, the research is descriptive.

Clearly, the more information about a study one has, the easier it is to categorize it. If all one has is the title of the study, words like *survey, comparison, relationship, historical, descriptive, effect,* and *qualitative* can suggest the type of study. If one has a description of the research strategy used in the study, one can often classify based on features such as large or small samples, qualitative or quantitative data, statistical (correlational, descriptive, comparative) or nonstatistical (interpretive, participants' viewpoint) analysis. Classifying a study by type is the first step in both conducting and reviewing a study, since each type entails different specific procedures and analyses.

The following examples should further clarify the differences among the types:

1. *Teachers' attitudes toward unions.* Probably descriptive. The study is determining the current attitudes of teachers. Data are probably collected through use of a questionnaire or an interview.
2. *Effect of socioeconomic status (SES) on self-concept.* Probably causal–comparative. The effect of SES on self-concept is being investigated. The independent variable, socioeconomic status, cannot be manipulated.
3. *Large-group versus small-group instruction on achievement.* Probably experimental. The effect of group size on achievement is being investigated. The independent variable, group size, can be manipulated by the researcher.
4. *The personal and educational interactions in a group of teachers developing social studies standards for a high school curriculum.* Probably qualitative. Teachers' interactions during the development of the standards are examined over time. A qualitative study provides a detailed description of the participants' perspectives.

F I G U R E   1 . 1

Decision Diagram for Determining the Type of Research Represented by a Particular Quantitative Study

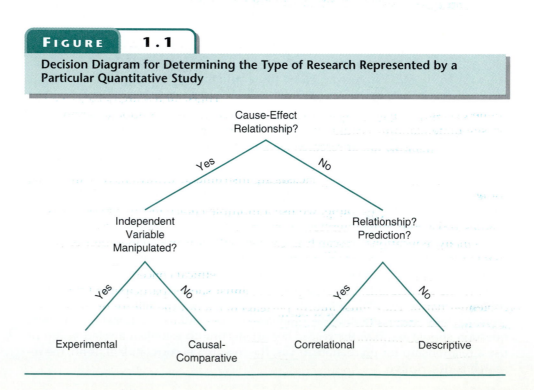

5. *The relationship of Graduate Record Examination (GRE) scores to graduate student performance.* Probably correlational. A relationship is involved, namely the relationship between GRE scores and success in graduate school (e.g., GPA).

6. *Participation of women in higher education, 1970–1990.* Probably historical. The study is investigating a trend established in the past.

7. *Characteristics of the drama–music clique in a suburban high school.* Probably qualitative. The topic is generally framed. The researcher would ferret out the beliefs, values, language, and activities of the chosen group. An account of the behavior of students in the drama–music clique would be described in terms of what they know and value that makes them successful in the culture.

Figure 1.1 can be used to determine types of quantitative research.

LIMITATIONS OF THE SCIENTIFIC AND DISCIPLINED INQUIRY APPROACH

The steps in the scientific and disciplined inquiry approach guide researchers in planning, conducting, and interpreting research studies. However, it is important to recognize some of the limitations of this approach. For example, it cannot provide answers to questions that seek to determine what *should* be done. Questions such as, "Should we adopt a new biology textbook or stay with the current one?" are not answerable by research studies. There is no way to solve questions like, "Should we legalize euthanasia?" by collecting data, because issues of philosophy, values, and ethics—in addition to data—go into the making of those decisions. Simply put, *should* questions are not researchable.

No research study can capture the full richness of the individuals and sites that they study. Although some research approaches lead to deeper understanding of the research context than others, no approach provides full comprehension of a site and its inhabitants. No matter how many variables one studies or how long one is immersed in a research context, there always will be other variables and aspects of context that were not examined. Thus, all research gives us a simplified version of reality; an abstraction from the whole. Additional variables and in-site understandings could always be added to a research study.

There are limits to our research technologies. Our data collection instruments and the available theories are primitive in comparison to the instruments and theories of, say, medicine. Our measuring instruments always have some degree of error. The variables that we study are often proxies for the real behavior we seek to examine. For example, we use a multiple-choice test to assess a person's values and a 20-minute interview to decide whether to hire a teacher.

Finally, educational research is carried out with the cooperation of participants who agree to provide researchers with data. Because researchers deal with human beings, they must consider a number of ethical concerns and responsibilities to the participants. For example, they must shelter participants from real or potential harm. They must inform participants about the nature of the planned research and address the expectations of the participants.

All of these limitations will be addressed in later sections of this book. For now, bear in mind both the advantages and limitations of adopting the scientific and disciplined inquiry approach as your approach to educational research.

Summary / Chapter 1

1. Knowledge of educational research methods is important because educators must be able to access, understand, and evaluate the findings of research and the claims of researchers.

Educational Research: Scientific and Disciplined Inquiry

2. Educational research is the application of the scientific and disciplined inquiry approach to the study of educational problems.
3. The primary goal of educational research is to explain or help understand educational issues, questions, and processes. Secondary goals of educational research are to help others understand, predict future outcomes, improve future research and practice, and raise new questions to research.
4. Rarely does any single study produce definitive answers to research questions. Rather, understandings accumulated from many studies are the basis for progress and understanding.
5. Compared to other methods of knowing, such as tradition, expert advice, personal experience, and inductive or deductive logic, a scientific and disciplined inquiry approach provides the most unbiased and verifiable understandings.
6. This approach is made up of many steps. The four most crucial steps are:
   1. Recognize and identify a question or problem to be studied;
   2. Describe and execute procedures to collect information about the questions or problem being studied;
   3. Analyze the collected information;
   4. State results or implications based on analysis of the information.
7. The scientific and disciplined inquiry approach encompasses many types of research topics, procedures to examine them, methods for analyzing data, and formats for reporting conclusions, implications, and findings.

Basic and Applied Research

8. Basic research is conducted to develop or refine theory, not to solve immediate practical problems. Applied research is conducted to find solutions to current practical problems.
9. Most educational research would be classified at the applied end of the basic–applied research continuum.

EVALUATION RESEARCH

10. The purpose of evaluation research is to aid decision making about educational programs and practices.

Quantitative and Qualitative Research

11. In general, the purpose of quantitative research is to generalize about or control phenomena, while qualitative research is to provide in-depth descriptions of unique settings and people.
12. Since the early 1920s, quantitative research methods have been the primary way educational researchers have sought understanding.
13. Because quantitative and qualitative researchers differ in their view of the world, they tend to utilize different methods to seek knowledge.
14. Quantitative and qualitative approaches should be thought of as complementary methods that, when taken together, provide broader options for investigating a wide range of important educational topics than either one alone.
15. Quantitative methods involve the collection and analysis of numerical data obtained from tests, questionnaires, checklists, and surveys.
16. Key features of quantitative research include defining the problem or question to be studied and hypotheses predicting the results of the research before the study begins; controlling contextual factors that might influence the results of the study; collecting data from

samples of participants; and using numerical, statistical approaches to analyze the collected data.

17. An important assumption that underlies the quantitative approach is that the world in which we live and carry out our research is relatively stable, uniform, and coherent; therefore, it can be measured, understood, and classified.

18. In recent years qualitative research methods have become popular and have attracted many advocates.

19. Qualitative methods involve the collection and analysis of primarily nonnumerical data obtained from observation, interviews, tape recordings, documents, and the like.

20. Key features of qualitative research include defining the problem or question to be studied, but not necessarily at the start of the study; taking into account contextual factors in the settings the research participants inhabit; collecting data from a small number of purposely selected participants; and using nonnumerical, interpretive approaches to provide narrative descriptions of the participants and their contexts.

21. An important belief that underlies qualitative research is that the world is neither stable, coherent, nor uniform, and therefore, "truth" as sought by quantitative researchers cannot be obtained because perspectives and understandings differ from group to group.

Descriptive Research

22. Quantitative research approaches are intended to describe current conditions, investigate relationships, and study cause–effect phenomena.

23. Descriptive research, also called survey research, collects numerical data to answer questions about the current status of the subject of study. Most descriptive studies obtain information about the preferences, attitudes, practices, concerns, or interests of some group. Data are collected by self-administered instruments or telephone polls.

24. An important and difficult aspect of descriptive research is that of constructing clear and consistent descriptive instruments.

25. A major problem complicating descriptive research is the failure of participants to return questionnaires or cooperate in telephone interviews.

Correlational Research

26. Correlational research examines the degree of relationship that exists between two or more variables. A correlation is a quantitative measure of the degree of correspondence between two or more variables (e.g., SAT scores and freshman college grades).

27. The degree of relationship is measured by a correlation coefficient, with a coefficient of ±1.00 indicating two variables are highly related and a coefficient of .00 indicating no relationship between the variables.

28. If two variables are highly related, it does not mean that one is the cause of the other; there may be a third factor that "causes" both the related variables.

Causal–Comparative Research

29. Causal–comparative research seeks to investigate cause and effect relations between two or more different programs, methods, or groups. The activity thought to make a difference (the program, method, or group) is called the *causal* factor, treatment, or independent variable. The *effect* is called the dependent variable.

30. In most causal–comparative research studies the researcher does not have control over the causal factor because it already has occurred or cannot be manipulated. This makes cause–effect conclusions tenuous and tentative.

31. Causal–comparative research is useful in those circumstances when it is impossible or unethical to manipulate the causal factor.

Experimental Research

32. Like causal–comparative research, experimental research seeks to investigate cause–effect relationships.

33. The experimental researcher controls the selection of participants by choosing them from a single pool and assigning them at random to different causal treatments. The

researcher also controls contextual variables that might interfere with the study.

34. Because it randomly selects and assigns participants into different treatments, experimental research permits true cause–effect statements to be made.

Historical Research Methods

35. Historical research is a form of qualitative research that involves interpreting past events. Most histories focus on individuals, important social issues, links between the old and new, and reinterpretations of prior historical work.

36. Historians work with data that already are available in a variety of forms.

37. Primary sources of data are provided by first-person eyewitnesses or authors, while non-first-person accounts are called secondary sources. Historians prefer to work with primary sources.

38. Historians use external criticism to assess the authenticity of their data and use internal criticism to assess the truthfulness of their data.

Qualitative Research Methods

39. Qualitative approaches include a number of specific methods such as ethnology, ethnomethodology, case study phenomenology, and symbolic interaction. The focus of these methods is on deep description of aspects of people's everyday perspectives and context.

40. Qualitative approaches provide field-focused, interpretive, detailed descriptions and interpretations of participants and their settings. Long-term immersion into the research setting is also a common feature of qualitative approaches because of the belief that participants and contexts are not independent.

41. Common methods of data collection include observation, interviewing, tape and video recording, examining artifacts, and participant observation (the researcher becomes part of the group being studied).

42. Data analysis is based on categorizing and interpreting the observations, conversations with participants, documents, tape recordings, and interviews collected to provide a description and explanation of the participants and their experiences.

43. The qualitative researcher writes from the perspective of the participants, not from the researcher's own perspective.

Guidelines for Classification

44. The type of research method needed for a given study depends on the problem to be studied. The same general problem can be investigated using many types of research. Knowing the type of research applied helps one identify the important aspects to examine in evaluating the study.

45. In classifying research, the more information available about the nature and procedures of a study, the easier it is to classify it.

46. A structured way to classify studies is to first determine whether it is a quantitative or qualitative study. If the former, try to identify the purpose of the study to determine whether it is descriptive, correlational, causal–comparative, or experimental. If it is qualitative, determine whether it is historical or qualitative. Look for key words in the title of the study: survey, description, relationship, historical, culture, and the like.

Limitations of the Scientific and Disciplined Inquiry Approach

47. Four factors put limitations on the use of a scientific and disciplined inquiry approach: inability to answer "should" questions, inability to capture the full richness of the research site and participants' complexity; limitations of measuring instruments; and need to address participants' ethical needs and responsibilities.

Task 1 *Performance Criteria* ■

On the following pages a published research report is reprinted. Following the report, spaces are provided for listing the components required by Task 1-A. Task 1-B requires classifying research topics according to the specific type of research they represent. If your responses differ greatly from the Suggested Responses in Appendix D, study the article again until you see why you were in error. Additional examples for these and subsequent tasks are included in the Student Guide that accompanies this text.

TASK 1-A

Read the article on pages 28–31. Then, on page 32, state the:

1. Topic studied
2. Procedures used to gather data
3. Method of data analysis
4. Major conclusion

One sentence should be sufficient to describe the topic. Six sentences or less will adequately describe the major procedures of most studies. Briefly describe the participants, instrument(s), and major steps. As with the topic, one or two sentences will usually be sufficient to state the major analysis. You are expected only to identify the analysis, not explain it. The major conclusion that you identify and state (one or two sentences should be sufficient) should directly relate to the original topic. Statements like "more research is needed in this area" do not represent major conclusions.

TASK 1-B

Six topic statements follow these instructions. Read each statement and decide whether it represents a descriptive, correlational, causal–comparative, experimental, historical, or qualitative research approach. State the research approach for each topic statement and indicate why you selected that approach. Your reasons should be related to characteristics that are unique to the type of research you have selected.

1. This study examines changes in the public schools' legal responsibilities regarding disabled students during the past 50 years.
2. This study used observation and interviewing to gather information about a 1-year trial of a model alternate-to-suspension program.
3. This study administered a questionnaire to determine how social studies teachers felt about teaching world history to fifth graders.
4. This study was conducted to determine whether the Acme Interest Test provided similar results to the Acne Interest Test.
5. This study compared the achievement in reading of fifth graders from single-parent families and those from two-parent families.
6. This study divided fifth-grade students in a school into two groups at random and compared the results of two methods of conflict resolution on students' aggressive behavior.

Motivational Effects on Test Scores of Elementary Students

STEVEN M. BROWN
Northeastern Illinois University

HERBERT J. WALBERG
University of Illinois at Chicago

ABSTRACT   A total of 406 heterogeneously grouped students in Grades 3, 4, 6, 7, and 8 in three K through 8 Chicago public schools were assigned randomly to two conditions, ordinary standardized-test instructions (control) and special instructions, to do as well as possible for themselves, their parents, and their teachers (experimental). On average, students given special instructions did significantly better ($p < .01$) than the control students did on the criterion measure, the mathematics section of the commonly used Iowa Test of Basic Skills. The three schools differed significantly in achievement ($p < .05$), but girls and boys and grade levels did not differ measurably. The motivational effect was constant across grade levels and boys and girls, but differed significantly ($p < .05$) across schools. The average effect was moderately large, .303 standard deviations, which implies that the special instructions raise the typical student's scores from the 50th to the 62nd percentile.

Parents, educators, business people, politicians, and the general public are greatly concerned about U.S. students' poor performance on international comparisons of achievement. Policy makers are planning additional international, state, district, and school comparisons to measure progress in solving the national crisis. Some members of those same groups have also grown concerned about the effects of students' high or low motivational states on how well they score on tests.

One commonly expressed apprehension is that some students worry unduly about tests and suffer debilitating anxiety (Hill, 1980). Another concern is that too much testing causes students to care little about how well they do, especially on standardized tests that have no bearing on their grades. Either case might lead to poorer scores than students would attain under ideal motivational states; such effects might explain, in part, the poor performance of U.S. students relative to those in other countries or in relation to what may be required for college and vocational success.

Experts and practicing educators have expressed a variety of conflicting opinions about motivational effects on learning and test scores (Association for Supervision and Curriculum Development, 1991, p. 7). Given the importance of testing policies, there is surprisingly little research on the topic. The purpose of the present study is to determine the effect of experimentally manipulated motivational conditions on elementary students' mathematical scores.

As conceived in this study, the term *motivation* refers to the commonsense meaning of the term, that is, students' propensity to engage in full, serious, and sustained effort on academic tests. As it has been measured in many previous studies, motivation refers to students' reported efforts to succeed or to excel on academic tasks. It is often associated with self-concept or self-regard in a successful student or test taker. A quantitative synthesis of the correlational studies of motivation and school learning showed that nearly all correlations were positive and averaged about .30 (Uguroglu & Walberg, 1979).

Previous Research

The National Assessment Governing Board (NAGB, 1990) recently characterized the National Assessment of Educational Progress (NAEP) as follows:

> . . . as a survey exam which by law cannot be reported for individual students and schools. NAEP may not be taken seriously enough by students to enlist their best efforts. Because it is given with no incentives for good performance and no opportunity for prior study, NAEP may understate achievement (NAGB, p. 17).

To investigate such questions, NAEP is adding items to ask students how hard they tried in responding to future achievement tests.

Motivation questions can be raised about nearly all standardized commercial tests, as well as state-constructed achievement tests. The content of those tests is often unrelated to specific topics that students have been recently studying; and their performance on such tests ordinarily does not affect their grades, college, or job prospects. Many students know they will not see how well they have done.

Address correspondence to Steven M. Brown, 924 South Austin, Apt. 2, Oak Park, IL 60304.

Some students admit deficient motivation, but surveys show reasonably favorable attitudes toward tests by most students. Paris, Lawton, and Turner (1991), for example, surveyed 250 students in Grades 4, 7, and 10 about the Michigan Educational Assessment Program. They found that most students reported that they tried hard, thought they did well, felt the test was not difficult or confusing, and saw little or no cheating. However, Karmos and Karmos's (1984) survey of 360 sixth- through ninth-grade student attitudes toward tests showed that 47% thought they were a waste of time, 22% saw no good reason to try to do well, and 21% did not try very hard.

Kellaghan, Madaus, and Arisian (1982) found various small fractions of a sixth-grade Irish sample disaffected by standardized tests, even though they are uncommon in Ireland. When asked about their experience with standardized tests, 29% reported feeling nervous, 19%, unconfident; 16%, bored; and 15% uninterested. Twenty-nine percent reported that they did not care whether they took the tests, and 16% said they did not enjoy the experience.

Paris, Lawton, and Turner (1991) speculated that standardized tests may lead both bright and dull students to do poorly: Bright students may feel heightened parental, peer, or self-imposed expectations to do well on tests, which makes them anxious. Slower, disadvantaged students may do poorly, then rationalize that school and tests are unimportant and, consequently, expend less effort preparing for and completing tests. Either case might lead to a self-reinforcing spiral of decelerating achievement.

Surveys, however, cannot establish causality. Poor motivation may cause poor achievement, or vice versa, or both may be caused by other factors such as deficiencies in ability, parental support of academic work, or teaching. To show an independent effect of motivation on achievement requires an experiment, that is, a randomized assignment of students to conditions of eliciting different degrees of motivation. Such was the purpose of our study.

Method

Sample

The subjects for the study included students from three K through 8 public schools in Chicago. The student populations of the schools are generally lower-middle, working class, mostly Hispanic and African-American. Two normal heterogeneous classes within the schools were sampled from Grades 3, 4, 6, 7, and 8; because of exigencies, we did not sample Grade 5 classes.

Instrument

We chose Form 7 of the Mathematics Concepts subtest of the Iowa Basic Skills (ITBS) 1978 edition, Levels 9–14, because it is a commonly used, highly reliable test. An earlier-than-contemporary edition was used so it would not interfere with current testing programs. In a review of the 1978 ITBS, Nitko (1985) judged that the reliability of its subtests is generally higher than .85 and that it contains content generally representative of school curriculum in Grades 3 though 9. "The ITBS," he concluded, "is an excellent basic skills battery measuring global skills that are likely to be highly related to the long-term goals of elementary schools" (p. 723).

Procedure

Pairs of classes at each grade level from each school were randomly chosen to participate. Classes were selected for experimental and control conditions by a flip of a coin.

The first author (Brown) met with all participating teachers in each school to explain the instructions from the ITBS test manual (see Appendix A). Then, the experimental teachers were retained for the following further instructions:

> We are conducting a research study to determine the effects of telling students that the test they are going to take is very important. It is extremely important that you read the brief script I have for you today EXACTLY as it is written to your students.

The following script was provided:

> It is really important that you do as WELL as you can on this test. The test score you receive will let others see just how well I am doing in teaching you math this year.
> Your scores will be compared to students in other grades here at this school, as well as to those in other schools in Chicago.
> That is why it is extremely important to do the VERY BEST that you can. Do it for YOURSELF, YOUR PARENTS, and ME.
> (Now read the instructions for the test.)

Following the administration of the test, teachers and the first author asked students for their reactions to the script that was read to them.

Analysis

An analysis of variance was run to test the effects of the experimental and normal conditions; the differences among the three schools and five grades; between boys and girls; and the interactions among the factors.

Results

The analysis of variance showed a highly significant effect of experimental condition ($F = 10.59$, $p < .01$), a significant effect of school ($F = 3.35$, $p < .05$), and an interaction between condition and school ($F = 5.01$, $p < .05$). No other effects, including grade level, were significant. The means and standard deviations of selected factors are shown in Table 1.

Table 1.—Normal Curve Equivalent Means and Standard Deviations

Grade	Condition	M	SD
3	Control	32.77	19.57
	Experimental	42.55*	16.59
4	Control	33.07	13.93
	Experimental	39.42*	13.12
6	Control	40.84	17.77
	Experimental	39.64	14.66
7	Control	43.21	16.07
	Experimental	41.21	16.48
8	Control	31.12	14.06
	Experimental	44.66**	15.94

*$p < .01$; **$p < .001$.

The mean normal curve equivalent test score of the 214 students in the experimental group was 41.37 ($SD = 15.41$), and the mean of the control group was 36.25 ($SD = 16.89$). The motivational effect is moderately large, .303 standard deviations, which implies that the special instructions raised the typical student's scores from the 50th to the 62nd percentile. The special instructions are comparable to the effects of better (though not the best) instructional practices over conventional classroom instruction (Walberg, 1986). If American students' average achievement in mathematics and science could be raised that much, it would be more comparable to that of students in other economically advanced countries.

The motivational effect was the same for boys and girls and constant across grade levels, but it differed among schools. Figure 1 shows a very large effect at School A, a large effect at School C, and the control group somewhat higher than the experimental group at School B.

Only 62 students (15% of the total sample) were tested at School B, which may account for the lack of effect in this school. At any rate, although the overall effect is moderately large and constant across grade levels and for boys and girls, the size of the effect varies from school to school. Such differences may depend on test-taking attitudes of teachers and students in the schools, motivational and cultural differences in the student populations, variations in conditions of administration, and other factors.

Several comments made by students and teachers during debriefing sessions illuminate the statistical findings. Student Comments 1, 2, and 3 illustrate students' motivation to do well to please their parents and teachers. Teacher Comments 1 and 2 also confirm the reasons for the effect. The last student and teacher comment, however, illustrate motivational states and conditions that diminish or vitiate the effect. When students are unthoughtful or when teachers keep constant pressures on for testing, special instructions may have little effect.

Conclusion

The results show that motivation can make a substantial difference in test scores. Students asked to try especially hard did considerably better than those who were given the usual standardized test instructions. The special conditions raised the typical student's score .303 standard deviation units, corresponding to a 12 percentile-point gain from the 50th to the 62nd percentile. Although the effect was the same for boys and girls and for students in different grade levels, it varied in magnitude among the three schools.

The results suggest that standardized commercial and state-constructed tests that have no bearing on students' grades may be underestimating U.S. students' real knowledge, understanding, skills, and other aspects of achievement. To the extent that motivation varies from school to school, moreover, achievement levels of some schools are considerably more underestimated than in others. Such motivational differences would tend to diminish the validity of comparisons of schools and districts.

We would be heartened to conclude that U.S. students' poor performance on achievement relative to students in other countries is attributable to the test-motivation effect. That conclusion is overly optimistic, however, because the effect may also operate to a greater or lesser extent in other countries. Further research is obviously in order.

The motivation effect might be reduced in several ways. Highly motivating instructions could be given to all students. The content of school lessons and standardized tests could be brought into closer correspondence, making the tests more plausible to students, and perhaps justifying their use in grading. Some students, moreover, may be unmotivated because they never see the results. Providing timely, specific, and useful feedback to stu-

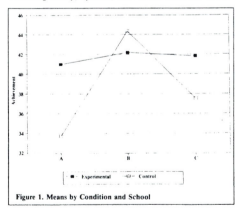

Figure 1. Means by Condition and School

dents, parents, and teachers on how well they have done might lead students to try harder.

APPENDIX A

Directions for Administering the Mathematics Concepts Subtest of the Iowa Test of Basic Skills (1979)

Now we are ready for the first mathematics test. Open your test booklets to page 73. (Pause) Find the section of your answer sheet for Test M-1: Mathematics Concepts. (Pause) Read the directions on page 73 silently while I read them aloud.

This is a test of how well you understand the number system and the terms and operations used in mathematics. Four answers are given for each exercise, but only one of the answers is right. You are to choose the one answer that you think is better than the others. Then, on the answer sheet, find the row of the answer numbered the same as the exercise. Fill in the answer space for the best answer.

Do not make any marks on the test booklet. Use your scratch paper for figuring. You will have 25 minutes for this test. If you finish early, recheck your work. Don't look at the other tests in the booklet. If you have questions, raise your hand, and I will help you after the others have begun. Now find your place to begin. (Pause)

Does everyone have the correct place? (Pause) Ready, BEGIN.

APPENDIX B

Selected Anecdotal Comments

Students

1. Third-Grade Girl: My teacher always tells us to get good scores on tests. I wanted to make her happy and my parents happy.

2. Fourth-Grade Boy: I think I did well. My teacher works hard with us. I also want my school to be the best.

3. Eighth-Grade Boy: I wanted to do really well for my teacher. She does a great job, and I didn't want to let her down.

4. Seventh-Grade Girl: I just took the test, and really didn't think much about the instructions she gave.

Teachers

1. I don't know what the results will show but my gut feeling is that students in the experimental groups will do better. I think it's probably because of motivational reasons.

2. The script gives me a feeling of *family*. I think if we told students just how much we want them to do well, and that it will not only benefit themselves but the whole school, they will probably do better.

3. I think all the students (control and experimental) will probably do equally well, because we always stress how important the tests are.

REFERENCES

Association for Supervision and Curriculum Development (1991). *Update, 33*(1), 1-8.

Hill, K. T. (1980). Motivation, evaluation, and testing policy. In L. J. Fyans, Jr. (Ed.), *Achievement motivation: Recent trends in theory and research*. New York, NY: Plenum Press.

Iowa Test of Basic Skills normal curve equivalent norms (1978). Boston, MA: Houghton Mifflin.

Karmos, A. H., & Karmos, J. S. (1984, July). Attitudes toward standardized achievement tests and their relation to achievement test performance. *Measurement and Evaluation in Counseling and Development, 12*, 56–66.

Kelleghan, T., Madaus, G. F., & Arisian, P. M. (1982). *The effects of standardized testing*. Boston, MA: Kluwer-Nijhoff.

National Assessment Governing Board (1991). Issues for the 1994–1996 NAEP. Washington, DC: Author.

Nitco, A. J. (1985). Review of the Iowa Test of Basic Skills. In James V. Mitchell (Ed.), *The ninth mental measurements yearbook*. Lincoln, NE: Buros Institute.

Paris, S. G., Lawton, T. A., & Turner, J. C. (1991). Reforming achievement testing to promote students' learning. In C. Collins & Mangieri (Eds.), *Learning in and out of school*. Hillsdale, NJ: Lawrence Erlbaum Associates.

Uguroglu, M. E., & Walberg, H. J. (1979). Motivation and achievement: A quantitative synthesis. *American Educational Research Journal, 16*, 375-390.

Walberg, H. J. (1986). Synthesis of research on teaching. In M. C. Wittrock (Ed.), *Handbook of research on teaching*. New York, NY: Macmillan.

MOTIVATIONAL EFFECTS ON TEST SCORES OF ELEMENTARY STUDENTS

SELF-TEST FOR TASK 1-A

The Topic

_____

_____

_____

_____

_____

The Procedures

_____

_____

_____

_____

_____

_____

_____

_____

The Method of Analysis

_____

_____

_____

_____

The Major Conclusion(s)

_____

_____

_____

_____

_____

_____

_____

SELF-TEST FOR TASK 1-B

Type

_____

Reasons

_____

_____

_____

_____

_____

_____

PART TWO

Research Problems

Selection and definition of a research topic is the first stage in applying the scientific and disciplined inquiry method. The research topic (also called the research question, problem, or purpose) focuses and provides structure for the remaining steps in the scientific and disciplined inquiry method; it is the thread that binds everything else together. The basic function of the research topic is to focus the domain of the study to a defined, manageable size. One of the common difficulties that arises among researchers seeking to develop a topic is the selection of one that is so broad and complex that the researcher is unable to implement and complete it. Usually the first topic identified is too broad to be manageable for study, so the researcher must engage in a process of refinement to narrow its scope. Selection and definition of a topic is a very important component of the research process and entails considerable time and thought. The statement of the topic, a review of literature related to the topic, and, in quantitative studies, the statement of hypotheses make up the introduction section of both the research plans and the report of the completed research.

The research topic that you ultimately select is the topic you will work with in succeeding stages of your study. Therefore, it is important that you select a problem that is relevant to your area of study and of particular interest to you. Given that you will be living with your study for a long time, it is especially important that you select a topic that will hold your interest through its completion.

The goal of Part Two is for you to acquire the ability to identify and define a meaningful topic, conduct an adequate review of related literature, and state the testable hypothesis. After you have read Part Two, you should be able to perform the following task.

TASK 2

Write an introduction for a research plan. This will include a statement of the specific topic to be investigated in the study, a statement concerning the significance of the problem, a brief review of related literature, and, if your topic involves quantitative methods, a testable hypothesis regarding the outcome of your study. Include definitions of terms where appropriate (see Performance Criteria, p. 82).

"Some graduate students spend many anxiety-ridden days and sleepless nights worrying about where they are going to 'find' the problem they need for their thesis or dissertation (p. 37)."

Selection and Definition of a Problem

■ OBJECTIVES

After reading chapter 2, you should be able to:

1. Make a list of at least three educational topics for which you would be interested in conducting a research study.
2. Select one of the topics and identify 10 to 15 complete references that directly relate to the selected problem. The references should include multiple sources (e.g., books, periodicals, Internet reports, etc.).
3. Read and abstract the references you have listed.
4. Formulate a testable hypothesis for your problem.

Note: These objectives will form the basis for Task 2.

IDENTIFYING A TOPIC TO RESEARCH

For most of our school careers we are taught to solve problems of various kinds. Ask most people to list the 10 most important outcomes of education, and somewhere on the list will invariably be problem solving. Now, after many years of emphasis on solving problems, you face a research task that asks you not to *solve* but to *find* a problem or topic to study. If you are like most people, you have had little experience in doing this. For this reason, beginning researchers often view the selection of a research topic as the most difficult step in the whole research process. Some graduate students spend many anxiety-ridden days and sleepless nights worrying about where they are going to find the problem they need for their thesis or dissertation.

Where do research topics or problems come from? Where should one look to ferret out topics to study? Three major sources of research topics are theories, personal experiences, and replications. One of the most meaningful sources of research topics is derived from theory. A *theory* is an organized body of concepts, generalizations, and principles that can be subjected to investigation. There are many educationally relevant theories from which problems can be drawn, such as theories of learning and behavior. For example, Piaget posited a theory of cognitive development that had four stages of development: sensorimotor stage (birth to age 2), preoperational stage (ages 2 to 7), concrete operational stage (ages 7 to 11), and formal operational stage (ages 11 to adulthood). At each level Piaget indicated what children could or could not do. Examining whether aspects of Piaget's theory operate as suggested could be the basis for many possible topics. For example, one could study whether children who receive a great deal of attention and verbal interaction reach the concrete operational stage earlier than students who received little attention and verbal interaction. If the high attention/verbal group did reach the concrete operational stage before the low attention/verbal group, it would suggest that entry into the stage varied not just on age, but also on the experiences of students. Think of two other theories that are popular in education and identify a few topics that could be investigated to examine features of the theories. Topics focused on aspects of a theory are not only conceptually rich, they also provide information that confirms or disconfirms some aspect of the theory. They also suggest additional studies that need to be done to further test the theory.

A second common way to identify research topics is to examine some of the questions we commonly ask ourselves. It is hard to imagine an educator who has never had a hunch concerning a better way to do something (e.g., a way to increase learning or improve student behavior) or asked questions about a program or materials whose effectiveness was untested (for example, questioning why a writing program was successful or science materials were not). We observe schools, teachers, programs, and news articles about schooling, and we ask ourselves questions that are usually stated in the following ways: "Why does that happen?" "What causes that?" "What would happen if . . . ?" and "How would a different group respond to this?" Normally we think briefly about such questions and get back to our everyday business. But such questions are probably the most common source of research topics. How do teachers structure their classroom cultures in the first few days of school? Would achievement go up if students were given quizzes each day on the prior day's instruction? Would I get the same results with high- and low-achieving students if I emphasized peer review in my instruction? What would happen to teacher performance if we evaluated teachers three times a year at unannounced times instead of at a single, preannounced time? Serendipity, also known as happenstance or being in the right place at the right time, is all around us and is often the source of research topics. Sensitivity to what is happening around us is an important inquiry skill to cultivate.

A veritable gold mine of research topics arises out of the questions we ask ourselves every day about education. Note, first, that this approach to finding research topics is appropriate for both qualitative (How do teachers structure their classroom culture?) and quantitative (Would achievement go up with more frequent use of quizzes?) topics. Note, also, that most of the initial topics need to be refined and clarified before they become suitable research topics.

A final source of research topics is replications. As the name suggests, *replication* means "doing it again." We noted in chapter 1 that no single study, regardless of its focus or format, provides the certainty and generalizability needed to assume that similar results will occur in all or most other situations. We also noted that progress through research usually comes from accumulated understandings and explanations. Replication is a means used to provide such accumulated information.

In most cases, a replication is not carried out identically with the original study. Rather, some feature or features of the original study are altered in an attempt to "stretch" the findings of the original study. Thus, the researcher might select a different sample of participants for the replication in the hope of determining whether the results obtained are the same as those of the original study. Or, the replication might examine a different kind of community, a different kind of student, a different classroom climate, a different questionnaire, or a different method of data analysis. There are many interesting and useful ways to replicate studies in the many domains of education.

E-Mail

When you think of e-mail, you probably think of a fast, convenient means of keeping up with friends, family, and co-workers, both far and near. E-mail serves other important functions, however. Researchers frequently use e-mail to solicit advice and feedback and conduct dialogue with peers and experts in their fields. The most common way to do so is by subscribing to a listserve.

A listserve is an electronic mailing list designed by an organization or special interest group to facilitate communication among its members. Through this list, you can expect to receive announcements and bulletins related to your area of interest. In addition, you can post comments or questions on the listserve. Your messages will be read by members of the listserve, who have the option of responding to you personally or to the mailing list as a whole.

A listserve is a good resource to consult when you are devising a research question. You can ask listserve members what they think of a particular topic, if they know of other research pertaining to your topic, or for links (electronic or otherwise) to resources of interest. You can also bounce ideas off of other listserve members at each stage of the research process. You can even ask for volunteers to read your work in progress!

To subscribe to a listserve, you generally are required to send a short e-mail message to the listserve. Once subscribed, you will receive detailed information about how to post messages on the listserve, how to unsubscribe, etc. Examples of useful education listserves include:

American Education Research Association List
   (AERA@ASUVM.INRE.ASU.EDU)

AERA-K Division K: Teaching and Teacher Education listserve
   (AERA-K@ASUVM.INRE.ASU.EDU)

Educational Administration Discussion List
   (EDAD-L@WVNVM.WVNET.EDU)

Educational Resources on the Internet
   (EDRES-L@LISTSERV.UNB.CA)

A useful Web site to consult in your search for appropriate listserves is http://www.lsoft.com/lists/listref.html. This site, which is sponsored by L-Soft International, contains a catalogue of listserve lists. At this site, you can browse over 20,000 public listserve lists on the Internet, search for mailing lists of interest, and get information about listserve host sites. A recent search for education listserves yielded 555 listserve mailing lists.

One commonly cited source of research topics is the library. Many students are encouraged to immerse themselves in the library and read voraciously in their area of study until a research topic emerges. Although some research topics do emerge from immersion in the library, they are considerably fewer than those emerging from theory, personal experience, and replications. Trying to identify a topic amid the enormous possibilities in a library is akin to looking for a needle in a haystack; sometimes we find it, but not very often. Clearly libraries are essential sources of information in the research process. However, the library is most useful after a topic has been identified. Then library resources can help the researcher gather information to place the topic in perspective, find what has already been done on the topic, and suggest methods for carrying out examination of a topic.

The first step in selecting a topic is to identify a general topic or problem that is related to your area of expertise and is also of particular interest to you. Examples of general topics might be: decision making in the schools, manipulatives for elementary mathematics, the effects of standardized testing, paraprofessionals in the elementary school, busing schoolchildren, and whole language reading. Note that these topic areas are very broad and inclusive, containing many, many more specific research topics. Such general areas have to be narrowed to a more focused and manageable research topic or problem. Remember, you will be spending a great deal of time reading about, planning, and carrying out your ultimate research topic. Choosing a topic that is of interest to you will help maintain your focus during the months of conducting and writing your study.

NARROWING THE TOPIC

For most quantitative researchers and some qualitative researchers, the next step is to narrow down the general topic area to a more specific, researchable topic. A topic that is too broad often leads to grief. First, a broad topic enlarges the scope of the review of related literature that one must inevitably conduct, likely resulting in many extra hours being spent in the library. Second, broad topics complicate the organization of the review itself. Finally, and more importantly, a topic that is too broad tends to result in a study that is too general, difficult to carry out, and difficult to interpret. Conversely, a well-defined manageable problem results in a well-defined, manageable study.

A quantitative research topic typically requires that the researcher spell out the topic to be studied, hypotheses related to the topic, strategies for conducting the research study, and methods of analyzing the collected data prior to initiating the study. Thus, for quantitative research, narrowing the general topic area into a more specific and manageable research topic is essential. Without a specific and manageable research topic, hypotheses, instruments, strategies, and analyses cannot be specified. Conversely, for qualitative research, it is appropriate to enter the research setting with only a general topic area in mind. Based on what is observed in the setting and the nature of the information that can be obtained (remember, qualitative research involves much more personal interaction with the participants than does quantitative research), the researcher will formulate a narrowed research topic after immersion in the selected setting. Eventually the qualitative researcher will narrow the research topic.

One way to narrow your topic is to talk to your advisors and to specialists in your area about specific suggestions for study. Another way is to read sources that provide overviews or summaries of the current status of research in your area. Search through handbooks that contain many chapters focused on research in a particular area (e.g., *Handbook of Research on Curriculum*; *Handbook of Research on Teaching*). You could also check the *Encyclopedia of Educational Research* or journals such as the *Review of Educational Research,* which provide reviews of research in many topic areas. These sources often identify "next-step" studies that need to be conducted. The suggested next step might involve a logical extension of another study or a replication of the study in a different setting. For example, a study investigating the effectiveness of microcomputer-assisted instruction in elementary arithmetic might suggest the need for similar studies in other curriculum areas. Bear in mind that at this stage in the research process you seek general research overviews that describe the nature of research in an area and that can suggest more specific topics in your chosen area.

In narrowing the problem area you should select an aspect of the general topic area that is related to your area of expertise. For example, the general problem area "the use of reviews to increase retention" could generate many specific problems, such as "the comparative effectiveness of immediate versus delayed review on the retention of geometric concepts" and "the effect of review games on the retention of vocabulary words by second graders." In your efforts to sufficiently delineate a problem, however, be careful not to get carried away; a problem that is too narrow is just as bad as a problem that is too broad. A study such as "the effectiveness of pre-class reminders in reducing instances of pencil sharpening during class time" would probably contribute little, if anything, to education knowledge.

Selecting a good problem is well worth the time and effort. As mentioned previously, there is no shortage of significant problems that need to be researched; there is really no excuse for selecting a trite problem. Besides, it is generally to your advantage to select a worthwhile problem; you will certainly get a great deal more out of it professionally and academically. If the subsequent study is well conducted and reported, not only will you earn a good grade and make a contribution to knowledge, but you might find your work published in a professional journal. The potential personal benefits to be derived from publication include increased professional status and job opportunities, not to mention tremendous self-satisfaction.

CHARACTERISTICS OF GOOD TOPICS

By definition, a research topic involves an issue in need of investigation. It follows that a fundamental characteristic of any research topic is that it is *researchable.* A researchable topic is one that can be investigated through the collection and analysis of data. Problems dealing with philosophical or ethical issues are not researchable. Research can assess how people "feel" about such issues but research cannot resolve them. Whether there is reward and punishment in the hereafter may be an important question to many people, but it is not researchable; there is no way to resolve it through the collection and analysis of data. Similarly, in education there are a number of issues that make great topics for debates (e.g., "Should prayer be allowed in the schools?" "Should students be grouped homogeneously or heterogeneously?" "Should students be held back in grade if they fail to meet defined standards of achievement?") but they are not researchable problems. In general, topics or questions that contain the word *should* cannot be answered by research of any kind, because they ultimately are a matter of opinion.

Note, however, that one could carry out research studies that examine the effects on teachers and students of school prayer, grouping practices, or being held back in grade. Such studies can tell us about the varied consequences of these practices, but the decision of what should be done in a school or classroom involves issues that go beyond the results of any research study. Issues of cost, educational philosophy, teacher and parental beliefs about the nature of schooling, and views about how students best learn are some of the other factors that would enter into the debate over what *should* be done. Research findings can inform decision making, but they cannot and should not be the sole or main determinant of what should or should not be done.

We have already stated that a good topic is interesting and researchable. Another characteristic of a good topic is that it has theoretical or practical significance. People's definitions of *significant* vary, but a general rule of thumb is that a significant study is one that contributes in some way to improvement or understanding of education or educational practice. A fourth major characteristic of a good topic is that it is a good topic for you. The fact that you have chosen a topic of interest to you, in an area in which you have expertise, is not sufficient. It must be a topic that you can adequately investigate given your (1) current level of research skill, (2) available resources, and (3) time and other restrictions. The availability of appropriate participants and measuring instruments, for example, is an important consideration.

The characteristics of a good topic are summarized for you in Table 2.1. Furthermore, as a beginning researcher, you likely have access to one or more faculty advisors. They can help you to assess the feasibility of your topic.

STATING RESEARCH TOPICS

The statement of research topics varies in form and specificity according to the type of research undertaken and the preferences of the student's advisor. For a quantitative study, a well-written statement of the topic generally indicates the variables of interest to the researcher, the specific relationship between those variables that will be investigated, and, ideally, the nature of the participants involved (i.e., gifted students, learning-disabled fourth graders, teenage mothers). An example of a problem statement might be: "The topic to be investigated in this study is the effect of positive reinforcement on the quality of 10th graders'

TABLE	**2.1**
Characteristics of a Good Research Topic	

1. *The topic is interesting.* It will hold the researcher's interest through the entire research process.

2. *The topic is researchable.* It can be investigated through the collection and analysis of data and it is not stated as a topic seeking to determine what *should* be done.

3. *The topic is significant.* It contributes in some way to the improvement or understanding of education theory or practice.

4. *The topic is manageable.* It fits the researchers' level or research skill, needed resources, and time restrictions.

English compositions." In this statement, the variables to be examined are "positive reinforcement" and "quality of English compositions." The sample will consist of 10th graders.

Other possible topic statements might be:

- "The topic to be investigated in this study is secondary teachers' attitudes toward required inservice activities."
- "The purpose of this study is to investigate the relationship between school entrance age and reading comprehension skills of primary-level students."
- "The problem to be studied is the effect of wearing required school uniforms on the self-esteem of disadvantaged sixth-grade students."
- "Does the effect of periodic home visits diminish the recidivism rate of juvenile offenders?"

Try to identify the variable or variables in each of these examples and suggest what type of quantitative research method would likely be employed to carry out the study.

Qualitative research topics often are stated later and more generally than quantitative ones, because in many cases, the qualitative researcher needs to be immersed in the research context before the focus of the study can emerge. Remember, the qualitative researcher usually is much more attuned to the specifics of the context in which the study takes place than is the quantitative researcher. Qualitative topic statements initially tend to be general, eventually becoming narrowed as more is learned about the research context and its inhabitants. Qualitative research topics are typically stated like the following examples:

- "The purpose of this study is to describe the nature of children's engagement with mathematics. The intention is to gather details about children's ways of entering into and sustaining their involvement with mathematics."
- "This qualitative study examines how members of an organization identify, evaluate, and respond to organizational change. The study examines what events members of an organization identify as significant change events and whether different events are seen as significant subgroups in the organization."
- "The purpose of this research is to study the social integration of disabled children in an integrated third-grade class."

A statement of the topic is the first component of the introductory sections of both a research plan and the completed research report. The topic statement gives direction to the remaining aspects of the research plan and report. The statement of the topic should be accompanied by a presentation of the background of the topic, a justification for the study in terms of its significance, and, often, a list of limitations of the study. The background of the topic includes information needed by readers to understand the nature of the topic. The topic should be justified in terms of its contribution to educational theory or practice. For example, an introduction might begin with a topic statement such as, "The purpose of this study is to compare the effectiveness of salaried paraprofessionals and non-salaried parent volunteers with respect to the reading achievement of first-grade children." This statement might be followed by a discussion concerning (1) the role of paraprofessionals, (2) increased utilization of paraprofessionals by schools, (3) the expense involved, and (4) the search for alternatives, such as parent volunteers. The significance of the problem would be that if parent volunteers and paid paraprofessionals are equally effective, volunteers can be substituted for salaried paraprofessionals at great savings. Any educational practice that might increase achievement at no additional cost is certainly worthy of investigation!

After a topic has been carefully selected, delineated, and clearly stated, the researcher is ready to attack the review of related literature. The researcher typically has a tentative hypothesis that guides the review. In the previous example, the tentative hypothesis would be that parent volunteers are equally effective as salaried paraprofessionals. It is likely that the tentative hypothesis will be modified, even changed radically, as a result of a more extensive review of the literature related to the topic. It does, however, give direction to the literature search and narrows its scope to include only relevant topics.

REVIEW OF RELATED LITERATURE

Having happily found a suitable topic, the beginning researcher is usually "raring to go." Too often the review of related literature is seen as a necessary evil to be completed as fast as possible so that one can get on with the "real research." This perspective is due to a lack of understanding about the purpose and importance of the review, and to a feeling of uneasiness on the part of students who are not sure exactly how to go about writing the review. The lack of practice that makes finding a topic difficult for many beginning researchers is revisited when they are faced with the need to write a literature review. They have had little or no prior experience writing a review. Nonetheless, the review of related literature is as important as any other component of the research, and it can be conducted quite painlessly if it is approached in an orderly manner. Some researchers even find the process quite enjoyable!

DEFINITION, PURPOSE, AND SCOPE

The review of related literature involves the systematic identification, location, and analysis of documents containing information related to the research problem. These documents include articles, abstracts, reviews, monographs, dissertations, books, other research reports, and electronic media. The review has several important functions that make it well worth the time and effort. The major purpose of reviewing the literature is to determine what has already been done that relates to your topic. This knowledge not only avoids unintentional duplication, but it also provides the understandings and insights necessary to develop a logical framework into which your topic fits. In other words, the review tells the researcher what has been done and, in so doing, also suggests what needs to be done. Earlier studies can provide the rationale for your research hypothesis, and indications of what needs to be done often form the basis for justifying the significance of your study.

Another important function of the literature review is to point out research strategies and specific procedures and measuring instruments that have and have not been found to be productive in investigating your topic. This information will help you to avoid other researchers' mistakes and to profit from their experiences. It may suggest approaches and procedures that you previously had not considered. For example, suppose your topic involved the comparative effectiveness of experiment-based versus traditional instruction on the achievement of eighth-grade physical science students. The review of literature might reveal 10 related studies already conducted that have found no differences in achievement. Several of the studies, however, might suggest that experiment-based instruction may be more effective for certain kinds of students than others. Thus, you might reformulate your topic to involve the comparative effectiveness of experiment-based versus traditional instruction on the achievement of low-aptitude eighth-grade physical science students.

Being familiar with previous research also facilitates interpretation of the results of your study. The results can be discussed in terms of whether and how they agree with previous findings. If the results contradict previous findings, differences between your study and the others can be described, providing a rationale for the discrepancy. If your results are consistent with other findings, your report should include suggestions for the next step; if they are not consistent, your report should include suggestions for studies that might resolve the conflict.

Beginning researchers seem to have difficulty in determining how broad their literature review should be. They understand that all literature directly related to their topic should be reviewed; they just don't know when to quit! They have trouble determining which articles are "related enough" to their topic to be included. Unfortunately, there is no statistical formula that can be applied; you must base your decisions on judgment and the advice of your advisor. These judgments become easier as you acquire experience.

Some general guidelines, however, can assist the beginner. First, avoid the temptation to include everything you find; bigger does not mean better. A smaller, well-organized review is definitely preferred to a review containing many studies that are peripherally related to the problem. Second, heavily researched areas usually provide enough references directly related to a specific problem to eliminate the need for relying on less related studies. For example, the role of feedback in learning has been extensively researched for both animals and human beings, for verbal learning and nonverbal learning, and for a variety of different learning tasks. If you were concerned with the relationship between frequency of feedback and chemistry achievement, you would probably not have to review, for example, feedback studies related to animal learning. Third, and conversely, new or little-researched problem areas usually require review of any study related in some meaningful way to the problem in order to develop a logical framework for the study and a sound rationale for the research hypothesis. For example, a study concerned with the effectiveness of the use of metal detectors for reducing incidents of injury-resulting violence would probably include in its literature search any study involving approaches to violence reduction. Five years from now there will probably be enough research on metal detectors to permit a much more narrowly focused literature review.

A common misconception among beginning researchers is the idea that the worth of their topic is a function of the amount of literature available on the topic. This is not the case. There are many new, important areas of research for which there is comparatively little available literature; use of metal detectors is one such area. The very lack of such research often increases the worth of the study. On the other hand, the fact that 1,000 studies have already been done in a given problem area does not mean there is no further need for research in that area. Such an area will generally be very well developed with additional needed research readily identifiable. Such an area is anxiety theory, which is concerned with the relationships between anxiety and learning.

GETTING STARTED

Since it will be a second home to you, at least for a while, you should become completely familiar with the library before beginning your review. Time spent initially will save time in the long run. You should find out what references are available and where they are located. You should also be familiar with services offered by the library, as well as the rules and regulations regarding the use of library materials. It also might be useful to identify three or so people who are actively conducting research in your topic areas. Once identified, you could contact them to request copies of their recent articles on your topic and suggestions for useful references in the area. They might even make suggestions.

A common question asked about a literature review is, "How should I start?" Eventually you will have to examine a wide range of sources that are pertinent to your topic. However, to start, it is better to narrow the initial search to educational encyclopedias, handbooks, and annual reviews that are pertinent to your study. These and similar resources provide broad overviews of issues in one or many subject areas, as well as initial references to examine. They allow you to get a picture of your topic in the broader context and provide you with understanding about where it fits in the field. Although not all fields have annual reviews, handbooks, or encyclopedias, it is well worth the effort to check whether your field does.

Significant library-related technological advances have been made in the last few years, and libraries vary greatly in their ability to capitalize on increasingly available options. Your library, for example, may or may not have an online computer search, CD-ROM access capability, or Internet hookups. Services also vary from library to library. One important service that is offered by most libraries is the interlibrary loan, which permits you to request references not available in your library from other libraries. Allow time for requested references to arrive. Most researchers happily pay the small fee often charged for this service. Libraries usually offer guided tours of the facilities, with instructions about how to access and use the various technology available. While librarians are usually very willing to help individuals, you should learn to use the library; the librarian might not be as cheerful the ninth time you approach as he or she was the first time!

Having formulated your problem and acquainted yourself with the library, there is one more thing you need to do before you go marching merrily off into the bookstacks—make a list of key words to guide your literature search. Most of the sources you consult will have alphabetical subject indexes to help you locate specific references. You will look in these indexes under the key words you have selected. For example, if your problem concerns the effect of interactive multimedia on the achievement of 10th-grade biology students, the logical key words would be *interactive multimedia* and *biology*. You will also need to think of alternative words under which your topic might be listed. For example, references related to this problem might be found using the key words *multimedia* or *interactive videodiscs* rather than just interactive. Usually, the key words will be obvious; sometimes you may have to play detective.

Some years ago a student was interested in the effect of artificial turf on knee injuries in football. He looked under every key word he could think of, such as *surface, playing surface, turf,* and *artificial turf.* He could find nothing. Since he knew that studies had been done, he kept trying. When he finally did find a reference, it was listed under, of all things, *lawns!* Identifying key words is usually not such a big deal. In looking in initial sources you might identify additional key words that will help you in succeeding sources. However, if you give some thought initially to possible key words, it will facilitate an efficient beginning to a task that requires organization. After you have identified your key words, you will finally be ready to begin to consult appropriate sources.

IDENTIFYING YOUR SOURCES

Many sources of literature might relate to a given problem. In general, however, there are a number of major sources commonly used by educational researchers. Some of these sources are primary sources and some are secondary. As with historical research, primary sources are definitely preferable because they describe a study written by the person who conducted it. A secondary source in the literature is generally a much briefer, abstracted description of a study written by someone other than the original researcher. The *Review of Educational Research,* for example, summarizes many research studies conducted on a given topic. Since secondary sources usually give complete bibliographic information on the references cited, they can direct the researcher to relevant primary sources. You should not be satisfied with the information contained in secondary sources; the corresponding primary sources will be considerably more detailed and will give you information "straight from the horse's mouth," as they say.

The number of individual references that could be consulted for a given problem is staggering. Fortunately, there are indexes, abstracts, and other retrieval mechanisms, such as computer searches, that facilitate identification of relevant references. In this section we will discuss the ones most often used in educational research; you should check the library for sources in your area of specialization. Following the discussion of the various sources, computer-assisted literature searches and World Wide Web searches will be described.

Examples of handbooks, encyclopedias, and reviews relevant to educational research are *Encyclopedia of Educational Research, National Society for the Study of Education (NSSE) Yearbooks, Review of Educational Research, The Encyclopedia of Human Development and Education: Theory, Research, and Studies, The Handbook of Research on Teaching, The International Encyclopedia of Education: Research and Studies, Handbook on Social Studies Teaching and Learning, Handbook of Research in Curriculum,* and *Review of Research in Education.* These and other similar works contain summaries of important topics in education, reviews of research on various topics, and complete bibliographic information on the references cited. It is useful to photocopy the bibliographic references in the summaries that you consult, to use later in the research process.

At this point, you may be asking, "How can I find such sources in my library?" Most libraries use a computer-based catalog system such as LUIS (Library User Information Service), which automatically indexes (by author, title, and subject) all the entries in the card catalog. In addition to the usual information such as the call number, most systems also provide other useful information, such as whether a given book is on the shelf or checked out. If you know the title

FIGURE 2.1

Opening Screen

```
                                                                  Introduction
-----------------------------------------------------------------------------


       To search by:         Use the command:        Example:

           Title                   T=                t=lives of the saints
           Author                  A=                a=shakespeare
           Keyword                 K=                k=computer and software
           Call Number             C=                c=pe1591.r73 1992
           Subject                 S=                s=television--censorship
           SuDoc Call Number       CS=               cs=c56.233:

       For more information on searching in the Catalog, press <RETURN>.
       For Library News, type NEWS and press <RETURN>.
       To return to the Main screen, type cho and press <RETURN>.
-------------------------------------------------- + Page 1 of 3 -------------
                    Enter search command                  <F8>  FORward page
                    NEWs              CHOose
                    CR for Course Reserve

  NEXT COMMAND:
  4-©              1 Sess-1     136.167.2.11
```

Source: Quest/Ameritech.

or author of the reference you are seeking, you will need to conduct a *title* or *author search*. The opening screen to most computer-based catalog systems allows you to search for sources in various ways: by title, key word, author, or call number, to name a few. Figure 2.1 shows a typical opening screen.

If you know the title of the resource that you are looking for, simply type t= and the title, omitting initial articles. For example, if you want to know if your library holds *Review of Research in Education,* type "t=review of research in education" and then press Enter. The resulting screen will inform you of whether the *Review of Research in Education* is held in your library. If it is held by your library, you will probably be required to enter the number corresponding to the title you have selected to find out what the call number is (if your library owns it). At this point, you will need to consult a floor map of your library to determine the location of books with the call number identified in your search. All you need to do at this point is go to the library shelves and get your book!

If you do not know the title of handbooks, encyclopedias, and research guides in your area of interest, you will need to conduct a keyword search. To do this, you will need to think of key words or phrases that are pertinent to the type of volume you seek. For example, if you would like to find summaries of research previously conducted in an area of psychology, you might choose key words such as *handbook* and *psychology.* You then will need to type "k=handbook and psychology" on the computer screen and then press Enter. An example of the sources identified by this search is shown in Figure 2.2.

If you decide that you would like to find out more about the 13th title displayed, *The Handbook of Psychology,* your next computer command will be the number 13 and then Enter. The next screen, shown in Figure 2.3, gives you full bibliographic information for the handbook, as well as where it is located (in the

FIGURE	2.2

Sources Identified by Keyword Search

```
Search Request: K=HANDBOOK AND PSYCHOLOGY
Search Results: 292 Entries Found                        Keyword Index
------------------------------------------------------------------------
      DATE  TITLE:                                    AUTHOR:
   1  1998  Behavioral medicine and women : a comprehe           OL
   2  1998  Handbook of child abuse research and treat           OL
   3  1998  Handbook of child behavior therapy                   OL
   4  1998  Handbook of child psychology                         OL
   5  1998  The handbook of social psychology                    OL
   6  1998  Measurement, judgment, and decision making           OL
   7  1997  Handbook of academic learning                        OL
   8  1997  Handbook of classroom assessment : learnin           OL
   9  1997  Handbook of cross-cultural psychology                OL
  10  1997  Handbook of Japan-United States environmen           OL
  11  1997  Handbook of modern item response theory              OL
  12  1997  Handbook of personality psychology                   OL
  13  1997  The handbook of psychology          Appleby, Drew     OL
  14  1997  The handbook of school art therapy : intro  Bush, Janet OL
------------------------------------------------ CONTINUED on next page ----
STArt over     Type number to display record        <F8>  FORward page
HELp           CHOose
OTHer options

NEXT COMMAND:
4-©              1 Sess-1    136.167.2.11
```

Source: Quest/Ameritech.

library stacks), the call number (BF131.A67 1997), and its availability. Then you need to go to the BF call number area and get the book.

After reading a few secondary sources to get a more informed overview of your topic, you should have a clearer idea of your topic. You may want to revise your initial topic to reflect a narrower focus. Once your topic has been restated, you should move beyond secondary sources to primary resources, including publications in which researchers report their own findings.

To recap what we have discussed so far, primary and secondary sources related to your topic may be found in a variety of ways.

1. Searching for books in the library
2. Consulting computer databases to locate journal articles, reports, and other publications
3. Obtaining the references listed in the bibliographies in the secondary sources you previously located
4. Searching the Internet and the World Wide Web for up-to-date information

In the following pages we will discuss these procedures in more detail.

Searching for Books on Your Topic in the Library

To locate primary sources, you need to conduct a library search much the same as the searches already illustrated. If, for example, you know the title of a book that you wish to obtain, you can conduct a title search by typing t= and the book title on the computer screen. If you want to find only books written by a specific author, you will conduct an author search by typing a= and the name of the

FIGURE 2.3

Bibliographic Information Display Screen

```
Search Request: K=HANDBOOK AND PSYCHOLOGY
BOOK - Record 13 of 292 Entries Found                        Brief View
-------------------------------------------------------------------------
Author:        Appleby, Drew.
Title:         The handbook of psychology / Drew Appleby.
Published:     New York : Longman, c1997.
Subjects:    S= Psychology--Handbooks, manuals, etc.
-------------------------------------------------------------------------
  LOCATION:            CALL NUMBER:          CIRC/ORD STAT:
   Library              BF131 .A67 1997       Not checked out
    Stacks




----------------------------------------------- Page 1 of 1 ---------------
  STArt over     LONg view                      <F6>  NEXt record
  HELp           INDex                           <F5>  PREvious record
  OTHer options  CHOose

  NEXT COMMAND:
 -------------------------------------------------------------------------
 4-ⓢ              1 Sess-1     136.167.2.11
```

Source: Quest/Ameritech.

author. If you want to find all of the books on a particular subject, you can conduct a subject search by typing s= and the subject you have in mind. If, somehow, you know the call number of a book for which you are looking, you can conduct a call number search by entering c= and as much of the call number as you have available. Table 2.2 gives useful tips for conducting searches.

If you are at the very beginning of your search for primary sources, you may not have any specific titles identified. In this case, you should conduct a keyword search. The ideal search strategy is one that gets you just the right number of references related to your topic but does not prevent you from locating one or more significant references.

A keyword search may be narrow or broad. If it is narrow, it is likely that all identified references will be related to your problem, but if it is too narrow, you may miss some important references. If a search is broad, it is likely that you will not miss any significant references, although you may get some that are not really related to your problem. How narrow or broad your search should be depends on factors such as the purpose of the search and the amount of material available on your topic. If you need a relatively small number of references and if much has been published about your topic, a narrow search will likely be appropriate. If you need a relatively large number of references and very little has been published about your topic, a broad search will be better. If you do not have a sense of what is available, your best strategy is to start narrow and broaden as necessary. For example, if you find that there are very few references related to the effect of interactive multimedia on the achievement of 10th-grade biology students, you could broaden your search by including all sciences or all secondary students.

TABLE	**2.2**

Useful Tips for Conducting Title, Author, Call Number, and Subject Searches

TYPE OF SEARCH	TITLE	AUTHOR	CALL NUMBER	SUBJECT
Examples	t=sun also rises t=color purple t=red badge	a=hemingway e a=shakespea a=symposium on atomic energy a=american nurses association	c=hv5800 c=pn1997m652x1988	s=astronomy s=greek art s=stein gertrude s=poetry--women authors s=latinos--boston
Comments	Omit initial articles If unsure of exact title, use shorter form	Use author's last name first An editor, organization, institution, or meeting can be an author	Depending on specificity of call #, will retrieve specific records or all items under a particular topic Not available on all systems	To search a complex subject heading, use two dashes between subdivisions When unsure of subject heading, try a keyword search Most records contain more than one subject heading

Adapted from Boston College Libraries Information System, "Guide to Using Quest." Used with permission of Trustees of Boston College.

A useful way to narrow or broaden a keyword search is to use Boolean (wow!) operators, which involve the use of *and, or,* and *not* connectors. Put simply, using the connections *and* or *not* narrow a search, while the connector *or* broadens it. Let's say you have two key words, Easter and rabbit. If you indicate that you are interested in obtaining references that relate to Easter *and* rabbit, you are saying that you only want references that refer to both Easter and rabbit. If you indicate that you are interested in obtaining references that relate to Easter but *not* to rabbit, your search is narrowed to references containing Easter, and references containing rabbit references will not be included in the search. If you indicate that you will take references related to Easter *or* rabbit, you are saying you will take references that relate to either or both concepts. For example, a search indicated that there were 603 references for multimedia instruction, 14,845 for science education, but only 22 for multimedia instruction and science education. By using various combinations of the *and* and *or* connectors, you can vary your search strategy as needed. Table 2.3 presents a summary of ways to limit keyword searches.

Consulting Computer Databases to Locate Journals, Articles, Reports, and Other Publications

Computerized databases are used to conduct literature searches. Available at most university and public libraries, computer databases facilitate the identification of relevant primary sources. General reference computer searches can be done

TABLE	2.3

Summary of Ways to Limit Keyword Searches

KEYWORD SEARCHES			
GENERAL	**FIELD CODES**	**BOOLEAN OPERATORS**	**FIELD QUALIFIERS**
k=assessment k=book review K=automa? (retrieves automatic, automation, automating, etc.)	Codes: k=dickonson.au k=criticism.su k=research.ti	k=assessment and alternative k=authentic or alternative k=assessment not standardized	k=1990.dt1,dt2. and assessment (books on assessment published in 1990) k=curriculum and fre.la (Books on curriculum in French)
Looks for word or phrase anywhere in a bibliographic record Adjacency is assumed (i.e., words will be next to each other unless specified) ? is used to retrieve singular, plural, or variant spellings	Codes limit searches to specific areas or fields in the bibliographic record, such as author, title, and subject	Used to expand or limit a search And: retrieves records containing *both* terms Or: retrieves records containing *either* term Not: retrieves records containing one term and not the other	Used with Boolean operators to limit searches Inquire in your library for available field qualifiers

Adapted from Boston College Libraries Information System, "Guide to Using Quest." Used with permission of Trustees of Boston College.

online or by using a CD-ROM. An online search is performed at a computer terminal that is directly connected via telephone lines to a central database system. A CD-ROM search involves using software onto which database information has been transferred. Both types are generally installed in university library computers and are available to researchers. In addition, literature search methods and results are identical in both formats.

The steps involved in conducting a computer database search, be it an online search or a CD-ROM search, are similar to those involved in a book search:

1. Identify key words related to your topic.
2. Select the databases you wish to search.
3. Specify your search strategy.

Your topic statement suggests obvious key words. Additional, or more useful, key words are identified by checking descriptors found in thesauruses belonging to each database. The resident search analyst in your library can assist you in identifying appropriate key words.

The most commonly used computer databases in education include:

ERIC. The ERIC (Educational Resources Information Center) database contains more than 800,000 references to thousands of educational topics. It is updated monthly and includes journal articles, books, theses, conference papers, curricula, standards, and guidelines. ERIC contains entries from two sources: the RIE (Resources in Education) file of document citations and the CIJE (Current Index to Journals in Education) file of journal article citations from more than 750 profes-

Bibliographic Software

One of the most tedious, yet important, tasks in the research process is keeping track of the references you are using and maintaining a bibliography of all of the sources you have referenced in your research. Quoting or referencing a source in your paper and then realizing later that you don't know the volume number of the journal it comes from or the exact page numbers of the article usually means returning to the library to locate journal articles and books all over again. Even when you have complete references on hand, formatting a bibliography according to a prescribed style—making sure every comma is correctly placed and the appropriate words are capitalized or underlined—can be an arduous process. Maintaining a complete and correctly formatted reference base can be a frustrating and time-consuming part of the research process.

Bibliographic software is a tool that many researchers use to alleviate the task of locating and formatting references. Bibliographic software simplifies the research process because it allows you to create stand alone bibliographies or bibliographies within your research paper by entering information into a template. These bibliographies can then be searched or sorted according to your needs.

One bibliographic software program that many researchers find useful is EndNote. EndNote comes with more than 300 predefined bibliographic styles that you can use, or you can create an unlimited number of your own styles. Depending on the word processing program you are using, you can either use the EndNote Add-in to create one-step bibliographies from within the word processing program or simply insert the necessary citations from your EndNote database into the text of your word processing document.

With EndNote, you can store a Web page within your EndNote record, providing a virtual map to full-text online information. EndNote will also automatically start your Web browser (e.g. Navigator, Internet Explorer) and link to online journals, full-text articles, or any other Web address stored within your EndNote record. As a result, your EndNote database becomes the card catalog of the electronic library.

While it will take a bit of time to learn how to use your bibliographic software, your efforts will be worthwhile. Not only will you have the chance to organize your references in a variety of creative ways, but you will gain access to online references in a manner that allows you to store information in a less haphazard way than if you were simply to surf from site to site and take note of where useful sites are located.

sional journals. The ERIC database provides bibliographic information and abstracts of educational sources, but not full texts. Complete ERIC documents are available in libraries, either in microfiche format or in ERIC journals on the library shelves.

The first step in using ERIC resources is to become familiar with the terms that ERIC uses to index references. The *Thesaurus of ERIC Descriptors*, also available in most libraries, is a compilation of the key words used in indexing ERIC documents. The ERIC thesaurus indicates the various terms under which a given topic is indexed.

ERIC references are labeled either with ED or EJ accession numbers. In most libraries, ED references are available on microfiche. In some libraries, you will need to ask a librarian to get the microfiche for you, while in other libraries, you are able to get it yourself. EJ references refer to literature that can be found on library shelves. To find out where an EJ reference is located at your library, do a title search on your library computer's online catalog. Enter t= and the name of the journal or book the ERIC reference is in. The resulting screen will tell you if your library owns the journal, where it is located, and whether it is available on the library shelves or on microfiche. Figure 2.4 shows the result of a sample ERIC search.

Education Index. The *Education Index* is an electronic index to educational periodicals with abstracts since 1983. It also includes yearbooks and selected monographs series, videotapes, motion picture and computer program reviews, and citations to law cases. The *Education Index* provides bibliographic information and abstracts of sources (not the full text of articles) pertaining to the topic(s) you have searched. To find an article listed in the *Education Index*, do a title search for the periodical in your library. Results of an *Education Index* search are shown in Figure 2.5.

FIGURE 2.4

Results of an ERIC Search

```
Record 1 of 1 - ERIC 1992-12/97
AN: ED410322
AU: Schwartz,-Wendy
TI: How Well Are Charter Schools Serving Urban and Minority Students? ERIC/CUE Digest, Number
    119.
CS: ERIC Clearinghouse on Urban Education  New York, N.Y.
PY: 1996
AV: ERIC Clearinghouse on Urban Education, Institute for Urban and Minority Education,
    Teachers College, Box 40, Columbia University, New York, NY 10027 (free).
NT: 6 p.
PR: EDRS Price - MF01/PC01 Plus Postage.
AB: Charter schools are created and managed by an entity composed of parents and/ or
    teachers, community and/or business leaders, nonprofit organizations, and for-profit
    businesses. Many people believe that charter schools can provide a high quality education
    without the regulatory constraints of the conventional public schools. This digest
    reviews many reports on the approximately 350 charter schools in the United States to
    show the various ways that charters approach funding, curriculum and instruction,
    assessment and accountability, parent involvement, and staffing. It focuses on the
    ability of charter schools to serve urban students. Many charter schools have been
    granted unprecedented freedom to implement their plans for a higher quality and more
    equitable educational system, and they have also tapped into funding sources previously
    unavailable to educators. Critics of charter schools are of the opinion that the freedom
    will not result in educational improvement, and that the lack of accountability may mean
    that a school's ineptitude will go unrecognized. It is too soon to evaluate the
    performance of students in charters, but it is apparent that charters are attracting
    urban students, in part because of their location. However, they are not attracting the
    most vulnerable and disadvantaged students. They are attracting dedicated and talented
    teachers but may not be able to offer them wages comparable to those of the public
    schools. Whether charter schools can provide a more effective public education remains to
    be seen, but their presence is at least serving to dramatize the need for educational
    improvement and increased community and business involvement and financial support. (
    Contains nine references.) (SLD)
```

Source: U.S. Department of Education.

FIGURE   2.5

Results of an *Education Index* Search

Record 1 of 1 in Education Abstracts 6/83-10/98

TITLEDeveloping academic confidence to build literacy: what teachers can do
AUTHOR(S)
     Colvin,-Carolyn; Schlosser,-Linda-Kramer
SOURCE
     Journal-of-Adolescent-and-Adult-Literacy.v. 41 (Dec. '97/Jan. '98) p. 272-81.
PUBLICATION YEAR
     1997
ABSTRACT
     A study examined how the classroom literacy behaviors of middle school students
relate to their academic success and reinforce students' evolving sense of self. The
participants were at-risk students, academically successful students, and teachers from a
middle school in southern California. It was found that when academically marginal
students call on literacy strategies, these strategies are limited in scope and offer little help.
However, more academically successful students seem well aware of the behaviors that are
likely to result in a successful literacy experience. The characteristics of academically
marginal and successful students are outlined, and suggestions for helping teachers create
classrooms where students behave with greater efficacy are offered.
ACCESSION NUMBER
     97030423 .

Psychological Abstracts. *Psychological Abstracts* presents summaries of completed psychological research studies. The sections on developmental psychology
and educational psychology are generally the most useful to educational researchers. The first step in using *Psychological Abstracts* is to refer to the *Thesaurus
of Psychological Index* to find the key words used in indexing *Psychological Abstracts* documents. For example, if your research topic concerns the effect of interactive multimedia on the achievement of 10th-grade biology students, you
would find that interactive multimedia is not a descriptor used by the *Thesaurus.*
You would have to try other descriptors such as instructional media. The procedure for using *Psychological Abstracts* is similar to the procedure for ERIC and the
Education Index. In addition to the key words, the word *bibliography* should be
checked. A bibliography related to your topic may exist and provide references.
You should locate those references of interest to you in the usual way, by doing a
title search on your university's computer catalog system.

Dissertation Abstracts. *Dissertation Abstracts* contains bibliographic citations
and abstracts from all subject areas for doctoral dissertations and master's theses
completed at more than 1,000 accredited colleges and universities worldwide.
The database dates back to 1861, with abstracts included from 1980 forward. If
after reading an abstract you wish to obtain a copy of the complete dissertation,
check to see if it is available in your library. If not, speak to a librarian about how
to obtain a copy of the dissertation. The results of a *Dissertation Abstracts* search
are shown in Figure 2.6.

Results of *Dissertation Abstracts* Search

```
Order No:    AAC 9535738  ProQuest - Dissertation Abstracts
Title:       SELF-CONCEPT AND CAREER DEVELOPMENT OF NON-COLLEGE-BOUND
             YOUTH IN THE PENNSYLVANIA YOUTH APPRENTICESHIP PROGRAM
Author:      DONOVAN-RICHARDSON, HELEN A.
School:      TEMPLE UNIVERSITY (0225)  Degree: EDD  Date: 1995  pp: 245
Advisor:     AMIDON, EDMUND
Source:      DAI-A 56/06, p. 2114, Dec 1995
Subject:     EDUCATION, GUIDANCE AND COUNSELING (0519); EDUCATION,
             VOCATIONAL (0747)
```

Abstract: The purpose of this study is to investigate the impact of
participation in the Pennsylvania Youth Apprenticeship Program (PYAP)
on students' self concepts and career development. Also examined in
relationship to the PYAP are the demographics, grades, attendance and
socioeconomic status. Additional analyses are performed regarding
student attitudes toward school, school outcomes, as well as choice
of job cluster and job values on self concept and career development.
   A second goal of the study is to do a more finely grained
analysis of differences between sample sites to explore additional
program implications.
   This was a quasi-experimental, post hoc comparison design study.
The respondents were 185, 11th and 12th grade students, 16 to 20
years of age, in six Pennsylvania locations representing urban,
suburban and rural school districts.
   The treatment group was 79 primarily white male students in
apprenticeships in the metalworking industry. The comparison group
was 106 primarily white male students in vocational and general track
programs.
   The Piers Harris Children's Self Concept Scale was converted to
two underlying factors, academic and social self concept. The
Harrington O'Shea Career Decision Making System Revised was converted
to Holland's theoretical concepts of Congruence, Differentiation and
Realism of Career Choice.
   The findings were unexpected. There were no differences between
the PYAP students and their non-participating comparison group on
self concept or career development. Membership on the academic track
was found to be the best predictor of higher academic self concept,
and being in the 12th grade was found to be the best predictor of
career development.
   Students' choice of Manual or Skilled Crafts job clusters, though
showing the highest levels of career development, showed negative
relationships to social self concepts. This finding reflects the
relationship between the two dependent variables which was small and
negative.
   It is concluded that self concept is too broad a construct for
career development. Future studies should explore the relationship of
self efficacy to career development (Bandura, 1977; Krumboltz, 1979;
and Betz, 1994).
   The researcher's recommendations for practice incorporate the
implications of the overall findings, the supplemental analysis by
location, and the positive relationships found between school
outcomes and student attitudes.

Readers' Guide to Periodical Literature. *Readers' Guide to Periodical Literature* is an index similar in format to the *Education Index*. Instead of professional publications, however, it indexes articles in nearly 200 widely read magazines. Articles located through the *Readers' Guide* will generally be nontechnical, opinion-type references. These can be useful in documenting the significance of your problem. The *Readers' Guide* lists bibliographic information for each entry. To obtain an article listed in the *Reader's Guide,* do a title search in your library of the magazine in which it appears. Then find out if your library holds that magazine.

Annual Review of Psychology. The *Annual Review of Psychology* includes reviews of psychological research that are often of relevance to educational research. It provides bibliographic information and abstracts for specific areas such as child development, educational administration, exceptional child education, and language teaching.

Obtaining the References Listed in the Bibliographies in Your Secondary Sources

Given the prior discussion and description of library resources, you should be able to access references listed in the secondary source bibliographies you examined to start your literature review. For references that are books, do a title search in your library's computerized catalog to find out if the books are held by your library and, if so, if they are available. For references that appear to be journal articles or reports, go to ERIC or the *Education Index*. Do a title search of the article or report. This should pinpoint the article or report directly. You can then use the usual means to determine if the publication in which the article or report appears is in your library.

Searching the World Wide Web

The Internet and the World Wide Web provide information and resources on many educational topics. The Internet is a computer network linking organizations and individuals all over the world by means of a communication protocol called TCP/IP. The World Wide Web is a service on the Internet that gives users access to text, graphics, and multimedia. To access the World Wide Web, you will need a computer with a modem that is hooked up to a telephone line. Your computer will also need a browser (such as Netscape or Mosaic, among many others). Typically, you need to sign up with an Internet Service Provider to access your browser and, hence, the World Wide Web. Most Internet Service Providers give customers unlimited usage of their services for about $20 per month. If you have these resources on your computer, you can conduct your search from the comfort of your own home. If not, most libraries have computers with Internet access.

The resources that you can find on the World Wide Web are almost limitless. With just a few clicks, you can access electronic educational journals that provide full-text articles, bibliographic information, and abstracts. You can also obtain up-to-the-minute research reports and information about educational research activities being undertaken at various research centers, and can access education home pages that provide "links" (connections) to a range of education resources that other researchers have found especially valuable. At times, the sheer volume of information that is on the World Wide Web can be overwhelming. The best way to become adept at searching the Web efficiently is simply by browsing the Web during your spare time. In this way, you will become familiar with maneuvering from site to site and implementing successful search strategies.

Here are some Web sites that are especially useful to educational researchers, along with each site's Internet address (in parentheses).

ERIC. *(http://www.aspensys.com/eric/)* Yes, ERIC is also available on the World Wide Web, and it functions very much the same as it does on a database in your library. In addition to the Research in Education (RIE) and Current Index to

ERIC Clearinghouses and Adjunct Clearinghouses on the WWW

CLEARINGHOUSE/ADJUNCT CLEARINGHOUSE	WWW ADDRESS	DESCRIPTION
ERIC Clearinghouse on Adult, Career and Vocational Education	http://ericae2.educ/cua/edu	Provides comprehensive information, publications, and services in adult and continuing education, all aspects of career education, and vocational and technical education, including work force preparation
ERIC Clearinghouse on Assessment and Evaluation	http://ericae.net	Seeks to provide balanced information concerning educational assessment and resources to encourage responsible test use
Adjunct Test Collection Clearinghouse		Database contains records on more than 10,000 tests and research instruments covering a wide range of subjects and fields
ERIC Clearinghouse for Community Colleges	http://www.gse.ucla.edu/ERIC/eric.html	Coordinates searches of the ERIC database on community college-related topics
Adjunct ERIC Clearinghouse on Entrepreneurial Education		Identifies sources of information on aspects of entrepreneurship education: K–12, post-secondary, nonprofit, commercial, and small business development
ERIC Clearinghouse on Counseling and Student Services	http://www.uncg.edu/~ericcas2/	Includes information on school counseling, school social work, school psychology, mental health counseling, marriage and family counseling, career counseling, and student development, as well as parent, student, and teacher education in the human resources area
ERIC Clearinghouse on Disabilities and Gifted Education	http://www.cec.sped.org/ericec.htm	Focuses on professional literature, information, and resources relating to the education and development of persons of all ages who have disabilities and/or are gifted
ERIC Clearinghouse on Educational Management	http://darkwing.uoregon.edu/~ericcem/	Prepares ERIC database information related to educational management and other topics of interest to educational policymakers, school administrators, researchers, and other personnel
ERIC Clearinghouse on Elementary and Early Childhood Education	http://ericps.crc.uiuc.edu/	Provides information for educators, parents, families, and others interested in the development, education, and care of children from birth through early adolescence
Adjunct ERIC Clearinghouse for Child Care		Promotes child care linkages and serves as a mechanism for supporting quality, comprehensive services for children and their families

Clearinghouse	URL	Description
ERIC Clearinghouse on Higher Education	http://www.gwu.edu/~eriche/	Covers information including students, faculty, graduate, and professional education, legal issues, financing, planning and evaluation, curriculum, teaching methods, and state–federal institutions related to higher education
ERIC Clearinghouse on Information Technology	http://ericir.syr.edu/ithome	Provides educational technology and library/information science at all academic levels and addresses all aspects of information management technology related to education
ERIC Clearinghouse on Languages and Linguistics	http://www.cal.org/ericcll/	Collects and disseminates information on current development in education research, instructional methods and materials, program design and evaluation, teacher training, and assessment of several language and literacy areas
National Clearinghouse for ESL Literacy Education		Provides literacy instructors, researchers, etc. with timely information on adult ESL literacy education with an emphasis on education for adults and out-of-school youth learning English as a second language
ERIC Clearinghouse on Reading, English, and Communication	http://www.indiana.edu/~eric_rec	Provides materials, services, and coursework to parents, educators, students, and others interested in the language arts
ERIC Clearinghouse on Rural Education and Small Schools	http://aelvira.ael.org/erichp.htm	Provides access to education-related resources about rural education, small schools, migrant education, and so on
ERIC Clearinghouse on Science, Math, and Environmental Education	http://www.ericse.org	Retrieves and disseminates printed materials related to science, mathematics, and environmental education
ERIC Clearinghouse on Social Studies/Social Science Education	http://www.indiana.edu/~ssdc/eric_chess.htm	Monitors issues about the teaching and learning of history, geography, civics, economics, and other subjects in the social studies/social sciences
Adjunct ERIC Clearinghouse on Service Learning		Contains an extensive database, a description of nationwide service-learning programs, grant information, books, articles, and publications
ERIC Clearinghouse on Teaching and Teacher Education	http://www.ericsp.org/	Responds to requests for information on teaching, teacher education, and health, physical education, recreation, and dance (HPERD), and produces special publications on current research, programs, and practices
ERIC Clearinghouse on Urban Education	http://eric-web.tc.columbia.edu/	Monitors curriculum and instruction of students of diverse racial, ethnic, social class, and linguistic populations in urban (and suburban) schools

Source: http://www.ed.gov/EdRes/EdFed/ERIC.html.

Journals in Education (CIJE), which we discussed earlier, the ERIC Web site also provides:

> *Extensive user assistance,* including AskERIC, an electronic question answering service for teachers on the Internet
>
> *National Parent Information Network,* which provides information and communications capabilities to parents and those who work with them
>
> *ERIC Clearinghouses,* which collect, abstract, and index education materials for the ERIC database; respond to requests for information in ERIC's subject specific areas; and produce special publications on current research, programs, and practices. There are 16 subject-specific clearinghouses.
>
> *Adjunct ERIC Clearinghouses,* which focus on narrower, more specialized topics than the rather general clearinghouses. Each adjunct identifies and acquires significant literature within its scope area. Like the larger clearinghouses, the adjuncts provide free reference and referral services in their subject areas. There are currently seven adjunct clearinghouses.
>
> *ERIC Digests,* which are two-page research syntheses. There are currently more than 1,000 *ERIC Digests,* with approximately 100 new titles produced each year. *ERIC Digests* can be accessed in each of the clearinghouses and adjunct clearinghouses.
> (Source: http://www.ed.gov/EdRes/EdFed/ERIC.html)

Web page addresses and short descriptions of the contents of the various clearinghouses and adjunct clearinghouses are found in Table 2.4.

UnCoverWeb. *(http://uncweb.carl.org)* UnCover is a database with brief descriptive information about articles from more than 17,000 multidisciplinary journals. If you register (for a fee) with UnCover REVEAL, an automated alerting service, you will receive monthly tables of contents from your favorite periodicals. The service also allows you to create search strategies for your research topics.

NewJour. *(http://gort.ucsd.edu/newjour/)* This site provides an up-to-date list of journals and newsletters available on the Internet on any subject. Using New Jour's search option, you can do a title search to see if a specific journal is currently on the World Wide Web or do a subject search to find out which journals in a particular subject are available on the Internet. Direct links are provided to journals available on the Internet.

Education Week. *(http://www.edweek.org/)* Full text articles from *Education Week,* a periodical devoted to education reform, schools, and policy, are available at this site. In addition to current and past articles, this site provides background data to enhance current news, resources for teachers, and recommended Web sites to investigate for other information.

Journal of Statistics in Education. *(http://www.stat.ncsu.edu/info/jse/)* This electronic journal provides abstracts and full-text articles that have appeared since 1993. Interesting features of the journal are "Teaching Bits: A Resource for Teachers of Statistics" and "Datasets and Stories."

CSTEEP: The Center for the Study of Testing, Evaluation, and Educational Policy. *(http://wwwcsteep.bc.edu/)* This educational research organization's Web page contains information on testing, evaluation, and public policy studies on school assessment practices and international comparative research.

National Center for Education Statistics. *(http://www.ed.gov/NCES/)* This site contains statistical reports and other information on the condition of American education. It also reports on education activities internationally.

Bill Huitt's Home Page. *(http://www.valdosta.peachnet.edu/~whuitt/educ.html)* This site was created by Dr. William G. (Bill) Huitt of the Department of Psychology, Counseling & Guidance at Valdosta State University in Georgia. It contains some interesting links to general, curriculum, technology, reform, and multicultural education.

Developing Educational Standards. *(http://putwest.boces.org/ Standards.html)* This site contains a multitude of up-to-date information regarding educational standards and curriculum frameworks from all sources (national, state, local, and other). The table of contents includes: Governmental and General Resources, Standards and Frameworks Documents Listed by Subject Area, Standards and Frameworks Documents Listed by State, and Updates and Information. Entire standards and frameworks are available.

Internet Resources for Special Education. *(http://specialed.miningco.com)* This site provides links to a variety of topics, including: teaching resources for regular and special education teachers; Web sites for students to visit; disability information, resources, and research; disability laws; special education laws; e-mail ideas; mailing lists and usenet information; assistive technology; clearinghouses; and Internet search engines and help topics.

U.S. Department of Education. *(http://www.ed.gov/)* This site contains links to the U.S. government's education databases (including ERIC). It also makes available (in full-text format) reports on current findings on education. In addition, it provides links to research offices and organizations, as well as research publications and products. The Department of Education has published a book titled *The Researcher's Guide to the Department of Education,* which helps researchers access the various resources that the Department has to offer.

WWW Library Resources: Education. *(http://www.csu.edu.au/education/library.html)* A section of the World Wide Web Virtual Library, this Web page contains education information on a number of different subjects.

Psych Web. *(http://www.psych-web.com/)* This site provides psychological information for students and teachers of psychology. Resources and links available include full-length books online, online pamphlets, discussion groups, university psychology departments on the Web, psychology journals on the Web, APA style resources, and other scholarly resources.

Using a Search Engine to Find Information Sources

It is entirely possible that you will want to access information on the World Wide Web that is not available in the Web addresses just given. The easiest, quickest way to find interesting new sites on the World Wide Web is to use a search engine to look for Web pages containing key words that you enter. Search

FIGURE 2.7

Search Options in Yahoo! Opening Screen

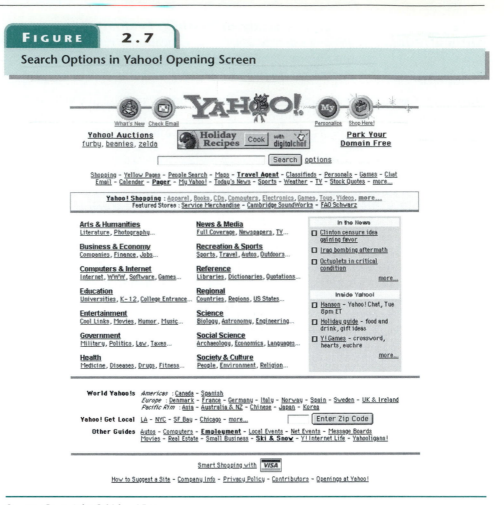

Source: Copyright © Yahoo! Inc.

engines are sites that allow you to search the entire Internet for specific information. Examples of search engines include Yahoo!, Lycos, Excite, and Alta Vista. Once you have entered a key word or key words in the appropriate place on the search engine's home page, the search engine examines the entire Internet (or a specific domain of the Internet, if you say so) for sites that contain your key word(s).

To facilitate your search, most search engines offer you the option of narrowing your search from the beginning so that only the most relevant sites are identified. An example using Yahoo! is shown in Figure 2.7.

Clicking on the subcategory "Education" in Figure 2.7 will significantly narrow your search to relevant sources in the field of education. After selecting the "Education" subcategory, a very useful page shown in Figure 2.8, appears.

You have the option of searching for a topic of your choice in all of Yahoo! or only in the Education subcategory. In addition, you can select any of the Education subtopics listed below the search option. Clicking on a subtopic will then take you to another Web page that provides links to numerous sites pertaining to your topic. For example, if you would like to find sites related to Early Childhood Education, you would click on that subcategory. The next page you would find is

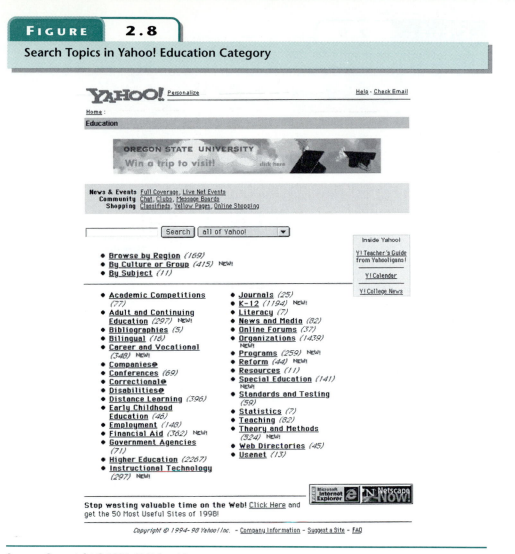

Source: Copyright © 1994–98 Yahoo! Inc.

as shown in Figure 2.9. Clicking on any of these links will access all of the information that those particular sites have to offer.

EVALUATING YOUR SOURCES

Once you have a source in hand, you will need to evaluate it. Obviously, the first thing to do is to determine if it really applies to your research topic. If it does, you then need to evaluate the quality of the information. For example, does the information come from a scholarly journal or a popular magazine? Is the information someone's personal opinion or the result of a research study? Clearly, sources of different types merit different weight in your review.

An initial appraisal of a source includes looking closely at the date of publication and where the source was found. Look at the copyright date of books that you find and the dates on which articles were published. Appropriate research in

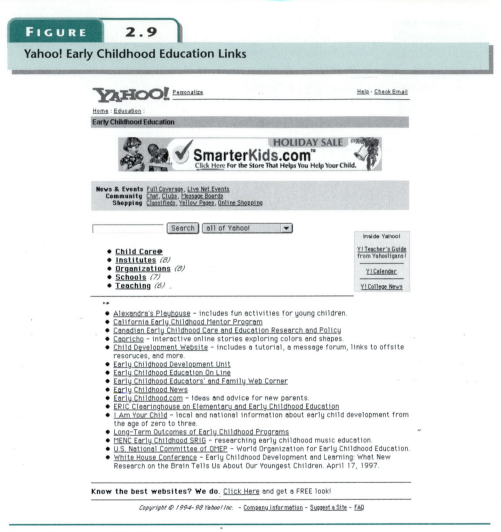

Source: Copyright © 1994–98 Yahoo! Inc.

topic areas of current interest and continuing development generally require recent, up-to-date references.

Next, identify where the source was found. For instance, did you find your source in a refereed or a nonrefereed journal? Research articles in refereed journals are required to comply with strict guidelines, not only in terms of format, but also in research procedures. Articles in refereed journals are reviewed by a panel of experts and thus tend to be more "trustworthy" than articles from nonrefereed or popular journals. The distinction between sources that are scholarly versus those that are popular is an important one.

It is also important to verify that the information presented in a particular source is objective and impartial. Does the author present evidence to support the interpretations made? Does the content of the article consist mainly of an individual's opinion or does it contain appropriately collected and analyzed data? Finally, does the source add to the information you have already gathered about your topic? If the source adds to your growing knowledge of your topic, it is useful and worth paying attention to.

Special care and caution must be taken when evaluating World Wide Web sources, because anyone can post information on the Web. Thus, just because an Internet search identifies a particular source does not mean that the source is accurate or credible. Sources from the World Wide Web must be closely examined for bias, subjectivity, intent, and accuracy.

Conducting effective library and Internet searches will yield an abundance of useful information about your topic. By combining the two, you will collect information that is at the same time up-to-date and comprehensive. As time goes on and you become more experienced at both, you will be able to conduct more efficient searches that are focused appropriately on your topic from the very start.

ABSTRACTING

After you have identified the primary references related to your topic using the appropriate resources, you are ready to move on to the next phase of a review of related literature—abstracting the references. Basically, this involves locating, reviewing, summarizing, and classifying your references. Students sometimes ask why it is necessary to read and abstract original, complete articles (or reports, or whatever) if they already have perfectly good abstracts. There are two basic reasons. First, abstracts are not necessarily "perfectly good." They may not be totally accurate interpretations or summaries of the articles' contents. And, second, there is a great deal of important information that can only be obtained by reading the complete article. (You'll see.)

Arrange the references you identified in each source in reverse chronological order, starting with the most recent. The abstracting process will be conducted in the same order. The main advantage of beginning with the latest references on a given topic is that in terms of research strategy, the most recent research is likely to have profited from previous research. Also, recent references may contain references to preceding studies you may not have identified. For each reference, a suggested procedure for abstracting is as follows:

1. If the article has an abstract or a summary, which most do, read it to determine the article's relevancy to your problem.
2. Skim the entire article, making mental notes of the main points of the study.
3. On a 4 × 6 in. index card write the complete bibliographic reference, including the library call number if it is a book. This is tedious but important. You will spend much more time trying to find the full citation of a reference you failed to abstract completely than you will abstracting it in the first place. If you know that your final report must follow a particular style, put your bibliographic reference in that form. If not, use the format of the American Psychological Association (APA). The APA format is becoming increasingly popular, primarily because it eliminates the need for formal footnotes. For a journal article, the APA bibliographic reference would be:

> Snurd, B. J. (1995). The use of white versus yellow chalk in the teaching of advanced calculus. *Journal of Useless Findings, 11,* 1–99.

In this example, 1995 refers to the date of publication, 11 to the volume, and 1–99 to the page numbers. If this reference were cited in the body of a paper (perhaps written by Goforth concerning the need for increased funding for useless research), then its description would be followed by (Snurd, 1995). The bibliography provides the full citation. If, however, the citation were a direct quote, the appropriate page number would need to be included, e.g., (Snurd, 1995, p. 45). Whatever format you use, use it consistently, and be certain the reference you copy is accurate. You never know when you might have to go back and get additional information from an article. Besides, even if you do not have to find it again, it is very unscholarly to have an incorrect reference in a research report. Also, if you are using index cards, put only one reference on each card. The purpose of using index cards is to facilitate sorting and organization of the articles prior to writing the review of the literature. An alternative strategy is to use a laptop computer for note taking. If you use this option, you still need to record correct and complete reference information. Many students prefer to photocopy articles, a strategy to be discussed shortly.

4. Classify and code the article according to some system and place the code on the same index card, or on the photocopy, in a conspicuous place, such as the upper right- or lefthand corner. If you are a laptop computer user, create a code that can be easily accessed when you want the computer to sort your notes into the categories you devise. For example, if your problem was concerned with salaried paraprofessionals versus parent volunteers (discussed earlier), you might use a three-part coding system to describe each article; the code might indicate whether the study was concerned with the use of paraprofessionals, parent volunteers, or both (PP versus PV versus B), whether it was an opinion article or a study (O versus S), and the degree of its relevance to your study (say 1, 2, or 3, with 3 meaning very relevant). Thus, PV/O/3 might be a code for an article describing the potential benefits to be derived from using parent volunteers. Any coding system that makes sense to you, given your problem, will facilitate your task later when you have to sort, organize, analyze, synthesize, and write your review of the literature. Useful computer programs that simplify the coding (and subsequent data retrieval) are HyperResearch[1] and EndNote.[2]

5. Abstract, or summarize, the reference. As neatly as you can (you're going to have to read them later!), write the essential points of the reference. If it is an opinion article, write the main points of the author's position—for example, "Jones believes parent volunteers should be used because . . ." and list the *becauses.* If it is a study, write the same kind of information you wrote for Task 1-A in chapter 1: the problem, the procedures (including the sample and instruments), and the major conclusions. Make special note of any particularly interesting or unique aspect of the study, such as a new measuring instrument that was utilized. Double-check the reference to make sure you have not omitted any pertinent information. If the abstract provided at the beginning of the article contains all the essential information (and that is a big if), by all means use it.

---

[1] Researchware. (1998). HyperRESEARCH 2.0. Randolph, MA.
[2] Niles and Associates. (1994). EndNotePlus. Berkeley, CA.

6. Indicate any thoughts that come to your mind, such as points on which you disagree (mark them with an X, for example) or components that you do not understand (put a ? next to them). For example, if an author stated that he or she had used a double-blind procedure, and you were unfamiliar with that technique, you could put a question mark in the margin next to that statement, either on your index card or on a photocopy of the page. Later, you can seek out a knowledgeable person, such as your advisor, and quickly identify points on which you need clarification or explanation.

7. Indicate any statements that are direct quotations or personal reactions: Plagiarism (intentional or not) is an absolute no-no, with the direst of consequences. If you do not put quotation marks around direct quotations on your index card, for example, you might not remember later which statements are, and which are not, direct quotations. Also, jot down the exact page number of the quotation in case you use the quotation later in your paper. Incidentally, direct quotations should be kept to a minimum in your research plan and report; both should be in your words, not other researchers'. Occasionally, however, a direct quotation may be quite appropriate.

8. As mentioned, an alternative strategy to taking notes on index cards is to photocopy references whenever feasible. You wouldn't want to copy a book, and if you did, you would probably get nasty treatment from those behind you in the copy machine line! More importantly, bear in mind that there is a copyright law that prohibits photocopying many resources. If it is appropriate to copy articles, you can take them home with you and make notes in the comfort of your home. The advantages of this approach are reduced time in the library and elimination of the possibility that you might have to go back and find a reference because you inadvertently left something out of your notes. Be sure, however, that you record all needed reference information (the volume number, for example) on your photocopy; not all journals list everything you need on each page (or even on the first page). Another alternative, for the truly technological among us, is to use a portable handheld scanner (with the same caveat concerning reference information). The main disadvantage of photocopying documents is the cost; photocopies cost a lot more than 4×6 in. index cards. Many researchers, however, feel that this approach is well worth it in terms of convenience. Probably some sort of compromise makes sense, such as using index cards for minor references and photocopying the articles that apply directly to your study, provide lots of information, or use very complicated procedures.

Whichever approach you use, guard your notes with your life. When you have completed your reviewing task, those notes will represent many hours of work. Students have been known to be literally in tears because they left their notes "on the bus" or "on a table in the cafeteria." Beyond being sympathetic, your instructor can do little more than to tell you to start over (ouch!). Also, when the research report is completed, the index cards can be filed (photocopies can be placed in notebooks), and saved for future reference and future studies (nobody can do just one!).

ANALYZING, ORGANIZING, AND
REPORTING THE LITERATURE

For beginning researchers, the hardest part of writing the literature review is thinking about how hard it is going to be to write the literature review. More time is spent worrying about doing it than actually doing it. Part of the reason for this hesitancy is lack of previous experience writing a literature review and part is the fact that writing a literature review is different from ordinary writing. A literature review is a technical form of writing that calls for different characteristics than most of the writing we normally do. In technical writing, facts must be documented and opinions must be substantiated. For example, if you say that the high school dropout percentage in Ohio has increased in the last 10 years, you must provide a source for this information. Technical writing is precise, requiring clarity of definitions and consistency in the use of terms. If the term *achievement* is important in your review, you must indicate what you mean by it and be consistent in using that meaning throughout the review. Table 2.5 identifies important characteristics of technical writing used in a literature review.

If you have efficiently abstracted the literature related to your problem, and if you approach the task in an equally systematic manner, then analyzing, organizing, and reporting it will be relatively painless. First, to get warmed up, read quickly through your notes. This will refresh your memory and help you identify

TABLE	**2.5**

Guidelines for Technical Writing

1. Document facts and substantiate opinions. Cite references to support your facts and opinions. Note that facts are usually based on empirical data while opinions are not. In the hierarchy of persuasiveness, facts are more persuasive than opinions. Differentiate between facts and opinions in the review.
2. Technical writing is precise, so clarity of definitions and consistency in the use of terms is required.
3. The review should be logically organized and aimed at a particular audience. Usually the review is aimed at a relatively naive reader, one who has some basic understanding of the topic but requires additional education to understand the topic or issue being studied. Do not assume your audience knows as much as you do about the topic and literature! They don't, so you have to write to educate them.
4. Technical writing is usually done using an accepted manual of style. The manual of style indicates the style in which chapter headings are set up, how tables must be constructed, how footnotes and bibliographies must be prepared, and the like. Follow the manual consistently. Commonly used manuals and their current editions are *Publication Manual of the American Psychological Association*, Fourth Edition, and *The Chicago Manual of Style*, Fourteenth Edition.
5. Evade affected verbiage and eschew obscuration of the obvious. Limit big words; avoid jargon.
6. Start each major section of the review with an introduction that provides a brief overview of the section. "In this section, three main issues are examined. The first is . . . ." This is also useful advice for introducing chapters in the report.
7. End major sections or chapters with a summary that indicates the main ideas, findings, or points.

some references that no longer seem sufficiently related to keep. Do not force references into your review that do not really "fit"; the review forms the background and rationale for your hypothesis and should only contain references that serve this purpose. It may hurt a little to discard references you worked so diligently to collect, but your review will be better for it. The following guidelines and suggestions are based on experience acquired the hard way and should be helpful to you:

1. Make an outline. Don't groan; your eighth-grade teacher was right about the virtues of an outline. However you do it, the time and thought you put into the outline will save you time in the long run and will increase your probability of having an organized review. The outline does not have to be excessively detailed. First, identify the main topics and the order in which they should be presented. For example, the outline formatted for this chapter started out as three main headings—Selection and Statement, Review of Related Literature, and Formulation and Statement of a Hypothesis. As another example, the outline of the review for the problem concerned with the effectiveness of salaried paraprofessionals versus parent volunteers might begin with the headings Literature on Salaried Paraprofessionals, Literature on Parent Volunteers, and Literature Comparing the Two. The next step is to differentiate each major heading into logical subheadings. In our outline, for example, Review of Related Literature was subdivided into the following:

   #### REVIEW OF RELATED LITERATURE
   Definition, Purpose, and Scope

   Getting Started

   Identifying Your Sources

   Evaluating Your Sources

   Abstracting

   Analyzing, Organizing, and Reporting

   The need for further differentiation will be determined by your topic and the literature you have reviewed; the more complex these are, the more subheadings will be required. When you have completed your outline you will invariably see topics that need rearranging. It is much easier, however, to reorganize an outline than it is to reorganize a document written in paragraph form.

2. Analyze each reference in terms of your outline; in other words, determine under which subheading each fits. Recognize that some references may fit in more than one subheading. Then sort your references into appropriate piles. If you end up with references without a home, there are three logical possibilities: (1) there is something wrong with your outline; (2) they do not belong in your review and should be discarded; or (3) they do not belong in your review but do belong somewhere else in your introduction. For example, a reference concerned with the problem of school vandalism might state that school vandalism costs U.S. taxpayers X thousands of dollars per year. Such a reference would belong either in the significance section of the statement of the problem—if the specific

problem to be investigated were concerned with several alternative methods of reducing school vandalism—or in the introductory paragraph to the review as an attention grabber. Opinion articles or reports of descriptive research often will be useful in the introductions, whereas formal research studies will be most useful in the review of related literature section.

3. Take all the references identified for a given subheading and analyze the relationships or differences between them. If three references say essentially the same thing, there is no need to describe each one; it is much better to make one summary statement followed by three references. For example:

> Several studies have found white chalk to be more effective than yellow chalk in the teaching of advanced mathematics (Snurd, 1995; Trivia, 1991; Ziggy, 1984).

Do not present your references as a series of abstracts or annotations (Jones found X, Smith found Y, and Brown found Z). Your task is to organize and summarize the references in a meaningful way. Do not ignore studies that are contradictory to most other studies or to your personal bias. Analyze and evaluate contradictory studies and try to determine a possible explanation. For example:

> Contrary to these studies is the work of Rottenstudee (1990), who found yellow chalk to be more effective than white chalk in the teaching of trigonometry. However, the size of the treatment groups (two students per group) and the duration of the study (one class period) may have seriously affected the results.

4. The review should flow in such a way that the references least related to the problem are discussed first, and the most related references are discussed last, just prior to the statement of the hypothesis. Think in terms of a big V. At the bottom of the V is your hypothesis; directly above your hypothesis are the studies most directly related to it, and so forth. For example, if your hypothesis stated that white chalk would be more effective than yellow chalk in teaching biology to 10th graders, immediately preceding it would be the studies indicating the effectiveness of white chalk in the teaching of mathematics. Preceding those studies might be studies indicating that students prefer to read white chalk. At the top of the V (the beginning of the review), several references might be cited expressing the belief that variables such as chalkboard color and color of chalk are important ones in the learning process, too often overlooked. These might be followed by similar references indicating that these variables might be even more critical in technical areas such as mathematics, which entail a lot of chalkboard usage. The idea is to organize and present your literature in such a way that it leads logically to a tentative, testable conclusion, namely your hypothesis. If your problem has more than one major aspect, you may have two Vs or one V that logically leads to two tentative, testable conclusions.

5. The review should conclude with a brief summary of the literature and its implications. The length of this summary depends on the length of the review. It should be detailed enough to clearly show the logic chain

you have followed in arriving at your implications and tentative conclusions. Having systematically developed and presented your rationale, you will now be ready to state your hypothesis.

It is important to note that literature reviews are constructed in both quantitative and qualitative research, because of the obligation to place a study in the context of similar or related research. However, there often is a difference between the two types of research in the approach to writing a literature review. A quantitative researcher normally follows the suggestions and steps for constructing a literature review just described. Some qualitative researchers also follows these, but most do not do a literature review until their study is well under way.

Most qualitative research requires expending substantial time in the research setting (e.g., a school or classroom) and relies heavily on the researcher's observation and questioning to collect data. Because of these features of qualitative research, there is a genuine concern on the part of qualitative researchers about the dangers of biasing their perceptions as a result of too early immersion in the topic's related literature. In addition, most qualitative researchers enter the research setting with a broad topic or very tentative hunches about what their study will be, and only lock in a specific topic after observing, questioning, and "living" in the setting. Thus, qualitative researchers often conduct literature reviews later in the process than do quantitative researchers, but ultimately, both develop a literature review for which the suggestions just noted become pertinent.

FORMULATION AND STATEMENT OF A HYPOTHESIS

Before you review the related literature, you have a tentative hypothesis that guides your search. Following the review, and preceding the actual execution of the study, the hypothesis is refined and finalized.

DEFINITION AND PURPOSE OF A HYPOTHESIS

A *hypothesis* is a researcher's tentative prediction of the results of the research findings. It states the researcher's expectations concerning the relationship between the variables in the research problem. Since many studies contain a number of variables, it is not uncommon to have more than one hypothesis for a research topic. The researcher does not then set out to *prove* his or her hypothesis, but rather, collects data to determine whether the hypothesis is supported or not supported by the data. Hypotheses are essential to all quantitative research studies, with the possible exception of some descriptive studies whose purpose is to answer certain specific questions.

The hypothesis is formulated from a theory or the review of related literature, prior to the execution of the study. It logically follows theory or the review, because it is based on the implications of the theory or the previous research. The related literature leads one to expect a certain relationship. For example, studies finding white chalk to be more effective than yellow chalk in teaching mathematics would lead a researcher to expect it to be more effective in teaching physics, if there were not other findings to the contrary. A theory that suggested that the ability to think abstractly was quite different for 10-year-olds versus 15-year-olds might suggest a hypothesis stating that there would be a difference in the performance of 10- and 15-year-olds on a test of abstract reasoning.

Hypotheses precede the study proper because the nature of the study is determined by the hypothesis. Every aspect of the research is affected by the hypothesis, including participants, measuring instruments, design, procedures, data analysis, and conclusions. Although all hypotheses are based on theory or previous knowledge and are aimed at extending knowledge, they are not all of equal worth. A number of criteria can and should be applied to a given hypothesis to determine its value.

CHARACTERISTICS OF A HYPOTHESIS

A good hypothesis has the following characteristics:

- It is based on sound reasoning.
- It provides a reasonable explanation for the predicted outcome.
- It clearly states the expected relationship between defined variables.
- It is testable within a reasonable time frame.

We will explore these characteristics in more detail in this section.

By now it should be clear that *a hypothesis should be based on a sound rationale.* It should follow from previous research or theory and lead to future research; its confirmation or disconfirmation should contribute to educational theory or practice. Therefore, a major characteristic of a good hypothesis is that it is consistent with theory or previous research. The chances of your being a Christopher Columbus of educational research who is going to show that something believed to be "flat" is really "round" are slim! Of course, in areas of research where there are conflicting results, you will not be able to be consistent with all of them, but your hypothesis should follow from the rule, not the exception.

The previously stated definition of a hypothesis indicated that it is a tentative prediction of the results of the research outcomes. *A good hypothesis provides a reasonable explanation for the predicted outcome.* If your telephone is out of order, you might hypothesize that it is because there are butterflies sitting on your telephone wires; such a hypothesis would not be a reasonable explanation. A reasonable hypothesis might be that you forgot to pay your bill or that a repair crew is working outside. In a research study, a hypothesis suggesting that children with freckles pay attention longer than children without freckles would not be a reasonable explanation for attention behavior. On the other hand, a hypothesis suggesting that children who have a good breakfast pay attention longer would be.

A good hypothesis states as clearly and concisely as possible the expected relationship (or difference) between two variables and defines those variables in operational, that is, measurable, terms. A simply but clearly stated hypothesis makes it easier for readers to understand, simplifies its testing, and facilitates formulation of conclusions. The relationship expressed between two variables may or may not be a causal one. For example, the variables anxiety and math achievement might be hypothesized to be significantly related (there is a significant correlation between anxiety and math achievement), or it might be hypothesized that on math problems high-anxiety students perform better than low-anxiety students.

This example also illustrates the need for operational definitions. What kind of math problems? What is a high-anxiety student? What does it mean to perform better? In this example, *high-anxiety student* might be defined as any student whose score on the Acme Anxiety Inventory is in the upper 30% of student scores. A *low-anxiety student* might be defined as any student who scores in the lowest 30% of students on the Acme Anxiety Inventory. Higher performance on "math problems" might be defined in terms of math subtest scores on the California Achievement Test. It is common to operationally define variables in terms of scores on a given test or inventory.

If the hypothesis variables can be operationally defined within the actual hypothesis statement without making it unwieldy, this should be done. If not, the hypothesis statement should be stated and the appropriate terms defined immediately following it. Of course, if all necessary terms have already been defined, either within or immediately following the topic statement, there is no need to repeat the definitions in the statement of the hypothesis. The general rule of thumb is to define terms the first time they are used, but it does not hurt to occasionally remind the reader of how terms are defined.

A well-stated and defined hypothesis must be testable (and it will be if it is well-formulated and stated). *It should be possible to test the hypothesis by collecting and analyzing data.* It would not be possible to test a hypothesis that indicated that some students behave better than others because some have an invisible little angel on their right shoulder and some have an invisible little devil on their left shoulder. There would be no way to collect data to support the hypothesis. In addition to being testable, *a good hypothesis should normally be testable within some reasonable period of time.* For example, the hypothesis that first-grade students who brush their teeth after lunch every day will have fewer false teeth at age 60 would obviously take a very long time to test. The researcher would very likely be long gone before the study was completed, not to mention the negligible educational significance of the hypothesis! A more manageable hypothesis with the same theme might be that first-grade children who brush their teeth after lunch every day will have fewer cavities than those who don't at the end of the first grade.

TYPES OF HYPOTHESES

Hypotheses can be classified in terms of how they are derived (inductive versus deductive hypotheses) or how they are stated (declarative versus null hypotheses). An inductive hypothesis is a generalization based on observed relationships. The researcher observes that certain patterns or associations among variables occur in a number of situations and uses these tentative observations to form an inductive hypothesis. For example, a researcher observes that in many eighth-grade classrooms students who are given essay tests appear to show less testing stress than those who are given multiple-choice tests. This observation could become the basis for an inductive hypothesis.

Deductive hypotheses are generally derived from theory. For example, a study conducted by Ausubel[3] (1966) found no significant differences in retention between a group receiving a review 1 day after learning and a group receiving a review 7 days after learning. Ausubel suggested that the timing of the review did not have a significant effect on retention because early and late reviews each contribute to retention in a different way. An early review consolidates material, while a delayed review promotes relearning of forgotten material. In a subsequent study, Gay[4] hypothesized that if Ausubel was correct, then two reviews,

---

[3]Ausubel, D. P. (1966). Early versus delayed review in meaningful learning. *Psychology in the Schools, 3,* 195–198.

[4]Gay, L. R. (1973). Temporal position of reviews and its effect on the retention of mathematical rules. *Journal of Educational Psychology, 74,* 171–182.

one early and one delayed, will be more effective than either two early reviews or two delayed reviews. The results of the study generally supported this hypothesis. In deriving a hypothesis from a theory, you should be sure that your hypothesis is a logical implication of theory, not a wild, unsupported inferential leap.

A research hypothesis states an expected relationship or difference between two variables. In other words, it specifies the relationship the researcher expects to verify in the research study. Research, or declarative, hypotheses can be nondirectional or directional. A *nondirectional hypothesis* simply states that a relationship or difference exists between variables. A *directional hypothesis* states the expected direction of the relationship or difference. For example, a nondirectional hypothesis might state:

> There is a significant difference in the achievement of 10th-grade biology students who are instructed using interactive multimedia and those who receive regular instruction only.

The corresponding directional hypothesis might state:

> Tenth-grade biology students who are instructed using interactive multimedia achieve at a higher level than those who receive regular instruction only.

The nondirectional hypothesis states that there will be a difference between the 10th-grade groups, while the directional hypothesis states that there will be a difference and that the difference will favor interactive media instruction.

A directional hypothesis should only be stated if you have a basis to believe that the results will occur in the stated direction. Nondirectional and directional hypotheses involve different types of statistical tests of significance, as will be examined in chapter 13.

Finally, a null hypothesis states that there is no significant relationship or difference between variables. For example, a null hypothesis might state:

> There is no significant difference in the achievement level of 10th-grade biology students who are instructed using interactive multimedia and those who receive regular instruction.

The null hypothesis is the hypothesis of choice when there is little research or theoretical support for a hypothesis. Also, statistical tests for the null hypothesis are more conservative than they are for directional hypotheses.

The disadvantage of null hypotheses is that they rarely express the researcher's true expectations based on literature, insights, and logic regarding the results of a study. One approach is to state a research hypothesis (either directional or nondirectional), analyze your data assuming a null hypothesis, and then make inferences concerning your research hypothesis based on your testing of a null hypothesis. Given that few studies are really designed to verify the nonexistence of a relationship, it seems logical that most studies should be based on a nonnull hypothesis.

Hypotheses are critical aspects of quantitative research approaches; they focus the study on the methods and strategies needed to collect data to test the hypotheses. As noted previously, the aims and strategies of qualitative research differ from those of quantitative research. As a general rule, qualitative researchers do not state hypotheses to guide the conduct of their studies. They rarely test hypotheses at all. Rather than testing a priori hypotheses, qualitative researchers are much more likely to generate new hypotheses as a result of their studies. The inductive processes used in qualitative research are based on observing patterns and associations in the natural setting without prior specification of what will be observed. The identification of patterns and associations in the setting often generate ideas and questions that lead to new hypotheses. For example, the repeated observation that early in the school year first-grade students can accurately identify who are the "smart" and who are the "not smart" students in class might suggest a hypothesis related to how teachers' actions and words communicate students' status in the classroom. In simple terms, it is generally appropriate to say that a strength of quantitative research is in testing hypotheses, while that of qualitative research is in generating hypotheses.

STATING THE HYPOTHESIS

As previously discussed, a good hypothesis is stated clearly and concisely, expresses the relationship between two variables, and defines those variables in measurable terms. A general model for stating hypotheses for experimental studies is as follows:

> P who get X do better on Y than
> P who do not get X (or get some other X)

If this model appears to be an oversimplification, it is because it is, and it may not always be appropriate. However, this model should help you to understand the statement of a hypothesis. Further, this model, sometimes with variations, will be applicable in many situations. In the model,

> P refers to the participants,
> X refers to the treatment, the causal or independent variable (IV), and
> Y refers to the observed outcome, the effect or dependent variable (DV).

Study the following topic statement and see if you can identify the P, X, and Y:

> The purpose of this study is to investigate the effectiveness of 12th-grade mentors on the absenteeism of low-achieving 10th graders.

In this example,

> P = low-achieving 10th graders,
>
> X = presence or absence of a 12th-grade mentor (IV), and
>
> Y = absenteeism (days absent or, stated positively, days present) (DV).

A review of the literature might indicate that mentors have been found to be effective in influencing younger students. Therefore, the directional hypothesis resulting from this topic might read:

> Low-achieving 10th graders *(P)* who have a 12th-grade mentor *(X)* have less absenteeism *(Y)* than low-achieving 10th graders who do not.

As another example, suppose your topic statement was as follows:

The purpose of the proposed research is to investigate the effectiveness of differ-ent conflict resolution techniques in reducing the aggressive behaviors of high school students in an alternative educational setting.

For this topic statement,

P = high school students in an alternative educational setting,

X = type of conflict resolution (punishment or discussion) (IV), and

Y = instances of aggressive behaviors (DV).

The related nondirectional hypothesis might read:

There will be a difference in the number of aggressive behaviors of high school students in an alternative educational setting who receive either punishment or discussion approaches to conflict resolution.

Got the idea? Let's try one more.
Topic Statement:

This study investigates the effectiveness of token reinforcement, in the form of free time given for the completion of practice worksheets, on the math computa-tion skills of ninth-grade general math students.

P = ninth-grade general math students,

X = token reinforcement in the form of free time for completion of practice worksheets, and

Y = math computation skills.

Hypothesis:

Ninth-grade general math students who receive token reinforcement in the form of free time for the completion of practice worksheets have higher math compu-tation skills than ninth-grade general math students who do not receive token re-inforcement for completed worksheets.

Of course, in all of these examples there are terms that would need to be de-fined (e.g., aggressive behaviors).
For a null hypothesis, the paradigm is:

There is no difference on Y between P who get X and P who do not get X (or get some other X).

See if you can write the null hypothesis for the following problem statement:

The purpose of this study is to assess the impact of formal versus informal preschool reading instruction on first graders' reading comprehension at the end of the first grade.

Testing the Hypothesis

The researcher selects the sample, measuring instruments, design, and procedures that will enable her or him to collect the data necessary to test the hypothesis. Collected data are analyzed in a manner that permits the researcher to determine whether the hypothesis is supported. Note that analysis of the data does not lead to a hypothesis being proven or not proven, only supported or not supported for this particular study. The results of analysis indicate whether a hypothesis was supported or not supported for the particular participants, context, and instruments involved. Many beginning researchers have the misconception that if their hypothesis is not supported by their data, then their study is a failure, and conversely, if it is supported, then their study is a success. Neither of these beliefs is true. It is just as important to know what variables are not related as it is to know what variables are related. If a hypothesis is not supported, a valuable contribution may be made in the form of a revision of some aspect of a theory; such revision will generate new or revised hypotheses. Thus, hypothesis testing contributes to the science of education primarily by expanding, refining, or revising its knowledge base.

Summary / Chapter 2

Identifying a Topic to Research

1. The first step in selecting a research topic is to identify a general area that is related to your area of expertise and is of particular interest to you.

2. There are three main sources of research topics: theory, personal experience, and replication.

3. Theories are composed of organized bodies of concepts, generalizations, and principles. Research studies commonly test or examine particular aspects of a theory to determine its applicability or generalizability.

4. A researcher's personal experiences and concerns often lead to useful and personally rewarding studies. Commonly asked questions, such as, "Why does that happen?" "What would happen if. . . ?" and "How would a different group respond to this approach?" can provide rich sources of topics if followed up.

5. Replication, that is, repeating an existing study, is also a common source of research topics. It is generally expected that some feature of the replication (e.g., sample, instruments) will differ from the original study.

6. Library immersion in the literature in a problem area is generally not an efficient way to identify a research topic unless one focuses on handbooks, encyclopedias, and yearbooks that cover many topics briefly. Of course, library resources will be an invaluable source of information once you have identified a topic to study.

7. Once an initial topic is identified, it usually needs to be narrowed and focused into a manageable topic to study.

8. Qualitative and quantitative research often differ in the timing of narrowing their topics. Quantitative research topics are usually narrowed as quickly as possible. Qualitative research topics are usually delayed until time is spent in the setting.

Characteristics of Good Topics

9. A basic characteristic of a research problem is that it is *researchable,* that is, it can be investigated through the collection and analysis of data. Topics related to philosophical and ethical issues or *should* questions are not researchable.

10. A good problem has theoretical or practical significance; its solution should contribute in some way to improvement of the educational process.

11. A good topic must be a good one for you. It must be a topic that you can adequately investigate given (1) your current level of research skill, (2) your available resources, and (3) your time and other restrictions.

STATING RESEARCH TOPICS

12. A well-written topic statement for a quantitative study generally indicates the variables of interest to the researcher, the specific relationship between those variables that is to be investigated, and, ideally, the type of participants involved.

13. A well-written quantitative topic statement also defines all relevant variables, either directly or operationally; operational definitions define concepts in terms of measurable characteristics.

14. The statement of the problem should be accompanied by a presentation of the background of the problem, including a justification for the study in terms of its significance.

15. Qualitative research topics often are stated later than those of quantitative research because the qualitative researcher needs to become attuned to the research context before narrowing the topic.

16. The topic statement is the first component in the introductory section of a research plan and provides direction for the remaining aspects of the study.

Literature Review: Definition, Purpose, and Scope

17. The review of related literature involves the systematic identification, location, and analysis of documents containing information related to the research topic.

18. The major purpose of reviewing the literature is to put your study in the context of what information already exists that relates to your topic.

19. Another important function of the literature review is that it points out research strate-gies, procedures, and instruments that have and have not been found to be productive in investigating your topic. It also facilitates interpretation of the results of the study.

20. A smaller, well-organized review is definitely to be preferred to a review containing many studies that are more or less related to the problem. This does not mean that important references are omitted from the review.

21. Heavily researched areas usually provide enough references directly related to a topic to eliminate the need for reporting less-related or secondary studies. Little-researched topics usually require review of any study related in some meaningful way in order to develop a logical framework and rationale for the study.

22. A common misconception among beginning researchers is the idea that the worth of their problem is a function of the amount of literature available on the topic. Unfortunately, there is no formula that indicates how much literature has to be reviewed for a given topic.

GETTING STARTED

23. Time spent initially will save time in the long run; you should find out what references are available and where they are located, especially the periodicals. Global resources such as handbooks, encyclopedias, and yearbooks are useful starting places to obtain an overview of your topic and useful references to examine.

24. You should also be familiar with services offered by the library as well as the rules and regulations. Most libraries have tours or written materials describing the resources and their use. Reference librarians will be of most help in planning and executing your literature review.

25. Before beginning the review, make a list of key words related to your problem to guide your literature search.

IDENTIFYING YOUR SOURCES

26. A primary source is a study written by the person who conducted it; a secondary source

is generally a much briefer description of a study written by someone other than the original researcher. Primary sources are preferred in the review.

27. There is a difference between the opinion of an author and the results of an empirical study. The latter is more valued in a review.

28. A good starting point to obtain a perspective on a topic and identify literature sources is to look at handbooks, encyclopedias, and reviews in your topic area.

Consulting Computer Databases

29. Most libraries use a computer catalog system that indexes all of the sources in the library by author, title, and subject.

30. The computer screen allows the user to find information about the topic, author, or subject by typing information about the topic, author, or subject of the search. The search provides information about the call number of the resource requested. The user can then seek out the resource in the library stacks.

31. If you are at the beginning of a literature search for primary references, you might not have identified specific titles or authors to search for. A keyword search uses terms or phrases pertinent to your topic to search and identify potentially useful literature sources.

32. Keyword searches can be focused by using the Boolean operators *and, or,* and *not.* Using *and* or *not* narrows a search and the number of sources identified, while *or* broadens the search and acquired sources. It is often best to start with a narrow search.

33. Computerized databases can facilitate the identification of relevant primary sources. An online search is performed at a computer terminal that is connected by telephone to the central database. Searching the database involves use of key words.

34. There are many useful databases pertinent to educational researchers. Among the most used are ERIC, *Education Index, Psychological Abstracts,* and *Dissertation Abstracts.* Most of these sources provide abstracts of literature, not the full text. Nonetheless, they are useful in identifying sources to investigate.

Searching the World Wide Web

35. The Internet is a computer network linking organizations and individuals all over the world. The World Wide Web is on the Internet. Users can converse with other users and access a variety of media, texts, and graphics.

36. To access the Internet you need a computer with a modem hooked to a telephone line and a browser to get you onto the World Wide Web. If you do not have the required parts, you can get on the Internet at most local libraries.

37. Since the available resources on the World Wide Web are virtually limitless, the best way to become familiar with its use is to "muck around" in your spare time. Also, talk to other Internet users when you have a question.

38. The World Wide Web contains a variety of sites relevant to an educational researcher. Each site is reached by using its Internet address. Addresses containing *ed* are related to educational institutions and those ending in *.com* are related to commercial enterprises.

39. Major Web sites include ERIC, which contains information on a variety of different educational areas. The U.S. Department of Education has a Web site, as do all state Departments of Education. Other sites focus on educational newspaper articles, curriculum, testing, ethics, and teaching methods.

40. Search engines are sites that allow the user to search the entire Internet. Most search engines list a variety of topics that can be used to focus a search. Search engines also allow keyword searches that encompass the entire World Wide Web.

41. It cannot be overemphasized that material on the World Wide Web is not screened for quality, honesty, bias, or authenticity. Virtually anyone can put anything on the Web. Thus, users must be careful not to assume that all material obtained from the Web is useful just because it comes from the Internet.

42. Combining a library search with a Web search will probably produce an abundance of sources to examine and rate for quality and relevance to your topic.

ABSTRACTING

43. Abstracting involves locating, reviewing, summarizing, and classifying your references.
44. The main advantage of beginning with the latest references on a given topic is that the most recent studies are likely to have profited from previous research. Also, references in more recent studies may contain references to preceding studies you had not identified.
45. For each reference, write a complete bibliographic record, including author's name, date of publication, title, journal name or book title, volume number, issue number, page numbers, and library call number. Identify main ideas. Put quotation marks around quotes taken from the reference and don't forget to get page numbers of the quote. Keep all references in the format required for research reports or dissertations.
46. Save your notes for future reference and future studies.

ANALYZING, ORGANIZING, AND REPORTING THE LITERATURE

47. Describing and reporting research call for a different style of writing than we commonly use. Technical writing requires documenting facts and substantiating opinions; clarifying definitions and using them consistently; using an accepted manual of style; starting sections with an introduction and ending them with a brief summary.
48. The following guidelines should be helpful: make an outline; sort your references into appropriate topic piles; analyze the relationships and differences between references in a given subheading; do not present your references as a series of abstracts or annotations; discuss references least related to the problem first; and conclude with a brief summary of the literature and its implications.
49. Both qualitative and quantitative researchers construct literature reviews, but the qualitative researcher is more likely to construct the review after starting the study, while the quantitative researcher is more likely to construct the review prior to starting the study.

Formulation and Statement of a Hypothesis

50. A hypothesis is the researcher's tentative predictions of the results of the research findings. Hypotheses are more common in quantitative than qualitative research.
51. The researcher does not set out to "prove" his or her hypothesis but rather, collects data that either support or do not support the hypothesis.
52. A hypothesis is formulated based on a theory or the review of related literature. It is stated prior to the execution of the study. The hypothesis logically follows the literature review and is based on the implications of previous research.
53. The hypothesis precedes the study because the hypothesis guides the conduct of the study.

CHARACTERISTICS OF A HYPOTHESIS

54. A critical characteristic of a good hypothesis is that it is based on a sound rationale. A hypothesis is a reasoned prediction, not a wild guess. It is a tentative, but rational, explanation for the predicted outcome.
55. A good hypothesis states as clearly and concisely as possible the expected relationship (or difference) between two variables and defines those variables in measurable terms.
56. A well-stated and defined hypothesis must be testable.

TYPES OF HYPOTHESES

57. An inductive hypothesis is a generalization made from a number of observations.
58. A deductive hypothesis is derived from theory and is aimed at providing evidence that supports, expands, or contradicts aspects of a given theory.
59. A research hypothesis states the expected relationship (or difference) between two variables. It states the relationship the researcher expects to verify through the collection and analysis of data. Research hypotheses can be nondirectional, directional, or null.
60. A nondirectional hypothesis indicates that a relationship or difference exists but does not

indicate the direction of the difference; a directional hypothesis indicates that a relationship or difference exists and indicates the direction of the difference. A null hypothesis states that there will be no significant relationship (or difference) between variables.

STATING THE HYPOTHESIS

61. A general paradigm, or model, for stating hypotheses for experimental studies is as follows: *P* who get *X* do better on *Y* than *P* who do not get *X* (or get some other *X*). *P* refers to participants, *X* refers to the treatment or independent variable (IV), and *Y* refers to the outcome or dependent variable (DV).

62. Hypotheses are tested using statistical analyses of data gathered in the study.

63. It is just as important to know which variables are not related as it is to know which variables are.

☐ **Task 2** *Performance Criteria*

The introduction that you develop for Task 2 will be the first part of the research report required for Task 8. Therefore, it may save you some revision time later if, when appropriate, statements are expressed in the past tense ("the topic investigated was" or "it was hypothesized," for example). Your introduction should include the following subheadings and contain the following types of information:

> INTRODUCTION (Background and significance of the problem)
> Statement of the Problem (Problem statement and necessary definitions)
> Review of Related Literature (Don't forget the big V)
> Statement of the Hypothesis(es)

As a guideline, three typed pages will generally be a sufficient length for Task 2. Of course for a real study you would review not just 10 to 15 references but all relevant references, and the introduction would be correspondingly longer.

Because of feedback from your instructor on Objective 4, and insight gained through developing your review of related literature, the hypothesis you state in Task 2 may very well be somewhat different from the one you stated for Objective 4 on page 37.

One final note: The hypothesis you formulate now will influence all further tasks—that is, who will be your participants, what they will do, and so forth. In this connection, the following is an informal observation based on the behavior of thousands of students, not a research-based finding. All beginning research students fall some place on a continuum of realism. At one extreme are the Cecil B. Demise students who want to design a study involving a cast of thousands, over an extended period of time. At the other extreme are the Mr. Magi students who will not even consider a procedure unless they know *for sure* they could actually execute it in their work setting, with their students or clients. Since you do not have to actually execute the study you design, feel free to operate in the manner most comfortable for you. Keep in mind, however, that there is a middle ground between Demise and Magi.

On the following pages an example is presented that illustrates the format and content of an introduction that meets the criteria just described (see the following Task 2 example). This task example (and task examples for succeeding parts), with few modifications, represents the task as submitted by a former student in an introductory educational research course—Sara Jane Caldron, Florida International University. While an example from published research could have been used, the example given more accurately reflects the performance that is expected of you at your current level of expertise. Additional examples for this and subsequent tasks are included in the *Student Guide* that accompanies this text.

1

Effect of Interactive Multimedia on the Achievement of
10th-Grade Biology Students

Introduction

One of the major concerns of educators and parents alike is the decline in student achievement (as measured by standardized tests). An area of particular concern is science education where the high-level thinking skills and problem solving techniques so necessary for success in our technological society need to be developed (Smith & Westhoff, 1992).

Research is constantly providing new proven methods for educators to use, and technology has developed all kinds of tools ideally suited to the classroom. One such tool is interactive multimedia (IMM). IMM provides teachers with an extensive amount of data in a number of different formats including text, sound, and video making it possible to appeal to the different learning styles of the students and to offer a variety of material for students to analyze (Howson & Davis, 1992).

When teachers use IMM, students become highly motivated, which results in improved class attendance and more completed assignments (O'Connor, 1993). Students also become actively involved in their own learning, encouraging comprehension rather than mere memorization of facts (Kneedler, 1993; Reeves, 1992).

Statement of the Problem

The purpose of this study was to investigate the effect of interactive multimedia on the achievement of 10th-grade biology students. Interactive multimedia was defined as "a computerized database that allows users to access infor-

2

mation in multiple forms, including text, graphics, video and audio" (Reeves, 1992, p. 47).

Review of Related Literature

Due to modern technology, students receive more information from visual sources than they do from the written word, and yet in school the majority of information is still transmitted through textbooks. While textbooks cover a wide range of topics superficially, IMM provides in-depth information on essential topics in a format that students find interesting (Kneedler, 1993). Smith and Westhoff (1992) note that when student interest is sparked, curiosity levels are increased and students are motivated to ask questions. The interactive nature of multimedia allows the students to seek out their own answers and by so doing they become owners of the concept involved. Ownership translates into comprehension (Howson & Davis, 1992).

Many science concepts are learned through observation of experiments. Using multimedia, students can participate in a variety of experiments that are either too expensive, too lengthy, or too dangerous to carry out in the laboratory (Howson & Davis, 1992; Leonard, 1989; Louie, Sweat, Gresham, & Smith, 1991). While observing the experiments the students can discuss what is happening and ask questions. At the touch of a button teachers are able to replay any part of the proceedings, and they also have random access to related information that can be used to completely illustrate the answer to the question (Howson & Davis, 1992). By answering students' questions in this detailed way the content will become more relevant to the needs of the student (Smith & Westhoff, 1992). When knowledge is relevant students are able to use it to solve problems and, in so doing, develop

3

higher-level thinking skills (Helms & Helms, 1992; Sherwood, Kinzer, Bransford, & Franks, 1987).

A major challenge of science education is to provide students with large amounts of information that will encourage them to be analytical (Howson & Davis, 1992; Sherwood et al., 1987). IMM offers electronic access to extensive information allowing students to organize, evaluate and use it in the solution of problems (Smith & Wilson, 1993). When information is introduced as an aid to problem solving, it becomes a tool with which to solve other problems, rather than a series of solitary, disconnected facts (Sherwood et al., 1987).

Although critics complain that IMM is entertainment and students do not learn from it (Corcoran, 1989), research has shown that student learning does improve when IMM is used in the classroom (Sherwood et al., 1987; Sherwood & Others, 1990). A 1987 study by Sherwood et al., for example, showed that seventh- and eighth-grade science students receiving instruction enhanced with IMM had better retention of that information, and O'Connor (1993) found that the use of IMM in high school mathematics and science increased the focus on students' problem solving and critical thinking skills.

Statement of the Hypothesis

The quality and quantity of software available for science classes has dramatically improved during the past decade. Although some research has been carried out on the effects of IMM on student achievement in science, due to promising updates in the technology involved, further study is warranted. Therefore, it was hypothesized that 10th-grade biology students whose teachers use IMM as part of their

4

instructional technique will exhibit significantly higher achievement than 10th-grade biology students whose teachers do not use IMM.

References

Corcoran, E. (1989, July). Show and tell: Hypermedia turns information into a multisensory event. <u>Scientific American, 261,</u> 72, 74.

Helms, C. W., & Helms, D. R. (1992, June). Multimedia in education (Report No. IR-016-090). Proceedings of the 25th Summer Conference of the Association of Small Computer Users in Education. North Myrtle Beach, SC (ERIC Document Reproduction Service No. ED 357 732).

Howson, B. A., & Davis, H. (1992). Enhancing comprehension with videodiscs. <u>Media and Methods, 28,</u> 3, 12-14.

Kneedler, P. E. (1993). California adopts multimedia science program. <u>Technological Horizons in Education Journal, 20,</u> 7, 73-76.

Lehmann, I. J. (1990). Review of National Proficiency Survey Series. In J. J. Kramer & J. C. Conoley (Eds.), <u>The eleventh mental measurements yearbook</u> (pp. 595-599). Lincoln: University of Nebraska, Buros Institute of Mental Measurement.

Leonard, W. H. (1989). A comparison of student reaction to biology instruction by interactive videodisc or conventional laboratory. <u>Journal of Research in Science Teaching, 26,</u> 95-104.

Louie, R., Sweat, S., Gresham, R., & Smith, L. (1991). Interactive video: Disseminating vital science and math information. <u>Media and Methods, 27,</u> 5, 22-23.

O'Connor, J. E. (1993, April). Evaluating the effects of

5

collaborative efforts to improve mathematics and science curricula (Report No. TM-019-862). Paper presented at the Annual Meeting of the American Educational Research Association, Atlanta, GA (ERIC
Document Reproduction Service No. ED 357 083).

Reeves, T. C. (1992). Evaluating interactive multimedia. <u>Ed-
ucational Technology, 32,</u> 5, 47-52.

Sherwood, R. D., Kinzer, C. K., Bransford, J. D., & Franks,
J. J. (1987). Some benefits of creating macro-contexts
for science instruction: Initial findings. <u>Journal of
Research in Science Teaching, 24,</u> 417-435.

Sherwood, R. D., & Others (1990, April). An evaluative study
of level one videodisc based chemistry program (Report No. SE-051-513). Paper presented at a Poster
Session at the 63rd. Annual Meeting of the National
Association for Research in Science Teaching, Atlanta, GA (ERIC Document Reproduction Service No. ED
320 772).

Smith, E. E., & Westhoff, G. M. (1992). The Taliesin project: Multidisciplinary education and multimedia. <u>Edu-
cational Technology, 32.</u> 15-23.

Smith, M. K., & Wilson, C. (1993, March). Integration of
student learning strategies via technology (Report
No. IR-016-035). Proceedings of the Fourth Annual
Conference of Technology and Teacher Education. San
Diego, CA (ERIC Document Reproduction Service No: ED
355 937).

PART THREE

Research Plans

Once you have identified your topic, examined pertinent literature, and, if appropriate, stated a hypothesis, the next step in the research process is to develop a research plan that delineates the methods and procedures you will use to carry out your study. Although research plans rarely are executed exactly as stated, having a plan provides an overview of your study and permits assessment of the impact of any changes that are needed.

Developing a complete research plan requires expertise in a number of areas. A research plan generally describes the nature of the sample, the nature of the variables you will study, the kind of data to be collected, the instruments used to collect the data, the conditions under which the data will be collected, and the techniques to be used to analyze the data. For example, a quantitative researcher whose topic concerns the attitude of students toward school might collect data from eighth graders using the Acme School Attitude Survey instrument with the teacher administering the instruments to the class. The researcher would score the survey and summarize the data into percentages of attitudes toward different aspects of schooling (recess, science class, study hall, etc.). A qualitative researcher interested in the attitude of students toward school might collect data from 10 articulate eighth graders who vary in school performance and future aspirations. Data might be collected by observing them in school and by a series of tape-recorded interviews about their attitudes toward aspects of

school. The researcher would collate his or her written observations and transcribe the tape recordings. The researcher would then search the transcriptions for important themes and issues prior to writing a narrative, including many student quotes about the students' and their perceptions of school. Clearly a researcher needs many competencies in order to create and carry out a viable quantitative or qualitative research plan.

The goal of Part Three is to help you to understand the importance of developing a research plan and to become familiar with the components of a plan. After you have read Part Three, you should be able to perform the following task.

TASK 3

For the hypothesis you have formulated, develop the remaining components of a research plan for a study you would conduct in order to test your hypothesis. Include the following:

    Method
        Participants
        Instruments
        Design
        Procedure
    Data Analysis
    Time Schedule

Note: Assumptions, limitations, and definitions should be included where appropriate (see Performance Criteria, p. 115).

"A written plan also allows others to both identify flaws and make suggestions about ways to improve the plan (p. 91)."

Preparation and Evaluation of a Research Plan

◼ OBJECTIVES

After reading chapter 3, you should be able to:

1. Briefly describe three ethical considerations involved in conducting and reporting educational research.
2. Describe two major pieces of legislation affecting educational research.
3. Briefly describe each of the components of a research plan.
4. Briefly describe two major ways in which a research plan can be evaluated.

DEFINITION AND PURPOSE OF A RESEARCH PLAN

A research plan is a detailed description of the procedures that will be used to investigate your topic or problem. It includes justification for hypotheses, a detailed presentation of the research steps that will be followed in collecting, choosing, and analyzing data, and an estimated time schedule for each major step. A research plan may be relatively brief and informal, such as the one that you will develop for Task 3, or very lengthy and formal, such as the proposals submitted to obtain governmental and private research funding. Most schools typically require that a proposal, or prospectus, be submitted for approval prior to the execution of a thesis or dissertation study. A student is expected to demonstrate that he or she has a reasonable research plan before being allowed to begin the study. Playing it by ear is all right for the piano, but not for conducting research.

After you have completed the review of related literature and, if needed, formulated your hypothesis, you are ready to develop the rest of the research plan. In quantitative research, the nature of the hypothesis will be the basis for determining the sample group,

measuring instruments, design, procedures, and statistical techniques used in your study.[1] The research plan serves several important purposes. First, it forces you to think through every aspect of the study. The very process of getting it down on paper usually makes you think of something you might otherwise have overlooked. A second purpose of a written plan is that it facilitates evaluation of the proposed study, by you and others. Problems become apparent and sometimes great ideas do not look so great after all when they have been written down and considered. A written plan also allows others to both identify flaws and make suggestions about ways to improve the plan. A third and fundamental purpose of a research plan is to provide detailed procedures to guide conduct of the study. Also, if something unexpected occurs that alters some phase of the study, a plan allows for assessment of the impact on the rest of the study. For example, suppose you ordered 60 copies

---

[1] Each of these parts of a research plan will be discussed in succeeding chapters.

91

of a test that was to be administered on May 1. If on April 15 you received a letter saying that, due to a shortage of available tests, your order could not be filled until May 15, your study might be seriously affected. At the very least it would be delayed several weeks. The deadlines in your research plan might indicate that you cannot afford to wait. You might decide to use an alternate measuring instrument. Or you might contact another vendor. The many benefits of a research plan are as viable for "old hands" as for beginning researchers. It is useful to document problems such as this to alert others to them.

Murphy's law states, essentially, that "if anything can go wrong, it will." Airasian and Gay's law states that "if anything can go wrong, it will—unless you make sure that it doesn't!" If your study is a disaster because of poor planning, you lose. If something that could have been avoided goes wrong, you might have to redo the whole study, at worst, or somehow salvage the remnants of a less-than-ideal study, at best. A well-thought-out plan saves time, provides structure for the study, reduces the probability of costly mistakes, and generally results in higher quality research.

Part of good planning is anticipation. Try to anticipate potential problems that might arise, and then do what you can to prevent them. For example, you might anticipate that some principals will be less than open to your using their students as participants in your study (a common occurrence). To deal with this contingency you should work up the best, but honest, sales pitch possible. Do not ask, "Hey, can I use your kids for my study?" Instead, tell them how the study will benefit their students or their schools. If there is still opposition, you might tell them how enthusiastic central administration is about the study. Got the idea? To avoid many problems and to obtain strategies for overcoming them, it is extremely useful to talk to more experienced researchers. Rarely will you be left totally to yourself when planning and carrying out a research plan or study.

You may tend to get frustrated at times when you find that you cannot do everything the way you would like to because of real or bureaucratic constraints.

Brainstorming

For many researchers, one of the most daunting tasks in the research process is identifying and organizing the many aspects of the problem being studied. Luckily, computer "brainstorming" programs can assist you in the process of generating ideas and examining the interrelationships among them. Some commonly used brainstorming software programs are Inspiration, Semantic Mapper, and Semnet.

Inspiration is perhaps the most well-known brainstorming software package. It is a visual development tool for creating ideas and plans. The program quickly produces mind maps, cluster diagrams, and idea maps as you brainstorm, helping the planning process by stimulating thinking and adding clarity.

Brainstorming software serves a valuable function both early and later on in the research process. Early on, it is a useful aid in narrowing down your research topic and organizing the ideas and information that you have collected in your literature review. Later in the process, brainstorming software can be used to visualize relationships among variables and codes in the data that you have collected. It can also assist you in making conclusions based on the analyses that you have performed.

Don't let such obstacles exasperate you. Just relax and do your best. Remember, a plan is a projection of what you hope will happen, not a guarantee that it will. On the positive side, a sound plan critiqued by others is likely to result in a sound study conducted with a minimum of grief. You cannot guarantee that your study will be executed exactly as planned, but you can guarantee that things will go as smoothly as possible.

GENERAL CONSIDERATIONS IN A RESEARCH PLAN

We have already noted a number of factors you should consider in planning your research. There are three additional factors that are important to all research studies. First is the ethics of conducting research. As a researcher you have ethical responsibilities for your participants. For example, any potential participant in your study should be given the right to refuse to be involved and the right to stop being involved at any time. Second, there are legal restrictions on access to student records. Third, you should be aware of strategies for achieving and maintaining cooperation—from school personnel, for example. Your research plan may not specifically address any of these factors, but the plan's chances of being properly and ethically executed will be increased if you are aware of them.

THE ETHICS OF RESEARCH

All researchers must be aware of and attend to the ethical considerations related to their studies. This need is important for all forms and methods of research. The ends do not justify the means in research, and the researchers must not put their need to carry out studies above their responsibility to maintain the well-being of the study participants. Research studies are built on trust between the researcher and the participants; researchers have a responsibility to maintain that trust, just as they expect participants to maintain it in the data they provide.

Many professional organizations have developed codes of ethical conduct for their members. Table 3.1, from *Ethical Principles of Psychologists*,[2] illustrates commonly agreed upon principles for the ethical conduct of research. Other professional organizations, such as the American Educational Research Association and the American Sociological Society, also have developed codes for ethical research.

In 1974, the U.S. Congress put the force of law behind codes of ethical research. The need for legal restrictions was graphically illustrated by a number of studies in which researchers lied to or put in harm research participants in order to carry out their studies. For example, in a study on the effects of group pressure (conducted some years ago) researchers lied to participants while they participated in and watched what they thought was the electric shocking of other human beings.[3] In another study, men known to be infected with syphilis were not treated for their illness because they were part of a control group in a comparative study.[4] Studies such as these prompted governmental regulations regarding research studies.

---

[2]Committee for the Protection of Human Participants in Research. (1990). *Ethical principles in the conduct of research with human participants.* Washington, D.C.: American Psychological Association.

[3]Milgram, S. (1964). Group pressure and action against a person. *Journal of Abnormal and Social Psychology, 69,* 137–143.

[4]Jones, J. H. (1998). *The Tuskegee Syphilis Experiment.* New York: Free Press.

TABLE	3.1

Ethical Principles of Psychologists

Research With Human Participants

The decision to undertake research rests upon a considered judgment by the individual psychologist about how best to contribute to psychological science and human welfare. Having made the decision to conduct research, the psychologist considers alternative directions in which research energies and resources might be invested. On the basis of this consideration, the psychologist carries out the investigation with respect and concern for the dignity and welfare of the people who participate and with cognizance of federal and state regulations and professional standards governing the conduct of research with human participants.

a. In planning a study, the investigator has the responsibility to make a careful evaluation of its ethical acceptability. To the extent that the weighing of scientific and human values suggests a compromise of any principle, the investigator incurs a correspondingly serious obligation to seek ethical advice and to observe stringent safeguards to protect the rights of human participants.

b. Considering whether a participant in a planned study will be a "subject at risk" or a "subject at minimal risk," according to recognized standards, is of primary ethical concern to the investigator.

c. The investigator always retains the responsibility for ensuring ethical practice in research. The investigator is also responsible for the ethical treatment of participants by collaborators, assistants, students and employees, all of whom, however, incur similar obligations.

d. Except in minimal-risk research, the investigator establishes a clear and fair agreement with research participants, prior to their participation, that clarifies the obligations and responsibilities of each. The investigator has the obligation to honor all promises and commitments included in that agreement. The investigator informs the participants of all aspects of the research that might reasonably be expected to influence willingness to participate and explains all other aspects of the research about which the participants inquire. Failure to make full disclosure prior to obtaining informed consent requires additional safeguards to protect the welfare and dignity of the research participants. Research with children or with participants who have impairments that would limit understanding and/or communication requires special safeguarding procedures.

e. Methodological requirements of a study may make the use of concealment or deception necessary. Before conducting such a study, the investigator has a special responsibility to (i) determine whether the use of such

Informed Consent and Protection from Harm

Two major pieces of legislation affecting educational research are the National Research Act of 1974 and the Family Educational Rights and Privacy Act of 1974, more commonly referred to as the Buckley Amendment. The National Research Act requires that, to ensure protection of participants, proposed research activities involving human participants be reviewed and approved by an authorized group prior to the execution of the research. Protection of participants is broadly defined and requires that they not be harmed in any way (physically or mentally) and that they participate only if they freely agree to do so (informed consent). If participants are not of age, informed consent must be given by parents or legal guardians.

Most colleges and universities have a review group, usually called the Human Subjects Review Board. By law, the Board must consist of at least five members, not all of one gender, include one nonscientist, and include one or more member who is mainly concerned with the welfare of the participants.

TABLE 3.1

continued

techniques is justified by the study's prospective scientific, educational, or applied value; (ii) determine whether alternative procedures are available that do not use concealment or deception; and (iii) ensure that the participants are provided with sufficient explanation as soon as possible.

f. The investigator respects the individual's freedom to decline to participate in or to withdraw from the research at any time. The obligation to pretest this freedom requires careful thought and consideration when the investigator is in a position of authority or influence over the participant. Such positions of authority include, but are not limited to, situations in which research participation is required as part of employment or in which the participant is a student, client, or employee of the investigator.

g. The investigator protects the participant from physical and research procedures. If risks of such consequences exist, the investigator informs the participant of that fact. Research procedures likely to cause serious or lasting harm to a participant are not used unless the failure to use these procedures might expose the participant to risk of greater harm, or unless the research has great potential benefit and fully informed and voluntary consent is obtained from each participant. The participant

should be informed of procedures for contacting the investigator within a reasonable time period following participation should stress, potential harm, or related questions or concerns arise.

h. After the data are collected, the investigator provides the participant with information about the nature of the study and attempts to remove any misconceptions that may have arisen. Where scientific or humane values justify delaying or withholding this information, the investigator incurs a special responsibility to monitor the research and to ensure that there are no damaging consequences for the participant.

i. Where research procedures result in undesirable consequences for the individual participant, the investigator has the responsibility to detect and remove or correct these consequences, including long-term effects.

j. Information obtained about a research participant during the course of an investigation is confidential unless otherwise agreed upon in advance. When the possibility exists that others may obtain access to such information, this possibility, together with the plans for protecting confidentiality, is explained to the participant as part of the procedure for obtaining informed consent.

Source: Principal 9 from "Ethical Principles of Psychologists," *American Psychologist 45,* 1990, pp. 390–395. Copyright 1990 by the American Psychological Association. Reprinted with permission. APA cautions that this reproduced material is drawn from the 1990 "Ethical Principles of Psychologists," which is an outdated document. The current version (1992) of the APA Ethics Code is entitled, "Ethical Principles of Psychologists and Code of Conduct."

Typically, the researcher submits a proposal to the chair of the Human Subjects Review Board, who, in turn, distributes copies to all the members. They review the proposal in terms of proposed treatment of participants. If there is any question as to whether participants might be harmed in any way, the researcher is usually asked to meet with the review group to answer questions and clarify proposed procedures. In rare cases the researcher is asked to rewrite the questionable or unclear areas of the research plan. When the review group is satisfied that the participants will not be placed at risk (or that potential risk is minimal compared to the potential benefits of the study), the committee members sign the approval forms. Members' signatures on the approval forms signify that the proposal is acceptable with respect to participant protection. Table 3.2 shows a typical Human Subjects Review Application. Note that the research plan is placed in one of three groups, depending on how intrusive the plan is on proposed participants. The criteria for plans in Categories II and III are more extensive,

TABLE	**3.2**

Human Subjects Review Form

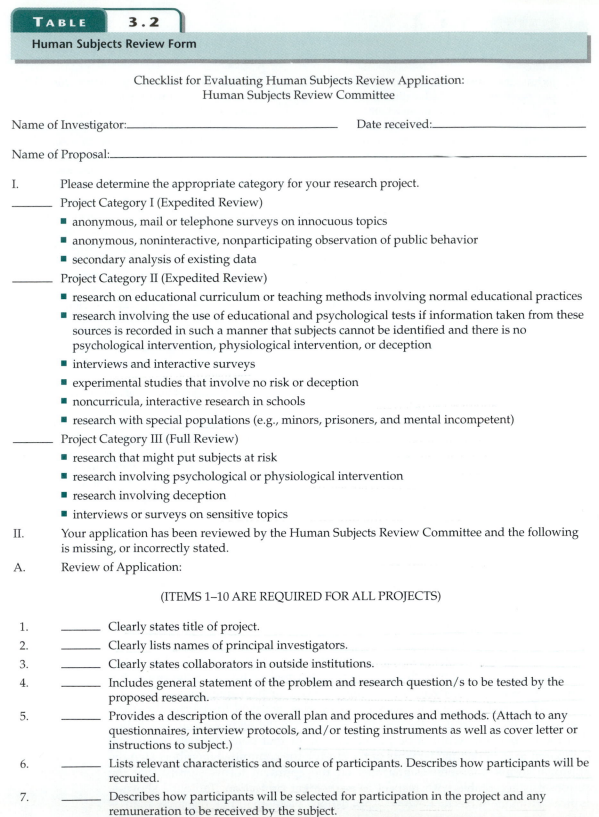

Checklist for Evaluating Human Subjects Review Application:
Human Subjects Review Committee

Name of Investigator:_____ Date received:_____

Name of Proposal:_____

I.   Please determine the appropriate category for your research project.

_____ Project Category I (Expedited Review)

- anonymous, mail or telephone surveys on innocuous topics
- anonymous, noninteractive, nonparticipating observation of public behavior
- secondary analysis of existing data

_____ Project Category II (Expedited Review)

- research on educational curriculum or teaching methods involving normal educational practices
- research involving the use of educational and psychological tests if information taken from these sources is recorded in such a manner that subjects cannot be identified and there is no psychological intervention, physiological intervention, or deception
- interviews and interactive surveys
- experimental studies that involve no risk or deception
- noncurricula, interactive research in schools
- research with special populations (e.g., minors, prisoners, and mental incompetent)

_____ Project Category III (Full Review)

- research that might put subjects at risk
- research involving psychological or physiological intervention
- research involving deception
- interviews or surveys on sensitive topics

II.   Your application has been reviewed by the Human Subjects Review Committee and the following is missing, or incorrectly stated.

A.   Review of Application:

(ITEMS 1–10 ARE REQUIRED FOR ALL PROJECTS)

1.   _____ Clearly states title of project.

2.   _____ Clearly lists names of principal investigators.

3.   _____ Clearly states collaborators in outside institutions.

4.   _____ Includes general statement of the problem and research question/s to be tested by the proposed research.

5.   _____ Provides a description of the overall plan and procedures and methods. (Attach to any questionnaires, interview protocols, and/or testing instruments as well as cover letter or instructions to subject.)

6.   _____ Lists relevant characteristics and source of participants. Describes how participants will be recruited.

7.   _____ Describes how participants will be selected for participation in the project and any remuneration to be received by the subject.

| **TABLE** | **3.2** |

continued

8. _____ Explains status and qualifications of research assistants.

9. _____ Explains source of funding for project.

10. _____ States expected starting and completion dates for projects.

(ITEMS 11–18 ARE REQUIRED FOR CATEGORIES II AND III ONLY)

11. _____ Outlines potential benefit of the project to the individual participant, group of participants, or society in general.

12. _____ Outlines potential risks to participants and the measures that will be taken to minimize such risks.

13. _____ Specifies procedures developed with respect to the anonymity of participants and the confidentiality of their responses. Indicates what personal identifying indicators will be kept on subjects. Specifies procedures for storage and ultimate disposal of personal information.

14. _____ Specifies how subjects will be informed of the nature of their participation in the project, that their participation is voluntary, and that their responses are confidential.

15. _____ Specifies any special populations involved in the project and describes the procedures for obtaining the appropriate consent.

16. _____ States that documentation of permission from the institution or organization which has the responsibility for the participants has been submitted to the Committee before final approval can be given.

17. _____ Specifies how the findings will be used or disseminated (e.g., professional publications, media, employers) and considers the policy implications of findings to the well-being of participants or constituent groups.

18. _____ Describes plan for researchers to provide some summary of findings to participants, or a rationale for why this is not tenable.

(ITEMS 19–20 ARE REQUIRED FOR CATEGORY III ONLY)

19. _____ Describes if the participants will be exposed to any psychological intervention such as deception, contrived social situations, manipulation of attitudes, opinions, or self-esteem, psychotherapeutic procedures, or other psychological influences. Describes procedures for follow-up and/or debriefing.

20. _____ Specifies any procedures that will be designed to address any adverse effects from participating in the study.

B. Informed Consent:

1. _____ Clearly invites the participant.

2. _____ States the reason the particular subject is asked to participate.

3. _____ Presents a clear statement that study is research (for dissertation, under supervision of advisor).

4. _____ Gives a clear description of study's purpose.

5. _____ Describes the procedures.

6. _____ States all possible risks.

7. _____ States benefits that are "hoped for," but not guaranteed.

8. _____ States financial consequences to the participant, or any payment to be given to the participants (when applicable).

TABLE 3.2

continued

9. _____ States alternative and standard intervention, advantages and disadvantages.
10. _____ States how confidentiality of responses and respondents will be secured.
11. _____ States that participants are free to ask questions.
12. _____ States participation is voluntary and indicates how the subject may withdraw from the study and the consequences of withdrawal, if appropriate.
13. _____ States how participants will be informed of or may have access to any summary of the findings or conclusions from the study.
14. _____ States informed consent in simple lay language.
15. _____ Includes the HSR application with the informed consent letter.
16. _____ Includes parental/guardian consent.
17. _____ Includes instruments to be used.
18. _____ Shows signature of faculty supervisor.
19. _____ Shows that proposal requires full review and has been sent to Committee.

Source: Boston College School of Education. Used with permission.

than those in Category I. Note, also, the many questions that have to be answered to obtain informed consent.

The Privacy Act of 1974, usually referred to as the Buckley Amendment, was designed to protect the privacy of students' educational records. Among its provisions is the specification that data that actually identify the students may not usually be made available unless written permission is acquired from the students (if of age), parents, or legal guardians. The consent must indicate what data may be disclosed, for what purposes, and to whom. Thus, if part of your study required obtaining information from individual students' record files, you would need to obtain permission from each student's parent, not a blanket approval from the principal or teacher. The researcher must obtain a signed and dated consent form from a parent or eligible student (18 or older). The form specifies the particular documents to be used, the purpose of the use, and the person to whom the disclosure is made. Note that if you are interested in using only class averages (in which no individual student is identified), individual consent from the principal would likely suffice. However, if you would calculate the class average from individual student records, individual permission would be necessary because you have access to individual records.

There are some exceptions to who is bound by the written consent provision. For example, school personnel with a "legitimate educational interest" in a student would not need written consent to examine student records. In other cases the researcher does not need to identify individual students by name. For example, the researcher could request that a teacher or guidance counselor either remove students' names from students' records completely or replace them with a coded number or letter. The researcher can then use the records without knowing the names of the individual students.

Perhaps the most basic and important ethical issues in research are concerned with participants' informed consent and freedom from harm. Informed consent focuses on ensuring that research participants enter the research of their free will and with understanding of the nature of the study and any possible obligations or dangers that may arise. It is intended to reduce the likelihood that participants will be exploited by the researcher persuading them to participate without full knowledge of the nature of the study and its requirements. Freedom from harm is focused on not exposing students to risks. It involves issues of confidentiality (to protect students from embarrassment or ridicule) and issues related to personal privacy. Collecting information on participants or observing them without their knowledge or without appropriate permission is not ethical. Furthermore, any information or data that are collected, either from or about a person, should be strictly confidential, especially if it is at all personal. Further, access to data should be limited to persons directly involved in conducting the research. An individual participant's performance should not be reported or made public using the participant's name, even for an innocuous measure such as an arithmetic test. For example, if a participant was named as a member of a group that performed poorly on a research instrument, that person might be subjected to ridicule, censure by parents, or lowered teacher expectations. Lack of privacy often creates the possibility of harm.

The use of confidentiality or anonymity to avoid privacy invasion and potential harm is common. Anonymity means that the researcher does not know the identities of the participants providing data for the study. It does not mean, as some people think, that the researcher knows the identities of participants but will not release them to anyone else. That is called confidentiality. If the researcher knows participants' identities, there can be confidentiality, but not anonymity. The preceding example of removing names or coding records is one commonly used way to maintain anonymity. When planning your study you must indicate to participants whether you will provide confidentiality or anonymity. Sometimes researchers seek access to data from a prior study to examine new questions based on the old data. In such cases, the original researcher has the responsibility to maintain the confidentiality or anonymity promised the participants of the original study.

Deception

An additional ethical dilemma occurs when a researcher poses a topic that, if given complete information to potential participants, would likely influence or change their responses. For example, studies concerned with participants' racial, gender, cultural, or medical orientation or attitudes are especially susceptible to such influences, so researchers often hide the true nature of the topic of study. Or, a researcher might want to study how a teacher interacts with high- and low-achieving students. If the researcher tells the teacher what the focus of the study is, it is likely that the teacher will change his or her normal behaviors more than if the researcher tells the teacher that the study is about how high- and low-achieving students perform on oral questioning. Nonetheless, such actions are intended to deceive study participants, and research topics that plan to use deception of participants must be seriously considered before being carried out. Some people believe that *any* study that requires deceitful practice should not be carried out. Others recognize that some important studies cannot be undertaken without deception. It is recommended that you not do your initial research study using a topic that requires deception to be carried out. If you do choose a topic that requires deception, your advisor and the Human Subjects Review Committee at your institution will provide suggestions about ethical ways to carry out your research plan.

Ethical Issues in Qualitative Research

The ethical issues and responsibilities discussed thus far pertain to both quantitative and qualitative research plans. However, there are features of qualitative research that raise additional issues not typically encountered in quantitative research. For the most part, quantitative research plans are specified before the researcher begins to carry out the study. The specifics of the plan and its presentation to the Human Subjects Review Committee provide a detailed examination of ethical issues. This does not mean that additional ethical issues will not arise, but because most quantitative researchers do not immerse themselves in the setting they study, the likelihood of such concerns is considerably lessened.

Qualitative research differs from quantitative in at least two major ways that produce additional ethical concerns. First, qualitative research plans typically evolve and change as the researcher's immersion in and understanding of the research setting grows. In a real sense, the research plan is "in process" and only generally formed when presented to the Human Subjects Review Committee. As the plan evolves with added understanding of the context and participants, there is increased likelihood that unanticipated and unreviewed ethical issues will arise and need to be resolved on the spot. For example, as participants become more comfortable with the researcher, they often will ask to see what has been written about them. They feel entitled to this, even though seeing what has been written may cause personal or data collection problems.

Second, unlike most quantitative researchers, qualitative researchers are personally involved and engaged with the research context and its inhabitants. That is one of the defining aspects of qualitative methods. Data collection methods such as interviews, debriefings, and the like bring the researcher and participants in close, personal contact with each other. Qualitative researchers often refer to participants as *informants* or *collaborators* rather than *subjects*, to indicate the intended bond between the two. The closeness between participants and researcher can create unconscious influences that raise issues for objectivity and data interpretation.

The focus on substantial immersion and detailed knowledge of the research context often leads the qualitative researcher to observe illegal or unprofessional behavior. This can occur in quantitative research also, but generally to a lesser degree because of its limited entry into the context. For example, the qualitative researcher might observe a janitor illegally loading school supplies into his or her car. Or the researcher might observe a teacher continually ridiculing a particular student for a speech impediment. In these and other similar situations, what is the researcher to do: make the school authorities aware of such activities, or keep silent on the assumption that the system will eventually identify and correct the problems? Should the researcher report the observations, knowing that it likely will end the study because participants will no longer be certain of the researcher's promise of confidentiality? Obviously if there is clear likelihood of physical or psychological danger, the researcher has a strong mandate to inform the school authorities. Unfortunately, not all situations present ethically clear actions.

There are many dimensions to the ethical conduct of research. The sources and advice noted in this chapter will help you conceive and conduct ethical studies. The suggestions provided do not cover all the ethical issues you are likely to encounter in your research. Perhaps the fundamental rule of ethics is that participants should not be harmed in any way, real or possible, in the name of science.

Respect and concern for your own integrity and for your participants' dignity and welfare are the bottom lines of ethical research.

GAINING ENTRY TO THE RESEARCH SITE

Very rarely is it possible to conduct educational research without the cooperation of a number of people. The first step in acquiring the needed cooperation is to identify and follow required procedures for approval to conduct the study in the chosen site. In schools, approval is usually granted by the superintendent, school board, or some other high-level administrator such as the associate superintendent for instruction. In other settings, such as hospitals or industry, there typically is someone charged with examining and deciding on requests to do research at the site. Regardless of the site, the approval process will involve the completion of one or more forms that describe the nature of the research, the specific request being made of the site personnel, and the benefits to the site. Once approval is obtained from the site authorities, it will be necessary to obtain permission from the research participants. For example, approval by a superintendent or school board may also require permission from the principal or principals whose schools will be involved. Even if such approval is not required it should be sought, both out of courtesy and for the sake of a smoothly executed study. The principal may refuse to participate—in most cases, the superintendent or board will support the principal's decision. Permission, or at least acceptance, should also be obtained from teachers who will participate in the study. If students under 18 are to be involved, written parental approval will be needed.

The potential complexity of obtaining permission to conduct your research at the chosen site or sites should indicate that you should not assume that permission will be granted easily ("we're too busy") or quickly (bureaucracies move slowly) and that you should prepare how you will explain your study to all those who must provide permission and approval. The key to gaining approval and cooperation is good planning. The key to good planning is a well-designed, carefully thought-out study and research plan. Some superintendents and principals are "gun shy" about people doing research in their schools because of a previous bad experience. They don't want anyone else running around their schools, disrupting classes, and administering poorly constructed questionnaires, or finding problems in the school. Unfortunately, many superintendents, principals, and teachers have experienced improperly trained, insensitive researchers who came into a school and left behind bad feelings about research and researchers. It is up to you to convince school personnel that what you are proposing is of value, that your study is carefully designed, and that you will work with teachers to minimize inconvenience.

Achieving full cooperation, and not just approval on paper, requires that you invest as much time as is necessary to discuss your study with the principal, the teachers, and perhaps even parents. These groups have varying levels of knowledge and understanding regarding the research process. Their concerns will focus mainly on the perceived value of the study, its potential affective impact, and the actual logistics of carrying it out. The principal, for example, will probably be more concerned with whether you are collecting any data that might be viewed as objectionable by the community than with the specific design you will be using. All groups will be interested in what you might be able to do for them. Potential benefits to be derived by the students, teachers, or principal as a result of your study should be explained fully. Your study, for example, might involve special instructional materials that are to be shared with the teachers and left with them after the study has ended. Even if all parties are favorably impressed, however, the spirit of cooperation will quickly dwindle if your study involves considerable extra work or inconvenience on their part. Bear in mind that principals and teachers are accommodating you, and are helping you complete your study without relief from their normal responsibilities. Thus, if changes can be made in the planned study to better accommodate their normal routine, they should be made in conjunction with consideration of its impact on the study as a whole.

Often, the principal or teachers will want something in return for their participation. The request may be related to your study, as when a principal asks to review your final draft for accuracy, requests that you return to the school to brief teachers on your findings, or requests that your results not be disseminated without the principal's approval. The first two requests are more easily agreed to than the third, which probably should be refused, but with an offer to discuss the principal's concerns, if any. Other principals or teachers might request activities unrelated to your study. For example, it is common to ask the researcher to provide a session or two of professional development for teachers in his or her content area.

Figure 3.1 presents a cover letter written by a principal in support of a doctoral student's proposed study. Note that the student secured not only the principal's permission, but also his strong support and cooperation, by sharing the potential benefits of the study to the principal's students. Figure 3.2 presents the parental consent form that accompanied the cover letter. It addresses many of the ethical and legal concerns discussed in this chapter.

Clearly, human relations is an important factor in conducting research in applied settings. That you should be your usual charming self goes without saying. But you should keep in mind that you are dealing with sincere, concerned educators who may not have your level of research expertise. Therefore, you must make a special effort to discuss your study in plain English (it is possible!) and to never give the impression that you are talking down to them. Also, your task is not over once the study begins. The feelings of involved persons must be monitored and responded to throughout the duration of the study if the initial level of cooperation is to be maintained.

COMPONENTS OF THE RESEARCH PLAN

Although they may go by other names, research plans typically include an introduction, a method section, a description of proposed data analyses, and a time schedule. Each component will be discussed in detail, but basically the format for a typical research plan is as follows:

INTRODUCTION

Statement of the Topic

Review of Related Literature

Statement of the Hypothesis (if appropriate)

FIGURE 3.1

Principal's Cover Letter of Support for a Proposed Research Study

THE SCHOOL BOARD OF BROWARD COUNTY, FLORIDA

The Nation's Largest Fully Accredited School System

BETHUNE ELEMENTARY
PERFORMING ARTS SCHOOL
Linda H. Arnold, Principal
2400 Meade Street
Hollywood, Florida 33020
(305) 926-0860

Robert D. Parks
Chairperson

Diana Wasserman
Vice Chairperson

Karen Dickerhoof
Donald J. Samuels
Eileen S. Schwartz
Toni J. Siskin
Neil Sterling

Virgil L. Morgan
Superintendent

January 23, 1999

Dear Parent/Guardian:

Country Isles Elementary School has been chosen to participate in a research study. Our school was selected out of the entire county as a result of our outstanding students and computer program. All third and fifth grade students will be able to participate. The results of this study will enable our teachers and parents to discover and understand the learning styles of our students. This knowledge will enable teachers and parents to provide special instruction and materials to improve student learning. It will also provide valuable information for the future development of effective professional computer software.

This study will take place from January 25 to March 30, 1999. It will be conducted by Mr. Joel Levine, a recognized and experienced computer educator. He has been Director of Computer Education at Barry University for six years. During that time he has participated in many projects in Dade and Broward Counties, which involved teacher training, computer curriculum development and computer assisted instruction implementation.

I have reviewed this research study and feel that it is a very worthwhile endeavor for our students and school. Please review the information on the following page in order to make a decision concerning parental consent for your child to participate in this study.

Sincerely,

Thos. J. Bardash

Thomas J. Bardash
Principal

Equal Opportunity Employer, Using Affirmative Action Guidelines

PARENTAL CONSENT FORM

The information provided on this form and the accompanying cover letter is presented to you in order to fulfill legal and ethical requirements for Florida International University (institution sponsoring this doctoral dissertation study) and the Department of Health and Human Services (HHS) regulations for the Protection of Human Research Subjects (45 CFR 46, as amended on January 26, 1983). The wording used in this form is utilized for all types of studies and should not be misinterpreted for this particular study.

The dissertation committee at Florida International University and the Research Review Committee of Broward County Public Schools have both given approval to conduct this study, "The Relationships Between the Modality Preferences of Elementary Students and Selected Instructional Styles of CAI as They Affect Verbal Learning of Facts." The purpose of this study is to determine the effect on achievement scores when the identified learning styles (visual, audio, tactile/kinesthetic) of elementary students in grade 3 and 5 are matched or mismatched to the instructional methods of specifically selected computer assisted instruction (CAI).

Your child will be involved in this study by way of the following:

1. Pretest on animal facts.
2. Posttest on animal facts.
3. Test on learning styles.
4. Interaction with computer-assisted instruction (CAI-software on the computer)—visual, audio, tactile CAI matching the student's own learning style.

All of these activities should not take more than two hours per student. There are no foreseeable risks to the students involved. In addition, the parent or researcher may remove the student from the study at any time with just cause. Specific information about individual students will be kept strictly confidential and will be obtainable from the school principal if desired. The results that are published publicly will not reference any individual students since the study will only analyze relationships among groups of data.

The purpose of this form is to allow your child to participate in the study, and to allow the researcher to use the information already available at the school or information obtained from the actual study, in order to analyze the outcomes of the study. Parental consent for this research study is strictly voluntary without undue influence or penalty. The parent signature below also assumes that the child understands and agrees to participate cooperatively.

If you have additional questions regarding the study, the rights of subjects, or potential problems, please call the principal, Mr. Tom Bardash or the researcher, Mr. Joel Levine (Director/Assistant Professor of Computer Education, Barry University, 463-1360).

_____

Student's Name

_____   _____

Signature of Parent/Guardian   Date

104

M ETHOD

   Participants

   Instruments

   Design

   Procedure

D ATA A NALYSIS

T IME S CHEDULE

B UDGET (IF APPROPRIATE)

Other headings may also be included, as needed. For example, if special materials are being developed for the study, or special equipment is being used (such as computer terminals), then headings such as Materials or Apparatus might be included under Method and before Design.

INTRODUCTION SECTION

If you have completed Task 2, you are familiar with the content of the introduction section: a statement of the topic, a review of related literature, and a statement of the hypothesis (if appropriate).

Statement of the Topic

Since the topic sets the stage for the rest of the plan, it should be stated as early as possible, given the nature of the particular research approach adopted. The statement should be accompanied by a description of the background of the topic and a rationale for its significance.

Review of Related Literature

The review of related literature should provide an overview of the topic and present references related to what is known about the topic. The literature sets a context for the topic and identifies prior research that can support the significance of your study. The literature review also can provide a basis for identifying hypotheses. The review should conclude with a brief summary of the literature and its implications. As with the statement of the topic, the timing of the review of related research may differ for quantitative and qualitative researchers.

Statement of the Hypothesis

For research plans that have one or more hypotheses, each hypothesis should have an underlying explanation for its prediction. That is, there should be some literature that supports the hypothesis. It should clearly and concisely state the expected relationship (or difference) between the variables in your study, and should define those variables in operational, measurable, or common-usage terms. The people reading your plan (and especially those reading your final report) may not be as familiar with your terminology as you are. Finally, each hypothesis should be clearly testable within a reasonable period of time.

METHOD SECTION

The specific method of research your study represents will affect the format and content of your method section. The method section for an experimental study, for example, typically includes a description of the experimental design, whereas a descriptive study may combine the design and procedure sections into one. The method section for a qualitative study may have varying forms and degrees of specificity, depending on when in the research process the method is written. In general, however, the method section includes a description of the research participants, measuring instruments, procedures, and data analysis.

Research Participants

The description of participants should identify the number, source, and characteristics of the sample.[5] It should also define the population, that is, the larger group, from which the sample will be selected. What are they like? How many do you have to choose from? For example, a description of participants might include the following:

> Participants will be selected from a population of 157 students enrolled in an algebra I course at a large urban high school in Miami, Florida. The population is tricultural, being composed primarily of Caucasian non-Hispanic students, African-American students, and Hispanic students from a variety of Latin American backgrounds.

The procedure for selecting the participants in the study can differ depending on whether a quantitative or qualitative study is being conducted. In general, quantitative research samples tend to be large and broadly representative, while qualitative research samples tend to be small and not necessarily broadly representative.

Instruments

This section describes the particular measures or instruments to be used in the study and how they will measure the variables stated in your hypothesis.[6] If you use instruments that are published, such as a standardized test, you should provide information about (1) the appropriateness of the chosen instruments for your study and sample; (2) the measurement properties of the instruments (especially validity[7] and reliability[8]); (3) the process of administering and scoring the instruments. If you are going to develop your own instrument, you should describe how the instrument will be developed, what it will measure, how you plan to evaluate its validity and reliability, and how it relates to your hypothesis and participants before its utilization in the actual study.

Of course, if more than one instrument is used—a common occurrence in many studies—each should be described separately and in detail. You may not

---

[5]Chapter 4 describes the process of sampling participants.

[6]Chapter 5 describes the nature of measures and instruments.

[7]Validity is concerned with whether the data or information being gathered is relevant to the decision to be made (see chapter 5).

[8]Reliability is concerned with the stability or consistency of the data or information (see chapter 5).

yet be able to identify and describe the instrument you would use in your study. Consequently, in Task 3, you should describe the kind of instrument that would be used rather than stating a specific instrument. For example, you might say that your instrument will be a questionnaire about teacher unions that will allow teachers to express different degrees of agreement or disagreement to statements regarding teacher unions. In writing this section of a research plan, you may discover that an appropriate instrument for collecting the needed data is not available. If this occurs, a decision to alter the hypothesis, change the selected variable, or develop one's own instrument needs to be made.

Qualitative research collects data using observation, note taking, and interviewing. If a formal instrument or test is used in conjunction with more qualitative data, it should be described in detail. Qualitative research should indicate the nature of evidence that will be collected and how it will be collected (e.g., observed field notes and tape recordings of teachers' perspectives on integrating special-needs students into the classroom, or photographs of dust-bowl children).

Materials/Apparatus

If special materials (such as booklets, training manuals, or computer programs) are to be developed for use in the study, they also should be described in the research plan. Also, if special apparatus (such as computer terminals) are going to be used, they should be described.

Design

A design is a general strategy for conducting a research study. The description of the design indicates the basic structure of the study. The nature of the hypothesis, the variables involved, and the constraints of the "real world" all contribute to the selection of the research design. For example, if the hypothesis involves comparing the effect of high-impact versus low-impact aerobic exercises with respect to exercise-related injuries, the study would involve comparing the number of injuries occurring in the two groups over some period of time. Thus, the design would involve two groups receiving different treatments and being compared in terms of number of exercise-related injuries. Depending upon whether participants were randomly assigned to treatment or already in treatment before the study, the design would be, respectively, an experiment or a causal-comparative design. There are a number of basic research designs to select from and a number of variations within each design. Both quantitative and qualitative research rely on designs that will be discussed in more detail in chapters 6, 7, 8, 9, 10, and 11.

Procedure

The procedure section describes all the steps that will be followed in conducting the study, from beginning to end, in the order in which they will occur. The procedure section typically begins with a detailed description of the technique to be used to select the study participants. If the design includes a pretest, the procedures for its administration—when it will be administered and how—will usually be described next. Any other measure to be administered at the beginning of the study will also be discussed. For example, in addition to a pretest on current skill in reading music, a general musical achievement test might be administered in order to check for the initial equivalence of groups. For a study designed to compare two different methods of teaching reading comprehension to third graders, the procedure section might state:

> In September, one week following the first day of school, the Barney Test of Reading Comprehension, Form A, will be administered to both reading method groups.

In research plans that do not include a separate instrument section, relevant information concerning the instrument will be presented here.

From this point on, the procedure section will describe what is going to occur in the study. The nature of what will occur depends greatly on the kind of research study planned. The procedures for conducting an experiment are different from those of conducting a survey and different from a historical study. Remaining chapters will examine these differences in detail.

The procedure section should also include any identified assumptions and limitations. An assumption is any important "fact" presumed to be true but not actually verified. For example, in a study involving reading instruction for preschool children, it might be assumed that, given the population, none of the children had received reading instruction at home. Limitations in the study also should be noted. A limitation is some aspect of the study that the researcher knows may negatively affect the study but over which he or she has no control. Two common limitations are sample size and length of the study. A research plan might state, for example: "Only one class of 30 students will be available for participation." or "While ideally participants should be exposed to the experimental treatment for a longer period of time in order to more accurately assess its effectiveness, permission has been granted to the researcher to be in the school for a maximum of two weeks." Such limitations have an impact on the study and should be openly and honestly stated so readers can judge for themselves how seriously the limitations might affect the study results.

For both quantitative and qualitative research, issues such as the procedures for gaining entry to the research site, the way participants are selected, the way data are collected and scored, and study limitations belong in the procedures section. Although there may be different emphasis on these areas depending on whether the procedure section is written for quantitative or qualitative research, both should discuss all of the areas to some degree.

The procedure section should be as detailed as possible, and any new terms introduced should, of course, be defined. The key to writing this section is precision; it should be precise to the point where someone else could read your plan and conduct your study in the same way as you intended it to be conducted. The reason that a detailed description of the procedures is critical for research studies is that without detailed information of *how* a study was carried out, external readers cannot make reasonable judgments about the usefulness of the results. It is the appropriateness of the procedures that permits external readers to judge the quality of the study and its conclusions. This is true for both quantitative and qualitative research studies.

DATA ANALYSIS

The research plan must include a description of the technique or techniques that will be used to analyze study data. For certain descriptive studies, data analysis may involve little more than simple tabulation and presentation of counts and percentages. For most quantitative studies, however, one or more statistical methods will be required. Identification of appropriate analysis techniques is extremely important. Very few situations cause as much "weeping and gnashing of teeth" as collecting data only to find that there is no appropriate statistical analysis or that the analysis that is appropriate requires sophistication beyond the researcher's level of competence. Note that this caution is appropriate for both quantitative and qualitative research. Once the data are collected, it usually is too late. That is one reason you should submit a detailed research plan before beginning your study.

The hypothesis of a study determines the nature of the research design, which in turn determines the analysis. An inappropriate analysis does not permit a valid test of the research hypothesis. Which analysis technique should be selected depends on a number of factors, such as how the groups will be formed (for example, by random assignment, by matching, or by using existing groups), how many different treatment groups will be involved, how many variables will be involved, and the kind of data to be collected (e.g., counts of the number of times fifth-grade students fail to turn in their homework on time; a pupil's test score; or pupil's placement into one of five socioeconomic categories). Although you may not be familiar with a variety of specific analytic techniques, you probably can describe in your research plan the kind of analysis you would need. For example, you might say:

> An analysis will be used appropriate for comparing the achievement, on a test of reading comprehension, of two randomly formed groups of second-grade students.

By the time you get to Task 7, you will know exactly what you need (honest!). Qualitative research sometimes combines qualitative (e.g., observation) and quantitative (e.g., test scores) data in studies, resulting in the need for statistical analysis. However, most qualitative research is heavily weighted towards interpretive, not statistical, data analysis. The researcher analyzes the qualitative data from interviews, field notes, observations, and the like by organizing and interpreting the data. Thus, qualitative research should describe the procedures for collating the various forms of data collected, the manner in which the data were categorized in terms of emergent themes in the data, and the rationale for the conclusions and interpretations made from the qualitative data. For example, an analysis that allows field notes and interview data to be organized into a limited number of concepts or issues will be used.

TIME SCHEDULE

A realistic time schedule is equally important for both beginning researchers working on a thesis or dissertation and for experienced researchers working under the deadlines of a research grant or contract. It is infrequent that a researcher has unlimited time to complete a study. The existence of deadlines typically necessitates careful budgeting of time. Basically, a time schedule includes a listing of major activities or phases of the proposed study and a corresponding expected completion time for each activity. Such a schedule in a research plan enables the researcher to assess the feasibility of conducting a study within existing time limitations. It also helps the researcher to stay on schedule during the

TABLE 3.3

Gantt Chart

SCHEDULE OF ACTIVITIES FOR PROPOSED STUDY

Activities	Dates										
	Jan.	Feb.	March	Apr.	May	June	July	Aug.	Sept.	Oct.	Nov.
1. Human Subjects Review	■										
2. Literature Review		■									
3. Selection of Participants			■								
4. Pre-testing				■							
5. Entry into Setting						■					
6. Treatment							■				
7. Post-testing								■			
8. Data Analysis									■		
9. Report Preparation											■

110

execution of the study. In developing a time frame, do not make the mistake of "cutting it too thin" by allocating a minimum amount of time for each activity. Allow yourself more time than you initially planned to account for unforeseen delays. (Some call research a process designed to take 3 to 6 months longer than the researcher thinks it will. Be advised!) For example, your advisor might not be available when needed, your computer might malfunction and need a lengthy repair, or the teacher who agreed to let you collect data in her class might become ill and be out of school for three weeks. Plan to set the completion date for your final study sometime *before* your actual deadline. Also recognize that your schedule will not necessarily be a series of sequential steps that require one activity to be completed before another is begun. For example, while the study is being conducted, you may also be working on the first part of the research report.

A useful approach for constructing a time schedule is a *Gantt chart*. A Gantt chart lists the activities to be completed down the lefthand side of a page and the time to be covered by the entire project across the top of the page. A bar graph format is used to indicate the beginning and ending date for each activity. Such a chart permits the researcher to easily see the "big picture" and to identify concurrent activities. Table 3.3 illustrates a Gantt chart. Note how some tasks overlap one another, indicating that they can be worked on simultaneously.

BUDGET

Proposals submitted to governmental or private agencies for research support almost always require the inclusion of a tentative budget. Although researchers not seeking external funding for their research are not required to create a budget, it is useful to anticipate costs that might occur in the study. For example, costs such as computer programs, travel, printing, and mailing are common research expenses. It is not necessary to have a detailed budget for these and similar expenses, but recognize that conducting your study will include some personal expenditures.

REVISING AND IMPROVING A RESEARCH PLAN

Judging the adequacy of a research plan can involve both informal and formal assessment. Informally, the plan should be reviewed and critiqued by you, your advisor, and another experienced researcher. A research plan should be reviewed by at least one skilled researcher and at least one expert in the study's area of investigation. No researcher, no matter how long she or he has been "in the business," cannot benefit from the insight of others. Rereading your own plan several days after having written it often identifies flaws or weaknesses.

Formally, aspects of the research plan can be field-tested in a pilot study in which the plan, or parts of it, are tried out on a small scale. A pilot study is best thought of as a dress rehearsal. In a pilot study all or part of the plan is tried out to identify unanticipated problems or issues. Beginning researchers gain valuable experience from conducting a pilot study; the quality of one's dissertation, for example, may be considerably improved as a result. Even a small-scale pilot study, based on a small number of participants, can help in refining procedures such as instrument administration, scoring routines, and analysis techniques. The research plan will almost always be modified as a result of a pilot study, and in some cases it may be substantially overhauled. One reason, aside from time, that more large-scale pilot studies are not conducted is lack of available participants. However, whenever feasible, conducting a pilot study—even a small one—should be considered a very worthwhile use of your time.

Summary / Chapter 3

Definition and Purpose of a Research Plan

1. A research plan is a detailed description of a proposed study; it includes justification for the study, a detailed description of the steps that will be followed in the study, and information about the analysis of the collected data. The plan provides a guide for conducting the study.

2. The research plans of quantitative and qualitative researchers often differ in their construction. Quantitative researchers typically develop their research plans prior to the start of the study, while qualitative researchers typically have general plans in which the details develop after immersion in the research settings. Both groups should have a research plan to guide their research activities.

3. Most quantitative studies are designed to test a hypothesis; the nature of the hypothesis influences decisions about the sample group, measuring instruments, design, procedures, and statistical techniques used in the study. Qualitative researchers rarely state and test hypotheses.

4. A written research plan helps you to think through the aspects of your study, facilitate evaluation of the proposed study, and generally improve the quality of the research.

5. Part of good planning is anticipation. Try to anticipate potential problems that might arise, do what you can to prevent them, and plan your strategies for dealing with them if they do occur.

General Considerations in a Research Plan

THE ETHICS OF RESEARCH

6. There are ethical considerations involved in all research studies, and all researchers must be aware of and attend to ethical considerations in their research.

7. Many professional organizations have developed ethical principles for their members and the federal government has enacted laws to protect research participants from harm and invasion of privacy.

8. The National Research Act of 1974 requires that proposed research activities involving human subjects be reviewed and approved by an authorized group in an institution, prior to the execution of the research, to ensure protection of the participants.

9. The two most overriding rules of ethics are that participants should not be harmed in any way (physically or mentally) and that the participants' privacy rights are maintained.

10. Probably the most definitive source of ethical guidelines for researchers is *Ethical Principles of Psychologists*, prepared for and published by the American Psychological Association (APA).

11. The Family Educational Rights and Privacy Act of 1974, more commonly referred to as the Buckley Amendment, basically protects the privacy of the educational records of students. It stipulates that data that identifies participants by name may not be made

available to the researcher unless written permission is granted by the participants.

12. Studies involving deception of participants are sometimes unavoidable, but should be examined critically for unethical practices.

13. Both quantitative and qualitative research are subject to ethical guidelines. Qualitative researchers, because their research plans typically evolve throughout the study and because they work very closely with their participants, must be aware continually of ethical issues.

GAINING ENTRY TO THE RESEARCH SITE

14. It is rarely possible to conduct research without the cooperation of many people. The first step in acquiring needed cooperation is to follow required procedures.

15. A formal approval process usually involves the completion of one or more forms describing the nature of the research and the specific request being made of the school system.

16. The key to gaining approval and cooperation is good planning and a well-designed, carefully thought-out study.

17. Once formal approval for the study is granted by the superintendent or school board, the researcher should invest as much time as is necessary to explain your study to the principal, the teachers, and perhaps even parents. If these groups do not cooperate, you will not be able to do your study.

18. If changes are requested and can be made to better accommodate the normal routine of participating personnel, these changes should be made unless the study will suffer as a consequence.

19. The feelings of involved persons must be monitored and responded to throughout the study if the initial level of cooperation is to be maintained. Human relations are an important aspect of conducting research in applied settings.

Components of the Research Plan

20. Research plans typically include an introduction, a method section, a time schedule, and a budget, if appropriate.

INTRODUCTION SECTION

21. The introduction includes a statement of the topic, a review of related literature, and a statement of the hypothesis (if necessary).

22. In writing these sections, use terms that are either common usage or are operationally defined to aid your reader's understanding.

METHOD SECTION

23. The specific method of research your study represents influences the content of your method section. Particular approaches to research—such as case study, causal–comparative, survey, and experiment—use different methods to carry out their unique purposes.

Research Participants

24. The description of participants should clearly define the number, source, and characteristics of the sample, as well as the population from which the sample was drawn.

Instruments

25. This aspect of the method section provides a description of the particular measures or instruments that will be used to collect data for the study. It is important to provide a rationale for the selection of the instruments.

26. If you are going to develop your own instrument, you should describe how the instrument will be developed, what it will measure, and how you plan to determine its validity and reliability.

27. Qualitative researchers are often their own data gathering instruments through the use of observations, field notes, and interviews. The qualitative researcher should describe the nature and method of the data collected.

Design

28. A design is a general strategy for conducting a research study. Depending upon the nature of the study's hypothesis, variables, and participants, the researcher selects an appropriate research design to structure the study. Both qualitative and quantitative research rely upon research designs.

Procedure

29. The procedure section describes all the steps that will be followed in conducting the study, from beginning to end, in the order in which they will occur.

30. The procedure section typically begins with a description of the technique to be used in selecting the sample, or samples, for the study. If the study includes a pretest, the procedure and timing of it should be described next.

31. From this point on, the procedure section will describe exactly what is going to occur in the study. The nature of what will occur depends on the kind of research study planned, since the procedures for different research approaches are different.

32. The procedure section should also include any identified assumptions and limitations. An assumption is any important "fact" presumed to be true but not actually verified, while a limitation is some aspect of the study that the researcher knows may negatively affect the results.

33. The procedure section should be as detailed as possible, and any new terms introduced should be defined. It should be precise to the point where someone else could read your plan and execute your study exactly as you intended it to be conducted.

DATA ANALYSIS

34. The research plan must include a description of the technique or techniques that will be used to analyze study data.

35. The hypothesis in a quantitative study determines the design, which in turn determines the statistical analysis.

36. Selection of an analysis technique depends on a number of factors, such as how the groups will be formed, how many there are, the number of variables that will be studied, and the kind of data to be collected.

37. Although qualitative researchers sometimes include quantitative data in their data collection, the main analysis for the qualitative researchers is their own analysis and interpretation of the qualitative data they have collected. They review their data, organize it into categories and themes, and interpret it in terms of the context and participants' perspectives.

TIME SCHEDULE

38. The construction of a time schedule listing major research activities and their corresponding expected completion date is a useful aid to planning.

39. Allow for more time than you think you will need to complete your study. Plan for down time, and set your finishing date earlier than the final deadline for completion that you have set.

Revising and Improving a Research Plan

40. A written research plan permits careful examination by you and others, including experienced researchers, regarding the quality of the plan and suggestions for how to improve it.

41. Formal evaluation of a research plan involves a pilot study. Even a small-scale pilot study based on a small number of participants can help in refining or changing procedures, such as instrument administration and scoring routines, and in trying out analysis techniques.

Task 3 *Performance Criteria* ■

The purpose of Task 3 is to have you construct a brief research plan. Your plan should state the topic you plan to study and a hypothesis you plan to examine. It should also provide information about the methods you will employ to carry out your study, including information about the research participants (sample), instruments, procedures, data analysis, and a time plan. While it is expected that your plan contain all the components of a research plan, it is not expected that your plan be extensive or technically accurate. Beginning with chapter 4, you will learn ways to formulate each of a research plan's components. Feedback from your instructor concerning your research plan will also help you identify and critique aspects of a plan.

On the following pages, an example is presented that illustrates the performance called for by Task 3 (see Task 3 example). This example is the task submitted by the same student whose task for Part Two was previously presented. Thus, in this example the research plan matches the introduction. Keep in mind that the proposed activities described in your plan (and in the example presented) do not necessarily represent ideal research procedure. Research plans are usually more detailed. The example given, however, does represent what you ought to be able to do at this point. Additional examples for this and subsequent tasks are included in the *Student Guide,* which accompanies this text.

1

Effect of Interactive Multimedia on the Achievement of
10th-Grade Biology Students

Method

Participants

Participants for this study will be 10th-grade biology students in an upper-middle-class, all-girl Catholic high school in Miami, Florida. Forty students will be selected and divided to two groups.

Instrument

The effectiveness of interactive multimedia (IMM) will be determined by comparing the biology achievement of the two groups as measured by a standardized test, if there is an acceptable test available. Otherwise, one will be developed.

Design

There will be two groups of 20 students each. Students in both groups will be posttested in May using a test of biology achievement.

Procedure

At the beginning of the school year, 40 tenth-grade biology students will be selected from a population of approximately 200. Selected students will be divided into two groups, and one group will be designated to be the experimental group. The same teacher will teach both classes.

During the school year, the nonexperimental group of students will be taught biology using traditional lecture and discussion methods. The students in the experimental group will be taught using IMM. Both groups will cover the same subject matter and use the same text. The groups will receive biology instruction for the same amount of time and in the same room, but not at the same time, as they will be taught by the same teacher.

2

       Academic objectives will be the same for each class and all tests measuring achievement will be identical. Both classes will have the same homework reading assignments. In May, a biology achievement test will be administered to both classes at the same time.

Data Analysis

The scores of the two groups will be compared statistically.

Time Schedule

	August	September . . . April	May	June
Select Participants	____			
Pretest	_____			
Execute Study		_____		
Posttest			_____	
Analyze Data				_____
Write Report		_____		

PART FOUR

Research Participants: Samples

The purpose of selecting a sample is to represent a population about which we seek some information. For example, if you were interested in the effect of daily homework assignments on the test scores of ninth-grade algebra students, it would not be possible for you to include all ninth-grade algebra students in the United States in your study. It would be necessary for you to select a sample, that is, a smaller group that represents the characteristics of the larger group, or population. The performance of a sample is used to make an inference about the performance of the larger group. As you shall see in this chapter, sampling strategies depend on the researcher's purpose and the selection of a research design. While all research involves the use of samples, the nature, size, and method of selecting samples vary with the research aim.

The goal of Part Four is to help you to understand the importance of selecting an appropriate sample and become familiar with various sampling techniques. The first section of the chapter deals with quantitative sampling, and the second section deals with qualitative sampling. After you have read Part Four, you should be able to perform the following task.

TASK 4

Having selected a problem, and having formulated one or more testable hypotheses or answerable questions, describe a sample appropriate for evaluating your hypotheses or answering your questions. This description will include:

1. A definition of the population from which the sample would be drawn
2. The procedural technique to select the sample and form it into groups
3. Sample sizes
4. Possible sources of sampling bias

(See Performance Criteria, p. 142.)

". . . every individual has the same probability of being selected and selection of one individual in no way affects selection of another individual (p. 123)."

Selection of a Sample

OBJECTIVES

After reading chapter 4, you should be able to:

1. Identify and describe four random sampling techniques.
2. Select a random sample using a table of random numbers.
3. Identify three variables that can be stratified.
4. Select a stratified sample.
5. Identify three possible clusters for cluster sampling.
6. Select a cluster sample.
7. Apply the procedures for selecting a systematic sampling.
8. Identify and briefly describe two major sources of sample bias.
9. Identify and describe three nonrandom sampling techniques.
10. Describe the strategies for selecting a sample for a qualitative study.

SAMPLING: DEFINITION AND PURPOSE

Sampling is the process of selecting a number of individuals for a study in such a way that they represent the larger group from which they were selected. A sample comprises the individuals, items, or events selected from a larger group referred to as a *population*. The purpose of sampling is to gain information about the population by using the sample. Rarely do studies gather data from the entire population. In fact, not only is it generally not feasible to study the whole population, it is also not necessary. If the population of interest is large or geographically scattered, study of it would not be feasible or would be prohibitively costly and time consuming. [TO use entire population] If a sample is well-selected, research results based on it will be generalizable to the population. The degree to which the sample represents the population is the degree to which results for one are applicable to the other.

As an example, suppose the superintendent of a large school system wanted to find out how the 5,000 teachers in that system felt about teacher unions, whether they would join one, and for what reasons. If interviews were selected as the best way to collect the desired data, it would take a very long time to interview each and every teacher. Even if each interview only took 15 minutes, it would take a minimum of 1,250 hours, 156 eight-hour days, or approximately 30 school weeks to collect interviews from all 5,000 teachers. On the other hand, if 10%, or 500, of the teachers were interviewed, it would take only 125 hours, or about 3 weeks to collect data. Assuming that the superintendent needed the information "now, not next year," the latter approach would definitely be preferable if the same information could be acquired. If the sample of 500 teachers is correctly selected, the conclusions based on the interviews of the sample of teachers would in all probability be the same or very close to the conclusions based on interviews of all the teachers. Of course, selection of just any 500 teachers would not do. Selecting and interviewing 500 elementary teachers, for example, would not be satisfactory. In the first place, there is a highly disproportionate number of female elementary teachers and males might feel differently about unions. In the second place, opinions of elementary teachers might not be the same as those of junior high teachers or senior high teachers. How about 500 teachers who were members of the National Education Association (NEA)? Although they would probably be more representative of all 5,000 teachers than just elementary teachers, they still would not do. Teachers who are already members of one professional organization would probably be more likely to join another organization. Nonmembers of the NEA *might* be more likely to join a different union, since it would approach certain problems differently. On the other hand, nonmembers of the NEA might hold a negative opinion of unions in general. In either case, however, it is reasonable to assume that the opinions toward unions of members and nonmembers of the NEA would be different. How, then, can we obtain an adequate sample; how could a representative sample be selected?

Give up? Don't! As you will see shortly, there are several relatively simple procedures or sampling techniques that could be applied to select a representative sample of teachers. These procedures would not guarantee that a sample was perfectly representative of the population, but they would definitely increase the odds. They would increase the degree of confidence that the superintendent could have regarding the generalizability of findings for the 500 teachers to all 5,000 teachers.

DEFINITION OF A POPULATION

The first step, then, in sampling is to define the population. The population is the group of interest to the researcher, the group to which she or he would like the results of the study to be generalizable. Generalizability is the extent to which the results of one study can be applied to other populations or situations. Examples of populations are all 10th-grade students in the United States, all elementary school gifted children in Utah, and all first-grade physically disabled students in Utopia County who have participated in preschool training. These examples illustrate two important points about populations. First, populations may be virtually any size and may cover almost any geographical area. Second, the entire group the researcher would really like to generalize to is rarely available. The population that the researcher would ideally like to generalize to is referred to as the *target population*. The population that the researcher can realistically select from is referred to as the *accessible,* or *available, population*. In most studies, the chosen population is generally a realistic choice (e.g., accessible), not an idealistic one (i.e., target).

For example, suppose you decide to do a study of high school principals' opinions about having their students attend school 6 days a week. Suppose, also, that you wish to generalize your results to all high school principals in the United States. You quickly realize the difficulty of getting information from every high school principal in the United States, so you decide to obtain a representative sample of high school principals in the United States. But even this would be a difficult, time-consuming, and expensive effort. Faced with these obstacles, your research plan will have to be brought into line with cold, hard reality, so you decide to study only principals in your home state. By selecting from a more narrowly defined population you would be saving time and money, but you would also be losing generalizability. Your results would be directly generalizable to all high school principals in your home state, but not to all high school principals in the United States. The key is to define your population in sufficient detail so that others may determine how applicable your findings are to their situation.

Regardless of what sampling approach is used, it is important to describe the characteristics of the sample. This description should include the number of participants in the sample and a description of the demographics of the sample (e.g., average number of years teaching, percentage of each gender or racial group, level of education, achievement level). The nature of demographic data varies with the sample; the demographic information used to describe a sample of teachers would be different from that used to describe a sample of students, parents, or administrators.

SELECTING A RANDOM SAMPLE

Selecting a sample is a very important step in conducting a research study. The "goodness" of the sample determines the meaningfulness and generalizability of the results. As discussed previously, a *good* sample is one that is representative of the population from which it was selected. As we saw with our superintendent who needed to assess teachers' attitudes, selecting a representative sample is not a haphazard process. There are several appropriate techniques for selecting a sample. Certain techniques are more appropriate for certain situations; the techniques provide different levels of assurance of sample representativeness. However, as with populations, we sometimes have to compromise the ideal for the real and do what is feasible. This is true for educational as well as for other areas of research. We can't always have what we want.

Regardless of the technique used, the steps in sampling are essentially the same: identify the population, determine the required sample size, and select the sample. There are four basic random sampling techniques or procedures: *simple random sampling, stratified sampling, cluster sampling,* and *systematic sampling.* They are referred to as *probability sampling techniques* because it is possible for the researcher to specify the probability, or chance, that each member of a defined population will be selected for the sample. These sampling techniques are all based on randomness in the selection of the sample.

SIMPLE RANDOM SAMPLING

Random sampling is the process of selecting a sample in such a way that all individuals in the defined population have an equal and independent chance of being selected for the sample. Randomness in sampling takes the selection of the sample completely out of the researcher's control by letting a random, or *chance,* procedure select the sample. In other words, every individual has the same probability of being selected and selection of one individual in no way affects selection of another individual. You may recall in physical education class the teacher occasionally formed teams by having the class line up and count off by twos—one-two-one-two, and so on. With this method, you could never be on the same team as the person next to you. This selection process was not random, because whether you were on one team or another was determined by where you were in line and the team for which the person next to you was on. If selection of teams had been random, you would have had an equal (50–50) chance of being on either team, regardless of the team status of the person next to you.

Random sampling is the best single way to obtain a representative sample. Although no technique, not even random sampling, guarantees a representative sample, the probability of achieving one is higher for this procedure than for any other. In most cases, the differences between the sample and the population are small. For example, you might not expect the exact same ratio of males and females in a sample as in a population, but random sampling assures that the ratio will be close and that the probability of having too many females is the same as the probability of having too many males. Also, differences that do occur are a function of chance, not of the researcher's conscious or unconscious bias in the selection process.

Another point in favor of random sampling is that it is required in many statistical analyses. This is very important, because these analyses permit the researcher to make inferences about a population based on the behavior of a sample. If samples are not randomly selected, then one of the major assumptions of many statistical analyses is violated, and inferences made from the research can be rendered suspect.[1]

Steps in Simple Random Sampling

In general, random sampling involves defining the population, identifying each member of the population, and selecting individuals for the sample on a completely chance basis. One way to do this is to write each individual's name on a separate slip of paper, place all the slips in a hat or other container, shake the container, and select slips from the container until the desired number of individuals is selected. This procedure is not exactly satisfactory if a population has 1,000 or more members. One would need a very large hat—and a strong writing hand! A much more satisfactory approach is to use a *table of random numbers* (also called a table of random digits). In essence, a table of random numbers selects the sample for you, each member being selected on a purely random, or chance, basis. Such tables are included in the appendix of most statistics books and some educational research books; they usually consist of columns of five-digit numbers which have been randomly generated by a computer to have no defined patterns or regularities. (See Table A.1 in the Appendix.) Using a table of random numbers to select a sample involves the following specific steps:

1. Identify and define the population.
2. Determine the desired sample size.
3. List all members of the population.
4. Assign all individuals on the list a consecutive number from zero to the required number, for example, 000 to 249 or 00 to 89. Each individual must have the same number of digits as each other individual.
5. Select an arbitrary number in the table of random numbers. (Close your eyes and point!)
6. For the selected number, look at only the number of digits assigned to each population member. For example, if a population has 800 members, you only need to use the last 3 digits of the number; if a population has 90 members, you only need to use the last 2 digits.

---

[1]In Part Seven, you will learn how to select and apply several commonly used inferential statistics. Don't you dare groan. You will be amazed at how easy statistics really is.

7. If the number corresponds to the number assigned to any of the individuals in the population, then that individual is in the sample. For example, if a population had 500 members and the number selected was 375, the individual assigned 375 would be in the sample; if a population had only 300 members, then 375 would be ignored.
8. Go to the next number in the column and repeat step 7 until the desired number of individuals has been selected for the sample.

Once the sample has been selected, it may be used as is for survey or correlational studies or randomly subdivided into two or more groups for use in experimental or causal–comparative studies. If there will be only two subgroups, the full sample may be divided by flipping a coin—heads one group, tails the other.

An Example of Simple Random Sampling

Actually, the random selection process is not as complicated as the step-by-step explanation might have made it sound. The following example should make the procedure clear.

It is now time to help our long-suffering superintendent who wants to select a sample of teachers so that their attitudes toward unions can be determined. We will apply each of the eight steps described to the solution of this problem:

1. The population is all 5,000 teachers in the superintendent's school system.
2. The desired sample size is 10% of the 5,000 teachers, or 500 teachers.
3. The superintendent has supplied a directory that lists all teachers in the system.
4. Using the directory, the teachers are each assigned a number from 0000 to 4999.
5. A table of random numbers[2] is entered at an arbitrarily selected number, such as the one underlined here.
    59058
    11859
    53634
    48708
    71710
    83942
    33278
    etc.
6. Since the population has 5,000 members, we only are concerned with the last four digits of the number, 3634.
7. There is a teacher assigned the number 3634; that teacher is therefore in the sample.
8. The next number in the column is 48708. The last four digits are 8708. Since there are only 5,000 teachers, there is no teacher assigned the number 8708. The number is therefore skipped.
9. Applying these steps to the remaining random numbers shown, teachers 1710, 3942, and 3278 are included. This procedure would be continued in succeeding columns until 500 teachers were selected.

---

[2]See Appendix A (pp. 605–620) for an example of a table of random numbers.

At the completion of this process the superintendent would in all probability have a representative sample of all the teachers in the system. The 500 selected teachers could be expected to appropriately represent all relevant subgroups of teachers, such as elementary teachers and male teachers. With simple random sampling, however, representation of subgroups is probable but not guaranteed. The probable does not always occur. If you flip a quarter 100 times, the probable outcome is 50 heads and 50 tails. You might get 53 heads and 47 tails, or 45 heads and 55 tails, but most of the time you can expect to get close to a 50–50 split. (You might want to try this during your next study break!) Other outcomes are possible, however; they may be less probable but they are possible. In tossing a quarter 100 times, 85 heads and 15 tails is a possible, low-probability outcome. Similarly, it would be possible, although less probable, for the sample of teachers to be unrepresentative of the total group on one or more dimensions. For example, if 55% of the 5,000 teachers were female and 45% were male, we would expect roughly the same percentages in the sample of 500. Just by chance, however, the sample might contain 30% females and 70% males.

The superintendent might not be willing to leave accurate representation to chance. If there were one or more variables that the superintendent believed might be highly related to attitudes toward unions, she might adopt a different sampling approach. She might decide, for example, that teaching level (elementary, middle, high) might be a significant variable and that elementary teachers might feel differently toward unions than middle or senior high school teachers. She would want a sample that would guarantee appropriate representation of the three teaching levels. To accomplish this she would probably use stratified sampling rather than simple random sampling.

STRATIFIED SAMPLING

Stratified sampling is the process of selecting a sample in such a way that identified subgroups in the population are represented in the sample in the same proportion that they exist in the population. It can also be used to select equal-sized samples from each of a number of subgroups if subgroup comparisons are desired. Proportional stratified sampling would be appropriate, for example, if you were going to take a survey prior to a national election in order to predict the probable winner. You would want your sample to represent the voting population. Therefore, you would want the proportion of Democrats and Republicans in your sample to be the same as in the population. For example, if Democrats made up 63 percent of registered voters and Republicans made up 37 percent of registered voters, you would want 63 percent of the sample to be Democrats and 37 percent to be Republicans. The group proportions in the sample are the same as in the population. Other likely variables for proportional stratification might include race, gender, and socioeconomic status.

Alternatively, equal-sized samples would be most useful if you wanted to compare the performance of different subgroups. Suppose, for example, that you were interested in comparing the achievement of students of different ability levels (high, average, and low) being taught by two methods of mathematics instruction (teacher and computer). Simply selecting a random sample of students and assigning one-half of the sample to each of the two methods would not (as you know!) guarantee equal representation of each of the ability levels in each method. In fact, just by chance, one of the methods might not have any students from one of the three ability levels. However, randomly selecting students separately for the three ability levels and then assigning half of each ability level to each of the methods would guarantee equal representation of each ability level in each method. The purpose of stratified sampling is to guarantee desired representation of relevant subgroups within the sample.

Steps in Equal-Sized Groups Stratified Sampling

The steps in stratified sampling are similar to those in random sampling except that selection is from subgroups in the population rather than the population as a whole. In other words, random sampling is done more than once; it is done for each subgroup. Stratified sampling involves the following steps:

1. Identify and define the population.
2. Determine desired sample size.
3. Identify the variable and subgroups (strata) for which you want to guarantee appropriate, equal representation.
4. Classify all members of the population as members of one of the identified subgroups.
5. Randomly select (using a table of random numbers) an "appropriate" number of individuals from each of the subgroups, *appropriate* in this case meaning an equal number of individuals.

As with simple random sampling, once the samples from each of the subgroups have been randomly selected, each may be randomly assigned to two or more treatment groups. If we were interested in the comparative effectiveness of two methods of mathematics instruction for different levels of ability, the steps in sampling might be as follows:

1. The population is all 300 eighth-grade students enrolled in general math at Central Junior High School.
2. The desired subgroups are three levels of ability—high, average, and low.
3. The desired sample size is 45 students in each of the two methods.
4. Classification of the 300 students indicates that there are 45 high-ability students, 215 average-ability students, and 40 low-ability students.
5. Using a table of random numbers, 30 students are randomly selected from each of the ability subgroups; that is, 30 high, 30 average, and 30 low students. This gives us three samples, one for each ability group.
6. The 30 students in each sample are randomly assigned to one of the two methods; that is, 15 of each 30 are randomly assigned to one of the two methods. Therefore, each method contains 45 students—15 high-ability students, 15 average-ability students, and 15 low-ability students (see Figure 4.1).

As you may have guessed, stratification can be done on more than one variable. In this example, we could have stratified on math interest or prior math grades. The following example, based on a familiar situation, should help to further clarify the process of stratified sampling.

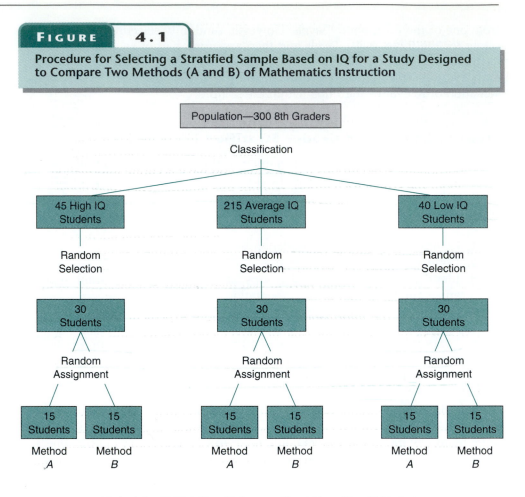

FIGURE   4.1

Procedure for Selecting a Stratified Sample Based on IQ for a Study Designed to Compare Two Methods (A and B) of Mathematics Instruction

Method *A* = 15 High IQ + 15 Average IQ + 15 Low IQ = 45 Students
Method *B* = 15 High IQ + 15 Average IQ + 15 Low IQ = 45 Students

An Example of Proportional Stratified Sampling

Let us suppose that our old friend the superintendent wanted to guarantee proportional representation of teaching level in the sample of teachers. We will apply each of the five steps previously described for selecting a stratified sample:

1. The population is all 5,000 teachers in the superintendent's school system.
2. Desired sample size is 10% of the 5,000 teachers, or 500 teachers.
3. The variable of interest is teaching level, and there are three subgroups—elementary, middle, and high.
4. We classify the teachers into the subgroups. Of the 5,000 teachers, 65%, or 3,250, are elementary teachers; 20%, or 1,000, are junior high teachers; and 15%, or 750, are senior high teachers.
5. We want 500 teachers. Since we want proportional representation, 65% of the sample (325 teachers) should be elementary teachers, 20% (100 teach-

ers) should be junior high teachers, and 15% (75 teachers) should be senior high teachers.

Therefore, using a table of random numbers, 325 of the 3,250 elementary teachers are randomly selected (makes sense, since we want a total sample of 10%), 100 of the 1,000 junior high teachers are selected, and 75 of the 750 senior high teachers are selected.

At the completion of this process, the superintendent would have a sample of 500 teachers (325 + 100 + 75), or 10% of the 5,000, and each teaching level would be proportionally represented. Note that using proportionally sized groups requires that you have accurate information about the size of each group. Without this information, proportional group studies are not recommended.

So far we have discovered two ways in which the superintendent could get a sample of teachers, simple random sampling and stratified sampling. Both of these techniques, however, would result in a sample scattered over the entire district. The interviewer would have to visit many, many schools; many of them containing only one or two teachers in the sample. In the event that the superintendent wanted the information quickly, a more expedient method of sampling would be needed. For the sake of convenience, cluster sampling might be used.

CLUSTER SAMPLING

Cluster sampling randomly selects groups, not individuals. All the members of selected groups have similar characteristics. For example, instead of randomly selecting from all fifth graders in a large school district, you could randomly select fifth-grade classrooms and use all the students in each classroom. Cluster sampling is most useful when the population is very large or spread out over a wide geographic area. Sometimes it is the only feasible method of selecting a sample. It is not always possible, for example, to obtain or compile a list of all members of the population, as is required by simple random sampling and stratified sampling. Also, educational researchers frequently cannot select and assign individual participants, as they may like. For example, if your population were 10th-grade biology students, it is very unlikely that you would obtain administrative approval to randomly select and remove a selected few students from different classrooms for your study. You would have a much better chance of securing permission to use several intact classrooms.

Any location within which we find an intact group of similar characteristics (population members) is a cluster. Examples of clusters include classrooms, schools, city blocks, hospitals, and department stores. Cluster sampling usually involves less time and expense and is generally convenient. Let us look at a few examples that illustrate this point. As the earlier example concerning 10th-grade biology students illustrated, it is easier to obtain permission to use all the students in several classrooms than several students in many classrooms. Similarly, in taking a survey, it is easier to use all the people in a limited number of city blocks than a few people in many city blocks. You should be able to apply this logic to the examples of clusters already mentioned. In each case you should note that cluster sampling would be easier (though not necessarily as good, as we shall see later!) than either simple random sampling or stratified sampling.

Steps in Cluster Sampling

The steps in cluster sampling are not very different from those involved in random sampling. The major difference, of course, is that random selection of groups (clusters) is involved, not individuals. Cluster sampling involves the following steps:

1. Identify and define the population.
2. Determine the desired sample size.
3. Identify and define a logical cluster.
4. List all clusters (or obtain a list) that make up the population of clusters.
5. Estimate the average number of population members per cluster.
6. Determine the number of clusters needed by dividing the sample size by the estimated size of a cluster.
7. Randomly select the needed number of clusters (using a table of random numbers).
8. Include in your study all population members in each selected cluster.

Cluster sampling can be done in stages, involving selection of clusters within clusters. For example, a district in a state, then schools in the district, and then classrooms in the schools could be randomly selected to sample classrooms for a study. This process is called *multistage sampling*.

One common misconception about cluster sampling is the belief that it is appropriate to randomly select only a single cluster. It is not uncommon, for example, for some researchers to define a population as all fifth graders in X County, a cluster as a school, and to randomly select only one school in the population. These same "researchers" would not dream of randomly selecting only one student! The principle is the same. Keeping in mind that a good sample is representative of the population from which it is selected, it is highly unlikely that one randomly selected student could ever be representative of an entire population. Similarly, it is unlikely that one randomly selected school could be representative of all schools in a population. Thus, one would normally have to select a number of clusters in order for the results of a study to be generalizable to the population. The following example should make the procedures involved in cluster sampling clear.

An Example of Cluster Sampling

Let us see how our superintendent would get a sample of teachers if cluster sampling were used. We will follow the steps previously listed:

1. The population is all 5,000 teachers in the superintendent's school system.
2. The desired sample size is 500.
3. A logical cluster is a school.
4. The superintendent has a list of all the schools in the district; there are 100 schools.
5. Although the schools vary in the number of teachers per school, there is an average of 50 teachers per school.
6. The number of clusters (schools) to be selected equals the desired sample size, 500, divided by the average size of a cluster, 50. Thus, the number of schools needed is $500 \div 50 = 10$.

7. Therefore, 10 of the 100 schools are randomly selected by assigning a number to each school and using a table of random numbers.
8. All the teachers in each of the 10 schools are in the sample (10 schools, 50 teachers per school on average, equals the desired sample size).

Thus, the interviewer could conduct interviews at 10 schools and interview all teachers in the school instead of traveling to a possible 100 schools. The advantages of cluster sampling are evident. As with most things, however, nothing is all good. Cluster sampling has several drawbacks. For one thing, the chances are greater of selecting a sample that is not representative of the population. The fewer the sampling points (individuals versus schools) selected, the more likely that the sample selected may not represent the population. For example, the teachers in this example are from a limited number of schools, so the possibility exists that the 10 schools selected are somehow different from the other 90 in the district (socioeconomic level of the students, teacher experience, and so forth). One way to compensate for this problem is by selecting a larger sample of clusters.

As another example, suppose our population were all fifth graders in 10 schools (each school having an average of 120 students in four classes of 30 students each), and we wanted a sample of 120 students. There are any number of ways we might select our sample. For example, we could: (1) randomly select one school and use all the fifth graders in that school, (2) randomly select two classes from each of two schools, or (3) randomly select 120 students from the 10 schools. In any of these ways we would wind up with 120 students, but our sample would probably not be equally "good" in each case. In case 1 we would have students from only one school. It is very likely that this school would be different from the other nine in some significant way (e.g., socioeconomic level or teacher experience). In case 2 we would be doing a little better, but we would still only have 2 of the 10 schools represented. Only in case 3 would we have a chance of selecting a sample containing students from all or most of the schools, and the classes within those schools. If random sampling were not feasible, as often is the case, selecting two classes from each of two schools would be preferable to selecting all the students in one school. Actually, if cluster sampling were used, it would be even better to select one class each from four of the schools. One way we could attempt to compensate for the loss of representativeness associated with cluster sampling would be to select more than four classes.

Another problem is that commonly used statistical methods are not appropriate for analyzing data resulting from a study using cluster sampling. Such statistics generally require randomly formed groups, not those selected in a whole cluster. The statistics that are available and appropriate for cluster samples are generally less sensitive to differences that may exist between groups. Thus, one should carefully weigh the advantages and disadvantages of cluster sampling before choosing this method of sampling.

SYSTEMATIC SAMPLING

Systematic sampling is not used very often, but it is appropriate in certain situations, and in some instances it is the only feasible way to select a sample. Systematic sampling is sampling in which individuals are selected from a list by taking every Kth name. So what's a "Kth" name? That depends on what K is. If $K = 4$, selection involves taking every 4th name, if $K = 10$, every 10th name, and so forth. What K actually equals depends on the size of the list and the desired sample size. The major difference between systematic sampling and the other types of sampling so far discussed is that all members of the population do not have an independent chance of being selected for the sample. Once the first name is selected, all the rest of the individuals to be included in the sample are automatically determined.

Even though choices are not independent, a systematic sample can be considered a random sample if the list of the population is randomly ordered. One or the other has to be random—either the selection process or the list. Since randomly ordered lists are rarely available, systematic sampling is rarely as "good" as random sampling. While some researchers argue this point, the major objection to systematic sampling of a nonrandom list is the possibility that certain subgroups of the population can be systematically excluded from the sample. A classic example is that certain nationalities have distinctive last names that tend to group together under certain letters of the alphabet; when taking every Kth name, if K is at all large, it is possible that certain nationalities can be skipped over completely.

Steps in Systematic Sampling

Systematic sampling involves the following steps:

1. Identify and define the population.
2. Determine the desired sample size.
3. Obtain a list of the population.
4. Determine what K is equal to by dividing the size of the population by the desired sample size.
5. Start at some random place in the population list. Close your eyes and stick your finger on a name.
6. Starting at that point, take every Kth name on the list until the desired sample size is reached.
7. If the end of the list is reached before the desired sample is reached, go back to the top of the list.

Now let us see how our superintendent would use systematic sampling.

An Example of Systematic Sampling

If our superintendent used systematic sampling, the process would be as follows:

1. The population is all 5,000 teachers in the superintendent's school system.
2. The desired sample size is 500.
3. The superintendent has a directory that lists all teachers in the system in alphabetical order. The list is not randomly ordered, but it is the best available.
4. K is equal to the size of the population, 5,000, divided by the desired sample size, 500. Thus $K = (5,000 \div 500) = 10$.
5. Some random name in the list of teachers is selected.
6. From that point, every following 10th name is automatically in the sample. For example, if the teacher selected in step 5 were the 3rd name on

TABLE	4.1		
Random Sampling Strategies			
TYPE	**PROCESS**	**ADVANTAGES**	**DISADVANTAGES**
simple random sampling	Select desired number of sample members using a table of random numbers.	Easy to conduct; strategy requires minimum knowledge of the population to be sampled.	Need names of all population members; may over- or under-represent sample members; there is difficulty in reaching all selected in sample.
stratified random sampling	Divide population into separate levels or strata and randomly sample from the separate strata.	More precise sample; can be used for both proportions and stratification sampling; sample represents the desired strata.	Need names of all population members; difficulty of reaching all selected in sample; researcher must have names of all populations.
cluster sampling	Select groups, not individuals; identify clusters and randomly select them to reach desired sample size.	Efficient; clusters are most likely to be used in school research; don't need names of all population members; reduces travel to sites.	Fewer sampling points make it less likely to have a representative sample.
systematic sampling	Using list of population, pick a name on list at random and select each Kth person on the list to the desired sample size.	Sample selection is simple.	All members of population do not have an equal chance to be selected; Kth person may be related to a periodic order in the population list, producing unrepresentative-ness in the sample.

the list, then the sample would include the 13th name, the 23rd, the 33rd, the 43rd, and so forth.

In this case, due to the nonrandom nature of the list, the sample might not be as representative as the samples resulting from application of the other techniques. Table 4.1 summarizes characteristics of the four random sampling approaches.

DETERMINING SAMPLE SIZE

The sampling question most frequently asked by beginning researchers is probably, "How large should my sample be?" And the answer is "large enough!" While the answer is not very comforting—or precise—the question is a difficult one. If the sample is too small, the results of the study may not be generalizable to the population. The results may be relevant only for the sample and not for the entire population of 300. A sample that is too small can affect the generalizability of the study regardless of how well it is selected. Suppose, for example, the population were 300 first graders. If we randomly selected only one student, clearly that student could not represent all the students. Nor could two, three, or four students, even if randomly selected, adequately represent the population. On the other hand, we would all agree that a sample of 299, 298, or 297 students would represent the population. How about 10? Too small, you say. OK, how about 30? 75? 100? At what point does the sample size stop being "too small" and become "big enough"? That is a question without an easy answer.

Knowing that the sample should be as large as possible helps some but still does not give any guidance as to what size sample is "big enough." In many cases, the researcher does not have access to large numbers of potential research participants. In fact, obtaining permission from potential study participants is generally not an easy task. Usually the problem is too few participants rather than too many.

Some guidelines can help you decide what size sample is "big enough." However, these guidelines are just that—*guidelines*—and are not endorsed by all researchers. As noted earlier, the size of the sample influences both the representativeness of the sample itself and the statistical analysis of study data. The smaller the sample, the more problematic these issues. Your advisor can help you think through the "how much is enough" issue in your own study.

The minimum sample size depends on the type of research involved. Some cite a sample size of 30 as a guideline for correlational, causal–comparative, and experimental research. Thus, for correlational studies at least 30 participants are needed to establish the existence or nonexistence of a relationship. For causal–comparative and experimental studies, a minimum of 30 participants in each group is recommended, although in some cases it might be difficult to attain this number for each group. The larger the sample, the more likely to detect a difference between the different groups. While we would not be super confident about the results of a single study based on small samples, if a number of such studies obtained similar results, our confidence in the findings would generally be higher.

For descriptive research, it is common to sample 10 to 20% of the population, although this range will change with the size of the population studied. In reality, the appropriate sample size depends on a number of factors such as the specific type of descriptive research involved, the size of the population, and whether data will be analyzed for given subgroups. Based on a formula originally developed by the United States Office of Education, Krejcie and Morgan generated the numbers shown in Table 4.2. For a given population size (*N*), Table 4.2 indicates the sample size (*S*) needed in order for the sample to be representative, assuming one is going to survey a random sample. Although it is true that in certain respects Table 4.2 represents an oversimplified approach to determining sample size, it does suggest some general rules of thumb. As with other types of research, statistical techniques and related software are available for determining sample size in a more precise way, given knowledge of relevant related variables.

Table 4.2 does, however, suggest the following generalities:

1. The larger the population size, the smaller the percentage of the population required to get a representative sample.
2. For smaller populations, say *N* = 100 or fewer, there is little point in sampling; survey the entire population.
3. If the population size is around 500 (give or take 100), 50% should be sampled.
4. If the population size is around 1,500, 20% should be sampled.

TABLE	4.2

Sample Sizes (S) Required for Given Population Sizes (N)

N	S	N	S	N	S	N	S	N	S
10	10	100	80	280	162	800	260	2800	338
15	14	110	86	290	165	850	265	3000	341
20	19	120	92	300	169	900	269	3500	346
25	24	130	97	320	175	950	274	4000	351
30	28	140	103	340	181	1000	278	4500	354
35	32	150	108	360	186	1100	285	5000	357
40	36	160	113	380	191	1200	291	6000	361
45	40	170	118	400	196	1300	297	7000	364
50	44	180	123	420	201	1400	302	8000	367
55	48	190	127	440	205	1500	306	9000	368
60	52	200	132	460	210	1600	310	10000	370
65	56	210	136	480	214	1700	313	15000	375
70	59	220	140	500	217	1800	317	20000	377
75	63	230	144	550	226	1900	320	30000	379
80	66	240	148	600	234	2000	322	40000	380
85	70	250	152	650	242	2200	327	50000	381
90	73	260	155	700	248	2400	331	75000	382
95	76	270	159	750	254	2600	335	100000	384

Source: R. V. Krejcie and D. W. Morgan (1970). Determining sample size for research activities. *Educational and Psychological Measurement, 30,* 608. Copyright © 1970 by Sage Publications. Reprinted by permission of Sage Publications, Inc.

5. Beyond a certain point (about $N = 5,000$), the population size is almost irrelevant and a sample size of 400 will be adequate. Thus, the superintendent from our previous examples would be relatively safe with a sample of 400 teachers, but would be even more confident with a sample of 500.

Of course, these numbers or percentages are suggested minimums. If it is at all possible to use more participants, you should do so. Using samples larger than these minimums is especially important in many situations. For example, in an experimental study the difference between groups is more likely to show up if the samples are large. There are relatively precise statistical techniques and computer programs that can be used to estimate required sample sizes given knowledge of certain facts about the population.

AVOIDING SAMPLING ERROR AND BIAS

Selecting random samples does not guarantee that they will be representative of the population. *Sampling error,* which is beyond the control of the researcher, is a reality of random sampling. Of course, no sample will have a composition precisely identical to that of the population. If well selected and sufficiently large, however, the chances are that the sample will closely represent the population. Occasionally, however, just by chance (remember, *random* means out of the researcher's control and at the mercy of chance), a sample will differ significantly from the population on some important variable. Usually this does not make a significant difference in the study, but if there is a variable for which nonrepresentation might really affect the outcome of the study, the researcher should stratify on that variable rather than leaving all to chance.

Sampling bias is quite different from sampling error. Sampling bias does not result from random differences between samples and populations. Sampling bias is nonrandom and is generally the fault of the researcher. Some aspect of the sampling creates a bias in the data. For example, suppose a researcher who wished to study the attitudes of college students toward alcohol stood outside bars and asked patrons leaving the bars to answer questions regarding their attitudes toward alcohol. This would be a biased sample. Remember, the study was to be about college students' attitudes—all types of college students. By sampling outside bars, the researcher systematically omitted college students who don't go to bars. The sampling bias in the study makes the study conclusions invalid. Similarly, when a survey researcher gets a return of only 45 percent of the questionnaires she sent out, the large number of nonreturns introduces a potential response bias in the results. In the presidential election of 1936, *The Literary Digest* poll predicted that Democrat Franklin Roosevelt would be defeated by Republican Alf Landon based on a poll of several million people. Unfortunately for *The Literary Digest*, the sample of people polled was selected primarily from automobile registration lists and telephone directories. In 1936, however, a sizable portion of the voting population did not own a car or have a telephone. Thus, the sample did not adequately represent the voting population. It was biased toward people who owned telephones or automobiles—a wealthier sample that tended to vote Republican. And guess what—people without cars and telephones voted anyway, and Roosevelt won!

As these examples illustrate, sample bias greatly affects the validity of the study. Researchers should be aware of sources of sampling bias and do their best to avoid it. Securing administrative approval to involve students in educational research studies is not easy, however. Of necessity, researchers often use whatever samples they can and whatever methods that are convenient to teachers and administrators. Cooperating with teachers and administrators is, of course, advisable, but not at the expense of good research. If your study cannot be conducted properly under the administrators' restrictions, the researcher should try hard to convince the administration to allow the study to be conducted in a way that will provide viable results. If this fails, the researcher should look elsewhere for participants. If suitable participants cannot be found or selected properly, the study probably should be temporarily or permanently abandoned.

If it is not possible to avoid sampling bias, the researcher must decide whether the bias is so severe that the study results will be seriously affected. If a decision is made to continue with the study, with full awareness of the existing bias, such bias should be completely reported in the final research report. The consumers of the research findings may then decide for themselves how serious they believe the bias to be.

SELECTING A NONRANDOM SAMPLE

Although random sampling techniques provide the best opportunity to obtain unbiased samples, it is not always possible for researchers to use random sampling. For example, we noted earlier that administrators often limit sampling to "these four classes, take them or leave them," or "you can only use intact class-rooms." Teachers may request to select the students or classes to be studied. Or, you might not find many people willing to participate in your study, so you have to solicit volunteers from wherever you can. Further, random samples consisting of a small number of participants cannot guarantee sample representation. These and similar factors can introduce sampling bias. Nonrandom samples—also called nonprobability samples—are sampling methods that do not have random sampling at any stage of sample selection.

When nonrandom samples are used, it is not possible to specify what probability each member of a population has of being selected for the sample. In fact, it is usually difficult, if not impossible, to even describe the population from which a sample was drawn and to whom results can be generalized. Nonrandom sampling approaches include *convenience sampling, purposive sampling*, and *quota sampling*. Of these sampling methods, convenience sampling is the most used in educational research, and is therefore the major source of sampling bias in educational research studies.

CONVENIENCE SAMPLING

Convenience sampling, also referred to as accidental sampling and haphazard sampling, basically involves including in the sample whoever happens to be available at the time. Two major examples of convenience sampling are the use of volunteers and the use of existing groups just because "they are there." For example, have you ever been stopped on the street or in a grocery store by someone who wants your opinion of an event or of a new kind of muffin? Volunteers are bound to be different from nonvolunteers. For example, they may be more motivated or more interested in the particular study. Since the population is composed of both volunteers and nonvolunteers, the results of a study based solely on volunteers are not likely generalizable to the entire population, and are tilted in favor of volunteers. Two examples should help to make this point clear. Suppose you send a questionnaire to 100 randomly selected people and ask the question, "How do you feel about questionnaires?" Suppose that 40 people respond and all 40 indicate that they love questionnaires. Should you then conclude that the group from which the sample was selected loves questionnaires? Certainly not. The 60 who did not respond may not have done so simply because they hate questionnaires! As a second example, suppose you want to do a study on the effectiveness of study-habit training on the achievement of college freshmen. You ask for volunteers from the freshman class and 80 students volunteer. Of course right off the bat they are not representative of all freshmen! For example, they may be students who are not doing well academically but wish that they were. In any event, suppose you then randomly assign the volunteers to two groups of 40, one group to receive study-habit training and one group to serve as a control. The experimental group is to receive study-habit training for 1 hour every day for 2 weeks, the control group is to do nothing special. Since they are all volunteers, the participants feel free to drop out of the study. Members of the control group have no need to drop out since no demands are made on their time. Members of the experimental group, on the other hand, may drop out after one or more sessions, not wishing to "donate" any more of their time. Suppose at the end of the study, only 20 of the original 40 students in the training group remain while all 40 members of the control group remain. Suppose a comparison of their subsequent achievement indicates that the group that received training achieved significantly higher grades. Could you then conclude that the training was effective?

Certainly not! In essence, we would be comparing the achievement of those in the control group with those members of the experimental group who chose to remain. The remaining 20 experimental group participants might very well be more motivated to achieve than the control group; the less motivated students dropped out of the study! It would be very difficult to determine how much of their achievement was due to the treatment (training) and how much was due to motivation.

PURPOSIVE SAMPLING

In *purposive sampling*, also referred to as judgment sampling, the researcher selects a sample based on his or her experience or knowledge of the group to be sampled. For example, if a researcher planned to study exceptional high schools, he or she would choose a group of schools to study based on his or her knowledge of exceptional schools. Prior knowledge or experience might lead the researcher to select exceptional high schools based on criteria such as high proportions of students going to four-year colleges, large numbers of AP students, extensive computer facilities, and high proportions of teachers with advanced degrees. Notice that there is an important difference between convenience samples in which participants who happen to be available are chosen and purposive sampling in which the researcher uses experience and prior knowledge to identify criteria for selecting the sample. Clear criteria provide a basis for describing and defending purposive samples. Much of the sampling in qualitative research is purposive. The main weakness of purposive sampling is the potential for inaccuracy in the researcher's criteria and resulting sample selections.

QUOTA SAMPLING

Quota sampling is most often used in survey research when it is not possible to list all members of the population of interest. When quota sampling is involved, data gatherers are given exact characteristics and quotas of persons to be interviewed (e.g., 35 working women with children under the age of 16, 20 working women with no children under the age of 16). This technique of sampling is widely used in large-scale surveys. Obviously, when quota sampling is used, data are obtained from easily accessible individuals. Thus, people who are less accessible (more difficult to contact, more reluctant to participate, and so forth), are underrepresented.

SAMPLING IN QUALITATIVE RESEARCH

The prior sections of this chapter focused on the selection of samples for quantitative studies, those based on large samples, generalization to a population, and statistical analyses of gathered data. Qualitative research samples are generally different from those of quantitative research because the two approaches have different aims and needs. Recall that qualitative research is characterized by in-depth inquiry, immersion in a setting, emphasis on context, concern with participants' perspectives, and description of a single setting, not generalization to many settings.

These characteristics call for sampling approaches that differ from those of quantitative research. For example, the qualitative researcher's interest in participants' perspectives of both their setting and the research topic being studied requires more in-depth data collection than that typically conducted in quantitative research. While a quantitative researcher might ask, "What teacher behaviors are correlated with the amount of time students will continue on a task?" a qualitative researcher might ask, "What are the meanings that students and teacher create together about time on task, and how are the perspectives of different students manifested when working on tasks?" To obtain the desired depth of information required by such topics, qualitative researchers must almost always deal with small samples. However, they normally interact with these samples over a long period of time and in great depth.

Because samples need to be small, and because many potential participants are unwilling to undergo the demands of participation, sampling in qualitative research is almost always purposive. That is, the experience and insight of the researcher is used to select a sample; randomness is rarely part of the process. One reason qualitative researchers spend time in the research setting before selecting a sample is to observe and obtain information that can be used to select a purposive sample of participants. Qualitative researchers choose participants whom they judge to be thoughtful and who have information, perspectives, and experiences related to the topic of research. The primary focus in qualitative research is on identifying participants who can provide information about the *particular* topic and setting being studied, not participants who necessarily represent some larger population. Remember, one of the basic tenets of qualitative research is that each research setting is unique in its own mix of people and contextual factors. Thus, the researcher's intent is to describe a particular context in-depth, not to generalize to a larger population. Representativeness is secondary to the quality of the participants' ability to provide the desired information about self and setting.

Within the domain of purposive sampling are a number of specific approaches that are useful in qualitative research. Among these are:

- *Intensity sampling:* selecting participants who permit study of different levels of the research topic; for example, the researcher might select some good and some bad students, some experienced and some inexperienced teachers, or teachers in self-contained classrooms and teachers in departmentalized teams.
- *Homogeneous sampling:* selecting participants who are very similar in experience, perspective, or outlook; this produces a narrow, homogeneous sample and makes data collection and analysis simpler.
- *Criterion sampling:* selecting all cases that meet some criterion or have some characteristic; for example, the researcher might pick students who have been held back in two successive years, teachers who left the field to raise children and then returned to teaching; female administrators with more than 15 years experience.
- *Snowball sampling:* selecting a few people who can identify other people who can identify still other people who might be good participants for a study; this approach is most useful when a study is carried on in a setting in which possible participants are scattered or not found in clusters.
- *Random purposive sampling* (with small sample): selecting by random means participants who were purposively selected and who are too numerous to include all in the study; for example, if 25 potential participants were purposively identified by the researcher, but only 10 partici-

pants could be studied, a random sample of 10 from the 25 potential participants would be chosen; this approach adds credibility to the sample, but is still based on an initial sample that was purposively selected.

In many qualitative studies combinations of these and other purposive sampling approaches may be used to identify and narrow a sample. For example, qualitative researchers can test the robustness of their findings by purposively selecting a few new participants and determining whether they provide similar information and perspectives as the original group of participants.

Qualitative research uses sampling strategies that produce samples that are predominantly small and nonrandom. This is in keeping with qualitative research's emphasis on in-depth description of participants' perspectives and context. The nature of data collection limits the number of research participants who can be accommodated in qualitative studies, typically leading to purposive sampling to insure that the "best" participants are included. In spite of the variety of purposive sampling techniques used by qualitative researchers, it is important to remember that purposive samples often do not provide information about the sample. This means that both qualitative and quantitative researchers who use samples must provide detailed information about the purposive research participants and how they were chosen.

Summary / Chapter 4

Sampling: Definition and Purpose

1. Sampling is the process of selecting a number of individuals for a study in such a way that the individuals represent the larger group from which they were selected.
2. The purpose of sampling is to gain information about a larger population. A population is the group to which a researcher would like the results of a study to be generalizable.
3. The population that the researcher would ideally like to generalize results to is referred to as the target population; the population that the researcher realistically selects from is referred to as the accessible, or available, population.
4. The degree to which the selected sample represents the population is the degree to which the research results are generalizable to the population.

Selecting a Random Sample

5. Regardless of the specific technique used, the steps in sampling include identification of

the population, determination of required sample size, and selection of the sample.

SIMPLE RANDOM SAMPLING

6. Simple random sampling is the process of selecting a sample in such a way that all individuals in the defined population have an equal and independent chance of being selected for the sample. It is the best single way to obtain a representative sample.
7. Random sampling involves defining the population, identifying each member of the population, and selecting individuals for the sample on a completely chance basis. Usually a table of random numbers is used to select the sample.

STRATIFIED SAMPLING

8. Stratified sampling is the process of selecting a sample in such a way that identified subgroups in the population are represented in the sample in the same proportion that they exist in the population.
9. Stratified sampling can also be used to select equal-sized samples from each of a number

of subgroups if subgroup comparisons are desired.

10. The steps in stratified sampling are similar to those in random sampling except that selection is from subgroups in the population rather than the population as a whole. In other words, random sampling is done for each subgroup.

CLUSTER SAMPLING

11. Cluster sampling is sampling in which groups, not individuals, are randomly selected. Clusters can be communities, states, school districts, and so on.
12. The steps in cluster sampling are similar to those in random sampling except that the random selection of groups (clusters) is involved, not individuals. Both stratified and cluster sampling often use multistage sampling.

SYSTEMATIC SAMPLING

13. Systematic sampling is sampling in which individuals are selected from a list by taking every Kth name, where K equals the number of individuals on the list divided by the number of participants desired for the sample.

Determining Sample Size

14. Samples should be as large as possible; in general, the larger the sample, the more representative it is likely to be, and the more generalizable the results of the study will be.
15. Minimum, acceptable sample sizes depend on the type of research, but there are no universally accepted minimum sample sizes.

Avoiding Sampling Error and Bias

16. Sampling error is beyond the control of the researcher and occurs as part of random selection procedures.

17. Sampling bias is systematic and is generally the fault of the researcher. Bias can result in research findings being invalid. A major source of bias is the use of nonrandom sampling techniques.

Selecting a Nonrandom Sample

18. Researchers cannot always select random samples and must rely on nonrandom selection procedures.
19. When nonrandom sampling techniques are used, it is not possible to specify what probability each member of a population has of being selected for the sample; and it is often difficult to even describe the population from which a sample was drawn and to whom results can be generalized.
20. Three types of nonrandom sampling are convenience sampling, which involves using as the sample whoever happens to be available; purposive sampling, which involves selecting a sample the researcher believes to be representative of a given population; and quota sampling, which involves giving interviewers exact numbers, or quotas, of persons of varying characteristics who are to be interviewed.
21. Any sampling bias present in a study should be fully described in the final research report.

Sampling in Qualitative Research

22. Qualitative research most often deals with small, purposive samples. The researcher's insights guide the selection of participants.
23. A variety of purposive sampling approaches are used in qualitative research, including intensity sampling, homogeneous sampling, criterion sampling, snowball sampling, and random purposive sampling.
24. The use of purposive sampling requires that the researcher describe in detail the methods used to select a sample.

◻ **Task 4** *Performance Criteria*

The definition of the population should describe its size and relevant characteristics (such as age, ability, and socioeconomic status).

The procedural technique for selecting study participants should be described in detail. For example, do not just say that stratified sampling will be used; indicate on what basis population members will be stratified and how they (and how many) will be selected from each subgroup. Also describe how selected participants will be placed into treatment groups; for example, by random assignment. If the entire population will be used in the study, say so and simply describe how population members will be assigned to groups.

Include a summary statement that indicates resulting sample size for each group. For example:

> Thus there will be two groups with a sample size of 30 each; each group will include 15 participants with above-average motivation and 15 participants with below-average motivation.

Any identifiable source of sampling bias should also be discussed; for example, small sample sizes.

On the following page, an example is presented that illustrates the performance called for by Task 4. (See Task 4 example.) Again, this example represents the task submitted by the same student whose tasks for Parts Two and Three were previously presented. Consequently, the sampling plan represents a refinement of the one included in Task 3.

Additional examples for this and subsequent tasks are included in the *Student Guide* that accompanies this text.

1

Effect of Interactive Multimedia on the Achievement of
10th-Grade Biology Students

Participants in this study will be selected from the population of 10th-grade biology students at an upper-middle-class all-girl Catholic high school in Miami, Florida. The student population is multicultural, reflecting the diverse ethnic groups in Dade County. The student body is composed of approximately 90% Hispanic students from a variety of Latin American backgrounds, the major one being Cuban, 9% Caucasian non-Hispanic students, and 1% African-American students. The population is anticipated to contain approximately 200 biology students.

Prior to the beginning of the school year, before students have been scheduled, 60 students will be randomly selected (using a table of random numbers) and randomly assigned to 2 classes of 30 each; 30 is the normal class size. One of the classes will be randomly chosen to receive IMM instruction and the other will not.

PART FIVE

Instruments

Whether you are testing hypotheses or seeking answers to questions, you must decide on a method or instrument to collect your data. In many cases this is a matter of selecting the best instrument for your purpose from those that already exist. Sometimes, however, you may have to develop your own data collection instrument. At other times you will be your own "instrument," observing and interacting with research participants. When selecting a method or instrument, a number of factors must be considered. The major point to remember, however, is that you should select or construct an approach that will provide pertinent data about the topic or hypothesis of your study.

The goals of Part Five are for you to (1) understand the link between constructs, variables, and instruments, (2) know criteria for selecting instruments, and (3) be able to select the best instrument for a given study from those available. After you have read Part Five, you should be able to perform the following task.

TASK 5

Having stated a topic to investigate, formulated one or more hypotheses or questions, and described a sample, describe three instruments appropriate for collection of data pertinent to the hypothesis or question. For each instrument selected, the description will include:

1. The name, publisher, and cost
2. A brief description of the purpose of the instrument
3. Validity and reliability data
4. The group for whom the instrument is intended
5. Administration requirements
6. Information regarding scoring and interpretation
7. Reviewers' overall impressions

Based on this information, indicate which instrument is most acceptable for your "study," and why. (See Performance Criteria, p. 194.)

"THE PICTURE OF DORIAN GRAY" © 1945 Turner Entertainment Co.

"The Thematic Apperception Test presents the individual with a series of pictures; the respondent is then asked to tell a story about what is happening in each picture (p. 161)."

Selection of Measuring Instruments

After reading chapter 5, you should be able to:

1. State the link between a construct, a variable, and an operationalized variable.
2. Describe different types of variables: nominal, ordinal, interval, and ratio; categorical and quantitative; dependent and independent.
3. Explain various testing terms: standardized test, assessment, measurement, selection, supply, performance assessments, raw scores, norm- and criterion-referenced scoring.
4. Describe the purposes of various types of tests: achievement, aptitude, attitude, interest, value, personality, projective, non-projective and self-report.
5. Describe various scales used to collect data for cognitive and affective variables.
6. Describe the purposes and ways to determine content, criterion-related, and construct validity.
7. Describe the purposes and ways to determine stability, equivalence, stability and equivalence, internal consistency, and rater reliability.
8. Define or describe standard error of measurement.
9. Know useful sources for finding information about specific tests.
10. State a strategy for test selection.
11. Identify and briefly describe three sources of test information.

CONSTRUCTS

Regardless of the type of research you do, you must collect data. The scientific and disciplined inquiry approach is based on the collection, analysis, and interpretation of data. Data are the pieces of information you collect and use to examine your topic or hypotheses. However, before you can collect data, you must determine what kind of data you need. To do this, you must understand the relationships among constructs, variables, and instruments.

Constructs are abstractions that cannot be observed directly; they are invented to explain behavior. Examples of educational constructs are intelligence, personality, teacher effectiveness, creativity, ability, achievement, and motivation. In order to measure constructs, they must be operationally defined, that is, defined in terms of processes or operations that can be observed and measured. To measure a construct, it is necessary to identify the scores or values it can assume. For example, the construct "personality" could be made measurable by defining two personality types, introverts and extroverts, as measured by scores on a 30-item questionnaire. Similarly, the construct "teacher effectiveness" might be operationally defined by observing a teacher in action and scoring effectiveness using four levels: unsatisfactory, marginal, adequate, and excellent. A variable is a construct that can take on two or more values or scores. We deal with variables in all our research studies.

As we shall see in this chapter, there are many different approaches and instruments to measure the same variable. For example, to measure sixth grade students' mathematics achievement, we can choose from a number of measuring instruments: the Stanford Achievement Test, California Achievement Test, Iowa Tests of Basic Skills, and others. Each of these measuring instruments is called a test or instrument.

Research topic statements and research hypotheses are usually stated in terms of variables. Read the following research topics and hypotheses and try to identify the variables in them.

1. Is there a relationship between middle students' grades and their self-confidence in science and math?
2. What do high school principals consider to be the most pressing administrative problems they face?
3. Do students learn more from our new social studies program than from the prior one?
4. What were the effects of the GI Bill on state colleges in the Midwest in the 1950s?
5. How do the first five weeks of school in Ms. Foley's classroom influence student activities and interactions in succeeding months?
6. There will be a statistically significant relationship between teachers' years teaching and their interest in taking new courses.
7. There will be a statistically significant difference in attitudes toward science between ninth grade girls and boys.

The variables in these examples are: (1) grades and self confidence; (2) administrative problems; (3) learning and the new social studies program (note that the social studies program has two forms [new and old programs] and thus is also a variable); (4) effects of the GI Bill; (5) student activities and student interactions; (6) years teaching and interest in taking new courses; and (7) attitudes toward science. Variables provide an indication of what will be examined in a research topic or hypothesis. The researcher will select or develop an appropriate instrument for each variable. Information about the instruments should be included in the Procedures section of the research proposal.

VARIABLES

For something to be a variable, it must have at least two values or scores. Height, weight, hair color, test score, age, teacher experience, and performance on the WWF motivation scale are all variables; people vary, or differ, on them. Variables themselves differ in many ways. For example, variables can be represented by different kinds of measurements, they can be identified as categorical or quantitative, or they can be divided into dependent and independent variables.

MEASUREMENT SCALES

There are four types of measurement scales: nominal, ordinal, interval, and ratio. It is important to know which type of scale is represented in your data because, as we shall see in chapters 12 and 13, different scales require different methods of statistical analysis. All variables are represented in at least one of the following measurement scales.

Nominal Variables

Nominal variables, also called categorical variables, represent the lowest level of measurement. They simply classify persons or objects into two or more categories where members of a category have at least one common characteristic. Nominal variables include gender (female, male); employment status (full-time, part-time, unemployed); marital status (married, divorced, single); and type of school (public, private, charter). For identification purposes, nominal variables are often represented by numbers. For example, the category "male" may be represented by the number 1 and "female" by the number 2. It is critically important to understand that such numbering of nominal variables does not indicate that one category is higher or better than another. That is, representing male with a 1 and female with a 2 does not indicate that males are lower or worse than females. The numbers are only labels for the groups. To avoid such confusion, it is often better to label nominal variables with letters (A, B, C, etc.), since they can only classify persons or objects into categories.

Ordinal Variables

Ordinal variables not only classify persons or objects, they also rank them in terms of the degree to which they possess a characteristic of interest. In other words, ordinal variables put persons or objects in order from highest to lowest or from most to least. For example, if 50 people were ranked from 1 to 50 on the ordinal variable height, the person with rank 1 would be the tallest and the person with rank 50 would be the shortest. Rankings make it possible to say that one person is taller or shorter than another. Class rank or order of finishing a marathon are ordinal variables. Although ordinal variables permit us to describe performance as higher, lower, better, or worse, they do *not* indicate how much higher or how much better one person performed compared to another. In other words, intervals between ranks are not equal; the difference between rank 1 and rank 2 is not necessarily the same as the difference between rank 2 and rank 3. For example, consider the ranking of these three heights:

RANK	HEIGHT
1	6 ft, 5 in.
2	6 ft, 0 in.
3	5 ft, 11 in.

The difference in height between the person ranked 1 and the person ranked 2 is 5 inches; the difference between rank 2 and rank 3 is 1 inch. Thus, while an ordinal variable can rank persons or objects, it does not have equal scale intervals. This characteristic limits the statistical methods used to analyze ordinal variables.

Interval Variables

Interval variables have all the characteristics of nominal and ordinal variables, but also have equal intervals. Most of the tests used in educational research, such as achievement, aptitude, motivation, and attitude tests, are treated as interval variables. When variables have equal intervals it is assumed, for example, that the difference between a score of 30 and a score of 40 is essentially the same as the difference between a score of 50 and a score of 60, and the difference between 81 and 82 is about the same as the difference between 82 and 83. Interval scales, however, do not have a true zero point. Thus, if Roland's science achievement test score was 0 on a scale of 0 to 100, his score does not indicate the total absence of science knowledge. Nor does Gianna's score of 100 indicate that she has complete possession of science knowledge. A score of 0 only indicates the lowest level of performance possible on that particular test and a score of 100 the highest level. Thus, we can say that a test score of 90 is 45 points higher than a score of 45, but we cannot say that a person scoring 90 knows twice as much as a person scoring 45. For most educational measurement it is sufficient to know only the score each person attained. Variables that have or are treated as having equal intervals utilize a broad array of statistical data analysis methods.

Ratio Variables

Ratio variables represent the highest, most precise, level of measurement. A ratio variable has all the properties of the types already discussed. In addition, it has a true zero point. Height, weight, time, distance, and speed are examples of ratio scales. The concept of "no weight," for example, is a meaningful one. Because of the true zero point, not only can we say that the difference between a height of 3 ft, 2 in. and a height of 4 ft, 2 in. is the same as the difference between 5 ft, 4 in. and 6 ft, 4 in., but also that a person 6 ft, 4 in. is twice as tall as one 3 ft, 2 in. Similarly, 60 minutes is three times as long as 20 minutes, and 40 pounds is four times as heavy as 10 pounds. Thus, with ratio variables we can say that Frankenstein is tall and Igor is short (nominal scale), Frankenstein is taller than Igor (ordinal scale), Frankenstein is 7 feet tall and Igor is 5 feet tall (interval scale), and Frankenstein is seven-fifths as tall as Igor (ratio scale). Since ratio variables encompass mainly physical measures, they are not used very often in educational research.

CATEGORICAL AND QUANTITATIVE VARIABLES

Categorical variables do not provide quantitative information about how people differ. They only provide information about qualitative differences. Nominal variables are categorical variables, in that they permit persons or things to be put into different categories that represent different qualities (e.g., eye color, religion, gender, political party) but not different quantities.

Quantitative variables are ones that exist on a continuum that ranges from low to high, or less to more. Ordinal, interval, and ratio variables are all quantitative variables, because they describe performance in quantitative terms.

DEPENDENT AND INDEPENDENT VARIABLES

We discussed dependent and independent variables in chapter 1. Recall this research topic statement from that chapter:

> What is the effect of positive versus negative reinforcement on elementary students' attitudes toward school?

Based on your knowledge, identify the variables in this topic.

You probably had little trouble identifying *attitudes toward school* as a variable, but did you also identify *type of reinforcement* as a variable? The variable "type of reinforcement" contains two levels or methods of reinforcement, positive and negative. Notice that attitudes toward school is a quantitative variable because it is measured in terms of more or less attitude. Notice, also, that type of reinforcement is a categorical variable because it represents categories, not quantitative degrees of difference.

Independent and dependent variables are primarily used in causal–comparative and experimental research studies. The independent variable (also called the treatment, causal, or manipulated variable) is the intended cause of the dependent variable (also called the effect, outcome, or criterion variable). The independent or treatment variable is manipulated by the researcher, while the dependent variable is not. For example, in this case, the researcher "manipulated" the two treatments by selecting them and then assigning participants to them. The dependent or outcome variable, attitudes toward school, is dependent on how well the two types of reinforcement function. The independent variable is the *cause* and the dependent variable is the *effect.* It is important to remember that the independent variable must have at least two levels or treatments. Thus, neither positive nor negative reinforcement is a variable by itself. It is only when both are included in the general variable (type of reinforcement) that we have two levels or treatments that vary and thus make up a variable.

COMBINATIONS OF VARIABLES

Most research in education fits into one of three variable combinations: two or more quantitative variables; one categorical and one quantitative; and two or more categorical variables. Studies consisting of two quantitative variables typically are correlational. For example, what is the correlation between family income and students' performance on a reading test? Studies consisting of a categorical and quantitative variable typically are experimental or causal–comparative. For example, will more homework or longer math classes be more successful in increasing fifth graders' interest in math? Studies consisting of two categorical variables typically are correlational or descriptive. For example, what is the relationship between the race of school principals and their political parties?

CHARACTERISTICS OF MEASURING INSTRUMENTS

The preceding pages introduced the role of and link between constructs, variables, and instruments. In this section we examine the wide range of measuring instruments that can be used to collect data in research studies. There are three major ways to collect research data:

1. Administer a standardized instrument.
2. Administer a self-developed instrument.
3. Record naturally occurring or already available data (such as observing or using existing grade point averages).

This chapter is concerned mainly with the selection of published, standardized tests. Although using already available data requires a minimum of effort and sounds very attractive, there are not many studies for which existing data are appropriate. Even when it is appropriate, there are other problems. For example, the same grade given by two different teachers does not necessarily represent the same level of achievement. On the other hand, developing an instrument for a particular study also has several major drawbacks. The development of a "good" instrument requires considerable time, effort, and skill. Total time for conducting a study usually is greatly increased if instrument development is involved. Also, at a minimum you need a course in measurement to acquire the skills needed for good instrument development. However, there are times when constructing your own instrument is necessary, especially if the research topic and concepts are original or relatively unresearched.

On the positive side, the time it takes to select an appropriate standardized instrument is invariably less than the time it takes to develop an instrument that measures the same thing. Further, standardized instruments tend to be developed by experts who possess needed test construction skills. From a research point of view, an additional advantage of using a standardized instrument is that results from different studies using the same instrument can be compared. Suppose, for example, that two separate studies were conducted to determine which method of teaching algebra results in higher end-of-course achievement, method A or method B. Suppose, further, that study 1 utilized a self-developed test of algebra achievement and study 2 used a standardized test of algebra achievement. Now if study 1 found no difference between methods A and B, but study 2 found method B to be superior, interpretation of these conflicting results would be difficult. It might be that the two tests were measuring different abilities, for example, application of formulas versus word-problem solving. It might also be that the test used in study 1 was inadequately constructed. In any event, it would be difficult to separate out differences due to the teaching method and differences due to the test used. Finally, use of a standardized instrument facilitates replication of a study by other researchers.

There are thousands of published and standardized instruments available that yield a wide variety of data for a wide variety of variables. Major areas for which numerous measuring instruments have been developed include achievement, personality, attitude, interest, and aptitude. Each of these can, in turn, be further divided into many subcategories. Personality instruments, for example, can be classified as nonprojective or projective; nonprojective instruments include measures of attitude and interest. Selection of an instrument for a particular research purpose involves identification and selection of the most appropriate one from among alternatives; a researcher does not find an instrument suited for his or her study, but rather selects the best one of those that are available. The selection process involves determination of the most appropriate type of instrument. In order to intelligently select an instrument, a researcher must be familiar with the wide variety of instruments that exist and must also be knowledgeable concerning the criteria that should be applied in selecting one from among alternatives.

Given the large array of instruments that are used in educational research, it is important to know some of the basic terminology used to describe them. We start with the terms "test," "assessment," and "measurement." A *test* is a formal, systematic, usually paper-and-pencil procedure for gathering information about peoples' cognitive (e.g., achievement, ability, reading) and affective (e.g., attitudes, emotions, interests, values) characteristics. Tests and instruments typically produce numerical scores. A *standardized test* is one that is administered, scored, and interpreted the same no matter where or when it is administered. They are typically developed by experts. For example, the SAT, ACT, Iowa Test, of Basic Skills, Stanford Achievement Test, and other nationally used tests are standardized in order to ensure that all test takers have the same conditions when taking the test. This allows comparisons among test takers from across the nation. You may remember taking a national standardized achievement test in school. They were the ones that every few pages has a stop sign that warned you to "Stop! Do not turn the page until instructed." *Assessment* is a broader term than test, or instrument, and encompasses the general process of collecting, synthesizing, and interpreting information, whether formal or informal. Tests are a subset of assessment, as are observations and interviews. *Measurement* is the process of quantifying or scoring persons' performance on assessments. Measurement occurs after data are collected.

There are three main methods of collecting data for a study: paper-and-pencil techniques, observations, and interviews. Paper-and-pencil methods are divided into two general categories: selection and supply. *Selection methods* include multiple-choice, true-false, and matching (one has to select from among the given answers). *Supply methods* include fill-in-the-blank, short answer, and essay (one has to supply one's own answer). Current emphasis on supply methods in schools has spawned the rise of so-called *performance assessments*, also know as authentic or alternative assessments. These assessments emphasize student processes (lab demonstration, debate, oral speech, or dramatic performances) or products (write an essay, construct a science fair project, write a research report). They typically are aimed at helping students perform more complex tasks than memorization. Paper-and-pencil instruments are the predominant form used in quantitative research. Observation and interviewing are important qualitative data collection approaches and will be described in detail in chapter 6.

Finally, there are four different ways of interpreting the instruments used in research. *Raw scores* are the number of items a person scored on a test or assessment. If Leron got 78 of 100 points on a test, his raw score is 78. In most quantitative research, raw scores are the basic data analyzed. However, using the bell curve, raw scores can be transformed into a variety of derived scores such as percentile ranks, stanines, and standard scores commonly used in many standardized tests.

Norm-referenced, criterion-referenced, and self-referenced scoring approaches represent three ways of interpreting performance on tests and measures. Norm-referenced scoring indicates how one student did compared to other students who took a test. For example, if we ask how well Rita did in science compared to other students in her grade from across the nation, we are asking for norm-referenced information. The interpretation of Rita's score will be based on how she performed compared to a national group of students in her grade. Norm-referenced scoring is also called *grading on the curve,* where the curve is the percentages of students who can receive each grade. Standardized tests and assessments frequently report norm-referenced scores in the form of derived scores such as percentile rank or stanines. *Criterion-referenced* scores also involve a comparison, but against predetermined levels of performance, not against the performance of other students. For example, if a teacher sets performance levels for grading test scores of 90 to 100 is an A, 80 to 89 is a B, 70 to 79 is a C, and so on, the teacher is using criterion-referenced grading. Students' test scores will be compared to the preestablished performance levels to determine the grade. Anyone who scores between 90 and 100 will get an A. If no one scores between 90 and 100, no one will get an A. If all students get between 90 and 100, they all will get As. This could not happen in norm-referenced grading, which requires that different scores, even very close ones, must get different grades. *Self-referenced* approaches involve measuring how a student's performance changes over time. Student performances at different times are compared to determine improvement or regression.

TYPES OF MEASURING INSTRUMENTS

There are many different kinds of tests available and many different ways to classify them. The Mental Measurements Yearbooks (MMYs) are a major source of test information for educational researchers. The Yearbooks provide information and reviews of published tests in various school subject areas such as English, mathematics, and reading, as well as personality, intelligence, aptitude, speech and hearing, and vocational tests.

COGNITIVE TESTS

Achievement Tests

Achievement tests are designed to provide information about how well test takers have learned what they have been taught in school. An individual's level of achievement on a standardized achievement test is usually determined by comparing it to the *norm,* the performance of a national group of students in the individual's grade or age level who took the same test. Thus, these tests can provide comparisons of a given student to similar students nationally. Standardized achievement tests are typically comprehensive batteries that measure achievement in a number of different curriculum areas. The Stanford Achievement Test, the Metropolitan Achievement Test, the California Achievement Test Battery, the SRA Survey of Basic Skills, and the Iowa Tests of Basic Skills are commonly used standardized achievement test batteries. Each includes subtests that measure achievement in many different areas such as reading comprehension, math computation, math problem solving, spelling, social studies, science, and listening comprehension. Depending on factors such as the number of different achievement areas tested, standardized achievement batteries take from 1 to 5 hours to complete.

Some achievement tests such as the Gates–McGinitie Reading Test focus on achievement in a single subject area. Sometimes diagnostic achievement tests are used to investigate specific weaknesses in a subject area that need remedial instruction. A diagnostic test is a type of achievement test that yields multiple scores to facilitate identification of a student's weak and strong areas. The Stanford Diagnostic Reading Test and the Key Math Diagnostic Inventory of Essential Mathematics Test are examples of widely used diagnostic achievement instruments.

Aptitude Tests

Aptitude tests measure intellect and abilities not normally taught in school and often are used to predict how well someone is likely to perform in the future. Tests of general aptitude are also referred to as scholastic aptitude tests and tests of general mental ability. Aptitude tests are standardized and are often administered as part of a school testing program; the results are useful to teachers, counselors, and administrators. They also are used extensively in job hiring.

General, multifactor aptitude tests typically require an individual to respond to a variety of verbal and nonverbal tasks intended to measure the individual's ability to apply knowledge and solve problems. Such tests often yield three scores—an overall score, a verbal score, and a quantitative score. A commonly used group-administered battery is the Columbia Mental Maturity Scale (CMMS). The CMMS has six versions and can be administered to school-age children, college students, and adults. It includes 12 subtests representing five aptitude factors: logical reasoning, spatial relations, numerical reasoning, verbal concepts, and memory. Another frequently administered group aptitude test is the Otis–Lennon School Ability Test, which has versions designed for school-age children in grades K–12. The Otis–Lennon School Ability Test measures four factors—verbal comprehension, verbal reasoning, figurative reasoning, and quantitative reasoning. The Sequential Tests of Educational Progress (STEP) battery, an academic aptitude battery, includes tests of reading, writing, mathematics, and science, among others. The Differential Aptitude Tests (DAT), on the other hand, include tests on space relations, mechanical reasoning, and clerical speed and accuracy, among others, and are designed to predict success in various job areas.

If there is ever a reason to question the appropriateness of group tests for a particular group of test takers (e.g., very young children), an individual test should be used. Probably the most well known of the individually administered tests are the Stanford–Binet Intelligence Scale and the Wechsler scales. The Stanford–Binet is appropriate for young children and adults. Wechsler scales are available to measure the intelligence of persons from the age of 4 to adulthood: the Wechsler Preschool and Primary Scale of Intelligence (WPPSI)—ages 3 to 7; the Wechsler Intelligence Scale for Children-Revised (WISC-R)—ages 5 to 15; and the Wechsler Adult Intelligence Scale-Revised (WAIS-R)—older adolescents and adults. As an example, the WISC is a scholastic aptitude test that includes verbal tests (e.g., general information, vocabulary) and performance tests (e.g., picture completion, object assembly). While the Stanford–Binet yields one overall score, the Wechsler scales yield a number of subscores. Other commonly used individually administered aptitude tests are McCarthy Scales of Children's Abilities and the Kaufman–Assessment Battery for Children (ABC) Test. Many of the individual aptitude tests use a combination of supply and performance-oriented items.

AFFECTIVE TESTS

Affective tests are designed to measure characteristics of individuals along a number of dimensions and to assess feelings, values, and attitudes toward self, others, and a variety of other activities, institutions, and situations. They are often used in educational research and exist in many different formats (performance versus paper and pencil, individual versus group, standardized versus nonstandardized, multiple-choice versus performance).

Most affective tests are nonprojective; that is, they are self-report measures. The individual responds to a series of questions or statements about him or herself. For example, a question that asked, "Which would you prefer, reading a book or playing basketball? Circle your answer." requires the individual to report his or her preference. Self-report tests are frequently used in descriptive studies (e.g., to describe the personality structure of various groups such as high school dropouts), correlational studies (e.g., to determine relationships between various personality traits and other variables such as achievement), and experimental studies (e.g., to investigate the comparative effectiveness of different instructional methods for different personality types).

Instruments that examine attitudes, interests, values, and personalities tap affective, emotive feelings, and perceptions. *Values* are deeply held beliefs about ideas, persons, or objects. For example, we may value our free time, our special friendships, or a vase given by our great-grandmother. *Attitudes* indicate what things we feel favorable or unfavorable about; our tendency to accept or reject groups, ideas, or objects. For example, Greg's attitude toward brussel sprouts is much more favorable than his attitude toward green beans (which puts Greg in a distinct minority). *Interests* indicate the degree to which we seek out or participate in particular activities, objects, and ideas. For example, I have very little interest in having my nose pierced (nor do I value or have a positive attitude toward nose piercing). *Personality*, also called temperament, is made up of a number of characteristics that represent a person's typical behaviors; it describes what we do in our natural life circumstances.

Attitude Scales

Attitude scales determine what an individual believes, perceives, or feels about self, others, and a variety of activities, institutions, and situations. There are five basic types of scales used to measure attitudes: Likert scales, semantic differential scales, rating scales, Thurstone scales, and Guttman scales. The first three are the most often used.

A Likert scale asks participants to respond to a series of statements by indicating whether they strongly agree (SA), agree (A), are undecided (U), disagree (D), or strongly disagree (SD) with each statement. Each response is associated with a point value, and an individual's score is determined by summing the point values of each statement. For example, the following point values are typically assigned to positive statements: SA = 5, A = 4, U = 3, D = 2, SD = 1. An example of a positive statement is "Short people are entitled to the same job opportunities as tall people." A score of 5 or 4 on this item would indicate a positive attitude toward equal opportunity for short people. A high total score across all items on the test would be indicative of an overall positive attitude. For negative statements, the point values should be reversed—that is, SA = 1, A = 2, U = 3, D = 4, and SD = 5. An example of a negative statement is "Short people are not entitled to the same job opportunities as tall people." On this item scores should be reversed; disagree or strongly disagree would indicate a positive attitude toward opportunities for short people.

A semantic differential scale asks an individual to give a quantitative rating to a topic such as attitude toward school or attitude toward smoking. A scale of a number of bipolar adjectives such as good–bad, friendly–unfriendly, and positive–negative are presented, and the respondent indicates the point on the continuum that represents her or his attitude. For example, on a scale concerning attitudes toward property taxes, the following items might be included:

Necessary	___	___	___	___	___	___	___	Unnecessary
Fair	___	___	___	___	___	___	___	Unfair
Better	___	___	___	___	___	___	___	Worse

Each position on the continuum has an associated score value; by totaling score values for all items, it can be determined whether the respondent's attitude is positive or negative. Semantic differential scales usually have 5 to 7 intervals with a neutral attitude assigned a score value of 0. For the above items, the score values would be as follows:

Necessary	___	___	___	___	___	___	___	Unnecessary
	3	2	1	0	−1	−2	−3	
Fair	___	___	___	___	___	___	___	Unfair
	3	2	1	0	−1	−2	−3	
Better	___	___	___	___	___	___	___	Worse
	3	2	1	0	−1	−2	−3	

A person who checked the first interval (i.e., a score of 3) on each of these items would be indicating a very positive attitude toward property taxes (fat chance!). Scores can be summed over items to get an overall score. Usually summed scores (interval data) are used in statistical data analysis.

A Thurstone scale asks participants to select from a list of statements that represent different points of view from those with which they are in agreement. Each item has an associated point value between 1 and 11; point values for each item are determined by averaging the values of the items assigned by a number of judges. An individual's attitude score is the average point value of all the statements checked by that individual. A Guttman scale also asks respondents to agree or disagree with a number of statements. A Guttman scale, however, attempts to determine whether an attitude is unidimensional. It is unidimensional if it produces a cumulative scale in which an individual who agrees with a given statement also agrees with all related preceding statements. For example, if you agree with statement 3, you also agree with statements 2 and 1.

Rating scales are also used to measure attitudes toward others. Such scales ask an individual to rate another individual on a number of behavioral dimensions. One form of rating scale provides descriptions of performance or preference and asks the individual to check the most appropriate description.

Select the choice that best describes your actions in the first five minutes of the classes you teach.
___ State lesson objectives and overview at start of the lesson
___ State lesson objectives but no overview at start of the lesson
___ Don't state objectives or give overview at start of the lesson

A second type of rating scale asks the individual to rate performance or preference using a numerical scale similar to a Likert scale.

Circle the number that best describes the degree to which you state lesson objectives and give an overview before teaching a lesson. A 5 = always, 4 = almost always, 3 = about half the time, 2 = rarely, and 1 = never.

1   2   3   4   5

Note that Likert, semantic differential, and rating scales are similar, requiring the respondent to provide a self-report along a continuum of choices. Note, also, that in certain situations such as observing performance or judging teaching competence, Likert, semantic differential, and rating scales can be used by others (a researcher, a principal, a colleague) to collect information about study participants. For example, in some studies it might be best to have the principal, rather than the teacher, use a Likert, semantic differential, or rating scale to collect data about the teacher.

Interest Inventories

An interest inventory asks participants to indicate personal likes and dislikes, such as the kinds of activities they prefer to engage in. Responses are generally compared to known interest patterns. The most widely used type of interest measure is the vocational interest inventory, which typically asks the respondent to indicate preferences in varied areas of occupational or occupational-related activities. The respondent's pattern of interest is then compared to the interest patterns typical of successful persons in various occupational fields. Interest inventories are widely used to suggest the fields in which respondents might be most happy and successful.

Two frequently used inventories are the Strong–Campbell Interest Inventory, and the Kuder Preference Record—Vocational. The Strong–Campbell Interest Inventory examines areas of interest in occupations, school subjects, activities, leisure activities, and day-to-day interactions with various types of people. Test takers are presented with many topics related to these five parts and are asked to indicate whether they like (L), dislike (D), or are indifferent to (I) each topic. A second part of the Strong–Campbell inventory consists of two sections. The first asks individuals to choose between two options such as "dealing with people or dealing with things." The second section presents a number of self-descriptive statements that the individual responds to by choosing Yes (like me), No (not like me), or ? (not sure). For example, an individual might be asked, "How like you is it to read a book in your spare time?"

The Kuder Occupational Interest Survey addresses ten broad categories of interest: outdoor, mechanical, computational, scientific, persuasive, artistic, literary, musical, social service, and clerical. Individuals are presented with three choices and must select the one they most like and the one they least like. For example, an individual would be presented with many items such as, "Would you rather: dig a hole, read a book, or draw a picture? Choose the one that you most would like to do and the one that you least would like to do."

The Strong–Campbell and the Kuder are both self-report instruments that provide information about persons' interests. Scoring the instruments requires sending data to the testing companies who produce them for computer analysis. *You cannot score them yourself.* While the Strong–Campbell and Kuder are among the most commonly used interest inventories, there are other interest instruments available. These, along with other attitudinal, value, and personality instruments, can be found in the Mental Measurement Yearbooks.

Values Tests

The Study of Values instrument is old, but is still used. It measures the relative strength of an individual's valuing of six different areas: theoretical (discovery of truth, empirical approach); economic (practical values); aesthetic (symmetry, form, and harmony); social (altruism, philanthropic); political (personal power, influence) and religious (unity of experience, cosmic coherence). Individuals are presented with items consisting of either two or four choices, based on the six test categories, and are asked to allocate points to the alternatives according to how much they value them.

For example, a two-alternative item might be, "Suppose you had the choice of reading one of two books first. If the books were titled *Making Money in the Stock Market* or *The Politics of Political Power,* which would you read first?" The respondent would have three points to allocate to the two choices. Three points could be allocated to one book and zero to another (indicating strong valuing of that area) or two points to one book and one point to the other (indicating a valuing of both books, with one slightly more valued). In no case could the two books be rated equally. Various combinations of the six areas are systematically mixed among the items. By counting up the points given to each of the six areas, an indication of an individual's preference among the six categories can be obtained. A second form of scoring provides four choices that the respondent must rank from 4 to 1 in order of preference.

Because the categories are too general to provide much specific direction to test takers, the Study of Values is used primarily in research studies to categorize individuals or measure the value orientation of different groups such as scientists and newspaper writers. Another values-based instrument is the Work Values Inventory.

Personality Inventories

Personality inventories present lists of questions or statements describing behaviors characteristic of certain personality traits. The individual is asked to indicate whether each statement describes him or her. Some inventories are presented as checklists; the individual simply checks items that characterize him or her. An individual's score is based on the number of responses characteristic of the trait being measured. An introvert, for example, would be expected to respond yes to the statement, "Reading is one of my favorite pastimes," and no to the statement, "I love large parties." Personality instruments may measure only one trait, such as introversion-extroversion, or may measure a number of traits. Since general inventories measure more than one trait at the same time, they take at least an hour or more to complete.

General inventories frequently used in educational research studies include the following: Personality Adjective Checklist, California Psychological Inventory, Minnesota Multiphasic Personality Inventory, Mooney Problem Checklist, Myers-Briggs Type Indicator, and the Sixteen Personality Factor Questionnaire. The Minnesota Multiphasic Personality Inventory (MMPI) alone has been utilized in hundreds of educational research studies. Its items were originally selected on the basis of response differences between psychiatric and normal patients. The MMPI measures many personality traits, such as depression, paranoia, schizophrenia, and social introversion. It contains more than 370 items to which a test-taker responds True (of me), False, or Cannot Say. It also has nearly 200 items that form additional scales such as anxiety, ego strength, repression, and alcoholism.

Self-report general personality instruments such as the MMPI are complex and require a substantial amount of knowledge of both measurement and psychology to score. It is recommended that beginning researchers avoid their use unless they have more than a passing knowledge of these areas.

Because they are generally self-report instruments, attitude, interest, values, and personality scales suffer from some problems. The researcher can never be sure that the individual is expressing his or her true attitude, interest, values, or personality, as opposed to a "socially acceptable" response. If this happens, the data gathered will not provide meaningful information. Every effort should be made, therefore, to increase honesty of response by giving appropriate directions to those completing the affective instruments.

Another serious problem, one particularly relevant when forced-choice items are used, is the problem of accurate responses. Scores are meaningful only to the degree that the respondent is honest and selects choices that truly characterize him or her. A common problem is the existence of a *response set*—that is, the tendency of an individual to continually respond in a particular way. One common response set is the tendency of an individual to select responses that he or she believes are the most socially acceptable, even if they are not necessarily characteristic of her or him. Another form of a response set is when a test taker continually responds "yes," "agree," or "true" to items because he or she believes that is what the test constructor desired. Whether response sets result from conscious or unconscious motivations, they can seriously distort an appraisal of the individual's affective characteristics. Therefore, in studies utilizing affective tests, every effort should be made to increase the likelihood that valid test results are obtained. One strategy to overcome the problem of response sets is to allow participants to respond anonymously.

Both affective and cognitive instruments are subject to biases that distort the data obtained. Bias is present when an individual's ethnicity, race, gender, language, or religious orientation distorts his or her test performance or responses. For example, low scores on reading tests by students who speak little English are probably due in large part to language disadvantages, not reading difficulties. For these students, test performance means something different than that of English-fluent students who also took the test. Or, if one's culture prohibits competition, or making eye contact, or speaking out, the responses on self-report instruments can differ according to cultural background, not personality, values, attitudes or interests. These issues need to be considered in selecting and interpreting the results of both cognitive and affective instruments.

PROJECTIVE TESTS

Projective tests were developed in part to eliminate some of the problems inherent in the use of self-report and forced-choice measures. Projective tests are intended to be ambiguous and not obvious to respondents. Since the purpose of the test is not clear, conscious dishonesty of response is reduced. Such tests are called projective because the respondent *projects* his or her true feelings or thoughts onto the ambiguous stimulus. The classic example of a projective test is the inkblot or Rorschach test. Respondents are shown a picture of an inkblot and are asked to describe what they see in it. The inkblot is really that, an inkblot made by putting a dab of ink on a paper and folding it in half to produce the blot. There are no right or wrong answers to the question, "What do you see in the inkblot?" (It's only an inkblot—honest.) The test taker's descriptions of such blots are a "projection" of his or her feelings and personality, which the administering clinician interprets.

The most commonly used projective technique is the method of association. Participants react to a stimulus such as a picture, inkblot, or word onto which they project a description. Word-association tests are probably the most well known of the association techniques (How many movies focused on a psychiatrist *haven't* included the line, "I'll say a word and you tell me the first thing that comes to your mind"?). Two of the most commonly used association tests are the Rorschach Inkblot Test and the Thematic Apperception Test. The Thematic Apperception Test presents the individual with a series of pictures; the respondent is then asked to tell a story about what is happening in each picture.

Until recently, all projective tests were required to be administered individually. There have been some recent efforts, however, to develop group projective tests. One such test is the Holtzman Inkblot Technique, which is intended to measure the same variables as the Rorschach Inkblot Test. Group projective instruments, including the Holtzman, are still in relatively early stages of development.

From the preceding comments, it should not be a surprise that projective tests are utilized mainly by clinical psychologists and very infrequently by educational researchers. This is due to the fact that administration, scoring, and interpretation of projective tests require lengthy and specialized training. One needs to be specially educated to use projective testing, and it is not recommended that beginning researchers utilize them.

There are other types and formats of measuring instruments beyond those discussed here. The intent of this section is to provide an overview of different types of tests, different formats for gathering data, different scoring methods, different interpretation strategies, and different limitations. To find more information about the specific tests described in this chapter and many other tests that were not described, refer to the Mental Measurement Yearbooks.

VALIDITY OF MEASURING INSTRUMENTS

Validity is the most important characteristic a test or measuring instrument can possess. It is concerned with the appropriateness of the interpretations made from test scores. When we test, we test for a purpose. For example, a researcher may administer a questionnaire to find out about people's opinions toward increasing funding for education. Or, an experimental research study may give a general science test to compare learning for science students taught by Method A and Method B. A key question for these and other test users is, "Does this test or instrument permit me to make the interpretation I wish to make?" That is, will responses to the opinion questionnaire or the science test allow the users to make appropriate interpretations about respondents' attitudes or learning?

Validity is important in all forms of research and all types of tests and measures. In some situations a test or instrument is used to make a number of different interpretations. For example, a high school chemistry achievement test may be used to assess students' end-of-year chemistry learning. It may also be used to predict students' future performance in science courses or to select students into advanced placement chemistry. Each of these uses calls for a different interpretation of the chemistry test scores: learning in the chemistry class, predicting future science achievement, and admission into advanced placement chemistry. Each intended interpretation requires its own validation. Further, the same test given to different groups of test takers may also have different validities. For example, if a reading achievement test were given to two fifth-grade classes, one that had been taught the test content and one that had not, the first group's scores would provide valid information about learning, but the second group's scores would be less valid because they did not have an opportunity to learn what was tested. The test did not measure their achievement and, therefore, interpretations about learning would be invalid. Thus, validity is specific to the interpretation being made and to the group being tested. Given this reality, it should be clear that validity does not refer to the test or instrument itself. That is, we do not say, "This test is valid." Rather, we say, "This test is valid for this particular interpretation and this particular group."

Clearly validity is a crucial feature of any test. If a test does not have high validity, if it does not allow users to make the interpretation desired, it should not be used. It is important to note that validation is a matter of degree; it does not exist on an all-or-nothing basis. Validity is best thought of in terms of degree: highly valid, moderately valid, and generally invalid. The validation process begins with an understanding of the interpretation(s) to be made from selected tests or instruments. It then requires the collection of evidence to support the desired interpretation.

For many years, validation was viewed as involving three distinct approaches to test validity: content validity, criterion-related validity, and construct validity. They focused on, respectively, the extent to which the test items or questions reflected the content area being measured; the extent to which the test predicted future performance or correlated with other measures; and the extent to which a construct like anxiety, personality, or intelligence is actually being measured. In recent years, the notion of separate types of validity has been replaced by a unitary concept of validity. That is, it is now recognized that content, criterion-referenced, and construct validity cut across and are pertinent to each others' focus.

Moreover, another dimension has recently been added to issues of validation: concern over the consequences that arise from use of tests and measures. As tests and measures have become increasingly used and important to test takers and others, concern over the consequences of testing has become common. Content, criterion-related, and construct validity pertain to the validity of test interpretations, which in some cases influence the consequences that ensue from testing. For example, test results are used to place students in special-education classrooms and to determine whether students will receive a high school diploma. Even if the tests used to make these two decisions are quite valid, they should be examined for the beneficial or deleterious consequences resulting from these test uses. Note that evidence of test consequences can be linked to evidence of test validity. The former is mainly concerned with the social or educational consequences of tests and measures, while the latter is mainly concerned with collecting evidence to validate test interpretations. Obviously, high test validity and beneficial test consequences are most desired. More specific information about testing in general and validity and reliability in particular can be found in the *Standards for Educational and Psychological Testing.*[1]

CONTENT VALIDITY

Content validity is the degree to which a test measures an intended content area. Content validity requires both item validity and sampling validity. Item validity is concerned with whether the test items are relevant to measurement of the intended content area. Sampling validity is concerned with how well the test samples the total content area being tested. A test designed to measure knowledge of biology facts might have good *item* validity because all the items are relevant to biology, but poor *sampling* validity, if, for example, all the test items were about vertebrates. A test with good content validity adequately samples the full content area. This is important because we cannot possibly measure each and every test item in a content area; the required test would be humongously long. And yet we do wish to make inferences about test takers' performance on the entire content area based on their performance on the sample of items included in the test. Such inferences are only possible if the test items adequately sample the domain of possible items. This sampling is, of course, easier for well-defined areas such as spelling than for fuzzier content areas such as social studies. Content areas come in different forms, breadth, and topics. For example, there are differences between all the topics studied in fifth-grade social studies, all the math topics taught in grades 1 to 8, all the spelling words in the second marking period, and all the lab experiments done in the introductory physics course. It is recommended that you clearly identify and examine for completeness the bounds of the content area to be tested before constructing or selecting a test or measuring instrument.

Content validity is of particular importance for achievement tests. A test score cannot accurately reflect a student's achievement if it does not measure what the student was taught and was supposed to learn. While this seems obvious, content validity can be compromised if the test covers topics not taught. If so, one no longer has a valid achievement test. Issues with achievement tests have been a problem in a number of research studies. Many studies are designed to compare the effectiveness of two (or more) different ways of teaching the same topic. Effectiveness is often measured in terms of the final achievement of the treatment groups. It is sometimes the case that the test used is more content valid for one of the groups than for the other. When this happens, final achievement differences may be at least partially attributable to the test used and not just to the teaching methods. This makes the scores of one group less content valid than those of the other group, making interpretation of study results also invalid. This phenomenon frequently occurs when an "innovative" approach is compared to a traditional approach. The different approaches often emphasize different areas of content.

A classic case is the early studies that compared the "new" math with the "old" math. These studies invariably found no achievement differences between

---

[1]American Educational Research Association, American Psychological Association, National Council on Measurement in Education. (1985) *Standards for Educational and Psychological Testing.* Washington, D.C., American Psychological Association.

students learning under the two approaches. The problem was that the "new" math was emphasizing concepts and principles, while the achievement tests were emphasizing computational skills. When tests were developed that contained an adequate sampling of items measuring concepts and principles, studies began to find that the two approaches to teaching math resulted in essentially equal computational ability, but that the "new" math resulted in better conceptual understanding. The moral of the story is, take care that the test measures what the students were expected to learn in the treatments. That is, be sure that the test is content valid for your study and for your research participants.

Content validity is determined by expert judgment. There is no formula by which it can be computed and there is no way to express it quantitatively. Usually experts in the area covered by the test are asked to assess its content validity. These experts carefully review the process used to develop the test as well as the test itself, and they make a judgment concerning how well items represent the intended content area. This judgment is based on whether all subareas have been included, in the correct proportions. In other words, a comparison is made between what ought to be included in the test, given its intended purpose, and what is actually included. When selecting a test for a research study, the researcher assumes the role of "expert" and determines whether the test is content valid for the study. The researcher compares what will be taught in the study with what is measured by the test. Information about test validity can be found in the MMY and other resources described later in this chapter.

The term *face validity* is sometimes used in conjunction with content validity in describing tests. Although its meaning is somewhat ambiguous, basically face validity refers to the degree to which a test *appears* to measure what it claims to measure. While determining face validity is not a psychometrically sound way of estimating validity, the process is sometimes used as an initial screening procedure in test selection. It should be followed up by content validation.

CRITERION-RELATED VALIDITY

Criterion-related validity has two forms, concurrent and predictive. The method of determining validity is the same for each form, but the time relations between them differ. Concurrent validity is the degree to which the scores on two tests taken at about the same time are correlated, and predictive validity is the degree to which the scores on two tests taken at different times are correlated. We deal with the two forms separately for clarity, but emphasize that both fit into the general category of criterion-related validity. The name *criterion-related* refers to the fact that this approach to validity involves correlating a test with a second test or measure. The second test is the criterion against which the validity of the initial test is judged.

Concurrent Validity

Concurrent validity is the degree to which scores on one test correlate to scores on another test when both tests are administered in the same time frame. Often, for example, a test is developed that claims to do the same job as some other tests, except easier or faster. One way to determine whether the claim is true is to administer the new and the old test (the criterion) to a group and correlate the scores. If there is a high correlation between the two tests, the concurrent validity of the new test is established and, in most cases, the new test will be utilized instead of the other test. A paper-and-pencil test that produces the same results as a performance test, or a short test that produces the same results as a longer test, would generally be preferred, especially in a research study.

Concurrent validity is determined by establishing a relationship or discrimination. The relationship method involves determining the correlation between scores on the test and scores on some other established test or criterion (e.g., grade point average). In this case, the steps involved in determining concurrent validity are as follows:

1. Administer the new test to a defined group of individuals.
2. Administer a previously established, valid criterion test (the criterion) to the same group, at the same time, or shortly thereafter.
3. Correlate the two sets of scores.
4. Evaluate the results.

The resulting correlation, or validity coefficient, indicates the degree of concurrent validity of the new test; if the coefficient is high (near 1.0), the test has good concurrent validity. Suppose, for example, that Professor Jeenyus developed a 5-minute group test of children's interest in school. If scores on this test correlated highly with scores on the Almost Never Ending School Interest Test (which must be administered to one child at a time and takes at least an hour), then Professor Jeenyus's test would definitely be preferable in a great many situations.

The discrimination method of establishing concurrent validity involves determining whether test scores can be used to discriminate between persons who possess a certain characteristic and those who do not, or those who possess it to a greater degree. For example, a test of personality disorder would have concurrent validity if scores resulting from it could be used to correctly classify institutionalized and noninstitutionalized persons.

When selecting a test for a given research purpose, you will usually be seeking a test that measures what you wish in the most efficient manner. If you select a shorter or more convenient test that allegedly measures the desired behavior, be careful that concurrent validity has been established using a valid criterion.

Predictive Validity

Predictive validity is the degree to which a test can predict how well individuals will do in a future situation. If an algebra aptitude test administered at the start of school can fairly accurately predict which students will perform well or poorly in algebra at the end of the school year (the criterion), the aptitude test has high predictive validity. Predictive validity is extremely important for tests that are used to classify or select individuals. An example with which many of you are all too familiar is the use of Graduate Record Examination (GRE) scores to select students for admission to graduate school. Many graduate schools require a minimum score for admission, often 1,000, in the belief that students who achieve that score have a higher probability of succeeding in graduate school than those scoring lower than 1,000. The predictive validity of the GRE has been the subject of many research studies. Results seem to indicate that the GRE has higher predictive validity for certain areas of graduate study than for others. For example, while the GRE appears to have satisfactory predictive validity for predicting success in graduate studies in English, its validity in predicting success in an art education program appears to be questionable. (Remember, a test can be used to make many interpretations, many having quite different validities.) Also, in general, GRE subject-specific tests in areas of graduate study tend to be better predictors of first-year grade point average (GPA) than the GRE General Test. Another example that illustrates the critical importance of predictive validity is the use of tests to determine which students should be assigned to special education classes. The decision to remove a child from the normal educational environment to place him or her in a special class is a serious one. In this situation it is imperative that the decision be based on the results of predictively valid measures. Also, in situations such as these, both predictive and consequential validity should be considered.

As the GRE example illustrates, the predictive validity of a given instrument varies with a number of factors. The predictive validity of an instrument may vary depending on such factors as the curriculum involved, textbooks used, and geographic location. The Mindboggling Algebra Aptitude Test, for example, may predict achievement better in courses using the *Brainscrambling Algebra I* text than in courses using other texts. Thus, if a test is to be used for prediction, it is important to compare the description of its validation with the situation in which it is to be used.

No test, of course, will have perfect predictive validity. Therefore, predictions based on the scores of any test will be imperfect. However, predictions based on a combination of several test scores will invariably be more accurate than predictions based on the scores of any single test. Therefore, when important classification or selection decisions are to be made, they should be based on data from more than one indicator. For example, we can use high school GPA to predict college GPA at the end of the freshman year. We can also use Scholastic Aptitude Test (SAT) score or rank in graduating class to predict college GPA. A prediction based on both SAT and grade point average, however, will provide more accurate prediction than one based on either one alone. A prediction based on three variables will be more accurate than a prediction based on two—provided the third variable is related to college GPA. Similarly, with respect to the GRE, predictions of graduate GPA that are based on both GRE scores and undergraduate GPA are more accurate than predictions based on GRE scores or undergraduate GPA alone.

The predictive validity of a test is determined by establishing the relationship between scores on the test and some measure of success in the situation of interest. The test used to predict success is referred to as the *predictor*, and the behavior predicted is referred to as the *criterion*. In establishing the predictive validity of a test, the first step is to identify and carefully define the criterion. The criterion selected must be a valid measure of the behavior to be predicted. For example, if we wished to establish the predictive validity of an algebra aptitude test, final examination scores at the completion of a course in algebra might be considered a valid criterion, but number of days absent during the course probably would not. As another example, if we were interested in establishing the predictive validity of a given test for predicting success in college, grade point average at the end of the first year would probably be considered a valid criterion, but number of extracurricular activities in which the student participated probably would not.

Once the criterion has been identified and defined, the procedure for determining predictive validity is as follows:

1. Administer the predictor variable to a group.
2. Wait until the behavior to be predicted, the criterion variable, occurs.
3. Obtain measures of the criterion for the same group.
4. Correlate the two sets of scores.
5. Evaluate the results.

The resulting correlation, or validity coefficient, indicates the predictive validity of the test; if the coefficient is high, the test has good predictive validity. For example, suppose we wished to determine the predictive validity of a physics aptitude test. First we would administer the test to a large group of potential physics students. Then we would wait until the students had completed a course in physics and would obtain a measure of their success, for example, final exam scores. The correlation between the two sets of scores would determine the predictive validity of the test; if the resulting correlation coefficient was high, the test would have high predictive validity.

As mentioned previously, often a combination of predictors is used to predict a criterion. In this case a prediction equation may be developed. A person's scores on each of a number of tests are inserted into the equation and her or his future performance is predicted. In this case the validity of the equation should be reestablished through cross-validation. Cross-validation involves administering the predictor tests to a different sample from the same population and developing a new equation. Of course, even if only one predictor test is involved, it is a good idea to determine predictive validity for more than just one sample of individuals. In other words, the predictive validity of a test should be reconfirmed.

You may have noticed that the procedures for determining concurrent validity and predictive validity are very similar. The major difference is in terms of when the criterion measure is administered. In establishing concurrent validity, it is administered at about the same time as the predictor, while in establishing predictive validity, one usually has to wait for a longer period of time to pass before criterion data can be collected. In the discussion of both concurrent and predictive validity there was a statement to the effect that if the resulting coefficient is high, the test has good validity. You may have wondered, "How high is high?" The question of how high the coefficient must be in order to be considered "good" is not easy to answer. There is no magic number that a coefficient should reach. In general, it is a comparative matter. A coefficient of .50 might be acceptable if there is only one test available designed to predict a given criterion; on the other hand, a coefficient of .50 might be inadequate if there are other tests available with higher coefficients. Comparing your correlation coefficient with similar ones in a *Mental Measurement Yearbook* will give you a sense of whether your correlation is high or low for that particular test area.

CONSTRUCT VALIDITY

Construct validity is the most important form of validity because it asks the fundamental validity question: What is this test really measuring? We have seen that all variables derive from constructs and that constructs are nonobservable traits, such as intelligence, anxiety, and honesty, "invented" to explain behavior. Constructs underlie the variables that researchers measure. You cannot see a construct, you can only observe its effect. "Why does that person act this way and that person a different way? Because one is intelligent and one is not—or one is dishonest and the other is not." We cannot prove that constructs exist, just as we cannot perform brain surgery on a person to "see" his or her intelligence, anxiety, or honesty.

Constructs, however, do an amazingly good job of explaining certain differences among individuals. For example, it was always observed that some students learn faster than others, learn more, and retain information longer. To explain these differences, a theory of intelligence was developed, and it was hypothesized that there is a construct called *intelligence* that is related to learning and that everyone possesses to a greater or lesser degree. Tests were developed to measure how much of it a person has. As it happens, students whose scores indicate that they have a "lot" of it—that is, they have high intelligence—tend to do better in school and other learning environments than those who have less of it. Other constructs that have been hypothesized to exist, and for which tests have been developed, include anxiety, creativity, and curiosity. Research studies that involve a construct are valid only to the extent that the test representing the construct is valid. That is, does the test really measure the intended construct, or is it measuring something else?

The process of determining construct validity is by no means easy. It usually involves gathering a number of pieces of evidence to demonstrate validity. If we wished to determine whether the Big Bob Intelligence Test was construct valid, we could carry out all or most of the following validation studies. First, we could see whether students who scored high on the Big Bob test learned faster, more, and with greater retention than low scorers. We could correlate scores on the Big Bob test taken at the beginning of the school year with students' grades at the end of the school year. We could also correlate performance on the Big Bob test with other, well-established intelligence tests to see whether the correlations were high. If they were, we'd have another piece of evidence to suggest that the Big Bob test is measuring the same things as other intelligence tests. We could have scholars in the field of intelligence examine the Big Bob test items to judge whether they represented typical topics in the field of intelligence. In addition to confirmatory evidence such as this, we could seek disconfirmatory validity information. For example, we would not expect scores on an intelligence test to correlate highly with self-esteem or height. If we correlated the Big Bob Intelligence Test with self-esteem and height and found low or moderate correlations, we could conclude that the Big Bob test is measuring something different from self-esteem or height. Thus, we would have evidence that the Big Bob test correlates highly with other intelligence tests (confirmatory validation) and does not correlate highly with self-esteem, personality, and height (disconfirmatory validation). Notice how content and criterion-related forms of validity are used in studies to determine a test's construct validity. No single validation study can establish the construct validity of a test. Rather, a series of studies would be needed to establish construct validity. Construct validity sheds light on the appropriateness of intended test interpretations and the justification of the test being used. When selecting a test for a given construct, the researcher must look for and critically evaluate evidence related to the construct validity of the test. Table 5.1 summarizes the three forms of validity.

TABLE 5.1		
Forms of Validity		
FORM	**METHOD**	**PURPOSE**
content validity	Compare content of the test to the domain being measured.	To what extent does this test represent the general domain of interest?
criterion-related validity	Correlate scores from one instrument to scores on a criterion measure, either at the same (concurrent) or different (predictive) time.	To what extent does this test correlate highly with another test?
construct validity	Amass convergent, divergent, and content-related evidence to determine that the presumed construct is what is being measured.	To what extent does this test reflect the construct it is intended to measure?

A number of factors can diminish the validity of tests and instruments used in research. They include:

- Unclear test directions
- Confusing and ambiguous test items
- Using vocabulary too difficult for test takers
- Overly difficult and complex sentence structures
- Inconsistent and subjective scoring methods
- Untaught items included on the achievement tests
- Failure to follow standardized test administration procedures
- Cheating, either by participants or by someone teaching the correct answers to the specific test items

All of these factors diminish the validity of tests because they distort or produce atypical test performance, which in turn distorts the desired interpretation of the test scores.

Validity is the most important characteristic a test or measure can have. Without validity, the desired interpretations of the variables measured have inappropriate meaning. There are multiple ways to establish the various forms of test validity. In the end, the test user makes the final decision about the validity and usefulness of a test or measure. The bases for that decision should be described in the Procedures section of your research plan.

RELIABILITY OF MEASURING INSTRUMENTS

In everyday English, reliability means dependability or trustworthiness. The term means the same thing with respect to measurements. *Reliability* is the degree to which a test consistently measures whatever it is measuring. The more reliable a test is, the more confidence we can have that the scores obtained from the test are essentially the same scores that would be obtained if the test were readministered to the same test takers. If a test is unreliable (i.e., if it provides inconsistent information about performance), then scores would be expected to be quite different every time the test was administered. For example, if an attitude test was unreliable, then a student getting a total score of 75 today might score 45 tomorrow and 95 the day after tomorrow. If the test was reliable, and if the student's total score was 75, then we would not expect his or her score to vary much if retested. If scores change greatly from one administration to another, the researcher does not know which score really represents a student's performance.

Of course, we also should not expect the student's score to be exactly the same on retestings. The reliability of test scores is similar to the reliability of one's golf, bowling, or shot-putting scores. Testing, as in golf, bowling, or shot-putting, rarely produces the identical score time after time after time. There is measurement error in all these activities, because we know that whatever score a person achieves in a single try will probably not be the exact same score achieved on another try. Tests and other performances will vary from time to time as a result of aspects of the individual or aspects of the test. For example, an individual's health, motivation, anxiety, guessing luck, attitude, and attention change from time to time and influence performance. Similarly, aspects of testing such as interruptions during test taking, changes in room comfort, time of day the test is taken, and errors in test scoring also introduce measurement error into performance.

Normally we don't expect such individual and testing factors to create large differences in scores, just as our golf, bowling, and shot-putting scores vary to some degree, but not wildly from time to time. However, all test scores have some degree of measurement error. The smaller the amount of error, the more reliable the scores and the more confidence we have in the consistency and stability of test takers' performances.

Reliability is expressed numerically, usually as a reliability coefficient, which is obtained by using correlation. A high reliability coefficient indicates high reliability. If a test were perfectly reliable, the reliability coefficient would be 1.00, meaning that a student's score perfectly reflected her or his true status with respect to the variable being measured. However, alas and alack, no test is perfectly reliable and, as noted, scores are invariably affected by errors of measurement resulting from a variety of causes. High reliability indicates minimum error variance; the effect of errors of measurement are small.

Although validity tells test users about the appropriateness of a test or measure, reliability tells about the consistency of the scores produced. Both are important criteria for examining and judging the suitability of a test or measuring instrument. If an achievement test is too difficult for a given group of students, all scores would be systematically lowered because the test was inappropriate; the test would have low validity for that group (remember, "valid for whom?"). However, the test might yield very consistent scores, that is, have high reliability. If the test was so hard that no test taker could answer even a single item, scores would be quite consistent, but not valid. Note that errors of measurement that affect reliability are random errors, while systematic or constant errors affect validity. A given student whose "true" achievement score was 80 and who scored 60 on a difficult test (invalidity) might score 60 every time he or she took the test (reliability). This illustrates an interesting relationship between validity and reliability: *a valid test is always reliable but a reliable test is not always valid.* In other words, if a test is measuring what it is supposed to be measuring, it will be reliable, but a reliable test can consistently measure the wrong thing and be invalid! Suppose an instrument that purported to measure social studies concepts really measured only social studies facts. It would not be a valid measure of concepts, but it could certainly measure the facts very consistently. To illustrate, suppose the reported reliability coefficient for a test were .24, which is definitely not good. Would this tell you anything about the test's validity? Yes, it would. It would tell you that the validity was not high because if it were, the reliability would be higher. What if the reported reliability coefficient were .92, which is definitely good. Would this tell you anything about the validity? H-m-m-m. The answer is—not really. It would only tell you that the validity might be good, because the reliability is good, but not necessarily; the test could be consistently measuring the wrong thing. To review, reliability is necessary but not sufficient for establishing validity. Got it?

All this talk about error might lead you to believe that measurement in education is pretty sloppy and imprecise to say the least. Actually it's not as bad as it may sound. There are many tests that measure their intended topics quite accurately. Measurement error is not unique to educational research. For example, consider the "test" of having your blood pressure measured by a doctor. Rarely do two blood pressures taken consecutively produce the identical readings. This physiological trait is subject to the same individual and "test" conditions as in educational testing, and in many cases is far less reliable than educational measures. Thus, a person's blood pressure reading is also the result of a combination of "true" blood pressure and error.

Like validity, there are different types of reliability, each of which deals with a different kind of test consistency. Each is determined in a different manner. Five general types of reliability will be discussed: stability, equivalence, equivalence and stability, internal consistency, and rater agreement.

STABILITY

Stability, also called test–retest reliability, is the degree to which scores on the same test are consistent over time. It indicates score variation that occurs from one testing session to another. In other words, it provides evidence that scores obtained on a test at one time (test) are the same or close to the same when the test is readministered some other time (retest). The more similar the scores on the test over time, the more stable or consistent are the test scores. Test stability is especially important for tests used as predictors, such as aptitude tests, and for affective and questionnaire instruments, since these measures are based heavily on the assumption that the scores will be stable over time. Such tests would not be useful if they produced very different scores at different times.

Determination of test–retest reliability is appropriate when alternate (equivalent) forms of a test are not available, and when it is unlikely that persons taking the test the second time will remember responses made on the test the first time. Test takers are more likely to remember items from a test with a lot of history facts, for example, than from a test with algebra problems.

The procedure for determining test–retest reliability is basically quite simple:

1. Administer the test to an appropriate group.
2. After some time has passed, say two weeks, administer the same test to the same group.
3. Correlate the two sets of scores.
4. Evaluate the results.

If the resulting coefficient, referred to as the coefficient of stability, is high, the test has good test–retest reliability. A major problem with this type of reliability is the difficulty of knowing how much time should elapse between the two testing sessions. If the interval is too short, the chances of students' remembering responses made on the test the first time are increased, and the estimate of reliability tends to be artificially high. If the interval is too long, students' test performance may increase due to intervening learning or maturation, and the estimate of reliability tends to be artificially low. Generally, though not universally, a period of from two to six weeks is used to determine a test's stability. When stability information about a test is given, the stability coefficient and the time interval between testings should be given. The problems associated with test–retest reliability are taken care of by equivalence reliability.

EQUIVALENCE

Equivalent or alternative forms of a test are two tests that are identical in every way except for the actual items included. The two forms measure the same variable, have the same number of items, the same structure, the same difficulty level, and the same directions for administration, scoring, and interpretation. In fact, if the same group takes both tests, the average score as well as the degree of score variability should be essentially the same on both tests. Only the specific items are not the same, although they do measure the same traits or objectives. The equivalent forms are developed by selecting, or sampling, two sets of items from the same, well-described behavior domain. The reliability issue is whether scores on the two forms are equivalent. If there is equivalence, the two tests can be used interchangeably. It is reassuring to know that a person's score will not be greatly affected by the particular form administered. Also, in some research studies two forms of a test are administered to the same group, one as a pretest and the other as a posttest. It is crucial, if the effects of the intervening activities are to be validly assessed, that the two tests be measuring essentially the same things.

The procedure for determining equivalent-forms reliability is similar to that for determining test–retest reliability:

1. Administer one form of the test to an appropriate group.
2. At the same session, or shortly thereafter, administer the second form of the test to the same group.
3. Correlate the two sets of scores.
4. Evaluate the results.

If the resulting coefficient of equivalence is high, the test has good equivalent-forms reliability. Equivalent-forms reliability is the most commonly used estimate of reliability for most tests used in research. The major problem involved with this method of estimating reliability is the difficulty of constructing two forms that are essentially equivalent. Lack of equivalence is a source of measurement error. Even though equivalent-forms reliability is considered to be a very good estimate of reliability, it is not always feasible to administer two different forms of the same test, or even the same test twice. Imagine telling your students that they had to take two final examinations! Imagine someone telling *you* to take the GRE or SAT twice! Fortunately, there are other methods of estimating reliability that require administering a test only once.

EQUIVALENCE AND STABILITY

This form of reliability is a combination of the equivalence and stability approaches. If the two forms of the test are administered at two different times (the best of all possible worlds!) the resulting coefficient is referred to as the coefficient of stability and equivalence. In essence, this approach assesses stability of scores over time as well as the equivalence of the two sets of items. Since more sources of measurement error are possible than with either method alone, the resulting coefficient is likely to be somewhat lower. Thus, the coefficient of stability and equivalence represents a conservative estimate of reliability.

The procedure for determining equivalence and stability reliability is:

1. Administer one form of the test to an appropriate group.
2. After a period of time, administer the other form of the test to the same group.
3. Correlate the two sets of scores.
4. Evaluate the results.

INTERNAL CONSISTENCY RELIABILITY

Internal consistency is a commonly used form of reliability that deals with one test at one time. It is obtained through three different approaches: split-half, Kuder–Richardson, and Cronbach's alpha. Each provides information about the consistency among the items in a single test. Because internal consistency approaches require only one test administration, sources of measurement errors, such as differences in testing conditions, are eliminated.

Split-Half Reliability

Split-half reliability involves breaking a single test into two halves. It is especially appropriate when a test is very long or when it would be difficult to administer either the same test at two different times or two different forms to a group. The procedure for determining split-half reliability is as follows:

1. Administer the total test to a group.
2. Divide the test into two comparable halves, or subtests—most commonly by dividing the test into odd and even numbered subtests.
3. Compute each subject's score on the two halves—each subject will have a score for the odd items and a score for the even items.
4. Correlate the two sets of scores.
5. Apply the Spearman–Brown correction formula.
6. Evaluate the results.

If the coefficient is high, the test has good split-half reliability. Most commonly, an odd–even strategy is used. This approach works out rather well regardless of how a test is organized. Suppose, for example, a test is a 20-item test in which the items get progressively more difficult. Items 1, 3, 5, 7, 9, 11, 13, 15, 17, and 19 as a group should be approximately as difficult as items 2, 4, 6, 8, 10, 12, 14, 16, 18, and 20. In effect, we are artificially creating two equivalent forms of a test and computing their equivalent-forms reliability. In split-half reliability, the two equivalent forms just happen to be in the same test—thus the label *internal consistency reliability.*

Since longer tests tend to be more reliable, and since split-half reliability represents the reliability of a test only half as long as the actual test, a correction formula must be applied to determine the reliability of the whole test. The correction formula used is the Spearman–Brown prophecy formula. For example, suppose the split-half reliability coefficient for a 50-item test were .80. The .80 would be based on the correlation between scores on 25 even items and 25 odd items and would therefore be an estimate of the reliability of a 25-item test, not a 50-item test. The Spearman-Brown formula provides an estimate of the full 50-item test. The formula is very simple and is applied to our example in the following way:

$$r_{total\ test} = \frac{2r_{split\ half}}{1 + r_{split\ half}}$$

$$r_{total\ test} = \frac{2(.80)}{1 + .80} = \frac{1.60}{1.80} = .89$$

Kuder–Richardson and Cronbach's Alpha Reliabilities

Kuder–Richardson (KR) and Cronbach's alpha estimate internal consistency reliability by determining how all items on a test relate to all other test items and to the total test. When its items or tasks are measuring similar things, they are internally consistent. Both KR-20 and Cronbach's alpha provide reliability estimates that are equivalent to the average of the split-half reliabilities computed for all possible halves. KR-20 is a highly regarded method of assessing reliability, but is useful only for dichotomously scored items such as in multiple choice items. If items have more than two scores, (e. g., 0, 1, 2, 3), then Cronbach's alpha (α) should be used. Cronbach's alpha is the general formula of which the KR-20 formula is a special case. Many affective instruments and performance tests are scored using more than two choices. For example, Likert scales are commonly used in many affective instruments. If numbers are used to represent the response choices, analysis for internal consistency can be accomplished by using Cronbach's alpha.

Kuder and Richardson provided an alternative, more easily computed form of their formula, called Kuder–Richardson 21, or KR-21. It requires less time than any other method of estimating reliability, although its results are a more conservative estimate of reliability.

The *KR*-21 formula is as follows:

$$r_{total\ test} = \frac{(K)(SD^2) - \overline{X}(K - \overline{X})}{(SD^2)(K - 1)}$$

where

K = the number of items in the test
SD = the standard deviation of the scores
$\overline{X}$ = the mean of the scores

In a later chapter you will learn how to compute the mean and standard deviation of a set of scores. For the moment, let it suffice to say that the mean ($\overline{X}$) is the average score on the test for the group that took it and the standard deviation (SD) is an indication of the amount of score variability, or how spread out the scores are. For example, assume that you have administered a 50-item test and

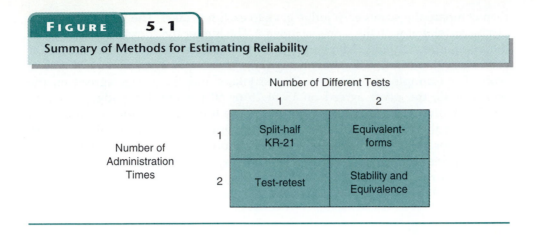

FIGURE 5.1

Summary of Methods for Estimating Reliability

| | | Number of Different Tests | |
		1	2
Number of Administration Times	1	Split-half KR-21	Equivalent- forms
	2	Test-retest	Stability and Equivalence

have calculated the mean to be 40 ($\overline{X} = 40$) and the standard deviation to be 4 ($SD = 4$). The reliability of the test (which in this example turns out to be not too hot!) would be calculated as follows:

$$r_{\text{total test}} = \frac{(50)(4^2) - 40\,(50 - 40)}{(4^2)(50 - 1)}$$

$$= \frac{(50)(16) - 40(10)}{(16)(49)} = \frac{800 - 400}{784} = \frac{400}{784} = .51$$

This formula should be more comprehensible after you have completed the task and objectives for chapter 12, but even at this stage the ease of application of KR-21 should be evident. Figure 5.1 summarizes the methods of estimating reliabilities.

Scorer/Rater Reliability

Reliability also must be investigated when scoring potentially subjective tests. Subjectivity occurs when different scorers or a single scorer over time do not agree on the scores of a single test. Essay tests, short-answer tests, performance and product tests, projective tests, and observations—almost any test that calls for more than a one-word response—raise concerns about the reliability of scoring. In such situations we are concerned with interjudge (interscorer, interrater, interobserver) reliability and/or intrajudge reliability. Interjudge reliability refers to the scoring reliability of two (or more) independent scorers; intrajudge reliability refers to the consistency of the scoring of a single judge over time (a kind of test–retest reliability).

Subjective scoring is a major source of errors of measurement, so it is important to determine the reliability of those who score open-ended tests. It is especially important to determine scorer/rater reliability when the results of the tests are consequential for test takers, such as the awarding of a high school diploma or promotion to the next grade on the basis of a test. Estimates of interjudge or intrajudge reliability are typically obtained by correlational techniques, but can also be expressed simply as a percentage of agreement. Interjudge reliability can be obtained by having two (or more) judges independently score the tests and then compare the scores each judge gave to each test taker. The scores of judge 1 can be correlated with the scores of judge 2. The higher the correlation, the higher the interjudge reliability. Alternatively, the two judges could compare scores for each student and determine how many times the judges agreed on a test taker's score. For example, if there were 25 test takers and the judges agreed on the scores of 15, the raters agreed on 15 of 25 or 60 percent. Interjudge reliability would involve a single judge scoring the same tests at two different times and correlating the two sets of scores or determining the percentage of agreement with him- or herself on the two scorings. The more open-ended test items are, the more important it is to seek consensus in scoring among judges. Subjective scoring reduces reliability and, in turn, diminishes the validity of the interpretations one wished to make from the scores. Table 5.2 summarizes the five types of reliability.

RELIABILITY COEFFICIENTS

What constitutes an acceptable level of reliability is to some degree determined by the type of test, although, of course, very high reliability coefficients would be acceptable for any test. The question really is concerned with what constitutes a minimum level of acceptability. This will differ among test types. For example, standardized achievement and aptitude tests have generally high reliability, often

TABLE 5.2

Methods of Determining Reliability

NAME	WHAT IS MEASURED	DESCRIPTION
stability (test-retest)	stability of scores over time	Give one group the same test at two different times and correlate the two scores.
equivalance (alternative forms)	relationship between two versions of a test intended to be equivalent	Give alternative test forms to a single group and correlate the two scores.
equivalance and stability	relationship between equivalent versions of a test given at two different times	Give two alternative tests to a group at two different times and correlate the scores.
internal consistency	the extent to which the items in a test are similar to one another in content	Give tests to one group and apply split-half, Kuder–Richardson, or Cronbach's alpha to estimate the internal consistency of the test items
scorer/rater	the extent to which independent scorers or a single scorer over time agree on the scoring of an open-ended test	Give copies of a set of tests to independent scorers or a single scorer at different times and correlate or compute the percentage of scorer agreement.

higher than .90. A user ought to expect a high reliability for such tests. On the other hand, personality measures do not typically report such high reliabilities (although certainly some do), and one would therefore be satisfied with a reliability somewhat lower than expected from an achievement test. Moreover, when tests are developed in new areas, reliability often is low initially. For example, instruments that measure curiosity are a relatively recent addition to the testing field. One would not necessarily expect high reliabilities for these instruments in the early stage of their development. If you are using a fairly new test, or using an established test with a group that is somewhat different than the test norm group, you should report reliability figures for your group. By doing so, you will verify that the test was reliable for your group, and you will provide valuable data for the test developers and for other researchers. It is a good practice to provide your own reliability information based on the participants in your research plan.

If a test is composed of several subtests that will be used individually in a study, then the reliability of each subtest should be evaluated, not just the reliability of the total test. Since reliability is a function of test length, the reliability of any particular subtest is typically lower than the total test reliability. You, as a researcher, should be a good consumer of test information. If a test manual or an entry in MMY (discussed shortly) states that "the total test reliability is .90, and all subtest reliabilities are satisfactory," you should immediately become suspicious. If subtest reliabilities are "satisfactory," the publisher will certainly want to tell you just how satisfactory they are. Most of the major, well-established tests report subtest reliabilities. This fact is no excuse for not reporting your own reliability based on your research participants.

It is extremely difficult to state appropriate reliability coefficients for different types of tests. Obviously, the higher the reliability the better, but what's a "high" or "low" reliability for an achievement, attitude, interest, personality, or curiosity test? One way to answer this question is to get information about the typical reliabilities for particular types of tests. For example, if you find that three curiosity tests had reliabilities between .60 and .75, you have an idea of what level of reliability to expect in other curiosity tests. It is also difficult to state appropriate reliability coefficients because reliability, like validity, is dependent on the group being tested. Groups with different characteristics will produce different reliabilities. For example, the more heterogeneous the test scores of a group, the higher the reliability will be. Thus, if Group A and Group B both took the same test, but Group A was made up of valedictorians (very homogeneous) and Group B was made up of students ranging from low to high performers (very heterogeneous), Group B will have a higher reliability than Group A. Also, the more items on a test and the more the scores range from high to low, the higher the reliability. That is why it is important for researchers to report reliability for their own research participants.

STANDARD ERROR OF MEASUREMENT

Reliability can also be expressed in terms of the standard error of measurement. You should be familiar with this concept, since such data are often reported for a test. Basically, the standard error of measurement is an estimate of how often you can expect test errors of a given size. Thus, a small standard error of measurement indicates high reliability, and a large standard error of measurement indicates low reliability.

If a test were perfectly reliable (which no test is), a person's test score would be his or her true score—that is, the score the person got would be perfectly reliable. However, we know that if you administered the same test over and over to the same group, the score of each individual would vary, like the golf, bowling, and shot-put examples discussed previously. The amount of variability in the individual scores would be a function of the test's reliability. The variability would be small for a highly reliable test (zero if the test were perfectly reliable) and large for a test with low reliability. If we could administer the test many times to the same group we could see how much variation actually occurred. Of course, realistically we can't do this; administering the same test even twice to the same group is tough enough. Fortunately, it is possible to estimate this degree of variation (the standard error of measurement) using the data from the administration of a single test. In other words, the standard error of measurement allows us to estimate how much difference there is between a person's obtained score and his or her true score. The size of this difference is a function of the reliability of the test. We can estimate the standard error of measurement using the following simple formula:

$$SEm = SD\sqrt{1-r}$$

where
SEm = standard error of measurement
SD = the standard deviation of the test scores
r = the reliability coefficient

For example, for a 25-item test we might calculate the standard deviation of a set of scores to be 5 ($SD = 5$) and the reliability coefficient to be .84 ($r = .84$). In this case the standard error of measurement would be calculated as follows:

$$SEm = SD\sqrt{1-r} = 5\sqrt{1-.84} = 5\sqrt{.16} = 5(.4) = 2.0$$

As this example illustrates, the size of the SEm is a function of both the SD and the reliability coefficient. Higher reliability is associated with a smaller SEm and a smaller SD is associated with a smaller SEm. If in the previous example $r = .64$, would you expect SEm to be larger or smaller? Right, larger, and in fact, it would be 3.0. Also, if in that example $SD = 10$, what would you expect to happen to SEm? Right, it would be larger—4.0, to be exact. While we prefer the SEm to be small, indicating less error, it is impossible to say how small is "good." This is because SEm is expressed in the same units as the test, and how small is "small" is relative to the size of the test. Thus $SEm = 5$ would be large for a 20-item test but small for a 200-item test. In our example, $SEm = 2.0$ would be considered moderate. To facilitate better interpretation of scores, some test publishers do not just present the SEm for the total group but also give a separate SEm for each of a number of identified subgroups.

SELECTION OF A TEST

A very important guideline for selecting a test is: Do not, repeat, do not stop with the first test you find that appears to measure what you want, say "Eureka, I have found it!" and blithely use it in your study! Instead, identify a group of tests that are appropriate for your study, compare them on relevant factors, and select the best one. If you become knowledgeable concerning the qualities a test should possess, and familiar with the various types of tests that are available, then the selection of an instrument will be a very orderly process. Given that you have defined the purpose of your study and the research participants, the first step in choosing a test is to determine precisely what type of test you need. The next step is to identify and locate appropriate tests. Finally, you must do a comparative analysis of the tests and select the best one. In order to locate appropriate tests, you need to be familiar with sources of test information.

SOURCES OF TEST INFORMATION

Mental Measurements Yearbooks

Once you have determined the type of test you need (e.g., a test of reading comprehension for second graders or an attitude measure for high schoolers), a logical place to start looking for specific tests to meet your needs is the Mental Measurements Yearbooks (MMYs). Currently produced by the Buros Institute of Mental Measurements at the University of Nebraska, the MMYs have been published periodically since 1938, and they represent the most comprehensive source of test information available to educational researchers. The MMYs were conceived by, and until relatively recently produced under, the auspices of Oscar Buros, who provided comprehensive test information for both researchers and practitioners. MMYs are available in the reference section at most university libraries. To locate a particular MMY in your library, do a title search and use the call number that is generated from the search to find out where the book is located.

The *Thirteenth Mental Measurements Yearbook* is the latest publication in a series which includes the *MMYs, Tests in Print,* and other related works such as *Vocational Tests and Reviews.* Table 5.3 lists the many volumes associated with the MMYs. An MMY is published every few years, and a Supplement is published between major revisions. The MMYs are expressly designed to assist users in making informed test selection decisions. The stated purposes are to provide: (1) factual information on all known new or revised tests in the English-speaking world; (2) objective test reviews written specifically for the MMYs; and (3) comprehensive bibliographies, for specific tests, of related references from published literature. Each volume contains information on tests that have been published or revised since the previous MMY, or have generated 20 or more references since the last MMY.

Getting maximum benefit from the MMYs requires becoming knowledgeable about their contents and the various ways of using them. At the very least, you should familiarize yourself with the organization and the indexes provided. The basic organization of the most recent MMYs is that all the test descriptions and reviews are presented *alphabetically by test title.* Thus, if you are looking for a particular test, you can go right to it without using any index. Perhaps the most important thing to know in using the MMYs is that the numbers given in the indexes are test numbers, not page numbers. For example, in the Classified Subject Index, under Achievement, you will find the following entry (among others): Iowa Tests of Basic Skills, Form J, grades K.1–1.5, K.8–1.9, 1.7–2.6, 2.5–3.5, 3, 4, 5, 6, 7, 8–9, see 184. The 184 means that the description of the Iowa Tests of Basic Skills is entry 184 in the main body of the volume; it does not mean that it is on page 184.

TABLE	**5.3**

Complete Listing of *Mental Measurements Yearbooks, Tests in Print,* and *Related Works*

Buros Desk Reference: Psychological Assessment in the Schools
Buros Desk Reference: Assessment Of Substance Abuse
Educational, Psychological and Personality Tests of 1933 and 1934
Educational, Psychological, and Personality Tests of 1933, 1934, and 1935
Educational, Psychological, and Personality Tests of 1936
The Nineteen Thirty-Eight Mental Measurements Yearbook
The Nineteen Forty Mental Measurements Yearbook
The Third Mental Measurements Yearbook
The Fourth Mental Measurements Yearbook
The Fifth Mental Measurements Yearbook
Tests in Print
The Sixth Mental Measurements Yearbook
Reading Tests and Reviews
Personality Tests and Reviews
The Seventh Mental Measurements Yearbook
Tests in Print II
English Tests and Reviews
Foreign Language Tests and Reviews
A Guide to 85 Tests for Special Education
Intelligence Tests and Reviews
Mathematics Tests and Reviews
Measures of Personality and Social Psychological Attitudes
Personality Tests and Reviews I
Personality Tests and Reviews II
Psychware Sourcebook
Reading Tests and Reviews
Science Tests and Reviews
Social Studies Tests and Reviews
Vocational Tests and Reviews
The Eighth Mental Measurements Yearbook
Tests: A Comprehensive Reference For Assessments in Psychology, Education, and Business
Test Critiques
Tests in Print III
The Ninth Mental Measurements Yearbook
Supplement to the Ninth Mental Measurements Yearbook
The Tenth Mental Measurements Yearbook
Supplement to the Tenth Mental Measurements Yearbook
The Eleventh Mental Measurements Yearbook
The Eleventh Mental Measurements Yearbook on CD-ROM
Supplement to the Eleventh Mental Measurements Yearbook
Tests in Print IV
The Twelfth Mental Measurements Yearbook
The Thirteenth Mental Measurements Yearbook

The MMY provides six indexes to help you find information about tests. The Index of Titles is simply an alphabetical listing of test titles. The Index of Acronyms gives full titles for commonly used test abbreviations. Unlike you, not everyone who has heard of the MMPI, for example, knows that MMPI stands for Minnesota Multiphasic Personality Inventory. The Classified Subject Index lists tests alphabetically under each classification heading (e.g., Achievement). The Publishers Directory and Index gives the names and addresses of the publishers of all the tests included in the MMY, as well as a list of test numbers for each publisher. The Index of Names includes the names of test developers and test reviewers, as well as authors of related references. So, for example, if you heard that Professor Jeenyus had developed a new interest test, but you did not know its name, you would look under Jeenyus; there you would be given test numbers for all tests developed by Professor Jeenyus that were included in the volume. Finally, the Score Index directs you to information concerning the types of scores obtained from tests in the MMY.

If you are looking for information on a particular test, you can find it easily using of the alphabetical organization of the most recent MMYs. If you are not sure of the title of the test you are seeking or have no specific test in mind, but know generally what kind of test you need, you may use the following procedure:

1. If you are not sure of the title of the test you are looking for or can't find it in the alphabetical list of tests, look through the Index of Titles for possible variants of the title or consult the appropriate subject area in the Classified Subject Index for that particular test or related ones.
2. If you know the test publisher, look up that publisher in the Publishers Directory and Index and look for the test you seek.
3. If you are looking for a test that yields a particular type of score, search for that type in the Score Index to find tests that include that type of score.
4. Using the entry numbers listed in all of the sections described above, locate the test descriptions in the Tests and Reviews section (the main body of the volume).

Entries for new tests in the Tests and Reviews section typically include the following information: title; purpose; acronym; a brief description; a description of groups for whom the test is intended; norming information; validity and reliability data; whether the test is a group or individual test; scoring; administration information; forms, parts, and levels; availability of a manual; distribution restrictions; foreign language and other special editions; author (developer); publisher; cost; cross references to reviews, excerpts, and references to that test in other MMYs; and critical reviews by qualified reviewers. Among other things, the reviews generally cite any special requirements or problems involved in test administration, scoring, or interpretation. Also, while your library may not yet have it, there is a CD-ROM version of the MMY. An example of an MMY entry is shown in Table 5.4.

Tests in Print

A very useful supplemental source of test information is *Tests in Print* (TIP). *TIP* is a comprehensive bibliography of all known commercially available tests that

[183]

The Hundred Pictures Naming Test.

Purpose: "A confrontation naming test designed to evaluate rapid naming ability."

Population: Ages 4-6 to 11-11.

Publication Date: 1992.

Acronym: HPNT.

Scores, 3: Error, Accuracy, Time.

Administration: Individual.

Price Data, 1992: $195 per complete kit including manual (84 pages), test book, and 25 response forms; $10 per 25 response forms.

Time: (6) minutes.

Authors: John P. Fisher and Jennifer M. Glenister.

Publisher: Australian Council for Educational Research Ltd. [Australia]

Review of The Hundred Pictures Naming Test by JEFFREY A. ATLAS, Deputy Chief Psychologist and Assistant Clinical Professor, Bronx Children's Psychiatric Center, Albert Einstein College of Medicine, Bronx, NY:

The Hundred Pictures Naming Test (HPNT) is introduced in its test manual as "a confrontation naming test designed to evaluate rapid naming ability across age groups" (manual, p. 1). Given this stated purpose, the HPNT seems to qualify as a "test," and a valuable one, for "preparatory" (preschooler) boys and girls aged 5 to 6½, a grouping that constituted roughly 66% of the test reference group of 275 children. The remaining group cells have too few children to provide truly normative data, but may be suggestive in screening subjects who may have language disability or in evaluating recovery of function after brain injury.

The manual and test plates are attractively packaged and sturdy (except for the cardboard test container which will likely be discarded after several uses), but a bit overpriced at $195 for a test with restricted norms and limited generalizability. My sample package contained repeats of the manual pages 1–6 and test plate 18. These are minor distractors that I hope do not reflect overall quality control.

The reference group has nearly equal sex distribution, satisfactory city-suburban-country stratification (64%, 25%, and 11%), but scant socioeconomic information. The fact the test was developed in Australia seems not to have resulted in much content sampling bias. Preliminary inspection for test items that might prompt minor concern suggest "unicorn" and "rake" are words that may be absent from the linguistic environment of preschoolers living in cinder-block projects in New York City, and "koala" and "crown" reflect Australian versus other English-language nationality locales.

The mean "accuracy" score for the reference group was 74.34 (sd = 15.67), with a range of 23 to 98. These numbers comprise expectable figures for a 100-item examination and the linearity of increased test scores by age was impressive, permitting some normative evaluation, especially for preschoolers. Useful indicators for evaluating poor test performance, with some error categories indicating the need for speech therapy, some response categories indicating psychological intervention (e.g., for Selective Mutism), and overall poor lexicon indicating language remediation. The inclusion of 31 speech-language problem youngsters in the reference group provides suggestive screening norms but the low sample number and uneven linearity of scores limits the usefulness of the HPNT as a test for this group. Similarly, the division of the reference group into English First, English Main(ly), and English Only is helpful in qualitative assessment of performance but inadequate in providing test norms.

A useful aspect of the HPNT may be as a monitor of recovery of function after brain injury. Test-retest data (r = .98, after about 1 month for a bit over a fifth of the reference pool) and interrater reliability (r = .97 using a little over a tenth of the pool) furnish adequate criteria for retest using the HPNT. A sample protocol in the manual illustrates 6-year-old Warren's notable improvements in accuracy and significant error reduction, reflecting good recovery of function approximately 7 months following brain injury suffered in a car accident.

In summary, The Hundred Pictures Naming Test offers a useful test of English-only preschoolers' expressive speech accuracy, of recovery of speech function in some aphasias, and a screening device for psychological, environmental, and second-language interferences. As such it represents itself as a useful addition to the armamentarium of speech-language pathologists, early childhood educators, and in a more limited way, English-as-Second-Language instructors.

Source: Conoley, J. C., and Impara, J. C. (Eds.), *The Twelfth Mental Measurements Yearbook*, pp. 380–81, Lincoln, NE: Buros Institute of Mental Measurements.

are currently in print. It also serves as a master index of tests that directs the reader to all original reviews that have appeared in the MMYs to date. It is most often used to determine a test's availability. Once you know that a test is available, you can look it up in the MMY to find out if it is appropriate for your purposes. The structure of *TIP* is similar to that of the Classified Subject Index of the MMYs, but considerably more information is given for each entry.

The main body of the latest *TIP* edition is organized alphabetically, like the latest MMYs. *TIP* also provides an Index of Titles, a Classified Subject Index, a Publishers Directory and Index, and an Index of Names, all of which are utilized in the same way as they are used in the MMYs. Also, as with the MMYs, it is beneficial to familiarize yourself with the format and content of *TIP* before attempting to use it. If you are seeking a particular test, you can find it easily since entries are listed alphabetically. If not, the following procedure may be utilized:

1. If you are not sure of the title of the test you are looking for or can't find it in the alphabetical list of tests, look through the Index of Titles for possible variants of the title or consult the appropriate subject area in the Classified Subject Index for that particular test or related ones.
2. If you know the test publisher, look up that publisher in the Publishers Directory and Index and look for the test you seek.
3. If you are looking for a test that yields a particular type of score, search for that type of score in the Score Index to find tests that include that type of score.
4. Read the descriptive entry for the test you have found.
5. If you are referred to additional information in MMYs, as you often will be, go to the suggested MMYs.

Thus, *TIP* provides information on many more tests than the MMYs, but is less comprehensive in terms of information given for each test. Table 5.5 shows sample *TIP* entries.

Both *TIP* and the MMYs are virtually indispensable tools for educational researchers. The two publications are interrelated and have extensive cross-referencing so they can be used as a system. The latest *Tests in Print* will be published soon. (Look for it at a library near you!)

PRO-ED Publications

Another source of test information is published by PRO-ED. Information on more than 3,000 tests in a number of areas such as psychology, education, and business are cited. Although no reviews are included, complete information about test publishers is provided to enable users to call or write for additional information. In addition, tests appropriate for individuals with physical, visual, and hearing impairments are listed, as well as tests that are available in a variety of languages. Visit http://www.proedinc.com/index.html on the World Wide Web to order a PRO-ED catalog or to order their most popular tests.

PRO-ED's *Test Critiques Compendium* includes reviews of 60 major psychological and educational test instruments, while the multivolumed *Test Critiques* contains reviews for more than 800 tests widely used in psychology, education, and business. The reviews are quite extensive. *Test Critiques* contains both subject and title indexes, and each volume provides a cumulative index.

TABLE	5.5

Sample *Tests in Print* Entries

[1155]

High Level Figure Classification Test.
Purpose: Designed to assess intellectual ability.
Population: Grades 10–12.
Publication Date: 1983.
Acronym: HL FCT.
Scores: Total score only.
Administration: Group.
Price Data: Available from publisher.
Foreign Language Edition: Test printed in both English and Afrikaans.
Time: 30(40) minutes.
Authors: M. Werbeloff and T. R. Taylor.
Publisher: National Institute for Personnel Research of the Human Sciences Research Council [South Africa].

[1156]

High School Career-Course Planner.
Purpose: Designed "to develop a high school course plan that is consistent with self-assessed career goals."
Population: Grades 8 and 9.
Publication Dates: 1983–90.
Acronym: HSCCP.
Scores: Total score only.
Administration: Group.
Price Data, 1992: $.50 per HSCCP folder and User's Guide ('90, 4 pages); $2 per Job-O dictionary; $16.50 per Occupational Outlook Handbook; $89.95 per HSCCP computer program.
Time: (50) minutes; 5–8 minutes for computer version.
Comments: Computer version also available.
Author: CFKR Career Materials, Inc.
Publisher: CFKR Career Materials, Inc.

[1149]

Henmon-Nelson Ability Test, Canadian Edition.
Purpose: "Designed to measure those aspects of cognitive ability which are important for success in academic work and in similar endeavors outside the classroom."
Population: Grades 3–6, 6–9, 9–12.
Publication Dates: 1957–1990.
Scores: Total score only.
Administration: Group.
Price Data, 1994: $49.45 per 35 reusable or consumable test booklets (specify level); $37.45 per 100 answer sheets (hand/machine scorable); $10.45 per scoring mask (all levels); $10 per examiner's manual ('90, 44 pages); $8.95 per 10 class record sheets; $12.45 per examination kit.
Time: (30) minutes.
Comments: Adapted from the 1973 U.S. edition of the test (The Henmon-Nelson Tests of Mental Ability, 1150).
Authors: Tom A. Lamke, M. J. Nelson, and Joseph L. French.
Publisher: Nelson Canada [Canada].
Cross References: See T3:1073 (13 references); for a review by Eric F. Gardner, see 8:190 (14 references); see also T2:391 (52 references); for a review by Norman E. Wallen and an excerpted review by John O. Crites of an earlier edition, see 6:462 (11 references); for reviews by D. Welty Lefever and Leona E. Tyler and an excerpted review by Laurance F. Shaffer, see 5:342 (14 references); for a review by H. M. Fowler, see 4:299 (25 references); for reviews by Anne Anastasi, August Dvorak, Howard Easley, and J. P. Guilford and an excerpted review by Francis N. Maxfield, see 2:1398.

ETS Test Collection Database

The ETS (Educational Testing Service) Test Collection Database is an extremely useful online resource. A joint project of the Educational Testing Service and the ERIC Clearinghouse on Assessment and Evaluation, the ETS Test Collection is a searchable database. The ETS Collection Database contains records for more than 9,500 tests and research instruments in virtually all fields. Like the Mental Measurements Yearbooks, its stated purpose is to make test information available to educational researchers and other interested professionals. In contrast to the MMYs, it includes unpublished as well as published tests, but provides much less information per test.

To access ETS Test Collection Database, go to http://ericae.net/testcol.htm on the World Wide Web. There you will be able to search through the ETS Test File for names, descriptions, and availability information on more than 10,000 tests and research instruments. Just enter the name of the test you are seeking or ERIC terms describing what you are looking for. You can specify a number of features of your search, such as the number of results you want. The search engine will then inform you of whether there are any tests matching your description. For each test included in the database, the following information is given: title; author; publication date; target population; publisher or source; and an annotation describing the purpose of the instrument. An example of an ETS Test Collection Database entry is found in Table 5.6.

TABLE 5.6

Sample ETS Test Collection Database Entry

Descriptive Information

Title: Career Beliefs Inventory.
Author: Krumboltz-John-D.
Abstract: An instrument designed to assist counselors, psychologists, and personnel administrators in assessing the career beliefs of clients or staff members. Instrument is based on the premise that people may hold inaccurate assumptions about themselves and their careers and that these assumptions may be preventing them from obtaining their career goals. On a five-point, Likert type scale, respondents indicate how strongly they agree or disagree with 96 statements concerning their beliefs about themselves and the workplace. Instrument is divided into 25 scales covering five areas: My Current Career Situation; What Seems Necessary for My Happiness; Factors That Influence My Decisions; Changes I Am Willing to Make; and Effort I Am Willing to Initiate. Results may be used to point out to clients and staff the inaccuracies in their beliefs which may be hindering them from solving career problems. Instrument may be used with individuals from the eighth grade level through retirement age. Contains an administrative index to detect inaccuracy in responses. Includes percentile ranks for each of the 25 scales arranged by the occupational status of the respondents as well as other technical data.

Subtests: Employment Status; Career Plans; Acceptance of Uncertainty; Openness; Achievement; College Education; Intrinsic Satisfaction; Peer Equality; Structured Work Environment; Control; Responsibility; Approval of Others; Self-Other Comparisons; Occupation/College Variation; Career Path Flexibility; Post-Training Transition; Job Experimentation; Relocation; Improving Self; Persisting While Uncertain; Taking Risks; Learning Job Skills; Negotiating/Searching; Overcoming Obstacles; Working Hard.
Number of Test Items: 96
Age Range: AGE 13–17, Adults.
Publication Date: 1991
Most recent update to the database: Oct 1992
ETS Tracking Number: TC017880

Contact Information

For more detailed information about this measure and its related materials, please contact or consult:

Consulting Psychologists Press, Inc.; 3803 E. Bayshore Road, Palo Alto, CA 94303.

Descriptors: *Attitude-Measures; *Career-Counseling; *Career Planning; *College-Students; *Employee-Attitudes; *Goal-Orientation; *Secondary-School-Students; *Student-Attitudes; *Work-Attitudes; Adults; Beliefs; Career-Development; Careers. Employment-Counselors; Higher-Education; Likert-Scales. Rating Scales; Secondary-Education Identifiers: Career Expectations; CBI

The ETS Test Collection also provides more than 200 annotated bibliographies representing eight major categories: achievement (e.g., reading readiness, psychology); aptitude (e.g., nonverbal aptitude, memory); attitudes and interests (e.g., attitudes toward curriculum, teacher attitudes); personality (e.g., leadership, stress); sensory-motor (e.g., auditory skills, motor skills); special populations (e.g., brain-damaged, juvenile delinquents); vocational/occupational (e.g., nurses, teacher assessment); and miscellaneous (e.g., culture-fair tests, moral development). The illustrative examples for each category just given indicate the scope of the Test Collection bibliographies.

The ETS Test Collection publishes two sources of test-related information, one on an ongoing basis. Upon request, anyone may receive, at no charge, a pamphlet that gives the names, addresses, and telephone numbers of major U.S. publishers of standardized tests. *News on Tests* is produced ten times a year and includes announcements of new tests, citations of test reviews, new reference materials, and other related items. Because of its publication frequency, it provides more current information on tests than the MMYs. The ETS Collection also provides another service to test users: *Tests in Microfiche. Tests in Microfiche* has copies of tests not available commercially. Test microfiche purchasers are given permission to make copies for their own use. For further information and current prices, visit the ETS Test Collection Web page or write ETS Test Collection, Princeton, NJ 08541. Also, check your library for the availability of ETS Collection materials and services.

ERIC/AE Test Locator

Two additional search features are available online in the ERIC/AE Test Locator at http://ericae.net/testcol.htm. (This is the same Web address as that of the ETS Test Collection Database.) These are the *Test Review Locator* and the *Buros/ERIC Test Publisher Directory*.

The *Test Review Locator* allows you to search for citations about a particular testing instrument in MMY and PRO-ED directories. Simply enter the test name or a portion of the name in the search boxes, and the *Test Review Locator* will tell you where citations about the test can be found. Once you know which volumes of the MMY or PRO-ED directories contain entries pertaining to your test, you can to go to your library to access them.

The *Buros/ERIC Test Publisher Directory* permits you to search for the names and addresses of more than 900 major commercial test publishers. Enter a word or phrase in the search boxes and the search engine will provide you with information enabling you to contact test publishers yourself for useful information regarding their tests.

Professional Journals

A number of journals regularly publish information of interest to test users, many of which are American Psychological Association publications. For example, *Psychological Abstracts* is a potential source of test information. Using the monthly or annual index, you can quickly determine if *Psychological Abstracts* contains information on a given test. Other journals of interest to test users include: *Journal of Applied Measurement; Journal of Consulting Psychology; Journal of Educational Measurement; Journal of Educational Psychology; Journal of Personnel Psychology;* and *Educational and Psychological Measurement.*

Test Publishers and Distributors

After narrowing your search to a few acceptable tests, a good source of additional information on tests is publishers' test manuals. Manuals typically include detailed technical information, a description of the population for whom the test is intended to be appropriate, a detailed description of norming procedures, conditions of administration, detailed scoring instructions, and requirements for score interpretation.

If no information can be found, or if available information is inadequate, you can generally obtain additional data by writing to the test developer, if known. Final selection of a test usually requires examination of the actual test. A test that appears from all descriptions to be exactly what you need may have one or more problems detectable only by inspection of the test itself. For example, it may contain many items measuring content not covered, or its language level may be too high or low for your participants. An initial inspection copy of a test, as well as additional required copies if you select that test for your study, can be acquired from the test publisher if it is commercially available. For many tests, the publisher's name and address are given in the Mental Measurements Yearbooks. If not commercially available, tests may usually be obtained either in microfiche form from the ETS Test Collection or directly from the test developer.

Above all, remember that in selecting tests you must be a good consumer. As the Romans used to say, caveat emptor.

SELECTING FROM ALTERNATIVES

Eventually you must reach a decision. Once you have narrowed the number of test candidates and acquired relevant information, you must make a comparative analysis of the tests. Although there are a number of factors to be considered in choosing a test, these factors are not of equal importance. For example, the least expensive test is not necessarily the best test! This principle is graphically illustrated by an experience a researcher had some years ago. A small school system had made improving the reading skills of its elementary students its number one priority. At the beginning of the school year, a reading test was administered to all elementary students in the system and, based on the results, students were placed in classes according to their test scores. It was not very long before teachers realized that something was amiss. A number of students in the highest reading groups apparently had very poor reading skills, while a number of students in the remedial groups could read quite well. The researcher was asked to meet with school system personnel to discuss the situation. One of the first questions the researcher asked the school administrators was, "What test did you use to form the groups?" The researcher had never heard of the test named—let's call it the Bozo Test—which seemed unusual, given the researcher's constant exposure to available tests. As a result of a little homework, the Bozo Test was located in a *Mental Measurements Yearbook*. There was no information on validity or reliability, but there was a review, which, in essence, stated that it was the worst instrument ever created, and that a person might just as well randomly assign students to groups as use the results of the Bozo. In a subsequent meeting with school personnel, the researcher diplomatically asked how the test had been identified and on what basis it had been selected. A book containing test information on a number of tests was produced and, sure enough, the Bozo was listed. Under validity and reliability data, the clear indication was that there was none. Perplexed, school personnel were again asked on what basis the Bozo had been selected. And there, stated in the test administration requirements section was the answer—"time to administer, five minutes." The bottom line was that some very sincere, hard-working, bright professionals had wasted considerable time, energy, and money because of lack of knowledge concerning test selection criteria.

As you undoubtedly know by now, the most important factor to be considered in test selection is validity. Is one of the tests more appropriate for your sample? If you are interested in prediction, does one of the tests have a significantly higher validity coefficient? If content validity is of prime importance, are the items of one test more relevant to the topic of your study than other tests? These are typical questions to ask. If, after the validity comparisons, there are still several tests that seem appropriate, the next factor to consider is reliability.

You would presumably select the test with the highest reliability, but there are other considerations. For example, a factor to be considered in relation to reliability is the length of the test and the time it takes to administer it. In general, a test that can be administered during one class period would be considerably more convenient than a 2-hour test. Shorter tests generally are also preferable in terms of test takers' fatigue and motivation. However, since longer tests have higher reliability, a shorter test will tend to be less reliable. So, questions to be considered are: How much shorter? How much less reliable? If one test takes half as long to administer as another and is only slightly less reliable, the shorter test is probably better. For example, suppose Test A has a reliability coefficient of .94 and takes 90 minutes to administer, and Test B has a reliability coefficient of .90 and takes 50 minutes to administer. Which would you choose? Most probably, Test B. If after comparing validity and reliability data, you still have more than one test candidate, you should consider factors such as administration time, complexity of scoring, and interpretation requirements.

By the time you get to this point, you have probably made a decision. It probably will be a group-administered test rather than an individually administered one. Most of the time, individually administered tests will not be necessary except for certain intelligence and personality testing situations. However, when they are, keep in mind the potential disadvantages associated with their use: additional cost, additional time, the need for trained administrators, and complicated scoring and interpretation procedures. Of course, if the nature of your research study requires it, by all means use an individually administered test, but be certain you have the qualifications needed to administer, score, and interpret the test. If you do not, can you afford to acquire the necessary personnel? If, after all this soul-searching, by some miracle you still have more than one test in the running, by all means pick the cheapest one!

There are two additional considerations in test selection that have nothing to do with their psychometric qualities. Both are related to the use of tests in schools. If you are planning to use schoolchildren in your study, you should check to see what tests they have already taken. You would not want to administer a test with which test takers are already familiar. Second, you should be sensitive to the fact that some parents or administrators might object to a test that contains "touchy" items. Certain attitude, values, and personality tests, for example, contain questions related to the personal beliefs and behaviors of the respondents. If there is any possibility that the test contains potentially objectionable items, either choose another test or acquire appropriate permissions before administering the test. There have been instances where researchers have been ordered to destroy (even burn!) test results. In this case, an ounce of prevention is truly worth a pound of cure.

On rare occasions a researcher may not be able to locate a suitable test. The solution is not to use an inadequate test with the rationale, "Oh well, I'll do the best I can!" One logical solution is to develop your own test. Good test construction requires a variety of skills. As mentioned previously, training at least equivalent to a course in measurement is needed. If you do develop your own test, you must collect validation data; a self-developed test should not be utilized in a research study unless it has been pretested first with a group similar to the group to be used in the actual study. In addition to collecting validity and reliability data, you will need to try out the administration and scoring procedures. In some cases, the results of pretesting will indicate the need for revisions and further pretesting. This procedure may sometimes be followed for an existing test. You may find a test that seems very appropriate but for which certain relevant types of validation data are not available. In this case you may decide to try to validate this test with your population rather than develop a test "from scratch."

TEST ADMINISTRATION

You should be aware of several general guidelines for test administration. First, if testing is to be conducted in a school setting, arrangements should be made beforehand with the appropriate person, usually the principal. Consultation with the principal should result in agreement as to when the testing will take place, under what conditions, and with what assistance from school personnel. The principal can be very helpful in supplying such information as dates for which testing is inadvisable (e.g., assembly days and days immediately preceding or following holidays). Second, whether you are testing in the schools or elsewhere, you should do everything you can to ensure ideal testing conditions; a comfortable, quiet environment is more conducive to participant cooperation. Also, if testing is to take place in more than one session, the conditions of the sessions should be as identical as possible. Third, follow the Boy Scout motto and be prepared. Be thoroughly familiar with the administration procedures presented in the test manual and follow the directions precisely. If they are at all complicated, practice beforehand. Administer the test to some group or stand in front of a mirror and give it to yourself!

As with everything in life, good planning and preparation usually pay off. If you have made all necessary arrangements, secured all necessary cooperation, and are very familiar and comfortable with the administration procedures, the actual testing situation should go well. If some unforeseen catastrophe occurs during testing, such as an earthquake or a power failure, make careful note of the incident. If it is serious enough to invalidate the testing, you may have to try again another day with another group. If in your judgment the effects of the incident are not serious, at least relate its occurrence in your final research report. Despite the possibility of unforeseen tragedies, it is certain that the probability of all going well will be greatly increased if you adequately plan and prepare for the big day.

Summary/Chapter 5

Constructs

1. All types of research require the collection of data; the scientific and disciplined inquiry approach is based on the collection, analysis, and interpretation of data. Data are the pieces of evidence used to examine a research topic or test a hypothesis.
2. Constructs are mental abstractions such as personality, creativity, and intelligence that cannot be observed or measured directly. Constructs become variables when different levels or scores can be used to measure the constructs.
3. Measurement scales describe four different levels of measurement: nominal, ordinal, interval, and ratio. Nominal variables categorize, ordinal variables rank, interval variables have equal scale intervals, and ratio variables have a defined zero point.
4. Categorical variables are nonnumerical variables that categorize persons or objects (nominal), while quantitative variables exist on a low to high continuum (ordinal, interval, and ratio).
5. Independent and dependent variables are relevant to causal–comparative and experimental research. The independent variable is the treatment or cause, while the dependent variable is the outcome or effect of the independent variable.

Characteristics of Measuring Instruments

6. There are three main ways to collect data for research studies: administer an existing instrument, construct one's own instrument, and record naturally occurring events (observation) or collect already existing data.
7. The time and skill it takes to select an appropriate instrument are invariably less than the time and skill it takes to develop an instrument that measures the same thing.
8. There are thousands of standardized and nonstandardized instruments available that encompass a broad range of variables. A standardized test is one that is administered, scored, and interpreted in the same

way no matter when and where it is administered.
9. Selecting an instrument involves the identification and selection of the most appropriate one from among alternatives.
10. Most tests are paper-and-pencil ones, using either selection approaches (multiple-choice, true-false, matching) or supply approaches (short answer, essay).
11. Raw scores indicate the number of items a person got correct. They can be transformed into derived scores such as percentile ranks, stanines, and standard scores. Derived scores are most often used with standardized tests.
12. Norm-referenced scoring compares a student's test performance to the performance of other test takers; criterion-referenced scoring compares a student's test performance to predetermined standards of performance; self-referenced scoring compares a student's performance over time.

COGNITIVE TESTS

Achievement Tests

13. Achievement tests measure the current status of individuals on school-taught subjects.
14. Standardized achievement tests are available for individual curriculum areas such as reading and mathematics, and also in the form of test batteries that measure achievement in many curriculum areas. Most standardized achievement tests are scored using norm-referencing.

Aptitude Tests

15. Aptitude tests are used to predict how well a test taker is likely to perform in the future. They normally do not measure school-taught topics.
16. Tests of general aptitude are referred to as scholastic aptitude tests and tests of general mental ability. They are standardized and used extensively in job hiring.
17. General aptitude tests typically ask the test taker to perform a variety of verbal and nonverbal tasks. Aptitude tests are also available

for a number of specific areas such as music, mechanical ability, and reading.

18. Readiness tests are administered prior to instruction in a specific area to determine whether and to what degree a student is ready for a given level of instruction. Reading readiness is the most common readiness test.

AFFECTIVE TESTS

19. Affective tests measure characteristics such as interest, values, attitude, and personality.
20. Most affective tests are nonprojective; that is, they are self-report measures in which the individual responds to a series of questions about him or herself.
21. Attitude scales indicate the things an individual feels favorable or unfavorable about.
22. There are five basic types of scales used to measure attitudes: Likert scales, semantic differential scales, rating scales, Thurstone scales, and Guttman scales. The first three are the most used.
23. Attitude scales ask respondents to state their feeling about various objects, persons, and activities. Likert scales are responded to by indicating strongly agree, agree, undecided, disagree, and strongly disagree; semantic differential scales present a continuum of attitudes on which the respondent selects a position to indicate the strength of attitude; and rating scales present statements that respondents must rate on a continuum from high to low. These are all self-report measures.
24. Interest inventories ask individuals to indicate personal likes and dislikes about activities they engage in. Responses are generally compared to existing interest patterns.
25. The most widely used interest measure is used for vocational interests.
26. Values are deeply held beliefs about ideas, persons, and objects.
27. Personality, also called temperament, describes characteristics that represent a person's typical behavior. Personality inventories present respondents with lists of statements describing human behaviors, and they must indicate whether each statement pertains to them.

28. Personality inventories may be specific to a single trait (introversion–extroversion) or may be general and measure a number of traits.
29. Personality measures require substantial knowledge of measurement and psychology, and should be used only by experienced researchers.
30. Use of self-report measures create the concern about whether an individual is expressing his or her true attitude, values, interests, or personality. Further, self-report, forced-choice items can lead to response sets, such as social desirability, which distort the data collected.
31. Test bias in both cognitive and affective measures also can distort the data obtained. Bias is present when one's ethnicity, race, gender, language, or religious orientation influences test performance.

PROJECTIVE TESTS

32. Projective tests are not self-report instruments. They present an ambiguous situation to the test taker that requires him or her to "project" his or her true feelings on the ambiguous situation.
33. Association is the most commonly used projective technique, and is exemplified by the inkblot and word association tests. Only the specially trained can administer and interpret projective tests.

Validity of Measuring Instruments

34. Validity is the most important quality of a test. It is the degree to which a test measures what it is supposed to measure and, consequently, permits appropriate interpretations of test scores.
35. A test is not valid per se; it is valid for a particular interpretation and for a particular group. Each intended score interpretation requires its own validation.
36. Validation is a matter of degree; tests are not valid or invalid, they are highly valid, moderately valid, or generally invalid.
37. The three main forms of validity are content, criterion-related, and construct. They are

viewed as interrelated, not independent aspects of validity.

Validity

✗① CONTENT VALIDITY

38. Content validity is the degree to which a test measures an intended content area. It requires both item validity and sampling validity. Item validity is concerned with whether the test items are relevant to the intended content area, and sampling validity is concerned with how well the test sample represents the total content area.
39. Content validity is of prime importance for achievement tests.
40. Content validity is determined by expert judgment of item and sample validity, not statistical means.

✗② CRITERION-RELATED VALIDITY

Concurrent

Predictive

41. Criterion-related validity has two forms, concurrent validity and predictive validity. Concurrent validity is the degree to which the scores on a test are related to scores on another test administered at the same time. Predictive validity is the degree to which scores on a test are related to scores on another test administered in the future. In both cases, a single group must take both tests.
42. Concurrent and predictive validity are determined by correlating one test with another, either at the same time or in the future, or by determining whether scores on a test differentiate between persons who possess a particular characteristic.

✗③ CONSTRUCT VALIDITY

43. Construct validity is the most important form of validity. Constructs underlie research variables and construct validity seeks to determine whether the construct underlying a variable is actually being measured.
44. Construct validity is determined by a series of validation studies that can include content and criterion-related approaches. Both confirmatory and disconfirmatory evidence are used in construct validation.
45. The validity of any test or measure can be diminished by factors such as unclear test

directions, inappropriate vocabulary, subjective scoring, and failing to follow administration procedures. These factors distort the meaning of test scores and therefore test validity.

Reliability of Measuring Instruments

study more

46. Reliability is the degree to which a test consistently measures whatever it measures. Reliability is expressed numerically, usually as a coefficient ranging from 0.0 to 1.0; a high coefficient indicates high reliability.
47. Reliability provides information about measurement error, that is, the inevitable fluctuations in scores due to person and test factors. No test is perfectly reliable, but the smaller the measurement error, the more reliable the test.
48. There are five different general approaches to reliability: stability, equivalence, equivalence and stability, internal consistency, and scorer/rater.
49. Stability, also called test–retest, determines the degree to which scores of one group of test takers on a test are consistent over time. It is determined by correlating scores of the group obtained at different times. *Stability*
50. Equivalence, also called equivalent forms, determines the degree to which two forms of a test produce similar scores from a single group of test takers. It is determined by correlating scores on the two equivalent forms. *Equivalence*
51. Equivalence and stability determine the degree to which two forms of a test given at two different times produce similar scores. Correlation is the method used to determine reliability.
52. Internal consistency deals with the reliability of a single test taken at one time. It measures the extent to which the items in the test are consistent among themselves and with the test as a whole. Split-half, Kuder–Richardson 20 and 21, and Cronbach's alpha are three main forms of internal consistency reliability. *Internal Consistency* 1. split 1/2 2. KR 3. Cronbach
53. Split-half reliability is determined by dividing a test into two equivalent halves (odd–even), correlating the two halves, and using the Spearman–Brown formula to determine the reliability of the whole test.

54. Kuder–Richardson reliability deals with the internal consistency of tests that are scored dichotomously (right, wrong), while Cronbach's alpha deals with the internal consistency of tests that are scored with more than two choices (agree, neutral, disagree or 0, 1, 2, 3).

55. Scorer/rater reliability is important when scoring tests that are potentially subjective. Interjudge reliability refers to the reliability of two or more independent scores; intrajudge reliability refers to the reliability of a single scorer/rater on two or more scorings.

56. Estimates of interjudge or intrajudge reliability are obtained by correlational means or by simply indicating percent agreement.

RELIABILITY COEFFICIENTS

57. What constitutes an acceptable level of reliability will differ among test types, with standardized achievement tests having very high reliabilities and projective tests having considerably lower reliabilities.

58. If a test is composed of several subtests that will be used individually in a study, the reliability of each subtest should be determined and reported.

STANDARD ERROR OF MEASUREMENT

59. The standard error of measurement is an estimate of how often one can expect test score errors of a given size. A small standard error of measurement indicates high reliability; a large standard error of measurement, low reliability.

60. The standard error of measurement allows us to estimate how much difference there probably is between a person's obtained and "true" score. The size of the difference is a function of the reliability of the test. Big differences indicate low reliability.

Selection of a Test

61. Do not choose the first test you find that appears to meet your needs. Do identify a few appropriate tests and compare them on relevant factors. The three most important factors, in order of importance, are validity, reliability, and ease of test use (administration, scoring, and interpretation).

62. Self-developed tests should be pretested before use to determine validity, reliability, and feasibility.

SOURCES OF TEST INFORMATION

63. The Mental Measurement Yearbooks (MMYs) are the most comprehensive sources of test information available for educational researchers. They provide (1) factual information on all known or revised tests, (2) test reviews, and (3) comprehensive bibliographies and indexes. The numbers given in the indexes are test numbers, not page numbers.

64. *Tests in Print* (*TIP*) is a comprehensive bibliography of all tests that have appeared in preceding MMYs. It also serves as a master index of tests, which directs the user to all original reviews that have appeared in the MMYs.

65. PRO-ED publications provide information on more than 3,000 tests in education, psychology, and business. The *Test Critiques Compendium* includes reviews of 60 major psychological and educational test instruments.

66. The ETS Test Collection is an extensive, growing library containing more than 10,000 tests intended to make test information available to researchers. It also includes unpublished tests.

67. Other sources of test information are professional journals and test publishers or distributors.

Test Administration

68. Every effort should be made to ensure ideal test administration conditions. Follow administration procedures precisely; altering the administration procedures, especially on standardized tests, lowers the validity of the test.

◻ **Task 5** *Performance Criteria*

All the information required for each test will be found in the Mental Measurements Yearbooks. Following the description of the three tests, you should present a comparative analysis of the tests that forms a rationale for your selection of the "most acceptable" test for your study. As an example, you might indicate that all three tests have similar reliability coefficients reported but that one of the tests is more appropriate for your participants.

On the following pages, an example is presented to illustrate the performance called for by Task 5. (See Task 5 example.) This example represents the task submitted by the same student whose tasks for Parts Two to Four were previously presented.

Additional examples for this and subsequent tasks are included in the *Student Guide* that accompanies this text.

1

Effect of Interactive Multimedia on the Achievement
of 10th-Grade Biology Students

Test One (from an MMY, test #160)

a)   High-School Subject Tests, Biology - 1980-1990
      American Testronics

      $33.85 per 35 tests with administration directions;
$13.25 per 35 machine-scorable answer sheets; $19.45 per
Teacher's Manual ('90, 110 pages).

b)   The Biology test of the High-School Subject Tests is
a group-administered achievement test that yields 10 scores
(Cell Structure and Function, Cellular Chemistry,
Viruses/Monerans/Protists/Fungi, Plants, Animals, Human Body
Systems and Physiology, Genetics, Ecology, Biological Analy-
sis and Experimentation).

c)   Reviewers state that reliability values (KR-20s) for
the various subject tests ranged from .85 to .93, with a
median of .88. Content validity should be examined using the
classification tables and objective lists provided in the
teacher's manual so that stated test objectives and research
objectives can be matched.

d)   Grades 9-12.

e)   Administration time is approximately 40 minutes.

f)   Scoring services are available from the publisher.

g)   Reviewers recommend the test as a useful tool in the
evaluation of instructional programs, recognizing that the
test fairly represents the content for biology in the high
school curriculum. However, they do caution that a match
should be established between stated test objectives and
local objectives.

2

Test Two (from an MMY, test #256)

a)   National Proficiency Survey Series: Biology (NPSS:B) –
1989

     The Riverside Publishing Company

     $34.98 per 35 test booklets including directions for
administration; $19.98 per 35 answer sheets; $9 per technical manual (26 pages) (1990 prices)

b)   The NPSS:B is a group-administered achievement test
with 45 items designed to measure "knowledge about the living world ranging from single-celled organisms to the human
body."

c)   Content validity is good; items were selected from a
large item bank provided by classroom teachers and curriculum experts. The manual alerts users that validity depends
in large measure upon the purpose of the test. Although the
standard error of measurement is not given for the biology
test, the range of KR-20s for the entire battery is from
.82 to .91 with a median of .86.

d)   Grades 9-12.

e)   Administration time is approximately 45 minutes.

f)   Tests can be machine scored or self scored. A program
is available on diskette so that machine scoring may be
done on site. Both percentile rank and NCE scores are used.
NCEs allow users to make group comparisons.

g)   The reviewer finds the reliability scores to be low if
the test is to be used to make decisions concerning individual students. However, he praises the publishers for
their comments regarding content validity, which state that
"information should always be interpreted in relation to the
user's own purpose for testing."

3

Test Three (from an MMY, test #135)

a)   End of Course Tests (ECT) - 1986

   CTB/McGraw-Hill

   $21 per complete kit including 35 test booklets (Biology 13 pages) and examiner's manual.

b)   The ECT covers a wide range of subjects in secondary school. Unfortunately, detailed information is not available for individual subjects. The number of questions range from 42 to 50 and are designed to measure subject matter content most commonly taught in a first-year course.

c)   No statistical validity evidence is provided for the ECT and no demographic breakdown is provided to understand the representativeness of the standardization samples. However, reliability estimates were given and ranged from .80 to .89 using the KR-20 formula.

d)   Secondary school students.

e)   Administration time is from 45 to 50 minutes for any one subject test.

f)   Both machine scoring and hand scoring are available. A Class Record Sheet is provided in the manual to help those who hand score to summarize the test results.

g)   Users must be willing to establish local norms and validation evidence for effectual use of the ECT, since no statistical validity evidence is provided.

Conclusion

All three batteries have a biology subtest; The High-School Subject Tests (HSST) and the NPSS:B are designed specifically for 10th-grade students, while the ECT is course, rather than grade, oriented. It is acknowledged that more data are needed for all three tests, but reported validity and reliability data suggest that they all would be at least

4

adequate for the purpose of this study (i.e., to assess the effectiveness of the use of interactive multimedia in biology instruction).

Since of the three tests the least validity evidence is provided for the ECT, it was eliminated from contention first. Both the HSST and the NPSS:B provide tables and objective lists in their manuals that may be used to establish a match between stated test objectives and research objectives. The HSST and the NPSS:B both have good content validity but the HSST does not cross-index items to objectives, as does the NPSS:B. Also, norming information indicates that Catholic school students were included in the battery norm group. Therefore, of the three tests, the NPSS:B seems to be the most valid for the study.

With respect to reliability, all three tests provide a comparable range of KR-20 values for battery subtests. While specific figures are not given for the biology subtests, the reported ranges (low eighties to low nineties) suggest that they all have adequate internal consistency reliability.

The NPSS:B appears to be the most appropriate instrument for the study. The items (which were provided by both classroom teachers and curriculum experts) appear to match the objectives of the research study quite well. The KR-20 reliability is good, both in absolute terms and as compared to that of the other available tests. Both machine- and self-scoring are options, but an added advantage is that machine scoring can be done on site using a program provided by the publisher.

Thus, the NPSS:B will be used in the current study. As a cross-check, internal consistency reliability will be computed based on the scores of the subjects in the study.

Types of Research

The prior sections provided an overview of the basic steps in conducting research and introduced tools of research that cut across varied research approaches. In this part, we examine in detail the procedures used to carry out a number of specific research methods. The discussion is divided into two sections, the first focused on general methods of collecting and analyzing data in qualitative research studies and the second focused on four quantitative research methods: descriptive, correlational, causal–comparative, and experimental.

The goal of Part Six is for you to be able to describe the data collection and analysis procedures involved in the various types of research discussed. After you have read Part Six, you should be able to perform the following task.

TASK 6

Having stated a problem, formulate one or more hypotheses (if appropriate), describe a sample, select one or more ways to collect data, and develop the methods section of your research report. This should include a description of participants, data collection methods, and research design. (See Performance Criteria, p. 425.)

"Meder hypothesizes quite simply that Dracula was (is?!) a woman—'a beautiful, seductive, evil noblewoman of highest society . . .' (p. 231)."

Qualitative Research: Data Collection

 **OBJECTIVES**

After reading chapter 6, you should be able to:

1. State the purposes of qualitative research.
2. Identify strategies for finding and selecting research participants.
3. Describe observation approaches for qualitative data collection.
4. Describe practices in obtaining and recording field notes.
5. Describe interview approaches for qualitative data collection.
6. State strategies to enhance the validity of data collected.
7. Describe the main steps in conducting historical research.

CHARACTERISTICS OF QUALITATIVE RESEARCH

Chapter 1 described a number of qualitative research characteristics and how qualitative research compares to quantitative research (Table 1.1). It provided a general introduction to qualitative research and some examples of qualitative studies. In considering qualitative research, it is useful to know some things about its underpinnings.[1] For example, qualitative research approaches are rooted in the disciplines of sociology, anthropology, and history. These disciplines rely heavily on deep verbal descriptions and interpretations in their research, not statistics. Similarly, these disciplines strive to capture the human meanings of social life as it is lived, experienced, and understood by the participants. Capturing this context is very important because it is assumed that each context examined is idiosyncratic. Because qualitative researchers rely heavily on verbal description, the main instrument of data collection, interpretation, and written explanation is the researcher him or herself. Note, however, that both qualitative and quantitative research emphasize disciplined inquiry.

Table 6.1 provides a brief description of some of the most commonly used qualitative approaches. Examination of Table 6.1 shows that the main difference among the approaches is in the particulars of the social context studied and the participants studied. For example, qualitative researchers focus on the characteristics of a single person or phenomenon (case study); a group's cultural patterns and perspectives (ethnography); the link between a group's everyday activities and its social structure (ethnomethodology); the link between participants' perspectives and social science theory (grounded theory); the meanings and perspectives gained by interactions (symbolic interaction); and how phenomena are experienced by participants (phenomenology). Taken together, a common generic name for these qualitative approaches is *interpretive research*.

---

[1]A useful and interesting description of the genesis of qualitative research can be found in Erickson, F. (1990). *Qualitative methods. Research in teaching and learning, volume 2.* New York: Macmillan. and Bogdan, R. C. and Biklen, S. K. (1998). *Qualitative research for education.* Chapter 1. Boston: Allyn and Bacon.

TABLE	6.1

Common Qualitative Research Approaches

APPROACH	KEY QUESTION
case study	What are the characteristics of this particular entity, phenomenon, or person?
ethnography	What are the cultural patterns and perspectives of this group in its natural setting?
ethology	How do the origins, characteristics, and culture of different societies compare to one another?
ethnomethodology	How do people make sense of their everyday activities in order to behave in socially accepted ways?
grounded theory	How is an inductively derived theory about a phenomenon grounded in the data in a particular setting?
phenomenology	What is the experience of an activity or concept from these particular participants' perspective?
symbolic interaction	How do people construct meanings and shared perspectives by interacting with others?

Source: Reprinted from Michael Quinn Patton, *Qualitative Evaluation and Research Methods,* Sage Publications, 1990. Copyright 1990 by Sage Publications. Reprinted by permission of Sage Publications, Inc.

For the most part, the methods used to conduct qualitative research in these areas are similar. They all involve (1) intensive participation in a field setting, (2) collecting detailed data from field activities, and (3) the researcher synthesizing and interpreting the meaning of the field data. Because of these commonalities across approaches, we will focus on general methods used to gather and analyze qualitative data rather than on the nuances of any particular qualitative research approach. The general methods presented will be appropriate for you to conduct your initial qualitative research studies.

QUALITATIVE RESEARCH QUESTIONS

Qualitative, interpretive research is useful for describing or answering questions about particular, localized occurrences or contexts and the perspectives of a participant group toward events, beliefs, or practices. It also is useful for exploring a complex research area about which little is known. Qualitative research is exceptionally suited for exploration, for beginning to understand a group or phenomenon. Such explorations often result in initial development of new theories.

Qualitative research questions encompass a broad range of topics, but most focus on participants' understanding of meanings and social life in a particular context. Table 6.1 illustrates the nature of qualitative research questions. However, these general questions would have to be focused and narrowed to become useful and researchable research questions. For example, the question, "What are the cultural patterns and perspectives of this group in its natural setting?" could be narrowed by asking, "What are the cultural patterns and perspectives of teachers during lunch in the teachers' room?" Or, "How do people make sense of their everyday activities in order to behave in socially acceptable ways?" might be focused by asking, "How do rival gang members engage in socially accepted ways when interacting with each other during the school day?" Clearly there are many ways to restate the questions in Table 6.1 to make them viable research questions.

Erickson[2] suggests why it is important to explore qualitative questions.

1. Qualitative questions have the potential to illuminate the "invisibility of everyday life," that is, to make the familiar strange and therefore more examined and understood.
2. Often, a general or generic answer to a research question is not useful; what is needed is specific, concrete details to guide understanding in a particular setting.
3. It is important to know the local meanings that activities and practices have for the groups engaged in them. Different settings or contexts may seem to carry out the same activities and practices, but may actually be quite different. How direct teaching or whole language is practiced in different classrooms might differ quite markedly, although teachers in those classrooms would indicate that they were using direct teaching or whole language.
4. Groups of qualitative research studies can help the comparative understanding of different settings. That is, a study focused on a particular fifth-grade classroom can be compared to another particular fifth-grade classroom in terms of common and uncommon aspects. However, qualitative research is not well suited to answer questions about research effects.

Qualitative research proposals (dissertation or otherwise) are usually more tentative than quantitative ones, mainly because it is expected that a qualitative study will evolve in focus once the researcher is in the research setting. This means that a qualitative proposal cannot provide the specificity and length of most quantitative proposals. However, the qualitative researcher cannot enter the selected research setting with no idea of what the study topic or research method is. The researcher must have thought about the topic and method prior to writing the proposal. A good proposal should answer the following questions, not necessarily in depth, but with some focus, rationale, and thought:

- What are you going to study?
- In what setting or context will you conduct the study?
- What kinds of data do you think you will collect?
- What methods do you plan to use?
- Why are you doing the study?
- What contribution might the study provide?

In general, the steps in the qualitative research process are: Select a topic or issue to study, obtain entry to the desired site and select participants, collect data, interpret the qualitative data, and describe the research conclusions. You must obtain permission from the Human Subjects Review Board at your institution before conducting your study.

---

[2]Erickson, F. (1990). *Qualitative methods. Research in teaching and learning, volume 2*. New York: Macmillan (pp. 83–85).

The view that qualitative researchers know nothing about the study prior to immersion in the setting is wrong and impossible. At the very least, the researcher must communicate information about the planned study to a doctoral advisor and/or to potential participants. As Yin[3] noted:

> When Christopher Columbus went to Queen Isabella to ask for support for his "exploration" of the New World, he had to have some reasons for asking for three ships (why not one? why not five?), and he had some rationale for going westward (why not north? why not south?). He also had some criteria for recognizing the New World when he actually encountered it. In short, his exploration began with some rationale and direction, even if his initial assumptions might later have been proved wrong.

A briefer way to say this is that your head is not empty when you approach qualitative research; it contains a number of thoughts, but you have not settled on a specific one you will follow. Qualitative proposals are not fixed contracts that cannot be altered, but neither are they so brief and general that they convey little about the proposed study.

QUALITATIVE RESEARCH STRUCTURE

The central focus of qualitative research studies is to provide understanding of a social setting or activity from the perspective of the research participants. To achieve this goal, qualitative research is guided by five general characteristics that cut across most types of qualitative studies. First, the *sources of data for qualitative research are real-world situations*, the study of natural, nonmanipulated settings. Researchers spend a great deal of time in the selected setting. Second, *qualitative research data are descriptive*. Data in the form of interview notes, observation records, documents, and field notes are the basis for analysis and interpretation. Numerical data are very rarely the main focus of a qualitative study. Third, *qualitative research emphasizes a holistic approach*, focusing on processes as well as final outcomes. The researcher is immersed in the details and specifics of the setting. It is the detailed recording of the processes occurring in the natural setting that provides the basis for understanding the setting, participants, and their interactions in their real-world setting. Without process data, the search for interpretation and understanding would elude the qualitative researcher. Fourth, *qualitative data are analyzed inductively*; that is, a generalization is reached from collecting or observing multiple specific instances. Thus, the qualitative researcher does not impose an organizing structure or make assumptions about the relationships among the data prior to collecting evidence. The specifics of the data are analyzed by the researcher, who seeks specific pieces of data that can be generalized. The more data collected, the more likely that inductive generalizations will be valid. Fifth, the researcher often seeks to *describe the meaning of the finding from the perspective of the research participants*, not the researcher him or herself.

Throughout, the focus is on the meanings participants hold in their natural setting. This focus is important because each setting and its participants are viewed as being unique, making the researcher's task to describe the reality of

---

[3]Yin, R. K. (1984). *Case study research: Design and methods.* Beverly Hills, CA: Sage.

the participants in their own, unique context. Table 6.2 shows the main aspects of qualitative inquiry.

GAINING ENTRANCE

Before a qualitative study can begin, the researcher must negotiate entry into the research setting and obtain the cooperation of potential participants. Because data collection in qualitative research is generally lengthy and in-depth, it

TABLE	**6.2**

Major Characteristics of Qualitative Research

1. Naturalistic inquiry	Studying real-world situations as they unfold naturally; nonmanipulative, unobtrusive, and noncontrolling; openness to whatever emerges—lack of predetermined constraints on outcomes
2. Inductive analysis	Immersion in the details and specifics of the data to discover important categories, dimensions, and interrelationships; begin by exploring genuinely open questions rather than testing theoretically derived (deductive) hypotheses
3. Holistic perspective	The *whole* phenomenon under study is understood as a complex system that is more than the sum of its parts; focus is on complex interdependencies not meaningfully reduced to a few discrete variables and linear, cause-effect relationships
4. Qualitative data	Detailed, thick description; inquiry in depth; direct quotations capturing people's personal perspectives and experiences
5. Personal contact and insight	The researcher has direct contact with and gets close to the people, situation, and phenomenon under study; researcher's personal experiences and insights are an important part of the inquiry and critical to understanding the phenomenon
6. Dynamic systems	Attention to process; assumes change is constant and ongoing whether the focus is on an individual or an entire culture
7. Unique case orientation	Assumes each case is special and unique; the first level of inquiry is being true to, respecting, and capturing the details of the individual cases being studied; cross-case analysis follows from and depends on the quality of individual case studies
8. Context sensitivity	Places findings in a social, historical, and temporal context; dubious of the possibility or meaningfulness of generalizations across time and space
9. Empathic neutrality	Complete objectivity is impossible; pure subjectivity undermines credibility; the researcher's passion is understanding the world in all its complexity—not proving something, not advocating, not advancing personal agendas, but understanding; the researcher includes personal experience and empathic insight as part of the relevant data, while taking a neutral nonjudgmental stance toward whatever content may emerge
10. Design flexibility	Open to adapting inquiry as understanding deepens and/or situations change; avoids getting locked into rigid designs that eliminate responsiveness; pursues new paths of discovery as they emerge

Source: Reprinted from Michael Quinn Patton (1990). *Qualitative evaluation and research methods* (2d ed.). Newbury Park, CA: Sage, pp. 40–41. Copyright 1990 Sage Publications. Reprinted by permission of Sage Publications, Inc.

involves a more-than-casual relationship between the researcher and participants. Thus, how the researcher enters the setting and makes contact with participants is extremely important. How the researcher gains access to a setting and makes contact with participants can influence the relationship between researcher and participants from the very beginning. For example, a researcher's poor initial impression can hamper the research study from start to finish, making participants hesitant to fully cooperate. Grandma was right: first impressions really *are* important and do influence the way others perceive you.

The first obstacle in the "gaining entrance" process is getting permission to carry out your research in the desired field setting. You have decided, at least in general, what your study will be about. If your research is to be conducted in a classroom, a clinic, or a hospital, you will likely have to deal with a *gatekeeper* who will either directly decide or strongly influence the decision to allow you to conduct your study in that setting. For example, in most schools, the principal is the most important gatekeeper in determining admission into the school for research. In large school districts there may be a central body that decides on the acceptability of proposed research study requests, although the school principal will still likely have substantial input in the decision to permit use of his or her school. Note that principals usually will not approve your request unless they know that the teachers or other participants agree. Note also that if you plan to gather data from students, you will probably need parental agreement. Most schools, hospitals, clinics, and other institutions have specific procedures that must be followed to gain entrance. You should identify the gatekeepers, find out about the procedures for requesting access to a desired site, and follow those procedures. You should also ask about how long the decision process typically takes.

The process of obtaining entrance to a field site can be tedious and lengthy. To avoid tedium and save time, you may be tempted to short circuit the process by studying participants you can access easily, such as people you supervise (teachers in your own school), students in your class, or acquaintances and friends whom you know will cooperate. This tempting alternative to institutional approval is not advised. People you supervise or students you teach will likely not feel free to express their true thoughts for fear of future repercussions. Acquaintances may be uncomfortable answering certain questions, and friends may assume they understand each other and thus not probe or question given responses.

Gaining permission to a site may require negotiation between yourself and the gatekeeper. For example, timing, access, use of results, and the like are common issues that may have to be negotiated. You should be prepared to answer questions from both the gatekeeper and, subsequently, the research participants. For example, they may wish to know:

■ *What are you trying to do in your study?* This question is logical and your response is important; participants want to know what you're planning to do and find out. Notice, to answer this question, you must have some idea about the purpose of your study. Few people will give access or agree to be participants if all you can tell them about your study is, "It's about teachers (or students, or aides, or parent involvement), but I don't know more than that at this time." You don't have to know the specifics of your topic and methods, but you will need to provide some focus in

your response. In describing your topic, avoid educational jargon. Anticipate their questions and prepare a two- or three-sentence description of
your aims. If pushed by participants for more details, it is appropriate to
respond that an important part of your study is to identify what's important and should be examined.

■ *How much will your presence disrupt my classroom and students?* Participants
have rhythms and routines to their activities and want to minimize their
disruption. It is important to be honest in answering this question. For example, don't water down what you expect teachers to do, because they
will be resentful and uncooperative when they find out (during the
study) that you were not truthful. However, you may also capitalize on
the fact that much of qualitative research involves data gathering that is
not disruptive.

■ *What will you do with the findings?* Gatekeepers and participants may have
concerns about how results of the study are reported, and to whom. For
example, they may worry about bad publicity or political use of the findings against the research site or its participants. Respond honestly. In
most cases you will be able to indicate that no participant's name or title
will be published and the site and location will be disguised for publication. Two things that you might face are the gatekeeper demanding a
copy of the results as a condition of providing the site and participants'
demanding access to the data during and at the end of the study. Agree-
ing to the former may affect the responses of participants; if I know the
principal will see the results, I may not give honest answers to questions
or may change my teaching practices. Allowing teachers access to data at
the end of the study can provide insights and corroboration of your interpretations, but may also make teachers self-conscious, leading to revisions
of interpretations and descriptions. Don't show data to participants during the study unless you have a compelling reason to do so.

■ *Why did you select our setting?* In answering this question try to say something positive about the setting as your basis for its selection. For example, I heard the teachers in this school are exceptional; there are many
new teachers in this school and I wanted to work in such a setting; you
have a unique science program that I wish to understand. It is important
that you indicate that your focus is on teachers or programs as a group,
not as individuals.

■ *What do we get out of this?* This is a valid and reasonable question. This is
a qualitative research study, so you will be spending a lot of time and
asking a lot of your participants. It is reasonable that they expect something in return. Think carefully about what you are willing to provide in
return for participation. Would you be willing to provide information
about your results, to meet with teachers and parents to summarize and
answer questions about the results, provide a written summary of the results? Would you teach teachers a course in teacher research? You should
give thought to this question.

There are many aspects to gaining entrance, and negotiation and compromise
usually are important aspects of the process. It might be useful for you to write
out brief answers to the prior questions, just to make you think about how you
will answer them when asked.

CONTACTING POTENTIAL RESEARCH PARTICIPANTS

Having obtained entry into the setting, you will want to contact the potential research participants. You should do this task yourself, because the initial communication with potential participants is the start of your relationship with them throughout the study. Make contact with potential participants by phone and set up a time when you can meet with them to discuss the study. It will usually be more convenient for the potential participants if you visit them in the setting, which is to your advantage because it gives you an initial look at the participant's setting. There are a number of benefits to the initial, face-to-face meeting. As noted, it gives you a view of the setting. It also shows the potential participant that you are willing to make a separate contact with him or her to discuss the study, showing your interest in him or her as a participant and starting the research relationship off in a good way. It allows you to explain your expectations for his or her participation and to find out if the potential participant is interested. A face-to-face discussion also lets you size-up the potential participant in terms of whether he or she is in a position to provide the data you seek. Finally, if the potential participant is interested and can provide appropriate data, mutually agreed upon times and places for interviewing, observing, and meeting can be arranged.

You probably will be asked, "Will your study disrupt my classroom and students?" "Will I be identified?" "Who will have access to the results?" and "What do you expect me to do for you?" Be prepared for such questions and answer them honestly. It is wise to assure teachers that they will not be identified by name and that their supervisors will not have access to their individual data. Ethically, you should protect the interests of potentially vulnerable participants. Be clear about issues of confidentiality or anonymity. Although it is true that the focus of a qualitative study grows and evolves as the study progresses, it is necessary that the researcher have a reasonably clear conception of the key research questions and the methods of data collection. If not, gaining access and participants' cooperation will be difficult. Gaining access and identifying the appropriate participants are critical aspects of qualitative research, but if a gatekeeper or the participants are not comfortable with you or if they are mistrustful of promises of confidentiality or anonymity, they may not provide or may even distort the information you seek, in order to protect themselves.

In sum, gaining entry and identifying potential participants is a complex process with many pitfalls. It depends much on the personal characteristics of the researcher and how others perceive him or her. Mutual trust underlies all research but especially qualitative research, because of the close and deep interactions between researcher and participant. Trust is earned, not given. The process begins with the first telephone call to potential participants and carries on during and after the study is completed.

> Trust and rapport in fieldwork are not simply a matter of niceness; a noncoercive, mutually rewarding relationship with key informants is essential if the researcher is to gain valid insights into the informant's point of view. Since gaining a sense of the perspective of the informant is crucial to the success of the research enterprise, it is necessary to establish trust and maintain it throughout the course of the study.[4]

---

[4]Erickson, F. (1990). *Qualitative methods. Research on teaching and learning, volume 2.* New York: Macmillan (p. 141).

SELECTING PARTICIPANTS

Qualitative research generally relies on purposive selection of participants; they are selected because they can provide pertinent information about the specific topic and setting investigated. The emphasis on in-depth inquiry and context, focus on participants' perspectives, and examination of single sites require different sampling approaches than those used in quantitative research. The quantitative researcher wants to generalize to a larger population, while the qualitative researcher wants to get the deepest understanding of the single setting studied. Because of the in-depth nature of the research and the deep understandings sought, qualitative researchers typically deal with small, purposely selected samples who can provide the insight and articulateness needed to attain the desired richness of data. Also, it often is difficult to obtain large numbers of participants who are willing to undergo the demands of participation. Thus, the focus of participant selection is to identify participants who can provide information about the particular topic and setting being studied.

Many purposive sampling strategies are useful in qualitative research, including intensity sampling, homogeneous sampling, criterion sampling, snowball sampling, and random purposive sampling. In selecting participants, be careful of potential participants who are extremely eager to be included in the study. They may have an ax to grind or have prior strong feelings concerning what they perceive the study to be about. You likely will get preformed, not reflective, responses. Table 6.3 describes the range of sampling strategies in qualitative research.

Inevitably you will face the question of how many participants are enough. As is usually the case with such questions, the answer is, "It depends." There is no hard and fast number that represents the "correct" number of participants in a study. It is usually true that sample sizes in quantitative research are larger than qualitative, for the reasons just noted. But qualitative studies can be done with a single participant, for example in a case study. Or they may be comparing perceptions across different settings and have a total of 60 or 70 participating across settings. Your resources—time, money, participant availability, participant interest, and the like—will influence the number of participants you use. You may want to select your participants at the start of the study and deal only with them, or you may start with a few participants and add new participants over time to corroborate and extend the perspectives of the initial few participants.

Two general indicators are commonly used to determine when the number of participants is adequate. The first is the extent to which the selected participants represent the range of potential participants in the setting. For example, if the research setting is a kindergarten to sixth grade school and the researcher only includes teachers from grades K, 1, and 2, the selected participants do not represent those in the chosen setting. To rectify this problem, the researcher could change the focus to the lower grades or add participants at the higher grade levels. The second indicator is the redundancy of the information gathered from the participants. When the researcher begins to hear the same thoughts, perspectives, and responses from most or all of the participants, he or she will know that little more is being learned and additional participants are not needed, at least for that particular topic or issue. This point is commonly known as *data saturation*.

Once participants are selected, it is useful to obtain their formal, informed consent for being part of the study. While this might seem like overkill, informed consent is useful for both the participants and the researcher and ensures that

TABLE	6.3

Typology of Sampling Strategies in Qualitative Inquiry

TYPE OF SAMPLING	PURPOSE
Maximum variation	Documents diverse variations and identifies important common patterns
Homogeneous	Focuses, reduces, simplifies, and facilitates group interviewing
Critical case	Permits logical generalization and maximum application of information to other cases
Theory-based	Finds examples of a theoretical construct and thereby elaborates on and examines it
Confirming and disconfirming cases	Elaborates on initial analysis, seeks exceptions, looks for variation
Snowball or chain	Identifies cases of interest from people who know people who know what cases are information-rich
Extreme or deviant case	Learns from highly unusual manifestations of the phenomenon of interest
Typical case	Highlights what is normal or average
Intensity	Looks at information-rich cases that manifest the phenomenon intensely but not extremely
Politically important cases	Attracts desired attention or avoids attracting undesired attention
Random purposeful	Adds credibility to sample when potential purposeful sample is too large
Stratified purposeful	Illustrates subgroups and facilitates comparisons
Criterion	Encompasses all cases that meet some criterion; useful for quality assurance
Opportunistic	Follows new leads; takes advantage of the unexpected
Combination or mixed	Triangulation, flexibility; meets multiple interests and needs
Convenience	Saves time, money, and effort, but at the expense of information and credibility

Source: M. B. Miles and A. M. Huberman (1994). *Qualitative Data Analysis: An Expanded Sourcebook, 2/e.* Copyright 1994 Sage Publications. Reprinted by permission of Sage Publications, Inc.

both know their reciprocal rights and expectations. Further, the depth of personal and sensitive information collected in qualitative studies calls for researcher–participant understandings prior to beginning the study. The emphasis is on *informed* consent. Participants should know, at least in general terms, about the nature and purpose of the study. They should know what they will be expected to do and if there are any risks in doing that. They should know about the conditions under which they may withdraw from the study. Issues of anonymity, confidentiality, and dissemination of results also should be made clear. It is best if the informed consent is signed by both the researcher and participant.

DATA COLLECTION

Observations, interviews, personal and official documents, photographs, recordings, drawings, e-mails, and informal conversations are all sources of qualitative data. The most commonly used sources are observations and interviews, sometimes together and sometimes individually. All these types of data have one key aspect in common: their analyses primarily depend on the integrative and interpretive skills of the researcher. Interpretation is necessary because the data gathered are rarely numerical and because the data are both rich in detail and lengthy. In this section we examine qualitative data collection, primarily observations and interviews. We examine these types individually for clarity, but in most cases, qualitative researchers employ more than one data collection method. Although the approaches we describe are the ones most commonly used, bear in mind that there are many options for data collection, including, in some cases, quantitative data. Any data collection approach that is ethical and feasible, and that contributes to understanding the phenomenon or individuals studied, may be used.

Having obtained entry into a setting and having selected participants, the qualitative researcher is ready to begin data collection, also commonly called fieldwork. Regardless of how much you read, think about, and discuss fieldwork with experienced researchers, you will not really know what fieldwork is like until you actually live it. Living an experience for a first time always means uncertainty in a new role—uncertainty about how to act and interact with others. It is common to feel nervous as you learn the ropes, try to establish rapport with participants, and get a feel for the setting. Bogdan and Biklen[5] suggest a number of cautions to make the initial days of entry into the setting less painful.

1. Do not take what happens in the field personally.
2. Set up your first visit so that someone is there to introduce you to the participants.
3. Don't try to accomplish too much in the first few days. Make your initial visit or observation short. You will have to take field notes after each data collection encounter, so start with brief data collection episodes to ease into the process of writing field notes.
4. Be relatively passive. Ask general, nonspecific, noncontroversial questions that allow participants to reply without being forced to provide answers they might find uncomfortable discussing with a relative "stranger." Ease your way into the context; don't storm in. The intent is for the participants to gradually become comfortable with you, and you with them. Then you can gradually increase your degree of involvement.
5. Be friendly and polite. Answer questions participants and others ask, but try not to say too much about the specifics of your presence and purpose, lest it influence the participants.

Your demeanor and personal characteristics will be as important in carrying out your research as your research skills. That is one of the realities of most qualitative research.

Decisions about methods and focus of data collection are usually made after site selection, examination of the site, and sizing up the participants. The researcher may even want to "get the feel" of the setting and participants before deciding on the data collection techniques to employ.

OBSERVATION

Observation can take many forms in qualitative research, depending on the involvement of the observer. The observer can be a participant observer who engages fully in the activities being studied but is known to the participants as a

---

[5]Bogdan, R. C. and Biklen, S. K. (1998). *Qualitative research in education*. Needham Heights, MA: Allyn and Bacon (pp. 79–81).

researcher. Alternatively, the observer can be an external or nonparticipant observer of the activities of the group being studied; that is, he or she watches, but does not participate. Between the participant observer and the external observer, there are a number of other possibilities, such as a combination of both approaches or external observer at the start of the study and participant observer in the latter stages of the study. It is also possible for the observer to be covert, disguising his or her identity from other participants. Although this approach may gather the most realistic data about participants and their setting, there are ethical issues regarding lack of awareness of other participants. The covert observer is a member of the group under false and unknown premises. Avoid covert observation.

The advantages of participant observation include the ability to gain insights and develop relationships with participants that cannot be obtained in any other way. Being a participant and having a "residence" in the field provides a broad breadth and depth of information about participants and setting. The drawbacks to participant observation are that the researcher may lose objectivity and become emotionally involved with the participants, and, more pragmatically, the researcher may have difficulty participating and taking detailed field notes simultaneously. Nonparticipant observers are less intrusive and less likely to become emotionally involved with the participants. On the other hand, information such as participants' opinions, attitudes, and emotional states are difficult to obtain.

Most qualitative observational research is naturalistic, encompassing holistic inquiry about participants' understanding of their natural setting or environment. The emphasis is on understanding the natural environment as lived by the participants, with no intent on the researcher's part to alter or manipulate the natural environment. Altering or manipulating the natural research setting destroys the reality of the researched setting and participants.

The amount and kind of observation that is appropriate for a given study will depend on the nature of the study. If it is not feasible for the researcher to become a true participant in the group being studied, it probably is best that he or she be an external observer. For example, the researcher may not have the background or needed expertise to meaningfully act as a participant. Or, in some cases, it might be awkward for a male researcher to enter as a participant observer in an all-female context or for a middle-aged researcher to be a true participant in a group of fifth graders. If the group studied is tight-knit and closely organized, participation may be difficult for both the researcher and the group. If participation is feasible, the researcher must decide how well he or she can simultaneously act as a participant and gather the desired data. In some measure the researcher's personality will influence whether he or she feels more comfortable being a participant or an external observer. Beginning qualitative researchers should consider this question carefully prior to deciding to adopt the role of a participant observer; balancing participation and observation can be difficult. There is much to think about in deciding the nature of observation to employ. Throughout observation of whatever type, Bogdan and Biklen[6] provide an important reminder.

> Becoming a researcher means internalizing the research goal while collecting data in the field. As you conduct research you participate with the subjects in var-

---

[6]Bogdan, R. C. and Biklen, S. K. 1998. *Qualitative research in education.* Needham Heights, MA: Allyn and Bacon, (p. 82).

ious ways. You joke with them and behave socially in many ways. You may even help them perform their duties. You do these things, but always from the purpose of promoting your research goals. You carry with you an imaginary sign that you hang over each subject and on every wall and tree. The sign says, "My primary purpose in being here is to collect data. How does what I am doing relate to that goal?"

This quote emphasizes the difference between a participant and a participant observer: a participant participates while a participant observer participates and collects data. This is, of course, a difficult and confusing exercise for the novice participant observer. There are so many things going on. What should be watched, written down, and ignored? How does one overcome this complexity? The same way one gets to Carnegie Hall: practice, practice, practice. With practice one learns to be aware of implicit agendas among participants, to try to experience the situation from the perspective of both an observer and a participant, to be introspective about what you see, and to provide records that richly describe observed situations. In a very real sense, one must learn to observe in a qualitative research way.

Field Notes

Field notes are the observer's record of what he or she has seen, heard, experienced, and thought about during an observation session. They contain a descriptive and a reflective aspect. The former describes what's seen and the latter provides the researcher's thoughts or ideas about the description. Field notes are the data that will be analyzed to provide the description and understanding of the research setting and participants. In each session, beginning with the first, observation should produce field notes that are as detailed as possible. If possible, notes should be made in the field, during the observation, when they are fresh to the researcher. The longer the interval between the observation and writing field notes, the more likely that there will be some distortion from the original observation, especially if you have an excellent, but short, memory.

Clearly, the longer an observation session, the more to digest and write up in the field notes. Although the researcher cannot always control the length of an observation (it may break up earlier or go on longer than anticipated), if the researcher has some control, it will be easier to develop field notes on shorter observation sessions. Over time, with practice, researchers often are surprised at how lengthy and detailed field notes produced from an observation session can be. Field notes should be entered into a computer for future examination and possibly for computer analysis.

Each observation session will have its unique focus and interactions, but it is useful to have a protocol or list of issues to guide observation. This has two benefits. It provides the researcher with a focus during the observation, and it provides a common framework for field notes, making it easier to organize and categorize across field notes. When making field notes, a simple protocol for observation might include these topics:

- Who is being observed? How many people are involved, who are they, and what individual roles and mannerisms are evident?
- What is going on? What is the nature of conversation? What are people saying or doing? What is the physical setting like? How are people

seated, and where? How do the participants interact with each other? What are the status or roles of people; who leads, who follows, who is decisive, who is not? What is the tone of the session? What beliefs, attitudes, values, etc. seem to emerge?
- How did the meeting end? Was the group divided, united, upset, bored, or relieved?
- What activities or interactions seemed unusual or significant?
- What was the researcher doing during the session?

Certainly different studies with different participants in a different setting would have alternative protocol questions. The aim here is not to be exhaustive, but to encourage readers to develop and refine some form of protocol for observations. Table 6.4 illustrates a simple protocol.

However, protocols are not useful if field notes are not extensive and descriptive. The term that describes extensive, clear field notes is *thick description*. Thick description is partially influenced by what is seen, but mainly by the detail and language the researcher uses in constructing the field notes. Be clear and descriptive. Don't write, "The class was happy." Instead, describe the activities of the students, the looks on their faces, the interactions with each other, the teachers' activities, and other observations that led you to think the class was happy. Don't write, "He turned to her and engaged her in conversation." Say instead, "Turning to face her, he asked, 'What are we doing here? Can't we leave now?' She seemed hardly to hear him and would not meet his eyes." Don't say that the teacher is "teaching." Provide a description that indicates what the teacher was doing and saying. Avoid words like "good," "happy," "useful," and the like; replace them with what was actually seen or heard. Figure 6.1 gives a portion of field notes that represent thick description. Note that Figure 6.1 shows the sixth set of field notes in the study and appears to be produced by a researcher with prior experience in constructing field notes. The sections labeled "O. C." indicate the observer's (researcher's) comments.

Figure 6.1 shows both the descriptive aspect of field notes and the reflective aspect of field notes. Each O. C. entry in the field notes represents a reflection that the researcher had while writing up the descriptive field notes. In reflective notes, the observer is free to express personal thoughts and issues. They represent a more personal and subjective aspect of the field notes, and should be distinguished from the descriptive material in the field notes. In reading Figure 6.1 you probably will identify times when the researcher's O. C.s were about something unusual, something that has recurred, something that had to be explored, and the like.

Good qualitative research requires simultaneous data collection and analysis. In the process of observing, writing, and reflecting on field notes, qualitative researchers engage in a process of evolving data analysis. These ongoing analyses lead to a form of data analysis referred to as *memo writing*. Memo writing is a form of thinking on paper; researchers write memos to themselves that describe their mental exploration of their ideas, themes, hunches, and reflections about the research topic. They are "thought pieces" that can range from a few sentences to many pages. The ideas, themes, hunches, and reflections contained in memos usually form the basis for much of the final research report. Figure 6.2 presents an example of a memo.

The reflective aspects of field notes serve a number of functions. First, they identify topics or issues the researcher wishes to explore in more detail (e.g., I

TABLE **6.4**

Protocol Example

Interview Protocol
Project: University Reaction to a Terrorist Incident

Time of interview:
Date:
Place:
Interviewer:
Interviewee:
Position of interviewee:

(Briefly describe the project)

Questions:
1. What has been your role in the incident?

2. What has happened since the event that you have been involved in?

3. What has been the impact on the university community of this incident?

4. What larger ramifications, if any, exist from the incident?

5. To whom should we talk to find out more about campus reaction to the incident?

(Thank individual for participating in this interview. Assure him or her of
confidentiality of responses and potential future interviews.)

Source: Creswell, J. W. (1998). *Qualitative Inquiry and Research Design Choosing among Five Traditions*,
p. 127. Copyright 1998 Sage Publications. Reprinted by permission of Sage Publications, Inc.

FIGURE **6.1**

Section of Field Notes

March 24, 1980
Joe McCloud
11:00 a.m. to 12:30 p.m.
Westwood High
6th Set of Notes

THE FOURTH-PERIOD
CLASS IN MARGE'S ROOM

I arrived at Westwood High at five minutes to eleven, the time Marge told me her fourth period started. I was dressed as usual: sport shirt, chino pants, and a Woolrich parka. The fourth period is the only time during the day when all the students who are in the "neurologically impaired/learning disability" program, better known as "Marge's program," come together. During the other periods, certain students in the program, two or three or four at most, come to her room for help with the work they are getting in other regular high school classes.

It was a warm, fortyish, promise of a spring day. There was a police patrol wagon, the kind that has benches in the back that are used for large busts, parked in the back of the big parking lot that is in front of the school. No one was sitting in it and I never heard its reason for being there. In the circular drive in front of the school was parked a United States Army car. It had insignias on the side and was a khaki color. As I walked from my car, a balding fortyish man in an Army uniform came out of the building and went to the car and sat down. Four boys and a girl also walked out of the school. All were white. They had on old dungarees and colored stenciled t-shirts with spring jackets over them. One of the boys, the tallest of the four, called out, "oink, oink, oink." This was done as he sighted the police vehicle in the back.

O.C.: This was strange to me in that I didn't think that the kids were into "the police as pigs." Somehow I associated that with another time, the early 1970s. I'm going to have to come to grips with the assumptions I have about high school due to my own experience. Sometimes I feel like Westwood is entirely different from my high school and yet this police car incident reminded me of mine.

Classes were changing when I walked down the halls. As usual there was the boy with girl standing here and there by the lockers. There were three couples that I saw. There was the occasional shout. There were no teachers outside the doors.

O.C.: The halls generally seem to be relatively unsupervised during class changes.

Two black girls I remember walking down the hall together. They were tall and thin and had their hair elaborately braided with beads all through them. I stopped by the office to tell Mr. Talbor's (the principal) secretary that I was in the building. She gave me a warm smile.

O.C.: I feel quite comfortable in the school now. Somehow I feel like I belong. As I walk down the halls some teachers say hello. I have been going out of my way to say hello to kids that I pass. Twice I've been in a stare-down with kids passing in the hall. Saying, "How ya' doin'?" seems to disarm them.

I walked into Marge's class and she was standing in front of the room with more people than I had ever seen in the room save for her homeroom which is right after second period. She looked like she was talking to the class or was just about to start. She was dressed as she had been on my other visits—clean, neat, well-dressed but casual. Today she had on a striped blazer, a white blouse and dark slacks. She looked up at me, smiled, and said: "Oh, I have a lot more people here now than the last time."

O.C.: This was in reference to my other visits during other periods where there are only a few students. She seems self-conscious about having such a small group of students to be responsible for. Perhaps she compares herself with the regular teachers who have classes of thirty or so.

There were two women in their late twenties sitting in the room. There was only one chair left. Marge said to me something like: "We have two visitors from the central office today. One is a vocational counselor and the other is a physical therapist," but I don't remember if those were the words. I felt embarrassed coming in late. I sat down in the only chair available next to one of the women from the central office. They had on skirts and carried their pocketbooks, much more dressed up than the teachers I've seen. They sat there and observed.

continued

Below is the seating arrangement of the class today:

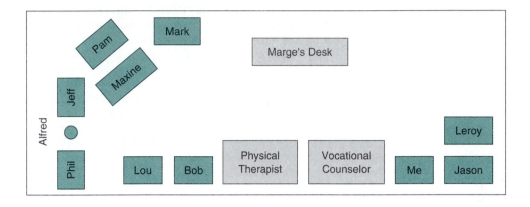

Alfred (Mr. Armstrong, the teacher's aide) walked around but when he stood in one place it was over by Phil and Jeff. Marge walked about near her desk during her talk which she started by saying to the class: "Now remember, tomorrow is a fieldtrip to the Rollway Company. We all meet in the usual place, by the bus, in front of the main entrance at 8:30. Mrs. Sharp wanted me to tell you that the tour of Rollway is not specifically for you. It's not like the trip to G.M. They took you to places where you were likely to be able to get jobs. Here, it's just a general tour that everybody goes on. Many of the jobs that you will see are not for you. Some are just for people with engineering degrees. You'd better wear comfortable shoes because you may be walking for two or three hours." Maxine and Mark said: "Ooh," in protest to the walking.

She paused and said in a demanding voice: "OK, any questions? You are all going to be there. (Pause) I want you to take a blank card and write down some questions so you have things to ask at the plant." She began passing out cards and at this point Jason, who was sitting next to me, made a tutting sound of disgust and said: "We got to do this?" Marge said: "I know this is too easy for you, Jason." This was said in a sarcastic way but not like a strong putdown.

O.C.: It was like sarcasm between two people who know each other well. Marge has known many of these kids for a few years. I have to explore the implications of that for her relations with them.

Marge continued: "OK, what are some of the questions you are going to ask?" Jason yelled out "Insurance," and Marge said: "I was asking Maxine not Jason." This was said matter of factly without anger toward Jason. Maxine said: "Hours—the hours you work, the wages." Somebody else yelled out: "Benefits." Marge wrote these things on the board. She got to Phil who was sitting there next to Jeff. I believe she skipped Jeff. Mr. Armstrong was standing right next to Phil. She said: "Have you got one?" Phil said: "I can't think of one." She said: "Honestly Phil. Wake up." Then she went to Joe, the white boy. Joe and Jeff are the only white boys I've seen in the program. The two girls are white. He said: "I can't think of any." She got to Jason and asked him if he could think of anything else. He said: "Yeah, you could ask 'em how many of the products they made each year." Marge said: "Yes, you could ask about production. How about Leroy, do you have any ideas Leroy?" He said: "No." Mr. Armstrong was standing over in the corner and saying to Phil in a low voice: "Now you know what kinds of questions you ask when you go for a job?" Phil said: "Training, what kind of training do you have to have?" Marge said: "Oh yes, that's right, training." Jason said out loud but not yelling: "How much schooling you need to get it." Marge kept listing them.

O.C.: Marge was quite animated. If I hadn't seen her like this before I would think she was putting on a show for the people from central office.

Source: From R. C. Bogdan and S. K. Biklen, *Qualitative Research for Education: An Introduction to Theory and Methods, 3/e.* © 1998 by Allyn & Bacon. Reproduced by permission.

FIGURE	6.2

Example of a Researcher's Memo

2. *Teachers' use of the concept of mainstreaming.* When I first started this study I thought that regular class teachers would or would not want to be involved with disabled children on the basis of their feelings and experiences with "labeled" kids. While this seems to be true in some cases, a lot of the disposition to the program seems unrelated to the particulars about it or the population served. Some teachers feel that the administration is in general not supportive and they approach what they consider "additional" problems with the disposition that "I have enough." When I say "the administration," I mean the central office, those whom they see as determining the outcome of the contract bargaining. Others concentrate on the principal and feel that he works hard to make things work for them so if he wants them to get involved in a new effort, they will. This needs a lot of working out but it may be fruitful to pursue looking at what one's position is on mainstreaming and how it is talked about as being a manifestation of conflict and competing interests in the school. Also, this reminds me of how particular teachers think of the various special education classes. Marge was telling me that she likes kids with learning disabilities because they aren't trouble-makers like those in the resource room who have emotional disturbances.

Source: From R. C. Bogdan and S. K. Biklen, *Qualitative Research for Education: An Introduction to Theory and Methods, 3/e.* © 1998 by Allyn & Bacon. Reproduced by permission.

have the feeling that tension among faculty members is growing). Second, they begin to identify areas that might be important to focus on in data analysis (e.g., I'm finding it hard to remain objective because of Mr. Hardnose's abrasive manner). Third, if categorized across field notes, they can be collected into reflective groups such as a group for reflections on method, on ethical issues, on areas for analysis, and on ways to improve the data collection process.

Guidelines for Field Notes

The following guidelines describe important aspects for successfully maintaining field notes in observational research.

- Do not assume you know what you're looking for until you "experience" the setting and participants for a while.
- Try to recognize and dismiss your own assumptions and biases and remain open to what you see; try to see things through the participants' perspectives.
- Write up your field notes as soon as possible. When you're done, list the main ideas or themes you've observed and recorded. Don't discuss your observation until the field notes are written; discussion may alter your initial perspective.
- List the date, site, time, and topic on every set of field notes. Leave wide margins to write in your impressions next to sections of the descriptive field notes. Write only on one side of a page. This will save you much photocopying when the time comes "to cut and paste" the field notes into different categories. Draw diagrams of the site.

■ In writing field notes, first list key words related to your observation, then outline what you saw and heard. Then, using the key words and outline, write your detailed field notes.

■ Although collected together, keep the descriptive and reflective sections of field notes separate. Focus on writing detailed descriptive field notes.

■ Write down your hunches, questions, and insights after each observation. Use memos.

■ Number the lines or paragraphs of your field notes. This will help you find particular sections when needed.

Field notes are obviously of prime importance in qualitative research studies of most kinds. Thus, it is important to understand the complexity involved in developing accurate and descriptive field notes. To appreciate the complexity, imagine yourself trying to write, *in detail*, what happened during just one class of your research methods course. What was the physical setting like? Who was present? How did they act? What was the instructor doing and saying and how was he or she interacting with the students? What took place? What was usual and unusual? The task appears even more daunting when you consider that you are expected to provide sharp, detailed descriptions that represent what was happening, not your interpretation of what was happening. Qualitative researchers can produce rich, deep descriptions and understandings of settings and participants, but it takes a great deal of hard and detailed work to do so.

INTERVIEWS

A second important qualitative data collection approach is the interview. An interview is a purposeful interaction, usually between two people, focused on one person trying to get information from the other person. Interviews permit the researcher to obtain important data that cannot be obtained from observation. For example, observation cannot provide information about past events, or the way things used to be before Mr. Hardnozed became principal, or why Ms. Haddit has had it and is considering transferring to another school. Information about these events cannot be observed; they must be obtained from peoples' own words. Interviewers can explore and probe participants' responses to gather more in-depth data about their experiences and feelings. They can examine attitudes, interests, feelings, concerns, and values more easily than using observation.

It is important to consider two additional aspects of interviews. First, not all qualitative researchers who gather data through interviews would accept the definition of interview stated above. Many researchers would not view the interview as a process of "pulling out" information from respondents about the topic studied. They would say that interviewing is a joint construction of meaning between the researcher and the participant, not just a construction of the participant. Second, while the concept of an interview study seems straightforward, it can be a complex and difficult undertaking when the gender, culture, and social lines of the interviewee and participant are quite different. Depending on the characteristics of the researcher and the participant, there can be issues of who "controls" the interview, the accuracy of responses provided, and the extent to which the language of the interviewee and the researcher are similar enough to permit meaningful inferences about the topic studied.

Interview methods can be used as a study's sole data collection method or used in conjunction with other data collection methods, such as participant observation. Combined with other data gathering approaches, interviews can lead to identifying new topics to explore and can help explain data collected from other methods. For example, issues that arise from observation may be clarified or expanded by interviewing participants.

Interviews vary in a number of ways. They may be a one-time interview or they may involve multiple interviews with the same participant. They may involve a single participant as in a case study, or a number of participants as in ethnographic research. Participants may be interviewed individually or in groups. Interviews may vary in length from a few minutes to up to 2 hours. They may be structured, with a specified set of questions to be asked, or they may be unstructured, with questions being prompted by the flow of the interview. Some qualitative studies employ both structured and unstructured approaches. For example, structured interviews may be used to gather basic information or a career history from participants at the start of a study, while an unstructured interview is used further into the study to obtain more complex or personal information. Semistructured interviews combine both structured and unstructured approaches. Interviews may be formal and planned (we'll meet Tuesday at 1:00 to discuss your perceptions) or informal and unplanned (I'm glad I caught you in the corridor, I've been meaning to ask you . . .).

Gaining Entry and Selecting Participants

Dealing with gatekeepers, obtaining permission, answering participants' questions about the study, contacting and selecting participants, and obtaining consent from participants are activities that occur in qualitative observation and interview studies. Similarly, important cautions such as entering the setting unobtrusively, building rapport and trust with participants before probing sensitive issues, and the importance of demeanor and personal characteristics for the success of qualitative research are similar for observation and interview studies. However, it should be noted that the interviewer will almost always be face to face with research participants, while some observers may not be. Thus, the cautions cited earlier are particularly important for the interviewer.

Types of Interviews

Interviews range from open-ended and spontaneous to closed-ended and prescribed, with various intermediate levels. In general, qualitative interviews tend to be on the unstructured rather than the structured side of Table 6.5. One of the emphases in qualitative research is its focus on depth of understanding. Usually the depth sought is more readily obtained from interviews that permit probing of participants' responses, exploring unplanned topics that arise, and obtaining clarification of participants' responses. Thus, qualitative interviews are more free-flowing and open than those of quantitative interviews.

Recognize, however, that it is easier to conduct structured interviews than less structured ones, because structured interviews contain the questions to be asked in the interview. Although an interviewer is always able to probe and explore during the interview, unstructured interviewing, even in small doses, requires insight, recognition of needed probing, and finesse in posing questions that will elicit the information sought. For researchers inexperienced in inter-

TABLE	**6.5**			

Continuum of Interviews with Increasing Amounts of Structure

UNSTRUCTURED	PARTIALLY STRUCTURED	SEMISTRUCTURED	STRUCTURED	TOTALLY STRUCTURED
Exploratory, only area of interest is chosen, interviewer "follows his/her nose" in formulating and ordering questions. Impromptu conversations that occur during observation are of this nature.	Area is chosen and questions are formulated but order is up to interviewer. Interviewer may add questions or modify them as deemed appropriate. Questions are open-ended, and responses are recorded nearly verbatim, possibly taped.	Questions and order of presentation are determined. Questions have open ends; interviewer records the essence of each response.	Questions and order are predetermined, and responses are coded by the interviewer as they are given.	Questions, order, and coding are predetermined, and the respondent is presented with alternatives for each question so that phrasing of responses is structured. Questions are self-coding in that each choice is preassigned a code.

Source: D. Krathwohl, *Methods of Educational and Social Science Research, 2/e,* 1998, p. 287. Copyright 1998. Reprinted by permission of Addison Wesley Educational Publications, Inc.

viewing, the use of an interview protocol is a helpful tool that can provide a safety net as the researcher refines his or her sensitivity to participants and interviewing technique (see Table 6.4). The focus of the interview can be on one or many areas. For example, interviews may focus on a participants' prior history (Where and when have you taught?), attitudes (How do you feel about parents' involvement in your classroom?), perceptions (What do you think are the main strengths and weaknesses of the first- and second-year teachers in this school?), knowledge (How much do you know about the planned rearrangement of the fifth-grade teams?), concerns (Are there any school policies or emphases that concern you?), and interpersonal relations (How would you describe your relationship with the principal and vice principal?). Asking questions that deal with values, feelings, and opinions, such as, "How did you feel when you found out that Mr. Hardcase was going to be appointed principal?" and "How has teacher morale been affected?" require both methodological and interpersonal skills on the part of the interviewer.

A good interviewer is always looking for openings to probe deeper. Although interviews often start with mundane questions and gradually ease into more sensitive and complex questions, the alert interviewer will respond to probing opportunities as they arise. If a response to an apparently innocuous question, "How long have you felt this way?" is "Too, too, too long!" the interviewer's antennae should go up, prompting a follow-up question such as, "Why do you say that?" Similarly, avoid posing questions that produce a yes or no answer; or, if such questions are asked, follow up with "Why?" or, "Tell me why you feel that way." Or, if a participant tells you that the reaction of the students today was "interesting," ask what the participant means by *interesting*, or ask for examples of what made the students' reactions interesting.

Remember, the aim of the qualitative interview is to find out about the participants, where they are "coming from," what they believe, experienced, felt, and so forth.

In addition to the range of structure that interviews can have, other aspects of interviews can vary. For example, the length of an interview can be short or long, although it is not recommended that interviews last more than 1 to 2 hours. The nature of the interview (structured versus unstructured), the amount and nature of the information desired (factual demographic information versus attitude and value personal information), and the attention span of the interviewer and interviewee (short versus long) all influence the nature of the interview. Also, you may interview each participant only once or more than once during the study. Single interviews are efficient, but cannot usually provide depth of data, nor allow for follow-up questions. Multiple participant interviews allow for follow-up questions and can build on one another to probe deeply and reveal changes over time. However, they are time-consuming and can produce voluminous data to organize and interpret. Interviews can be with a single participant or a group of participants (often called a focus group). A focus group is especially useful in obtaining a variety of views or opinions about a topic or issue, which can then be used in interviews with single participants.

Collecting Data from Interviews

Interviewers have three basic choices for collecting their data: taking notes during the interview, writing notes after the interview, and tape recording the interview. The last choice is the most viable, although all can be used in a study. Taking notes during the interview is distracting and can alter the flow of the session. Writing notes after the interview is better than trying to write during the interview, but it is difficult to remember the contents of the interview. Plus, long interview sessions limit the usefulness of these two approaches. Thus, the data collection method of choice is tape recording the interview, which provides a verbatim account of the session. Also, tapes provide researchers with the original data for use at any time. Although a few participants may balk at the use of a tape recorder during the interview, most participants will not, especially if you promise them confidentiality. Make sure that the recording machine is in good working order (new batteries, too) prior to entering the interview setting.

To work most productively, it is useful to transcribe the tape recordings. This is a time-consuming task, especially for long interviews. If the researcher chooses to do the transcribing instead of hiring someone to transcribe (a costly alternative), it would help the researcher to use short interview sessions, if feasible. Transcribing one 60-minute tape may take 4 or 5 more hours. When transcribing, write the date, subject discussed, and participant (using a coded name) on the transcript. Number all pages. Make sure a different indicator is given and used to identify the various persons speaking on the tape.

The transcripts are the field notes for interview data. Interview transcripts are voluminous and usually have to be reduced to focus on the data pertinent to the study. Sometimes this is difficult to do. During data analysis the transcript will be read and important (or thought to be important) sections labeled to indicate their importance. This process of culling the transcripts will be described in the next chapter.

Guidelines for Interviewing

There are a number of actions that can improve the collection of interview data.[7]

- Listen more, talk less. Listening is the most important part of interviewing.
- Follow up on what participants say and ask questions when you don't understand.
- Avoid leading questions; ask open-ended questions.
- Don't interrupt. Learn how to wait.
- Keep participants focused and ask for concrete details.
- Tolerate silence. It means the participant is thinking.
- Don't be judgmental about participants' views or beliefs. You're there to learn about their perspectives, whether you agree with them or not.
- Don't debate with participants over their responses. You are a recorder, not a debater.

THREATS TO THE QUALITY OF OBSERVATIONS AND INTERVIEWS

Two main threats to the validity of observation and interview studies are observer bias and observer effects. For example, the very presence of the researcher in the setting may create potential problems. The situation may be "seen" differently than it would have been through the eyes of a different researcher (observer bias) or may be a somewhat different situation than it would have been if the researcher were not present (observer effect). Although these problems are not unique to qualitative research, they are potentially more serious because of the more intimate involvement of the researcher and the participants.

Observer bias refers to invalid information that results from the perspective the researcher brings to the study. Each researcher brings to a setting a highly individual background, set of experiences, preferences, attitudes, and the like, which, in turn, affect not only what and how he or she observes, but also his or her personal reflections and interpretations. The qualitative researcher runs the risk of identifying with one or more participants or being negative toward others, which can influence the way the researcher weights information from different groups. For example, after attending a number of faculty meetings a researcher might tend to identify with the values of the teachers, and observations and interpretations of principal–teacher interactions would be affected by this role identification. In other words, no two researchers in the same situation would have identical field notes. (No, not even identical twins!) This apparently inevitable subjectivity is, however, both a weakness and a strength of participant observation. The more involved the researcher is, the greater the degree of subjectivity likely to creep into the observations. On the other hand, the greater the involvement, the greater the opportunity for acquiring in-depth understanding and insight.

Thus, qualitative researchers must walk a fine line in their attempt to be at the same time both involved and unbiased. What is important is that they be

---

[7]Seidman, I. E. (1991). *Interviewing as qualitative research.* New York: Teachers College, Columbia University.

aware of this challenge and make every effort to meet it. For example, they may try to minimize the effects of their personal biases on their findings by conscientiously recording their thoughts, feelings, and reactions about what they observe. Of course detecting bias and eliminating it are not the same thing. Qualitative researchers, however, do not claim that they can eliminate all bias. They do maintain, however, and rightfully so, that they have a number of strategies for minimizing its effect on the results of their research. These strategies are discussed in the next section.

The other side of the coin is called the *observer effect* and refers to the impact of the observer's participation on the setting or participants being studied. In other words, the situation is somewhat different than it would have been if the observer did not participate; and, of course, the greater the researcher's participation, the greater the likely observer effect. It is not news that persons being observed may behave atypically simply because they are being observed. Would you behave exactly the same as you normally would on a given day if you knew you were being observed? Probably not. Again, while this problem is by no means unique to qualitative research, it is potentially more serious, since the researcher is trying to study how people naturally behave in their natural setting. The larger the observer effect, the less "natural" the setting is.

Thus, once again we see that qualitative researchers must walk a fine line, as they attempt to be involved enough to gain the cooperation and insights they are seeking while at the same time they try to be as unobtrusive, or inconspicuous, as possible. One of their major strategies to lessen observer effect is to be unassuming and nonthreatening initially and gradually increase participation and entry into the setting. Thus, for example, at the first faculty meeting the researcher may simply observe and appear cordial, but by the fourth or fifth faculty meeting, people will become used to his or her presence and tend to be their usual selves. As noted, it also helps if the exact nature of the researcher's inquiry is not described in any more detail than is necessary, ethically or legally. The fact that persons being observed may initially behave differently than usual is a problem, but focusing participants on the specific research targets to be examined can be much worse! So, for example, it would probably be sufficient if the *official* reason given for the researcher's presence were "to observe high school faculty meetings," rather than "to observe principal–teacher interactions." Qualitative researchers are well aware that they cannot totally eliminate observer effects. They do, however, make every effort to recognize, minimize, record, and report them.

ENHANCING VALIDITY AND REDUCING BIAS

The data collected from and about participants in qualitative research studies are voluminous, generally nonquantitative, and rich in detail. Because qualitative data extend far beyond superficial issues, and because each researcher brings his or her own perspectives and biases to the study, important questions that all qualitative researchers must ask and answer are, "How much confidence can I place in the data I have collected? What is the quality of the data I have obtained from participants? Have my personal biases intruded into the data collection process?" These questions relate to the validity of the data collected.

Qualitative researchers use several strategies to check on and enhance a study's validity. Used in combination, the following strategies can reduce researcher bias and improve the validity of the data collected.

- Extend the study by staying in the field for a longer period to obtain additional data that can be compared to earlier data or to compare participant's consistency of responses.
- Include additional participants to broaden the representativeness of the study and thus the database.
- Make a concerted effort to obtain participant trust and comfort, thus providing more detailed, honest information from participants.
- Try to recognize one's own biases and preferences and be honest with oneself in seeking them out.
- Work with another researcher and independently gather and compare data collected from subgroups of the participants.
- Allow participants to review and critique field notes or tape recordings for accuracy and meaning, but only at the end of the entire data collection period. Doing this in the middle of data collection may influence participants' responses or actions in subsequent data collections. Note that the comments and reactions of participants at the end of the study provide additional data for the researcher.
- Use verbatim accounts of observations or interviews by collecting and recording data with tape recordings or detailed field notes, including quotes.
- Record in a journal one's own reflections, concerns, and uncertainties during the study and refer to them when examining the data collected.
- Examine unusual or contradictory results for explanations; ignoring such "outliers" may represent a bias in the researcher's perspective toward the more "conventional" data collected.
- Triangulate by using different data sources to confirm one another, as when an interview, related documents, and recollections of other participants produce the same descriptions of an event, or when a participant responds similarly to a personal question asked on three different occasions. Examining documents to corroborate participant information is useful because documents are "unobtrusive" measures that are not affected by the presence of the researcher. Participant absenteeism records, for example, might be one unobtrusive measure of stress that could be compared to the participant's interview comments on stress. It is not likely that data derived from different sources will all be biased in the same way.

In reality, it is virtually impossible to obtain totally unbiased and perfectly valid data in a qualitative research study. The same can be said for quantitative researcher studies. However, the evolving design of the study, the volume and nature of the data collected, and the personal interpretive role the researcher takes in qualitative research make bias and invalid data serious concerns. Interpretation is desired and expected of qualitative research, and efforts to change this would defeat the purpose of such research. Nonetheless, attention to issues of bias and validity are important for maintaining the integrity of qualitative research.

LEAVING THE FIELD

There is always a quandary about when to exit the field. Sometimes the decision is easy (e.g., my sabbatical ends next week and I have to return home to Boston.

Or, school is ending for the year and my participants are about to disperse. Or, I have no more money to support data gathering so I must quit). In most cases, the answer to the when-to-leave-the-field quandary is less clear. How much is enough data? How many pages of field notes are enough? These are hard questions to answer in general, since each study is different from others in some respects. Leaving the field is also complicated, because the bonds formed with the participants throughout the study usually will be severed upon leaving the site. So, there are no simple rules for disengagement.

Some say that the researcher will just "know" when it's time to stop. Others say that the search for the researcher's grail—that one more piece of evidence that will "make" the study—keeps many researchers in the field for too long. In the end, however, the more practical bases for leaving the field are when your field notes become similar or redundant or when more recent data adds little to older data. In some circumstances, the researcher can also observe similar, but new, participants from the site to see whether the observations are similar to the prior participants. It may also be psychologically better for both the researcher and the research participants if the researcher "eases out" over time, rather than abruptly leaving.

HISTORICAL RESEARCH

Historical research is another common form of qualitative research. In fact, until recently, it was the sole form of qualitative research recognized by many. Historical research has most of the same characteristics common to other forms of qualitative research, except that it has a retrospective focus, seeking to understand and describe past characters, events, and settings. It uses data collection and interpretation procedures quite similar to those already described in this chapter, but its main, though not sole, method tends to be literature review. Historical research is the systematic collection and evaluation of data related to past occurrences for the purpose of describing causes, effects, or trends of those events. It helps to explain current events and to anticipate future ones.

Many current educational practices, theories, and issues can be better understood in light of past experiences. Issues of grading, cooperative learning, testing, and reading methods are not new in education, nor is cooperative learning an innovation of the 1970s, and a knowledge of their history can yield insight into the evolution of the current educational system, as well as into practices and approaches that have been found to be ineffective or unfeasible. In fact, studying the history of education might lead one to believe that there is little new under the educational sun, although some practices seem to appear and disappear with regularity. For example, for more than 150 years individualized instruction and group instruction have seemingly taken turns being the favored approach of the day.

The steps involved in conducting a historical research study are similar to other types of research: identify a topic or problem, formulate questions to be answered or hypotheses to be tested, collect data, interpret the data, and produce a verbal synthesis of the findings or interpretations. In conducting a historical study, the researcher can neither manipulate nor control any of the variables. On the other hand, there is no way the researcher can affect events of the past; what has happened has happened. The researcher can, however, describe the documents used and provide bases for his or her interpretations. Not everyone may agree with the researcher's interpretations, but the researcher will have provided information about the bases of his or her reasoning and interpretations. These will need to be confronted by anyone criticizing the work.

SELECTION OF A TOPIC

The purpose of historical research is, as in all qualitative research, to help the reader understand a person or event by providing in-depth description and interpretation of the data. Clearly, the purpose of a historical research study should not be undertaken to prove the researcher's prior beliefs or to support a pet position of the researcher. One can easily verify almost any point of view by consciously or unconsciously "overlooking" evidence to the contrary. There are probably data available to support almost any position; the historical researcher's task is to weigh and interpret existing evidence in arriving at a tenable description or conclusion. For example, one could cite data that would seemingly support the position that having more highly educated and trained teachers has led to increased school vandalism. One could do a historical study describing how requirements for teacher certification and recertification have increased over the years and how school vandalism has correspondingly increased. Of course such a study would indicate very poor critical analysis, since two separate, independent sets of factors are probably responsible for each of these trends rather than one being the cause or effect of the other. To avoid this sort of biased data collection and analysis, one should probably avoid topics about which one has strong feelings. It is a lot easier to be even-handed and open-minded about the topic when you are not emotionally involved.

Worthwhile historical research topics are identified and evaluated in much the same way as topics for other types of qualitative research. The *History of Education Quarterly* is one special resource for acquainting researchers with the range of historical research studies that have been conducted and for suggesting future studies. Given the qualitative focus of historical research, it is important to formulate a manageable, well-defined topic to study. Otherwise, it is likely that an overwhelming amount of data will be collected, considerably increasing the analysis and synthesis of the data and drawing adequately documented interpretations. This is a problem we saw in the discussion of observation and interview studies. On the other hand, a concern unique to historical research is the possibility that a problem will be selected for which insufficient data are available. Historical researchers cannot "create" historical data. They are basically limited to whatever data are already available. Thus, if insufficient data are available, the problem will be inadequately investigated. For example, you may have difficulty studying the influence of Charles Dickens's flat feet on the themes he chose to write about. Select topics less esoteric than Dickens and his feet. There are plenty of better documented historical studies to be studied.

DATA COLLECTION

In historical research, the review of related literature and the study procedures are part of the same process. The term *literature* takes on a broad meaning in a historical study and refers to all sorts of communications, including tape recordings, movies, photographs, documents, oral history, books, pamphlets, journal articles, and so on. The literature may be in the form of legal documents, records, minutes of meetings, letters, and other documents, many of which are not normally indexed alphabetically by subject, author, and title in a library. Thus, identification of such data often requires considerably more "detective work" on the part of the researcher. Further, given the nature of the topic, it is not uncommon for relevant literature to be available only at distant locations (e.g., in a special library collection). In such cases, proper examination of the data requires either considerable travel or, when feasible, extensive reproduction. Each of these approaches presents the researcher with problems. Travel requires that the researcher have a healthy bank account (which very few do!), unless, of course, the effort is supported by a funding agency. Acquiring photocopies of documents in a private collection can also become costly, and a 50-page document might turn out to contain only one or two paragraphs directly related to the research topic.

A historical research study in education might also involve interviews with persons who observed an event or knew a person being written about. Remember, however, that the use of interviews has limitations; it would be pretty tough to interview an observer of the Boston tea party! If a historical study focuses on changes in high school social studies textbooks from 1880 to 1945, artifacts such as textbooks would be important data. The range of useful data in a historical study can be quite broad and varied.

Sources of data in a historical research study are classified as either primary or secondary sources. Primary sources include firsthand information, such as original documents and eye-witness observation reports. Secondary sources include secondhand information, such as encyclopedias or textbooks or reports by persons who were not actual participants or eye-witness observers. If you see an automobile crash on the highway, your description of it is a primary source. If you go home and tell your mother what you saw and she describes it to a newspaper reporter who had to talk with your mother because you were not home, her description is that of a secondary source. Similarly, a student who participated in the takeover of the president's office at Rowdy U. would be a primary source of data concerning the event; the student's roommate who was not in the president's office would be a secondary source. Primary sources are definitely preferred; in general, the further removed from the primary source the evidence is, the less comprehensive and accurate the resulting data. You may have played a party game, usually called *telephone,* that illustrates how the facts get twisted as a story is passed from person to person. The first person hears the "true" story and whispers it to the second person, who whispers it to the third person, and so on until finally the last person tells out loud the story he or she was told. There is generally a considerable discrepancy between the first and the last version: "Greg and Muffy were seen holding hands at Bigger Burger" may well end up as "Greg and Muffy were kicked out of Club Yuppee because of their behavior on the dance floor!"

Because primary sources are often more difficult to acquire, a common criticism of historical research is excessive reliance on secondary sources. It is better to select a "less grand" problem for which primary sources are available and accessible than to inadequately investigate the "problem of the year." Of course the further back in time the event under study occurred, the more likely it is that secondary sources may also have to be used. As a general rule, however, the more primary sources, the better.

The process of obtaining, reviewing, and abstracting data from primary and secondary sources is described in chapter 2, and includes assessing the source's relevancy to your topic; recording complete bibliographic information; coding the data from each source with respect to the areas of the study to which it relates; summarizing the pertinent information; and noting questions, comments, and quotations. Due to the nature of historical sources, several different note cards may be required for any one source. Also, one source may provide information for more than one aspect of the study. One critical aspect of historical sources is that they must be subjected to a careful analysis to determine both their authenticity and accuracy.

DATA ANALYSIS: EXTERNAL AND INTERNAL CRITICISM

Historical sources exist independently of your study; they were not written or developed for use in a research project. Thus, while they may very well serve the purpose for which they were created, they may not serve your purpose. Consider a letter, allegedly written by Albert Einstein, containing an expression of concern regarding the amount of physical punishment of students in schools. Even if the letter were determined to be authentic, that is, written by Einstein, unless it could be shown that Albert Einstein was a reliable source concerning educational practices of his day, his letter should not be used as evidence to support a position concerning widespread corporal punishment during his era.

All sources of historical data must be subjected to rigorous scientific analysis to determine both their authenticity (external criticism) and their accuracy (internal criticism). As with Aristotle and his fly with five legs, too often statements are uncritically accepted as factual statements if they are made by well-known persons. An authority in one area may have opinions about other areas, but they are not necessarily true or accurate. Similarly, the fact that records are "official" does not necessarily mean that all information contained in those records is accurate. A school board member, for example, might state that teachers are losing control of their classrooms. This would be an opinion, which would have to be put to the authenticity and accuracy tests. Thus, for each source of historical data, it must be determined whether it is authentic (was this letter really written by Albert Einstein?) and accurate (was Einstein in a position to provide such an observation?).

External criticism—establishment of authenticity—is generally not the problem in educational research. The researcher does not usually have to worry about possible hoaxes or forgeries; there is not a big market for forged school board minutes! If the researcher is dealing with a problem for which sources are relatively old, and for which authenticity is not necessarily a given, there are a number of scientific techniques available. Age of document or relic, for example, can be fairly accurately estimated by applying various physical and chemical tests. Rarely are historical researchers driven to this extreme, however.

Internal criticism—establishing the accuracy of the content of the source—is considerably more difficult to determine. In determining the accuracy of documents, for example, at least four factors must be considered:

1. *Knowledge and competence of the author.* It must be determined that the person who wrote the document is, or was, a competent person and in a position to be knowledgeable concerning what actually occurred.
2. *Time delay.* An important consideration is how much time is likely to have elapsed between the event's occurrence and the recording of the facts. As with observational and interview field notes, historical reports written while an event is occurring (such as minutes of meetings), or shortly after (such as entries in a diary), are more likely to be accurate

than reports written some time after, such as an anecdote in an autobiography.

3. *Bias and motives of the author*. People often report or record incorrect information. Such distortion of the truth may be intentional or unintentional. People, for example, tend to remember what they want to remember. People also tend to amplify, or add little details, in order to make a story more interesting. A more serious problem occurs when the recorder has motives for consciously or unconsciously misinterpreting the facts; accounts of the same event given by the plaintiff and the defendant on *The People's Court* often differ considerably.

4. *Consistency of data*. Each piece of evidence must be compared with all other pieces to determine the degree of agreement. If one observer's account disagrees with those of other observers, his or her testimony may be suspect. Thus, in a sense, by the very fact that they agree, sources may validate their accuracy.

Having reviewed, abstracted, and evaluated the data, the researcher then organizes and synthesizes the findings and prepares a research report.

DATA SYNTHESIS

As with a review of related literature, historical data should be organized, synthesized, and interpreted. As with other qualitative methods, analysis is based on the researcher's interpretations. Also, just as a review of literature should not be a series of annotations, a historical study should not be presented as a chronological listing of events. Critics of historical research question the researcher's interpretations based on events that can never be exactly duplicated. However, the interpretation problem is not unique to historical research, it is a critical aspect of qualitative research. For the qualitative researcher, the focus is on interpretation in a given context, event, or individual. Unique *understanding* is critical, not whether the *results* of the study generalize beyond the context, event, or individual studied.

Since integration of historical research data involves interpretive analysis rather than statistical analysis, the researcher must take care to avoid observer bias. It is very easy to overlook or to discard evidence that does not support, or that contradicts, the research's view. One may, for example, subconsciously apply stricter criteria to unwanted data when engaged in internal criticism. One way to avoid this is to adopt a caveat from the medical field; if in doubt, get a second opinion. From time to time even the most experienced experts in any field feel uncomfortable with a particular issue and find it helpful to seek out an unbiased and respected colleague just to say, "Take a look at this and tell me what you think."

You may realize by now that there is a lot more to historical research than getting a bunch of articles to describe. A historical research study contains many of the characteristics, processes, and difficulties encountered in other forms of qualitative research.

AN EXAMPLE OF HISTORICAL RESEARCH

Many beginning researchers tend to have a preconceived notion that historical research (and history in general) is really quite dull. As the example to be discussed will illustrate, nothing could be further from the truth. Conducting a historical study can be a very challenging, exciting pursuit. Many of the characteristics that would make one a good detective—such as a desire to collect reliable evidence and pursue clues—also make a good historical researcher. The following example is not presented as a model of historical research; by the researcher's own admission, it is based primarily on secondary sources, and it is of very little educational significance. It is presented because it does represent a fascinating area of research in which primary sources are hard to come by, or, as the researcher himself puts it, "It is fun to be in sort of scholarly disagreement in such a 'fun' area as this Dracula business . . ."[8]

Based on his experiences as a youth in Transylvania, his knowledge of the Romanian language, translations of court records, and other documentary evidence, Meder hypothesizes quite simply that Dracula was (is?!) a woman—"a beautiful, seductive, evil noblewoman of highest society. . . ."[9] As one piece of evidence, Meder cites the fact that "Dracula" translates into English literally as "the female devil." Further, there is a known historic figure, Countess Elizabeth Bathory of Transylvania, who in the 17th century was proven guilty in the highest court of the direct blood-ritual murders of more than 600 young girls. Convinced that the blood of beautiful young virgins was the key to eternal beauty and youth, the Countess would bathe in the warm blood drained from their main blood vessel. According to Meder, "scores of legal documents still exist in the Hungarian archives to attest to the truth of these blood orgies." Because of her high rank, she was only locked up in her bed-chamber where she was later found dead, lying face down on the floor, the characteristic position of the undead in the Dracula legend. Since nobody actually saw her die, and since the guard who found her only saw her lying face down, it is easy to see how stories could be originated suggesting that she did not really die, but rather escaped to continue her ghastly pursuits. As further evidence, Meder describes a painting titled Elizabeth Bathory, by István Csók, that seems to depict preparations for a blood bath. The female image of Dracula is also supported by another painting by Csók, titled The Vampires, showing a woman sucking blood from the neck artery of a young victim.

In his work, Meder also refutes the evidence presented by McNally and Florescu in *In Search of Dracula* identifying Dracula with a male Wallachian ruler who was known as Vlad the Impaler[10]. Meder questions not their evidence or its veracity, but rather its consistency with the Dracula legend. Regardless of who is correct, the question of Dracula's sex is, as Meder puts it, definitely a "fun" area of historical research[11].

An example of historical research is presented on the following pages. Note that the study was based on primary sources of data.

---

[8]Z. Meder. (personal communication, November 17, 1974)

[9]Meder, Z. *Dracula is a woman*. Manuscript in preparation. Note: When the first edition of this text was being written, Dr. Meder was contacted for additional information on his theory. During a lengthy visit, he was kind enough to share the picture of Elizabeth Bathory, which appears at the beginning of this chapter, and to discuss his work. He had spent his youth in Transylvania and, more recently, his summers. His goal was to spend an extended period of time there, collecting information related to his theory. Since then, attempts to contact him, in order to update this footnote and determine the status of his manuscript, have been futile. Letters sent to his last known address have been returned, and the university at which he taught claims no knowledge of his whereabouts. Honest.

[10]McNally, R. T., & Florescu, R. (1972). *In search of Dracula*. Greenwich, CT: New York Graphic Society.

[11]Following publication of an earlier edition of this text, it was discovered that in 1983 McGraw-Hill published a book titled *Dracula was a Woman*(!), written by R. T. McNally (!!), which includes the same information as the Meder manuscript. McNally (personal communication, June 21, 1990) claims no knowledge of Meder's existence or work. We swear, we're not making this up.

Summary/Chapter 6

Characteristics of Qualitative Research

1. There are a variety of qualitative approaches, including case studies, ethnography, phenomenology, historical research, ethology, and grounded theory. The differences among most of these approaches is the particulars of the social context they study.

2. The common features of qualitative research are a reliance on interpretation involving intensive field participation, rich data collected in the field, and the researcher as the primary synthesizing and interpretive agent of data analysis.

Qualitative Research Questions

3. Qualitative research is useful for describing particular, localized settings and for exploratory analyses. Understanding, not generalization, is the emphasis in qualitative research studies.

4. Qualitative research proposals are usually shorter than quantitative ones. Entry into the field is needed to define aspects of the study. Nonetheless, qualitative researchers should have at least a general idea of the topic and methods of their study.

Qualitative Research Structure

5. Five characteristics of qualitative research are: real-world setting for the study; descriptive not numerical data; holistic approach to the setting and participants; inductive data analysis, and an emphasis on the perspectives of the research participants.

Gaining Entrance

6. Gaining entry to the desired research setting usually requires obtaining permission from gatekeepers and acceptance by the potential participants.

7. Qualitative researchers should be prepared to answer the following questions in a general way to gatekeepers and potential participants: What is the purpose of your study? How much will your presence disrupt my setting and activities? What will you do with the findings? Why did you select us? and What do we get out of this?

Contacting Potential Research Participants

8. Meet potential participants face to face and explain what is expected of them and what protections you will provide them (e.g., anonymity, confidentiality, no reporting to supervisors). If selected, try to obtain a signed informed consent document.

Selecting Participants

9. Selection of participants is usually done with purposive sampling. Obtaining rapport with participants is essential to the tone of the study and the quality of the data collected. Enter the setting gradually.

Data Collection

10. There are many sources of qualitative data, including observation, interviews, artifacts, photographs, documents, drawings, and e-mails. Often multiple sources are used in a study.

Observation

11. Observation takes many forms and levels of interaction with participants, ranging from participant observer to covert observer. Covert observation is not recommended because its participants are not informed that they are being observed.

12. Although participant observers can gain insights from their contact with participants, they also may lose objectivity and become emotionally engaged with participants.

13. Field notes describe what the observer has heard, seen, experienced, and thought during an observation. Because field notes will

be the basis for data analysis, they must be detailed and descriptive, seeking to capture the reality of the setting and participants.

14. Field notes contain rich descriptions of what was observed and reflections of the researcher about what he or she has seen. The description and reflection sections should be separated. Both of these are important in data analysis.

15. Field notes should be written as soon as possible after the observation, and should include the date, time, site, and topics recorded. Number pages of the field notes to keep them in order.

16. Novice observers should use a structured, written protocol to guide and focus their observations. The protocol should be treated as a guide, not something to be slavishly followed.

INTERVIEWS

17. An interview is a purposive interaction between two or more persons, one trying to obtain information from the other. Interviews permit researchers to obtain information that cannot be obtained from observation, such as past events or participants' emotions.

18. Interviews vary in a number of ways: they can be focused on one or many interviewees, of varying length, structured or unstructured.

19. Generally, qualitative interviews are free flowing and open-ended, with the interviewer probing to clarify and extend the participant's comments. This interview format requires insight, tact, and timing to accomplish successfully. An important aspect of good interviewing is the interviewer's ability to "read" the interviewee. Inexperienced interviewers should have a general protocol of questions as a safety net.

20. Multiple-participant interviews are mainly useful for exploring ideas, topics, and perspectives of participants. Group interviews are commonly called focus groups.

21. It is difficult to simultaneously interview participants and record the data they provide, so use of recording devices during interviews is recommended. Tapes provide the researcher with a verbatim account of the interview.

22. It is expensive and time-consuming to transcribe interview recordings, especially long ones. Nonetheless, transcribing is strongly encouraged. Beginning researchers should keep their interviews relatively short.

23. The transcriptions of the interviews become the data that will be analyzed.

THREATS TO THE QUALITY OF OBSERVATIONS AND INTERVIEWS

24. There are two main threats to the validity of qualitative data: observer bias and observer effect.

25. Observer bias occurs when the perspective or beliefs of the researcher influences what he or she sees or hears while gathering data. It is probably true that no researcher can be totally unbiased about what he or she sees or hears, but the researcher should try as much as possible to avoid observer bias.

26. Observer effect occurs when the presence of the researcher leads participants to behave in an atypical manner. Qualitative researchers walk a fine line between being involved with participants and affecting or biasing what participants say or do.

ENHANCING VALIDITY AND REDUCING BIAS

27. A number of strategies can be used to improve validity and reduce bias. For example, the researcher can work hard to obtain participant trust and comfort, recognize his or her own biases, use verbatim observation and interview data, work with a co-researcher when collecting and reviewing data, and triangulate varied data sources.

LEAVING THE FIELD

28. Disengagement from the field and participants is not an easy task, either to decide when to leave or to actually leave. There are no simple rules to determine when to disengage, except when data collection becomes redundant. However, whenever one leaves the setting and participants, it may be helpful to "ease out" gradually.

Historical Research

29. Historical research is another common qualitative approach. Its emphasis is on a retrospective description and understanding of past people and events.

30. Many educational practices can be better understood by examination of their historical roots.

31. The steps in conducting historical research are similar to other forms of qualitative research: identify a topic or issue, collect data, organize the data, and produce an interpretive synthesis of the topic. In most cases, the historical researcher relies on documents, articles, photographs, artifacts, books, and the like for data collection. In some cases, however, interviews and tape recordings will be useful, as when a "living history" is obtained from live persons who have lived through an event.

32. Different researchers will have different views and interpretations of the same event or person. Although it is not expected that all researchers will similarly view a topic, it is expected that the researcher can provide evidence to support his or her interpretation.

33. Historical sources are classified into two categories. Primary sources include firsthand information, that is, eye-witness accounts of events or the author who had the original thought or approach. Secondary sources are secondhand, non-eye-witness accounts. Primary sources are more valued in historical research.

34. Historical data are examined for both its authenticity (external criticism) and for its accuracy (internal criticism). Authenticity is concerned with whether the data were actually authored by the stated author. For example, did Michelangelo really paint this picture, or was it painted by one of his assistants? Accuracy is concerned with whether the author was in a position to provide the data. For example, was Burke actually present in France at the time of the French Revolution, or was his description written in England based on newspaper articles? If the latter, a historical researcher would be suspicious of Burke's description and interpretation.

". . . no qualitative researcher can be amazing enough, brilliant enough, or experienced enough to observe and grasp *everything* of interest in a given setting (p. 237)."

Qualitative Research: Data Analysis

■ OBJECTIVES

After reading chapter 7, you should be able to:

1. Describe the purpose of qualitative research data analysis.
2. Describe six processes involved in analyzing, interpreting, and reporting qualitative data.
3. Indicate the role of field notes and transcriptions in data analysis.
4. State the role of categories in structuring qualitative data analysis.
5. State approaches to qualitative data analysis.
6. Describe the role of data analysis at various stages of the research process.
7. Distinguish between data analysis and data interpretation.
8. Identify guidelines that can provide information about the quality of the data analyzed.
9. Identify characteristics of a good qualitative research report.

PREPARING TO ANALYZE DATA

Analyzing qualitative data is a formidable task for all qualitative researchers, especially those just starting their qualitative careers. As a novice researcher you have followed the urgings of your qualitative mentors who have emphasized the need to collect rich, thick, and deep data that reveal the perspectives and understandings of the participants studied. And here you now stand (or sit), looking over piles of field notes, piles of verbatim interview transcriptions, or piles of both. Your data are not only rich and thick and deep, they are voluminous and unorganized. You face the task of bringing order to your data, of separating the wheat from the chaff among your field notes and transcripts. Unlike the quantitative researcher whose data produces numbers that can be organized and "crunched" in fairly routine ways, you must find your own, idiosyncratic path to the meaning of your data. However, it may be consoling to know that no qualitative researcher can be amazing enough, brilliant enough, or experienced enough to observe and grasp *everything* of interest in a given setting.

You must systematically search, categorize, integrate and interpret the data you have collected, and ultimately provide your own understandings of them. The process is lengthy and time-consuming, not only because the quantity of data to be analyzed is large, but also because the data typically are not organized in a manner that facilitates analysis. You must organize your data before you can begin to analyze and interpret them.

DATA ANALYSIS DURING DATA COLLECTION

Bogdan and Biklen[1] suggest a number of steps that can be accomplished during data collection that aid data analysis. For example, they recommend that during data collection the researcher try to progressively narrow the focus of what will be studied. As the researcher sees aspects of the setting and participants that are of interest, a focus to the study begins to emerge. Having such a focus is hugely beneficial in determining what data are important and what data are not. Also, having a focus to the study makes it possible to design data collection sessions that are built on prior sessions, thereby allowing the researcher to gather richer, more focused data for analysis. It also is important to reexamine the research topic to identify if and how it has changed during data collection.

Another of their suggestions is to write observer's comments, reflections, and memos during data collection. These also help organize and focus the data analysis. Bogdan and Biklen recommend that the literature begin to be explored after the researcher has been in the field for a while. Although this suggestion is not universally endorsed by all qualitative researchers, it is true that knowing what other researchers have found may help you conceptually and methodologically by guiding the direction of your data analysis. Finally, the use of metaphors, analogies, and visual devices can provide the researcher with alternative perspectives of the data collected. To make links between the data and more familiar analogies, ask yourself, "What does this remind me of?" or, "Is this activity like some other activity I'm familiar with?" Similarly, making charts, diagrams, or matrices is useful in identifying relations between or among topics of the data. The point is to use strategies in the data collection process to help you focus and think about aspects of the data analysis process.

Notice that following the steps recommended during data collection implies that the researcher is doing more than just collecting data. The process of data collection, either by observation or interview, interacts with the processes of data interpretation and analysis. It is difficult, if not impossible, for researchers to completely divorce data collection from data interpretation and analysis. And they should not. Data analysis begins with data collection. The fact that researchers write memos to themselves demonstrates that they are thinking about what the data mean or how they relate to one another. Further, a researcher observing a group interaction or listening to a participant's responses to interview questions cannot help but form opinions, interpret activities, and identify patterns. Whether done consciously or unconsciously, the researcher will inevitably bring perceptions, interpretations, and viewpoints from the data collection process to the data analysis process. So, analysis does not begin when data collection finishes; it goes on during data collection. In qualitative research, data collection and data analysis are intertwined, iterative processes.[2] This is an important characteristic of qualitative research.

DATA ANALYSIS AFTER DATA COLLECTION

After the data have been collected, the "romance" of field research is over and the difficult task of data analysis and interpretation begins. Guided by insights

[1]Bogdan, R. C. and Biklen, S. K. (1998). *Qualitative research for education*. Needham Heights, MA: Allyn and Bacon.

[2]Wolcott, H. F. (1994). *Transforming qualitative data*. Thousand Oaks, CA: Sage.

gained during data collection, data analysis is concerned with describing what is in the data. Interpretation is concerned with making sense of what the descriptions mean. Data analysis and interpretation are based on induction; the researcher discovers patterns that emerge from the data and makes sense of them. There are no predefined variables to focus analysis, as there are in quantitative research. The qualitative researcher identifies his or her own variables from examination of the field notes or interview transcripts.

An immediate problem that faces the qualitative researcher is the lack of agreed-upon approaches to analyzing qualitative data. There are some guidelines and general strategies for analysis, but few specific rules for their application. Thus, once data are collected, the qualitative researcher undertakes a multistaged process of organizing, categorizing, synthesizing, interpreting, and writing about the data. Each of these processes is iterative; in most cases the researcher will cycle through the stages more than once, in a continual effort to narrow and make sense of what he or she sees in the data.

ANALYZING QUALITATIVE RESEARCH DATA

This chapter describes steps for analyzing qualitative data: data managing, reading/memoing, describing, classifying, interpreting, and representing the findings in a written report.[3] Although these steps are not exhaustive of the many qualitative research approaches, they are used in most qualitative approaches.

Bearing in mind that data analysis takes place simultaneously with data collection, the first step in data analysis is managing the data so they can be studied. Once the data are organized, data analysis begins in earnest. The researcher cannot interpret data until the data are broken down and classified in some way, so the analysis itself requires four iterative steps: reading/memoing, describing, classifying, and interpreting. This cyclical process focuses on (1) becoming familiar with the data and identifying main themes in it (reading/memoing); (2) examining the data in depth to provide detailed descriptions of the setting, participants, and activities (describing); (3) categorizing and coding pieces of data and physically grouping them into themes (classifying); and (4) interpreting and synthesizing the organized data into general conclusions or understandings (interpreting). Figure 7.1 lists the four data analysis processes and the relationships among them.

Figure 7.1 shows that the interrelationships among reading/memoing, describing, classifying, and interpreting are not necessarily linear. At the start of data analysis, the logical sequence of activities is from reading/memoing to description, to classifying, to interpretation. However, as the researcher begins to internalize and reflect on the data, the initial ordered sequence loses its structure and becomes less predictable. For example, describing may lead to interpretation without the intermediate step of classifying. Or, interpretation may lead to reclassifying some areas. If you've ever been driving home pondering some issue or problem you've not solved and have had a sudden flash of understanding that provides a solution, you have a sense of how qualitative data analysis takes place. Once into the data, it is not the four steps that lead to understanding and

---

[3]Creswell, J. W. (1998). *Qualitative inquiry and research design*. Thousand Oaks, CA: Sage.

FIGURE	7.1

The Integration of Qualitative Data

4 steps in analyzing data

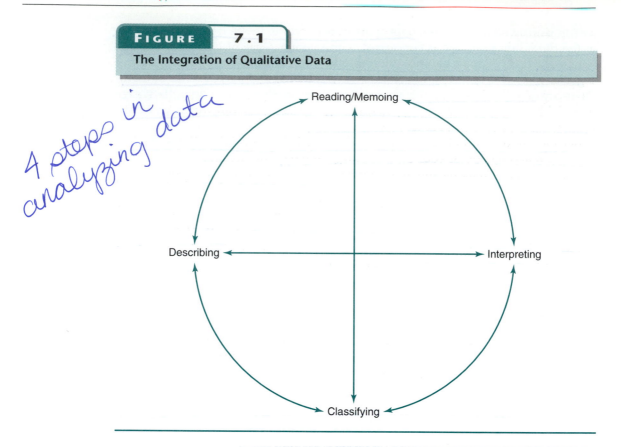

interpretation, it is the researcher's ability to think, imagine, hypothesize, and analyze that prods the data analysis. Knowing the steps is not enough; the thinker, imaginer, hypothesizer, and analyzer—that is, the researcher—is the data interpreter, and the quality of the analysis and interpretation depends heavily on the intellectual qualities he or she brings to the research. Said in more blunt terms, if you are unable to integrate, analyze, and interpret, you will find the inductive nature of qualitative research difficult to master and frustrating to pursue.

Let us be very clear about the process being discussed. It is a process of digesting the contents of qualitative data and finding common threads in it. You will not meaningfully accomplish these tasks with one or two or three readings of your data. To make the kinds of connections you need to analyze and interpret qualitative data, you must know your data—really know and live it, in your head, not just on paper. Thus, the process of data analysis and interpretation can be tedious, time consuming, and necessarily iterative. With this proviso in mind, we can discuss actions that help organize and interpret qualitative data, always bearing in mind that the insights and qualities of the researcher are the main influence on the quality of the study.

DATA MANAGING

Data managing involves creating and organizing the data collected during the study. Try to envision what the data from an observation or interview study looks like. Piles of field notes or transcripts and numerous computer files await order and organization. Before you can begin the process of interpreting the data, you must put the data in a form that will facilitate analysis. For example, you might need to "tidy up" the data you have collected to make sure that you have dated, organized, and sequenced all field notes, transcripts, observer's comments, memos, and reflections. You can also organize your computer files and create separate folders for different data types and stages of analysis. You would probably want to make copies of your field notes and transcripts so that you can mark or underline important sections or cross out unneeded ones while still retaining a clean, unmarked copy of your precious original data. Put one unmarked copy in a really safe place, making sure that *all* the data are there. It is also useful to make backup copies of the computer files containing your data in the event that you lose some data by mistake. You may also read through the data and note tentative issues or activities that relate to your research topic. Arranging the data so that it can be easily managed and "milked" is an important first step in analysis.

There are two main purposes for data managing. The first is to organize the data and check it for completeness. The second is to start the researcher on the process of analyzing and interpreting the data. In organizing the data the researcher also examines observer's comments, memos, notes and the like that were made on the field notes or interview transcripts. The researcher also begins the initial questioning of the data by noting themes, patterns, regularities, and issues that have previously emerged or that currently attract his or her attention. At this early stage, data questioning is general and rudimentary. A more detailed analysis is needed to uncover the meaning of the data.

READING/MEMOING

The first step in analysis is reading/memoing; reading the field notes, transcripts, memos, and observer comments to get a sense of your data. Find a quiet place and plan on reading for a few hours at a time during the initial reading of the data. Krathwohl[4] wisely points out that "the first time you sit down to read your data is the only time you come to that particular set fresh." It is important that you write notes in the margins or underline sections or issues that seem important to you so that you will have a record of your initial thoughts and sense of the data. You might find that many of these early impressions will not be useful once you are deeper into analysis, but you will also find some initial impressions that do hold up through analysis. In addition to recording initial impressions from the data, at this stage of analysis you also will begin the search for themes or common threads that reoccur throughout the notes.

DESCRIPTION

Description addresses this issue: What is going on in this setting and among these participants? It is based on the observations and field notes collected by the qualitative researcher. The aim is to provide a true picture of the settings and events that took place in it so the researcher and the reader will have an understanding of the context in which the study took place. Description is often held in less esteem than analytical or theoretical aspects of research, but in qualitative research

---

[4]Krathwohl, D. R. (1998). *Methods of educational and social science research.* New York: Longmans, (p. 309).

description is an integral and important aspect. Early in the analysis process, the researcher develops thorough and comprehensive descriptions of the phenomena studied. Such description is often called *thick* or *thorough* description, to contrast it to *thin* description that only contains facts. Description focuses on painting a verbal picture of the context, processes, and the world as viewed from the participants' perspective.

Attention to features of the research context is a common and important theme in qualitative research, because the context influences participants' actions and understandings. Meaning is influenced by context; without a thorough description of the context, actions, and interactions of participants real interpretation is hampered. Another important concern of qualitative researchers is portraying the views of the participants. How participants define situations and explain their actions are important to describe thoroughly. Finally, ongoing descriptions of the interactions and social relations among the participants is important because social processes can change over time. Thus, the focus of description is on social and contextual conditions and consequences. The descriptions of the research context, meanings, and social relations can be presented in a number of forms. Among the possibilities are chronological ordering of setting and events, description of a typical "day in the life" of participants in the setting, emphasizing key contextual episodes, and illuminating different perspectives of participants.

Description also leads to the separation and grouping of pieces of data related to different aspects of the setting, events, and participants. As Dey[5] notes,

> One distinctive feature of description is its integrative function. By summarizing data, for example, we strip away unnecessary detail and delineate more clearly the more central characteristics of the data. Moreover, it is in pulling together and relating these central characteristics through a reasoned account that description acquires its unity and force.

Description enhances and leads to classifying the data.

CLASSIFYING

Qualitative data analysis is basically a process of breaking down the data into smaller units, determining the import of these units, and putting the units together again in an interpreted form. The typical way qualitative data are broken down and organized is through the process of classifying, which means ordering field notes or transcriptions into categories that represent different aspects of the data. A category is a classification of ideas or concepts. When concepts in the data are examined and compared to one another and connections are made, categories are formed. Categories are used to organize similar concepts into separate groups. Note, also, that lower-level categories can themselves be organized into even higher, more abstract conceptual categories.

To get a feel for the nature of classification, imagine you are in a large room that contains hundreds and hundreds of books. Your task is to organize the books into categories that differentiate among the many characteristics (concepts) of the books. Think about some possible categories that can be used to differentiate among book characteristics. With that thought, you probably would identify cat-

---

[5]Dey, I. (1993). *Qualitative data analysis*. New York: Routledge, (p. 39).

egories of fiction and nonfiction, categories for each of the various book publishers, categories for the length of books, categories for the age of books, categories for children and adult books, and so on.

But did you identify categories for male and female authors, for the print type used in the books, or for the cities in which they were published? Probably not, which points out the fact that there are many, many ways to categorize books. Now consider qualitative data and think of the potential categories that can be identified from, say, 20 observations or 20 interviews. The researcher's task is to choose categories that will help make sense out of the collected data. Without data that are classified, there is no feasible way to analyze the qualitative data, because the categories provide the basis for structuring analysis and interpretation. Are you beginning to get a sense of the meaning of *interpretive research*? Think of completing a 1,000-piece jigsaw puzzle.

However, unlike the jigsaw puzzle, the categories you identify to organize your data would not necessarily be the same ones another researcher would identify. There is no one correct way to organize the data. There are many reasons why different researchers would not produce the same categories from the same data. Among these are researcher biases, interests, style, and interpretive focus. Another important reason for variations among researchers is the different research topics they pursue. Clearly, the topic or focus of the study should have a major effect on categories chosen and categories ignored. This is one reason why having a clear study topic or focus is useful in data analysis.

Three strategies are used to analyze qualitative data: constant comparison, negative case analysis, and analytic induction.[6] Each is important in making comparisons among the data for the purpose of identifying and categorizing concepts related to the research categories and patterns. The **constant comparison method** involves the constant comparison of identified topics and concepts to determine their distinctive characteristics so they can be placed in appropriate categories. Throughout the study the researcher is involved in making constant comparisons. As each new topic or concept is identified, it is compared to existing categories. The researcher asks "Is this topic or concept similar to or different from existing categories?" Categories are modified as needed to fit new data and are further tested by additional new data. New categories might be defined. Categories can be compared to develop more general patterns of data. The aim of the constant comparative method is to understand and explain the qualitative data.

Negative case and discrepant data methods are, as the names suggest, based on the search for data that are negative or discrepant from the main data collected in a study. A negative case is one that contradicts an emerging category or pattern and a discrepant case is one that provides a variant perspective on an emerging category or pattern. It is often easy for a researcher (any researcher) to adopt or cling to an initial hypothesis or hunch and fail to examine counter evidence that might negate or weaken the hypothesis or hunch. The search for negative and discrepant data provides an important counterbalance to the researcher's tendency to stick with first impressions or hunches.

Although the constant comparative, negative case, and discrepant data methods are typically iterative processes carried out during data collection and analysis, **analytic induction** is a process concerned with the development and test of a theory. It is aimed at the generalizability of a study. It starts with a preliminary

---

[6]Strauss, A. & Corbin, J. (1990). *Basics of qualitative research.* Newbury Park, CA: Sage.

hypothesis or explanation of a phenomenon being studied. For example, early in a study of teachers' perspective on merit pay, the researcher may hypothesize that teachers who do not receive merit pay are those who have little allegiance to their school and students. A hypothetical explanation of the hypothesis is formed. For example, *lack of merit pay angers teachers and their anger is taken out on the school and students.* Given this hypothesis, data are gathered to test it. If the hypothesis is upheld, more data are gathered to determine whether the hypothesis is still upheld. If the initial hypothesis is not upheld, it is reformulated based on the contrary evidence. For example, *lack of merit pay does not make teachers angry, it lowers their self-esteem and this is translated into teachers distancing themselves from the school and students.* Data are then gathered to examine the revised hypothesis. The process continues with the refining of the hypothesis until there are no examples of the revised hypothesis not being upheld. However, one failure to uphold requires additional revision. This process is very rigorous, but the hypothesis ultimately arrived at will generally be quite generalizable. The constant comparative, negative/discrepant case, and analytic induction are commonly used qualitative data analysis methods.

Where do categories come from? One answer is from commonly used, predefined categories. For example, Miles and Huberman[7] suggest the use of these categories to order data: participant acts, activities, participant meanings, relationships among participants, and setting. Bogdan and Biklen[8] recommend the use of categories such as research setting, perspectives of participants, participants' ways of thinking, regularly occurring activities, infrequently occurring activities, and methods. Clearly these categories could be subdivided into narrower categories. In fact, the researcher might start with Miles and Huberman's or Bogdan and Biklen's general categories and put as many pieces of data as will fit into the selected general categories and then, in succeeding iterations, break down the contents of the more general categories into more specific and narrower categories. For example, "participant acts" could be subdivided into "group acts" and "individual acts." Or, "regularly occurring activities" could be subdivided into "teacher regularities," "student regularities," and "joint regularities." Categories can also be defined by the researcher, based on the focus of his or her study, the data that were collected, and other guides such as observation or interview protocols. Obviously, categories can also be defined by a combination of predefined and researcher-defined categories. Note, also, that relying on predefined categories may increase substantially the likelihood that researchers will overload or miss important categories in their data. In the end, these decisions are guided by theory, that is, the perspectives of the researcher or participants.

For example, consider Table 7.1, which shows a portion of a researcher's field notes obtained during an observation. Two aspects of the field notes stand out: (1) some sections are underlined or bracketed, and (2) brief labels in the margins are linked to each underlined or bracketed section. The underlined/bracketed sections are individual pieces of data from the field session. Similar individual data pieces can and must be identified in all qualitative data. The marginal labels are categories or topics; that is, they are more general placeholders for organizing

[7]Miles, M. B. and Huberman, A. M. (1994). *Qualitative data analysis: An expanded sourcebook.* Thousand Oaks, CA: Sage, (p. 51).

[8]Bogdan, R. C. and Biklen, S. K. (1998). *Qualitative research in education.* Needham Heights, MA: Allyn and Bacon, (pp. 172–177).

> | **TABLE** | **7.1** |
>
> **Coded Field Notes**

Field Notes
Vista City Elementary School Teachers' Lounge
February 3, 1981

teachers' work

Then I went down to the teachers' lounge to see if anybody might happen to be there. I was in luck. Jill Martin sat at the first table, correcting papers; Kathy Thomas was also there, walking around and smoking. I said, "Hi Jill, hi Kathy. Okay if I join you?" "Sure," Jill said. "You and your husband have been to China, right?" I said, "Yes. Why?" Jill then turned to Kathy and said, "Have you studied China yet? Sari has slides that she can show." Kathy said

authority

to me that she was going to study world communities, even though "they" had taken them out of the sixth-grade social studies curriculum. "Now can you tell me who 'they' are?" I asked her. She said, "You know, 'them': 'they.'"

autonomy

Both Jill and Kathy were upset at how they had mandated what the teachers could teach in their rooms. "They" turned out to be the central office who had communicated the state's revised sixth-grade social studies curriculum. The state has "taken out all the things that we think are important" from the curriculum and have substituted the theme of "economic geography" for the sixth-graders to study.

doing your own thing

Both Jill and Kathy think that "sixth-graders can't comprehend economic geography well," and think world communities of Africa and Asia are more important. They said they planned to teach what they wanted to anyway. Kathy said, "They'll come around one of these days." "Oh, Kathy, are you a rebel?" I asked. "No," she replied, "I'm just doing my own thing."

parents

After we chatted for a little while, Jill turned to me: "You're interested in what concerns us. I guess one thing is parents." She proceeded to describe a parent conference she had participated in yesterday afternoon with a child's parents and a

parents

child's psychiatrist. She said, "What really upsets me is how much responsibility they placed on me to change the child's behavior." They seemed to give lip service, she reported, to have "controls" come from the child when they said, "It's so difficult for parents to see that kids need to take responsibility for their actions."

Source: From R. C. Bogdan and S. K. Biklen, *Qualitative Research for Education: An Introduction to Theory and Methods*, 3/e. © 1998 by Allyn & Bacon. Reproduced by permission.

and accumulating related data pieces. Thus, the data piece *correcting papers* would fit into a more general category called "teachers' work." Other data pieces related to teachers' work (e.g., writing lesson plans, dealing with parents) found in other field notes would also be placed in that category. Two different data pieces related to parents were identified in the last section of the field notes.

How were these data pieces and categories identified? What is the process that uncovers the important data pieces and categories from among all the possible data pieces and categories that could be derived from a set of field notes or transcripts? The answer is that there are a number of ways and strategies for dissecting and reorganizing the data. For example, the topic or focus of the study can provide initial ideas about relevant data pieces and more general categories. Thus, the researcher in Table 7.1 might have been interested in the activities of teachers and thus identified the categories shown before analysis actually began. He or she would then scour the data trying to find examples in the field notes that fit into the previously identified categories. In this case, the categories precede the data pieces. Alternatively, while reading through a few of the field notes, the researcher in Table 7.1 might have encountered some themes or common issues that cut across the field notes. For example, the researcher might have noted that various kinds of teachers' work as well as comments about parents occurred in a number of the field notes. From these common multiple data pieces, general descriptive categories (e.g., teachers' work and parents) could be identified. In this case, the field notes preceded the categories. Categories can also be identified as a result of observer's comments or memos. For example, a researcher's memo regarding the number of discipline events teachers referred to in their transcription could suggest the need for a category for discipline. Reflections, anomalies, and commonalities noted during data analysis may also lead to useful categories. Finally, any mix of these approaches may also guide data organization.

> Probably the most fundamental operation in the analysis of qualitative data is that of discovering significant *classes* of things, persons, and events and the *properties* which characterize them. In this process, which continues throughout the research, the analyst gradually comes to reveal his own "is's" and "because's": he names classes and links one with another, at first with "simple" statements (propositions) that express the linkages, and continues this process until his propositions fall into sets, in an ever-increasing density of linkages.[9]

The development and verification of categories is not done with a single reading of the data. The quantity and complexity of qualitative data require more than one pass through the data. In fact, one strategy that is useful for both learning one's data and verifying the usefulness of potential categories is to stagger the reading of field notes and transcripts. For example, a portion of the field notes or transcripts, perhaps one quarter, are read carefully. If a preexisting set of categories is available, the researcher can try to classify data pieces from the selected field notes or transcripts into the categories. If some data pieces cannot be classified into the preexisting categories, additional ones likely should be added. If some categories are empty, the possibility of eliminating those categories can be considered. If there are no preexisting categories, the researcher can read a portion of the field notes or transcripts and identify tentative categories based on the data examined.

The categories identified from either of these approaches should be considered provisional. One should not become overly attached to initial categories until they have been tested more rigorously. For example, one approach to sharpen and validate categories is to apply the categories derived from the first quarter of the data to the second quarter of the data. Do the initial categories hold up? Can one classify all data pieces in these categories? Are additional categories

[9]Schatzman, L. & Strauss, A. (1973). *Field research*. Englewood Cliffs, NJ: Prentice Hall, (p. 110).

needed? Is one category so broad that it should be divided into two categories instead of one? As noted, the process of data analysis is iterative.

Even when one has continued to refine and validate the categories by using them to examine additional data, the categorization task may not be completed. If you have identified 60 categories, you probably should winnow the 60 down to 10 or 20. Too many categories, especially for beginning qualitative researchers, often make data analysis and description difficult, time consuming, and superficial. Ask questions such as: Can two or more categories be collapsed into one? Are some categories secondary to the main focus of the study? Is the category with only three data pieces really needed? A great deal of data are generated in qualitative research; focusing on the most important data is sometimes difficult, but is very important. It may even be useful to reread the field notes or transcripts to make sure important data were not overlooked and that you are still "comfortable" with your categories upon another reading.

We have seen that categories help organize data and that identifying and inferring the categories that best represent the data can take multiple examinations of the data. We have also seen that categories can be identified before or after data analysis. In the end, the aim is to analyze data into a pyramid with at least three levels: data pieces, categories, and patterns. At each level, the pyramid narrows, signifying more integration and abstraction of the qualitative data. Just as some data pieces can be subsumed into categories, so too can some categories or data pieces with a category be subsumed into patterns. Patterns are links among categories that further integrate the data and usually become the primary basis for organizing and reporting the outcomes of the study. Figure 7.2 shows a simple form of a data pyramid, relating features of schools into a narrowing organization. Theoretically, there is no limit to the levels of data classification, but three to five levels should be the goal of beginning qualitative researchers.

Patterns are identified in the same way pieces of data are organized into categories—the researcher seeks and finds connections among the categories. There is, of course, no guarantee that there will be patterns to be induced from the categories, but seeking relations among activities, time usage, or links among categories can help focus the search for patterns. For example, Figure 7.2 shows a pattern linking the nature of instructional materials and the characteristics of students as they relate to instructional activities. Also, parent–teacher interactions are often linked to teachers' assessments and parents' reactions to them.

How long should data analysis of this type go on? Frankly, it's hard to say, since the analysis depends on the nature of the study, the amount of data collected, and the analytic and synthetic abilities of the researcher. The qualitative researcher must both deconstruct the field notes or transcriptions into data pieces and then reconstruct them into meaningful and relevant data categories and patterns. The ability of the researcher to induce or construct meaning from the data greatly influences the duration and quality of the data analysis. Qualitative data analysis typically requires substantially more time to complete than quantitative data analysis.

Using Computers in Qualitative Data Analysis

Many computer programs for both the Mac and PC are available to aid in the analysis of qualitative data. Although programs differ in the features they provide, there are a number of common features that one can expect when using al-

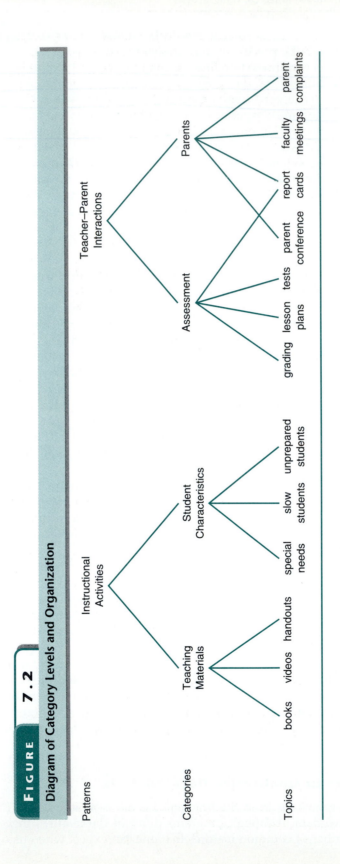

FIGURE 7.2

Diagram of Category Levels and Organization

Patterns

Instructional
Activities

Teacher–Parent
Interactions

Categories

Teaching
Materials

Student
Characteristics

Assessment

Parents

Topics

books

videos

handouts

special
needs

slow
students

unprepared
students

grading

lesson
plans

tests

parent
conference

report
cards

faculty
meetings

parent
complaints

most any qualitative data analysis program. See Weitzman and Miles[10] and Kelle[11] for reviews of the many qualitative analysis programs available.

Most qualitative analysis programs provide the following capabilities:

- storing and organizing data files and text
- inputting data and diagrams from word processors
- creating an index system for data
- searching for words, phrases, or categories
- organizing data by categories or patterns
- producing counts of words and phrases
- constructing data diagrams
- displaying information about aspects of the study

There are some drawbacks to using computers for qualitative analyses. For example, the researcher must learn how to use the program. The more features the program provides, the longer it will take to master it. Programs differ in their features. Most programs provide little help with the interpretive process of analyzing data, although their search capabilities can be a useful prod to researcher interpretation. However, the main drawback of computer analyses is that they diminish the likelihood of the researcher's reexamination of the data set once the computer-generated organization is produced. A fundamental aspect of qualitative research is frequent reexamination of the entire data set. Thus, the programs do support data analysis, but they cannot do everything for the researcher. The important interpretive judgments inherent in qualitative research studies must be made by the researcher

Table 7.2 shows the use of one popular qualitative data analysis program, NUD-IST,[12] for helping the researcher to analyze and write qualitative data. In reviewing this table, note that the use of the term *node* is equivalent to the term *category*. As can be seen in Table 7.2, the primary benefit of the use of a computer program it its ability to organize and structure analysis and writing. This ability can be exceptionally helpful to the researcher, but, as noted, does not eliminate the researcher's need to interpret and make decisions about both the data and what to write about the data.

INTERPRETING

What you cannot explain to others, you do not understand yourself. Producing an account of our analysis is not just something we do for an audience. It is also something we do for ourselves. Producing an account is not just a question of reporting results; it is also another method of producing these results. Through the challenge of explaining ourselves to others, we can help to clarify and integrate the concepts and relationships we have identified in our analysis.[13]

These comments contain a number of important insights about data analysis, interpretation, and writing. Dey emphasizes the need to understand one's data as

---

[10]Weitzman, E. A. and Miles, M. B. (1995). *Computer programs for qualitative data analysis*. Thousand Oaks, CA: Sage.

[11]Kelle, E. (ed.). (1995). *Computer-aided qualitative analysis*. Thousand Oaks, CA: Sage.

[12]Scolari Software. (1997). Thousand Oaks, CA: Sage

[13]Dey, I. (1993). *Qualitative data analysis*. New York: Routledge, (p. 237).

TABLE	7.2

Data Analysis Elements, Writing Objectives, and NUD-IST Procedures

DATA ANALYSIS ELEMENT	WRITING OBJECTIVE	NUD-IST PROCEDURE
Create a template for analysis	Develop a visual of data analysis plan	Create a tree of steps in analysis into which data segments are placed
Create headings in the manuscript for major themes	Create four or five major themes in the study in words of participants	Create a node for each heading and put text that applies into the node
Title the manuscript	Create a title in the words of the participants—to make report realistic, to catch attention of readers	Create a node based on short phrases found in the text; create alternative titles in this node as they appear in analyzing the texts
Include quotes in the manuscript	Identify good quotes that provide sound evidence for the themes, description, interpretation, and so forth	Create a general node and place all good quotes in that node; create a node for quotes under each theme or category of information
Phrase study in words of participants	Locate commonly used words or phrases and develop them into themes	Use word search procedure, string or pattern search, and place contents into a node; spread text around the word (or phrase) to capture the context of the word (or phrase)
Create a comparison table	Compare categories of information	Use matrix feature of program
Show levels of abstraction in the analysis	Present a visual of the categories in the analysis	Present the "tree" diagram
Discuss metaphors	Find text in which metaphors are presented and group into categories	Set up one node for metaphors with children of different types of metaphors; place text in nodes by types of metaphors

Source: Creswell, J. (1998). *Qualitative inquiry and research design: Choosing among five traditions*. Thousand Oaks, CA: Sage Publications, p. 162. Copyright 1998 Sage Publications. Reprinted by permission of Sage Publications, Inc.

a prerequisite to describing it to others. He notes that data interpretation continues on after the data collection, analysis, and interpretive stages of a study; interpretation is also a part of the process of writing the results of the study. Dey reminds us that explaining ourselves to others is an excellent way to clarify and integrate for ourselves. Interpreting is the reflective, integrative, and explanatory aspect of dealing with a study's data. At this stage the question is not, "What is in the data?" but rather, "What are the meanings in the data?"

Data interpretation is based heavily on the connections, common aspects, and linkages among the data, especially the identified categories and patterns. One cannot classify data into categories without thinking about the meaning of the categories. Thus, implicitly or explicitly, the researcher is interpreting data whenever he or she uses some conceptual basis or understanding to cluster a variety of data pieces into a category. To aid interpretation, it is important to make explicit what the conceptual bases or understandings of the categories are and what makes one category different from another. Thus, interpretation requires more conceptual and integrative thinking than data analysis, since interpretation involves identifying and abstracting important understandings from the detail and complexity of the data.

All researchers, but qualitative researchers in particular, must face the prospect of not reporting all of the data they have collected in the analysis. This is a difficult reality for any researcher, but more so for qualitative researchers because of the time and effort it typically takes them to obtain their data. Nonetheless, if only to make analysis and reporting manageable, data must be examined for relevance and deleted if necessary. Rarely is every piece of data incorporated into the interpretation and report of a study. Remember, the task of interpreting data is to identify the important themes or meanings in the data. The search is for clarity and the essential features of the data. It is those features and meanings that should be focused on, not only because they are the most meaningful, but also because trying to interpret and integrate every piece of data will ultimately detract from the major, more important interpretations.

It is also important to note that the nature of the qualitative research employed in a study provides a strong influence on what areas of interpretation the study will emphasize. For example, if the study is an ethnography, interpretation will focus on the cultural patterns and perspectives of the participants. If the study is a case study, interpretation will focus on the characteristics of a single person or group. If the study is phenomenologic, the focus will be on how individuals experienced a given phenomenon. Thus, as noted earlier in this chapter, the processes used among many qualitative approaches are quite similar, but the focuses of the studies vary.

Regardless of the research approach, the implicit issue in data interpretation is the answer to these questions: "What is important in the data; why is it important; and what can be learned from it?" The researcher's task, then, is to determine how one identifies what is important, why it is important, and what it indicates about the participants and context studied. As we have stated numerous times in this and the prior chapter, the process for answering these questions is to a large extent idiosyncratic. Interpretation is personal. Thus, the process is difficult to teach because there are no hard and fast rules for how to go about the task of interpreting the meaning of the data. It is, as in most qualitative studies, dependent upon the perspective and interpretive abilities of the researcher.

There are, however, some strategies that can help guide data interpretation. For example, pay attention to your topic or research focus; it should guide you when selecting important portions of your data for interpretation. Examine closely categories that contain large amounts of data; they are likely to identify important concepts or practices for interpretation. Also, because they contain a great deal of data, look within the categories for links or sequences. Patterns represent the highest level of data integration, so identify the interrelations between the categories that are linked to a pattern. What do the links suggest? How do they relate to one another? What meaning do they have for the study's topic? A similar search for interpretations can involve the data pieces that link to a particular category. Also, examining existing studies related to your topic may identify interpretations pertinent to your study, although a danger of this practice is over-reliance on others' interpretations. Talk with colleagues or co-investigators about the data and its meaning, focusing on discussion of areas of agreement and disagreement. Finally, step back from the data every now and then to give yourself time to reflect on what you've seen and thought about the data. All of these strategies are merely suggestions that may help in deriving interpretations from the data. In the end, these or other approaches to making sense of the data will only be as successful as the researcher's interpretive and integrative skills.

At this point we must stop for a caveat. Throughout this chapter the centrality of the researcher as the integrator and interpreter of data has been emphasized. You might infer that this emphasis means that researchers have carte blanche when analyzing and interpreting data; that is, they can rely strictly on their feelings or preferences when analyzing and interpreting data. This is definitely not the case. If qualitative research were based solely on producing unsubstantiated opinions, ignoring data that did not confirm the researcher's expectations, and failing to examine biases of research participants, it would be of little value. Thus, while researchers do have substantial control over data analysis and interpretations, that control should be exercised within guidelines.

For example, Dey[14] identifies six questions intended to help researchers check the quality of their data:

- Are the data based on one's own observation, or is it hearsay?
- Is there corroboration by others of one's observation?
- In what circumstances was an observation made or reported?
- How reliable are those providing the data?
- What motivations might have influenced a participant's report?
- What biases might have influenced how an observation was made or reported?

Triangulation is another important and powerful approach used to establish the credibility of a qualitative research study. Triangulation is a form of cross-validation that seeks regularities in the data by comparing different participants, settings, and methods to identify recurring results. The aim is to obtain similar information from different independent sources. Denzin[15] identified three types of triangulation: (1) comparing multiple sources of data across participants, times, and sites; (2) comparing the results of multiple independent investigators; and (3) comparing multiple methods of data analysis. Other approaches to triangulation include observing participants' consistency in different situations or comparing participants' consistency in their verbal statements and actual performance. In each case, the ability to produce similar results from different times or methods enhances the credibility of the data.

A number of researchers have attempted to identify criteria suitable for qualitative data analysis (Lincoln and Guba,[16] Marshall and Rossman,[17] Miles and Huberman[18]). One criterion is *credibility* or *plausibility*, which is to demonstrate that the inquiry was conducted in such a manner as to ensure that the subject was accurately identified and described. Credibility can be attained by demonstrating that the concepts used to describe the study are congruent with the data selected to gather information about the concepts. For example, if the purpose of a study was to examine perceptions of participants' social justice in a community college, credibility would be demonstrated by showing that the data gathered matched the researcher's definition of social justice. Credibility also may be attained by eliminating rival explanations of the data and by showing that the study results

---

[14]Dey, I. (1993). *Qualitative data analysis*. New York: Routledge, (p. 224).

[15]Denzin, N. (1978). *The research act*. Newbury Park, CA: Sage

[16]Lincoln, Y. S. and Guba, E. G. (1985). *Naturalistic inquiry*. Beverly Hills, CA: Sage.

[17]Marshall, C. and Rossman, G. (1995). *Designing qualitative research*. Thousand Oaks, CA: Sage.

[18]Miles, M. B. and Huberman, A. M. (1994). *Qualitative data analysis: An expanded source book*. Thousand Oaks, CA: Sage.

are similar to other, similar studies. Of course, triangulation is a paramount approach to qualitative research credibility.

A second criterion is *transferability*, which is concerned with transferring or generalizing the results of a study to other contexts. Transferability may relate to demonstrating that the results generalize to others in the original research context or to contexts beyond the original study. Recognize, however, that many qualitative researchers have no desire to generalize beyond the research setting, not feeling the necessity to leap beyond the initial study. In multisite qualitative studies, generalization may be an important intent.

A third criterion is *including a methods section* that describes in-depth the processes and methods used in the study. This criterion is commonly required of quantitative studies and is beginning to be recognized as an important aspect of qualitative research. In order to judge the credibility, transferability, and conclusions of a research study, it is important to know the methods applied to collect and interpret data. Without this information, it is difficult to judge the quality of the study and the meaningfulness of the results. For example, without information of how participants were selected, why particular data collection methods were chosen, how and how much data were collected, and how data were organized and analyzed, it is difficult to judge the quality and usefulness of the reported results. Thus, while data analysis and interpretation are heavily determined by the researcher, there are criteria that researchers should respect and respond to in conducting their own studies.

WRITING THE REPORT

The final stage in the qualitative research process is the writing of a report to describe the study and its findings.[19] Of course, the characteristics and length of the report will depend on the type of report being written. If you are writing a dissertation, the report will be lengthy and structured by the dissertation format at your university. If you are preparing a journal article or a conference paper, it will be relatively short, often limited by the number of pages available to the journal's editor or minutes you have to present your report. Oddly, in most instances, the shorter the report, the harder it is to write because of the large amounts of data obtained in qualitative studies. The form of the report may be based on a thesis, a theme, or a topic. A thesis is a position you state and then argue—for example, "Researchers have claimed that . . . this report demonstrates that they have overlooked important information." A theme is some conceptual issue or finding that emerges from your data—for example, "This study describes a phenomenon called the 'pork barrel effect' in a first-grade classroom." A topic is a descriptive presentation of some process or activity in your data—for example, "This report describes the process of acculturation among kindergarten children in an inner city school." Notice that in each instance, the title of the report provides a helpful indication of its focus.

Regardless of the form of writing you choose, it will serve a dual purpose. It will lead to reexamination of your data interpretation as well as producing the

---

[19]For a good primer, see Wolcott, H. F. (1990). *Writing up qualitative research*. (Qualitative research methods, series 20.). Newbury Park, CA: Sage.

report. The process of writing a report describing your study will inevitably force you to reexamine your data interpretations. Unless you are astoundingly atypical, you probably have found that the writing process raises questions, concerns, and anomalies that were not questions, concerns, and anomalies when you were planning your writing. The concrete process of writing our thoughts in a logical and explanatory manner inevitably identifies flaws in our thinking, missing links in our descriptions, and new interpretations of our concepts and understandings. That is the reality and the importance of writing a report. So, as you strive to produce your report, recognize that your writing is also a test of your thoughts and interpretations. If something you write doesn't "feel" right or doesn't logically fit into a chain of reasoning you are developing, go back to your data and interpretations to try to understand why, so you can provide a more coherent, logical description.

There are many pieces of information that can be included in a research report. Obviously, the type of report will influence the number and depth of these pieces. Typically, pieces such as an introduction, purpose or focus of the study, information about existing literature, and the background of the study are placed in the introductory section of the report. Pieces such as descriptions of the data, the methods used to collect it, descriptions of the participants and context, development of categories and patterns, quotes and examples to illustrate the data, methods of data analysis, and major interpretations and findings are usually included in the body of the report. Finally, major conclusions, implications of your findings, and perhaps suggestions for future research belong in the ending or conclusion section of the report.

Dey[20] provides a useful metaphor relating writing a qualitative report to storytelling. He notes that qualitative report writing has three main features analogous to storytelling: a setting in which data are collected, characters who are informants, and a plot in the form of the social action in which the characters are engaged. Continuing the metaphor, he describes a good report as one that "provides an authentic context in which characters and plot can unfold," one that "engages our attention by making us care about what happens to the characters," and one in which there is "evolution of the plot toward some sort of climax or resolution." To keep the "story" coherent, the researcher must keep track of major activities and decisions made as the story unfolds and must integrate them into a report that flows logically and ends with some resolution or generalization. Note that keeping the story coherent and integrated may require elimination of data that are not central to the "plot."

To make the metaphor more descriptive, Dey provides six guidelines for writing the report:

1. Engage interest through description and dramatization.
2. Trace the evolution of the account.
3. Develop overall coherence.
4. Select key themes.
5. Use simple language.
6. Make concepts and connections explicit.

Qualitative reports can be organized in numerous ways, all intended to aid the readers' understanding. First-person voice is acceptable.

---

[20]Dey, I. (1993). *Qualitative data analysis.* New York: Routledge, (pp. 238–249).

Although the style of the report is one matter, the issue of what makes an acceptable qualitative report is another. Throughout this chapter, characteristics of what makes an acceptable report have been identified, particularly in the section on "Interpreting." Table 7.3 provides a more comprehensive list of characteristics that are important in producing an acceptable report. Although not every qualitative study will require each of the criteria listed in Table 7.3, it will be useful for qualitative researchers to consider the list when planning a report in order to identify the criteria that should be addressed in the report.

> On the pages following Table 7.3 an example of qualitative research is presented. Note that the study involved document analysis (specifically, analysis of reflective journals), multiple observations, and descriptive statistics. Also note the study relied heavily on conversation and interviews to collect data. Which sections of the study are analagous to categories of Figure 7.2 on page 248?

> **TABLE 7.3**
>
> **Common Criteria for Qualitative Reports**

(1) The method is explicated in detail so the reader can judge whether it was adequate and makes sense. An articulate rationale for the use of qualitative methods is given so that skeptics will accept the approach. The methods for attaining entry and managing role, data collection, recording, analysis, ethics, and exit are discussed. There is an audability trail—a running record of procedures (often done in an appendix)—and there is description of how the site and sample were selected. Data collection and analysis procedures are public, not magical.

(2) Assumptions are stated. Biases are expressed, and the researcher does a kind of self-analysis for personal biases and a framework analysis for theoretical biases.

(3) The research guards against value judgments in data collection and in analysis.

(4) There is abundant evidence from raw data to demonstrate the connection between the presented findings and the real world, and the data are presented in readable, accessible form, perhaps aided by graphics, models, charts, and figures.

(5) The research questions are stated, and the study answers those questions and generates further questions.

(6) The relationship between this study and previous studies is explicit. Definitions of phenomena are provided, with explicit reference to previously identified phenomena, but it is clear that the research goes beyond previously established frameworks—challenging old ways of thinking.

(7) The study is reported in a manner that is accessible to other researchers, practitioners, and policy makers. It makes adequate translation of findings so that others will be able to use the findings in a timely way.

(8) Evidence is presented showing that the researcher was tolerant of ambiguity, searched for alternative explanations, checked out negative instances, and used a variety of methods to check the findings (i.e., triangulation).

(9) The report acknowledges the limitations of generalizability while assisting the readers in seeing the transferability of findings.

(10) It is clear that there was a phase of "first days in the field" in which a problem focus was generated from observation, not from library research. In other words, it is a study that is an exploration, not merely a study to find contextual data to verify old theories.

(11) Observations are made (or sampled) of a full range of activities over a full cycle of activities.

(12) Data are preserved and available for reanalysis.

(13) Methods are devised for checking data quality (e.g., informants' knowledgeability, ulterior motives, and truthfulness) and for guarding against ethnocentric explanations.

(14) In-field work analysis is documented.

(15) Meaning is elicited from cross-cultural perspectives.

(16) The researcher is careful about sensitivity of those being researched—ethical standards are maintained.

(17) People in the research setting benefit in some way (ranging from getting a free meal or an hour of sympathetic listening to being empowered to throw off their chains).

(18) Data collection strategies are the most adequate and efficient available. There is evidence that the researcher is a finely tuned research instrument, whose personal talents, experiential biases, and insights are used consciously. The researcher is careful to be self-analytical and recognize when she or he is getting subjective or going native.

(19) The study is tied into "the big picture." The researcher looks holistically at the setting to understand linkages among systems.

(20) The researcher traces the historical context to understand how institutions and roles have evolved.

Source: Marshall, C., and Rossman, G. (1995). *Designing qualitative research* (2nd ed.), Thousand Oaks, CA: Sage Publications, (pp. 146–148). Copyright 1995 Sage Publications. Reprinted by permission of Sage Publications, Inc.

QUALITATIVE STUDIES IN EDUCATION. 1997, VOL. 10, NO. 2, 221–235

Identity work by alternative high school students

JIM FRASER
Department of Sociology, University of Utah

PHILLIP W. DAVIS
Department of Sociology, Georgia State University

RAVINDER SINGH
Center for Policy Studies in Education, Florida State University

This article examines the adaptive strategies of institutionally marginalized students in an alternative high school setting. Snow and Anderson's (1987) model of "identity work" is used to analyze the ways in which students symbolically distance themselves from certain features of their "home" school and embrace certain features of their alternative school. Drawing upon semistructured interviews with 25 students, it is argued that these distancing and embracement processes lie at the heart of their struggle to assemble a sense of self that is congruent with their former "problem" and consistent with their current institutional status. Key distancing themes are identified, including institutional controls, teacher competence, peer evaluations, educational quality, and alternative school images. Embracement strategies revolve around organizational, associational, and atmospheric themes. The policy implications for a more contextualized understanding of alternative school experiences are examined, and the theoretical implications of an interactionist model for a better understanding of the intersection of institutional arrangements and student identities are discussed.

> People should know that alternative high schools aren't that bad. My mom's friends were telling her, "Don't let Julie go to Forest 'cause it's nothing but drug addicts and people with babies and kids that drop out of school and don't have a life." Alternative schools, at least this one, aren't like that. If you make a mistake here you can correct yourself... If you feel you didn't fit in [at] your home school, at least you can fit in at this school. (Julie: a student at Forest Alternative High School)

Stained student identities vary widely, and some discolorations penetrate the self more deeply than others. Some sources of taint are academic in nature when, for example, students are put on probation because of low grades. Others are more structural when, for example, students are alleged to have broken rules or defied authority. Still other sources involve group standing when, for example, some students are labelled "nerds," "brainiacs," "bullies," "loners," and so on. While the effects of these discolorations are far from irreversible (Evans & Eder, 1993), students labeled in these ways often face problems of acceptance and performance (Carlton-Ford, Reef, Black, & Simmons, 1989). Marginalized, isolated, and devalued, they are often lonely and have low self-esteem (Asher & Wheeler, 1985; Carlton-Ford et al., 1989).[1] Research on student reactions to marginalization shows that some of them affiliate with devalued groups while others conform to conventional standards, perhaps by using available resources such as athletic programs and campus organizations (Kinney, 1993). But there are

0951-8398/97 $12·00 © 1997 Taylor & Francis Ltd

many other ways students can react to educational marginality and dislocation. The success or failure of those reactions may depend in part on the sense they make of themselves and their surroundings and in part on the adaptive strategies they use to accept, modify, or resist the institutional identities made available to them.

In this paper our primary concern is with one type of adaptation called "identity work." Identity work refers to, "the range of activities individuals engage in to create, present, and sustain personal identities that are congruent with and supportive of the self-concept" (Snow & Anderson, 1987, p. 1348). Mehan (1992) argues that identity work is a part of the internal life of schools that is often neglected or given a residual status in educational analyses. Identity work is especially significant when people become the objects of discrediting attributes. Such identity work can make the difference between someone who accepts a denigrating, stigmatized status and someone who resists it (Goffman, 1963).

Our approach to identity work is informed by symbolic interactionism, a sociological theory that is based on the following notions: that social action, behavior, and self-concepts arise in the course of ongoing interaction with people who share a symbolic world; that people develop interpretations or "definitions" of their immediate situations; that identities, interaction, and definitions develop in a sociopolitical context; and that definitions and self-concepts have causal status (Blumer, 1969; Denzin, 1984; LaRossa & Reitzes, 1993). According to this model, interpretations and identities are ongoing, tentative, changing, and dynamic.[2] Similarly, identities are assembled or constructed by selves and others. Personal identities are characteristics that actors impute to themselves, while social identities are the traits imputed by others to the actor. The development of both personal and social identities rests on the relationship people have with their cultural and social environments. Selves are actively represented to others through scripted talk and strategic action, usually in favorable ways that may or may not reveal the actor's personally held views (Goffman, 1959). Finally, actors "work" on their identities in the sense they revise biographies according to new circumstances, to changing audiences, and to alternative surroundings.[3] One implication of this model is that students in alternative educational surroundings will engage in identity work to make sense of their new surroundings.

Some educational surroundings are designed to give students new ways of looking at themselves, to provide them with new possibilities instead of the stains and restrictions that come with traditional viewpoints. The emancipatory possibilities of schools have received substantial attention in recent theoretical statements based on cultural and educational studies frameworks (Levinson, Foley, & Holland, 1996; McFadden, 1995; Wexler, 1992). A central concern in those statements is the interaction among different cultures within particular school settings. For example, McFadden (1995), drawing on Walker (1993), states that the central issue is:

> ...convergence and divergence of intercultural relations in concrete problem contexts (for example, in schools between teacher and student cultures), and therefore is a question of intercultural articulations and connections and how they structure social options for individuals and groups in certain social settings. (p. 295)

Resistance to institutionally supplied identities is complex (Wexler, 1992), and is generally situated and dependent upon context and form. Students have various vantage points from which they evaluate their educational experiences. Accordingly, student selves can be seen as a conversation between students' experiences in schools and their larger orientations towards society. This conversation requires sense-making activities that provide continuity across a multitude of lived experiences in diverse social settings.

Additionally, a school's atmosphere affects the students' sense of identity and self-image in relation to their other social positions. For example, a pregnant student does not solely respond to schooling as a site of accomplishing utilitarian goals, but rather, the school may be a site of social interaction in which gender identity work occurs (Wexler, 1992). And, in addition to developing gendered ideas about themselves, students also develop biographies in which former problems and current standing take on meaning.

Our empirical strategy is to examine student identity work in unconventional rather than conventional surroundings in order to analyze the interplay between identity and environment when students have fewer resources and when their environment is associated with widespread negative images. This strategy also allows us to address student well-being, resistance, and change in specialized educational settings. One important and fairly recent type of specialized setting is the alternative high school. Alternative schools usually offer nontraditional programs aimed at reducing local drop-out rates. Having spread quickly during the 1970s, alternative schools typically provide individualized programs, small classes, increased opportunities for family involvement, and an open or more democratic organizational structure (Franklin, McNeil, & Wright, 1992). They are described as "schools of choice" with progressive philosophies (Everhart, 1985) and as educational sites, "that contest hegemonic curriculum by setting up alternatives outside of it" (Connell, 1988, p. 67). Therefore, many alternative schools are structured to be more cooperative than traditional environments, some of them giving students greater freedom and input concerning school rules (Kaczynski, 1989).

Past and current research on alternative high schools focuses primarily on delinquency prevention, institutional reform, background causation, and predictors of success. These studies generally highlight important differences between traditional and alternative school environments and argue that students who do not do well in traditional settings prefer the alternative setting (Kaczynski, 1989; Ruby & Law, 1983; Williamson, Tobin, & Fraser, 1986). For example, researchers suggest that many students in traditional schools become alienated and subsequently their performance suffers (Everhart, 1985; Foley & McConnaughy, 1982). In contrast, alternative settings, according to Perry and Duke (1978) and Gold (1978), may help improve the academic performance of students because the school's size, the staff's treatment of students as "young adults," the teachers' realistic view of student behavior, and the administrators' recruitment of teachers with more experience contribute to creating an environment that is conducive to learning for students. Further, students tend to prefer cooperative environments, and those who view their alternative school as especially cooperative do better in English and mathematics (Hattie, Bryne, & Fraser, 1986). Additionally, Gold (1978) indicates that self-image in alternative schools is associated positively with achievement and negatively with delinquency.[4]

After a description of our methods and materials, we analyze the identity work of a sample of alternative high school students. We discuss how they view themselves, including their ideas about their former problems and their current standing. We place special emphasis upon their strategies of distancing and embracing certain features of their home schools and their alternative schools as part of a sense-making process that is important in sustaining self-respect, organizing personal history, and resisting

224   JIM FRASER ET AL.

institutional denigration. We then discuss the implications of our analysis for a more contextualized understanding of identity work, alternative school life, and institutional change.

Method and materials

Our analysis is based on interviews and observations at a public alternative high school in a mostly middle-class suburb of a large southeastern city. Founded in 1978 to help reduce the county's public school dropout rate, Forest High initially enrolled about 100 students from other high schools in the area.[5] It quickly grew to more than 400 students. Forest is open to all students in the county from the ages of 16 through 19, although some exceptions are made for older students. The racial composition of the school is about 75% European-American, 20% African-American, and 5% Hispanic or Asian. Approximately 55% of the student body is female. Students attend one to four classes a day depending on the number of credit hours they are taking. Classes are 100 minutes rather than the traditional 50 so that material can be covered more quickly and students can graduate as soon as possible. Administrators say the school operates on a "trust system," giving students considerable freedom to come and go as they please during breaks and at lunch as long as they show signs of academic progress and follow school rules. Forest High's stated mission is to provide a "school of choice" for students who have special personal or educational needs.

In 1993 the first and third authors spent approximately 100 hours observing school activities and joining casual conversations with students and teachers during breaks in the class schedule as well as during some classes. Their membership role was more peripheral than active (Adler & Adler, 1987). They were known observers (Lofland & Lofland, 1994) at all times; presenting themselves as "sociologists doing a project" from a nearby university. They also interviewed 25 students.[6] There were 13 women and 12 men in the sample, and the racial composition was fairly consistent with the school's racial breakdown. The students were chosen largely on the basis of convenience, but a few were selected on the basis of student and teacher referrals. Students were interviewed away from teachers, usually in empty classrooms, the dining hall, hallways, or the plaza. Most students were interviewed individually, although a few wanted to be interviewed with two or three of their friends present. We followed a flexible format and avoided leading questions. Students were asked to describe their home school, the reasons they left, and their general experiences at Forest High. While these questions gave structure to the interviews, we gave students considerable freedom to shape the direction of our discussions. After obtaining informed consent from all interviewees, we taped-recorded the interviews that ranged from 20 to 50 minutes and averaged 25 to 30 minutes.

During the period at Forest High, the first and third authors developed some fairly personalized relationships with teachers and students. One characteristic of the second author that seemed to be salient for the students was his ethnicity. The third author is a Sikh, and the students became fascinated with the traditional turban he wore at all times. Additionally, the first author shared his own history of "dropping out" of traditional high school and eventually obtaining a GED. These qualities that the researchers brought to their interactions with students at Forest High created opportunities for casual conversation and revealing interviews. In a sense, both researchers had characteristics that placed them closer to the periphery than the center of "mainstream" culture. Perhaps for these reasons many students turned to the researchers as sources of information about how to navigate their way into college. During the project the first and third authors had numerous conversations with students about university life and the way it differed from high school. These encounters, we believe, fostered a sense of community between the first two authors and the students.

Distancing from a former problem

Students at Forest High viewed themselves as having had any number of problems at their home school, and the way they described them closely resembles the adaptive strategy Snow and Anderson (1987) call "distancing work."[7] All of the students we talked to held largely negative views of their home school, most of them saying that their home schools failed to give them what they needed, wanted, or deserved. We will discuss the five most common distancing themes that emerged from our interviews, including social controls, teacher competence, peer evaluations, educational quality, and negative stereotypes.

Home school controls

Students at Forest High generally viewed home schools as intrinsically flawed and fundamentally deficient institutions characterized by an inordinate emphasis on rules, regimen, and order. Most students said their home schools were overwhelmingly concerned with controlling students rather than educating them, and some likened their home schools to jails or detention centers. John, a student at Forest, noted:

> The teachers would only care about the rules and controlling people ... it was like a jail because there were fences and guards around the school. You needed a pass to walk down the halls and teachers would watch you.

Penny made a similar analogy:

> I felt like I was in prison because you were not allowed to – you had to follow these stupid rules. You got your upper classmen who can beat on the lower classmen without a big problem ... During lunch time, you had guards at each door so you couldn't leave.

The real problem from the standpoint of many alternative students was not that they got into trouble, but that home schools had too many walls, rules, and guards. They distanced themselves from the idea that they were failed troublemakers or academic incompetents by pointing to these institutional preoccupations.

Much of their resentment was rooted in their home school's emphasis on rules and controls that restricted personal liberties. Erica remembered the rules at her home school this way:

> They were real strict. The dress code was real strict. It was like they took more care of the lawn and the trees than they did the students. You couldn't walk on the grass. You couldn't wear shorts. We couldn't wear fleece sweat pants ... It was like they were strict, and at the same time, they had the "I don't care" attitude about them.

While these and other dissatisfactions about school controls are commonplace in any number of educational settings, home school rules had special significance for these students. Rules and controls at their home schools are part of a symbolic world that students experience, at least in retrospect, as wrongful and fateful factors in the development of their educational and personal problem. They are central rather than peripheral features of schools that, from the students' point of view, were settings in which conformity and regimen were valued over education and inner lives.

Home school teachers

Another way students distanced themselves from the stained self implied by their unconventional student status was by characterizing home school teachers as professionally and morally misguided or incompetent. Not only did the teachers not invest enough time, attention, and energy into their teaching, from the students' point of view, they also were not concerned with students beyond the classroom as "whole individuals." Teachers were also described as inattentive, indifferent, and biased; consequently, students who needed extra help were ignored, and some students seemed to be arbitrarily valued more than others. Some alternative students felt that their home school teachers should have dispensed attention and rewards more impartially. Fran described her home school teachers as playing "favorites" in the following way:

> The teachers were always lecturing. What can you do if there are so many students and short periods of time to be in them [classes]. You know the teachers did not really care about us unless you were one of the football players or a cheerleader. It was like, if you didn't like what was going on or needed some extra help to understand, you could forget it.

Je Quette had a similar view of home school teachers as lacking in impartiality:

> In my drama class, she played favorites really bad. She had the same people for the same parts, for all the big parts, and she chose. I thought she chose all the good actors for the good parts and ... that really discouraged me because, well, I mean, I guess that's not true, right?

She said that, while home school controls were the real problem, there were a few dramatic "last straws" that ended her home school career. Angry with the emphasis on control, she said she threw a chair at one teacher and told another to "fuck off."

Another student, Mindy, said that all the rules at her home school caused her to do things she defined as "rebellion." In trouble with the principal, she eventually was kicked out:

> It made me angry, and I just did everything to piss them off.... It made me not ever want to go to school. It [rebelling] made me feel like I was getting something accomplished, but really, you know, it just made me get set back a couple of years, until I came here [to Forest].

She went to private school for a year before returning to her home school. Back in the same situation, she had one especially bad experience with another teacher:

> A teacher heard that my grandfather was in the S.S. [a Nazi] 'cause he's from Germany, and she told me that people like me should be killed. And I do not even believe that way! She told me that we should be shot down for all the Jews that my relatives have killed and that I would be sure to fail in her class. And I did fail her class.

Derrick felt that his teachers were condescending in their attitude towards him because he chose to associate with unpopular student groups:

The teachers judged you by who you were with. The teachers downtalked to me 'cause I hung out with kids who sat at "this table." The kids sat at different lunch tables, and I would sit at the "little junkies" lunch table. And the teachers would talk down to me 'cause of that. I sat at the skin-head table. I did that once. I'd sit at the handicapped kids table, 'cause nobody would sit with them. I felt sorry for them. The teachers would talk down to me 'cause of who I was friends with, and that really upset me. They wouldn't give me the same chances they would to the football players and the kids that hung out with the football players and the cheerleaders.

Home school peers

Students also distanced themselves from their home school problems by pointing to the judgmental tendencies of their former peers. Overall, Forest students said that, because they did not adhere to the social or moral guidelines of the traditional school, they were treated badly by conventional students. Some Forest students said they were harassed by other students at their home school and were made to feel less than normal. Sarina recalled:

A peer did come up to me, I mean just came up to me and called me a dyke.... I was really mad, and then they started going around and making fun of just like anyone, you know, is homosexual or anything, and I am really against making fun of that ... I got really mad, and I went up to this guy, and I just started beating him up. That was kind of funny, but I was really mad.

She added that it was not only the other students who would "spread rumors about people who were thought to be homosexual, but also teachers." She said that she could not understand how students could be so mean to her and how teachers and administrators could allow it to continue:

The reason I dropped out of that school was because I was being harassed really bad by students and teachers ... awfully bad; not just a little teasing, but people would trip me and throw things at me and not sit with me and move away from where I sat.

Tara commented that at the traditional school you are taught to compete for scarce rewards and that "if you didn't buy into the same game like other students," you were on the outside. For her, that game involved participation in sports and other traditionally valued activities:

At my home school you didn't get noticed unless you were on the football team or a cheerleader or in the student government ... [Y]ou had to be in some club that was considered important ... I don't think anyone really noticed me or knew my name because the students that were in all the activities were in the same clique. They were pretty much the kids with money in their family. I guess I got noticed when I stopped going to school for a month ... I got kicked out.

Home school education

Students also distanced themselves from their former educational problem by pointing to the lack of meaning and purpose of the learning process at their home schools. Interactions with teachers and peers coupled with the controlling structure of their

228   JIM FRASER ET AL.

home schools led to the view that their home school "education" lacked purpose, direction, or value. Students at Forest said that the things they were made to learn at their home school were not preparing them for the next part of their lives. They said they could see no reason to go to the home school for four or more years, only to learn material that was personally irrelevant and unimportant. A few students also defined their home school's curriculum as unchallenging. Derrick, for example, was an academic anomaly in our sample because he was doing quite well academically before he came to Forest:

> I was an honour student, and I had better than a 3·0 grade point average. I didn't get along there too well because of the rules, and I'm kind of an abstract thinker… I ended up skipping thirty days and dropped out of school.

He went on to say that there was nothing he could do about his lack of enthusiasm because students were not permitted to challenge the teachers and the curriculum. He said that he thought that the restrictive atmosphere of the school caused problems for students who were bright because the school did not allow students to pursue knowledge for its own sake. Other students said that they were just learning facts in order to spout them back.

Alternative school images

Another aspect of our interviewees' distancing work pertains to their ideas of what outsiders (e.g., those not attending) think about Forest students. Outsiders' negative images of alternative schools stand in sharp contrast with what students believe are the more positive realities of Forest life. Students insist, for example, that many people in their families, community, and home schools think Forest is for delinquents, toughs, drug users, pregnant women, and dumb students. Tim said:

> I think this school has gotten a bad name 'cause of what's happened in the past. They used to have a bit of a drug problem here. Not violence – I think we've had like two fights all year. They don't realize that the regular schools are much worse than here.

Similarly, Julie noted:

> People should know that alternative schools aren't that bad. 'Cause my mom's friends were telling her, "Don't let Julie go to Forest cause it's nothing but drug addicts and people with babies and kids that drop out of school and don't have a life." Alternative schools, at least this one, aren't like that. If you make a mistake, here you can correct yourself… If you feel you didn't fit in your home school, at least you can fit in at this school.

Some students said they used to hold some of those same views themselves. Angela said:

> My mom was like, "Oh you don't want to go there cause it's an alternative school, all the students there use drugs." They think [we] toke weed. They think everybody can run around and do whatever they want to. I used to think you could come here and get high with the teachers and do whatever you want.

Trent described his first day at Forest this way:

> As I was walking up, I was thinking, "All the bad kids go here. I'm gonna get my butt kicked." I got my schedule. I go to my class. I sit down. And there were all the kids I used to hang out with at [home school] that just disappeared.

Victor said, "People at the home school say it's really easy here, but it's not. It's harder than a regular school."

In these ways the students we interviewed differentiated between the selves they preferred and the selves their home schools implied. They felt they had been marginalized and made out to be "different" at their home schools, not because the academic standards were too stringent for them, but because the social climate was too punitive, the teachers too partial, the peers too abusive, and the curriculum too meaningless. They created a symbolic and moral distance from their former problem and the self it implied by pointing to the ways that their problems were rooted in the institutional, interpersonal, and educational features of their home school experiences. But the value of distancing themselves from the negative identities implied by their former problem is only half the picture. Alternative high school students also find ways of uplifting their moral selves and personal identities by identifying positive features of their current location.

Embracing the alternative status

An important aspect of alternative students' identity work is their selective embracing of the alternative situation.[8] It is one thing for students to identify the ways their former school failed them, but it is another thing to identify what currently validates their worth and defines their value in their new surroundings. We will discuss three environmental features – organizational, associational, and atmospheric – that students embrace *en route* to constructing essentially competent, basically normal, and potentially successful selves.[9]

Organizational embracement

Many of the students we interviewed formed linkages between their personal identities and the daily routines of their new surroundings. The meanings they attached to these organizational qualities centered on the open structure, flexible schedules, and individualized programs of Forest High School. Overall, students indicated that Forest was better than their home school. Either the problems they had experienced at their home schools had not arisen at Forest, or, if they had, they were more manageable within the alternative setting. Tabrina, for example, said she had trouble, especially in the mornings, at her home school. She felt the only thing to do about the problem there was to skip because she sees herself as more of an "afternoon person." And when she skipped, she got into trouble. At Forest she says she is given some flexibility, is able to take less than the full six-hour class load, and feels more personal responsibility for doing the work:

> I think I am better prepared because you can only take four classes a day, and there [home school] you take up to six, and…if I was taking classes until 3:45 in the afternoon, I don't think I could do it. But you can determine how many classes you want to take…if you're a better afternoon person you can come in after lunch and take third and fourth hour…and so I think I am better prepared because my attendance is better. I am always scared to miss class because we do so much more in a class period.

Coming to define themselves as being responsible for their futures is a real challenge for some students who already think that they are not "good" students. It is not surprising, then, that many of the students we spoke to described the process of identity management as a combination of success and failure. Many admitted that the new environment did not solve problems, but they were afforded the responsibility of managing their own affairs. Geraldo praised the no-cut policy at Forest:

> You get more prepared for college here because you have an open campus, number one. You have an attendance policy – five cuts and you're cut. Here they put more responsibility on you... The responsibility is that if you leave, you have to come back. If you take your five cuts, you are withdrawn: so it is pretty cool.

Jud was having difficulty keeping up with his courses at Forest, but defined himself as the cause of the problem:

> When I got here, I was thinking I could graduate by this time, and I was going to take four class every time. But then I started taking three classes, and then two, and now I'm only taking one class, and that's gotta stop. There is a slack part of it because if you don't keep check on yourself, you ain't doing nothing... It just jumped up in my face recently that I was being a real slack-ass.

Even though Jud was going slower than he originally intended, it was not for lack of organizationally structured opportunities to move quickly towards his diploma.

Associational embracement

In addition to embracing the alternative school's organizational features, some students placed special emphasis on the associational and interpersonal aspects of their new school lives. More specifically, they pointed to the unique qualities of their teachers and the accepting attitude of their peers. Cheryl defined her transition from home school to alternative school as initially difficult. For her, it was the personal qualities of her teachers that soon made alternative school a wonderful place. She saw her new teachers as especially accessible, caring, and considerate:

> At first, the change was hard. I was nervous. It wasn't but a few days before I felt at home... it was great to be accepted. And it wasn't just by the students, it was by the teachers and other faculty. It was great. I love it here. I really do.

Dennis felt that while classroom dynamics at his home school did not match his personal style of learning, the alternative school dynamics did:

> At a regular school they might not review as much and not try to help you as much... they assign the work and half the time don't explain it fully. I didn't understand something [at Forest] and as long as you keep asking questions, they keep on going... if I'd done this at a regular school, they would have kicked me out of class because when I don't understand something, I keep on asking questions, a lot of questions, until they explain it to me fully.

Other students were less "categorical" (Snow & Anderson, 1987, p. 1357) in their associational embracement and do not find the transition so uncomplicated. Sharon, who flunked two years in a row at her home school before enrolling at Forest, described her home teachers as uncaring and only wanting to "just do their job." At Forest the same problem with some teachers continued, but she believed most teachers were ready for problems with new students:

I think here people come in with bad attitudes, and they are prepared for it, so they want to help. And if you go to a regular high school and have a bad attitude they don't even want to help.[10]

Another student, Matt, said, "We are all here for one reason, and that is to graduate. I don't like everybody, but there is no one that I am against." This type of response was typical at Forest. The same student who offered the jail metaphor in portraying his home school said that Forest was a place where he could really "be myself" and that the cliques that characterized traditional settings were absent at Forest.

Atmospheric embracing

In addition to embracing the organizational and associational dimensions of alternative high school life, students identified strongly with the overall spirit, ethos, and mystique of their new school. We call this aspect of their personal identity work "atmospheric embracement," and at Forest it revolves around the general feeling that there is an air of freedom, opportunity, salvation, and responsibility.[11] More than an ideology, this kind of identity work links values to local settings and attaches self-meanings to what is perceived as the essence or spirit characteristic of the setting. Students viewed these atmospheric qualities as real, external, typical, and consequential. Petra, who was one week away from graduation at the time of her interview, saw the alternative school as her educational salvation:

Coming here teaches you about life, people, and responsibility... The education I have gotten here is just as good or better in some respects than what I got at a regular school because... you learn how to run your own life and how to relate to people, and just everything you need to know to survive... Overall if it hadn't been for Forest, I wouldn't have graduated from high school and wouldn't be continuing my education.

Some students viewed the alternative ethos as a two-edged sword, as posing a new kind of identity problem should they fail at Forest after their lack of home school success. Rodrick commented:

You're given this freedom, and if you take advantage of this freedom, you're gonna mess up, and the only person that can be blamed is you. Then if you do it good, the only person that can be looked at as "you did this good" is you. So you're given that opportunity to better yourself or worsen yourself.

These feelings of freedom and opportunity are part of the ethos at Forest. Students speak of them as though they were "in the air." And this atmospheric quality stands in sharp contrast in their minds with the restrictive arrangements and limited possibilities they experienced at their home schools.

Discussion

We have examined how a group of alternative high school students contend with their marginal status and stained identities. Their identity work generally involves imposing a moral and symbolic wedge between their view of themselves and the self implied by

232   JIM FRASER ET AL.

home school failure. These students distance themselves from home school controls, students, teachers, and education. In addition, they also distance themselves from the negative images they believe other people have of their alternative school. Finally, their identity work includes embracing certain features of their new alternative school environment. They embrace the organizational structure, teachers, peers, and atmosphere school.

When unconventional schools provide identities for institutionally marginalized students, the intent is usually to communicate morally neutral meanings, i.e., the idea that there is nothing wrong with the student as a person. But students do not passively or automatically accept those meanings or assume those identities. Instead, they engage in a complex and creative process in which they modify and make sense of what they are told about themselves. They utilize both their previous educational experiences and their current definitions of those situations. They actively manage the moral, social, and political meanings associated with old and new situations. And, they resist the idea that they need the new arrangements because they failed in the old setting.

The significance of their resistance derives from the cognitive, interactive, and symbolic lens through which they look back on, and account for, their earlier problems. This interpretive lens is fashioned in large part by their current social position. In short, they view their former problem from the standpoint of what they believe is a contemporary solution. That standpoint organizes the problem and defines it as having external origins.

However, the identity work of these students may or may not be similar to what students in other unconventional settings experience. The identity work of students in other environments, including alternative schools, boot-camp style schools, continuation schools, and perhaps home schooling situations, also requires close and careful study. It should be noted, though, that not all marginalized students end up resisting institutionally supplied identities and definitions of educational "failure." Some are unable to distance themselves from situations and experiences that to others look like individual deficiencies. And their identity work, and key points of departure from the work of resistive students, should be examined as well. Similarly, the identity work of the students in this study may or may not be akin to the efforts of marginalized students who remain in conventional settings. These latter students may be better able to distance themselves from certain features of their stigmatized social identity. They may embrace other aspects of their social lives and experiences, because of the resources available in conventional settings (Kinney, 1993).

Nonetheless, the identity work of alternative students is important, not only for creating and sustaining positive selves, but also for developing educational institutions. Identity work establishes linkages between individuals and their student role, the educational institution, and other actors in the new environment. Thus, their interpretive work creates identities that make them feel different but not deviant. Although this study did not examine the relationship between identity work and school performance, it would seem that the more identity work students do, the more they put their past behind them and take advantage of the new institutional setting. The important identity work they do may help prepare them to do the classroom work needed to matriculate. While it would not be advisable for unconventional schools to define home schools negatively, they can help students put their earlier negative school experiences in perspective.

While such students' views may seem to be an effect of the alternative environment, we must remember that identity work is a creative process. Students may value their new environment because they do not see anywhere else they can go. Many people believe, for example, that these schools are the last resort. "Last resorts," according to Emerson (1981), are remedies to problems that are pursued on the assumption that the person has exhausted other, less fateful, solutions. They may no longer qualify for less serious solutions to the problem in what Goffman (1971) calls a "remedial cycle." The students generally preferred the open campus and caring teachers at Forest, but they may also see it as a "last-resort school" that saves them from the streets. Regrettably, our interviews did not explore student beliefs about failure at alternative schools. Future research might focus on the ways that both mainstream and nonmainstream students incorporate the idea of last resorts into their personal identity work.

Finally, the identity work of these students is carried out with the aid of institutionally supplied designations and meanings. These students have entered a new social arena formally designated as an "alternative environment," with distinctive institutionalized ideas, definitions, values, sentiments, and beliefs. Forest supplied students with the idea that an alternative school is a morally neutral place where they are different but equal to students in conventional schools. This allowed Forest students to embrace their school in a way that many students of devalued statuses cannot "organizationally embrace" their conventional home schools. Nevertheless, not all students view the alternative school positively, and future research might focus on those that do not. In addition, much more research must be done to find out how students acquire spoiled identities, and educators must develop intervention strategies before despair sets in and damages the life chances of these young people.

Ultimately, what may be needed is an expanded notion of what it means to educate youth. Identity is not a traditional measure of "educational success," but this research suggests that its significance should not be overlooked. To understand more fully the poverty that some students experience in terms of rejection and self-esteem, educators need a better understanding of how students "become somebody" (Wexler, 1992) through creative identity work. These interviews show how human agency and subjective interpretations in the realm of identity work affect educational experiences, and, thus, it behooves concerned educators to know more fully the student point of view.

Notes

1. This varies considerably by socioeconomic status and social class (see Berndt, 1983).

2. Symbolic interaction is premised on the philosophy of George Herbert Mead's (1934) theory of the past, present, and future as they relate to identity work. Postmodern thinkers in education and sociology have not often been explicit in the origins of their claim that people reinvent themselves in a nonlinear fashion. The present study takes to heart Mead's understanding of self and postmodern consciousness.

3. Social identities are the ways that others perceive and cast the person. Personal identities are imputations, designations, and attributions by the person about themselves, and may or may not hinge on biographical events and meanings (Snow & Anderson, 1987). Identities, both personal and social, make up selves that are symbolic, contingent, and encompassing (Fine, 1993; Gecas, 1982).

4. School life is important because in no other setting, "are the standards of achievement so clear [and] the means to attain them so narrow ... a derogated self-image is naturally aversive and it will set into motion psychic forces to dispel it" (Gold, 1978, p. 292).

5. The name of the school is a pseudonym, as are the names of students used in our analysis.

6. This sample size is fairly typical for small-scale qualitative studies (Lofland & Lofland, 1994). We believe that these interviews provided especially revealing commentaries for two reasons. First, there was a relative lack of distance between the interviewers and students. The interviewers look young for their age (24 and 26), and they related stories of their own experiences in high school. We think students generally saw them as "hip" to the student point of view (Lugones & Spelman, 1983). Second, the interviews were impromptu, usually arranged not far in advance, giving them an unrehearsed quality.

234   JIM FRASER ET AL.

7. Snow and Anderson (1987) argue that when social and personal identities are inconsistent, people distance themselves from the negative implications of their social identity by differentiating between themselves and the negative and the implied associations, roles, and institutions (see also Coser, 1966; Stebbins, 1967, 1975). In their study of homeless men, for example, they found that the men's personal identity work revolved around distancing themselves from devalued themes and embracing certain positive themes. Three types of distancing were identified: associational, role, and institutional. The men distanced themselves from their devalued peers, the vagrant role, and the agencies that "served" them.

8. Snow and Anderson (1987) identity role, associational, and ideological embracement. Of these, associational embracement is the most apparent in the identity work of alternative high school students we interviewed. We find that the organizational context is important since they are enrolled in small but formal structures with set routines, tasks, channels, and hierarchies. We also see them embracing a more intangible and atmospheric quality of the alternative school.

9. This does not imply that all students at Forest see themselves as competent and potentially successful. Many, no doubt, do not, but only a few of our interviewees identified with devaluing labels.

10. Many students, despite their widespread embracement of the organizational, associational, and atmospheric qualities of the alternative school, point out that Forest is not a perfect place. Most of them had encountered a few of "traditional" types of teachers and administrative policies at Forest that reminded them of their home school experiences.

11. Some aspects of atmospheric embracement are similar to what Snow and Anderson (1987) call ideological embracement, especially the idea that Forest gives students freedom and instills responsibility. Everhart (1985) identifies a practical ideology found at many alternative schools that involves beliefs about the virtues of self-reliance and personal responsibility for success.

References

Adler, P. A., & Adler, P. (1987). *Membership roles in field research.* Newbury Park: Sage.

Asher, S. R., & Wheeler, V. A. (1985). Children's loneliness: a comparison of rejected and neglected peer status. *Journal of Consulting and Clinical Psychology, 53*(4), 500–505.

Berndt, T. J. (1983). Correlates and causes of sociometric status in childhood: a commentary on six current studies of popular, rejected, and neglected children. *Merrill-Palmer Quarterly, 29*(4), 449–458.

Blumer, H. (1969). *Symbolic interactionism: perspective and method.* Englewood Cliffs, NJ: Prentice-Hall.

Carlton-Ford, S., Reef, M. J., Black, A., & Simmons, R. (1989, April). *Problem behavior, verbal ridicule, victimization, and self-esteem during the transition to early and middle adolescence in two school contexts.* Paper presented at the annual meeting of the Midwest Sociological Association, St Louis, MO.

Connell, R. W. (1988). Curriculum politics, hegemony and strategies of social change. *Curriculum and Teaching, 3*(1–2), 63–71.

Coser, R. (1966). Role distance, sociological ambivalence, and transitional status systems. *American Journal of Sociology, 72*, 173–187.

Denzin, N. (1984). Toward a phenomenology of domestic, family violence. *American Journal of Sociology, 90*, 483–513.

Emerson, R. (1981). Last resorts. *American Journal of Sociology, 23*(3), 213–223.

Evans, C., & Eder, D. (1993). No exit: processes of social isolation in the middle school. *Journal of Contemporary Ethnography, 22* 139–170.

Everhart, R. B. (1985). On feeling good about oneself: practical ideology in schools of choice. *Sociology of Education, 58*, 251–260.

Fine, G. A. (1993). The sad demise, mysterious disappearance, and glorious triumph of symbolic interactionism. *Annual Review of Sociology, 19* 61–87.

Foley, E. M., & McConnaughy, S. B. (1982). *Towards school improvement: lessons from alternative high schools* (Public Education Association Reports-Research Technical). New York: Morgan Guaranty Trust Co. And New York Community Trust.

Franklin, C., McNeil, S., & Wright, R. (1992). School social work works: findings from an alternative school for dropouts. *Social Work in Education, 12*(3), 177–194.

Gecas, V. (1982). The self-concept. *Annual Review of Sociology, 8*, 1–33.

Giroux, H. (1983). *Theory and resistance in education: a pedagogy for the opposition.* S. Hadley, MA: Bergin & Garvey.

Goffman, E. (1959). *The presentation of self in everyday life.* New York: Doubleday Anchor.

Goffman, E. (1963). *Stigma: some notes on the management of spoiled identity.* New York: Prentice-Hall.

Goffman, E. (1971). *Relations in public.* New York: Harper & Row.

Gold, M. (1978). Scholastic experience, self-esteem, and delinquent behavior: a theory for alternative schools. *Crime and Delinquency, 24*(3), 290–302.

Hattie, J. A., Byrne, D., & Fraser, B. J. (1986, April). *Research into students' perceptions of preferred and actual learning environment.* Paper presented at the annual meeting of the American Educational Research Association, San Francisco, CA.

IDENTITY WORK   235

Kaczynski, D. J. (1989, March). *Traditional high school dropouts: a qualitative study at an alternative high school.* Paper presented at the annual meeting of the American Educational Research Association. San Francisco, CA.

Kinney, D. A. (1993). From nerds to normals: the recovery of identity among adolescents from middle school to high school. *Sociology of Education, 66,* 21–40.

LaRossa, R., & Reitzes, D. C. (1993). Symbolic interactionism and family studies. In P. G. Boss, W. J. Doherty, R. LaRossa, W. R. Schumm, & S. K. Steinmetz (Eds.), *Sourcebook of family theories and methods: a contextual approach* (pp. 135–166). New York: Plenum Press.

Levinson, B., Foley, D., & Holland, D. (1996). *The cultural production of the educated person: critical ethnographies of school and local practice.* New York: SUNY Press.

Lofland, J., & Lofland, L. H. (1994). *Analyzing social settings: a guide to qualitative observation and analysis* (3rd ed.). Belmont, CA: Wadsworth.

Lugones, M., & Spelman, E. (1983). Have we got a theory for you! Feminist theory, cultural imperialism, and the demand for 'the women's voice'. *Women's Studies International Forum, 6* (6), 573–581.

McFadden, M. G. (1995). Resistance to schooling and educational outcomes: questions of structure and agency. *British Journal of Sociology of Education, 16* (3), 293–308.

Mead, G. H. (1934). *Mind, self, and society.* Chicago: University of Chicago Press.

Mehan, H. (1992). Understanding inequality in schools: the contribution of interpretive studies. *Sociology of Education, 65,* 1–20.

Perry, C. L., & Duke, D. L. (1978). Lessons to be learned about discipline from alternative high schools. *Journal of Research and Development in Education, 11* (4), 78–91.

Ruby, T., & Law, R. (1983, August). *Potential school dropouts – the attitude factor.* Paper presented at the Annual Convention of the American Psychological Association, Anaheim, CA.

Snow, D. A., & Anderson, L. (1987). Identity work among the homeless: the verbal construction and avowal of personal identities. *American Journal of Sociology, 92,* 1337–1371.

Stebbins, R. (1967). A note on the concept of role distance. *American Journal of Sociology, 73,* 247–250.

Stebbins, R. (1975). Role distance behavior and jazz musicians. In D. Brissett & C. Edgley (Eds.), *Life As Theater: A Dramaturgical Sourcebook* (pp. 133–141). Chicago: Aldine.

Walker, J. C. (1993). Girls, schooling, and sub-culture of resistance. In R. White (Ed.), *Youth subcultures: theory, history and the American experience.* New York: Hobart.

Wexler, P. (1992). *Becoming somebody: toward a social psychology of school.* London: Falmer Press.

Williamson, J. C., Tobin, K. G., & Fraser, B. J. (1986, April). *Use of classroom and school environment scales in evaluating alternative high schools.* Paper presented at the annual meeting of the American Educational Research Association, Boston, MA.

Summary/Chapter 7

Preparing to Analyze Data

1. Qualitative data analysis requires the researcher to systematically search, categorize, integrate, and interpret the data collected in a study.

2. Because qualitative data are typically voluminous, the researcher should try to narrow the focus of the study to facilitate analysis.

3. A great deal of data analysis occurs before formal data collection. Researchers think about and make hunches about what they see and hear during data collection.

4. Analysis involves describing what's in the data. Interpretation involves making sense of what the data mean.

5. There is no single, agreed upon approach for qualitative data analysis. The method selected will depend in part on the topic chosen and the researcher's analytic abilities. The researcher has the key role in data analysis.

Analyzing Qualitative Research Data

6. Data analysis typically involves six processes: data managing; reading/memoing; describing; classifying; interpreting; and representing the results. These processes do not have to be applied sequentially during analysis.

7. Data analysis is a cyclical, iterative process of reviewing data for common topics or themes. The analytic focus is on the context, events, and participants, with a focus on describing from the perspective of the participants. Three approaches to data analysis are the constant comparative, negative case, and analytic induction.

8. Classifying small pieces of data into more general categories is the qualitative researcher's way to make sense and find connections among the data. The categories used may be predetermined before data collection, developed during data collection, or a combination of both.

9. Field notes and transcriptions are broken down to small pieces of data, and these pieces are integrated into categories and often to more general patterns.

10. Typically, data analysis results in a pyramid, with small data pieces at the bottom layer linked to larger and more general categories, and categories linked to even more general patterns.

11. The length of data analysis is difficult to state. It depends mainly on the nature of the study, the amount of data to be analyzed, and the analytic and synthetic abilities of the researcher.

12. Data interpretation is based heavily on the connections, common aspects, and linkages among the data pieces, categories, and patterns. Interpretation cannot be meaningfully accomplished unless the researcher knows his or her data in great detail.

13. The aim of interpretation is to answer three questions: "What is important in the data; Why is it important; and What can be learned from it?"

14. There are some strategies that can help answer these questions: pay attention to your research topic when searching for interpretations; examine closely categories that contain a large amount of data pieces because they likely identify important concepts or practices; examine the findings of other researchers to identify interpretations; and talk to co-investigators and colleagues.

15. Much of the analysis and interpretation relies on the skills of the researcher. However, while the researcher is the main analyst and interpreter, he or she must act within guidelines that help maintain the integrity of the analysis and interpretation.

16. Guidelines for analysis and interpretations include: (1) the credibility of the link between the topic studied and the data used to examine the topic; (2) the description of the methods used to collect, analyze, and interpret the data; (3) expressing researcher and participant biases; and (4) checking data quality.

17. Many computer programs are available for qualitative data analysis. However, the main advantage of the programs is their ability to store, retrieve, and search the database.

Writing the Report

18. The nature of the final report of the study differs with the type of report needed (e.g., dissertation, speech, journal article, etc.).
19. Data analysis and interpretation also go on during the writing of the report. Writing tests the quality and meaningfulness of our ideas and logic. Inevitably we must return to the data to clarify a thought or to verify a logical connection in our report.
20. The report should focus on the key themes and interpretations in the data, not on every theme or interpretation. Language should be straightforward and nonjargony. First-person voice is acceptable. Qualitative reports are often more like a story than a formal report.

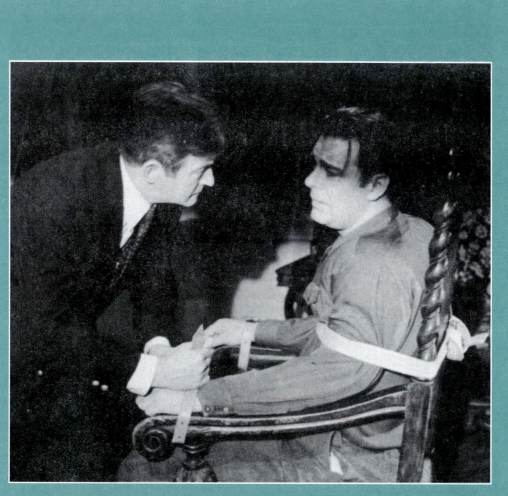

"The responses given by a respondent may be biased and affected by her or his reaction to the interviewer . . . (p. 291)."

Descriptive Research

OBJECTIVES

After reading chapter 8, you should be able to:

1. Briefly state the purpose of descriptive research.
2. List the major steps involved in designing and conducting a descriptive research study.
3. State the major difference between self-report and observational research.
4. List and briefly describe the steps involved in conducting a questionnaire study.
5. Identify and briefly describe four major differences between an interview study and a questionnaire study.
6. Briefly describe two types of observational research.
7. Briefly describe the steps involved in conducting an observational study.

DESCRIPTIVE RESEARCH: DEFINITION AND PURPOSE

A descriptive study determines and describes the way things are. It may also compare how subgroups such as males and females or experienced and inexperienced teachers view issues and topics. We discuss descriptive research in some detail for two major reasons. First, a high percentage of research studies are descriptive in nature. Descriptive research, also called survey research, influences what TV programs we see, the types of automobiles that will be produced, the foods found on grocery shelves, the fashions we wear, and what issues will confront us next year. Second, the descriptive method is useful for investigating a variety of educational problems and issues. Typical descriptive studies are concerned with the assessment of attitudes, opinions, preferences, demographics, practices, and procedures. Examples of educational survey topics are: How do teachers in our school district rate the qualities of our new teacher evaluation program? What do high school principals consider their most pressing administrative problems? Descriptive data are usually collected by questionnaire, interview, telephone, or observation.

Chapter 6 also discussed issues of descriptive research, mainly interviews and observations, as they pertain to qualitative research. While there is some overlap between chapter 6 and this chapter, there are important differences that highlight distinctions between qualitative and quantitative research approaches. For example, the descriptive research plan as described in this chapter is much more structured and standardized than that described in chapter 6. Further, while the qualitative researchers described in chapter 6 interviewed and observed research participants, they did so primarily to identify what the important issues to study were from the participants' perspective. In this more quantitatively oriented chapter, we observe that the researcher predetermines what variables will be surveyed before selecting or observing the research participants. The two approaches have a different conception of whose view is more important, the researcher's or the participants'. Also, the sample sizes and the methods of data analysis differ across the two research approaches. It is important to recognize these differences, but it is also important to understand that both are viable approaches to descriptive research.

Descriptive research sounds very simple—just ask some people some questions and count responses—but there is considerably more to it than just asking questions and reporting answers. A set of basic steps should guide descriptive research studies. Each step must be conscientiously executed: identify a topic or problem, select an appropriate sample of participants, collect valid and reliable data, and analyze and report conclusions. In addition, descriptive studies involve a number of unique problems. For example, self-report studies, such as those utilizing questionnaires or interviews, often suffer from lack of participant response; many potential participants do not return mailed questionnaires or attend scheduled interviews. This makes it difficult to interpret findings, since people who do not respond may feel very differently than those who do. Twenty percent of survey participants might feel very negatively about the year-round school concept and might avail themselves of every opportunity to express their unhappiness, including on your questionnaire. The other 80%, who are neutral or positive toward the concept, might not be as motivated to respond. Thus, if conclusions were based only on those who responded, very wrong conclusions might be drawn concerning the population's feelings about year-round schooling. Further, the researcher is seldom able to explain to research participants who are filling out a questionnaire what exactly a particular question or word really means. One of the hardest things questionnaire researchers must do is to write or select questions that are clear and unambiguous. Descriptive studies that utilize observational techniques often require training observers and developing recording forms that permit data to be collected objectively and reliably. There is more to survey research than first meets the eye.

Once a descriptive problem has been defined, related literature reviewed, and, if appropriate, hypotheses or questions stated, the researcher must give careful thought to selection of the research participants and data collection procedures. It is not always easy to identify the population that has the desired information, for example, and there are many methods for collecting data. Suppose, for example, your problem was concerned with how elementary school teachers spend their time during the school day. You might hypothesize that they spend one quarter of their time on noninstructional activities such as collecting book money and maintaining order. Your first thought might be to mail a questionnaire about how teachers spend their time to a sample of principals. Doing this, however, assumes that principals know how teachers spend their daily time. Although principals would, of course, be familiar with the duties and responsibilities of their teachers, it is not likely that they could provide the data needed for the study. Thus, directly asking the teachers themselves would probably result in more accurate information. However, it is possible that teachers might tend to subconsciously exaggerate the amount of time they spend on activities they consider to be distasteful, such as clerical operations like grading papers. (More to think about!) Further thought might suggest that direct observation would probably yield the most accurate data (but that is very time consuming), or that allowing teachers to respond anonymously would increase the likelihood of accurate answers.

Having decided on a target population and a data collection strategy, the next steps are to identify your accessible population, determine needed sample size, select an appropriate sampling technique, and select or develop a data collection instrument. Because descriptive studies often seek information that is not already available, the development of an appropriate instrument is usually needed. Of course if there is a valid and reliable instrument available, it can be used, but using an instrument just "because it is there" is not a good idea. If you want the appropriate answers, you have to ask the appropriate questions. If instrument development is necessary, the instrument should be tried out and revised where necessary before it is used in the actual study.

Having identified an appropriate sample of participants, and selected or developed a valid data collection instrument, the next step is to carefully plan and execute the specific procedures of the study (when the instrument will be administered, to whom, and how) and the data analysis procedures. In general, the basic steps in conducting a descriptive study will be similar across studies, with specific details such as the research question, the participants, and data collection instruments differing across studies.

Surveys are often viewed with some disdain because many people have encountered poorly planned and poorly executed survey studies utilizing poorly developed instruments. You should not condemn survey research, however, just because it is often misused. After all, you do not stop using telephones just because some people use them to make annoying phone calls. Descriptive research at its best can provide very valuable data.

TYPES OF SURVEYS

Surveys are used in many fields, including political science, sociology, economics, and education. In education their most common use is for the collection of data by schools or about schools. Surveys conducted by schools are usually prompted by a need for certain kinds of information related to the instruction, facilities, or student population. For example, school surveys may examine variables such as community attitudes toward schools, institutional and administrative personnel, curriculum and instruction, finances, and physical facilities. School surveys can provide necessary and valuable information to both the schools studied and to other agencies and groups whose operations are school-related.

The results of various public opinion polls are frequently reported by the media. Such polls represent an attempt to determine how all the members of a population (be it the American public in general or citizens of Skunk Hollow) feel about political, social, educational, or economic issues. Public opinion polls are almost always descriptive surveys. Samples are selected to properly represent relevant subgroups (in terms of such variables as socioeconomic status, gender, and geographic location) and results are often reported separately for each of those subgroups as well as for the total group.

Developmental surveys are concerned primarily with variables that differentiate children at different levels of age, growth, or maturation. Developmental studies may investigate progression along a number of dimensions, such as intellectual, physical, emotional, or social development. The children studied may be a relatively heterogeneous group, such as fourth graders in general, or a more narrowly defined homogeneous group, such as the study of academically gifted children. Knowledge of developmental patterns of various student groups can be used to make the curriculum and instruction more appropriate and relevant for students. Knowing that 4-year-old and 5-year-old children typically enjoy skill-testing games (such as jumping rope and bouncing balls) but do not enjoy group

> ### Tabulating Questionnaire Responses
>
> The easiest way to tabulate questionnaire responses is to have participants mark responses to closed-ended questions on a scannable answer sheet. This option involves locating a scanner and possibly paying a fee to have questionnaires scanned.
>
> If scannable answer sheets are not an option, then each respondent's answers will have to be entered one by one into a computer spreadsheet (e.g., Excel or Lotus) or a statistical program (e.g., SPSS or SAS). Remember this when designing your questionnaire. Make sure that the format is easy to follow and allows respondents to mark answers clearly. This will ensure that you can enter data quickly, without having to search for information.
>
> If your questionnaire contains open-ended questions, you will need to code answers according to patterns in the responses provided. It is very useful to use a qualitative software program to examine your textual data, code it, and generate information regarding the frequency and nature of various codes. Many qualitative software programs also allow the researcher to export coded qualitative data into statistical programs, where advanced statistical analyses can be performed.

work or activities involving competition would certainly be helpful to a preschool teacher in developing lesson plans.

Follow-up studies are conducted to determine the status of a group after some period of time. Like school surveys, follow-up studies are often conducted by educational institutions for the purpose of internal or external evaluation of their instructional program. Colleges and accreditation agencies, for example, typically require systematic follow-up of their graduates. Such follow-up efforts seek objective information regarding the current status of the former students (Are you currently employed?) as well as attitudinal and opinion data concerning the graduates' perceptions of the adequacy of their education. If a majority of graduates should indicate that they think the career counseling they received at old Alma Mater University was poor, this would suggest an area for improvement. Follow-up studies may also be conducted solely for research purposes. A researcher may be interested, for example, in assessing the degree to which initial treatment effects have been maintained over time. A study might demonstrate that students participating in preschool education are better adjusted socially and demonstrate higher academic achievement in the first grade. A follow-up study could be conducted to determine if this initial advantage is still in evidence at the end of the third grade. Often, treatments have an initial impact that does not last; initial differences "wash out" or disappear after some period of time. Conversely, some treatments do not result in initial differences but may produce long-range effects. In many areas of research, a follow-up study is essential to a more complete understanding of the effects of a given approach or technique.

CLASSIFYING DESCRIPTIVE RESEARCH

There are many ways to classify descriptive research, but the two most common are in terms of how often a particular group is surveyed—through cross-sectional or longitudinal surveys—and how data are collected—through self-report instruments or observation.

The first general classification of descriptive research differentiates *cross-sectional surveys* from *longitudinal surveys*. A cross-sectional survey involves the collection of data from selected individuals in a single time period (however long it takes to collect data from the participants). It is a single, stand-alone study. One limitation of cross-sectional studies is that often, a single point in time does not provide sufficient perspective to make needed decisions. When a cross-sectional study includes the entire population, as in the U. S. census, the survey is called, oddly enough, a census. Longitudinal surveys collect data at two or more times in order to measure changes over time. Developmental surveys frequently rely on longitudinal data to measure growth or development.

There are four kinds of longitudinal surveys. All collect data multiple times, but all study different sample groups. To illustrate the difference among the four types, consider how each could be used to collect information about California female valedictorians' attitudes toward female/male equality.

1. *A trend survey* would sample from the general population of female valedictorians in California. To provide information about the trend of the valedictorians' attitudes over time, the researcher would annually select a sample of the female valedictorians in the current year. Each succeeding year the sample would be made up of that year's female valedictorians. A trend survey consists of different groups and different samples over time.

2. *A cohort survey* would select a specific population of female California valedictorians, such as the valedictorians in 1997. Over time, the researcher would select samples of the 1997 valedictorians. Each sample would be composed of different valedictorians, but all samples would be selected only from the 1997 valedictorian group. The members stay the same, but different groups of them are sampled over time. A cohort survey consists of the same group but different samples from that group over time.

3. *A panel survey* would select a single sample of valedictorians from a particular year and study the attitudes of that sample over time. If the researcher were conducting a three-year panel study, the same individuals would respond in each of the three years of the study. A panel survey consists of the same group and the same sample over time. A frequent problem with panel studies, and to a lesser degree cohort studies, is loss of individuals from the study because of their relocation, name change, lack of interest, or death. This is especially problematical the longer the longitudinal survey continues.

4. *A follow-up survey* is similar to a panel study, except that it is undertaken after the panel study is completed and seeks to examine subsequent development or change. It typically is undertaken to determine subsequent development or perceptions. For example, if a researcher wished to study female valedictorians in California a number of years after the original study was concluded, he or she would find individuals from the prior study and survey them to examine changes in their attitudes.

Longitudinal surveys are useful for studying the dynamics of a topic or issue over time. Suppose, for example, you were interested in studying the development of abstract thinking in elementary school students in grades 1 to 4. If you used a cross-sectional approach, you could study samples of children at each of the four grade levels, including first graders to fourth graders. The children studied at one grade level would be different children from those studied at another grade level. The advantage of the cross-sectional method is convenience. If you used a longitudinal approach such as a panel study, you could select a sample of first graders and study the development of their abstract thinking as they progressed from grade to grade; the children who were studied at the fourth-grade level would be the same children who were studied at the first, second, and third grade levels. In longitudinal studies, samples tend to shrink as time goes by; keeping track of participants over time can be difficult, as can maintaining their participation in the study. A major concern in a cross-sectional study is selecting samples of children that truly represent children at their level. A further related problem is selecting samples at different levels that are comparable on relevant variables such as intelligence. An advantage of the longitudinal method is that this latter concern about comparability is not a problem in that the same group is involved at each level. A major disadvantage of the longitudinal method is that an extended commitment must be made by the researcher, the subjects, and all others involved.

The second classification of descriptive research is based on how the data are collected. As noted in chapter 5, *self-report approaches* require individuals to respond to a series of statements or questions about themselves. For example, a survey about local schools might ask respondents questions such as, "Do you believe the cost for the education of children in our community is too high?" Respondents would self-report their views by marking "yes," "uncertain," or "no." Note that questionnaires, telephone surveys, and interviews are all self-report methods, differing only in the ways the self-report data are collected.

Conversely, in an *observation study*, individuals are not directly asked for information. Rather, the researcher obtains the desired data by watching participants. As stated in chapter 6, observation permits various levels of involvement, ranging from participant observer (very involved) to uninvolved observer (least involved). In descriptive research, observers tend to be uninvolved with the participants. Also, survey researchers typically observe predetermined activities, unlike qualitative researchers, who usually do not have predetermined topics to observe.

It is possible, but not typical, for a descriptive study to employ both self-report and observation methods. The following pages discuss both methods in greater detail.

CONDUCTING SELF-REPORT RESEARCH

Self-report research requires the collection of standardized, quantifiable information from all members of a population or sample. In order to obtain comparable data from all research participants, the same questions must be asked. Many of the types of tests described in chapter 5 are used in survey self-report research studies. A collection of such questions is called a *questionnaire*.

CONDUCTING A QUESTIONNAIRE STUDY

Most criticisms of questionnaires are related not to their use but to their misuse. Carelessly and incompetently constructed questionnaires have unfortunately been administered and distributed too often. Development of a sound questionnaire requires both skill and time. The use of a paper-and-pencil questionnaire has some definite advantages over other methods of collecting data such as interviews. In comparison to an interview, a questionnaire requires less time, is less expensive, and permits collection of data from a much larger sample. Questionnaires may be individually administered to each respondent, but for efficiency they are usually mailed. Although a personally administered questionnaire has some of the same advantages as an interview, such as the opportunity to establish rapport with respondents and explain unclear items, it also has some drawbacks. It is very time consuming, especially if the number of respondents is large and geographically scattered. An often-used alternative to the mailed questionnaires is the telephone interview. The steps in conducting a questionnaire study are essentially the same as for other types of research, although data collection involves some unique considerations.

Statement of the Problem

The problem or topic studied and the contents of the questionnaire must be of sufficient significance to both motivate potential respondents to respond and justify the research effort in the first place. Questionnaires dealing with trivial issues such as what color pencils fifth graders prefer or what make of car teachers most favor, usually end up in potential respondents' circular file. Further, the topic must be defined in terms of specific objectives indicating the kind of information needed. Specific aspects of the topic should be described, as well as the kind of questions to be formulated.

Suppose a school superintendent wanted to know how high school teachers perceive their schools. She wanted to conduct a study to help identify areas in the high schools that might be improved. Since a survey questionnaire is made up of a number of questions related to the research topic, it would be useful for the superintendent to identify important aspects of her general question. For example, the following four subareas of the topic might be used to focus the study: (1) respondent demographics (in order to compare the perceptions of males and females, experienced and new teachers and teachers in different departments); (2) teacher perceptions of the quality of teaching; (3) teacher perceptions of available educational resources; and (4) teacher perceptions of the school curriculum. Breaking the general topic into a few main areas helps to focus the survey and aid decision making in succeeding steps in the research sequence.

Selection of Participants

Survey participants should be selected using an appropriate sampling technique. Although simple random and stratified random sampling are most commonly used in survey research, cluster, systematic, and nonrandom samples are also used. In some cases, when the population is very small, the entire group may make up the sample. The selected research participants must be (1) able to provide the desired information sought and (2) willing to provide it to the researcher. Individuals who possess the desired information but are not sufficiently interested, or for whom the topic under study has little meaning, are not likely to respond. It is sometimes worth the effort to do a preliminary check of a few potential respondents to determine their receptivity.

The target population for the superintendent's study is likely to be all high school teachers in the state. Practically speaking, this may be too large a group to reasonably survey, so the superintendent will select participants from the accessible population. In this case, the likely accessible population would be high school teachers from the high schools in the superintendent's district. A sample of high school teachers in the district, perhaps stratified by gender and department, would be randomly selected and asked to complete the questionnaire.

In some cases it is useful to send the questionnaire to a person of authority, rather than directly to the person with the desired information. If a person's boss passes along a questionnaire and asks the person to complete and return it, that person may be more likely to do so than if you ask him or her directly. However, this assumes that the boss cares enough to pass the questionnaire along and that the fact that the boss requested its completion does not influence the respondent's responses.

Construction of the Questionnaire

As a general guideline, the questionnaire should be attractive, brief, and easy to fill out. Respondents are turned off by sloppy, crowded, misspelled, and lengthy questionnaires, especially ones that require long written responses to each question. Turning people off is certainly not the way to get them to respond. To meet this guideline you must carefully plan both the content and the format of the questionnaire. No item should be included that does not directly relate to the topic of the study, and structured, selection-type items should be used if at all possible. It is easier to respond by circling a letter or word than writing out a lengthy response. Identifying subareas of the research topic can greatly help in developing the questionnaire. For example, the four areas identified by our superintendent could make up the four sections of a questionnaire.

An important decision that all survey researchers face is: What method should be used to collect data? As noted, there are four approaches: mail, telephone, personal administration, and interview. The bulk of educational surveys rely on mailed questionnaires. Each approach has its advantages and disadvantages. For example, telephone surveys tend to have high response rates and fairly quick data collection, but require phone numbers and administrator training. Personal administration is efficient if participants are closely situated, but requires time and training for questionnaire administrators. Personal interviews allow rich, more complete responses, but have the least standardization and take the longest to administer. Mail surveys provide the greatest standardization and least training to administer, but can have low response rates and do not permit follow-up or questions regarding unclear responses. Table 8.1 summarizes the strengths and weaknesses of the four survey methods.

Many types of items are commonly used in questionnaires, including scaled items (Likert and semantic differential), ranked items (rank the following activities in order of their importance), checklist items (check all of the following that characterize your principal), and free response items (write in your own words the main reasons you became a teacher). These item types are all self-report measures. Most surveys consist of closed-ended items (i.e., items that are answered by circling a letter, checking a list, or numbering preferences).

Questionnaires rarely contain large numbers of free response items, but in many cases one or two free response questions can be included to give respon-

TABLE	8.1

Comparison of Descriptive Data Collection Methods

METHOD	ADVANTAGES	DISADVANTAGES
questionnaire	inexpensive can be confidential or anonymous easy to score most items standardized items and procedures	response rate may be small cannot probe or explain items only used by people who can read possibility of response sets
interview	can probe and explain items usually high return rate can be recorded for later analysis flexibility of use	time-consuming to use no anonymity bias of interviewer complex scoring of unstructured items training needed
observation	usually unobtrusive examines naturalistic behaviors tends to provide a true picture of observees	time consuming and expensive interpretation can be difficult training needed observer bias and effects
telephone	high response rate quick data collection can reach a wide range of locales and respondents	requires phone numbers difficult to get in-depth data requires training

dents opportunity to add information not tapped by the closed-end items. An unstructured item format, in which the responder has complete freedom of response (questions are posed and the responder must construct his or her own responses), is sometimes defended on the grounds that it permits greater depth of response and insight into the reasons for responses. While this may be true, and unstructured items are simpler to construct, their disadvantages generally outweigh their advantages. Heavy reliance on free response items creates two important problems for the researcher: (1) many respondents won't take the time to respond to free response items and many that do will give unclear or useless responses, and (2) scoring free response items is more difficult and time consuming than scoring closed-ended items. For certain topics or purposes unstructured items may be necessary, and some questionnaires do contain both structured and unstructured items. In general, however, structured items are to be preferred.

Consider the superintendent who wished to conduct a survey to identify areas in high schools that could be improved. She was interested in four areas: the demographics of high school teachers, and teachers' perceptions of teaching quality, educational resources, and school curriculum. She might have developed items such as the following for her questionnaire. Each of the four item types relates to one of the superintendent's areas of interest. Note that these items are examples and the full questionnaire would likely have more items under each of the four areas. It is also desirable to include an open-ended question for respondents to provide additional information.

DEMOGRAPHIC INFORMATION

For each of the following items, put an X beside the choice that best describes you.
1. Gender: Male ___   Female ___
2. Total years teaching: 1–5 ___ 6–10 ___ 11–15 ___ 16–20 ___ 21–25 ___ more than 25 ___
3. Department (please list) _____

CHECKLIST

Below is a list of educational resources. Put a check in front of each resource you think is adequately available in your school.
4. ___ up-to-date textbooks
5. ___ VCRs
6. ___ classroom computers
7. ___ games
8. ___ trade books

LIKERT

Following are a number of statements describing a school's curriculum. Read each statement and circle whether you strongly agree (SA), agree (A), are uncertain (U), disagree (D), or strongly disagree (SD) that it describes your school.
In my school the curriculum:

9. is up to date	SA A U D SD
10. emphasizes outcomes more complex than memory	SA A U D SD
11. is familiar to all teachers	SA A U D SD
12. is followed by most teachers	SA A U D SD
13. can be adapted to meet student needs	SA A U D SD

FREE RESPONSE

14. Circle how you would rate the quality of teaching in your school:
    very good   good   fair   poor
15. Write a brief explanation of why you feel as you do about the quality of teaching in your school.
16. Please indicate other additional comments you have about this topic.

Test items should also be constructed according to a set of guidelines. Include only items that relate to the purpose of the study. Collect demographic information about the sample if you plan to make comparisons between different subgroups of the sample. Each question should deal with a single concept and be worded as clearly as possible. The item, "Although labor unions are desirable in most fields, they have no place in the teaching profession. Agree or disagree," really is asking two questions: Do you agree or disagree that labor unions are desirable, and do you agree or disagree that there should be no teachers' unions? This creates a problem for the respondents and for the researcher. If respondents agree with one part of the item but disagree with the other, how should they respond? Also, if a respondent selects agree, can the researcher assume that means agreement to both statements or to only one—and which one?

Avoid jargon! Any term or concept that might mean different things to different people should be defined or restated. Be specific! Do not ask, "Do you spend a lot of time each week preparing for your classes?" because one teacher might consider one hour per day "a lot," while another might consider one hour per week "a lot." Instead, ask, "How many hours per week do you spend preparing for your classes?" or "How much time do you spend per week preparing for your classes? (a) less than 30 minutes, (b) between 30 minutes and 1 hour, (c) between 1 and 3 hours, (d) between 3 and 5 hours, (e) more than 5 hours."

Also, when necessary, questions should indicate a point of reference. For example, do not ask, "How much time do you spend preparing for your classes?" Instead, specify a particular time reference such as, "How much time do you spend per day (or week) preparing for your classes?" Or, if you were interested in how many hours were actually spent in preparation and also in teachers' perceptions concerning that time, you would not ask, "Do you think you spend a lot of time preparing for classes?" Instead, you would ask, "Compared to other teachers in your department, do you think you spend a lot of time preparing for your classes?" If you don't provide a point of reference, different respondents will use different points, thereby confusing interpretations of responses. Avoid words like *several* or *usually;* be specific about what you mean by *several,* for example. Underlining (in a typed questionnaire) or italicizing (in a printed one) key phrases may also help to clarify questions.

There are a few more don'ts to keep in mind when constructing items. First, avoid leading questions, which suggest that one response may be more appropriate than another. Don't use items that say: "Do you agree with the experts that . . ." or "Would you agree with most people that . . ." Second, avoid touchy questions to which respondents might not reply honestly or at all. For example, asking teachers if they set high standards for achievement is like asking mothers if they love their children; the answer in both cases is going to be "of course!" Don't ask a question that assumes a fact not necessarily true. For example, suppose you asked, "Have you stopped stealing from the church poor box?" The question calls for a simple "yes" or "no" response, but how does one who has never stolen respond? If a respondent answers "yes," it suggests that he or she used to steal but has stopped; if the respondent answers "no," it suggests that he or she is still stealing! Typically, unwarranted assumptions are more subtle and difficult to spot. For example, a questionnaire item sent to high school foreign language teachers in a state asked, "How many hours per week do you use your foreign language laboratory?" This question assumes that all high schools in the state have a foreign language lab. A better way to ask this question is first to ask whether the school has a language lab and then ask those who do have one to indicate how many hours per week it is used.

Remember that the questionnaire items must stand on their own. In most cases you will not be present to explain to respondents what you meant by a particular word or item. That is why it is important to make your questions clear and unambiguous. Table 8.2 summarizes important aspects of writing questionnaire items.

After the questionnaire items have been constructed, they must be placed in the questionnaire and directions for respondents must be written. Even though respondents will have received a cover letter describing the study and asking for their participation, it is good practice to include a brief statement describing the study and its purpose at the top of the questionnaire. Ask general items first and then move to more specific items. Start with a few interesting and nonthreatening items. If possible—and it often is not—put similar item types together. Provide information about how to respond to items (e.g., "Select the choice that you most agree with," "Circle the letter of choice," "Rank the choices from 1 to 5, where 1 is the most desirable and 5 the least," and "Darken your choice on the answer sheet provided. Please use a pencil to record your choices.") Standardized directions promote standardized, comparable responses. Also, providing

TABLE	**8.2**
Criteria for Writing Questionnaire Items	

- Know what information you need
- Know why you need each item
- Write items that make sense
- Define or explain ambiguous terms
- Include only items respondents can answer
- Focus items on a single topic or idea
- Use short questions; do not require a great deal of reading
- Word questions as briefly and clearly as possible
- Word questions in positive, not negative, terms
- Avoid leading questions
- Organize items from general to specific
- Use examples if item format is unusual
- Try to keep items that are clustered on a single page; if a second page is needed, put the response options at the top of the second page
- If using open-ended items, leave sufficient space for respondents to write their responses
- Avoid or carefully word items that are potentially controversial or embarrassing
- Subject items to a pretest review of the questionnaire

clear directions for respondents helps them in completing the questionnaire and helps you in getting ready to conduct data analysis. Don't jam items together; a lot of white should show on questionnaire pages. Number pages and items to help with organizing your data for analysis. Don't put very important questions at the end; respondents often do not finish questionnaires.

Preparation of the Cover Letter

Every mailed questionnaire must be accompanied by a cover letter that explains what is being asked of the respondent and why. The letter should be brief, neat, and, if at all possible, addressed specifically to the potential responder (Dear Dr. Jekyll, not Dear Sir). Mercifully, there are database management computer programs that can assist you with the chore of personalizing your letters. However, recognize that it is not always possible to identify each potential respondent by name. The letter should also explain the purpose of the study, emphasizing its importance and significance. Give the responder a good reason for cooperating—the fact that you need the data for your thesis or dissertation is not a good reason. Good reasons relate to how the data gathered will help the respondent and/or the field in general. If at all possible, the letter should state a commitment to share the results of the study when completed. Include an address, a phone number, or an e-mail address where you can be reached in case potential respondents want to ask questions. In some cases, prior contact with potential research participants is useful, such as a brief letter or phone call indicating that they will be receiving a request for participation in a study. The letter or phone call should briefly note the nature of the study, who the researcher(s) are, and when the formal request is likely to arrive.

It usually helps and adds credibility if you can obtain the endorsement of an organization, institution, group, or administrator that the responder is likely to recognize. For example, if you are seeking principals as respondents, you should try to get a principals' professional organization or the state's chief school officer to endorse your study. If you are seeking parents as respondents, then school principals or school committees would be helpful endorsers of your study. Ideally, you would like to have them cosign the cover letter, but even having them agree to state their endorsement in the cover letter will be helpful. If the planned respondents are heterogeneous, or have no identifiable affiliation in common, a general appeal to professionalism can be made.

If the questions to be asked are at all threatening (such as items dealing with gender or attitudes toward colleagues or the local administrators), anonymity or confidentiality of responses must be assured. *Anonymity* means that no one, including the researcher, knows who completed a given questionnaire. *Confidentiality* means that the researcher knows who completed each survey, but promises not to divulge that information. It is recommended that one of these approaches be used, with its use explained in the cover letter. The promise of anonymity or confidentiality will increase the truthfulness of responses, as well as the percentage of returns. One way to promise anonymity and still be able to utilize follow-up efforts with nonrespondents is to include a preaddressed, stamped postcard with the questionnaire sent to respondents. Request that they sign their name on the postcard and mail it separately from the questionnaire. The postcards allow the researcher to know who has and has not responded, but maintain the anonymity of the separately mailed questionnaire. Anonymity also makes subgroup comparisons impossible unless specific demographic items such as grade taught, gender, and years on the job are included in the questionnaire.

A specific deadline date by which the completed questionnaire is to be returned should be given. This date should give participants enough time to respond but should discourage procrastination; two to three weeks will usually be sufficient. Each letter to be sent should be signed individually. When many questionnaires are to be sent, individually signing each letter will admittedly take considerably more time than making copies of one signed letter, but it adds a personal touch that might make a difference in the potential responder's decision to comply or not comply. Finally, the act of responding should be made as painless as possible. A stamped, addressed, return envelope should be included; if not, your letter and questionnaire will very likely be placed into the circular file, along with the mail addressed to "occupant"! Figure 8.1 shows an example of a cover letter.

Pretesting the Questionnaire

Before distributing the questionnaire to participants, try it out in a pilot study. The cover letter can be pilot tested at the same time. Few things are more disconcerting and injurious to a survey than sending out a questionnaire only to discover that the participants didn't understand the directions or many of the questions. Pretesting the questionnaire provides information about deficiencies and suggestions for improvement. Having three or four individuals read the cover letter and complete the questionnaire will help identify problems. Choose individuals who are thoughtful and critical, as well as similar to the research participants. That is, if research participants are superintendents, then individuals critiquing the cover letter and questionnaire should be superintendents. The pretest group should be encouraged to make comments and state suggestions concerning the survey directions, recording procedures, and specific items. They should

FIGURE **8.1**

Sample Cover Letter

SCHOOL OF EDUCATION

BOSTON COLLEGE

April 10, 1998

Mr. Dennis Yacubian
Vice-Principal
Westside High School
Westside, MA 00001

Dear Mr. Yacubian,

The Department of Measurement and Evaluation at Boston College is interested in determining the types of testing, evaluation, research and statistical needs high school administrators in Massachusetts have. Our intent is to develop a Master's level program that provides graduates who can meet the methodological need of high school administrators. The enclosed questionnaire is designed to obtain information about your needs in the areas of testing, evaluation, research, and statistics. Your responses will be anonymous and seriously considered in developing the planned program. We will also provide you a summary of the results of the survey so that you can examine the responses of other high school administrators. This study has been approved by the university's Human Subjects Review Committee.

We would appreciate your completion of the questionnaire by April 30. We have provided a stamped, addressed envelope for you to use in returning the questionnaire. You do not need to put your name on the questionnaire, but we request that you sign your name on the enclosed postcard and mail it separately from the questionnaire. That way we will know you have replied and will not have to bother you with follow-up letters.

We realize that your schedule is busy and your time is valuable. However, we hope that the 15 minutes it will take you to complete the questionnaire will help lead to a program that will provide a useful service to school administrators.

Thank you in advance for your participation. If you have questions about the study, you can contact me at 555-555-4444.

Yours truly,

James Jones
Department Chair

note issues of both commission and omission. For example, if they think that certain important questions have been left out or if they think that some existing topics are not relevant, they should note this. Having reviewers examine the completeness of the questionnaire is one way to determine its content validity. All feedback provided should be carefully studied and considered. The end product of the pretest will be a revised instrument and cover letter that are ready to be mailed to the already-selected research participants.

Follow-Up Activities

Not everyone to whom you send a questionnaire is going to return it. (What an understatement!) Some recipients have no intention of completing it, others mean to but put it off so long that they either forget it or lose it. It is for this latter group that follow-up activities are mainly conducted. The higher your percent of returned questionnaires, the better your data. Although you should not expect 100% responses, you should not be satisfied with whatever you get after your first mailing. Given all the work you have already done, it makes no sense to end up with a study of limited value because of low returns when some additional effort on your part can make a big difference.

An initial follow-up strategy is to simply send out a reminder postcard. Remember, if you decide upon anonymity in your survey, you will have to send out reminders and questionnaires to all participants, unless you use some procedure that allows you to know who has responded, but not what their responses were. If responses are confidential but not anonymous, you can mail a card only to those who have not responded. Follow-up will prompt those who meant to fill it out but put it off and have not yet lost it! Include a statement like the ones used by finance companies—"If you have already responded, please disregard this reminder and thank you for your cooperation." Follow-up activities are usually begun shortly after the cover letter deadline for responding has passed. After the reminder postcard, a second set of questionnaires is sent to participants who have not responded, but with a new cover letter, and, of course, another stamped envelope. The new letter should suggest that you know they meant to respond but that they may have misplaced the questionnaire or maybe they never even received it. In other words, do not scold them; provide them with an acceptable reason for their nonresponse. The significance and purpose of the study should be repeated and the importance of their input should be reemphasized. The letter should suggest subtly that many others are responding, thus implying that their peers have found the study to be important and so should they.

If the second mailing does not result in an overall acceptable percentage of return, be creative. Magazine subscription agencies have developed follow-up procedures to a science and have become very creative, sending several gentle reminders and "sensational one-time-only offers," as well as phone calls from sweet-voiced representatives suggesting that your mail was apparently not getting through since you failed to renew your subscription. The point is that phone calls, if feasible, may be used with any other method of written, verbal, or personal communication that might induce additional participants to respond. They might grow to admire your persistence!

If your topic is of interest, your questionnaire well constructed, and your cover letter well written, you should get at least an adequate response rate. Research suggests that first mailings will typically result in a 30% to 50% return rate, and a second mailing will increase the percentage by about 20%; mailings beyond a second are generally not cost-effective, in that they each increase the percentage by about 10% or less. After a second mailing, it is usually better to use other approaches to obtain an acceptable percentage of returns.

Dealing with Nonresponse

Despite all your efforts and follow-ups, you may find yourself with an overall response rate of 60%. This raises concern about the generalizability of results, since you do not know how well the 60% responding represent the population from which the sample was originally selected or from the sample actually surveyed. If you knew that those responding were quite similar to the total sample, there would be no problem with generalizablilty; but you do not know that. Those who responded may be different in some systematic way from the nonresponders. After all, they chose not to reply, which already makes them different. They may be better educated, feel more strongly about the issue, or be more concerned about other issues than those responding.

The usual approach to dealing with such nonresponders is to try to determine if they are different from responders in some systematic way. This can be dome by randomly selecting a small sample of nonresponders and interviewing them, either in person or by phone. This allows the researcher not only to obtain responses to questionnaire items, but also to gather demographic information to determine if nonrespondents are similar to respondents. If responses are essentially the same for the two groups, it may be assumed that the response group is representative of the whole sample and that the results are generalizable. If the groups are significantly different, the generalizability across both groups is not present and must be discussed in the research report. Information describing the return rate and its impact on study interpretations should be provided in the final report.

In addition to nonresponse to the questionnaire in general, there also can be nonresponse to individual items in the questionnaire. If respondents do not understand an item or if they find it offensive in some way, they may not respond to it. The nonresponse of the entire questionnaire is usually more frequent and more critical than individual item nonresponse. The best defense for item nonresponse is the careful examination of the questionnaire during the pretest activities. It is at that time that problems with items are most likely to show up. If you follow the item-writing suggestions in Table 8.2 and subject the questionnaire to rigorous examination, item nonresponses will be few and pose no problem in analysis.

Analysis of Results

When presenting the results of a questionnaire study, the response rate for each item should be given, as well as the total sample size and the overall percentage of returns, since not all respondents will answer all questions. The simplest way to present the results is to indicate the percentage of responders who selected each alternative for each item. For example, "On item 4 dealing with possession of a master's degree, 50% said yes, 30% said no, and 20% said they were working on one." In addition to simply determining choices, comparisons can be investigated by examining the responses of different subgroups in the sample. For example, it might be determined that 80% of those reporting possession of a master's degree expressed favorable attitudes toward personalized instruction, while only 40% of those reporting lack of a master's degree expressed a favorable attitude. Thus, possible explanations for certain attitudes and behaviors can be explored by identifying factors that seem to be related to certain responses. Note that the questionnaire must obtain demographic information about the respondents in order to make desired comparisons.

Although item-by-item descriptions provide one form of reporting the results of a survey, it can produce an overload of information that is difficult to absorb and condense. A better way to report is to group items into clusters that address the same issue and develop total scores across an item cluster. For example, recall the four issues our school superintendent had, and also recall the nature of the items she included for the four issues, especially the ones related to Likert and checklist items (see p. 284). Instead of reporting each Likert or checklist item separately, each type can be summed into a total score. For example, if the Likert items were scored from 5 (SA) to 1 (SD), a score for each item could be obtained and the scores could be summed across the Likert items. The total scores or their average could be reported and demographic comparisons could be made using the average score of each group being compared (e.g., males and females). Not only does developing and analyzing clusters of items related to the same issue make it easier and more meaningful to report survey results, it also improves the reliability of the scores themselves—in general, the more items, the higher the reliability.

CONDUCTING AN INTERVIEW STUDY

An interview is essentially the oral, in-person administration of a questionnaire to each member of a sample. The interview has a number of unique advantages and disadvantages. When conducted well it can produce in-depth data not possible with a questionnaire; on the other hand, it is expensive and time consuming. The interview is most appropriate for asking questions that cannot effectively be structured into a multiple-choice format, such as questions of a personal nature or questions that require lengthy responses. In contrast to the questionnaire, the interview is flexible; the interviewer can adapt the situation to each subject. By establishing rapport and a trust relationship, the interviewer can often obtain data that respondents would not give on a questionnaire. The interview may also result in more accurate and honest responses, since the interviewer can explain and clarify both the purposes of the research and individual questions. Another advantage of the interview is that it allows follow-up on incomplete or unclear responses by asking additional probing questions. Reasons for particular responses can also be determined.

Direct interviewer-interviewee contact also has disadvantages. The responses given by a respondent may be biased and affected by her or his reaction to the interviewer, especially if there is not a long-time relationship with the interviewer. For example, a respondent may become hostile or uncooperative if the interviewer reminds him of the dentist who performed five root canals on him last Wednesday! However, another respondent may try hard to please the interviewer because she looks like her sister. Another disadvantage is that interviews are time consuming and expensive, with the consequence that the number of respondents is generally a great deal fewer than the number that can be surveyed with a questionnaire. Interviewing 500 people would be a monumental task compared to mailing 500 questionnaires.

Also, the interview requires a level of skill usually beyond that of the beginning researcher. It requires not only research skills, such as knowledge of sam pling and instrument development, but also a variety of communication and interpersonal relation skills.

An alternative to face-to-face interviewing that is widely used is telephone interviewing. The telephone interview is most useful and effective when the interview is short, specific, not too personal, and contains mainly selection-type questions. Other advantages of telephone interviews are that they are less expensive because there is no travel; they can be used to gather data from national samples; and data are collected and summarized easily in a single location. Telephone interviews also have some drawbacks. For example, it is difficult to build rapport with the interviewee; it is difficult to obtain detailed information over the telephone; interviewees are often bombarded by phone interviews and unwilling to participate. In general, telephone interviews, like face-to-face interviews, require a clearly stated interview questionnaire and training for interviewers.

The steps in conducting an interview study are basically the same as for a questionnaire study, with some unique differences. The process of selecting and defining a problem and formulating hypotheses is essentially the same. Potential respondents who possess the desired information are selected using an appropriate sampling method. An extra effort must be made to get a commitment of cooperation from selected respondents, because their failure to attend interviews is more serious since the interview sample size is small to begin with. The major differences between an interview study and a questionnaire study are the nature of the instrument involved (an interview guide versus a questionnaire), the need for human relations and communication skills, the methods of recording responses, and the nature of pretest activities.

Construction of the Interview Guide

The interviewer must have a written guide that indicates what questions are to be asked, in what order, and how much additional prompting or probing is permitted. In order to obtain standardized, comparable data from each respondent, all interviews must be conducted in essentially the same manner. As with a questionnaire, each question in the interview should relate to a specific study topic. Also, as with a questionnaire, interview questions may be structured, semistructured, or unstructured, but generally are semi- or unstructured to take advantage of the strengths of interviews. Structured questions tend to defeat the purpose of an interview. Completely unstructured questions, such as "What do you think about life in general?" or "Tell me about yourself," allow absolute freedom of response, but tend to be time consuming and unproductive. Therefore, most interviews use a semistructured approach that focuses respondents on more narrow questions and issues. However, sometimes it is useful to ask a structured question to focus in on a desired topic and then use semistructured questions to follow up on the structured question. For example, "Are you in favor of or against the death penalty?" "Why do you feel that way?" The semi-structured questions facilitate explanation and understanding of the responses to the structured question. Thus, a combination of objectivity and depth can be obtained, and results can be tabulated as well as explained.

Many of the guidelines for constructing questionnaires apply to the construction of interview guides. The interview should be as brief as possible and questions should be worded as clearly as possible. Terms should be defined when necessary and a point of reference given when appropriate. Also, leading questions should be avoided, as should questions based on the assumption of a fact not in evidence ("Tell me, are you still stealing from the church poor box?").

Communication During the Interview

Effective communication during the interview is critical, and interviewers should be well-trained before the study begins. Since first impressions are important, getting the interview "off on the right foot" is desirable. Before asking the first formal question, you should spend some time establishing rapport and putting the interviewee at ease. Explain the purpose of the study and assure confidentiality or anonymity of responses. Note that it is hard to provide anonymity when you are face to face with the respondent. As the interview proceeds, make full use of the advantages of the interview situation. The interviewer can, for example, explain the purpose of any question that is unclear to the respondent. The interviewer should also be sensitive to the reactions of the respondent and should proceed accordingly. For example, if a respondent appears to be threatened by a particular line of questioning, you should move on to other questions and return to the threatening questions later, when perhaps the interviewee is more relaxed. Or, if the participant gets carried away with a question and gets "off the track," you can gently get him or her back on target. Above all, the interviewer should avoid words or actions that may make the respondent unhappy or feel threatened. Frowns and disapproving looks have no place in an interview!

Recording Responses

Responses made during an interview can be recorded manually by the interviewer or mechanically by a recording device. If you as the interviewer write the responses, space on the interview form should be provided after each question. Responses can be written during the interview or shortly after the interview is completed. Writing responses during the interview may tend to slow things down, especially if responses are at all lengthy. It also may make some respondents nervous to have someone writing down the words they say. If responses are written after the interview, you are not likely to recall every response exactly as given, especially if many questions are asked. On the other hand, if an audiocassette recorder or video camcorder is used, the interview moves more quickly, and responses are recorded exactly as given. If a response needs clarifying, several persons can listen to or view the recordings independently and make judgments about the response. A recorder or VCR may make respondents nervous, but they tend to forget its presence as the interview progresses. In general, mechanical recording leads to more objective interpretations and scoring. However, if a mechanical recording device is used, it is very important that the respondent know that and agree to its use.

Pretesting the Interview Procedure

The interview guide, procedures, and planned analysis should be tried out before the main study begins, using a small group from the same population or a similar population to the one being studied. As with written questionnaires, feedback from a small pilot study can be used to add, remove, or revise interview questions. Insights into better ways to handle certain questions can also be acquired. Finally, the pilot study will determine whether the resulting data can be quantified and analyzed in the manner intended. As with the pretesting of a questionnaire, feedback should be sought from the pilot group as well as from the interviewers. As always, a pretest is a good use of the researcher's time.

CONDUCTING OBSERVATIONAL RESEARCH

In an observational study, the current status of a phenomenon is determined not by asking but by observing. For certain research questions, observation is clearly the most appropriate approach. For example, you could ask teachers how they handle discipline in their classrooms, but more objective information would probably be obtained by actually observing teachers' classes. The value of observational research is illustrated by a study conducted in the Southwest on the classroom interaction between teachers and Mexican-American students. Many teachers claimed that Mexican-American children are difficult to teach due to their lack of participation in classroom activities and their failure to ask or answer questions. However, systematic observation revealed that the main reason they did not answer questions was that they were not asked very many! Observation revealed that teachers tended to talk less often and less favorably to Mexican-American children and to ask them fewer questions. Thus, observation not only provided more accurate information than teacher reports, but also made the teachers aware that they were unintentionally part of the problem.

Observational techniques may also be used to collect data in nondescriptive studies. For example, in an experimental study designed to determine the effect of behavior modification techniques on disruptive behavior, students could be observed prior to and following the introduction of behavior modification in order to determine if instances of disruptive behavior were reduced in number. In either case, an observational study must be planned and executed just as carefully as any other type of research study.

NONPARTICIPANT OBSERVATION

The major type of quantitative observational research is nonparticipant observation. Recall from chapter 6 that participant observation is usually associated with qualitative research. In nonparticipant observation, the observer is not directly involved in the situation to be observed. In other words, the observer is on the outside looking in and does not intentionally interact with, or affect, the object of the observation. Nonparticipant observation includes both naturalistic observation and simulation observation, and typically involves observation of human subjects.

Naturalistic Observation

Certain kinds of behavior can only be (or best be) observed as they occur naturally. In such situations the observer purposely does not control or manipulate the setting being observed. In fact, the researcher works very hard at not affecting the observed situation in any way. As noted in chapter 6, naturalistic observation is also an important qualitative method. The main difference between a quantitative and qualitative approach to naturalistic observation is that the quantitative researcher approaches the observation with a predetermined idea of what behaviors will be observed, while the qualitative researcher tends not to have a preformed focus. The intent is to record and study behavior as it normally occurs. As an example, classroom behavior of the teacher, student, and the interactions between teacher and student can best be studied through naturalistic observation. Insights gained as a result of naturalistic observation often form the foundation for more controlled research in an area. The work of Piaget, for example, involved primarily naturalistic observation of children. His research and the research that it stimulated have provided education with many important findings regarding concept development in children.

Simulation Observation

In simulation observation the researcher creates a situation to be observed and tells participants what activities they are to engage in. This technique allows the researcher to observe behavior that occurs infrequently in natural situations or not at all—for example, having a teacher trainee role-play a teacher–parent conference. The major disadvantage of this type of observation is that it is not natural, and the behaviors exhibited by those observed may not be the behaviors that would occur in a natural setting. Those being observed may behave the way they think they should behave, rather than the way they normally would behave. In reality, this problem is not as serious as it may sound. Individuals being observed often get carried away with their roles and often exhibit very true-to-life emotions. Besides, even if those observed "fake it," at least they show that they are aware of the correct way to behave or perform. A student who demonstrates the correct way to interact with an irate parent at least knows what should be done.

Two major types of simulation are individual role-playing and team role-playing. In individual role-playing the researcher is interested in the behavior of one person, although other "players" may be involved. The individual is given a role, a situation, and a problem to solve. The observer records and evaluates the person's solution to the problem and the way in which she or he executed it. As an example, a teacher trainee might be told:

> Yesterday Billy Bungle was caught drawing pictures on his desk. You made him stay after school and wash and wax all the desks. The principal has just informed you that a very upset Mrs. Bungle is on her way to see you. What will you say to Mrs. Bungle?

In a team role-playing situation, a small group is presented with a situation and a problem, and the group solution is recorded and evaluated. As an example, a group might be told: The faculty has appointed you a committee of six. Your charge is to come up with possible solutions to the problem of student fights in the halls, an occurrence that has been increasing.

CONSTRUCTING OBSERVATIONAL RESEARCH

The steps in conducting observational research are essentially the same as for other types of descriptive research. Selection and definition of the problem are essentially the same, as is participant selection. Like the interview technique, observation is time consuming and typically involves smaller samples than questionnaire and interview studies. The following discussion focuses on nonparticipant observational studies. Specific guidelines for conducting meta-analyses are beyond the scope of this text, but the subject is touched on at the end of this chapter. (Hey, do you want a 1,000-page text?)

Definition of Observational Variables

There is no way that an observer can observe and record everything that goes on during an observation session, especially in a natural setting such as a classroom.

The research hypothesis or question determines what will be observed. Thus, in a study concerned with the effectiveness of assertive discipline in reducing instances of disruptive behavior, attention would be focused only on "disruptive behavior." The term *disruptive behavior*, however, does not have universal meaning, so the researcher must clearly define (operationalize) what specific behaviors do and do not make up disruptive behavior. In the earlier example, "disruptive behavior" might include talking out of turn, making extraneous noises, throwing things, making offensive noises, and getting out of one's seat, whereas doodling during class would probably not be considered disruptive.

Once an observational topic is defined, observations must be quantified so that all observers will count the behavioral activities in the same way. If Gorgo screams and tips over his chair at the same time, that could be considered as one instance of disruptive behavior or as two instances. Researchers typically divide observation sessions into a number of specific observation periods. That is, they define a time unit for observation. Thus, for a 1-hour session, a time unit of 30 seconds might be agreed upon, resulting in a total of 120 observations per hour. The length of the time unit will usually be a function of both the behavior to be observed and the frequency with which it normally occurs. If observation is simply a matter of observing and recording a high-frequency behavior, the time unit may be as small as 10 seconds. If any judgments or inferences are required on the part of the observer, or if the behavior is a low-frequency behavior, the time unit is typically longer, perhaps 30 seconds or 1 minute. There should be correspondence between actual frequency and recorded frequency. Once the time unit has been established, the observer records what occurred in each observation period. If during a 15-second interval a student exhibits disruptive behavior, this would be indicated, regardless of how often disruptive behavior occurred. After the variables have been defined and the time unit established, a decision must be made as to when observations will be made. For example, if behavior varies with factors such as day of the week and time of day, it would be unwise to observe every Tuesday morning only. One solution is to randomly select observation times so that different days and different times of day are reflected in the observations.

Recording Observations

One point, which at first reading may seem obvious, is that observers should not only observe but also record observed behavior. Even if you are interested in two types of behavior (e.g., teacher behavior and student behavior), the observer should only have to make one decision at a time. Thus, if two types of behavior are to be observed they should probably be observed alternately. In other words, for the teacher–student observation example, teacher behavior might be observed during the first, third, fifth, seventh (and so forth) observation periods, and student behavior might be observed during the second, fourth, sixth, and eighth periods. Such a procedure would present a fairly accurate picture of what occurred in the observed classroom. It is also a good idea to alternate observation periods and recording periods, especially if any inference is required on the part of the observers. Thus, we might have the observers observe for 15 seconds, record for 5 seconds, observe for 15 seconds, record for 5 seconds, and so forth. This approach controls for the fact that the observer is not paying complete attention while recording, and tends to increase the reliability of observations.

Although the point is debatable, as a general rule it is probably better to record observations at the time the behavior occurs. Since each observation must be made within a set period of time, for example 15 seconds or 5 minutes, the recording process should be as simplified as possible. Most observation studies facilitate recording by using an agreed-upon code and a recording instrument. Often the task is not just to determine whether a behavior occurred but to record what actually occurred. The classic Flanders System, for example, which is widely used for classroom observation, classifies all teacher behavior and all student behavior into 1 of 10 categories, each of which is represented by a number. Figure 8.2 describes the 10 categories. Thus, if a teacher praises a student, the observer records that 2 occurred.

FIGURE 8.2

Flanders Interaction Analysis Categories (FIAC)

Teacher Talk	Response	1. *Accepts feeling.* Accepts and clarifies an attitude or the feeling tone of a student in a nonthreatening manner. Feelings may be positive or negative. Predicting and recalling feelings are included. 2. *Praises or encourages.* Praises or encourages students; says "um hum" or "go on"; makes jokes that release tension, but not at the expense of a student. 3. *Accepts or uses ideas of students.* Acknowledges student talk. Clarifies, builds on, or asks questions based on student ideas.
		4. *Asks questions.* Asks questions about content or procedures, based on teacher ideas, with the intent that a student will answer.
	Initiation	5. *Lectures.* Offers facts or opinions about content or procedures; expresses *his* own ideas, gives *his* own explanation, or cites an authority other than a student. 6. *Gives directions.* Gives directions, commands, or orders to which a student is expected to comply. 7. *Criticizes students or justifies authority.* Makes statements intended to change student behavior from nonacceptable to acceptable patterns; corrects student behaviors; bawls someone out. Or, states why the teacher is doing what he is doing; uses extreme self-reference.
Student Talk	Response	8. *Student talk—response.* Student talk in response to teacher contact which structures or limits the situation. Freedom to express own ideas is limited.
	Initiation	9. *Student talk—initiation.* Students initiate or express own ideas either spontaneously or in response to teacher's soliciting initiation. Freedom to develop opinions and a line of thought; going beyond existing structure.
Silence		10. *Silence or confusion.* Pauses, short periods of silence, and periods of confusion in which communication cannot be understood by the observer.

Researchers have developed some very good coding systems. Go to the ETS Test Collection Database (http://ericae.net/testcol.htm) and search under "observation" to see brief descriptions of many observational instruments.

There are a number of different types of observation recording forms. Probably the most often and easily used one is a checklist of all behaviors to be observed so that the observer can simply check each behavior as it occurs. This permits the observer to spend his or her time thinking about what is occurring rather than how to record it. Figure 8.3 shows the recording form for the Flanders observational instrument. It is basically a checklist in which the 10 categories shown in Figure 8.2 are listed on the vertical axis and the observation periods are indicated across the top (1–30). With the exception of categories 1 and 2, which must be described in writing, other categories are indicated with a checkmark. The time line shows the sequence of events that occurred over a period of time. During observation periods 1 and 2, the teacher was asking questions. During the next four periods students were expressing their ideas, and so forth. Thus, Figure 8.3 represents a classroom interaction in which the students are doing most of the talking and the teacher is encouraging and supporting their participation. In addition to time sampling, other data collection approaches include observing the duration of a behavior or the number of times a behavior occurs.

Rating scales are also sometimes used in observational research. These require the observer to observe, evaluate, and rate the observed performance. For example, an observer might rate a teacher's explanation to a student as 1 (not very clear), 2 (clear), or 3 (very clear.) Although as many as five rating categories are used, three is probably the ideal number. Do not use more than five rating categories, because the more categories, the more difficult it becomes to reliably classify performance. An observer could probably discriminate between "not very clear" and "clear" fairly easily, but deciding between "very unclear" and "not very clear" would not be as simple and would lower reliability.

Before developing your own observation form, you should check to see if there is a standardized observation form that is appropriate for your study. Check the ETS Test Collection Database or other sources cited in chapter 5. Using a standardized observation form has the same advantages as using a standardized test in terms of time saved, validity, and reliability. Also, as with standardized tests, the results of your study can be compared with the results of other

	FIGURE	**8.3**

Recording Form for Flanders Interaction Analysis Categories

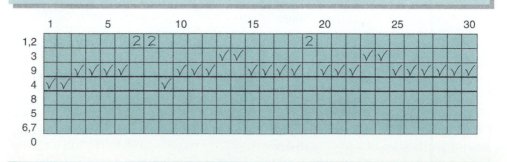

studies that have used the same form. The Flanders System, for example, has been used in a number of studies.

Assessing Observer Reliability

Unreliable observations are as useless as an unreliable test. Determining observer reliability generally requires that at least two observers independently make observations so that their recorded judgments can then be compared to determine agreement. If we wanted to estimate the reliability of scoring for a short-answer test, we could correlate the scores resulting from two independent scorings of the same answers. In other words, all of the tests would be scored twice, and the correlation between the two sets of scores would be our estimate of the reliability of scoring. When we observe behavior, however, we are not typically dealing with scores, but rather with frequencies; that is, how frequently certain behaviors occurred. In these cases reliability is generally calculated based on percent agreement. For example, we might have two independent observers recording the number of disruptive behaviors exhibited by a selected student during a 1-hour period. One observer recorded 20 incidents and the other observer recorded 25 incidents. We can compute interobserver reliability by dividing the total number of agreed observations by the total number of agreed and disagreed observations. That is, suppose that 18 observations were common across the two observers. That means that one observer had two disagreed upon observations and the other had seven disagreed observations. The percent agreement is 18 (number of agreements) divided by 27 (total of agreements and disagreements), or .67 reliability.

Sometimes it is not possible for several observers to observe the same situation at the same time. One solution is to record the observation with a VCR or cassette recorder to play back at a time convenient for the observers. Another advantage to recording observations is that you can replay it as often as you like. If the behaviors observed are at all complex or occur at a fairly rapid rate, it may be difficult to obtain reliable observations from a single observation. If you record the behavior, you can play it back to your heart's content, as can other observers. This is especially useful if important judgments or evaluations are required of the observer. You want such judgments and evaluations to be as reliable as possible. Assuming usage of a valid, reliable observation system, regardless of whether observations are written as they occur or while viewing or listening to a tape, the best way to increase observer reliability is by thoroughly training and monitoring observers.

Training Observers. The most important effect on the reliability and validity of observations is that of the observers. In order to determine agreement among observers, at least two observers are required. That means that there will be at least one other person besides yourself (or two, if you are not going to personally observe) who needs to be familiar with the observational procedures. Additional observers need to be trained in order to have assurance that all observers are observing and recording the same behaviors in the same way. Thus, they must be instructed as to what behaviors to observe, how behaviors are to be coded, how behaviors are to be recorded, and how often (time unit). Observers should participate in numerous practice sessions at which they observe and score situations similar to those to be involved in the study. Then observers should compare their recordings. Each point of disagreement should be discussed so that the observer who differs from the expected understands why. Practice sessions using recordings of behavior are most effective, because segments with which observers have difficulty can be replayed for discussion and feedback purposes. Estimates of observer reliability should be calculated periodically to determine the effectiveness of the training and practice; observer reliability should increase with each session. Training may be terminated when a satisfactory level of agreement is achieved (say 80%).

Monitoring Observers. Training observers only guarantees that the desired level of interobserver reliability is attained. It does not guarantee that this level will be maintained throughout the study. Observers can get tired, bored, overconfident, and forgetful over time. The major way to ensure continued satisfactory levels of reliability is to monitor the observers. The ideal would be to constantly monitor all observers, but this is usually not feasible. At the very least, however, spot checks of observer agreement should be made. As a general rule, the more monitoring that can reasonably be managed, the better.

Reducing Observation Bias

Bias in observations affects the validity of the interpretations. Observers should be made aware of two factors that may seriously affect the validity of observations—observer bias and observer effect. *Observer bias* refers to invalid observations that result from the way in which the observer observes. *Observer effect* refers to invalid observations that result from the fact that those being observed (let's call them observees, with apologies to Webster!) behave differently simply because they are being observed. Each observer brings to the observation setting a unique background that may affect the way he or she perceives the situation and his or her role. Having more than one observer recording independently helps to detect the presence of bias but does not eliminate it. Training and practice sessions should help to reduce it by making observers aware of its existence and by providing feedback when it appears to be occurring. Other types of observer bias are similar to those described as response sets in chapter 5. A response set is the tendency of an observer to rate the majority of observees as above average, average, or below average regardless of the observees' actual behavior. A related problem is the *halo effect*, whereby initial impressions concerning an observee (positive or negative) affect subsequent observations. A final major source of observer bias occurs when the observer's knowledge of the observees or the purposes of the study affect observations. The observer might tend to see what he or she expected or wanted to see. In this instance, having observers view recordings rather than observe live behavior would help, since observers would not have to be told which recordings were made early and which were made late.

The other side of the problem, observer effect, occurs when persons being observed behave atypically simply because they are being observed. For example, a new face in the classroom often leads to teachers and students doing things they normally wouldn't do. Solutions to this problem such as those depicted on television crime shows (one-way mirrors, for example) may seem intriguing but are hardly ever practical, never mind ethical, in observational settings. The best way to handle the problem is to make observers aware of it so that they can attempt to be as unobtrusive (inconspicuous) as possible. Observees usually will ignore the presence of an observer after a few sessions. Thus, simply observing a few sessions prior to recording any data is an effective technique, but watch out for the halo effect. Observers should also be instructed not to discuss the purpose of their observations with the observees. The fact that they may be behaving differently is bad enough; having them behave the way they think you want them to behave is worse!

Another approach to the problem of observer effect is to eliminate observees. If the same information can be determined by observing existing data, use them. For example, school suspension lists have never been known to act differently because they were being observed, and such lists might be a useful, unobtrusive measure of students' disruptive behavior. The following example, although not necessarily sufficient to withstand the scrutiny of economics professors, does illustrate the concept of unobtrusive measures: Mike T. Researcher wanted to know which of the exhibits in the local science museum was most visited by those who come to the museum. Instead of developing a questionnaire, an interview schedule, or an observational study, he decided to use an unobtrusive measure. He measured the wear on the floor beside various exhibits to find the ones that had the most wear. These were the most visited. Unobtrusive measures remove concerns of observer bias and observer effect.

META-ANALYSIS

Meta-analysis is a statistical approach to summarizing the results of many studies that have investigated basically the same problem. Given a number of studies, meta-analysis provides a numerical way of expressing the "average" result of the studies. As you may have noticed when you reviewed the literature related to your problem, numerous variables have been the subject of literally hundreds of studies—ability grouping and cheating, for example. Traditional attempts to summarize the results of many related studies have basically involved classifying the studies in some defined way, noting the number of studies in which a variable was and was not significant, and drawing one or more conclusions. Thus, it might be stated that since in 45 of 57 studies the Warmfuzzy approach resulted in greater student self-esteem than the Nononsense approach, the Warmfuzzy approach appears to be an effective method for promoting self-esteem.

There are two major problems associated with this traditional approach to summarizing studies. The first is that subjectivity is involved. Different authors use different criteria for selecting the studies to be summarized. They apply different review strategies and often come to different (sometimes opposite) conclusions. Thus, for example, some reviewers might conclude that the Warmfuzzy method is superior to the Nononsense method, while other reviewers might conclude that the results are inconclusive. The second major problem is that as the number of research studies available on a topic increases, so does the difficulty of the reviewing task. During the 1970s, the need for a more efficient and more objective approach to research integration, or summarization, became increasingly apparent.

Meta-analysis is the alternative that was developed by Glass and his colleagues.[1] While much has been written on the subject, Glass's *Meta-Analysis in Social Research* remains the classic work in the field. It delineates specific procedures for finding, describing, classifying, and coding the research studies to be included

[1]Glass, G. V., McGaw, B., & Smith, M. L. (1981). *Meta-analysis in social research*. Beverly Hills, CA: Sage.

in a meta-analytic review, and for measuring and analyzing study findings. A central characteristic that distinguishes meta-analysis from more traditional approaches is the emphasis placed on having the review be as inclusive as possible. Thus, reviewers are encouraged to include results typically excluded, such as those presented in dissertation reports and unpublished works. Critics of meta-analysis claim that this strategy results in the inclusion in a review of a number of "poor" studies. Glass and his colleagues counter that there is no evidence that such is the case or that final conclusions are negatively affected, and further, there is evidence that on average, dissertations exhibit higher design quality than many published journal articles. They also note that experimental effects reported in journals are generally larger than those presented in dissertations; thus, if dissertations are excluded, effects will appear to be greater than they actually are.

The key feature of meta-analysis is that each study's results are translated into an effect size (ES), symbolized as Δ. Effect size is a numerical way of expressing the strength or magnitude of a reported relationship, be it causal or not. For example, in an experimental study the effect size expresses how much better (or worse) the experimental group performed as compared to the control group. The basic formula for effect size is:

$$ES = \frac{\bar{X}_e - \bar{X}_c}{SD_c}$$

where

$\bar{X}_e$ = the mean (average) score for the experimental group
$\bar{X}_c$ = the mean (average) score for the control group
SD_c = the standard deviation (variability) of the scores for the control group

The formula may differ, depending upon the statistics actually presented in a study, but the objective is the same. After effect sizes have been calculated for each study, they are averaged, yielding one number that summarizes the overall effect of the studies. Effect size is expressed as a decimal number and, while numbers greater than 1.00 are possible, they do not occur very often. Thus, an effect size near .00 means that, on average, experimental and control groups performed the same; a positive effect size means that, on average, the experimental group performed better; and a negative effect size means that, on average, the control group did better. For positive effect sizes, the larger the number the more effective the experimental treatment.

Although there are no hard and fast rules, it is generally agreed that an effect size in the twenties (e.g., .28) indicates a treatment that produces a relatively small effect, whereas an effect size in the eighties (e.g., .81) indicates a powerful treatment. Just to give you a couple of examples, Walberg[2] has reported that for cooperative learning studies the effect size is .76. This indicates that cooperative learning is a very effective instructional strategy. Walberg also reports that the effect size for assigned homework is .28, and for graded homework, .79. This suggests that homework makes a difference in achievement and that graded homework makes a big difference. (Many of you can probably use this information to your advantage!) As suggested earlier, meta-analysis is not without its critics. It

[2]Walberg, H. J. (1984). Improving the productivity of America's schools. *Educational Leadership, 41*(8), 19–27.

must be recognized, however, that despite its perceived shortcomings, it still represents a significant improvement over traditional methods of summarizing literature. Further, it is not a fait accompli, but rather an approach in the process of refinement.

> On the following pages an example of descriptive research is presented. Note that the study involved a stratified random sample, a mailed questionnaire, a procedure for assuring anonymity of responses, a follow-up mailing, and telephone interviews to assess response bias (i.e., differences between mail responders and nonresponders).

Reading Instruction: Perceptions of Elementary School Principals

JOHN JACOBSON
The University of Texas at Arlington

D. RAY REUTZEL
Brigham Young University

PAUL M. HOLLINGSWORTH
Brigham Young University

ABSTRACT   A stratified random sample of 1,244 U.S. elementary public school principals was surveyed to determine perceptions of their understanding of current issues in elementary reading instruction and the information sources that they use to learn about current issues in reading. The principals reported four major unresolved reading issues: (a) whole language versus basal approaches; (b) assessment of students' reading progress; (c) the use of tradebooks in place of basals; and (d) ability grouping students for reading instruction. Principals' priority ranking of the four most important unresolved reading issues were (a) whole language versus basal approaches; (b) effective alternative assessment of students' reading progress; (c) alternatives to ability grouping students for reading instruction; and (d) the necessity of phonics instruction as a prerequisite to formal reading instruction. The most frequently consulted reading information sources used by elementary school principals within the past 12 months included (a) professional education magazines, (b) personal contacts with specialists and colleagues, and (c) newspapers. Although college classes were the least used information resource of U.S. elementary school principals within the past 12 months, college courses in reading education rated high in utility along with personal contacts with reading specialists. The study concluded that U.S. elementary school principals report awareness of the important reading issues of the day, but that they may need readily accessible and practical information to significantly impact implementation of the current innovations in reading education.

No other area of the curriculum receives as much attention and generates as much debate as does reading instruction. For many years, research and practice have indicated that the success or failure of a school's reading program depends largely upon the quality of school principals' knowledge of and involvement in the school reading program (Ellis, 1986; McNinch & Richmond, 1983; McWilliams, 1981; Weber, 1971). One may conclude, then, that it is important for elementary principals to be informed, active participants in the national conversation about reading instructional issues. It is also an ipso facto conclusion that the quality of school principals' instructional leadership in school reading programs is directly linked to the quality of their knowledge about reading instruction (Barnard & Hetzel, 1982; Kean, Summers, Raivetz, & Tarber, 1979; McNinch & Richmond, 1983; Nufrio, 1987; Rausch & Sanacore, 1984). When principals lack necessary understanding of reading instruction, they tend to shun or delegate responsibility to others for the school reading program (Nufrio). Even worse, some researchers have determined that principals who lack sufficient knowledge of reading instruction tend to resort to misguided means for making decisions instead of grounding their decisions in reliable information and research (Roser, 1974; Zinski, 1975).

A synthesis of past and current research strongly suggests that elementary school principals should bear a major responsibility for the school reading program and have an ethical and professional obligation to be conversant in the same curriculum areas as those expected of elementary classroom teachers (Wilkerson, 1988). To do this, elementary school administrators must stay abreast of current critical reading issues to be effective instructional leaders in their own schools' reading programs.

Past research related to elementary school principals' understanding of reading instruction has been based primarily on surveys of teachers' impressions of principals' reading leadership capabilities. In other related studies, elementary school administrators have been queried about their familiarity with specific reading instructional concepts, their professional reading instruction preparation, and the amount of their own classroom reading teaching experience. Some past research has determined that principals understand reading instructional concepts fairly well (Aldridge, 1973; Gehring, 1977; Panchyshyn, 1971; Shelton, Rafferty, and Rose, 1990), while other research concluded that principals' reading instructional understanding is insufficient and their preparation inadequate to assume leadership roles for elementary school reading programs (Berger & Andolina, 1977; Kurth,

Address correspondence to Paul M. Hollingsworth, Brigham Young University, Department of Elementary Education, 215 McKay Building, Provo, UT 84602.

Jacobson, J., Reutzel, D. R. & Hollingsworth, P. M. (1992). Reading perceptions of elementary school principals. *The Journal of Educational Research, 85,* 370–380. Reprinted with the permission of the Helen Dwight Reid Educational Foundation. Published by Heldref Publications, 1319 Eighteenth St., N. W., Washington, DC 20036-1802. Copyright © 1992.

July/August 1992 [Vol. 85(No. 6)]

1985; Laffey & Kelly, 1983; Lilly, 1982; Moss, 1985; Nufrio, 1987; Rausch & Sanacore, 1984; Zinski, 1975).

Several problems have been associated with past attempts to research principals' knowledge of reading instruction. First, most past studies have been limited to a local area or single state. Few past studies go beyond state lines, and none of them have attempted to describe elementary school principals' perceived knowledge of reading instructional issues nationwide. Second, past survey studies have generally had marginally acceptable return rates, and no checks for response bias by comparing responders with nonresponders were made, thus severely limiting the generalizability of their conclusions.

An exhaustive search of the extant literature indicated that no national research study of principals' perceived knowledge of current critical issues in reading education has been conducted to date. Thus, little is known about the state of contemporary elementary school administrators' perceptions of current, critical issues in reading education. Furthermore, no research data are available on how these important leaders of school reading programs commonly access information regarding current issues in reading education. Thus, the purpose of this study focused on three research questions: (a) What do practicing elementary prinicipals perceive are the critical and unresolved issues in reading education? (b) What level of understanding do practicing elementary principals perceive that they have of each issue? (c) What sources do practicing elementary principals use and find helpful to inform themselves about current issues in reading education?

Method

Survey Instrument

A survey questionnaire consisting of several sections was constructed (see Appendix A). The first section requested the following standard demographic information from the elementary school principals surveyed: (a) school size and type (1–299, 300–599, or 600 or more students, and Grades K–3, K–6, etc.), (b) years of experience as a principal and educator, (c) state, and (d) type of reading approaches used in their schools. The second section of the survey instrument included three tasks. Task 1 presented principals with 11 reading issues and asked them to indicate whether each issue was resolved, unresolved, or never had been an issue in their own minds, experiences, or schools.[1] Task 2 requested that principals rank order from 1 to 3 the top three issues that they had classified as unresolved in Task 1. Task 3 requested that the principals perform a self-rating of their understanding level of each reading issue on a 4-point forced-choice scale: (a) understand well enough to describe underlying issues and give a reasoned argument, (b) understand most of the underlying issues and give a rationale in taking a position, (c) know problem exists, but not sure of basic issue, and (d) not aware of a problem.

In the third section of the questionnaire, Task 4 listed 16 different information sources that principals could use to learn about current reading instructional issues and related research. Principals were asked to respond whether they "had" or "had not" used each of the 16 information sources within the past 12 months. Finally, Task 5 asked principals to rate the usefulness of each reading information resource that they had used on a 3-point forced-choice scale: (1) quite helpful, (2) moderately helpful, and (3) not very helpful.

Procedures

Subjects for this study were randomly selected from a computerized list obtained from Quality Educational Data (QED) of elementary public school principals in the United States during the 1989–90 school year. A total of 1,261 principals from a possible population of 41,467 were selected. The sample represented approximately 3% of the total target population. A stratified random sampling design was used to increase the precision of variable estimates (Fowler, 1988). Elementary school principals were proportionately selected from school size and school types to yield 95% confidence intervals of within ± 1% for the total population from schools with a population of 1 through 299, 300 through 599, and 600 or more. Other subject schools included those having only Grades K through 3 and K through 6 (Fowler, 1988, p. 42).

To track the responses anonymously, we included a postcard (giving the principal's name and a code indicating the size of school) in the mailing. Respondents were asked to return the questionnaire and postcard to separate return addresses. The first mailing was sent in February 1990. Four weeks later, a second mailing (with an updated cover letter and survey form) was sent to those who had not responded to the initial mailing (Heberlein & Baumgartner, 1981).

Return rates on mailed educational survey instruments are frequently in the 40 to 60% range (Could-Silva & Sadoski, 1987). An unbiased final sample of 500 responses would still yield 95% confidence intervals of within ± 3% for the entire target population of U.S. elementary school administrators surveyed (Asher, 1976). To check for response bias among responders, a trained graduate student randomly selected and interviewed over the telephone a sample of 31 (5%) of the nonrespondents (Frey, 1989). The telephone interview consisted of 16 questions selected from the mailed questionnaire (11 questions relating to reading issues and 5 questions on reading information sources used). Telephone responses were then compared with mailed responses by using chi-square analyses of each item to learn if any systematic differences existed between the answers of the two groups. If significant differences were not found between the two groups, then responses for those who returned their survey by mail may be generalizable to the larger

Journal of Educational Research

population of elementary school principals (Borg & Gall, 1989).

Results

Of the 1,261 surveys sent, 17 were returned because of inaccurate addresses. Thus, a total of 1,244 possible responses remained. Thirty percent (373) of the principals responded to the first mailing. The second mailing yielded an additional 17% or 208 principals, giving a total response rate of 47%, or 581 principals. In Table 1, we report the number of principals receiving and returning questionnaires from each state.

Because a 47% survey return rate is a figure that is minimally adequate to accurately reflect the perceptions of the target population (Dillman, 1978), a follow-up telephone interview of 5% of the nonrespondents was conducted. Responses to the telephone interview were compared with the mailed responses by constructing contingency tables from the responses of the two groups (responders and nonresponders). Chi-square statistics were calculated for each of the 16 questions. No significant differences ($p < .05$) were found for responses on 7 of 11 reading issues and 4 of 5 reading information sources. In other words, 64% of the responses between those who responded by telephone and those who responded by mail did not vary significantly on the 11 reading issues. And 80% of the responses between those who responded by

telephone and those who responded by mail did not vary significantly on the sources of information that principals use to remain informed about reading issues. The differences between responders and nonresponders are described in Table 2.

In addition, chi-square analyses of responders from the first and second mailings yielded no significant differences, nor were measurable differences found between respondents resulting from school type or size ($p < .05$). Overall, the similarities between the two groups were determined sufficient to enable reasonably confident generalizations to the target population to be made by using the mail responses only (deVaus, 1986). Therefore, only the mail response data are reported.

Summary of Research Questions

Research Question 1: What do practicing elementary school principals perceive are the critical and unresolved issues in reading education? Of the 11 issues surveyed, 40% or more of the principals perceived 6 issues as *unresolved*: (a) use of whole language approaches instead of basal-reader approaches (73%); (b) assessment of students' reading progress (63%); (c) use of tradebooks instead of basal readers (56%); (d) use of ability grouping for reading instruction (48%); (e) whether kindergarten children should pass a screening test to enter kindergarten (46%); (f) whether at-risk readers should spend increased time reading or practicing skills (40%).

Table 1.—Number of Principals Receiving and Returning Questionnaires, by State

State	Sent	Returned	State	Sent	Returned
Alabama	21	5	Missouri	29	16
Alaska	5	3	Montana	7	3
Arizona	14	6	Nebraska	17	7
Arkansas	17	6	Nevada	6	2
California	125	38	New Hampshire	7	4
Colorado	23	12	New Jersey	36	13
Connecticut	18	7	New Mexico	11	8
Delaware	2	0	New York	68	27
District of Columbia	3	2	North Carolina	31	12
Florida	39	16	North Dakota	4	1
Georgia	27	16	Ohio	62	28
Hawaii	4	3	Oklahoma	21	10
Idaho	9	8	Oregon	21	8
Illinois	53	30	Pennsylvania	57	30
Indiana	33	19	Rhode Island	7	3
Iowa	25	12	South Carolina	17	5
Kansas	22	7	South Dakota	17	4
Kentucky	16	8	Tennessee	22	8
Louisiana	23	8	Texas	92	45
Maine	9	3	Utah	10	7
Maryland	24	12	Vermont	7	2
Massachusetts	32	11	Virginia	21	10
Michigan	56	24	Washington	24	12
Minnesota	24	12	West Virginia	19	10
Mississippi	12	6	Wisconsin	23	11
Total				1,244[a]	581

July/August 1992 [Vol. 85(No. 6)]

Table 2.—Percentage of Responders and Nonresponders Whose Answers Differed Significantly (Chi-Square) for the Resolvedness Question About Reading

Issue	Unresolved (%)	Resolved (%)	Never an issue (%)	No response	Total
Should schools be required to adopt a basal series?					
Responders	38.9	35.1	26.0	3	581
Nonresponders	48.4	51.6	.0	0	31
Should reading instruction be mastery based?					
Responders	37.3	46.0	16.7	5	581
Nonresponders	38.7	61.3	0.0	0	31
Should children's entry into kindergarten be delayed until they perform successfully on a screening test?					
Responders	45.7	29.1	25.3	3	581
Nonresponders	45.2	48.4	6.5	0	31
Should schools be required to use the same program in all grades (e.g., same basal series)?					
Responders	35.0	41.1	23.9	7	581
Nonresponders	51.6	45.2	3.2	0	31

Note. Critical value of chi-square = 5.99, $df = 2$, $p < .05$.

Of the 11 issues, 40% or more of the principals surveyed perceived the following 6 issues as *resolved*: (a) whether reading skills should be taught in isolation or integrated with the remaining language arts (63%); (b) whether phonics should be taught as a prerequisite to formal reading instruction (48%); (c) whether at-risk readers should spend increased time reading or practicing skills (47%); (d) whether reading instruction should be mastery based (46%); (e) use of ability grouping for reading instruction (43%); and (f) whether schools should be required to use the same reading instructional program in all grades (41%).

In 24% or more of the principals' responses, they indicated that certain reading issues had never been an issue in their perception. In order of *never been an issue*, the principals indicated (a) whether schools should be required to adopt basal reading series (26%); (b) whether tradebooks should be used in place of basal readers (25%); (c) whether kindergarten children should pass a screening test to enter kindergarten (25%); and (d) whether schools should be required to use the same reading instructional program in all grades (24%).

Of the issues that principals rated as unresolved, the top four items receiving the highest *priority ranking* in terms of their relative importance to improving reading instruction were (a) use of whole language approaches instead of basal reader approaches; (b) assessment of students' reading progress; (c) use of ability grouping for reading instruction; and (d) whether phonics should be

taught as a prerequisite to formal reading instruction. Of the 11 reading issues surveyed, the principals perceived the issue of requiring schools to use the same program in all grades (e.g., the same basal series) to be the issue of least importance. Table 3 gives the rankings of the surveyed elementary school principals for each reading issue.[2]

In summary, from among the 11 reading issues surveyed, elementary school principals rated the following as the single most important *unresolved* issue: use of whole language approaches instead of basal reader approaches (73%). The issue that the prinicipals perceived as most *resolved* was whether reading skills should be taught in isolation or integrated with the remaining language arts (63%). The *unresolved* issue that the principals ranked highest in relative importance was use of whole language approaches instead of basal reader approaches. Finally, the issue that most of the principals felt had *never been an issue* was whether schools should be required to adopt basal reading series (26%).

Research Question 2: What level of understanding do practicing elementary principals perceive they have of each issue? After the principals were asked to rank order the unresolved issues in terms of importance, we requested that they rate their understanding level for each of the 11 reading issues using a 4-point scale (1 being the highest). Therefore, the lower the mean score, the higher the principals rated their personal understanding of each reading issue. Percentages, along with means and standard deviations, are also presented in Table 3.

Journal of Educational Research

Table 3.—Classification, Rating, and Ranking of Reading Issues by U.S. Elementary School Principals

Reading issues	Unresolved (%)	Resolved (%)	Never an issue (%)	Issue ranking	Understanding of the issues[a]					
					1 (%)	2 (%)	3 (%)	4 (%)	M	SD
How should student reading progress be assessed?	65	26	9	2	60	33	5	2	1.48	.68
Should the whole language approach be used instead of the basal reader approach?	73	21	6	1	52	39	8	1	1.58	.67
Should tradebooks be used in place of basals?	56	19	25	7	43	15	31	11	1.93	1.0
Should reading skills be taught in isolation or integrated with other language arts curriculum?	23	63	14	8	76	18	3	3	1.34	.70
Should phonics be taught as a prerequisite to formal reading instruction?	39	48	13	4	67	27	4	2	1.42	.67
Should students be grouped by ability for reading instruction?	48	43	9	3	67	28	2	3	1.42	.69
Should schools be required to adopt a basal series?	39	35	26	10	57	26	6	11	1.72	1.0
Should at-risk readers spend more time reading connected text or on practicing isolated reading skills?	40	47	13	6	57	33	8	2	1.54	.71
Should reading instruction be mastery based?	37	46	17	9	45	39	11	5	1.76	.84
Should children's entrance into kindergarten be delayed until they perform successfully on a screening test?	46	29	25	5	58	28	9	5	1.62	.86
Should schools be required to use the same program in all grades (e.g., the same basal series)?	35	41	24	11	61	24	5	10	1.64	.96

[a]1 = understand well enough to describe underlying issues and give a reasoned argument; 2 = understand most of underlying issues and give a rationale in taking a position; 3 = know problem exists, but not sure of basic issue; 4 = not aware of problem.

Principals expressed *greatest* understanding of the following four issues: (a) teaching reading skills in isolation or integrated with other language arts curriculum ($M = 1.34$); (b) grouping students by reading ability for instruction in reading ($M = 1.42$); (c) teaching phonics as a prerequisite to reading instruction ($M = 1.42$); and (d) assessing students' reading progress. Principals expressed *least* confidence in their understanding of the following three issues: (a) using tradebooks in place of basals ($M = 1.93$); (b) using mastery-based reading instruction ($M = 1.76$); and (c) requiring schools to adopt a basal series ($M = 1.72$). Though principals reported a lack of confidence in their understanding of certain reading education issues, an overall mean score of 1.59 indicated that, generally, elementary school principals believed they understood most of the underlying issues, but, according to the survey criteria, they did not feel confident enough in their understanding of reading issues to give a good rationale for taking one side or the other.

Research Question 3: What sources do practicing elementary principals use and find helpful to inform themselves about current issues in reading education? Sixteen different information sources were listed on the questionnaire. Principals were to indicate if they had used each of the information sources in the past 12 months. They were asked also to rate the helpfulness of the sources that they had used. Percentages, along with means and standard deviations, were calculated and are reported in Table 4.

The principals reported that the top four reading information sources *used most* were (a) magazines for professional educators that carry articles about reading and literacy (96.6%); (b) personal contacts with specialists in the field (95.9%); (c) newspaper articles about reading issues (93.6%); and (d) magazines or newsletters focusing on reading issues (88.6%). The five reading information sources *used least* were, in order, (a) college or university reading courses (14.3%); (b) college textbooks focused on reading (24.9%); (c) reading articles in professional

July/August 1992 [Vol. 85(No. 6)]

Table 4.—Utility of Reading Education Information Sources as Rated by U.S. Elementary School Principals

Source	Percentage used	Rated utility in percentages			M	SD
		Quite	Moderately	Not very		
Personal contacts with specialists in the field	95.9	79.1	20.7	.2	1.2	.41
Professional association conventions	61.0	62.0	35.4	2.5	1.4	.54
Magazines or newsletters focusing on reading issues	88.6	52.5	46.3	1.2	1.5	.52
Literacy articles in magazines for professional educators	96.6	61.3	36.6	2.1	1.4	.53
Reading articles in magazines focused on techniques and instructional methods	81.3	46.2	51.5	2.3	1.6	.54
Reading articles in popular national magazines	74.4	17.6	55.4	27.0	2.1	.66
Journal articles reporting results of research	49.3	53.3	42.1	4.6	1.5	.59
Reading articles in professional handbooks	38.8	50.0	46.4	3.6	1.5	.57
College textbooks focused on reading	24.9	42.0	49.0	9.1	1.7	.64
Books about reading published by popular press	64.4	36.3	53.8	9.9	1.7	.63
TV or radio broadcasts about reading issues	77.7	19.3	55.6	25.1	2.1	.67
Newspaper articles about reading issues	93.6	18.3	55.8	25.9	2.1	.66
Reading reports from research agencies	42.3	49.6	46.7	3.7	1.5	.57
Reading reports and publications sponsored by governmental agencies	76.2	47.0	46.6	6.4	1.6	.61
College or university reading courses	14.3	61.3	35.0	3.8	1.4	.57
Workshops or organized study groups focused on reading issues	67.5	71.5	27.9	.5	1.3	.47

Note. Data represent only those principals who reported using the information resources in the past 12 months.

handbooks (38.8%); (d) reading reports from research agencies (42.3%); and (e) journal research articles (49.3%).

Also shown in Table 4 are the principals' rankings of the relative helpfulness of each used source. To calculate means and standard deviations for the relative helpfulness rating of each information resource, we converted category responses to numeric values, using a 3-point scale. The closer each mean approximated the value of 1, the higher the mean helpfulness utility rating for the information source. From an examination of the means, the following five reading information sources were reported as *most helpful: (a) personal contacts with specialists in the field (M = 1.2);* (b) workshops or organized study groups focused on reading (M = 1.3); (c) attendance at professional association conventions (M = 1.4); (d) literacy articles in magazines for professional educators (M = 1.4); and (e) college or university reading courses (M = 1.4). Three information sources rated *least helpful* by elementary principals were (a) reading articles in popular national magazines (M = 2.1); (b) watching

or listening to TV or radio broadcasts about reading issues (M = 2.1); and (c) reading newspaper articles about reading issues (M = 2.1).

Discussion

Among elementary school principals surveyed across the United States, the most unresolved reading issue is the controversy between the whole language versus basal approaches to reading instruction. The reading education issue rated least understood by principals was the use of tradebooks in place of basals. These findings are most interesting because of their immediate relationship to each other and to the whole language versus basal reader approaches to reading instruction issue. Explaining this finding is difficult because principals were not asked *why* they indicated that this issue is unresolved. One speculation might be that, in the minds of principals, part of the problem associated with deciding whether to implement tradebooks in reading instruction is the question of *how* to use tradebooks either to supplant or supplement the

Journal of Educational Research

basal reader. However, further research is needed to determine the reasons *why* the issue surrounding the use of whole language versus basal readers is an issue of such great importance.

Also of note, the principals ranked as the second and third most important *unresolved* national reading issues, assessment of reading progress and use of ability grouping. Yet, when asked to rank their understanding of reading issues, the principals gave the second and most important unresolved issue, assessment of student reading progress, the fourth highest rating of understanding, indicating that although it is an unresolved issue, they understand it well. Additionally, the third most important unresolved issue, ability grouping students for reading instruction, received the second highest rating of understanding. Though principals rated their perceived understanding of the issue of ability grouping as being high, it remains an unresolved issue in the minds of principals nationally. Again, these issues share close philosophical proximity with the whole language versus basal reader issue. Because tradebook use calls into question accepted assessment practices and the use of ability groups, one can understand that these issues would loom as critical issues in the minds of U.S. principals.

Principals' perceived lack of understanding and priority rating of the whole language versus basal reader issue as unresolved reflects a widespread concern among principals nationally regarding this issue. One positive sign that principals may be attempting to deal with the whole language versus basal reader issue is the fact that only 77% of the principals surveyed reported that their schools used the basal reader as the major approach for reading instruction, as compared with other recent estimates indicating that basal reader use in American schools exceeds 90% (Goodman, Shannon, Freeman, & Murphy, 1988).

Although the principals rated their understanding of the whole language versus basal reader issue as one of the least understood issues, they reported less use of basal readers and greater use of tradebooks in schools than previous national estimates indicated. This finding suggests that the principals' perceived lack of understanding regarding the whole language versus basal reader issue may not be precluding their attempts to make greater use of tradebooks in their school reading programs. The means by which principals are learning to make these changes *may* be related to their use of reading information resources.

With respect to the information resources used and valued most by principals, this study revealed that the majority of principals surveyed relied on (a) professional education magazines, (b) personal contacts with specialists in reading, and (c) newspapers as their major sources for gaining information about reading education issues and practices. Nearly 90% of those principals surveyed indicated that they had used one of those top three information sources about reading education in the past 12 months. Of note, those sources tend to be interpretive sources and may give only surface-level information, as opposed to more in-depth original research sources. However, considering the constraints exigent upon principals' time, less formal research synthesis may be the most pragmatic means of acquiring current information regarding critical reading instructional issues and promising practices. This fact is substantiated in part by the information sources that the principals used least.

During the past 12 months, the information sources that principals used least were (a) college or university reading courses, (b) college textbooks on reading, (c) articles in professional handbooks, and (d) research reports from research agencies. Those sources tend to focus on theories, practices, techniques, and approaches verified by in-depth original research studies, and they require greater time commitments than do the less formal information resources used most by practicing principals. The finding that enrolling in college or university reading courses was least used was rather curious when juxtaposed against principals' rankings of the most helpful information sources. Although the principals tended not to enroll in college and university reading course work during the past 12 months, they ranked college and university reading courses in the top four reading information sources as most helpful ($M = 1.4$, on a 3-point, with 1 being the highest).

In summary, the principals chose print informational sources that were interpretive, informal, and less technical information sources, that is, newsletters, newspaper articles, and magazines. They tended not to use detailed research reports found in texts, journals, handbooks, and reading reports from research agencies. However, the principals' selection and use of less technical, more interpretive reading information sources, as well as accessible reading specialists, seems logical given the constraints upon their time. Although the principals tended to rate college courses as extremely helpful, enrolling in university course work might not always be accessible, convenient, or even feasible for many practicing principals.

Implications

From this study, one might conclude that the vast majority of U.S. elementary school principals do attempt to keep current on issues related to reading education. Although principals appear to be aware of current trends and issues in reading education, they may not feel sufficiently confident about their understanding of the issues to implement innovative changes in school reading programs. This conclusion is sustained by the principals' ranking of the issue regarding using whole language versus basal readers as the most unresolved issue while also ranking this issue as least understood.

July/August 1992 [Vol. 85(No. 6)]

The conclusion of this study, that U.S. elementary school principals prefer obtaining information about critical reading issues and practices from practical and accessible sources, suggests that authors of educational literature and reading specialists should be aware that principals not only need to understand the issues but also to receive specific guidance on *how* to select promising reading practices for use in their schools and *how* to implement reading program changes.

One paradoxical finding should give strong signals to colleges and universities. Although the principals valued university-level reading courses, many of them had not used that information resource within the past 12 months. This finding may indicate a need for institutions of higher learning to design more accessible means for disseminating current, practical information into schools and classrooms.

In conclusion, the majority of U.S. elementary principals perceived that they were aware of current, critical, and unresolved issues in reading education, that is, tradebooks, reading assessment, and ability grouping. However, according to the survey criteria, many principals did not have enough confidence in their understanding of reading issues to give a reasoned rationale for taking one side or the other. Finally, if principals are to remain informed, information related to innovative reading practices must be disseminated in easily accessible and understandable ways.

APPENDIX A

Reading Education in the United States: Elementary Principals' Involvement

ELEMENTARY SCHOOL PRINCIPALS' QUESTIONNAIRE

(This questionnaire takes approximately 10–15 minutes to complete)

Section 1. IMPORTANT Demographic Information

Please complete the following:
(Check)

School Size: _____1–299 _____300–599 _____600+

School Type: _____K–3 _____K–6 _____Other _____
(Specify)

Years of experience as an elementary school principal_____

Total years of experience as an educator_____

State in which your school is located_____

Give, in percentage, the kinds of reading approaches that are currently being used in your school.
(e.g., 70% basal 20% literature based 10% whole language _____other_____)
_____basal _____literature based _____whole language _____other _____
(Specify)

SECTION 2. THIS SECTION ASKS YOU TO CONSIDER ELEVEN READING INSTRUCTION ISSUES. YOU WILL BE ASKED TO COMPLETE THREE TASKS RELATED TO THESE ELEVEN ISSUES.

Task 1. Classify
Eleven reading education issues are listed below. In your mind, which of these are:
UI: An *Unresolved Issue* (research is not conclusive)
RI: A *Resolved Issue* (research is conclusive—was once an issue but is no longer)
NI: *Never has been an issue* as far as I am concerned.
For each concern, circle the letter which designates the category you selected.

Task 2. Rank
After you have classified each statement, rank order the top three *unresolved issues* in terms of their relative importance to improving reading instruction from your point of view. Use the number "1" to indicate the issue which you believe is most important. Then use the numbers "2," "3," and so on to indicate the issues that are second, third. . . . Rank only the issues you classified as *unresolved*.

Task 3. Rate
Please rate your understanding of each issue (including any issues you added) as follows:
A. I understand this problem well enough to describe the underlying issues and can give a reasoned argument explaining my position.
B. I believe that I understand most of the underlying issues, but I can't give a good rationale for taking one side or the other.
C. I know that this problem exists, but I'm unsure of what the basic issues are.
D. I'm not aware of any problems in this area.

Journal of Educational Research

READING ISSUES:

	Task 1: Classify			Task 2: Rank	Task 3: Rate
1. How should students' reading progress be assessed?	UI	RI	NI	___	___
2. Should the whole language approach be used instead of the basal reader approach?	UI	RI	NI	___	___
3. Should tradebooks be used in place of basals?	UI	RI	NI	___	___
4. Should reading skills be taught in isolation or integrated with other language arts curriculum?	UI	RI	NI	___	___
5. Should phonics be taught as a prerequisite to reading instruction?	UI	RI	NI	___	___
6. Should students be grouped by reading ability for instruction in reading?	UI	RI	NI	___	___
7. Should schools be required to adopt a basal reading series?	UI	RI	NI	___	___
8. Should at-risk readers spend more time on reading connected text or on practicing isolated reading skills?	UI	RI	NI	___	___
9. Should reading instruction be mastery based?	UI	RI	NI	___	___
10. Should children's entry into kindergarten be delayed until they perform successfully on a screening test?	UI	RI	NI	___	___
11. Should schools be required to use the same program in all grades (e.g., the same basal series)?	UI	RI	NI	___	___
12. (Other)_____	UI	RI	NI	___	___

SECTION 3. THIS SECTION ASKS YOU TO CONSIDER SIXTEEN READING INFORMATION SOURCES AVAILABLE TO PRINCIPALS. YOU WILL BE ASKED TO DO TWO TASKS IN THIS SECTION.

Task 4
Which of the activities listed below have you personally participated in during the past 12 months as a means of keeping yourself informed about current issues in reading. Mark an "X" in the blank "Have Done" or "Have Not Done" for each source.

Task 5
After completing Task 4, rate the degree to which each source you have used was helpful by placing an "X" in the blank "Quite Helpful," "Moderately Helpful," or "Not Very Helpful." **DO NOT** rate sources that you have not used in the last 12 months.

SOURCES:	Task 4 Have Done	Have Not Done	Task 5 Quite Helpful	Moderately Helpful	Not Very Helpful
1. Personal contacts with specialists in the field (e.g., informal contacts with friends, colleagues, professors, and educators who have specialized in reading education)	___	___	___	___	___
2. Attendance at conventions of professional associations (e.g., local, state, or national: International Reading Association, National Reading Conference)	___	___	___	___	___
3. Reading magazines or newsletters which focus on reading issues (e.g., *Language Arts, Reading Teacher, Journal of Reading, Reading Horizons*)	___	___	___	___	___
4. Reading articles about literacy issues in magazines for professional educators (e.g., *Phi Delta Kappan, The Principal, Elementary School Journal, Educational Leadership*)	___	___	___	___	___
5. Reading articles in magazines focused on teaching techniques and instructional methods (e.g., *Instructor, Teacher, K–12 Learning*)	___	___	___	___	___
6. Reading articles in popular national magazines (e.g., *Atlantic Monthly, Time, U.S. News, Reader's Digest, Parents, Family Circle*)	___	___	___	___	___
7. Reading journal articles which focus on reporting the results of reading research (e.g., *Reading Research Quarterly, Journal of Reading Behavior, Journal of Educational Psychology, Journal of Educational Research*)	___	___	___	___	___
8. Reading articles in professional handbooks (e.g., *Handbook of Reading Research, Handbook of Research on Teaching, Encyclopedia of Educational Research, Review of Research in Education*)	___	___	___	___	___

July/August 1992 [Vol. 85(No. 6)]

Sources continued . . .

	Task 4			Task 5		

9. Reading college textbooks focused on reading (e.g., Books on teaching language arts, reading)

10. Books about reading which have been published by popular press (e.g., *Cultural Literacy, Illiterate American, Why Johnny Still Can't Read, Closing of the American Mind, All I Ever Needed to Know I Learned in Kindergarten*)

11. Watching or listening to radio and television broadcasts about reading issues (e.g., news reports, documentaries, debates, interviews, commentaries)

12. Reading newspaper articles about reading issues.

13. Reading reports about reading from research agencies (e.g., Center for the Study of Reading, regional labs)

14. Reading reports and publications about reading sponsored by governmental agencies (e.g., *What Works, Becoming a Nation of Readers*)

15. Enrollment in college or university courses related to reading education.

16. Participation in workshops, seminars, or organized study groups focused on reading issues.

17. Other: _____

NOTES

1. The 11 issues included in the survey were selected by a panel of reading experts. Issues were selected based on attention that each has received in the recent reading education and research literature.

2. In the ranking of the reading issues, some respondents did not follow directions. They ranked all issues, instead of ranking only issues that they felt were unresolved. To adjust for the problem, we included only unresolved issues in the data analysis.

REFERENCES

Aldridge, T. (1973). *The elementary principal as an instructional leader for reading instruction.* Unpublished doctoral dissertation, University of Missouri.

Asher, J. W. (1976). *Educational research and evaluation methods.* Boston: Little, Brown.

Barnard, D., & Hetzel, R. (1982). *Principals handbook to improve reading instruction.* Lexington, MA: Ginn and Company.

Berger, A., & Andolina, C. (1977). How administrators keep abreast of trends and research in reading. *Journal of Reading, 21,* 121-125.

Borg, W. R., & Gall, M. D. (1989). *Educational research, 5th ed.* New York: Longman.

Could-Silva, C., & Sadoski, M. (1987). Reading teachers' attitudes toward basal reader use and state adoption policies. *Journal of Educational Research, 81,* (1), 5-16.

deVaus, D. A. (1986). *Surveys in social research.* Boston: George Allen and Unwin.

Dillman, D. A. (1978). *Mail and telephone surveys: The total design method.* New York: Wiley.

Ellis, T. (1986). The principal as instructional leader. *Research-Roundup, 3*(1), 6.

Fowler, F. J. (1988). *Survey research methods.* Newbury Park, CA: Sage.

Frey, J. H. (1989). *Survey research by telephone* (2nd ed.). Newbury Park, CA: Sage.

Gehring, R. (1977). *An investigation of knowledge of Clark County, Nevada, elementary school principals about the teaching of reading in primary grades.* Unpublished doctoral dissertation, University of Colorado, Boulder.

Goodman, K., Shannon, P., Freeman, Y., & Murphy, S. (1988). *Report card on basal readers.* Katohah, NY: Richard C. Owen Publishers.

Heberlein, T. A., & Baumgartner, R. (1981). Is a questionnaire necessary in a second mailing? *Public Opinion Quarterly, 45,* 102-108.

Kean, M., Summers, A., Raivetz, M., & Tarber, I. (1979). *What works in reading.* Office of Research and Evaluation, School Districts of Philadelphia, PA.

Kurth, R. J. (1985, December). *Problems court: The role of the reading educator in the training of elementary school principals.* Paper presented at the annual meeting of the American Reading Forum, Sarasota, FL.

Laffey, J., & Kelly, D. (1983). Survey of elementary principals. *The Journal of the Virginia State Reading Association* (a special edition), James Madison University, Harrisonburg, VA.

Lilly, E. R. (1982, September). *Administrative leadership in reading: A professional quagmire.* Paper presented at the meeting of the District of Columbia Reading Council of the International Reading Association, Washington, DC.

McNinch, G. H., & Richmond, M. G. (1983). Defining the principals' roles in reading instruction. *Reading Improvement, 18,* 235-242.

McWilliams, D. R. (1981). *The role of the elementary principal in the management of the primary reading program.* Unpublished doctoral dissertation, University of Pittsburgh, PA.

Moss, R. K. (1985). *More than facilitator: A principal's job in educating new and experienced reading teachers.* Paper presented at the annual meeting of the National Council of Teachers of English Spring Conference, Houston, TX. (ERIC Document Reproduction Service No. ED 253 856)

Nufrio, R. M. (1987). *An administrator's overview for teaching reading.* Opinion paper. (ERIC Document Reproduction Service No. ED 286 287)

Panchyshyn, R. (1971). *An investigation of the knowledge of elementary school principals about the teaching of reading in primary grades.* Unpublished doctoral dissertation, University of Iowa, Iowa City.

Rausch, S., & Sanacore, J. (1984). The administrator and the reading program: An annotated bibliography on reading leadership. *Reading World, 23,* 388-393.

Roser, N. L. (1974, February). Evaluation and the administrator: How decisions are made. *Journal of Education, 156*, 48–49.

Shelton, M., Rafferty, C., & Rose, L. (1990, Winter). The state of reading: What Michigan administrators know. *Michigan Reading Journal, 23*, 3–14.

Weber, G. (1971). *Inner-city children can be taught to read: Four successful schools.* New York: Council for Basic Education, Occasional Papers No. 18.

Wilkerson, B. (1988). A prinicipal's perspective. In J. L. Davidson (Ed.), *Counterpoint and beyond: A response to becoming a nation of readers.* Urbana, IL: National Council of Teachers of English.

Zinski, R. (1975). *The elementary school principals and the administration of a total reading program.* Unpublished doctoral dissertation, University of Wisconsin, Madison.

Summary/Chapter 8

Descriptive Research: (Survey Research) Definition and Purpose

1. Descriptive research involves collecting data in order to test hypotheses or to answer questions about the opinions of people about some topic or issue. Descriptive research is also called survey research.

2. A high percentage of all research studies are descriptive in nature. Surveys are used in many fields, including education, political science, sociology, and economics.

3. Descriptive research is not as simple as it appears. It is guided by the basic steps of the scientific and disciplined inquiry approach.

4. Descriptive studies are commonly classified in terms of how data are collected, through self-report or observation. The most common self-report approaches are questionnaires, telephone surveys, and interviews. Self-report research requires the collection of standardized, quantifiable information from all members of a population or sample.

5. Descriptive research is also categorized in terms of cross-sectional or longitudinal. Cross-sectional research collects data at one point in time while longitudinal research collects data at more than one time in order to measure growth or change.

CONDUCTING A QUESTIONNAIRE STUDY

6. In comparison to use of an interview procedure, a questionnaire is much more efficient in that it requires less time, is less expensive, and permits collection of data from a much larger sample.

7. Questionnaires may be administered to respondents by mail, telephone, or in person, but are usually mailed.

Statement of the Problem

8. The problem under investigation, and the topic of the questionnaire, must be of sufficient significance to motivate subjects to respond.

9. The problem must be defined in terms of specific objectives or subtopics concerning the kind of information needed; questions must be formulated and every item on the questionnaire should directly relate to them.

Selection of Participants

10. Participants should be selected using an appropriate sampling technique (or an entire population may be used), and identified participants must be persons who (1) have the desired information and (2) are likely to be willing to give it.

Construction of the Questionnaire

11. As a general guideline, the questionnaire should be attractive, brief, and easy to fill out. No item should be included that does not directly relate to the objectives of the study.

12. Structured, or closed-form, items should be used if at all possible. A structured item consists of a question and a list of alternative responses from which the respondent selects. In addition to facilitating responses, structured items also facilitate data analysis; scoring is objective and efficient.

13. Common structured items used in questionnaires are scaled items (Likert and semantic differential), ranked items, and checklists. Often it is useful to obtain demographic information about the participants (e.g., gender, occupation, years teaching) to make comparisons of the respondents in different subgroups.

14. In an unstructured item format, the respondent has complete freedom of response; questions are asked but the respondent must construct his or her own answers. Unstructured items permit greater depth of response that may permit insight into the reasons for responses, but they often are difficult to analyze and interpret.

15. With respect to item construction, the number one rule is that each question should deal with a single concept and be worded as clearly as possible. Any term or concept that might mean different things to different people should be defined.

16. Avoid leading questions, questions that assume a fact not necessarily in evidence, and questions that do not indicate a point of reference.

Preparation of the Cover Letter

17. Every mailed questionnaire must be accompanied by a cover letter that explains what is being asked of the respondent and why. The cover letter should be brief, neat, and addressed specifically to the potential respondent if possible.
18. The letter should explain the purpose of the study, emphasizing its importance and significance, and give the responder a good reason for cooperating.
19. It usually helps to obtain the endorsement of an organization, institution, group, or administrator with which the responder is associated or views with respect (such as a professional organization).
20. It should be made clear whether anonymity or confidentiality of responses is assured.
21. A specific deadline date by which the completed questionnaire is to be returned should be given. Include a stamped, addressed, return envelope for the respondents to return their surveys.

Pretesting the Questionnaire

22. The questionnaire and cover letter should be tried out in a field test using a few respondents who are similar to those who will respond to the questionnaire.
23. Pretesting the questionnaire yields data concerning instrument deficiencies as well as suggestions for improvement. Omissions or unclear or irrelevant items should be revised.
24. A too-often-neglected procedure is validation of the questionnaire in order to determine if it measures what it was developed to measure.

Follow-Up Activities

25. If your percentage of returns is low, the validity of your conclusions may be weak. An initial follow-up strategy is to simply send out a reminder postcard.
26. Full-scale follow-up activities are usually begun shortly after the deadline for responding has passed.

Dealing with Nonresponse

27. If your total response rate is quite low (40% or lower) you may have a problem with the generalizability of your results. You should try to determine if the persons who did not respond are similar to the persons who did respond. This can be done by randomly selecting a small subsample of nonresponders and interviewing them, either in person or by phone.

Analysis of Results

28. The simplest way to present the results is to indicate the percentage of responders who selected each alternative for each item. However, analyzing summed item clusters, that is, groups of items focused on the same issue, is more meaningful and reliable.
29. Relationships between variables can be investigated by comparing the summed cluster scores of different subgroups (e.g., males–females).

CONDUCTING AN INTERVIEW STUDY

30. An interview is essentially the oral, in-person administration of a questionnaire to each member of a sample.
31. When well conducted, an interview can produce in-depth data not possible with a questionnaire; but it is expensive, time consuming, and generally involves smaller samples.

Construction of the Interview Guide

32. The interviewer must have a written guide that indicates what questions are to be asked, in what order, and what additional prompting or probing is permitted. In order to obtain standardized, comparable data from each subject, all interviews must be conducted in essentially the same manner.
33. As with a questionnaire, each question in the interview should relate to a specific study objective. Most interviews use a semistructured approach that asks structured questions and follows them up with explanatory, open-ended questions.
34. Many of the guidelines for constructing a questionnaire apply to the construction of interview guides.

Communication During the Interview

35. Before the first formal question is asked, some time should be spent establishing rapport and putting the interviewee at ease. The interviewer should also be sensitive to the reactions of the respondent and proceed accordingly.

36. Responses made during an interview can be recorded manually by the interviewer or mechanically by a recording device. In general, mechanical recording is more objective and efficient.

Pretesting the Interview Procedure

37. Feedback from a small pilot study can be used to revise questions in the interview guide. Insights into better ways to handle certain questions can also be acquired.

38. The pilot study will determine whether the resulting data can be quantified and analyzed in the manner intended.

Conducting Observational Research

39. In nonparticipant observation, the observer is not directly involved in the situation to be observed.

40. In naturalistic observation, the observer purposely does not control or manipulate the setting so that observations will reveal the natural state of activity in the setting.

41. In simulation observation the researcher creates a situation to be observed and tells participants what activities they are to engage in. This technique allows the researcher to observe behavior that occurs infrequently in natural situations or not at all. Two major types of simulation are individual and team role-playing.

CONSTRUCTING OBSERVATIONAL RESEARCH

42. The steps in conducting observational research are essentially the same as for other types of descriptive research. Once the behavior to be observed is determined, the researcher must clearly define what specific actions do and do not match the intended behavior.

43. Once a behavioral unit is defined, observations must be quantified so that all observers will observe and count the same way.

44. Researchers typically divide observation sessions into a number of timed periods. Observation times may be regular or randomly selected, depending on the nature of the behavior being observed. There should be correspondence between actual behavior frequency and recorded frequency.

Recording Observations

45. Observers should have to observe and record only one behavior at a time. It is also a good idea to alternate observation periods and recording periods, especially if inferences are required on the part of the observers.

46. As a general rule, it is probably better to record observations as the behavior occurs. Most observation studies facilitate recording by using an agreed-upon code, or set of symbols, and a recording instrument.

47. Probably the most often and efficiently used type of recording form is a checklist that lists all behaviors to be observed so that the observer can simply check each behavior as it occurs. Rating scales are also sometimes used.

Assessing Observer Reliability

48. Determining observer reliability generally requires two observers independently making observations. Their recorded judgments about what occurred are compared to see how well they agree.

49. One approach to increasing reliability is to use shorter observation periods and to base reliability calculations on both observer agreements and disagreements. This approach makes it is easier to determine whether observers are recording the same events at the same time.

50. Mechanical recording allows observers to play back tapes as often as needed. They can improve both validity and reliability.

51. Observers need to be trained to assure that all observers are observing and recording the same behaviors in the same way. Observers must be instructed as to what behaviors to observe, how behaviors are to be coded, how behaviors are to be recorded, and how often.

52. Practice sessions using recordings of behaviors are most effective since segments with which observers have difficulty can be replayed for discussion and feedback purposes. Training may be terminated when a satisfactory level of reliability is achieved (say 80%).

53. The main way to ensure continued high levels of reliability is to periodically monitor the activities of observers. As a general rule, the more monitoring that can reasonably be managed, the better.

Reducing Observation Bias

54. Observer bias refers to invalid observations that result from the observer's perceptions, beliefs, and biases, rather than from what is objectively observed.

55. Observer effect occurs when the presence of the observer makes the persons being observed behave atypically because they are being observed. The best way to handle the problem is to make observers aware of it so that they can attempt to be as unobtrusive as possible.

56. Another approach is to substitute unobtrusive measures for observees. If the same information can be obtained by using unobtrusive measures, use them.

Meta-Analysis

57. Meta-analysis is a statistical approach to summarizing the results of many studies that have investigated a similar topic problem. Given a number of studies, it provides a numerical way of expressing the "average" result.

58. The key feature of meta-analysis is that the results of each study are translated into an effect size (ES), symbolized as Δ. Effect size is a numerical way of expressing the strength, or magnitude, of a reported relationship, be it causal or not.

59. After effect size has been calculated for each study, they are averaged, yielding one number that summarizes the overall, or typical, effect. Low effect scores (0.00 to 0.30) indicate that a treatment does not make a difference, whereas a high effect size (0.70 to 1.00) indicates a strong treatment effect.

CHAPTER | 9

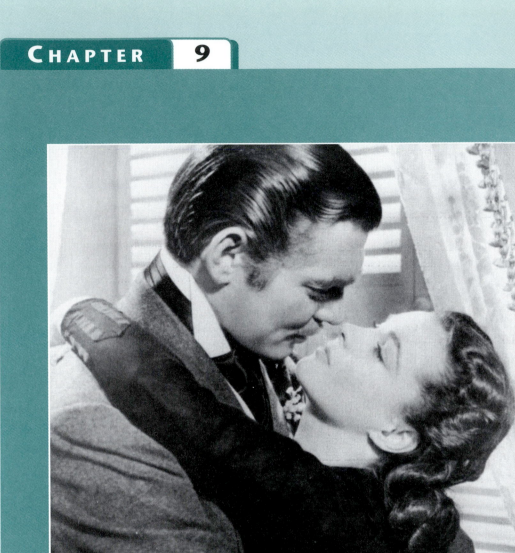

"GONE WITH THE WIND" © 1939 Turner Entertainment Co.

"Correlational research involves collecting data in order to determine whether, and to what degree, a relationship exists . . . (p. 321)."

Correlational Research

 **OBJECTIVES**

After reading chapter 9, you should be able to:

1. Briefly state the purpose of correlational research.
2. List and briefly describe the major steps involved in the basic correlational research process.
3. Describe the size and direction of values associated with a correlation coefficient.
4. Describe how the size of a correlation coefficient affects its interpretation with respect to (a) statistical significance, (b) its use in prediction, and (c) its use as an index of validity and reliability.
5. State two major purposes of relationship studies.
6. Identify and briefly describe the steps involved in conducting a relationship study.
7. Briefly describe four different types of correlation and the nature of the variables they are used to correlate.
8. Describe the difference between a linear and a curvilinear relationship.
9. Identify and briefly describe two factors that may contribute to an inaccurate estimate of relationship.
10. Briefly define or describe predictor variables and criterion variables.
11. State purposes of prediction studies.
12. State the major difference between data collection procedures in a prediction study and a relationship study.

CORRELATIONAL RESEARCH: DEFINITION AND PURPOSE

Correlational research is sometimes treated as a type of descriptive research, primarily because it does describe an existing condition. However, the condition it describes is distinctly different from the conditions typically described in survey or observational studies. Correlational research involves collecting data in order to determine whether, and to what degree, a relationship exists between two or more quantifiable variables. The degree of relationship is expressed as a correlation coefficient. If a relationship exists between two variables, it means that scores within a certain range on one variable are associated with scores within a certain range on the other variable. For example, there is a relationship between intelligence and academic achievement; persons who score highly on intelligence tests tend to have high grade point averages, and persons who score lowly on intelligence tests tend to have low grade point averages.

The purpose of a correlational study is to determine relationships between variables or to use these relationships to make predictions. Correlational studies typically investigate a number of variables believed to be related to a major, complex variable, such as achievement. Variables found not to be highly related to achievement will be dropped from further examination, while variables that are highly related to achievement may be examined in causal–comparative or experimental studies to determine the nature of relationships. As noted in chapter 1, the fact that there is a high correlation between two variables does not imply that one causes the other. A high correlation between self-concept and achievement does not mean that achievement causes self-concept or that self-concept causes achievement. However, even though correlational relationships are not cause–effect ones, the existence of a high correlation does permit prediction. For example, high school grade point average (GPA) and college GPA are highly related; students who have high GPAs in high school tend to have high GPAs in college, and students who have low GPAs in high school tend to have low GPAs in college. Therefore, high school GPA can, and is, used in college admission to predict college GPA. As discussed in chapter 5, correlational procedures are also used to determine various types of validity and reliability.

Correlational studies provide a numerical estimate of how related two variables are. Clearly, the higher the correlation, the more the two variables are related and the more accurate are predictions based on the relationship. Rarely are two variables perfectly correlated or perfectly uncorrelated, but many are sufficiently related to permit useful predictions.

THE CORRELATIONAL RESEARCH PROCESS

Although relationship and prediction studies have unique features that differentiate them, their basic processes are very similar.

PROBLEM SELECTION

Correlational studies may be designed either to determine whether and how a set of variables are related, or to test hypotheses regarding expected relationships. Variables to be correlated should be selected on the basis of some rationale. That is, the relationship to be investigated should be a logical one, suggested by theory or derived from experience. Having a theoretical or experiential basis for selecting variables to be correlated makes interpretation of results more meaningful. Correlational "treasure hunts" in which the researcher correlates all sorts of variables to see "what turns up" are strongly discouraged. This research strategy (appropriately referred to as a *shotgun* or *fishing* approach) is both very inefficient and difficult to interpret.

PARTICIPANT AND INSTRUMENT SELECTION

The sample for a correlational study is selected using an acceptable sampling method, and 30 participants are generally considered to be a minimally acceptable sample size. There are, however, some factors that influence the size of the sample. The higher the validity and reliability of the variables to be correlated, the smaller the sample can be, but not less than 30. If validity and reliability are low, a larger sample is needed, because errors of measurement may mask the true relationship. As in any study, it is important to select or develop valid and reliable measures of the variables being studied. Also, if the measures used in correlation do not represent the intended variables, the resulting correlation coefficient will not accurately indicate the degree of relationship. Suppose, for example, you wanted to determine the relationship between achievement in mathematics and achievement in physics. If you administered a valid, reliable test of math computational skill and a valid, reliable test of physics achievement, the resulting correlation coefficient would not be an accurate estimate of the intended relationship, since computational skill is only one aspect of mathematical achievement. The resulting coefficient would indicate the relationship between physics achievement and only one aspect of mathematical achievement, computational skill. Thus, care must be taken to select measures that are valid and reliable for your purposes.

DESIGN AND PROCEDURE

The basic correlational research design is not complicated. Two (or more) scores are obtained for each member of the sample, one score for each variable of interest, and the paired scores are then correlated. The result is expressed as a correlation coefficient that indicates the degree of relationship between the two variables. Different studies investigate different numbers of variables, and some utilize complex statistical procedures, but the basic design is similar in all correlational studies.

DATA ANALYSIS AND INTERPRETATION

When two variables are correlated the result is a correlation coefficient. A correlation coefficient indicates the size and direction of a relationship. A correlation coefficient is a decimal number ranging from −1.00 to 0.00 to +1.00. A coefficient near +1.00 has a high size and a positive direction. This means that a person with a high score on one of the variables is likely to have a high score on the other variable, and a person with a low score on one variable is likely to have a low score on the other. An increase on one variable is associated with an increase on the other variable. If the coefficient is near .00, the variables are not related. This means that a person's score on one variable provides no indication of what the person's score is on the other variable. A coefficient near −1.00 has a high size and a negative or inverse direction. This means that a person with a high score on one variable is likely to have a low score on the other variable, and a person with a low score on one is likely to have a high score on the other. An increase on one variable is associated with a decrease on the other variable, and vice versa. Note that correlations near +1.00 and near −1.00 represent the same size of relationship. The + and − represent different directions of relationship.

Table 9.1 presents four scores for each of eight 12th-grade students: IQ, GPA, weight, and errors on a 20-item final exam. Table 9.1 shows that IQ is highly and positively related to GPA ($r = +.95$), not related to weight ($r = +.13$), and negatively, or inversely, related to errors ($r = -.89$). The students with progressively higher IQs have progressively higher GPAs. On the other hand, students with higher IQs tend to make fewer errors (makes sense!). The relationships are not perfect, but then again, variables rarely are perfectly related or unrelated. One's GPA, for example, is related to other variables besides intelligence, such as motivation. The data do indicate, however, that IQ is one major variable related to both GPA and examination errors. The data also remind us of an important concept that is often misunderstood. A high negative relationship is just as strong as a high positive relationship; −1.00 and +1.00 indicate equally perfect relationships. The farther away from .00 the coefficient is, in either direction, the stronger the relationship. Both high positive and high negative relationships are equally useful for making predictions; knowing that Iggie has a low IQ score would enable you to predict both a low GPA and a high number of errors.

TABLE	9.1

Hypothetical Sets of Data Illustrating a High Positive Relationship Between Two Variables, No Relationship, and a High Negative Relationship

	HIGH POSITIVE RELATIONSHIP		NO RELATIONSHIP		HIGH NEGATIVE RELATIONSHIP	
	IQ	GPA	IQ	WEIGHT	IQ	ERRORS
1. Iggie	85	1.0	85	156	85	16
2. Hermie	90	1.2	90	140	90	10
3. Fifi	100	2.4	100	120	100	8
4. Teenie	110	2.2	110	116	110	5
5. Tiny	120	2.8	120	160	120	9
6. Tillie	130	3.4	130	110	130	3
7. Millie	135	3.2	135	140	135	2
8. Jane	140	3.8	140	166	140	1
correlation	$r = +.95$		$r = +.13$		$r = -.89$	

Figure 9.1 shows a scatterplot for each of the three correlations shown in Table 9.1. The top scatterplot shows that students who score low on IQ also tend to score low on GPA, while students who score high on IQ also tend to score high on GPA. This pattern illustrates a high, positive correlation. The bottom scatterplot shows that students who score high on IQ tend to score low on errors, while students who score low on IQ tend to score high on errors. This pattern illustrates a high, negative correlation. The lack of any systematic relationship between IQ and weight in the middle scatterplot illustrates a lack of relation between the two variables.

One way to interpret correlation coefficients is: coefficient below plus or minus .35, low or not related; coefficient between plus or minus .35 and .65, moderately related, and coefficient higher than plus or minus .65, highly related. These are approximations and should not be blindly used. A correlation coefficient much below plus or minus .50 is generally useless for either group prediction or individual prediction, although a combination of several variables in this range might yield a reasonably satisfactory prediction. Coefficients of plus or minus .60 or .70 are usually considered adequate for group prediction purposes, and coefficients of plus or minus .80 and above are adequate for individual prediction purposes. A correlational criterion-related validity of .60 for an affective measuring instrument may be considered high, since many affective instruments have lower validities. Conversely, we would consider a stability reliability of .74 for an achievement test to be low. A researcher would be very happy with observer reliabilities in the .90s, satisfied with the .80s, minimally accepting of the .70s, and would be progressively more unhappy with the .60s, .50s, and so forth. Thus, a correlation coefficient of .40, for example, would be considered useful in a relationship study, not useful in a prediction study, and terrible in a reliability study. A coefficient of .60 would be considered useful in a prediction study but would still probably be considered unsatisfactory as an estimate of reliability.

What a correlation coefficient means is difficult to explain. However, one thing it does *not* indicate is the percentage of relationship between variables. Unfortunately, many beginning researchers erroneously think that a correlation co-

FIGURE   9.1

Data Points for Scores Presented in Table 9.1 Illustrating a High Positive Relationship (IQ and GPA), No Relationship (IQ and Weight), and a High Negative Relationship (IQ and Errors)

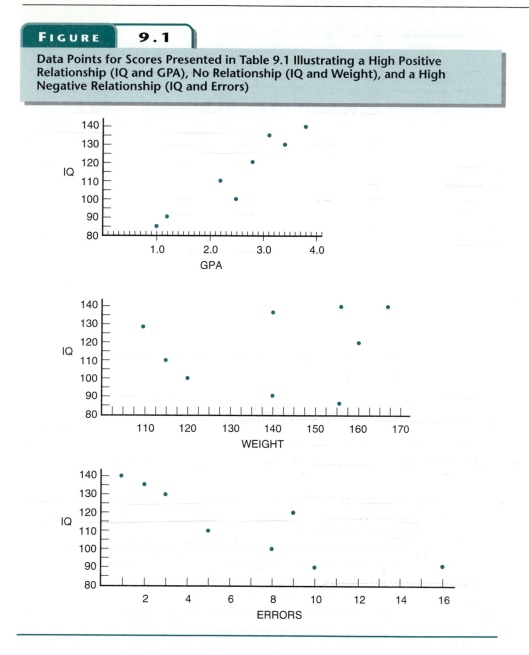

efficient of .50 means that two variables are 50% related. Not true. In research talk, a correlation coefficient squared indicates the amount of common variance shared by the variables (WHAT??!!). Now, in English: When two or more variables are correlated, each variable will have a range of scores and a score variance (i.e., everyone will not get the same score). In Table 9.1, for example, IQ scores vary from 85 to 140 and GPAs vary from 1.0 to 3.8. Common, or shared, variance indicates the extent to which variables vary in a systematic way. The more systematically two variables vary, the higher the correlation coefficient. If two variables do not systematically vary, then the scores on one variable are unrelated to the scores on the other variable. In this case, there is no common variance and the correlation coefficient will be at or near .00. If two variables are perfectly related (positively or negatively), then the variability of one set of scores is very similar to the variability in the other set of scores. There is a great deal of common variance and the correlation coefficient will be near plus or minus 1.00. Thus, the more the common variance, the higher the correlation coefficient. In Table 9.1, a great deal of the score variance of IQ and GPA and IQ and errors is common, whereas the shared variance of IQ and weight is quite small.

The percent of common variance is less than the numerical value of the correlation coefficient. In fact, to determine common variance you simply square the correlation coefficient. A correlation coefficient of .80 indicates $(.80)^2$ or .64, or 64% common variance. A correlation coefficient of .00 indicates $(.00)^2$ or .00, or 00% common variance, and a coefficient of 1.00 indicates $(1.00)^2$ or 1.00, or 100% common variance. Thus, a correlation coefficient of .50 may look pretty good at first but it actually means that the variables have 25% common variance; 75% of the variance is unexplained, not common, variance.

Interpretation of a correlation coefficient depends on how it is to be used. In other words, how large it needs to be in order to be useful depends on the purpose for which it was computed. In a prediction study, the value of the correlation coefficient should be high to facilitate accurate predictions. In a study designed to explore or test hypothesized relationships, a correlation coefficient is interpreted in terms of its statistical significance. Heads up! Statistical significance is an important new concept that you will be seeing more of in the next few chapters. It refers to whether an obtained correlation coefficient is really different from a correlation of zero, or no relation. That is, does a correlation reflect a true statistical relationship, or is it only a chance one with no meaning? Decisions concerning statistical significance are made at a given level of probability.[1] Based on a correlation with a sample of a given size, a statistical significance test does not allow you to determine with perfect certainty that there is or is not a true, meaningful relationship between the variables. However, the statistical test does indicate the probability that there is or is not a significant, true relationship. To determine statistical significance, consult a table that tells you how large your coefficient needs to be in order to be significant at a given probability level and given sample size. See Table A.2 in the Appendix. See also the article at the end of this chapter, especially Tables 2 and 3.

Statistical significance depends on the sample size. To demonstrate a true relationship, small sample sizes require higher correlation coefficients than large sample sizes. This is because we can generally have a lot more confidence in a correlation coefficient based on 100 participants than one based on only 10 participants. Thus, for example, to be 95% confident that a correlation represents a true relationship (not a chance one), with a small sample of only 12 participants you would need a correlation of at least .58 in order to conclude the existence of a significant relationship. On the other hand, using a sample of 102 participants you would need a correlation of only .19 to conclude that the relationship is significant.[2] This concept makes sense if you consider the case when you could collect data on every member of a population. In this case, no inference would be needed because the whole population was in the sample. Thus, regardless of how

---

[1]The concepts of statistical significance, level of significance, and degrees of freedom will be discussed further in chapter 14.

[2]In case you are trying to read Table A.2, a 95% level of confidence corresponds to $p = .05$, and 12 cases correspond to $df = 8$; degrees of freedom, df, are equal to N (number in the sample) − 2, thus, $12 - 2 = 10$. For 102 cases, $df = 102 - 2 = 100$.

small the actual correlation coefficient was, it would represent the true degree of relationship between the variables *for that population*. Even if the coefficient were only .11, for example, it would still indicate the existence of a significant relationship. As noted, the larger the sample, the more closely it approximates the population, and therefore, the more probable it is that a given correlation coefficient represents a significant relationship.

You may also have noticed that for a given sample size, the value of the correlation coefficient needed for significance increases as the level of confidence increases. The level of confidence, commonly called the significance level, indicates how confident we wish to be that we have a significant relationship. Usually we choose a significance level of .05 or .01, meaning that we wish to be 95% or 99% sure that we have a real, significant relationship. As the significance level increases, the p value (probability level) in the table gets smaller; the 95% confidence level corresponds to $p = .05$ and the 99% level to $p = .01$. Thus, for a sample of 12 ($df = 10$), and $p = .05$, a coefficient of .58 is required; for a sample of 12 and $p = .01$, a correlation of .71 is required. In other words, the more confident you wish to be that your decision concerning significance is the correct one, the larger the coefficient must be. Beware, however, of confusing significance with strength. No matter how significant a coefficient is, a low coefficient represents a low relationship. The level of significance only indicates the probability that a given relationship is a true one, regardless of whether it is a weak relationship or a strong relationship.

When interpreting a correlation coefficient you must always keep in mind that you are talking about relationship, not causality. When one observes a high relationship between two variables, it is often very tempting to conclude that one variable "causes" the other. In fact, it may be that neither one is the cause of the other; there may be a third variable that "causes" both of them. The existence of a positive relationship between self-concept and achievement could mean one of three things: a higher self-concept leads to higher achievement, higher achievement leads to higher self-concept, or there is a variable such as parent–child interaction that underlies both self-concept and higher achievement. A significant correlation coefficient may suggest a cause–effect relationship but does not establish one. The only way to establish a cause–effect relationship is to conduct experimental research.

RELATIONSHIP STUDIES

Relationship studies attempt to gain insight into variables that are related to complex variables such as academic achievement, motivation, and self-concept. For example, a researcher might be interested in whether a variable such as hyperactivity is related to motivation, or whether parental punishment is related to elementary schoolchildren's self-concept. Identification of related variables serves several purposes. First, correlational studies suggest subsequent examination using causal–comparative and experimental studies to determine whether there is a causal connection between the variables. Since experimental studies are costly and often time consuming, the use of correlational studies to suggest potentially productive experimental studies is efficient. Second, in both causal–comparative and experimental research studies, the researcher may need to control for variables that might be related to performance on the dependent variable. In other words, the researcher identifies variables that are correlated with the dependent variable and removes their influence so that they will not be confused with that of the independent variable. Relationship studies help the researcher to identify such variables, to control for them, and therefore to investigate the effects of the intended variable. For example, if you were interested in comparing the effectiveness of different methods of reading instruction on first graders, you would probably want to control for initial differences in reading readiness. You could do this by selecting first graders who were homogeneous in reading readiness or by using stratified sampling to ensure similar levels of reading readiness in each method.

The strategy of attempting to understand a complex variable like self-concept by identifying variables correlated with it has been more successful for some variables than others. For example, while a number of variables correlated with achievement have been identified, factors significantly related to success in areas such as administration and teaching have not been as easy to pin down. If nothing else, however, relationship studies that have not uncovered useful relationships have at least identified variables that can be excluded from future studies, a necessary step in science.

DATA COLLECTION

In a correlational study the researcher first identifies the variables to be correlated. For example, if you were interested in factors related to self-concept, you might identify variables such as introversion, academic achievement, and socioeconomic status. As noted previously, you should have a reason for selecting variables in the study. A "shotgun approach" is very inefficient and often misleading. Also, the more correlation coefficients that are computed at one time, the more likely it is that some wrong conclusions about the existence of a relationship will be reached. If only 10 or 15 correlation coefficients are computed, this is not a major problem. On the other hand, if 100 coefficients are computed, it is likely that there will be relationships that are erroneously suggested as true. Thus, a smaller number of carefully selected variables is much preferred to a larger number of carelessly selected variables.

The next step in data collection is to identify an appropriate population of participants from which to select a sample. The population must be one for which data on each of the identified variables can be collected. Although data on some variables such as past achievement can be collected without direct access to participants, many relationship studies require the administration of one or more instruments and, in some cases, observations. Any of the types of measuring instruments so far discussed in this text can be used in a correlation study. One advantage of a relationship study is that all the data may be collected within a relatively short period of time. Instruments may be administered at one session or several sessions in close succession. If schoolchildren are the participants, as is often the case, time demands on students and teachers are relatively small compared to those required for experimental studies, and it is usually easier to obtain administrative approval.

DATA ANALYSIS AND INTERPRETATION

In a correlational study, the scores for one variable are correlated with the scores for another variable. If a number of variables are to be correlated with some particular variable of primary interest, each of the variables would be correlated with the variable of primary interest. Each correlation coefficient represents the relationship between a particular variable and the variable of primary interest. The end result of data analysis is a number of correlation coefficients, ranging from −1.00 to +1.00.

There are a number of different methods of computing a correlation coefficient. Which one is appropriate depends on the type of data represented by each variable. The most commonly used technique is the product moment correlation coefficient, usually referred to as the Pearson r. The Pearson r is used when both variables to be correlated are expressed as continuous data such as ratio or interval data. Since most instruments used in education, such as achievement measures and personality measures, are treated as being interval data, the Pearson r is usually the appropriate coefficient for determining relationship. Further, since the Pearson r results in the most precise estimate of correlation, its use is preferred even when other methods may be applied.

If the data for a variable are expressed as rank or ordinal data, the appropriate correlation coefficient to use is the rank difference correlation, usually referred to as the Spearman rho. Rank data are used when participants are arranged in order of score and each participant is assigned a rank from 1 to however many participants there are. For a group of 30 participants, for example, the participant with the highest score would be assigned a rank of 1, the participant with the second highest score 2, and the participant with the lowest score 30. If two participants have the same score, their ranks are averaged. Thus, if two participants have the same highest score, they are each assigned the average of rank 1 and rank 2, namely 1.5. If only one of the variables to be correlated is in rank order, such as class standing at the time of graduation, the other variable or variables to be correlated with it must also be expressed in terms of ranks in order to use the Spearman rho technique. For example, if intelligence were to be correlated with class standing, students would have to be ranked from high to low in terms of intelligence. Actual IQ scores would not be used. Although the Pearson r is more precise, with a small number of participants (less than 30) the Spearman rho is much easier to compute and results in a coefficient very close to the one that would have been obtained had a Pearson r been computed. When the number of participants is large, however, the process of ranking becomes more time consuming and the Spearman rho loses its only advantage over the Pearson r.

There are also a number of other correlational techniques that are encountered less often but that should be used when appropriate. Some variables can only be expressed in terms of a categorical dichotomy, such as gender (male or female). Other variables that may be expressed as a dichotomy include political affiliation (Democrat versus Republican), smoking status (smoker versus nonsmoker), and educational status (high school graduate versus high school dropout). The two parts typically are labeled 1 or 0 (female versus male) or 1 or 2 (female versus male). Recall that for nominal variables, a 2 does not mean more of something than a 1, and 1 does not mean more than 0. The numbers only indicate different categories, not different amounts. These examples illustrate "true" dichotomies in that a person is or is not a female, a Democrat, a smoker, or a high school graduate. Such dichotomies are correlated using a phi coefficient.

Artificial dichotomies may also be created by operationally defining a midpoint and categorizing participants as falling above it or below it. For example, participants with test scores of 50 or above could be classified as "high achievers" and those below 50 as "low achievers." Such artificial classifications are typically

TABLE	9.2

Types of Correlation Coefficients

NAME	VARIABLE 1	VARIABLE 2	COMMENTS
Pearson r	continuous	continuous	most common correlation
Spearman's rho; or rank-difference	rank	rank	easy to compute for small samples
Kendall's tau	rank	rank	used with samples less than 10
Biserial	artificial dichotomy	continuous	used to analyze test items; may have r greater than 1.00 if score distribution is oddly shaped
Point biserial	genuine dichotomy	continuous	maximum when dichotomous variable split 50–50
Tetrachoric	artificial dichotomy	artificial dichotomy	should not be used with extreme splits or sample
Phi coefficient	true dichotomy	true dichotomy	used in determining inter-item relationships
Intraclass	continuous	continuous	useful in judging rater agreement
Correlation ratio or eta	continuous	continuous	used for nonlinear relationships

translated into scores of 1 and 0. These are called *artificial dichotomies* because variables that were ordinal, interval, or ratio are artificially turned into nominal variables. Table 9.2 describes a number of different correlations and the conditions under which they are used.

Most correlational techniques are based on the assumption that the relationship being investigated is a linear one. If a relationship is linear, then plotting the scores of the two variables will result in a straight line. If a relationship is perfect (+1.00 or −1.00), the line will be perfectly straight, but if there is no relationship, the points will form a scattered, random plot. Refer back to Figure 9.1. The top and bottom scatterplots illustrate the concept of a linear relationship. However, not all relationships are linear; some are curvilinear. If a relationship is curvilinear, an increase in one variable is associated with a corresponding increase in another variable up to a point, at which further increases in the first variable result in corresponding decreases in the other variable (or vice versa). For example, the relationship between age and agility is a curvilinear one. As Figure 9.2 illustrates, agility increasingly improves with age, peaks or reaches its maximum somewhere in the twenties, and then progressively decreases as age increases. Two other examples of curvilinear relationships are age of car and dollar value, and anxiety and achievement. A car decreases in value as soon as it leaves the lot and continues to do so over time until it becomes an antique (!) and then it increases in value as time goes by. In contrast, increases in anxiety are associated with increases in achievement to a point; but at some point, anxiety becomes counter-

FIGURE   9.2

The Curvilinear Relationship between Age and Agility

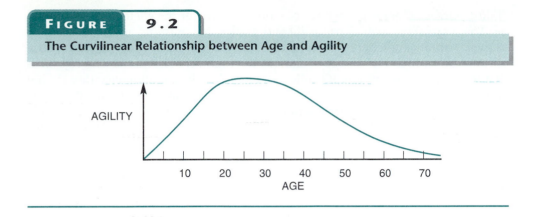

productive and interferes with learning in that as anxiety increases, achievement decreases. If a relationship is suspected of being curvilinear, then an eta correlation is appropriate. If you try to use a correlational technique that assumes a linear relationship when the relationship is in fact curvilinear, your measure of the degree of relationship will be way off base. Use of a linear correlation coefficient to determine a curvilinear correlation will reveal little or no relationship.

In addition to computing correlation coefficients for a total participant group, it is sometimes useful to examine relationships separately for certain defined subgroups. For example, the relationship between two variables may be different for females and males, college graduates and non–college graduates, or high-ability students and low-ability students. When the subgroups are lumped together and correlated, differential relationships may be obscured. However, regardless of whatever worthwhile knowledge may come from subdividing a sample and correlating the subgroups separately, a few cautions must be recognized. For example, subdivision and correlation can only be carried out if the original sample is large enough to permit sufficient numbers in the subgroups. Suppose a researcher starts with a correlation sample of 30 participants (15 males and 15 females) and subsequently wishes to compare separately the correlations of males and females on the selected variables. Upon subdividing the sample into male and female groups, the researcher has only 15 participants per group to study. The resulting samples are too small to obtain stable results. Sometimes researchers recognize this problem and select a larger sample to permit analysis of subgroups. However, if there are unequal numbers in the subgroups (for example 55 females and 15 males), comparative analyses still cannot be carried out. If you think you want to study subgroups of your sample, select larger samples and use stratified samples to ensure similar numbers in the subgroups.

There are other factors that may contribute to inaccurate estimates of relationship. Attenuation, for example, refers to the fact that correlation coefficients tend to be lowered if the measures being correlated have low reliability. In correlational studies a correction for attenuation (unreliability) can be applied that provides an estimate of what the coefficient would be if both measures were perfectly reliable. If such a correction is used, it must be kept in mind that the resulting coefficient does not represent what was actually found. Such a correction should not be used in prediction studies since predictions must be made based on existing measures, not on hypothetical, perfectly reliable, measures. Another factor that may lead to a correlation coefficient being an underestimate of the true relationship between two variables is a restricted range of scores. The more variability (spread) there is in each set of scores, the higher the coefficient is likely to be. The correlation coefficient for IQ and grades, for example, tends to decrease as these variables are measured at higher educational levels. Thus, the correlation will not be as high for college seniors as for high school seniors. The reason is that there are not many low-IQ college seniors; low-IQ individuals either do not enter college or drop out long before their senior year. In other words, the range of IQ scores is smaller, or more restricted, for college seniors, and a correlation coefficient based on a narrow range of scores will tend to be lowered. There is also a correction for restriction in range that may be applied to obtain an estimate of what the coefficient would be if the range of scores were not restricted. It should be interpreted with the same caution as the correction for attenuation, since it does not represent what was actually found.

PREDICTION STUDIES

If two variables are highly related, scores on one variable can be used to predict scores on the other variable. High school grades, for example, can be used to predict college grades. Or, scores on a teacher certification exam can be used to predict principals' evaluations of teachers' classroom performance. The variable used to predict (high school grades or certification exam) is called the *predictor*, and the variable that is predicted (college grades or principals' evaluations) is called the *criterion*. Prediction studies are conducted to facilitate decisions about individuals or to aid in various types of selection. Prediction studies are also conducted to test variables believed to be good predictors of a criterion, and to determine the predictive validity of measuring instruments. Prediction studies are used to predict an individual's likely level of success in a specific course like first-year algebra, to predict which of a number of individuals are likely to succeed in college or in a vocational training program, and to predict in which area of study an individual is most likely to be successful. Thus, the results of prediction studies are used by a number of groups such as counselors, admissions directors, and employers, in addition to researchers.

More than one variable can be used to make predictions. If several predictor variables each correlate well with a criterion, then a prediction based on a combination of those variables will be more accurate than a prediction based on any one of them. For example, a prediction of probable level of GPA success in college based on high school grades will be less predictive than basing the prediction on high school grades, rank in graduating class, and scores on college entrance exams. Although there are several major differences between prediction studies and relationship studies, both involve determining the relationship between a number of identified variables.

DATA COLLECTION

As in all correlation studies, research participants must be able to provide the desired data and must be available to the researcher. Valid measuring instruments should be selected to represent the variables. It is especially important that the measure used as the criterion variable be valid. If the criterion were "success on the job," the researcher would have to carefully define *success* in quantifiable terms in order to carry out the prediction study. For example, size of desk would probably not be a valid measure of job success (although you never know!), whereas number of promotions or salary increases probably would be. The major difference in data collection procedures for a relationship study and a prediction study is that in a relationship study all variables are collected within a relatively short period of time, whereas in a prediction study the predictor variables are generally obtained earlier than the criterion variable. The researcher must have data that spans a sometimes-lengthy time period, which, in turn, can create problems of participant loss. In determining the predictive validity of a physics aptitude test, for example, success in physics would probably be measured by end of course grade, whereas the aptitude test would be administered some time prior to the beginning of the course.

Once the strength of the predictor variable is established, the predictive relationship will be tested on a new group of physics students to determine how well it will predict for other groups. An interesting characteristic of prediction studies is *shrinkage*; that is, the tendency of a prediction equation to become less accurate when used with a group other than the one on which the equation was originally developed. The reason for shrinkage is that an initial equation may be the result of chance relationships that will not be found again with another group of participants. Thus, any prediction equation should be validated with at least one other group, and variables no longer found to be related to the criterion measure should be taken out of the equation. This procedure is referred to as cross-validation.

DATA ANALYSIS AND INTERPRETATION

Data analysis in prediction studies differs somewhat from that of relational studies. It is beyond the scope of this text to discuss the statistical processes related to the analysis of prediction studies, but we will provide examples of how to interpret them. There are two types of prediction studies, single prediction studies and multiple prediction studies. The former predict using a single predictive variable and the latter predict using more than one predictive variable. In both cases, data analysis is based on a prediction equation.

For single variable predictions, the form of the prediction equation is

$$Y = a + bX$$

where
  Y = the predicted criterion score for an individual
  X = an individual's score on the predictor variable
  a = a constant calculated from the scores of all participants
  b = a coefficient that indicates the contribution of the predictor variable to the criterion variable

Suppose, for example, that we wished to predict a student's college GPA using the student's high school GPA. We want to know the student's predicted score. Suppose that the student's high school GPA is 3.0, the coefficient b is .87, and the constant a is .15. The student's predicted score would be

$$Y = .15 + .87(3.0) = .15 + 2.61 = 2.76 \text{ predicted college GPA}$$

We can compare the student's predicted college GPA to the student's actual college GPA at some subsequent time to determine how accurately the prediction equation is.

A multiple prediction equation—also called a multiple regression equation—is similar to a single predictive equation except that it contains more predictors.

For example, suppose we wished to predict college GPA from high school GPA, SAT verbal score, and the rated quality of the student's admission essay. The student's high school GPA is 3.0, SAT verbal is 450, and rated admission essay is 10. If a is .15, and the coefficients b for the three predictors are .87, .0003, and .4, the multiple regression prediction equation would be

$$Y = .15 + .87(3.0) + .0003(450) + .4(10)$$
$$= .15 + 2.61 + .135 + .2 = 3.095 \text{ predicted college GPA}$$

We would validate the accuracy of the multiple regression equation by comparing the predicted GPA of 3.095 to the student's actual college GPA.

Predictive studies are influenced by factors that affect the accuracy of prediction. For example, if the predictor and criterion variables are not reliable, error of measurement is introduced and the accuracy of the prediction is diminished. Also, the longer the length of time between the measurement of the predictor and the criterion, the lower the prediction accuracy is. This is because many intervening variables can influence the link between predictor and criterion variables over time. Finally, general criterion variables such as success in business or teacher effectiveness tend to have lower prediction accuracy than narrower criterion variables because so many factors make up broad, general criterion variables.

Since relationships are rarely perfect, predictions made by single or multiple prediction equations are not perfect. Thus, predicted scores are generally reported as a range of predicted scores using a statistic called the standard error. For example, a predicted college GPA of 2.20 might be placed in an interval of 1.80 to 2.60. In other words, students with a predicted GPA of 2.20 would be predicted to earn a GPA somewhere in the range of 1.80 to 2.60. Thus, for most useful interpretation, the prediction should be viewed as a range of possible scores, not any single score. A college that does not accept all applicants will probably as a general rule fail to accept any applicants with such a projected GPA range, even though it is very likely that some of those students would be successful if admitted. Although the predictions for any given individual might be way off (either too high or too low), for the total group of applicants predictions are quite accurate on the whole; most applicants predicted to succeed, do so. As with relationship studies, and for similar reasons, prediction equations may be formulated for each of a number of subgroups as well as for a total group.

As in relational studies, predictive studies can provide an indication of the common variance shared by the predictor(s) and the criterion variables. This statistic is called the coefficient of determination and indicates the percentage of variance in the criterion variable that is predicted by the predictor(s) variable. The coefficient of determination is the squared correlation of the predictor and the criterion. For example, if the correlation between high school GPA and college GPA is .80, the coefficient of determination is $(.80)^2 = .64$ or 64%. This is a moderately high coefficient of determination, and the higher the coefficient of determination, the better the prediction.

OTHER CORRELATION-BASED ANALYSES

There are many sophisticated statistical analyses that are based on correlational data. We will briefly describe a number of these, recognizing that they are statistically complex. *Discriminant function analysis* is quite similar to multiple regression analysis, with one major difference. The criterion variable is categorical, not continuous. In multiple regression, continuous predictor variables are used to predict a continuous criterion variable. In discriminant function analysis, continuous predictor variables are used to predict a categorical variable, such as introverted/extroverted, high anxiety/low anxiety, or achiever/nonachiever. Thus, the predictions made are about categorical group membership. For example, based on the predictor variables, discriminant function analysis allows us to classify whether an individual manifests the characteristics of an introvert or an extrovert. Having identified groups who are introverts and extroverts, a researcher might want to compare the two groups on other variables.

Path analysis allows us to see the relationships and patterns among a number of variables. The outcome of a path analysis is a diagram that shows how variables are related to each other. Suppose, for example, that we wanted to examine the connections (paths) between variable X and variables A, B, and C. A path analysis based on the correlations among the variables will produce a path diagram such as that shown in Figure 9.3. In this diagram, single arrows indicate connections among variables and double arrows (A to B) indicate no direct link. Thus, variables A and B are individually linked to D and A and B are linked to variable C. C is not linked to D. Path analyses are useful both for showing what variables influence a given variable (like X) and also for testing theories about the ways groups of variables are related to a given variable. A more sophisticated, powerful extension of path analysis is called *structural equation modeling, or LISREL,* for the computer program used to perform the analysis. This approach provides more theoretical validity and statistical precision in the model diagrams it produces than those of path analysis. Like path analysis, it clarifies the direct and indirect interrelations among variables relative to a given variable.

Canonical correlation is an extension of multiple regression analysis. As noted, multiple regression uses multiple predictors to predict a single criterion variable. Canonical correlation produces a correlation based on a group of predictor variables and a group of criterion variables. For example, if we had a group of predictors related to achievement (GPA, SAT scores, teachers' ratings of ability, and number of AP courses passed) and we wanted to see how these predictors related to a group of criterion variables also related to achievement (job success, work income, and college GPA), we would use canonical correlation. A single correlation will be produced to indicate the correlation among both groups of variables.

Trying to make sense of a large number of variables is difficult, simply because there are so many variables to be considered. *Factor analysis* is a way to take

FIGURE	**9.3**

Example of a Path Analysis Model: The Connections of Variables *A*, *B*, and *C* to Variable *D*

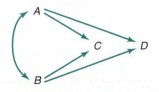

a large number of variables and group them into a smaller number of clusters called *factors*. Factor analysis computes the correlations among all the variables and then derives factors by finding groups of variables that are correlated highly among each other, but lowly with other variables. The factors identified, not the many individual items within the factors, are then used as variables. Factor analysis produces a manageable number of factor variables to deal with and analyze.

PROBLEMS TO CONSIDER IN INTERPRETING CORRELATION COEFFICIENTS

The quality of the information provided in correlation coefficients depends on the data from which they are calculated. It is important to ask the following questions when interpreting correlation coefficients.

- Was the proper correlation method used to calculate the correlation? (see Table 9.2)
- Do the variables being correlated have high reliabilities? Low reliabilities lower the chance of finding significant relationships.
- Is the validity of the variables strong? Invalid variables produce meaningless results.
- Is the range of scores to be correlated restricted or extended? Narrow or restricted score ranges lower correlation coefficients, while broad or extended score ranges raise them.
- How large is the sample size? The larger the sample size, the smaller the value needed to reach statistical significance. Large sample sizes may be statistically significant, but practically unimportant.

The following pages present an example of correlational research. Note that the alpha reliability coefficients for the instruments used are given and that they are satisfactory.

Explorations in Parent-School Relations

KATHLEEN V. HOOVER-DEMPSEY
OTTO C. BASSLER
JANE S. BRISSIE
Peabody College of Vanderbilt University

ABSTRACT Grounded in Bandura's (1976, 1986) work, parent efficacy was defined as a parent's belief that he or she is capable of exerting a positive influence on children's school outcomes. Parents' sense of efficacy and its relationship to parent involvement were examined in this study. Parents (*n* = 390) of children in kindergarten through fourth grade in a metropolitan public school district responded to questionnaires assessing parent efficacy and parent involvement in five types of activities: help with homework, educational activities, classroom volunteering, conference participation, and telephone calls with teachers. Teachers (*n* = 50) from the same schools also participated, responding to questionnaires assessing teacher efficacy, perceptions of parent efficacy, and estimates of parent involvement. Findings revealed small but significant relationships between self-reported parent efficacy and three of the five indicators of parent involvement. Results for teachers revealed significant relationships among teacher efficacy, teacher perceptions of parent efficacy, and teacher reports of parent involvement in four areas. Results are discussed in relation to the patterns of involvement activities reported by parents and implications for research and intervention in parent-school relationships.

Bandura's (1977, 1984, 1986) work on personal efficacy considers the influence of beliefs that one is capable of achieving specific outcomes on behavior choices. In general, his work suggests that persons higher in efficacy will be more likely to engage in behaviors leading to a goal and will be more persistent in the face of obstacles than will persons with a lower sense of efficacy.

Hoover-Dempsey, Bassler, and Brissie (1987) earlier examined relationships between teacher efficacy and parent involvement. Building on Bandura's work and studies of the role of teacher efficacy in various educational outcomes (Ashton, Webb, & Doda, 1983; Dembo & Gibson, 1985), the authors defined teacher efficacy as "teachers' certainty that their instructional skills are effective" (p. 425). Hoover-Dempsey, Bassler, and Brissie found that teacher efficacy was significantly related to teacher reports of parents' involvement in conferences, volunteering, and home tutoring, as well as teacher perceptions of parent support.

Examination of specific parent variables often related to children's school performance suggests a complementary avenue of exploration in efforts to understand and improve parent-school relations. Some evidence that *parent* efficacy beliefs may be important in parent behaviors and child outcomes are reported in Baumrind's (1971, 1973) work on parenting styles, which established clear linkages between patterns of parenting behaviors and patterns of children's social and cognitive development. For example, the characteristics of Baumrind's authoritative style include consistent parental willingness to give reasons and explanations for requests and to consider and discuss alternative points of view. Because children of authoritative parents have consistent access to their parents' thinking—and because authoritative parents listen and take into account their children's reasoning— the children tend to develop higher levels of social and cognitive competence than do peers raised in other parenting styles.

Dornbusch, Ritter, Leiderman, Roberts, and Fraleigh (1987) recently demonstrated another specific outcome of an authoritative parenting style; they found that adolescents raised by authoritative parents, when compared with adolescents raised by authoritarian parents, have higher levels of academic performance in high school. In a related line of inquiry, Mondell and Tyler (1981) reported significant positive relationships between elements of parental competence and characteristics of parents' teaching interactions with their children, for example, more competent parents treat the child as an "origin," offer more approval and acceptance, and offer more helpful problem-solving questions and strategies.

In each set of findings, the qualities of parental behavior suggest the presence of strong parental beliefs in the abilities and "worthiness" of the child, for example, giving children reasons for requests and treating them as capable of solving problems. These behaviors suggest that parents believe in the abilities of the child and have

Address correspondence to Kathleen V. Hoover-Dempsey, Department of Psychology and Human Development, Box 512, Peabody College, Vanderbilt University, Nashville, TN 37203.

Hoover-Dempsey, K. V., Bassler, O. C., & Brissie, J. S. (1992). Explorations in parent-school relations. *The Journal of Educational Research, 85,* 287–294. Reprinted with the permission of the Helen Dwight Reid Educational Foundation. Published by Heldref Publications, 1319 Eighteenth St., N. W., Washington, DC 20036-1802. Copyright © 1992.

Journal of Educational Research

confidence in their own ability to guide the child's learning. Such attitudes and the behaviors that they enable are central to a parental sense of efficacy—parents' belief and knowledge that they can teach their children (content, processes, attitudes, and values) and that their children can learn what they teach.

Applied in this manner, Bandura's (1977, 1984, 1986) theory suggests that parents will hold personal efficacy beliefs about their ability to help their children learn. These efficacy beliefs will influence their decisions about the avenues and timing of efforts to become involved in their children's education. For example, parents with a strong sense of efficacy are more likely than low-efficacy parents are to help their children resolve a misunderstanding with the teacher, because they believe that they are capable of offering, and helping their child to act on, appropriate guidance. Overall, parents most likely become involved when they believe that their involvement will "make a difference" for their children.

Following Bandura's (1986) suggestion that assessments of perceived self-efficacy are appropriately "tailored to the domains of functioning being analyzed" (p. 360), the present study was designed to explore parent efficacy and the nature of its relationship to specific indicators of parents' involvement in their elementary school children's education. Although parent efficacy is likely only one of several contributors to parents' involvement decisions (Bandura 1986), we believe that it may operate as a fundamentally important mechanism, explaining variations in involvement decisions more fully than do some of the more frequently referenced status variables (e.g., parent income, education, employment). We believe that self-efficacy is more significant than such status variables because self-efficacy beliefs, far more than variables describing an individual's status, "function as an important set of proximal determinants of human motivation, affect, and action" (Bandura, 1989, p. 1175). Support for this position comes from related bodies of work, for example, Greenberger and Goldberg's (1989) findings that adults' commitment to parenting is "more consequential" for other parenting practices than is their involvement in work (30).

We also explored the replicability of previous results indicating a significant positive relationship between teachers' sense of efficacy and parent involvement. That relationship is grounded in the logical probability that teachers with a higher sense of personal teaching efficacy, being more confident of their teaching skills, are more likely to invite parent involvement and to accept parents' initiation of involvement activities (Hoover-Dempsey et al., 1987). Finally, we explored teachers' perceptions of parents' efficacy and involvement, based, in part, on earlier findings of a significant relationship between an "other's" perceptions of teacher efficacy and selected teacher outcomes (Brissie, Hoover-Dempsey, & Bassler, 1988). In general, we expected that higher levels of parent involvement would be associated with higher levels of parent efficacy, teacher efficacy, and teacher perceptions of parent efficacy. We expected to find those relationships because higher efficacy parents and teachers, being more confident of their skills and abilities related to children's learning, would more likely initiate and invite parent involvement in children's school-related learning activities.

Sample, Methods, and Procedures

Four elementary schools in a large public school district participated in the study. The schools varied in geographic location within the district, size (300 to 500 students), and mean annual family income reported by parents ($15,000 to $37,000). Because the purpose of the study was to examine a group of parents across varied school settings, data are not reported for individual schools.

We contacted principals from each school and obtained permission to solicit parent and teacher participation. Letters describing the study were put in teacher mailboxes at each school. Teachers choosing to participate were asked to complete a questionnaire that contained all teacher data needed for the study and to leave it in a sealed envelope in a collection box in the school office. All the teachers at each school, whether they choose to participate in the study or not, were asked to send parent letters and questionnaire packets home with students in their classes. The letter explained the study, solicited voluntary participation, and asked parents to complete an accompanying questionnaire and return it to school in a sealed envelope. We collected the sealed return envelopes from parents and teachers at the schools.

Parent Sample

Three hundred ninety parents participated in the study. The number represented approximately 30% of the children served by the four schools. Individual school response rates ranged from 24% to 36%. Given the relatively low response rate, the results must be interpreted with caution. It seemed probable that bias in the sample favored participation by parents who had stronger opinions about the issues involved. As a check on that possibility, we reviewed parents' comments at the end of the questionnaire (in a "comments" space used by approximately half of the participants). The comments revealed a wide range of positive and negative statements, indicating a varied set of parent experiences and attitudes (e.g., "I would appreciate more news on what the children are doing and why from teachers to parents, plus how to assist with that at home." "Conference times are inaccessible to people who work. Teachers do not like phone calls from parents in their off time and I understand this. You never hear from the schoolteacher unless they have a complaint or want something." "Our son's teacher this

May/June 1992 [Vol. 85(No. 5)]

year and last has been a very positive influence on him. We're grateful for her caring the way she does." "She never has homework. What is this teacher's problem? Is she too lazy to grade extra papers? My child is making Cs and Ds. Please help."). Although the respondents may have had a higher-than-average level of interest in parent involvement issues, the variety of experiences reflected in their comments suggested that their reports would be useful in understanding many parents' patterns of school-related involvement.

In general, the respondents appeared to be an average group of elementary school parents (Table 1). Most of the respondents were mothers, most were married, and most were employed outside of the home. Education and income levels spanned a wide range. A comparison of that group with national data suggests that those parents were typical of many public school districts' parent population (e.g., compare Table 1 figures with national percentages for marital status in 1987—63% married, 36% not married—and for education—among the 25- to 34-year-old age group in 1984, 34% had a high school education and 16% had a college degree; U.S. Bureau of the Census, 1989).

Table 1.—Parent Characteristics

Elementary school parents	n	% of sample
Sex		
Female	326	84
Male	54	14
No response	8	2
Education		
Grade school	27	7
High school	131	34
Some college	125	32
BA/BS degree	50	13
Some graduate work	22	6
Graduate degree (MA/MS, PhD/MD)	24	7
No response	9	2
Marital status		
Married	259	67
Not married (includes single, separated, divorced, widowed)	124	32
No response	5	1
Employment status		
Employed out of the home	253	65
Not employed out of the home	118	30
No response	17	4
Family income		
≤ $5,000	25	6
$5,001–$10,000	42	11
$10,001–$20,000	78	20
$20,001–$30,000	76	20
$30,001–$40,000	75	20
$40,001–$50,000	36	9
$50,001 +	23	6
No response	10	8
Age of respondent	$M = 33.37$	$SD = 6.61$

Teacher Sample

Fifty teachers in the four schools (63% of the total possible) participated in the study and returned usable questionnaires. All the teachers were women, and their class enrollments averaged 21.06 ($SD = 5.20$). They had been teaching for an average of 15.76 years ($SD = 7.57$) and had been in their present schools for approximately 6.5 years ($SD = 5.73$). Their average age was 41.21 years ($SD = 8.73$). The majority of the teachers held a master's degree, and many had credits beyond the MA/MS degrees.

Measures

All data on the parents and teachers were derived from questionnaires returned by the respondents. The questionnaire for each set of respondents contained demographic items, a set of requests for estimates of participation in specific parent involvement activities, and a series of items designed to assess respondents' perceptions of parent or teacher efficacy.

Parent Questionnaire. The Parent Questionnaire asked participants to give specific information about themselves (employment status, education, family income, marital status, age, and sex) and estimates of their levels of involvement in various forms of parent-school activities—help with homework (hours in average week); other educational activities with children (hours in average week); volunteer work at school (hours in average week); telephone calls with teachers (number in average month); and parent-teacher conferences (average number in semester). Similar estimation procedures have been used successfully in other investigations (Grolnick & Ryan, 1989; Hoover-Dempsey, et al., 1987; Stevenson & Baker, 1987).

The Parent Questionnaire contained Likert-scale response items designed to assess parents' perceptions of their own efficacy. We developed the 12-item Parent Perceptions of Parent Efficacy Scale on the basis of the teaching efficacy and parenting literature cited earlier. Although efforts to develop an assessment of general parenting efficacy have been reported (Johnston & Mash, 1989), the teaching efficacy literature was used as the basis for this measure because interest in this study focused on parents' perceptions of personal efficacy specifically in relation to children's school learning. The scale included such items as "I know how to help my child do well in school" and "If I try hard, I can get through to my child even when he/she has trouble understanding something." Following the model set by previously reported scales of teacher efficacy, items in this scale focused on assessment of parents' general abilities to influence children's school outcomes and specific effectiveness in influencing children's school learning. Items were scored on a 5-point scale ranging from *strongly disagree* (1) to *strongly agree* (5). Negatively worded items were subsequently rescored so that higher scores uniformly reflected higher efficacy.

Journal of Educational Research

Possible total scores for the scale ranged from 12 to 60. Similarity to selected items of the Teacher Perceptions of Efficacy Scale (see below) and its grounding in related literature support the validity of this scale. Alpha reliability for this sample, .81, was judged satisfactory.

Teacher Questionnaire. The Teacher Questionnaire asked for specific information about teachers and their classes (grade, enrollment, percentage of students qualifying for free lunch, total years taught, years at present school, highest degree earned, sex, and age). Teachers were also asked to estimate the number of students in their classes whose parents participated in scheduled conferences, volunteer work at school, regular assistance with homework, regular involvement in other educational activities with children (e.g., reading and playing games), and telephone calls with the teacher. Again, such procedures have been used successfully in other investigations (Hoover-Dempsey et al., 1987; Stevenson & Baker, 1987).

We developed a seven-item Teacher Perceptions of Parent Efficacy Scale on the basis of the literature cited earlier. Items included such statements as "My students' parents help their children learn," and "My students' parents have little influence on their children's academic performance." All the items were scored on a scale ranging from *strongly disagree* (1) to *strongly agree* (5); negatively worded items were rescored so that higher scores consistently reflected more positive teacher perceptions of parent efficacy. Possible scores for the scale ranged from 7 to 35. Similarity to selected items of the Parent Perceptions of Parent Efficacy Scale and its grounding in the literature reviewed earlier support the validity of this scale. Alpha reliability of .79 for this sample was adequate.

Items on the 12-item Teacher Perceptions of Teacher Efficacy Scale (Hoover-Dempsey et al., 1987) included such statements as "I am successful with the students in my class" and "I feel that I am making a significant educational difference in the lives of my students." Items were scored on a scale ranging from *strongly disagree* (1) to *strongly agree* (5); negatively worded items were subsequently rescored so that higher scores uniformly reflected higher efficacy. Total scale scores ranged from 12 to 60. The scale's grounding in related literature, and its earlier successful use after substantial pretesting for clarity and content, support the validity of the scale. An alpha reliability of .83 for the scale with this sample was judged satisfactory.

Results

Correlations between parent efficacy and three indicators of parent involvement were statistically significant. Higher levels of parent efficacy were associated with more hours of classroom volunteering, more hours spent in educational activities with children, and fewer telephone calls with the teacher (see Table 2).

Parent efficacy scores did not reveal significant variations related to parents' sex, marital status, employment status, or family income. Parent education, however, was linked to some variations in efficacy scores, $F(5, 353)$ = 4.59, $p < .01$). Parents with a grade school education had significantly lower efficacy scores than did parents with all levels of college education, and parents with a high school education were significantly lower than parents with some college work beyond the bachelor's degree.

Table 2.—Means, Standard Deviations, and Intercorrelations: Parent Involvement Variables and Parent Efficacy ($N = 354$)

	Homework	Educational activities	Volunteering	Telephone calls	Conferences	Parent efficacy
Homework (hours per week)	—					
Educational activities (hours per week)	.38**	—				
Volunteering (hours per week)	.07	.14**	—			
Telephone calls (number per month)	.09	.02	.02	—		
Conferences (number per semester)	.10*	.08	.08	.34**	—	
Parent efficacy	.06	.11*	.15**	−.14**	.02	—
M	4.54	4.84	.66	.49	1.45	45.71
SD	3.58	3.58	.21	1.06	1.99	5.82

*$p < .05$ (.11). **$p < .01$ (.14).

May/June 1992 [Vol. 85(No. 5)]

Parent reports of involvement were linked to some parent status characteristics. More hours of classroom volunteering were reported by females (0.74 hours per week v. 0.25 for males, $F[1, 352] = 8.53$, $p < .01$), married parents (0.81 hours per week v. 0.32 for not married, $F[1, 352] = 7.90$, $p < .01$), and unemployed parents (1.27 hours per week v. 0.34 for employed, $F[1, 352] = 8.82$, $p < .01$). More hours of homework help were reported by parents with lower education (high school at 4.80 hours per week v. college degree at 3.33, $F[5, 348] = 3.18$, $p < .01$), lower family income (3 lower income groups = 6.52 − 5.33 hours per week v. 3 higher income groups = 3.62 − 3.09, $F[6, 326] = 7.97$, $p < .01$), and single parent status (not married = 5.51 hours per week v. married = 4.05, $F[1, 352] = 13.83$, $p < .01$). More phone calls were reported by the lowest income parents (lowest income group = 1.38 calls per month v. 0.58 − 0.20 for all other income groups, $F[6, 326] = 3.90$, $p < .01$).

Teacher efficacy and teacher perceptions of parents' efficacy were both positively linked to teacher reports of parent involvement in homework, educational activities, volunteering, and conference participation (see Table 3). Teacher efficacy was also positively linked to teacher perceptions of parent efficacy. Although teacher efficacy did not show a significant relationship with the number of students qualifying for free lunch ($r = -.16$, ns), teacher perceptions of parent efficacy were significantly linked to the free lunch figure ($r = -.59$, $p < .01$).

Discussion

The finding that parent efficacy is related, at modest but significant levels, to volunteering, educational activities, and telephone calls suggests that the construct may contribute to an understanding of variables that influence parents' involvement in decisions and choices. Defined as a set of beliefs that one is capable of achieving desired outcomes through one's efforts and the effects of those efforts on others, parent efficacy appears to facilitate increased levels of parent activity in some areas of parent involvement. The correlational nature of our results suggests that just as efficacy may influence involvement choices, these varied forms of involvement may influence parents' sense of efficacy (e.g., parents may feel increased effectiveness when they observe, during their involvement activities, that their children are successful). Regardless of the direction of influence, however, the observed linkages seem logically based in dynamic aspects of the relationship between many parents and teachers.

Classroom volunteering, for example, may be linked to efficacy, because the decision to volunteer requires some sense that one has educationally relevant skills that can and will be used effectively. Similarly, the experiences implicit in classroom volunteering may offer parents new and positive information about their effectiveness with their own child. The decision to engage in educational activities with one's children at home may reflect a sense of personal efficacy ("I will do this because it will help my child learn."); in like manner, the activities undertaken may show up, from the parent's perspective, in improved school performance that, in turn, may enhance parent efficacy. The negative relationship between efficacy and telephone calls probably reflects the still-prevalent reality that calls to and from the school signal child difficulties. Lower efficacy parents, less certain of their ability to exert positive influence on their children's learning, may seek contact more often. Similarly, more school-initiated calls may signal to the parent that he or she is offering the child less-than-adequate help.

Overall, our findings suggest that the construct of parent efficacy warrants further investigation. Grounded in the teaching efficacy literature and theoretical work on personal efficacy, the Parent Perceptions of Parent Efficacy Scale achieved satisfactory reliability with this sample and emerged, as predicted, with modest but significant relationships with some indicators of parent involvement. Parents' average efficacy score, 45.71 ($SD = 5.82$) in a scale range of 12 to 60, indicated that those parents as a group had relatively positive perceptions of their own efficacy. The variations in efficacy by parental status characteristics suggested that, at least in this group, sex, marital status, employment status, and family income were *not* related to efficacy. The finding that parental education was significantly linked to efficacy is not surprising, given the probability that parents' own school experiences contribute to their sense of school-focused efficacy in relation to their children.

Parent efficacy may differ from parent education in the way it operates, however. Whereas higher levels of education may give parents a higher level of skill and knowledge, efficacy—a set of attitudes about one's ability to get necessary resources and offer effective help—increases the likelihood that a parent will *act* on his or her knowledge (or seek more information when available resources are insufficient). The explanatory function of efficacy is suggested by the finding that parent education was related to fewer and different outcomes than parent efficacy was. Parent efficacy was related to educational activities, volunteering and telephone calls, whereas education was significantly linked to homework alone. In that finding, parents with a high school education reported spending more time helping their children with homework than did parents with a college education. The fact that a group with lower education reported *more* homework help may reflect several different possibilities: the lower efficacy parents may be more determined to see their children succeed; they may use a set of less efficient helping strategies; or they may be responding to a pattern of greater school difficulty experienced by their children.

Although our data do not permit an assessment of those possibilities, we suspect that the finding reflects less adequate knowledge of effective helping strategies. Be-

Journal of Educational Research

Table 3.—Means, Standard Deviations, and Intercorrelations Among Teacher Variables

	Homework	Educational activities	Volunteering	Telephone calls	Conferences	Free Lunch	Teacher efficacy	Perceptions of parent efficacy
Parents help with homework (number of students)	—							
Parents engage in educational activities with children (number of students)	.69**	—						
Parents do volunteer work at school (number of students)	.58**	.67**	—					
Telephone calls with parents (average number per month)	.25	.30	.12	—				
Parents attend scheduled conferences (number of students)	.62**	.52**	.49**	.10	—			
Number of students qualifying for free lunch	−.34*	−.48**	−.45**	−.25	−.38**	—		
Teacher efficacy	.42**	.39**	.54**	.17	.41**	−.16	—	
Perceptions of parent efficacy	.56**	.75**	.65**	.27	.59**	.44**	−.59**	—
M	8.72	8.06	2.96	4.74	9.98	9.94	43.28	24.09
SD	4.59	4.58	2.48	5.03	5.83	8.39	6.38	4.57

*$p < .05$ (.30). **$p < .01$ (.38).

cause many of our low-education parents were also unemployed, the finding may also reflect that they simply had more time for their children's homework activities than did the other parent groups. Whatever the explanations, the finding that education was related to fewer and different outcomes than efficacy suggests that the construct of parent efficacy warrants further investigation, perhaps particularly as it is distinguished from parent education.

Results for teachers support earlier findings (Hoover-Dempsey et al., 1987) of significant positive relationships between teacher efficacy and teacher reports of parent involvement. The general pattern—higher efficacy teachers reported high levels of parent participation in help with homework, educational activities, volunteering, and conferences—suggests that higher efficacy teachers may invite and receive more parent involvement or, conversely, that teachers who perceive and report higher levels of parent involvement develop higher judgments of personal teaching efficacy. It is also possible that both perceptions are operating. The absence of a significant positive relationship between teacher efficacy and the number of students in a school using the free lunch program also supports previous findings, suggesting again that teachers' personal efficacy judgments are to some extent independent of school socioeconomic status (SES). We suspect that the absence of a significant relationship reflects the probability that teacher judgments of personal ability to "make a difference" are related more powerfully to variables other than the status characteristics of their stu-

dents—for example, teaching skills, organizational support, and relations with colleagues (Brissie et al., 1988).

The strong positive linkages between teacher judgments of parents' efficacy and teacher reports of parent involvement likely point to the important role that parents' involvement efforts (and perhaps the visibility of those efforts) play in teachers' judgments of parents' effectiveness. In contrast to the absence of a significant relationship between teacher efficacy and school SES, teachers' judgments of *parent* efficacy were strongly and positively linked to school SES. Thus, although teachers appeared to distinguish between their own efficacy and the socioeconomic circumstances of the families that they serve, they did not appear to draw such boundaries between parents' SES and their judgments of parents' efficacy.

The further linkage between teacher efficacy and teacher judgments of parent efficacy suggests both that teachers with higher efficacy were likely to judge parents as more efficacious and that teachers who see their students' parents as more effective experience higher levels of efficacy themselves. We suspect that this relationship is an interactive one in reality, because, for example, high efficacy in each party would tend to allow each to act with more confidence and less defensiveness in the many forms of interaction that parents and teachers often routinely undertake.

The relationships between parent efficacy and some parent involvement outcomes, as well as those between teacher perceptions of parent efficacy and teacher effi-

May/June 1992 [Vol. 85(No. 5)]

cacy, suggest the potential importance of intervention strategies designed to increase parents' sense of efficacy and involvement. Bandura's (1977, 1984, 1986) work offers specific points of entry into the development of such interventions. For example, parents' *outcome expectancies*—their general beliefs that engaging in certain involvement behaviors will usually yield certain outcomes —should be examined in relation to parents' *personal efficacy* expectancies (beliefs that one's *own* involvement behaviors will yield desired outcomes). Future investigations might focus on parents' expectations about the outcomes of involvement, for example, do most parents really believe that their involvement is directly linked to child outcomes? If they believe so, what makes parents think that their *own* involvement choices are—or are not —important?

The findings reported here suggest the possibility that high-efficacy parents are more likely than those with low efficacy to believe that their efforts pay off. Therefore, the schools' best interests may be served by designing parent involvement approaches that focus specifically on increasing parents' sense of positive influence in their children's school success. This could be accomplished in a number of ways. For example, schools might regularly send home relatively specific instructions for parents about strategies for helping children with specific types of homework assignments. Schools might issue specific invitations related to volunteering for specific assignments (e.g., making posters, doing classroom aide work) and follow up with brief notes of thanks for a valued job well done. Teachers might routinely link some student accomplishments and positive characteristics to parent efforts as they conduct scheduled conference discussions. Many schools already engage in such practices, but the frequency and focus of such efforts might be increased in other schools as one means of communicating a basic efficacy-linked message to parents: "We think you're doing a good job of _____, and this is helping your child learn."

Similarly, the role and functions of teacher efficacy in the parent involvement process should be explored further. Is it the case, for instance, that higher efficacy teachers—more secure in and confident of their own roles in children's learning—invite (explicitly and implicitly) more frequent and significant parent involvement? Do more efficacious teachers, aware of children's specific learning needs, offer more specific suggestions or tasks for parent-child interaction? It may be true that teachers in schools with stronger parent involvement programs tend to receive more (and more positive) feedback on the value and impact of their teaching efforts. Also, teachers with varying levels of teaching efficacy perceive parent involvement and comments from parents differently (e.g., high-efficacy teachers may hear legitimate questions in a parent comment, whereas low-efficacy teachers hear criticism and threat).

The role and function of teachers' perceptions of parent efficacy also appear to warrant further examination. Teachers in this sample appeared able to give reliable estimates of their assessments of parents' efficacy. Of future interest would be an examination of the bases on which teachers make such evaluations and the role of those evaluations in teacher interactions with parents. Lightfoot (1978) suggested that parents and teachers participate in children's schooling with different interests and roles; the roles often engender conflict, but they may also be construed as complementary. Implicit in these relationships, whatever their form, is the assumption that parents and teachers watch and evaluate the actions of the other, equally essential, players in the child's school success. Closer examination of teachers' and parents' perceptions of their own roles and the "others' " roles in children's learning may yield information about an important source of influence on parent involvement and its outcomes.

The many calls over recent decades for increased parent involvement in children's education (Hess & Holloway, 1984; Hobbs, Dokecki, Hoover-Dempsey, Moroney, Shayne, & Weeks, 1984; Phi Delta Kappa, 1980) appear to have produced public and professional belief that parent involvement is one means of increasing positive educational outcomes for children. As yet, however, there has been little specific examination of the ways in which parent involvement—in general or in its varied forms—functions to produce those outcomes. With few exceptions (Epstein, 1986), little information on patterns of specific forms of parent involvement is available, underscoring the relatively unexamined nature of the causes, manifestations, and outcomes of parent involvement. The findings of this study suggest that further examination of parents' and teachers' sense of efficacy in relation to children's educational outcomes may yield useful information as both sets of participants work to increase the probabilities of children's school success.

NOTES

We appreciate the cooperation and support of the parents, teachers, principals, and other administrators who participated in this research.
We also gratefully acknowledge support from the H. G. Hill Fund of Peabody College, Vanderbilt University.

REFERENCES

Ashton, P. T., Webb, R. B., & Doda, N. (1983). *A study of teachers' sense of efficacy: Final report, executive summary.* Gainesville, FL: University of Florida.
Bandura, A. (1977). Self-efficacy: Toward a unifying theory of behavioral change. *Psychological Review, 84*, 191–215.
Bandura, A. (1984). Recycling misconceptions of perceived self-efficacy. *Cognitive Therapy and Research, 8*, 231–255.
Bandura, A. (1986). The explanatory and predictive scope of self-efficacy theory. *Journal of Social and Clinical Psychology, 4*, 359–373.

Journal of Educational Research

Bandura, A. (1989). Human agency in social cognitive theory. *American Psychologist, 44,* 1175–1184.

Baumrind, D. (1971). Current patterns of parental authority. *Developmental Psychology Monographs, 4,* 1–103.

Baumrind, D. (1973). The development of instrumental competence through socialization. In A. D. Pick (Ed.), *Minnesota Symposium on Child Psychology, Vol. 7,* 3–46. Minneapolis, MN: University of Minnesota Press.

Brissie, J. S., Hoover-Dempsey, K. V., & Bassler, O. C. (1988). Individual and situational contributors to teacher burnout. *Journal of Educational Research, 82,* 106–112.

Dembo, M. H., & Gibson, S. (1985). Teachers' sense of efficacy: An important factor in school achievement. *The Elementary School Journal, 86,* 173–184.

Dornbusch, S. M., Ritter, P. L., Leiderman, P. H., Roberts, D. F., & Fraleigh, M. J. (1987). The relation of parenting style to adolescent school performance. *Child Development, 58,* 1244–1257.

Epstein, J. L. (1986). Parents' reactions to teacher practices of parent involvement. *Elementary School Journal, 86,* 277–294.

Greenberger, E., & Goldberg, W. A. (1989). Work, parenting and the socialization of children. *Developmental Psychology, 25,* 22–35.

Grolnick, W. S., & Ryan, R. M. (1989). Parent styles associated with children's self-regulation and competence in school. *Journal of Educational Psychology, 81,* 143–154.

Hess, R. D., & Holloway, S. D. (1984). Family and school as educational institutions. In R. D. Parke, R. M. Emde, H. P. McAdoo, & G. P. Sackett (Eds.), *Review of child development research: Vol. 7. The family* (pp. 179–222). Chicago: University of Chicago Press.

Hobbs, N., Dokecki, P. R., Hoover-Dempsey, K. V., Moroney, R. M., Shayne, M. W., & Weeks, K. A. (1984). *Strengthening families.* San Francisco: Jossey-Bass.

Hoover-Dempsey, K. V., Bassler, O. C., & Brissie, J. S. (1987). Parent involvement: contributions of teacher efficacy, school socioeconomic status, and other school characteristics. *American Educational Research Journal, 24,* 417–435.

Lightfoot, S. L. (1978). *Worlds apart: Relationships between families and schools.* New York: Basic Books.

Johnston, C., & Mash, E. J. (1989). A measure of parenting satisfaction and efficacy. *Journal of Clinical Child Psychology, 18,* 167–175.

Mondell, S., & Tyler, F. B. (1981). Parental competence and styles of problem-solving/play behavior with children. *Developmental Psychology, 17,* 73–78.

Phi Delta Kappa (1980). *Why do some urban schools succeed?* Bloomington, IN: Author.

Stevenson, D. L., & Baker, D. P. (1987). The family-school relation and the child's school performance. *Child Development, 58,* 1348–1357.

U.S. Bureau of the Census (1989). *Statistical abstract of the United States.* Washington, DC: U.S. Government Printing Office.

Summary/Chapter 9

Correlational Research: Definition and Purpose

1. Correlational research involves collecting data to determine whether and to what degree a relationship exists between two or more variables. The degree of relationship is expressed as a correlation coefficient.

2. If a relationship exists between two variables, it means that the scores on the variables vary in some nonrandom, related way.

3. The fact that there is a relationship between variables does not imply that one is the cause of the other. Correlations do not describe causal relationships.

4. If two variables are highly related, a correlation coefficient near +1.00 (or −1.00) will be obtained; if two variables are not related, a coefficient near .00 will be obtained. The more highly related two variables are, the more accurate are predictions based on their relationship.

The Correlational Research Process

PROBLEM SELECTION

5. Correlational studies may be designed either to determine which variables of a list of likely candidates are related or to test hypotheses regarding expected relationships. The variables to be correlated should have some theoretical or experimental basis for selection.

PARTICIPANT AND INSTRUMENT SELECTION

6. A common, minimally accepted sample size for a correlational study is 30 participants. However, if the variables correlated have low reliabilities and validities or if the participants will be subdivided and correlated, a higher sample size is necessary.

DESIGN AND PROCEDURE

7. The basic correlational design obtains two (or more) scores from all members of a selected sample and one score for each variable, and the paired scores are correlated.

DATA ANALYSIS AND INTERPRETATION

8. A correlation coefficient describes both the size and direction of a relationship. A decimal number between −1.00 and +1.00 indicates the size of the relationship between the two variables. If the correlation coefficient is near .00, the variables are not related

9. A correlation coefficient near +1.00 indicates that the variables are highly and positively related. A person with a high score on one variable is likely to have a high score on the other variable, and a person with a low score on one is likely to have a low score on the other. An increase on one variable is associated with an increase on the other.

10. If the correlation coefficient is near −1.00, the variables are highly and negatively or inversely related. A person with a high score on one variable is likely to have a low score on the other variable, and a person with a low score on one is likely to have a high score on the other. An increase on one variable is associated with a decrease on the other variable, and vice versa.

11. Correlations of +1.00 and −1.00 represent the same high degree of association, but in different directions.

12. The squared correlation coefficient indicates the amount of common or shared variation between the variables. The higher the shared variation is, the higher the correlation.

13. How large a correlation coefficient needs to be in order to be useful depends on the purpose for which it was computed. Exploring or testing hypothesized relationships, predicting future performance, or determining validity and reliability require different correlation sizes.

14. Statistical significance refers to whether the obtained coefficient is really different from zero and reflects a true relationship, not a chance relationship. To determine statistical significance you consult a table that tells you

how large your correlation coefficient needs to be in order to be significant, given a level of significance and the size of your sample.

15. For a given level of significance, the smaller the sample size the larger the coefficient required. For a given sample size, the value of the correlation coefficient needed for significance increases as the level of confidence increases.

16. No matter how significant a coefficient is, a low coefficient represents a low relationship.

17. A correlation coefficient much below .50 is not generally useful for either group prediction or individual prediction. However, using a combination of correlations below .50 may yield a useful prediction.

18. Coefficients in the .60s and .70s are usually considered adequate for group prediction purposes, and coefficients in the .80s and above are adequate for individual prediction purposes.

19. Although all reliabilities in the .90s are acceptable, for certain kinds of instruments, such as personality measures, a reliability in the low .70s might be acceptable.

20. When interpreting any correlation coefficient you must always keep in mind that you are talking about a relationship only, not a cause–effect relationship.

Relationship Studies

21. Relationship studies are conducted to gain insight into the variables that are related to complex variables such as academic achievement, motivation, and self-concept. Such studies give direction to subsequent causal–comparative and experimental studies.

DATA COLLECTION

22. In a relationship study the researcher first identifies, either inductively or deductively, the variables to be related. An approach that involves unexamined collection and correlation of large numbers of variables is very inefficient and often misleading. A smaller number of carefully selected variables is much to be preferred to a large number of carelessly selected variables.

23. The population must be one for which data on each of the identified variables can be collected, and one whose members are available to the researcher. One advantage of a relationship study is that all the data may be collected within a relatively short period of time.

DATA ANALYSIS AND INTERPRETATION

24. In a relationship study, the scores for each variable are correlated among themselves or with the scores of a complex variable of interest.

25. There are many types of correlation, distinguished mainly by the type of data that are being correlated. The most commonly used correlation is the product moment correlation coefficient (Pearson r), which is used when both variables are continuous (i.e., ratio or interval data). The Spearman rho correlation is used when ordinal data (ranks) are being correlated. See Table 9.2.

26. Most correlational techniques are concerned with investigating linear relationships. If a relationship is curvilinear, an increase in one variable is associated with a corresponding increase in another variable to a point, at which point further increase in the first variable results in a corresponding decrease in the other variable (or vice versa).

27. In addition to computing correlation coefficients for a total sample group, it is sometimes profitable to examine relationships separately for certain defined subgroups. In doing this you must be sure you have a large enough sample size to obtain reliable results.

28. Attenuation refers to the fact that correlation coefficients tend to be lowered due to the use of less-than-perfectly-reliable measures. In relationship studies, a correction for attenuation can be applied that indicates what the correlation coefficient would be if both measures were perfectly reliable.

29. A narrow or restricted range of scores is another factor that can lead to a correlation coefficient underrepresenting the true relationship. There is a correction for restriction in range that may be applied to obtain an esti-

mate of what the coefficient would be if the range of scores were not restricted.

Prediction Studies

30. If two variables are highly related, scores on one variable can be used to predict scores on the other variable. Prediction studies are often conducted to facilitate decision making concerning individuals or to aid in the selection of individuals.
31. The variable upon which the prediction is made is referred to as the predictor, and the variable predicted is referred to as the criterion.
32. If several predictor variables each correlate well with a criterion, then a prediction based on a combination of those variables will be more accurate than a prediction based on any one of them.

DATA COLLECTION

33. As with a relationship study, participants must be selected from whom the desired data can be collected and from those who are available to the researcher.
34. The major difference in data collection procedures for a relationship study and a prediction study is that in a relationship study data on all variables are collected within a relatively short period of time, whereas in a prediction study predictor variables are measured some period of time before the criterion variable is measured.
35. Once a prediction study is completed, it should be cross-validated on a new group of participants to determine its usefulness for groups other than the original one.

DATA ANALYSIS AND INTERPRETATION

36. As with a relationship study, each predictor variable is correlated with the criterion variable.

37. There are two types of prediction studies, single predictor variable studies and multiple predictor studies.
38. Since a combination of variables usually results in a more accurate prediction than any one variable, prediction studies often result in a prediction equation referred to as a multiple regression equation. A multiple regression equation uses all variables that individually predict the criterion to make a more accurate prediction.
39. The accuracy of prediction can be lowered by unreliable variables, length of time between gathering data about the predictor(s) and the criterion variable, and broadness of the criterion.
40. Since relationships are not perfect, predictions made by a multiple regression equation are not perfect. Predictive studies can provide an indication of the common variance shared by the predictor(s) and the criterion variables by using the coefficient of determination.
41. Predicted scores should be interpreted as intervals, not as a single number.
42. As with relationship studies, and for similar reasons, prediction equations may be used for both the total group and subgroups.
43. Shrinkage is the tendency of a prediction equation to become less accurate when used with a group other than the one on which the equation was originally formulated. Thus, any prediction equation should be validated with at least one other group to assess shrinkage.
44. A number of more sophisticated and statistically complex procedures are based on correlations and relationships.

". . . the resulting matched groups are identical or very similar with respect to the identified extraneous variable (p. 355)."

Causal–Comparative Research

After reading chapter 10, you should be able to:

1. Briefly state the purpose of causal–comparative research.
2. State the major differences between causal–comparative and correlational research.
3. State one major way in which causal–comparative and experimental research are the same and one major way in which they are different.
4. Diagram and describe the basic causal–comparative design.
5. Identify and describe three types of control procedures that can be used in a causal–comparative study.
6. Explain why the results of causal–comparative studies must be interpreted very cautiously.

CAUSAL–COMPARATIVE RESEARCH: DEFINITION AND PURPOSE

Like correlational research, causal–comparative research is sometimes treated as a type of descriptive research, since it, too, describes conditions that already exist. Causal–comparative research, however, also attempts to determine reasons, or causes, for the existing condition. This emphasis, as well as differences in research procedures, qualifies causal–comparative as a separate type of research.

In causal–comparative research, the researcher attempts to determine the cause, or reason, for preexisting differences in groups of individuals. In other words, it is observed that groups are different on some variable and the researcher attempts to identify the main factor that has led to this difference. Such research is referred to as *ex post facto* (Latin for "after the fact"), since both the effect and the alleged cause have already occurred and must be studied in retrospect. For

example, a researcher might hypothesize that participation in preschool education is the major contributing factor for differences in the social adjustment of first graders. To examine this hypothesis the researcher would select a sample of first graders who had participated in preschool education and a sample of first graders who had not, and then compare the social adjustment of the two groups. If the group that did participate in preschool education exhibited a higher level of social adjustment, the researcher's hypothesis would be supported. Thus, the basic causal–comparative approach involves starting with an effect and seeking possible causes.

A variation of the basic approach starts with a cause and investigates its effect on some variable. Such research is concerned with the question, "What is the effect of X?" For example, a researcher might wish to investigate what long-range effect failure to be promoted to the seventh grade has on the self-concept of children not promoted. The researcher might hypothesize that children who are "socially promoted" have higher self-concepts at the end of the seventh grade than children who are retained or "held back" in the sixth grade. At the end of a school year, the researcher would identify a group of seventh graders who had been socially promoted to the seventh grade the year before, and a group of sixth graders who had been made to repeat the sixth grade. The self-concepts of the two groups would be compared. If the socially promoted group exhibited a higher level of self-concept, the researcher's hypothesis would be supported. The basic approach is sometimes referred to as retrospective causal–comparative research (since it starts with effects and investigates causes), and the variation is called prospective causal–comparative research (since it starts with causes and investigates effects). Retrospective causal–comparative studies are by far more common in educational research.

Beginning researchers often confuse causal–comparative research with both correlational research and experimental research. Correlational and causal–comparative research are probably confused because of the lack of manipulation common to both and the similar cautions regarding interpretation of results. There are definite differences, however. Causal–comparative studies *attempt* to identify cause–effect relationships; correlational studies do not. Causal–comparative studies typically involve two (or more) groups and one independent variable, whereas correlational studies typically involve two (or more) variables and one group. Also, causal–comparative studies involve comparison, whereas correlational studies involve relationship.

It is understandable that causal–comparative and experimental research are at first difficult to distinguish, since both attempt to establish cause–effect relationships and both involve group comparisons. In an experimental study the researcher selects a random sample from a population and then randomly divides the sample into two or more groups. These groups are assigned to the treatments by the researcher and the study is carried out. In causal–comparative research there is also a comparison, but individuals are not randomly assigned to treatment groups because they already were selected into groups before the research began. To put it as simply as possible, the major difference is that in experimental research the independent variable, the alleged cause, is manipulated by the researcher, whereas in causal–comparative research it is not because it has already occurred. In experimental research, researchers can randomly form groups and manipulate the independent variable; that is, they can determine "who" is going to get "what treatment" of the independent variable. In causal–comparative research, the groups are *already formed* and are already different on the independent variable. The difference between the groups (the independent variable) was not brought about by researchers.

Independent variables in causal–comparative studies are variables that cannot be manipulated (such as socioeconomic status), should not be manipulated (such as number of cigarettes smoked per day), or simply are not manipulated but could be (such as method of reading instruction). There are a number of important educational problems for which it is impossible or unfeasible to manipulate the independent variable. For example, it is not possible to manipulate organismic variables such as age or gender. Ethical considerations often prevent manipulation of a variable that *could be* manipulated but *should not be*, such as smoking or drug use. If the nature of the independent variable is such that it may cause physical or mental harm to participants, the ethics of research dictate that it should not be manipulated. For example, if a researcher were interested in determining the effect of mothers' prenatal care on the developmental status of their children at age one, it would not be ethical to deprive a group of mothers-to-be of prenatal care for the sake of a research study when such care is considered to be extremely important to both the mother's and the child's welfare. Thus, causal–comparative research permits investigation of a number of variables that cannot be studied experimentally.

Table 10.1 shows independent variables often studied in causal–comparative research. These variables are used to compare two or more levels of a given variable. For example, a causal–comparative study might compare participants younger than 50 to participants older than 50 in terms of their retention of facts. Students with high anxiety could be compared to students with low anxiety on attention span, or the difference in achievement between first graders who attended preschool and first graders who did not could be examined. In each case, preexisting participant groups were compared on a dependent variable.

As mentioned previously, experimental studies are costly in more ways than one and should be conducted only when there is good reason to believe the effort will be fruitful. Like correlational studies, causal–comparative studies help to identify variables worthy of experimental investigation. In fact, causal–comparative studies are sometimes conducted solely for the purpose of identifying the probable outcome of an experimental study. Suppose, for example, a superintendent was considering the implementation of computer-assisted remedial math

TABLE 10.1

Examples of Independent Variables Investigated in Causal–Comparative Studies

Organismic Variables
Age
Sex
Ethnicity

Ability Variables
Intelligence
Scholastic aptitude
Specific aptitudes
Perceptual ability

Personality Variables
Anxiety level
Introversion/extroversion
Agression level
Self-concept
Self-esteem
Aspiration level
Brain dominance
Learning style (e.g.,
    field independence/
    field dependence)

Family-Related Variables
Family income
Socioeconomic status
Employment status (of)
    Student
    Mother
    Father
Marital status of parents
Family environment
Birth order
Number of siblings

School-Related Variables
Preschool attendance
Size of school
Type of school (e.g., public
    vs. private)
Per pupil expenditure
Type of curriculum
Leadership style
Teaching style
Peer pressure

Note: A few of the variables *can be* manipulated (e.g., type of curriculum), but are frequently the object of causal–comparative research.

instruction. Before initiating total implementation in the school system, the superintendent might consider trying it out for a year in a number of schools or classrooms. However, even such limited adoption would be costly in terms of equipment and teacher training. Thus, as a preliminary measure to inform her decision, the superintendent might conduct a causal–comparative study and compare the math achievement of students in school districts or classrooms currently using computer-assisted remedial math instruction with the math achievement of students in school districts or classrooms not currently using computer-assisted remedial math instruction. Since most districts have yearly testing programs to assess students' achievements, including math, obtaining information on math achievement would not be difficult. If the results indicated that students' learning through computer-assisted remedial math instruction were greater, the superintendent would probably decide to go ahead with an experimental tryout of computer-assisted remedial math instruction in her own district. If no differences were found, the superintendent would probably not go ahead with the experimental tryout, preferring not to waste time, money, and effort.

Despite its many advantages, causal-comparative research does have some serious limitations that should also be kept in mind. Since the independent variable has already occurred, the same kinds of controls cannot be exercised as in an experimental study. Extreme caution must be applied in interpreting results. An apparent cause–effect relationship may not be as it appears. As with a correlational study, only a *relationship* is established, not necessarily a causal connection. The alleged cause of an observed effect may in fact be the effect itself, or there may be a third variable that has caused both the identified cause and the effect. For example, suppose a researcher hypothesized that self-concept is a determinant of reading achievement. The researcher would identify two groups, one group with high self-concepts and one group with low self-concepts. The dependent variable would be reading achievement. If the high self-concept group did indeed show higher reading achievement, the temptation would be to conclude that self-concept influences high reading achievement. However, this conclusion would not be warranted, since it is not possible to establish whether self-concept precedes achievement or vice versa. It might be that achievement influences self-concept. Since both the independent and dependent variables would have already occurred, it would not be possible to determine which came first, and thus, which influenced the other. If the study were reversed, and a group of high achievers was compared with a group of low achievers, it might well be that they would be different on self-concept, thus suggesting that achievement causes self-concept. Even worse, it would be possible (in fact, very plausible) that some third variable, such as parental attitude, might be the main influence on *both* self-concept and achievement. Parents who praise and encourage their children might produce high self-concept and high academic achievement. Thus, caution must be exercised in attributing cause–effect relationships based on causal–comparative research. Only in experimental research is the degree of control sufficient to establish cause–effect relationships. Only in experimental research does the researcher randomly assign participants to treatment groups. In causal–comparative research the researcher cannot assign participants to treatment groups because they are already in those groups. However, causal–comparative studies do have their place among research methods, since they permit investigation of variables that cannot or should not be investigated experimentally, facilitate decision making, provide guidance for experimental studies, and are less costly on all dimensions.

CONDUCTING A CAUSAL–COMPARATIVE STUDY

The basic causal–comparative design is quite simple, and although the independent variable is not manipulated, there are control procedures that can be exercised to improve interpretation of results. Causal–comparative studies also involve a wider variety of statistical techniques than the other types of research thus far discussed.

DESIGN AND PROCEDURE

The basic causal–comparative design involves selecting two groups differing on some independent variable and comparing them on some dependent variable (see Figure 10.1). As Figure 10.1 indicates, the researcher selects two groups of participants usually referred to as experimental and control groups, but more accurately referred to as comparison groups. The groups may differ in one of two ways: first, one group possesses a characteristic that the other does not (case A), or second, each group has the characteristic but to differing degrees or amounts (case B). An example of case A would be a comparison of two groups, one that was composed of brain-damaged children and the other that was composed of non-brain-damaged children. An example of case B would be a comparison of two groups, one group composed of high self-concept individuals and one group composed of low self-concept individuals. Another case B example is a comparison of the algebra achievement of two groups, one that had learned algebra via traditional instruction and one that had learned algebra via computer-assisted instruction. In both case A and case B, the performance of the groups should be compared using some valid dependent variable measure selected from the types of instruments discussed in chapter 5.

FIGURE	10.1

The Basic Causal–Comparative Design

	Group	Independent Variable	Dependent Variable
Case A	(E)	(X)	O
	(C)		O

OR

	Group	Independent Variable	Dependent Variable
Case B	(E)	(X_1)	O
	(C)	(X_2)	O

Symbols:
(E) = Experimental group; ( ) indicates no manipulation
(C) = Control group
(X) = Independent variable
 O = Dependent variable

Definition and selection of the comparison groups is a very important part of the causal–comparative procedure. The independent variable differentiating the groups must be clearly and operationally defined, since each group represents a different population. The way in which the groups are defined will affect the generalizability of the results. If a researcher were to compare a group of students with an "unstable" home life to a group of students with a "stable" home life, the terms *unstable* and *stable* would have to be operationally defined. An unstable home life could refer to any number of things, such as a home with an alcoholic parent, a violent parent, child neglect, or a combination of such factors. The operational definitions will help define the populations and guide sample selection.

Random selection from the defined populations is generally the preferred method of participant selection. The important consideration is to select samples that are representative of their respective populations. Note that in causal–comparative research the random sample is selected from two already-existing populations, not from a single population, as in experimental research. This is key in differentiating the two approaches. As in experimental studies, the goal is to have groups that are as similar as possible on all relevant variables except the independent variable. In order to determine the equality of groups, information on a number of background and current status variables may be collected and compared for each group. For example, information on age, years of experience, gender, prior knowledge and the like may be obtained and examined for the groups being compared. The more similar the two groups are on such variables, the more homogeneous they are on everything but the independent variable. This makes a stronger study and reduces the possible alternative explanations of the research findings. There are a number of control procedures to correct for identified inequalities on such variables.

CONTROL PROCEDURES

Lack of randomization, manipulation, and control are all sources of weakness in a causal–comparative study. Random assignment of participants to groups is probably the single best way to try to ensure equality of groups. This is not possible in causal–comparative studies, because the groups already exist and have already received the independent variable. A problem already discussed is the possibility that the groups are different on some other important variable (e.g., gender, experience, age) besides the identified independent variable. It may be that this other variable is the real cause of the observed difference between the causal–comparative groups.

For example, if a researcher simply compared a group of students who had received preschool education to a group who had not, he might draw the conclusion that preschool education results in higher first-grade reading achievement. However, what if all preschool programs in the region in which the study was conducted were private and required high tuition. If this were the case, the researcher would really be investigating the effects not just of preschool education, but also of membership in a well-to-do family. It might very well be that parents in such families provide early informal reading instruction for their children. This could make it very difficult to disentangle the effects of attending preschool from the effects of affluent families on first-grade reading. If, however, the researcher was aware of the situation, he could control for the affluence variable by studying only children of well-to-do parents. Thus, the two groups to be compared would be equated with respect to the extraneous variable of parents' income level. This example is but one illustration of a number of statistical and nonstatistical methods that can be applied in an attempt to control for extraneous variables.[1]

Matching

Matching is another control technique. A researcher who has identified a variable likely to influence performance on the dependent variable may control for that variable by pair-wise matching of participants. In other words, for each participant in one group, the researcher finds a participant in the other group with the same or very similar score on the control variable. If a participant in either group does not have a suitable match, the participant is eliminated from the study. Thus, the resulting matched groups are identical or very similar with respect to the identified extraneous variable. For example, if a researcher matched participants in each group on IQ, a participant in one group with an IQ of 140 would have a matched participant with an IQ at or near 140. As you may have deduced (if you have an IQ of 140!), a major problem with pair-wise matching is that there are invariably participants who have no match and must therefore be eliminated from the study. The problem becomes even more serious when the researcher attempts to simultaneously match participants on two or more variables.

Comparing Homogeneous Groups or Subgroups

Another way to control extraneous variables is to compare groups that are homogeneous with respect to the extraneous variable. For example, if IQ were an identified extraneous variable, the researcher might limit the groups to only participants with IQs between 85 and 115 (average IQ). Of course this procedure may lower the numbers of participants in the study and, of course, it limits the generalizability of the findings.

A similar but more satisfactory approach is to form subgroups within each group that represent all levels of the control variable. For example, each group might be divided into high (116 and above), average (85 to 115), and low (84 and below) IQ subgroups. The existence of comparable subgroups in each group controls for IQ. In addition to controlling for the variable, this approach also permits the researcher to determine whether the independent variable affects the dependent variable differently at different levels of IQ, the control variable. That is, the researcher can examine whether the effect on the dependent variable is different for the different subgroups. If this information is of interest, the best approach is not to do separate analyses for each of the subgroups but to build the control variable right into the research design and to analyze the results with a statistical technique called *factorial analysis of variance*. A factorial analysis (see chapter 11) allows the researcher to determine the effect of the independent variable and the control variable on the dependent variable, both separately and in combination. In other words, it permits the researcher to determine if there is an interaction between the independent variable and the control variable such that the independent variable operates differently at different levels of the control variable. For example, IQ might be a control variable in a causal–comparative study of the

---

[1]Several of these methods will be discussed further, and in more detail, in regard to their use in experimental research.

effects of two different methods of learning fractions. It might be found that a method involving manipulation of blocks is more effective for low IQ students who may have difficulty thinking abstractly.

Analysis of Covariance

Analysis of covariance is used to adjust initial group differences on variables used in causal–comparative and experimental research studies. In essence, analysis of covariance adjusts scores on a dependent variable for initial differences on some other variable related to performance on the dependent. For example, suppose we were doing a study to compare two methods, X and Y, of teaching fifth graders to solve math problems. When we gave the two groups a pretest of math ability, we found that the group in method Y scored much higher than the group in method X. This difference suggests that method Y will be superior to method X at the end of the study just because the group in method Y has higher math ability than the other group. Covariate analysis statistically adjusts the scores of method Y to remove the initial advantage so that the results at the end of the study can be fairly compared as if the two groups started equally.

DATA ANALYSIS AND INTERPRETATION

Analysis of data in causal–comparative studies involves a variety of descriptive and inferential statistics. All of the statistics that may be used in a causal–comparative study may also be used in an experimental study, and a number of them will be described in Part Seven. Briefly, however, the most commonly used descriptive statistics are the mean, which indicates the average performance of a group on a measure of some variable, and the standard deviation, which indicates how spread out a set of scores is around the mean (i.e., whether the scores are relatively homogeneous or heterogeneous around the mean). The most commonly used inferential statistics are the t test, used to determine whether the means of two groups are significantly different from one another; analysis of variance, used to determine if there is significant difference among the means of three or more groups; and chi square, used to compare group frequencies (i.e., to see if an event occurs more frequently in one group than another).

As repeatedly pointed out, interpretation of the findings in a causal–comparative study requires considerable caution. Due to lack of randomization, manipulation, and control factors, it is difficult to establish cause–effect relationships with any great degree of confidence. The cause–effect relationship may in fact be the reverse of the one hypothesized (the alleged cause may be the effect and vice versa), or there may be a third factor which is the "real" underlying cause of both the independent and dependent variables. Note, however, that there are some cases in which reversed causality is not a reasonable alternative. For example, preschool training may "cause" increased reading achievement in first grade, but reading achievement in first grade cannot "cause" preschool training. Similarly, one's gender may affect one's achievement in mathematics, but one's achievement in mathematics certainly does not affect one's gender! In other cases, however, reversed causality is more plausible and should be investigated. For example, as pointed out, it is equally plausible that achievement affects self-concept as it is that self-concept affects achievement. It is also equally plausible that excessive absenteeism produces, or leads to, involvement in criminal activities as it is that involvement in criminal activities produces, or leads to, excessive absenteeism. The way to determine the correct order of causality (i.e., which variable caused which) is to determine which one occurred first. If, in the previous example, it could be demonstrated that a period of excessive absenteeism was frequently followed by a student getting in trouble with the law, then it could more reasonably be concluded that excessive absenteeism leads to involvement in criminal activities. On the other hand, if it were determined that prior to a student's first involvement in criminal activities his or her attendance was good, but following it, was poor, then the hypothesis that involvement in criminal activities leads to excessive absenteeism would be more reasonable.

The possibility of a third, common explanation in causal–comparative research is plausible in many situations. Recall the example of parental attitude affecting both self-concept and achievement. One way to control for a potential common cause is to equate groups on that variable. For example, if students in both the high self-concept group and the low self-concept group could be selected from parents who had similar attitudes, the effects of parents' attitudes are removed because both groups have the same parental attitudes. It is clear that in order to investigate or control for alternative hypotheses, researchers must be aware of them and must present evidence that they are not in fact the true explanation for the behavioral differences being investigated.

The following pages present an example of causal–comparative research. Note that even though survey forms were used to collect data, the study was not descriptive because the purpose of the study was to investigate existing differences between groups.

Differing Opinions on Testing Between Preservice and Inservice Teachers

KATHY E. GREEN
University of Denver

ABSTRACT   Studies of teachers' use of tests suggest that classroom tests are widely used and that standardized test results are rarely used. What is the genesis of this lack of use? A previous comparison of pre- and inservice teachers' attitudes toward assessment suggested no differences. This study assessed the different opinions among sophomores (n = 84), seniors (n = 152), and inservice teachers (n = 553) about the use of classroom and standardized tests. Significant differences were found; preservice teachers had less favorable attitudes toward classroom testing than teachers did and more favorable attitudes toward standardized testing.

This study assessed differences among college students entering a teacher education program, students finishing a teacher education program, and inservice teachers concerning their opinions of some aspects of classroom and standardized testing. Although numerous studies of inservice teachers' attitudes toward testing have been conducted, little research is available regarding preservice teachers' views of testing and of the genesis of teachers' views of testing.

Interest in this topic stemmed from research findings suggesting that the results of standardized tests are not used by most teachers. If standardized testing is to continue, the failure to use results is wasteful. Other studies have identified some of the reasons for the lack of use. This study's purpose was to determine whether opinions about the usefulness of standardized and other tests were negative for students before they even entered the teaching profession. When were those attitudes developed? Are attitudes fixed by students' educational experiences *prior* to entry into a teacher education program? Are preservice teachers socialized by their educational programs into resistance to testing? Do negative attitudes appear upon entry into the profession because of socialization into the school culture? Or do they appear after several years of service as a teacher because of personal experiences in the classroom?

I found only one study that addressed differences in opinions of pre- and inservice teachers (Reeves & Kazelskis, 1985). That study examined a broad range of issues salient to first-year teachers; only one item addressed testing specifically. Reeves and Kazelskis found no significant differences between pre- and inservice teachers' opinions about testing, as measured by that item. In this study, I sought more information pertinent to the development of opinions about testing.

Test use in U.S. schools has been and continues to be extensive. It has been estimated that from 10 to 15% of class time is spent dealing with tests (Carlberg, 1981; Newman & Stallings, 1982). Gullickson (1982) found that 95% of the teachers he surveyed gave tests at least once every 2 weeks. The estimated percentage of students' course grades that are based on test scores is 40 to 50%, ranging from 0 to 100% (Gullickson, 1984; McKee & Manning-Curtis, 1982; Newman & Stallings). Classroom tests, thus, are used frequently and may, at times, be used almost exclusively in determining students' grades.

In contrast, a review of past practice suggests minimal teacher use of *standardized* test results in making instructional decisions (Fennessey, 1982; Green & Williams, 1989; Lazar-Morrison, Polin, Moy, & Burry, 1980; Ruddell, 1985). Stetz and Beck (1979) conducted a national study of over 3,000 teachers' opinions about standardized tests. They noted that 41% of the teachers surveyed reported making little use of test results, a finding consistent with that of Goslin (1967) from several decades ago and that of Boyd, McKenna, Stake, and Yachinsky (1975). Test results were viewed as providing information that was supplemental to the wider variety of information that the teachers already possessed. Reasons offered for why standardized tests are given but results not always used by teachers include resistance to a perceived narrowing of the curriculum, resistance to management control, accountability avoidance (Darling-Hammond,

Address correspondence to Kathy E. Green, University of Denver, School of Education, Denver, CO 80208.

Journal of Educational Research

1985), and a limited understanding of score interpretation resulting from inadequate preservice training (Cramer & Slakter, 1968; Gullickson & Hopkins, 1987). Marso and Pigge (1988) found that teachers perceive a lower need for standardized testing skills than for classroom testing skills. They also found that teachers reported lower proficiencies in standardized test score use and interpretation than in classroom test score use and interpretation.

The results of those studies suggest that inservice teachers use classroom tests extensively but make little use of standardized test results. This suggests that inservice teachers, in general, hold positive attitudes toward classroom tests and less positive attitudes toward standardized tests. The literature does not lead to any predictions about preservice teachers' attitudes toward tests.

This study assessed differences between preservice and inservice teachers' opinions about testing and test use. The following research hypotheses were formulated to direct the study.

H1. There are significant differences in opinions about the testing and test use between preservice and inservice teachers.
H2. There are significant differences in opinions about testing between students beginning their preparation (sophomores) and students finishing their preparation (seniors).
H3. There are significant differences among inservice teachers with differing years of experience.

Method

Samples

Three samples were drawn for this study. They were samples of (a) practicing teachers, (b) college sophomores beginning a teacher education program, and (c) college seniors completing a teacher education program (but prior to student teaching). For the first sample, survey forms were mailed in a rural western state to 700 teachers randomly selected from the State Department of Education list of all licensed educators. During the spring semester of 1986, teachers were sent a letter explaining the nature of the study, a survey form, and a stamped return envelope. With two follow-up mailings, a total of 555 questionnaires were received, or 81% of the deliverable envelopes. (Twelve questionnaires were undeliverable, 4 persons refused to respond, and 133 persons did not reply.) No compulsory statewide standardized testing program was in place in the state.

The second sample was a convenience sample of three sections of an educational foundations class typically taken by college sophomores who have just enrolled in a teacher preparation program (*n* = 84). The course examines educational thought and practice in the United States. The classes were taught in an 8-week block, meeting for 50 min per day, 4 days per week. Survey forms were distributed in class and completed during class time.

The third sample was also a convenience sample of four sections of a tests and measurement class taken by college seniors (*n* = 152). The course is typically taken after coursework is almost complete, but prior to student teaching. The course provides instruction in basic statistics, classroom test construction and analysis, and standardized test use and interpretation. The course was also taught in an 8-week block, with the same schedule as the foundations course. Survey forms were distributed during the first week of class and completed during class time. Survey forms took from 10 to 30 min to complete. Responses were anonymous. Both sophomores and seniors were attending a public university in a small western town.

Table 1 presents descriptive information for the three samples.

Instruments

Three different forms with overlapping questions were used in this study. The survey form sent to the teachers contained questions regarding training in tests and measurement, subject and grades taught, tests given, and attitudes toward both standardized and classroom tests. The questionnaire was two pages in length, double-sided and contained 49 questions. The form given to the sophomores had 43 questions and was one page in length, double-sided. The form given to the seniors was three pages in length, single-sided. The latter two forms differed by the inclusion of an evaluation anxiety scale and items eliciting importance of contemporary measurement practices for the seniors. Although different formats may have affected responses to some extent, all the forms began with several demographic questions followed by the items relevant to this study. Any form differences would, then, likely be minimized for those initial items.

There were 18 items common to the three forms. Sixteen of the items were Likert items with a 1 to 6 (*strongly disagree* to *strongly agree*) response format. Likert-scale items were drawn from a previously developed measure of attitudes toward both standardized and classroom testing (Green & Stager, 1986). Internal consistency reliabilities of the measures ranged from .63 to .75. The re-

Table 1.—Description of Samples

Item	Sophomores (*n* = 84)	Seniors (*n* = 152)	Teachers (*n* = 553)
Percentage female	84	152	553
Mean age	73.0	75.9	63.6
Age range	18–33	20–45	—
Mean years in teaching	—	—	12

September/October 1992 [Vol. 86(No. 1)]

maining two items asked how many hours per week teachers spend in testing activities and how much of a student's grade should be based on test results. The study examined differences found among groups on those items. Item content is presented in Table 2, in which items are grouped by content (opinions about standardized tests, classroom tests, and about personal liking for tests).

Data were analyzed using multivariate analyses of variance, followed by univariate analyses of variance. If univariate results were significant, I used Tukey's HSD test to assess the significance of pairwise post hoc differences. Samples of both items and persons were limited; therefore, results may not be widely generalizable.

Results

Significant multivariate differences were found across opinion items (Wilks's lambda = .70, $p < .001$) when the three samples were compared (Table 2). Hypothesis 1 was supported. Differences were found between teachers and students for all items, with significance levels varying from .02 to .001 for individual items. Opinions were not consistently more positive across all items for teachers or for students. For instance, whereas teachers were most likely to feel that standardized tests address important educational outcomes, teachers were least likely to find that standardized tests serve a useful purpose. In general, though, students favored use of standardized tests for student or teacher evaluation more than teachers did. Al-

Table 2.—Means and Standard Deviations for Opinions About Testing by Group

Variable	Sophomores ($n = 84$)	Seniors ($n = 152$)	Teachers ($n = 553$)	p	1	2	3
Hours spent in testing/week	10.43 (6.72)	9.18 (6.43)	4.37 (4.05)	.001	*	*	—
Percentage grade based on test	49.63 (15.48)	46.94 (18.71)	41.31 (22.68)	.001	*	*	—
Standardized test items							
Standardized tests are the best way to evaluate a teacher's effectiveness.	2.79 (1.03)	2.83 (1.10)	2.12 (1.18)	.001	*	*	—
Teachers whose students score higher on standardized tests should receive higher salaries.	2.53 (1.07)	2.33 (1.17)	1.74 (1.01)	.001	*	*	—
Requiring *students* to pass competency tests would raise educational standards.	4.14 (1.13)	3.89 (1.09)	3.69 (1.26)	.001	*	*	—
Requiring *teachers* to pass competency tests would raise educational standards.	4.35 (.90)	4.09 (1.27)	3.30 (1.34)	.001	*	*	—
Standardized tests assess important educational outcomes.	3.47 (1.04)	3.54 (.87)	3.95 (.88)	.001	*	*	—
Standardized tests serve a useful purpose.	4.02 (.83)	3.97 (.81)	2.93 (.97)	.001	*	*	—
Standardized tests force teachers to "teach to the test."	3.05 (1.19)	2.74 (.98)	3.11 (1.22)	.02	—	*	—
Classroom test items							
Test construction takes too much teacher time.	4.57 (1.02)	4.36 (.85)	3.97 (.88)	.001	*	*	—
Test scores are a fair way to grade students.	3.42 (1.02)	3.32 (1.13)	4.04 (.84)	.001	*	*	—
Testing has a favorable impact on student motivation.	4.00 (.71)	3.88 (1.00)	4.16 (.88)	.01	—	*	—
Tests are of little value in identifying learning problems.	1.76 (.96)	1.43 (.84)	1.44 (1.05)	.01	*	—	*
It is relatively easy to construct tests in my subject area.	4.11 (1.25)	3.51 (1.34)	4.35 (.89)	.001	—	*	*
Tests measure only minor aspects of what students can learn.	2.92 (1.13)	3.01 (1.13)	3.24 (1.00)	.01	*	—	—
Personal reflections							
I do(did) well on tests.	4.05 (1.04)	4.00 (1.10)	4.46 (.94)	.001	*	*	—
I personally dislike taking tests.	3.13 (1.35)	3.12 (1.14)	3.46 (1.16)	.01	—	*	—
The tests I have taken were generally good assessments of my knowledge of an area.	3.65 (1.08)	3.41 (1.10)	4.09 (.82)	.001	*	*	—

Note. For opinion items, the scale ranged from *strongly disagree* (1) to *strongly agree* (6). Standard deviations are presented in parentheses. Asterisks(*) indicate significant ($p < .05$) differences between groups: 1 = teachers versus sophomores, 2 = teachers versus seniors, 3 = sophomores versus seniors.

Journal of Educational Research

though the students were less likely to say that they do well on tests and that tests previously taken were good assessments of their ability, the students were also less likely to say that they disliked taking tests. Students' opinions about classroom testing were less favorable than were teachers' opinions for all but one item. Differences were also found between teachers and students in estimates of time spent in testing and in the percentage of students' grades based on test scores.

Hypothesis 2 was not supported. Only two significant differences in means were found between the sophomores and the seniors. One difference was found for the item "It is relatively easy to construct tests in my subject area." Sophomores tended to agree with that statement more than the seniors did. Because the seniors were required to complete a task involving test construction, the impending course requirement may have influenced their opinions. The second difference was found for the item "Tests are of little value in identifying learning problems," with more positive opinions expressed by seniors than by sophomores.

Hypothesis 3 was tested by dividing teachers into three groups: 0 to 1 years, 2 to 5 years, and 5+ years of experience as a teacher. No significant multivariate or univariate differences were found, so Hypothesis 3 was not supported. However, there were few teachers with 0 to 1 years of experience in the sample. Because of the small number of teachers with 0 to 1 years of teaching (46 teachers; 8.7% of the data file), groups were reformed as follows: 0 to 3 years, 4 to 6 years, and 6+ years of experience. Still, no significant multivariate or univariate differences were found. (In addition, no differences were found between teachers with 0 to 3 years of experience and those with 6 or more years of experience.)

Discussion

This study was undertaken to examine whether differences in opinions about testing would be discerned between preservice and inservice teachers and whether those differences would suggest a progression. The differences found suggest that teacher education students are less favorable to classroom testing and more favorable to standardized testing than teachers are. Differences were *not* found between sophomores and seniors, however. Nor were opinions about testing found to depend upon years of experience in teaching. Those results do not reflect a developmental progression. The shift in opinion seems to occur when beginning a teaching position, suggesting effects that result from job requirements or socialization as a teacher more than from a developmental trend. Differences between students and teachers, then, seem likely to be caused by direct teacher experience with creating, administering, and using tests or by acculturation into life as a teacher in a school. That conclusion suggests that if

one wishes to affect teachers' opinions about testing, provision of inservice experiences may be a more profitable avenue than additional preservice education.

Test use. The teachers sampled in this study reported spending an average of about 11% of their time in testing, which is consistent with estimates reported in the literature (10 to 15%). The finding in this study that an average of 41% of the students' grades was based on test results is also consistent with estimates reported in the literature (40 to 50%). Estimates of the time needed for testing activities obtained from students sampled in this study were much higher (23% and 26% for seniors and sophomores, respectively) than the estimates obtained from the teachers' reports. Although students' estimates of the percentage of grade based on test scores were significantly higher than those of teachers, they were within the range reported in the literature. Students, then, who lack an experiential base, seem either to have exaggerated views regarding the time that teachers spend on testing-related activities or think that it will take them longer to construct tests.

Beginning teachers also lack an experiential base. One might ask whether beginning teachers spend more time in test-related activities than do teachers with more experience, because beginning teachers may not have files of tests to draw upon. Mean reported time spent in testing was higher for first- and second-year teachers (means of 5.4 and 5.7 hours per week) than for teachers with more experience (mean for third year = 2.3, 4th year = 2.8, 5th year = 3.8). Thus, students may be accurate in their perception of the time needed by novices for testing-related activities.

Standardized testing. The students' opinions ranged from neutral to positive regarding the use of standardized tests and were, on average, significantly more positive than the teachers' opinions. One explanation for the positive opinions may be that students have extremely limited personal experience with standardized tests (their own or their friends') and so have a limited basis upon which to judge test effectiveness. By college level, most students have taken a number of standardized tests but may not be aware of the results, may not have been directly affected by the results, or may have been affected by the results at a time when they were too young to understand or argue. Students may believe that the tests must be useful because "authorities and experts" sanction their administration. Students' opinions may, then, be shaped by the positive *public* value placed on tests, as well as by their educational programs. The tests and measurement course taken by many preservice teachers emphasizes how tests can be valuable if used properly. One can argue that most students view themselves as intending to use tests properly. In contrast, many teachers are required to give standardized tests, and they may also be required to take them.

September/October 1992 [Vol. 86(No. 1)]

Preservice–inservice differences might be even more extreme in states where the stakes attached to standardized test use are higher—where the teacher's job or salary depends upon test results. Teachers develop a broader base of experience with standardized testing, and they may be more aware of the limitations of the tests and of the controversy surrounding standardized testing. The measurement profession is unclear about the value of standardized testing; it is not surprising that teachers also have reservations.

Classroom testing. Differences were also found between teachers and teacher education students for most classroom test items, though differences were not as pronounced for these items. The result is in contrast to Reeves and Kazelskis's (1985) finding of no differences between similar groups. The result of somewhat less favorable opinions of preservice than inservice teachers toward classroom testing may have stemmed from the frequent test taking by students versus the frequent use of tests by teachers. By the time students are seniors in college, they will have taken a larger number of classroom tests than standardized tests and thus will have considerably more experience in evaluating their effectiveness. Students undoubtedly encounter classroom tests and test questions that they consider to be unfair assessments of their knowledge. Such experiences may temper their opinions toward classroom tests. In contrast, because most teachers rely to some extent on test results in assigning grades and in evaluating instruction, opinions may change to conform with this behavior. Teachers' opinions may also be influenced by an experiential understanding of testing gained through learning how informative test results can be.

Because it is unlikely that the widespread use of classroom and standardized tests will diminish, teachers will continue to be called upon to use tests to make decisions that are important in the lives of students. Teachers need to be competent in test construction and interpretation. However, if tests are to be used effectively as part of the instructional process, teachers must perceive the positive aspects of test use. If a teacher finds that task impossible, that teacher should discontinue traditional test use and seek alternative assessment techniques, within the boundaries allowed by the district. Teachers should communicate positive feelings about the tests they give to their students. Teachers will probably be more likely to do so if they have positive opinions of tests. Tests are often viewed as evaluative; they may more effectively be viewed as informative and prescriptive.

If teacher educators wish to affect prospective teachers' views, they may need to both clarify their own views about the place of testing in instruction and clearly present arguments about testing, pro and con, to their classes. Well-constructed classroom assessments, whether paper-and-pencil, portfolio, or performance measures, provide diagnostic and prescriptive information about the students' progress and about the effectiveness of instruction. This information is valuable. Poorly constructed or standardized measures that do not address the curriculum provide little information of use in the classroom. The reasons for giving tests that do not provide information useful in instruction must be clearly explained. Such tests may be mandated to provide legitimate administrative, state, or national information.

But to what extent can teacher educators shape *prospective* teachers' views? The results of this study suggest that opinions held prior to and following preservice instruction may not survive the transition to the real world of the classroom. If this is the case, the preservice course —no matter how good it is—would be ineffective in influencing attitudes. (It may, however, be highly effective in influencing the quality of testing practices by providing basic skills in test construction and interpretation.) Inservice instruction may be a better vehicle to use to produce attitude change.

This study was cross-sectional in design. A longitudinal study that examined opinions over time (from preservice to inservice) is required to identify the extent to which opinions are shaped by school requirements. Additional information regarding school characteristics affecting preservice and inservice teachers' attitudes toward testing would be of interest, as would information about differences in testing skill levels between pre- and inservice teachers.

NOTES

An earlier version of this paper was presented at the 1990 annual meeting of the National Council on Measurement in Education, held April 1990 in Boston.

Appreciation is expressed to the *Journal of Educational Research* reviewers for their helpful suggestions.

REFERENCES

Boyd, J., McKenna, B. H., Stake, R. E., & Yachinsky, J. (1975). *A study of testing practices in the Royal Oak (MI) public schools.* Royal Oak, MI: Royal Oak City School District. (ERIC Reproduction Service No. 117 161)

Carlberg, C. (1981). South Dakota study report. Denver, CO: Midcontinent Regional Educational Laboratory.

Cramer, S., & Slakter, M. (1968). A scale to assess attitudes toward aptitude testing. *Measurement and Evaluation in Guidance, 1*(2).

Darling-Hammond, L., & Wise, A. E. (1985). Beyond standardization: State standards and school improvement. *Elementary School Journal, 85,* 315–336.

Fennessey, D. (1982). Primary teachers' assessment practices: Some implications for teacher training. Paper presented at the annual conference of the South Pacific Association for Teacher Education, Frankston, Victoria, Australia.

Goslin, D. A. (1967). *Teachers and testing.* New York: Russell Sage Foundation.

Green, K. E., & Stager, S. F. (1986–87). Testing: Coursework, attitudes, and practices. *Educational Research Quarterly, 11*(2), 48–55.

Green, K. E., & Stager, S. F. (1986). Measuring attitudes of teachers toward testing. *Measurement and Evaluation in Counseling and Development, 19,* 141–150.

Green, K. E., & Williams, E. J. (1989, March). Standardized test use by

Journal of Educational Research

classroom teachers: Effects of training and grade level taught. Paper presented at the annual meeting of the National Council on Measurement in Education, San Francisco.

Gullickson, A. R. (1982). The practice of testing in elementary and secondary schools. (ERIC Reproduction Service No. ED 229 391)

Gullickson, A. R. (1984). Teacher perspectives of their instructional use of tests. *Journal of Educational Research, 77*, 244–248.

Gullickson, A. R, & Hopkins, K. D. (1987). The context of educational measurement instruction for preservice teachers: Professor perspectives. *Educational Measurement: Issues and Practice, 6*, 12–16.

Karmos, A. H., & Karmos, J. S. (1984). Attitudes toward standardized achievement tests and their relation to achievement test performance. *Measurement and Evaluation in Counseling and Development, 17*, 56–66.

Lazar-Morison, C., Polin, L., Moy, R., & Burry, J. (1980). A review of the literature on test use. Los Angeles: Center for the Study of Evaluation, California State University. (ERIC Reproduction Service No. 204 411)

Marso, R. N., & Pigge, F. L. (1988). Ohio secondary teachers' testing needs and proficiencies: Assessments by teachers, supervisors, and principals. *American Secondary Education, 17*, 2–9.

McKee, B. G., & Manning-Curtis, C. (1982, March). Teacher-constructed classroom tests: The stepchild of measurement research. Paper presented at the National Council on Measurement in Education annual conference, New York.

Newman, D. C., & Stallings, W. M. (1982). Teacher competency in classroom testing, measurement preparation, and classroom testing practices. Paper presented at the American Educational Research Association annual meeting. New York. (ERIC Reproduction Service No. ED 220 491)

Reeves, C. K., & Kazelskis, R. (1985). Concerns of preservice and inservice teachers. *Journal of Educational Research, 78*, 267–271.

Ruddell, R. B. (1985). Knowledge and attitudes toward testing: Field educators and legislators. *Reading Teacher, 38*, 538–543.

Stetz, F. P., & Beck, M. D. (1979). Comments from the classroom: Teachers' and students' opinions of achievement tests. Paper presented at the annual meeting of the National Council on Measurement in Education, San Francisco.

Summary/Chapter 10

Causal–Comparative Research: Definition and Purpose

1. In causal–comparative, or ex post facto, research, the researcher attempts to determine the cause, or reason, for existing differences in the behavior or status of groups.

2. The basic causal–comparative approach is retrospective; that is, it starts with an effect and seeks its possible causes. A variation of the basic approach is prospective; that is, it starts with a cause and investigates its effect on some variable.

3. An important difference between causal–comparative and correlational research is that causal–comparative studies involve two or more groups and one independent variable, while correlational studies involve two or more variables and one group.

4. The major difference between experimental research and causal–comparative research is that in experimental research the independent variable, the alleged cause, is manipulated, and in causal–comparative research it is not, because it has already occurred. In experimental research the researcher can randomly form groups and manipulate the independent variable. In causal–comparative research the groups are already formed and already divided on the independent variable.

5. Independent variables in causal–comparative studies are variables that cannot be manipulated (such as socioeconomic status), should not be manipulated (such as number of cigarettes smoked per day), or simply are not manipulated, though they could be (such as method of reading instruction).

6. Causal–comparative studies identify relationships that may lead to experimental studies, but only a relationship is established. Cause–effect relationships established through causal–comparative research are at best tenuous and tentative. Only experimental research can truly establish cause–effect relationships.

7. The alleged cause of an observed causal–comparative effect may in fact be the effect, the supposed cause, or a third variable that has "caused" both the identified cause and effect.

Conducting a Causal–Comparative Study

DESIGN AND PROCEDURE

8. The basic causal–comparative design involves selecting two groups differing on some independent variable and comparing them on some dependent variable.

9. The groups may differ in a number of ways. One group may possess a characteristic that the other does not, one group may possess more of a characteristic than the other, or the two groups may have had different kinds of experiences.

10. It is important to select samples that are representative of their respective populations and similar with respect to critical variables other than the independent variable.

CONTROL PROCEDURES

11. Lack of randomization, manipulation, and control are all sources of weakness in a causal–comparative design. A threat is the possibility that the groups are different on some other major variable besides the identified independent variable, and it is this other variable that is the real cause of the observed difference between the groups.

12. A number of strategies are available to overcome problems of initial group differences on an extraneous variable. Three approaches to overcome such group differences: matching, comparing homogeneous groups or subgroups, and covariate analysis.

13. Analysis of covariance adjusts scores on a dependent variable for initial differences on some other variable (assuming that performance on the "other variable" is related to performance on the dependent variable, which is what control is all about, anyway).

DATA ANALYSIS
AND INTERPRETATION

14. Analysis of data in causal–comparative studies involves a variety of descriptive and inferential statistics.

15. The most commonly used descriptive statistics are the mean, which indicates the average performance of a group on a measure of some variable, and the standard deviation, which indicates how spread out a set of scores is, (i.e., whether the scores are clustered together around the mean or widely spread out around the mean).

16. The most commonly used inferential statistics are the *t* test, which is used to determine if there is a significant difference between the means of two groups; analysis of variance, which is used to determine if there is a significant difference among the means of three or more groups; and chi square, which is used to compare group frequencies (i.e., to see if an event occurs more frequently in one group than another).

17. As repeatedly pointed out, interpretation of the findings in a causal–comparative study requires considerable caution. The alleged cause may be the effect and vice versa. There may be a third factor that is the real "cause" of both the independent and dependent variables.

18. The way to determine the correct order of causality (which variable caused which) is to determine which one occurred first.

19. One way to control for a potential common cause is to equate groups on the suspected variable.

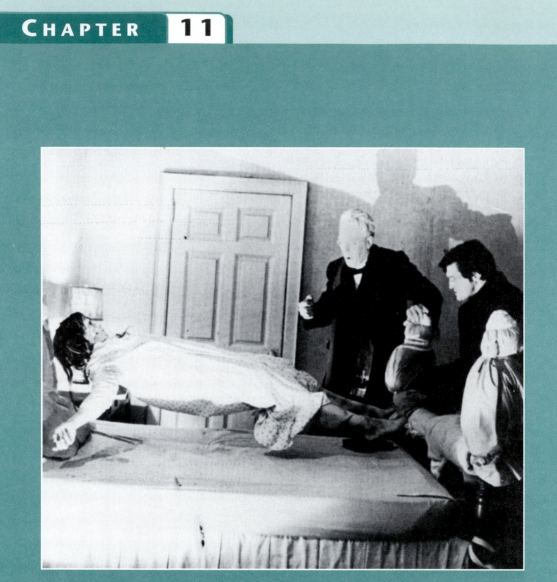

Single-subject experimental designs ". . . are typically used to study the behavior change an individual exhibits as a result of some treatment (p. 400)."

Experimental Research

OBJECTIVES

After reading chapter 11, you should be able to:

1. Briefly state the purpose of experimental research.
2. List the basic steps involved in conducting an experiment.
3. Explain the purpose of control.
4. Briefly define or describe internal validity and external validity.
5. Identify and briefly describe eight major threats to the internal validity of an experiment.
6. Identify and briefly describe seven major threats to the external validity of an experiment.
7. Briefly discuss the purpose of experimental design.
8. Identify and briefly describe five ways to control extraneous variables (and you better not leave out randomization!).
9. For each of the pre-experimental, true experimental, and quasi-experimental group designs discussed in this chapter, (a) draw a diagram, (b) list the steps involved in its application, and (c) identify major problems of invalidity.
10. Briefly describe the definition and purpose of a factorial design.
11. Briefly explain what is meant by the term interaction.
12. For each of the A–B–A single-subject designs discussed in this chapter, (a) draw a diagram, (b) list the steps involved in its application, and (c) identify major problems with which it is associated.
13. Briefly describe the procedures involved in using a multiple-baseline design.
14. Briefly describe an alternating treatments design.
15. Briefly describe three types of replication involved in single-subject research.

EXPERIMENTAL RESEARCH: DEFINITION AND PURPOSE

Experimental research is the only type of research that can test hypotheses to establish cause-and-effect relationships. It represents the strongest chain of reasoning about the links between variables. In an experimental study, the researcher manipulates at least one independent variable, controls other relevant variables, and observes the effect on one or more dependent variables. The researcher determines "who gets what"—that is, the researcher has control over the selection and assignment of groups to treatments. The manipulation of the independent variable is the one characteristic that differentiates experimental research from other types of research. The independent variable, also called the treatment, causal, or experimental variable, is the treatment or characteristic believed to make a difference. In educational research, independent variables that are frequently manipulated include method of instruction, type of reinforcement, arrangement of learning environment, type of learning materials, and length of treatment. This list is by no means exhaustive. The dependent variable, also called the criterion, effect, or outcome variable, shows the result of the study, the change or difference in groups that occurs as a result of the independent variable. It is referred to as the dependent variable because it is "dependent" on the independent variable. The dependent variable may be measured by a test or some other quantitative measure or by variables such as attendance, number of suspensions, and attention span. The only restriction on the dependent variable is that it represents an outcome that is measurable.

Experimental research is the most structured of all research types. When well conducted, experimental studies produce the soundest evidence concerning cause–effect relationships. The results of experimental research permit prediction, but not the kind characteristic of correlational research. A correlational prediction predicts a particular score for a particular individual. Predictions based on experimental findings are more global and often take the form, "If you use approach A you will probably get better results than if you use approach B." Of course it is unusual for a single experimental study to produce broad generalization of results, because any single study is limited in context and participants. However, replications of a study using different contexts and participants often produce cause–effect results that can be generalized widely.

THE EXPERIMENTAL PROCESS

The steps in an experimental study are basically the same as in other types of research: selection and definition of a problem, selection of participants and measuring instruments, selection of a research plan, execution of the plan, analysis of data, and formulation of conclusions. An experimental study is guided by at least one hypothesis that states an expected causal relationship between two variables. The experiment is conducted to confirm (support) or disconfirm the experimental hypothesis. In an experimental study, the researcher is in on the action from the very beginning. He or she selects the groups, decides what treatment will go to which group, controls extraneous variables, and measures the effect of the treatment at the end of the study.

It is important to note that the experimental researcher controls *both* the selection and the assignment of the research participants. That is, the researcher randomly selects participants from a single, well-defined population and then randomly assigns these participants into the different treatment conditions. It is the ability to randomly select and randomly assign participants to treatments that makes experimental research unique. The random assignment of participants to treatments, which is also called the researcher's manipulation of the treatments, is the distinguishing aspect of experimental research and the feature that distinguishes it from causal–comparative research. It is important for you to understand the difference between random selection and random assignment. Experimental research has both, whereas causal–comparative research has only random selection not assignment, because causal–comparative participants are obtained from two or more already existing populations. There can be *no* random assignment to treatment from a single population in causal–comparative studies.

An experiment typically involves a comparison of two groups (although as you will see later, there may be only one group, or there may be three or more groups). The experimental comparison is usually one of three types: (1) comparison of two different approaches (A versus B); (2) comparison of a new approach and the existing approach (A versus no A); and (3) comparison of different amounts of a single approach (a little of A versus a lot of A). An example of an A versus B comparison would be a study that compared the effects of a computer-based and a teacher-based approach to teaching first-grade reading. An example of an A versus no A comparison would be a study that compared a new hand-writing method and the classroom teachers' existing handwriting approach. An example of a little of A versus more of A comparison would be a study that compared the effect of 20 minutes of daily science instruction to 40 minutes of daily science instruction on fifth graders' attitudes toward science. Experimental designs may get quite complex and involve simultaneous manipulation of several independent variables. At this stage of the game, however, it is recommended that you stick to just one!

The group that receives the new or novel treatment is often called the experimental group, while the other group is called the control group. An alternative to using experimental and control groups is to simply describe the treatments as comparison groups, treatment groups, or Group A and B. The terms are commonly used interchangeably. A common misconception is that a control group always receives no treatment. This is not true and would hardly provide a fair comparison. For example, if the independent variable was type of reading instruction, the experimental group might be instructed with a new method, while the control group might continue instruction with the currently used method. The control group would still receive reading instruction; it would not sit in a closet while the study was being conducted. Otherwise, you would not be evaluating the effectiveness of a new method as compared to a traditional method, but rather, the effectiveness of a new method as compared to no reading instruction at all! Any method of instruction is bound to be more effective than no instruction at all.

The groups that are to receive the different treatments should be equated on all variables that might influence performance on the dependent variable. For example, in the previous reading example, initial reading readiness should be equated or should be very similar in each treatment group at the start of the study. In other words, the researcher makes every effort to ensure that the two groups start as equivalently as possible on all variables except the independent variable. The main way that groups are equated is through simple random or stratified random sampling.

After the groups have been exposed to the treatment for some period, the researcher collects data on the dependent variable from the groups and determines whether there is a real or significant difference between their performances. In other words, using statistical analysis, the researcher determines whether the treatment made a real difference. Chapters 12 and 13 discuss statistical analysis of experimental studies in detail. For now, suppose that at the end of an experimental study one group had an average score of 29 on the dependent variable and the other group had an average score of 27. There clearly is a difference between the groups, but is a two-point difference a meaningful or significant difference, or is it just a chance difference produced by measurement error? Statistical analysis helps answer this question.

Experimental studies in education often encounter two problems, a lack of sufficient exposure to treatments and failure to make the treatments substantially different from each other. In most cases, no matter how effective a treatment is, it is not likely to be effective if students are exposed to it for only a brief period. To adequately test a hypothesis concerning the effectiveness of a treatment, the experimental group would need to be exposed to it over a period of time so that the treatment is given a fair chance to work. Also of concern is the difference between treatments. In a study comparing team teaching and traditional lecture teaching it would be vital that team teaching be operationalized in a manner that clearly differentiated it from the traditional method. If team teaching meant two teachers taking turns lecturing, it would not be very different from traditional teaching and the researcher would be very unlikely to find a meaningful difference between the two study treatments. Also, if teachers using different treatments converse with and borrow from each other's treatments, the original treatments become diluted and similar to each other. These problems have detrimental effects on the outcome of the study.

MANIPULATION AND CONTROL

Direct manipulation by the researcher of at least one independent variable is the one single characteristic that differentiates experimental research from other types of research. Manipulation of an independent variable is often a difficult concept to grasp. Quite simply, it means that the researcher decides what treatments will make up the independent variable and which group will get which treatment. For example, if the independent variable was number of annual teacher reviews, the researcher might decide that there should be three groups, one group receiving no review, a second group receiving one review, and a third group receiving two reviews. In addition, having selected research participants from a single, well-defined population, the researcher would randomly assign participants to treatments. Thus, manipulation means being able to select the number and type of treatments and to randomly assign participants to treatments.

Independent variables in education are either manipulated (active variables) or not manipulated (assigned variables). You can manipulate such variables as method of instruction, number of reviews, and size of group. You cannot manipulate variables such as gender, age, or socioeconomic status. You can place participants into one method of instruction or another (active), but you cannot place participants into male or female categories because they already are male or female (assigned). Although the design of an experimental study may or may not include assigned variables, at least one active variable that can be manipulated must be present.

Control refers to the researcher's efforts to remove the influence of any extraneous variable (other than the independent variable itself) that might affect scores on the dependent variable. In other words, the researcher wants the groups to be as similar as possible, so that the only major difference between them is the treatment variables manipulated by the researcher. To illustrate the importance of research control, suppose you conducted a study to compare the effectiveness of student tutors versus parent tutors in teaching first graders to read. Student tutors might be older children from higher grade levels, and parent tutors might be members of the PTA. Suppose also that student tutors helped each member of their group for 1 hour per day for a month, while the parent tutors helped each member of their group for 2 hours per week for a month. Would the comparison be fair? Certainly not. Participants with the student tutors would have received two and one half times as much help as from the parents group (5 hours per week versus 2 hours per week). Thus, one variable that would need to be controlled would be amount of tutoring. Otherwise, if the student tutors produced higher reading scores than the parent tutors, the researcher would not know whether this result indicated that student tutors were more effective than parent tutors, that longer periods of tutoring were more effective than shorter periods, or that type and amount of tutoring combined are more effective. For the comparison to be fair and interpretable, both students and parents should tutor for the same amount of time. Then time of tutoring would be controlled and the researcher could truly compare the effectiveness of the student and parent tutors.

This example is just one of the many kinds of factors that must be considered in planning an experimental study. Some variables that need controlling may be relatively obvious; in the previous example, in addition to time tutoring, other variables such as reading readiness and prior reading instruction would need to be examined and controlled if necessary. Some variables that need to be controlled may not be as obvious; for example, the researcher would need to ensure that both groups used similar reading texts and materials. Thus, there are really two different kinds of variables that must be controlled: participant variables (such as reading readiness) on which participants in the different groups might differ; and environmental variables (such as learning materials) that might cause unwanted differences between groups. The researcher strives to ensure that the characteristics and experiences of the groups are as equal as possible on all important variables except the independent variable. If relevant variables can be controlled, group differences on the dependent variable can be attributed to the independent variable.

Control is not easy in an experiment, especially in educational studies where real live participants are involved. It certainly is a lot easier to control solids, liquids, and gases! Our task is not an impossible one, however, since we can concentrate on identifying and controlling only those variables that might really affect the dependent variable. For example, if two groups differed significantly with respect to shoe size or height, the results of most education studies would probably not be affected by these differences. Other techniques that can be used to control for extraneous variables will be discussed later in the chapter. Bear in mind, however, that even though experimental research is the only type of research that can truly establish cause–effect relationships, it is not universally appropriate for all educational research problems or studies. The experimental method is only one of many ways to examine important educational questions and problems.

THREATS TO EXPERIMENTAL VALIDITY

As already noted, any uncontrolled extraneous variables affecting performance on the dependent variable are threats to the validity of an experiment. An experiment is valid if results obtained are due only to the manipulated independent variable and if they are generalizable to individuals or contexts beyond the experimental setting. These two criteria are referred to, respectively, as the internal validity and external validity of an experiment. Internal validity is concerned with threats or factors other than the independent variable that affect the dependent variable. In other words, internal validity focuses on threats or rival explanations that influence the outcomes of an experimental study but are not part of the independent variable. In the former example of student and parent tutors, a plausible threat or rival explanation for the research results would have been differences in the amount of time the two groups tutored. The degree to which experimental research results are attributable to the independent variable and not to some other rival explanation is the degree to which an experimental study is internally valid.

External validity, also called ecological validity, is concerned with the extent to which the study results can be generalized to groups and settings beyond those of the experiment. In other words, external validity focuses on threats or rival explanations that would not permit the results of a study to be generalized to other settings or groups. For example, if a study was conducted using groups of gifted ninth graders, the results should be applicable to other groups of gifted ninth graders. If research results are not generalizable outside of the experimental setting, then no one could profit from the research. Each and every study would have to be reestablished over and over and over. An experimental study can only contribute to educational theory or practice if there is some assurance that results and effects are replicable and generalize to other places and groups. If results cannot be replicated in other settings by other researchers, the study has low external or ecological validity.

So, all one has to do in order to conduct a valid experiment is to maximize internal and external validity, right? Wrong. Unfortunately, there is a "catch-22" complicating the researcher's experimental life. Maximizing internal validity requires the use of very rigid controls over participants and conditions, similar to a laboratory-like environment. However, the more a research situation is narrowed and controlled, the less realistic and generalizable it becomes. A study can contribute little to educational practice if there is no assurance that a technique effective in a highly controlled setting will also be effective in a less controlled classroom setting. On the other hand, the more natural the experimental setting becomes, the more difficult it is to control extraneous variables. It is very difficult, for example, to conduct a well-controlled study in an actual classroom. Thus, the researcher must strive for balance between control and realism. If a choice is involved, the researcher should err on the side of control rather than realism,[1] since a study that is not internally valid is worthless. A useful strategy to address this problem is first to demonstrate an effect in a highly controlled environment (with maximum internal validity) and then to redo the study in a more natural setting (to examine external validity). In the final analysis, however, the researcher seeks a compromise between a highly controlled and highly natural environment.

In the following pages many threats to internal and external validity will be discussed. Some extraneous variables are threats to internal validity, some are threats to external validity, and some may be threats to both. How potential threats are classified is not of great importance; what is important is that you be aware of their existence and how to control for them. As you read, you may begin to feel that there are just too many threats for one little researcher to control. However, the task is not as formidable as it may at first appear, since a number of experimental designs *do* control many or most of the threats you are likely to encounter. Also, remember that each threat to be discussed is only a potential threat that may not be a problem in a particular study.

THREATS TO INTERNAL VALIDITY

Probably the most authoritative source regarding experimental design and threats to experimental validity is the work of Donald Campbell and Julian Stan-

---

[1]This is a clear distinction between the emphasis of quantitative and qualitative research.

ley and Thomas Cook and Donald Campbell.[2] They have identified eight main threats to internal validity:

- history
- maturation
- testing
- instrumentation
- statistical regression
- differential selection of participants
- mortality
- selection–maturation interaction *not in notes*

However, before describing these threats to internal validity, it is useful to note the role of experimental research in overcoming these threats. You are not rendered helpless when faced with them. Quite the contrary; the use of random selection of participants, the researcher's assignment of participants to treatments, and control of other variables are powerful approaches to overcoming the threats. As you read the threats, note how experimental research's random selection and assignment to treatments can control most threats.

History

History refers to the occurrence of events that are not part of the experimental treatment but that occur during the study and affect the dependent variable. The longer a study lasts, the more likely it is that history will be a threat. Happenings such as a bomb scare, an epidemic of measles, or even current events are examples of the history effect. For example, suppose you conducted a series of in-service workshops designed to increase the morale of the teacher participants. Suppose that between the time you conducted the workshops and the time you administered a posttest measure of morale, the news media announced that, due to state-level budget problems, funding to the local school district was going to be significantly reduced and that it was likely that promised pay raises for teachers would have to be postponed. Such an event could easily wipe out any effect the workshops might have had, and posttest morale scores might well be considerably lower than they otherwise might have been (to say the least!).

Maturation

Maturation refers to natural physical, intellectual, and emotional changes that occur in the participants over a period of time. These changes may affect the participants' performance on the dependent variable. Especially in studies that last a long time, participants may become older, more coordinated, unmotivated, anxious, or just plain bored. Maturation is more likely to be a problem in a study designed to test the effectiveness of a psychomotor training program on three-year-olds than in a study designed to compare two methods of teaching algebra.

---

[2]Campbell, D. T. & Stanley, J. C. (1971). *Experimental and quasi-experimental designs for research.* Chicago: Rand McNally.

Cook, T. D. & Campbell, D. T. (1979). *Quasi-experimentation: Design and analysis issues for field settings.* Chicago: Rand McNally.

Younger participants would typically be undergoing rapid biological changes during the training program, raising the question of whether changes were due to the training program or to maturation.

Testing

Testing, also called pretest sensitization, refers to improved scores on a posttest as a result of having taken a pretest. Taking a pretest may improve performance on a posttest, regardless of whether there is any treatment or instruction in between. Testing is more likely to be a threat when the time between testings is short; a pretest taken in September is not likely to affect performance on a posttest taken in June. The testing threat to internal validity is more likely to occur in studies that measure factual information that can be recalled. For example, taking a pretest on algebraic equations is less likely to improve performance on a similar posttest than if the information were factual.

Instrumentation

The instrumentation threat refers to unreliability, or lack of consistency, in measuring instruments that can result in an invalid assessment of performance. Instrumentation may occur in several different ways. If two different tests are used, one for pretesting and one for posttesting, and if the tests are not of equal difficulty, instrumentation may become a threat. For example, if the posttest is more difficult than the pretest, it may mask improvement that is actually present. Alternatively, if the posttest is less difficult than the pretest, it may indicate improvement that is not really present. If data are collected through observation, the observers may not be observing or evaluating behavior the same way at the end of the study as at the beginning. In fact, if they are aware of the nature of the study, they may unconsciously tend to see and record what they know the researcher is hypothesizing. If data are collected through the use of a mechanical device, the device may be poorly calibrated, resulting in inaccurate measurement. Thus, the researcher must take care in selecting tests, observers, and mechanical devices to measure the dependent variable.

Statistical Regression

Statistical regression usually occurs when participants are selected on the basis of their extremely high or extremely low scores. It refers to the tendency of participants who score highest on a test to score lower on a second, similar test, and of participants who score lowest on a test to score higher on a second, similar test. The tendency is for scores to regress, or move toward, a mean (average) or expected score. Thus, extremely high scorers regress (lower) to the mean and extremely low scorers regress (higher) to the mean. For example, suppose a researcher wished to determine the effectiveness of a new method of spelling instruction on the spelling ability of poor spellers. The researcher might administer a 100-item, four-alternative, multiple-choice spelling pretest. Each question might read, "Which of the following four words is spelled incorrectly?" The researcher might then select for the study the 30 students who scored lowest. Now suppose none of the pretested students knew any of the words and guessed on every single question. With 100 items, and four choices for each item, a student would be expected to receive a score of 25 just by guessing. Some students, however, just due to rotten guessing, would receive scores much lower than 25, and other students, just by chance, would receive much higher scores than 25. If they were administered the test a second time, without any instruction intervening, their expected score would still be 25. Thus, students who scored very low the first time would be expected to have a second score closer to 25, and students who scored very high the first time would also be expected to score closer to 25 the second time. Whenever participants are selected on the basis of their extremely high or extremely low performance, statistical regression is a viable threat to internal validity.

Differential Selection of Participants

Differential selection of participants usually occurs when already formed groups are compared, thereby raising the threat that the groups were different before the study even begins. Initial group differences may account for posttest differences. Suppose, for example, you received permission to use two of Ms. Onomatopoeia's English classes in your study. There is no guarantee that the two classes are at all equivalent. If your luck was really bad, one class might be the honors English class and the other class might be the remedial English class. It would not be too surprising if the first class did much better on the posttest! Thus, using already formed groups should be avoided if possible. If they must be used, groups should be selected that are as similar as possible, and a pretest should be administered to check for initial equivalence.

Mortality

First, let us make it perfectly clear that mortality does not mean that participants die! Mortality, or attrition, refers to the case in which participants drop out of a study. Mortality is a particular problem when different groups drop out for different reasons and with different frequency. The change in the characteristics of the groups due to mortality can significantly affect the results of the study. For example, participants who drop out of a study may be less motivated or uninterested in the study than those who remain. This is especially a problem when volunteers are used or when a study compares a new treatment to an existing treatment. Participants rarely drop out of control groups or existing treatments because few or no additional demands are made on them. However, volunteers or participants using the new, experimental treatment may drop out because too much effort is required for participation. The experimental group that remains at the end of the study then represents a more motivated group than the control group. As another example of mortality, suppose Suzy Shiningstar (a high IQ and all that student) got the measles and dropped out of your control group. Suppose that before Suzy dropped out she managed to infect her friends in the control group. Since birds of a feather often flock together, Suzy's control group friends might also be the "high IQ and all that" type students. The experimental group might end up looking pretty good when compared to the control group simply because many of the good students dropped out of the control group. The researcher cannot assume that participants drop out of a study in a random fashion and should, if possible, select a design that controls for mortality.

One way to assess the mortality of groups is to obtain demographic information about the participant groups prior to the start of the study and compare the groups at the end of the study. Another approach is to provide some incentive to participants to remain in the study. Finally, one can identify the kinds of participants who drop out of the study and remove similar portions from the other groups.

Selection–Maturation Interaction, Etc.

The *etc.* means that selection may also interact with history and testing as well as maturation, although the selection–maturation interaction is most common. What this means is that if already-formed groups are used, one group may profit more (or less) from a treatment, or have an initial advantage, because of maturation, history, or testing factors. Suppose, for example, that you received permission to use two of Ms. Doppler's English classes, and both classes were average and apparently equivalent on all relevant variables. Suppose, however, that for some reason Ms. Doppler had to miss one of her classes but not the other (maybe she had to have a root canal), and Ms. Alma Mater took over Ms. Doppler's class. Suppose, further, that as luck would have it, Ms. Mater covered much of the material now included in your posttest (remember history?). Unbeknownst to you, your experimental group would have a definite advantage to begin with, and it might be this initial advantage, not the independent variable, that caused posttest differences in the dependent variable. Thus, the researcher must select a design that controls for this potential problem or make every effort to determine if it is operating in the study. Table 11.1 summarizes the threats to internal validity.

TABLE 11.1

Threats to Internal Validity

history	Unexpected events occur between the pre- and posttest, affecting the dependent variable.
maturation	Changes occur in the participants, from growing older, wiser, more experienced, etc. during the study.
testing	Taking a pretest alters the result of the posttest.
instrumentation	The measuring instrument is changed between pre- and posttesting, or a single measuring instrument is unreliable.
statistical regression	Extremely high or extremely low scorers tend to regress to the mean on retesting.
differential selection of participants	Participants in the experimental and control groups have different characteristics that affect the dependent variable differently.
mortality	Different participants drop out of the study in different numbers, altering the composition of the treatment groups.
selection–maturation interaction	The participants selected into treatment groups have different maturation rates. Selection interactions also occur with history and instrumentation.

THREATS TO EXTERNAL VALIDITY

Seven major threats to external validity can limit generalization of experimental results to other populations:

- pretest–treatment interaction
- selection–treatment interaction
- multiple treatment interference
- specificity of variables
- treatment diffusion
- experimenter effects
- reactive effects

Building on the work of Campbell and Stanley, Bracht and Glass[3] refined and expanded discussion of threats to external validity. Bracht and Glass classified these threats into two categories. Threats affecting "generalizing to whom," that is, to what groups research results can be generalized, make up threats to population validity. Threats affecting "generalizing to what," that is, to what settings, conditions, variables, and contexts results can be generalized, are referred to as threats to ecological validity. The following discussion incorporates the contributions of Bracht and Glass into Campbell and Stanley's original conceptualizations.

Pretest–Treatment Interaction

Pretest–treatment interaction occurs when participants respond or react differently to a treatment because they have been pretested. Pretesting may sensitize or alert participants to the nature of the treatment, potentially making the treatment effect different than had participants not been pretested. Thus, the research results would only be generalizable to other pretested groups. The results are not even generalizable to the unpretested population from which the sample was selected. The seriousness of the pretest–treatment interaction threat is dependent on the research participants, the nature of the independent and dependent variables, and the duration of the study. Studies involving self-report measures such as attitude and interest are especially susceptible to this threat. Campbell and Stanley illustrate this effect by pointing out the probable lack of comparability of a group viewing the antiprejudice film *Gentleman's Agreement* right after taking a lengthy pretest dealing with anti-Semitism, and another group viewing the movie without a pretest. Individuals not pretested could quite conceivably enjoy the movie as a good love story and be unaware that it deals with a social issue. Pretested individuals would be much more likely to see a connection between the pretest and the message of the film. Conversely, taking a pretest on algebraic algorithms would probably have very little impact on a group's responsiveness to a new method of teaching algebra. The pretest–treatment interaction would also be expected to be minimized in studies involving very young children, who would probably not see or remember a connection between the pretest and the subsequent treatment. Similarly, for studies conducted over a period of months

---

[3]Bracht, G. H. & Glass, G. V. (1968). The external validity of experiments, *American Educational Research Journal, 5,* 437–474.

or longer, the effects of the pretest would probably have worn off or been greatly diminished by the time a posttest was given. Thus, for some studies the potential interactive effect of a pretest is a more serious consideration than others. In such cases the researcher should select a design that either controls for the effect or allows the researcher to determine the magnitude of the effect. In studies in which there is a strong possibility that pretest sensitization may occur, unobtrusive measures are recommended, if feasible.

Multiple-Treatment Interference

Multiple-treatment interference occurs when the same research participants receive more than one treatment in succession. The carryover effects from an earlier treatment may make it difficult to assess the effectiveness of a later treatment. Suppose you were interested in comparing two different approaches to improving classroom behavior—behavior modification and corporal punishment (admittedly an extreme example used to make a point!). Let us say that for 2 months behavior modification techniques were systematically applied to the participants, and at the end of this period behavior was found to be significantly better than before the study began. Now suppose that for the next 2 months the same participants were physically punished whenever they misbehaved (hand slappings, spankings, and the like), and at the end of the 2 months behavior was equally as good as after the 2 months of behavior modification. Could you then conclude that behavior modification and corporal punishment are equally effective methods of behavior control? Cer-tain-ly not. In fact, the goal of behavior modification is to produce behavior that is self-maintaining; that is, it continues after direct intervention is stopped. Thus, the good behavior exhibited by the participants at the end of the corporal punishment period could well be due to the effectiveness of previous exposure to behavior modification and exist in spite of, rather than because of, exposure to corporal punishment. If it is not possible to select a design in which each group receives only one treatment, the researcher should try to minimize potential multiple-treatment interference by allowing sufficient time to elapse between treatments and by investigating distinctly different types of independent variables. Multiple-treatment interference may also occur when participants who have already participated in a study are selected for inclusion in another, apparently unrelated, study. If the accessible population for a study is one whose members are likely to have participated in other studies (psychology majors, for example), then information on previous participation should be collected and evaluated before participants are selected for the current study. If any members of the accessible population are eliminated from consideration because of previous research activities, a note should be made of this limitation in the research report.

Selection–Treatment Interaction

Selection–treatment interaction is similar to the "differential selection of participants" problem associated with internal invalidity. It mainly occurs when participants are not randomly selected for treatments. Interaction effects aside, the very fact that participants are not randomly selected from a population severely limits the researcher's ability to generalize, because what population the sample represents is in question. Even if intact groups are randomly selected, the possibility exists that the experimental group is in some important way different from the control group, and/or from the larger population. Nonrepresentativeness of groups may also result in a selection–treatment interaction, such that the results of a study apply only to the groups involved and are not representative of the treatment effect in the extended population. The interaction of personological variables and treatment effects creates another population validity threat. This interaction occurs when *actual* study participants at one level of a variable react differently to a treatment than other *potential* participants in the population, at another level, would have reacted. For example, a researcher might conduct a study on the effectiveness of microcomputer-assisted instruction on the math achievement of junior high students. Classes available to the researcher (the accessible population) may represent an overall ability level at the lower end of the ability spectrum for all junior high students (the target population). If a positive effect is found, it may be that it would not have been found if the participants were truly representative of the target population. And similarly, if an effect is not found, it might have been. Thus, extra caution must be taken in stating conclusions and generalizations based on studies involving existing, nonrandomized groups.

Selection–treatment interaction is also an uncontrolled variable in designs involving randomization. For example, one's accessible population is often quite different from one's target population, creating another population validity problem when one attempts to generalize the results of the accessible population to the target population. Thus, the way a given population becomes available to a researcher may make generalizability of findings questionable, no matter how internally valid an experiment may be. If, in seeking a sample, a researcher is turned down by nine school systems and finally accepted by a 10th, the accepting system is very likely to be different from both the other nine and the population of schools to which the researcher would like to generalize the results. Administrators and instructional personnel in the 10th school likely have higher morale, less fear of being inspected, and more zeal for improvement than personnel in the other nine schools. It is recommended that researchers report problems involved in acquiring participants, including the number of times they was turned down, so that the reader can judge the seriousness of a possible selection–treatment interaction.

Specificity of Variables

Like selection–treatment interaction, specificity of variables is a threat to generalizability of research results regardless of the particular experimental design used. Specificity of variables refers to the fact that any given study is conducted (1) with a specific kind of participant; (2) based on a particular operational definition of the independent variable; (3) using specific dependent variables; (4) at a specific time; and (5) under a specific set of circumstances. We have also discussed the need to describe research procedures in sufficient detail to permit another researcher to replicate your study. Such detailed descriptions also permit interested readers to assess how applicable findings are to their situation. Experimental procedures require operational definition of the variables. When a group of studies that supposedly manipulated the same independent variable get quite different results, it is often difficult to determine the reasons for the differences because researchers have not provided a clear, operational description of their independent variables. When clearly stated operational descriptions of independent variables are available, it often is found that two independent variables with the same name are quite differently operationalized, thus explaining why results differed.

Since terms like *discovery method*, *whole language*, and *computer-based instruction*, mean different things to different people, it is impossible to know what a researcher means by these terms without clear operationalized descriptions. Without operationalized descriptions it is not clear to what populations a study can be generalized. Generalizability of results is also tied to the clear definition of the dependent variable, although in most cases the specific measure selected (e.g., the Baloney Achievement Test) is the operational definition. When there are several dependent variable measures to select from, questions about the comparability of these instruments are raised, just as with the definition of the independent variables.

Generalizability of results may also be affected by short- or long-term events that occur while the study is taking place. This threat is referred to as the interaction of history and treatment effects. It describes the situation in which events extraneous to the study alter the research results. Short-term, emotion-packed events, such as the firing of a superintendent, the release of district test scores, or the impeachment of a president, for example, might affect the behavior of participants. Usually, however, the researcher is aware of such happenings and can assess their possible impact on results. Of course, accounts of such events should also be included in the research report. The impact of more long-term events, such as wars and depressions, however, is more subtle and tougher to evaluate. Another threat to external validity is the interaction of time of measurement and treatment effect. This threat results from the fact that posttesting may yield different results, depending on when it is done. A treatment effect based on the administration of a posttest immediately following the treatment may not be the same if a delayed posttest is given some time after treatment. Conversely, a treatment may have a long-term, but not a short-term, effect. Thus, the only way to assess the generalizability of findings over time is to measure the dependent variable at various times following treatment. To deal with the threats associated with specificity, the researcher must (1) operationally define variables in a way that has meaning outside of the experimental setting and (2) be careful in stating conclusions and generalizations.

Treatment Diffusion

Treatment diffusion occurs when different treatment groups communicate with and learn from each other. Knowledge of each other's treatments often leads to the groups borrowing aspects from each other so that the study no longer has two distinctly different treatments, but two overlapping treatments. The integrity of each treatment is diffused. Often, it is the more desirable treatment, the experimental treatment or the treatment with additional resources, that is diffused into the less desirable treatment. For example, Mr. Darth and Ms. Vader's classes were trying out two different treatments to improve spelling. Mr. Darth's class received videos, new and colorful spelling texts, and prizes for improved spelling. Ms. Vader's class received the traditional approach to spelling, list words on the board, copy them into notebooks, use each word in a sentence, and study at home. After the first week of treatments, the students began talking to their teachers about the different ways spelling was being taught. Ms. Vader heard about Mr. Darth's spelling treatment and asked if she could try out the videos in her class. Her students liked them so well that she incorporated them into her spelling program. The diffusion of Mr. Darth's treatment into Ms. Vader's treatment produced two overlapping treatments that did not represent the initial intended treatments. Requesting teachers who are implementing different treatments not to communicate with each other about their treatments until the study is completed or to carry out the study in different locales are strategies to reduce treatment diffusion.

Experimenter Effects

There is evidence that researchers themselves may present potential threats to the external validity of their own studies. In a number of ways the experimenter may unintentionally affect study procedures, the behavior of participants, or the assessment of their performance. Experimenter effects may be passive or active. Passive elements include characteristics or personality traits of the experimenter such as gender, age, race, anxiety level, and hostility level. These influences are collectively called the *experimenter personal-attributes effects*. Active experimenter effects occur when the researcher's expectations of the study results affect his or her behavior and the research outcomes. This effect is referred to as the *experimenter bias effect*. Thus, the way an experimenter looks, feels, or acts may unintentionally affect study results, typically in the direction desired by the researcher. One form of experimenter bias occurs when the researcher affects participants' behavior because of previous knowledge of the participants. Suppose a researcher hypothesizes that a new reading approach will improve reading skills. If the researcher knows that Suzy Shiningstar is in the experimental group and that Suzy is a good student, the researcher might give Suzy's reading skills a higher rating than it actually warrants. This example illustrates another way a researcher's expectations may actually contribute to producing those outcomes: Knowing which participants are in the experimental and control groups may cause the researcher to unintentionally evaluate their performances differently. It is difficult to identify experimenter bias in a study, which is all the more reason for researchers to be aware of its consequences on the external validity of their study. The moral is that researchers should strive to avoid communicating emotions and expectations to participants in the study. Experimenter bias effects can be reduced by doing things such as scoring dependent variables "blind," that is, without the researcher knowing whose variable is being scored.

Reactive Arrangements

Reactive arrangements, also called *participant effects*, refer to a number of factors associated with the way in which a study is conducted and the feelings and attitudes of the participants involved. As discussed previously, in order to maintain a high degree of control to obtain internal validity, a researcher may create an experimental environment that is highly artificial and hinders generalizability to nonexperimental settings. Another type of reactive arrangement results from the participants' knowledge that they are involved in an experiment or their feeling that they are in some way receiving "special" attention. The effect that such knowledge or feelings can have on the participants was demonstrated at the Hawthorne Works of the Western Electric Company in Chicago in 1927. Studies were conducted to investigate the relationship between various working conditions and productivity. As part of their study, researchers investigated the effect of light intensity and worker output. The researchers increased light intensity and production went up. They increased it some more and production went up some more. The brighter the place became, the more production rose. As a check, the researchers decreased the light intensity, and guess what, production went up! The darker it got, the more workers produced. The researchers soon realized that it was the attention given the workers, and not the illumination, that was affecting production. To this day, the term *Hawthorne effect* is used to describe any situation in which participants' behavior is affected not by the treatment per se, but by their knowledge of participating in a study.

A related reactive effect is known as *compensatory rivalry*, or the *John Henry effect*. Folk hero John Henry, you may recall, was a "steel drivin' man" who worked for a railroad. When he heard that a steam drill was going to replace him and his fellow steel drivers, he challenged, and set out to beat, the machine. Through tremendous effort he managed to win the ensuing contest, dropping dead at the finish line. Compensatory rivalry occurs when the control group is informed that they will be the control group for a new, experimental method. Like John Henry, they decide to challenge the new method by putting extra effort into their work, essentially saying (to themselves), "We'll show them that our old ways are as effective as their new-fangled ways!" By doing this, however, the control group performs atypically and thus becomes a rival explanation for the study results. When this effect occurs, the treatment under investigation does not appear to be very effective, since posttest performance of the experimental group is not much (if at all) better than that of the control group.

A so-called *placebo effect* is often used as an antidote to the Hawthorne and John Henry effects. Medical researchers discovered that any "medication," even sugar and water, could make participants feel better. To counteract this effect, a placebo approach was developed in which half of the participants receive the true medication and half receive a placebo (sugar and water, for example). The use of a placebo is, of course, not known by the participants; both groups think they are taking a real medicine. The implication of the placebo effect for educational research is that all groups in an experiment should appear to be treated the same. Suppose, for example, you have four groups of ninth graders, two experimental and two control, and the treatment is a film designed to promote a positive attitude toward a vocational career. If the experimental participants are to be excused from several of their classes in order to view the film, then the control participants should also be excused and shown another film whose content is unrelated to the purpose of the study (*Drugs and You: Just Say No!*, would do). As an added control you might have all the participants told that there are two movies and that eventually all of them will see both movies. In other words, it should appear as if all the students are doing the same thing.

Another related participant effect is the *novelty effect*, which refers to increased interest, motivation, or engagement on the part of participants simply because they are doing something different. In other words, a treatment may be effective because it is different, not because it is better. To counteract the novelty effect, the study should be conducted over a period of time sufficient to allow the treatment "newness" to wear off. This is especially true if the treatment involves activities very different from the participants' usual routine. Table 11.2 summarizes the threats to external validity.

Obviously there are many internal and external threats to the validity of an experimental (and causal–comparative) study. You should be aware of likely validity threats to validity of your research study and strive to nullify them. One main way to overcome many threats to validity is to choose a research design that controls for such threats. We examine some of these designs in the following sections.

TABLE **11.2**	
Threats to External Validity	
pretest–treatment interaction	The pretest sensitizes participants to aspects of the treatment and thus influences posttest scores.
selection–treatment interaction	The nonrandom or volunteer selection of participants limits the generalizability of the study.
multiple treatment interference	When participants receive more than one treatment, the effect of prior treatment can affect or interact with later treatments, limiting generalizability.
specificity of variables	Poorly operationalized variables make it difficult to identify the setting and procedures to which the variables can be generalized.
treatment diffusion	Treatment groups communicate and adopt pieces of each other's treatment, altering the initial status of the treatments comparison.
experimenter effects	Conscious or unconscious actions of the researcher affects participants' performance and responses.
reactive effects	The fact of being in a study affects participants from their normal behavior. The Hawthorne and John Henry effects are reactive responses to being in a study.

GROUP EXPERIMENTAL DESIGNS

The validity of an experiment is a direct function of the degree to which internal and external variables are controlled. If these variables are not controlled, it is difficult to interpret the results of a study and the groups to which it can be generalized. The term *confounding* is sometimes used to refer to the fact that the effects of the independent variable may intertwine with extraneous variables, such that it is difficult to determine the unique effects of each. This is what experimental design is all about, the control of extraneous variables. Good designs control many sources of invalidity, poor designs control few. If you recall, two types of extraneous variables in need of control are participant variables and environmental variables. Participant variables are characteristics of the participants (such as gender) that cannot be altered but that can be controlled. Environmental variables are variables that intervene between the independent and the dependent variables (such as anxiety or boredom) that cannot be directly observed, but can be controlled.

CONTROL OF EXTRANEOUS VARIABLES

Randomization is the best single way to simultaneously control for many extraneous variables. Thus, randomization should be used whenever possible; participants should be randomly selected from a population and they should be randomly assigned to treatment groups. Recall that random selection and assignment mean that participants' selection and assignment to treatments is done by pure chance, usually with a table of random numbers. Other randomization methods are also available. For example, you could flip a coin or use odd and even numbers on a die to assign participants to two treatments; heads or even number to treatment 1 and tails or odd number to treatment 2.

Randomization is effective in creating equivalent, representative groups that are essentially the same on all relevant variables. As noted, randomly formed treatment groups are a unique characteristic of experimental research; it is a control factor not possible with causal–comparative research. The underlying rationale for randomization is that if participants are assigned at random (by chance) to groups, there is no reason to believe that the groups will be greatly different in any systematic way. Thus, the groups would be expected to perform essentially the same on the dependent variable if the independent variable makes no difference. Therefore, if the groups perform differently at the end of the study, the difference can be attributed to the independent variable. It is important to remember that the larger the groups, the more confidence the researcher can have in the effectiveness of randomization. Randomly assigning six participants to two treatments is much less likely to equalize extraneous variables than assigning 50 participants to two treatments. In addition to equating groups on variables such as ability, gender, or prior experience, randomization can also equalize groups on environmental variables. Teachers, for example, can be randomly assigned to treatment groups so that the experimental groups will not have all the "Carmel Kandee" teachers or all the "Hester Hartless" teachers (and neither will the control groups). Clearly, the researcher should use as much randomization as possible. If participants cannot be randomly selected, those available should at least be randomly assigned. If participants cannot be randomly assigned to groups, then at least treatment condition should be randomly assigned to the existing groups.

In addition to randomization, there are other ways to control for extraneous variables. Certain environmental variables, for example, can be controlled by holding them constant for all groups. Recall the example of the student tutor versus parent tutor study. In that example, help time was an important variable that had to be held constant, in order for them to be fairly compared. Other such variables that might need to be held constant include learning materials, prior exposure, meeting place and time (students might be more alert in the morning than in the afternoon), and years of teacher experience. Controlling participant variables is critical. If the groups are not the same to start with, you have not even given yourself a fighting chance to obtain valid, interpretable research results. Even if groups cannot be randomly formed, there are a number of techniques that can be used to try to equate groups.

Matching

Matching is a technique for equating groups on one or more variables, usually ones highly related to performance on the dependent variable. The most commonly used approach to matching involves random assignment of pairs, one participant to each group. In other words, the researcher attempts to find pairs of participants similar on the variable or variables to be controlled. If the researcher is matching on gender, obviously the matched pairs must be of the same gender. However, if the researcher is matching on variables such as pretest, GRE, or ability scores, the pairs should be based on having similar scores. Unless the number of participants is very large, it is unreasonable to try to make exact matches or matches on more than one or two variables. Once a matched pair is identified, one member of the pair is randomly assigned to one treatment group and the other member to the other treatment group. If a participant does not have a suitable match, he or she is excluded from the study. The resulting matched groups are identical or very similar with respect to the variable being controlled. A major problem with such matching is that there are invariably participants who do not have a match and must be eliminated from the study. This may cost the researcher many participants, especially if matching is attempted on two or more variables (imagine trying to find a match for a male with an IQ near 140 and a GPA between 1.00 and 1.50!). Of course, one way to combat loss of participants is to match less stringently. For example, the researcher might decide that if two ability test scores are within 20 points they will constitute an acceptable match. This procedure may increase participants, but it tends to defeat the purpose of matching.

A related matching procedure is to rank all of the participants, from highest to lowest, based on their scores on the variable to be matched. The two highest ranking participants, regardless of score, are the first pair. One member of the first pair is randomly assigned to one group and the other member to the other group. The next two highest ranked participants (third and fourth ranked) are pair two, and so on. The major advantage of this approach is that no participants are lost. The major disadvantage is that it is a lot less precise than pair-wise matching. Advanced statistical procedures, such as analysis of covariance, have greatly reduced the research use of matching.

Comparing Homogeneous Groups or Subgroups

Another previously discussed way to control an extraneous variable is to compare groups that are homogeneous with respect to that variable. For example, if IQ were an identified extraneous variable, the researcher might select only participants with IQs between 85 and 115 (average IQ). The researcher would then randomly assign half the selected participants to the experimental group and half to the control group. Of course this procedure also lowers the number of participants in the population and additionally restricts the generalizability of the findings to participants with IQs between 85 and 115. As noted in the discussion of causal–comparative research, a similar, more satisfactory approach is to form different subgroups representing all levels of the control variable. For example, the available participants might be divided into high (116 or above), average (85 to 115), and low (84 and below) IQ subgroups. Half of the participants from each of the subgroups could then be randomly assigned to the experimental group and half to the control group. The procedure just described should sound familiar, because it describes stratified sampling. (You knew that!) If the researcher is interested not just in controlling the variable but also in seeing if the independent variable affects the dependent variable differently at different levels of IQ, the best approach is to build the control variable right into the design. Thus, the research design would have six cells, two treatments by three IQ levels. Draw the design for yourself, and label each cell with its treatment and IQ level.

Using Participants as Their Own Controls

Using participants as their own controls involves exposing a single group to different treatments one treatment at a time. This strategy helps to control for participant differences, since the same participants get both treatments. Of course this approach is not always feasible; you cannot teach the same algebraic concepts to the same group twice using two different methods of instruction (well, you could, but it would not make much sense). A problem with this approach is a carryover effect from one treatment to the next. To use a previous example, it would be very difficult to evaluate the effectiveness of corporal punishment in improving behavior if the group receiving corporal punishment was the same group that had previously been exposed to behavior modification. If only one group is available, a better approach, if feasible, is to randomly divide the group into two smaller groups, each of which receives both treatments but in a different order. Thus, the researcher could at least get some idea of the effectiveness of corporal punishment because there would be a group that received it before behavior modification. In situations in which the effect of the dependent variable disappears quickly after treatment, or when a single participant is the focus of the research, participants can be used as their own control.

Analysis of Covariance

The analysis of covariance is a statistical method for equating randomly formed groups on one or more variables. In essence, analysis of covariance adjusts scores on a dependent variable for initial differences on some other variable, such as pretest scores, IQ, reading readiness, or musical aptitude. The covariate variable should be one related to performance on the dependent variable. Although analysis of covariance can be used in studies when groups cannot be randomly formed, its use is most appropriate when randomization is used. In spite of randomization, it might be found that two groups still differ significantly in terms of pretest scores. Analysis of covariance can be used in such cases to "correct" or adjust posttest scores for initial pretest differences. However, analysis of covariance is not universally useful. For example, the relationship between the independent and covariate variables depends on their being linear (straight line). If the relationship is curvilinear, analysis of covariance is not useful. Also, analysis of covariance is often called upon when a study deals with intact groups, uncontrolled variables, and nonrandom assignment to treatments, all of which weaken the results of covariance analysis. Calculation of an analysis of covariance is a complex procedure.

TYPES OF GROUP DESIGNS

The experimental design you select dictates to a great extent the specific procedures of your study. Selection of a given design influences factors such as whether there will be a control group, whether participants will be randomly selected and assigned to groups, whether the groups will be pretested, and how data will be analyzed. Particular combinations of such factors produce different designs that are appropriate for testing different types of hypotheses. Designs vary widely in the degree to which they control various threats to internal and external validity. Of course there are certain threats to validity, such as experimenter bias, that no design can control. However, some designs clearly do a better job than others. In selecting a design, you first determine which designs are appropriate for your study and for testing your hypothesis. You then determine which of these are also feasible given the constraints under which you may be operating. If, for example, you must use existing groups, a number of designs will automatically be eliminated. From the designs that are appropriate and feasible, you select the one that will control the most sources of internal and external invalidity and will yield the data you need to test your hypothesis or hypotheses.

There are two major classes of experimental designs, single-variable designs, which involve one manipulated independent variable, and factorial designs, which involve two or more independent variables with at least one being manipulated. Single-variable designs are classified as pre-experimental, true experimental, or quasi-experimental, depending upon the degree of control they provide for threats to internal and external invalidity. *Pre-experimental designs* do not do a very good job of controlling threats to validity and should be avoided. In fact, the results of a study based on a pre-experimental design are so questionable that they are not useful for most purposes except, perhaps, as a preliminary investigation of a problem. *True experimental designs* provide a very high degree of control and are always to be preferred. *Quasi-experimental designs* do not control as well as true experimental designs, but do a much better job than pre-experimental designs. If we were to assign letter grades to experimental designs, true experimental designs would get an A, quasi-experimental designs would get a B or a C (some are better than others), and pre-experimental designs would get a D or an F. Thus, if you have a choice between a true experimental design and a quasi-experimental design, select the true design. If your choice is between a quasi-experimental design and a pre-experimental design, select the quasi-experimental design. If your choice is between a pre-experimental design or not doing the study at all, do not do the study at all, or do a follow-up study using an acceptable (C or better!) design. The less useful designs are discussed here only so that (1) you will know what not to do, and (2) you will recognize their use in published research reports and will be appropriately critical of their findings.

Factorial designs are basically elaborations of single-variable experimental designs except that they permit investigation of two or more variables, individually and in interaction with each other. After an independent variable has been investigated using a single-variable design, it is often useful to study the variable in combination with one or more other variables. Some variables work differently when paired with different levels of another variable. The designs to be discussed represent the basic designs in each category. Campbell and Stanley and Cook and Campbell[4] present a number of variations (for those of you who are getting "hooked" on research).

Pre-Experimental Designs

Here is a research riddle for you: Can you do an experiment with only one group? The answer is . . . yes, but not a really good one. As Figure 11.1 illustrates, none of the pre-experimental designs does a very good job of controlling extraneous variables that jeopardize validity.

The One-Shot Case Study. The one-shot case study (it even sounds shoddy) involves a single group that is exposed to a treatment (X) and then posttested (O). None of the sources of invalidity are controlled in this design. As Figure 11.1

[4]Campbell, D. T. & Stanley, J. C. (1971). *Experimental and quasi-experimental designs for research*. Chicago: Rand McNally.

Cook, T. D. & Campbell, D. T. (1979). *Quasi-experimentation: Design and analysis issues for field settings*. Chicago: Rand McNally.

<table>
<tr>
<td rowspan="3">Designs</td>
<td colspan="10">Sources of Invalidity</td>
</tr>
<tr>
<td colspan="8">Internal</td>
<td colspan="2">External</td>
</tr>
<tr>
<td>History</td>
<td>Maturation</td>
<td>Testing</td>
<td>Instrumentation</td>
<td>Regression</td>
<td>Selection</td>
<td>Mortality</td>
<td>Selection Interactions</td>
<td>Pretest-X Interaction</td>
<td>Multiple-X Interference</td>
</tr>
<tr>
<td>One-Shot Case Study
$X\ O$</td>
<td>–</td>
<td>–</td>
<td>(+)</td>
<td>(+)</td>
<td>(+)</td>
<td>(+)</td>
<td>–</td>
<td>(+)</td>
<td>(+)</td>
<td>(+)</td>
</tr>
<tr>
<td>One-Group Pretest–
Posttest Design
$O\ X\ O$</td>
<td>–</td>
<td>–</td>
<td>–</td>
<td>–</td>
<td>–</td>
<td>(+)</td>
<td>+</td>
<td>(+)</td>
<td>–</td>
<td>(+)</td>
</tr>
<tr>
<td>Static Group
Comparison
$X_1\ O$
$X_2\ O$</td>
<td>+</td>
<td>–</td>
<td>(+)</td>
<td>(+)</td>
<td>(+)</td>
<td>–</td>
<td>–</td>
<td>–</td>
<td>(+)</td>
<td>(+)</td>
</tr>
</table>

FIGURE 11.1

Sources of Invalidity for Pre-Experimental Designs

Symbols:

X or X_1 = Unusual treatment
X_2 = Control treatment
O = Test, pretest or posttest

+ = Factor controlled for
(+) = Factor controlled for because not relevant
– = Factor not controlled for

Each line of Xs and Os represents a group.

Note: Figures 11.1 and 11.2 basically follow the format used by Campbell and Stanley and are presented with a similar note of caution: The figures are intended to be supplements to, not substitutes for, textual discussions. You *should not* totally accept or reject designs because of their +s and –s; you *should* also be aware that which design is most appropriate for a given study is determined not only by the controls provided by the various designs but also by the nature of the study and the setting in which it is to be conducted.

While the symbols used in these figures, and their placement, vary somewhat from Campbell and Stanley's format, the intent, interpretations, and textual discussions of the two presentations are in agreement (Personal communication with Donald T. Campbell, April 22, 1975).

indicates, the only threats to validity that are controlled are those that are automatically controlled because they are irrelevant in this design. None of the relevant validity threats (such as history, maturation, and mortality) are controlled. Even if the research participants score high on the posttest, you cannot attribute their performance to the treatment, since you do not even know what they knew before you administered the treatment. So, if you have a choice between using this design and not doing a study, select another study.

The One-Group Pretest–Posttest Design. This design involves a single group that is pretested (O), exposed to a treatment (X), and posttested (O). The success of the treatment is determined by comparing pretest and posttest scores. This design controls some areas of invalidity not controlled by the one-shot case study, but a number of additional factors relevant to this design are not controlled. If participants do significantly better on the posttest than on the pretest, it cannot be assumed that the improvement is due to the treatment. History and maturation are not controlled. Something may happen to the participants that makes them perform better the second time, and the longer the study takes, the more likely these become threats. Testing and instrumentation also are not controlled; the participants may learn something on the pretest that helps them on the posttest, or unreliability of the measures may be responsible for the apparent improvement. Statistical regression is also not controlled. Even if participants are not selected on the basis of extreme scores (high or low), it is possible that a group may do very poorly on the pretest, just by poor luck. For example, participants may guess badly just by chance on a multiple-choice pretest and improve on a posttest simply because their score based on guessing is more in line with an expected score. The external validity threat of pretest–treatment interaction is also not controlled. Pretest–treatment interaction may cause participants to react differently to the treatment than they would have if they had not been pretested.

To illustrate the problems associated with this design, let us examine a hypothetical study. Suppose Professor I. R. Scwaird teaches a very "heavy" statistics course and is concerned that the high anxiety level of students interferes with their learning. The kindly professor (aren't they all) prepares a 100-page booklet that explains the course, tries to convince students that they will have no problems, and promises all the help they need to successfully complete the course, even if they have a poor math background. The professor wants to see if the booklet "works." At the beginning of the term, Professor Scwaird administers an anxiety test and then gives each student a copy of the booklet with instructions to read it as soon as possible. Two weeks later Professor Scwaird administers the anxiety scale again and, sure enough, the students' scores indicate much less anxiety than at the beginning of the term. The professor is satisfied and proud of the booklet's effectiveness in reducing anxiety. But wait: Is this self-satisfaction warranted? If you think about it, you will see that there are a number of alternative factors or threats that could explain the students' decreased anxiety. For example, students are typically more anxious at the beginning of a course because they do not know exactly what they are in for (fear of the unknown!). After being in a course for a couple of weeks, students usually find that it is not as bad as they imagined (right?), or they have dropped the class (remember mortality?). Also, the professor doesn't even know whether the students read her masterpiece! The only situation for which the one-group pretest–posttest design is even remotely appropriate is when the behavior to be measured is not likely to change by itself. Certain prejudices, for example, are not likely to change unless a concerted effort is made.

The Static-Group Comparison. The static-group comparison at least involves two groups, one that receives a new, or experimental, treatment and another that receives a traditional, or control treatment. Both groups are posttested. In this case, although the terms *experimental* and *control* groups are commonly used, it is probably more appropriate to call both groups comparison groups, since each really serves as the comparison for the other. Each group receives some form of the independent variable (the treatments). So, for example, if the independent variable is type of drill and practice, the "experimental" group (X_1) may receive computer-assisted drill and practice, and the "control" group (X_2) may receive worksheet drill and practice. Occasionally, but not often, the experimental group may receive something while the control group receives nothing. For example, a group of teachers may receive some type of in-service education while the comparison group of teachers does not. In this case, X_1 = in-service training and X_2 = no in-service training. The purpose of a control group is to indicate what the performance of the experimental group would have been if it had not received the experimental treatment. Of course, this purpose is fulfilled only to the degree that the control group is equivalent to the experimental group.

The static group comparison design can be expanded to deal with any number of groups. For three groups the design would take the form:

$$X_1 \quad O$$
$$X_2 \quad O$$
$$X_3 \quad O$$

Which group is the control group? Basically, each group serves as a control or comparison group for the other two. For example, if the independent variable were number of minutes of review at the end of math lessons, then X_1 might represent 6 minutes of review, X_2 might represent 3 minutes of review, and X_3 0 minutes of review. Thus X_3 (no minutes) would help us to assess the impact of X_2 (3 minutes), and X_2 would help us to assess the impact of X_1 (6 minutes). As already emphasized, but worthy of repeating, the degree to which the groups are equivalent is the degree to which their comparison is reasonable. In this design, participants are not randomly assigned to groups, and since there are no pretest data, it is difficult to determine just how equivalent the groups are. That is, it is possible that posttest differences are due to initial group differences in maturation, selection, and selection interactions, rather than the treatment effects. Mortality is also a problem, since if you lose participants from the study you have no information regarding what you have lost because you have no pretest data. On the positive side, the presence of a comparison group does control for history, because it is assumed that events occurring outside of the experimental setting will equally affect both groups.

In spite of its limitations, the static-group comparison design is occasionally employed in a preliminary or exploratory study. For example, one semester, early in the term, a teacher wondered if the kind of test items given to educational research students affects their retention of course concepts. For the rest of the term students in one section of the course were given multiple-choice tests, and students in another section were given short-answer tests. At the end of the term, group performances were compared. The group receiving short-answer test items had higher total scores than the multiple-choice item group. Based on this exploratory study, a formal investigation of this issue was undertaken (with randomly formed groups and everything!).

True Experimental Designs

True experimental designs control for nearly all sources of internal and external invalidity. As Figure 11.2 indicates, all of the true experimental designs have one characteristic in common that none of the other designs have—random

FIGURE 11.2

Sources of Invalidity for True Experimental Designs and Quasi-Experimental Designs

Designs	Internal								External	
	History	Maturation	Testing	Instrumentation	Regression	Selection	Mortality	Selection Interactions	Pretest-X Interaction	Multiple-X Interference
TRUE EXPERIMENTAL DESIGNS										
1. Pretest–Posttest Control Group Design R O X_1 O R O X_2 O	+	+	+	+	+	+	+	+	–	(+)
2. Posttest-Only Control Group Design R X_1 O R X_2 O	+	+	(+)	(+)	(+)	+	–	+	(+)	(+)
3. Solomon Four-Group Design R O X_1 O R O X_2 O R X_1 O R X_2 O	+	+	+	+	+	+	+	+	+	(+)
QUASI-EXPERIMENTAL DESIGNS										
4. Nonequivalent Control Group Design O X_1 O O X_2 O	+	+	+	+	–	+	+	–	–	(+)
5. Time Series Design $O O O O X O O O O$	–	+	+	–	+	(+)	+	(+)	–	(+)
6. Counterbalanced Design $X_1 O$ $X_2 O$ $X_3 O$ $X_3 O$ $X_1 O$ $X_2 O$ $X_2 O$ $X_3 O$ $X_1 O$	+	+	+	+	+	+	+	–	–	–

New Symbol:

R = Random assignment of subjects to groups

assignment of participants to treatment groups. Ideally, participants should be randomly selected and randomly assigned; however, to qualify as a true design, at least random assignment must be involved. Notice, too, that all the true designs have a control group. Finally, although the posttest-only control group design looks like the static-group comparison design, random assignment in the former makes it very different in terms of control.

The Pretest–Posttest Control Group Design. This design requires at least two groups, each of which is formed by random assignment. Both groups are administered a pretest and each group receives a different treatment. Both groups are posttested at the end of the study. Posttest scores are compared to determine the effectiveness of the treatment. The pretest–posttest control group design may also be expanded to include any number of treatment groups. For three groups, for example, this design would take the following form:

$$R \quad O \quad X_1 \quad O$$
$$R \quad O \quad X_2 \quad O$$
$$R \quad O \quad X_3 \quad O$$

The combination of random assignment and the presence of a pretest and a control group serve to control for all sources of internal invalidity. Random assignment controls for regression and selection factors; the pretest controls for mortality; randomization and the control group control for maturation; and the control group controls for history, testing, and instrumentation. Testing is controlled because if pretesting leads to higher posttest scores, the advantage should be equal for both the experimental and control groups. The only weakness in this design is a possible interaction between the pretest and the treatment, which may make the results generalizable only to other pretested groups. The seriousness of this potential weakness depends on the nature of the pretest, the nature of the treatment, and the length of the study. When this design is used, the researcher should assess and report the probability of a pretest–treatment interaction. For example, a researcher might indicate that possible pretest interaction was likely to be minimized by the nonreactive nature of the pretest (chemical equations), and by the length of the study (9 months).

There are a number of ways in which the data from this and other experimental designs can be analyzed in order to test the research hypothesis regarding the effectiveness of the treatments. The best way to analyze these data is to compare the posttest scores of the two treatment groups. The pretest is used to see if the groups are essentially the same on the dependent variable at the start of the study. If they are, posttest scores can be directly compared using a statistic called the t-test. If the groups are not essentially the same on the pretest (random assignment does not guarantee equality), posttest scores can be analyzed using analysis of covariance. Recall that covariance adjusts posttest scores for initial differences on any variable, including pretest scores. This approach is superior to using gain or difference scores (posttest minus pretest) to determine the treatment effects.

A variation of the pretest–posttest control group design involves random assignment of matched pairs to the treatment groups, in order to more closely control for one or more extraneous variables. There is really no advantage to this technique, however, since any variable that can be controlled through matching can be better controlled using other procedures such as analysis of covariance.

Another variation of this design involves one or more additional posttests. For example:

$$R \quad O \quad X_2 \quad O \quad O$$
$$R \quad O \quad X_3 \quad O \quad O$$

This variation has the advantage of providing information about the effect of the independent variable both immediately following treatment and at a later date. Recall that the interaction of time of measurement and treatment effects is a threat to external validity because posttesting may yield different results depending on when it is done. A treatment effect (or lack of same) that is based on the administration of a posttest immediately following the treatment may not be found if a delayed posttest is given after treatment. Although this variation does not completely solve the problem, it does greatly minimize it by providing information about group performance subsequent to the initial posttest.

The Posttest-Only Control Group Design. This design is exactly the same as the pretest–posttest control group design except there is no pretest. Participants are randomly assigned to groups, exposed to the different treatments, and posttested. Posttest scores are then compared to determine the effectiveness of the treatment. As with the pretest–posttest control group design, the posttest-only control group design can be expanded to include more than two groups. The combination of random assignment and the presence of a control group serves to control for all sources of internal invalidity except mortality. Mortality is not controlled because of the absence of pretest data on participants. However, bear in mind that mortality may or may not be a problem, depending on the duration of the study. In this case the researcher may report that while mortality is a potential threat to validity with this design, it did not prove to be a threat in this study because the group sizes remained constant or nearly constant throughout the study. If the probability of differential mortality is low, the posttest-only design can be very effective. However, if there is any chance that the groups may be different with respect to pretreatment knowledge related to the dependent variable, the pretest–posttest control group design should be used. Which design is "best" depends on the study. If the study is to be short, and if it can be assumed that neither group has any knowledge related to the dependent variable, then the posttest-only design may be the "best" choice. If the study is to be lengthy (good chance of mortality), or if there is a chance that the two groups differ on initial knowledge related to the dependent variable, then the pretest–posttest control group design may be the best.

What if, however, you face the following dilemma:

1. The study is going to last 2 months.
2. Information about initial knowledge is essential.
3. The pretest is an attitude test and the treatment is designed to change attitudes.

This is a classic case where pretest–treatment interaction is probable. Do we throw our hands up in despair? Of course not. One solution is to select the lesser of the two evils by taking our chances that mortality will not be a threat. Another solution, if enough participants are available, is to use the Solomon four-group design, which will be discussed next. Figure 11.2 shows that the Solomon four-group design is simply a combination of the pretest–posttest control group design (the top two lines) and the posttest-only control group design (the third and fourth lines). A variation of the posttest-only control group design involves random assignment of matched pairs to the treatment groups, one member to each group, to control for one or more extraneous variables. However, there is really no advantage to this technique, since any variable that can be controlled by matching can better be controlled using other procedures.

The Solomon Four-Group Design. The Solomon four-group design involves random assignment of participants to one of four groups. Two of the groups are pretested and two are not. One of the pretested groups and one of the unpretested groups receive the experimental treatment. All four groups are posttested with the dependent variable. As Figure 11.2 indicates, this design is a combination of the pretest–posttest control group design and the posttest-only control group design, each of which has its own major source of invalidity (pretest–treatment interaction and mortality, respectively). The combination of these two designs results in a design that controls for pretest–treatment interaction and for mortality. The correct way to analyze data resulting from application of this design is to use a 2 × 2 (two by two) factorial with treatment and control groups crossed with pre- and nonpretesting. There are two independent variables in this design, treatment/control and pretest/no pretest. The 2 × 2 factorial analysis tells the researcher whether the treatment is effective and whether there is an interaction between the treatment and the pretest. To put it simply, if the pretested experimental group performs differently on the posttest than the unpretested experimental group, there is probably a pretest–treatment interaction. If no pretest-treatment interaction is found, then the researcher can have more confidence in the generalizability of treatment differences across pre- and nonpretested treatments.

A common misconception is that since the Solomon four-group design controls for so many sources of invalidity, it is always the "best" design to choose. This is not true. For one thing, this design requires twice as many participants as most other true experimental designs, and participants are often hard to find. Further, if mortality is not likely to be a problem, and pretest data are not needed, then the posttest-only design may be the best choice. If pretest–treatment interaction is unlikely, and testing is a normal part of the participants' environment (such as when classroom tests are used), then the pretest–posttest control group design may be the "best." Thus, which design is the "best" depends on the nature of the study and the conditions under which it is to be conducted.

Quasi-Experimental Designs

Sometimes it is just not possible to randomly assign individual participants to groups. For example, in order to receive permission to use schoolchildren in a study, a researcher often has to agree to keep students in existing classrooms intact. Thus, entire classrooms, not individual students, are assigned to treatments. When this situation occurs there are still a number of designs that provide adequate control of sources of invalidity. These designs are referred to as quasi-experimental designs. Although there are many such designs, we discuss only three of the major ones here. Keep in mind that designs such as these are only to be used when it is not feasible to use a true experimental design.

The Nonequivalent Control Group Design. This design should be familiar to you since it looks very much like the pretest–posttest control group design. The only difference is that the nonequivalent control group design involves random assignment of intact groups to treatments, not random assignment of individuals. Two (or more) treatment groups are pretested, administered a treatment, and posttested. For example, suppose a school volunteered six intact classrooms for a study. Three of six classrooms may be randomly assigned to the experimental group (X_1) and the remaining three assigned to the control group (X_2). The inability to randomly assign individuals to treatments (we're stuck with whole classes), adds validity threats such as regression and interactions between selection maturation, history, and testing. The more similar the intact groups are, the stronger the study, so the researcher should make every effort to use groups that are as equivalent as possible. Comparing an advanced algebra class to a remedial algebra class, for example, would not be comparing equivalent groups. If differences between the groups on any major extraneous variable are identified, analysis of covariance can be used to statistically equate the groups. An advantage of this design is that since classes are selected "as is," possible effects from reactive arrangements are minimized. Groups may not even be aware that they are involved in a study. As with the pretest–posttest control group design, the nonequivalent control group design may be extended to include more than two groups.

The Time-Series Design. The time series design is actually an elaboration of the one-group pretest–posttest design. One group is repeatedly pretested until pretest scores are stable, then the group is exposed to a treatment, and after treatment implementation, repeatedly posttested. If a group scores essentially the same on a number of pretests and then significantly improves following a treatment, the researcher can be more confident about the effectiveness of the treatment than if just one pretest and one posttest were administered. To use a former example, if our statistics professor measured anxiety several times before giving the students her booklet, she would be able to see if anxiety was declining naturally, and thus not a result of the booklet per se. History is still a problem with this design because some event or activity might occur between the last pretest and the first posttest. Instrumentation may also be a problem, but only if the researcher changes measuring instruments during the study. Pretest–treatment interaction is also a validity problem. If one pretest can interact with a treatment, more than one pretest can only make matters worse. If instrumentation or pretest–treatment interaction occurs, however, you will probably be aware of the problem because scores will change prior to treatment.

Although statistical analyses appropriate for this design are quite advanced, determining the effectiveness of the treatment basically involves analysis of the pattern of the test scores. Figure 11.3 illustrates some of the possible patterns that might be found with the time-series design. In Figure 11.3 the vertical line between O_4 and O_5 indicates the point at which the treatment was introduced. Pattern A, at the top, does not indicate a treatment effect; performance was increasing before the treatment was introduced, and continued to increase at the same rate following introduction of the treatment. In fact, pattern A represents the reverse situation to that encountered by Professor Scwaird and the anxiety-reducing booklet. Patterns B and C do indicate a treatment effect, with pattern C more permanent than in pattern B. Both B and C increased after the treatment

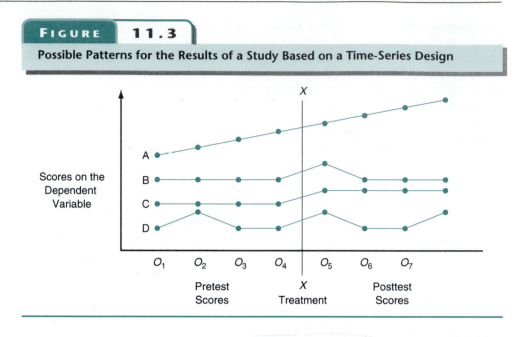

FIGURE   11.3

Possible Patterns for the Results of a Study Based on a Time-Series Design

was applied, but B's scores dropped back while C's stayed up. Pattern D does not indicate a treatment effect even though student scores are higher on O_5 than O_4. The pattern is too erratic to make a decision about treatment effect. Scores appear to be fluctuating up and down, so the O_4 to O_5 fluctuation cannot be attributed to the treatment. These four patterns illustrate that just comparing O_4 and O_5 is not sufficient; in all four cases O_5 indicates a higher score than O_4, but in only two of the patterns does it appear that the difference is due to a treatment effect.

A variation of the time-series design is the multiple time-series design, which involves the addition of a control group as shown here.

$$O \quad O \quad O \quad O \quad X_1 \quad O \quad O \quad O \quad O$$
$$O \quad O \quad O \quad O \quad X_2 \quad O \quad O \quad O \quad O$$

This variation eliminates history and instrumentation as validity threats and thus represents a design with no likely sources of internal invalidity. This design can be more effectively used in situations where testing is a naturally occurring event, such as research involving school classrooms.

Counterbalanced Designs. In a counterbalanced design, all groups receive all treatments but in a different order. Although the sixth example in Figure 11.2 represents the design for three groups and three treatments, any number of groups more than one may be studied. The only restriction is that the number of groups be equal to the number of treatments. The order in which the groups receive the treatments is randomly determined. Although participants may be pretested, this design is usually employed when intact groups must be used and when administration of a pretest is not possible. The pre-experimental static group comparison also can be used in such situations, but the counterbalanced design controls several additional sources of invalidity. Figure 11.2 shows that there are three treatment groups and three treatments. The first horizontal line indicates that group A receives treatment 1 and is posttested, then receives treatment 2 and is posttested, then treatment 3 and is posttested. The second line indicates that group B receives treatment 3, then treatment 1, and then treatment 2, and is posttested after each treatment. The third line indicates that group C receives treatment 2, then treatment 3, then treatment 1, and is posttested after each treatment. To put it another way, the first column indicates that at time 1, while group A is receiving treatment 1, group B is receiving treatment 3 and group C is receiving treatment 2. All three groups are posttested and the treatments are shifted to produce the second column. The second column indicates that at time 2, while group A is receiving treatment 2, group B is receiving treatment 1, and group C is receiving treatment 3. The groups are then posttested again and the treatments are again shifted to produce the third column showing that at time 3, group A is receiving treatment 3, group B is receiving treatment 2, and group C is receiving treatment 1. All groups are posttested again. (Note that this design is *not* a research variation of the old comedy routine "Who's on First?") In order to determine the effectiveness of the treatments, the average performance of the groups on each treatment can be calculated and compared. In other words, the posttest scores for all the groups for the first treatment can be compared to the posttest scores of all the groups for the second treatment, and so forth, depending on the number of groups and treatments.

A unique weakness of this design is potential multiple-treatment interference that results when the same group receives more than one treatment. Thus, a counterbalanced design should really only be used when the treatments are such that exposure to one will not affect the effectiveness of another. Unfortunately, there are not too many situations in education where this condition can be met. You cannot, for example, teach the same geometric concepts to the same group using several different methods of instruction. Sophisticated analysis procedures that are beyond the level of this text can be applied to determine both the effects of treatments and the effects of the order of treatments.

Factorial Designs

Factorial designs involve two or more independent variables, at least one of which is manipulated by the researcher. Factorial designs are basically elaborations of single-variable true experimental designs that permit investigation of two or more variables individually and in interaction with each other. In education, variables rarely operate in isolation. After an independent variable has been investigated using a single-variable design, it is often useful to study that variable in combination with one or more other variables. Some variables work differently at different levels of another variable. For example, one method of math instruction may be more effective for high-aptitude students while a different method may be more effective for low-aptitude students. The term *factorial* refers to a design that has more than one independent variable, or factor. In the preceding example, method of instruction is one independent variable or factor and student aptitude is another independent variable or factor. In the example, the factor "method of instruction" has two levels because there are two types of instruction, and the factor "student aptitude" also has two levels, high aptitude and low aptitude. Thus, a 2×2 factorial design has two factors and each factor has two levels. This four-celled example is the simplest possible factorial design. As another example, a 2×3 factorial design has two factors; one factor has two levels and the other factor has three levels (such as high, average, and low apti-

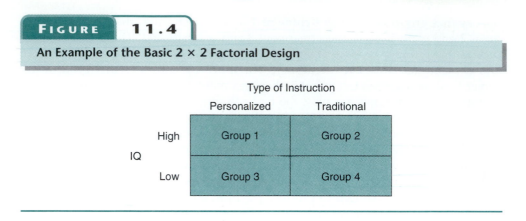

FIGURE **11.4**

An Example of the Basic 2 × 2 Factorial Design

tude). Suppose we have three independent variables, or factors: homework (required homework, voluntary homework, no homework); ability (high, average, low); and gender (male, female). How would you symbolize this study? Right, it is a 3 × 3 × 2 factorial design. Note that multiplying the factors indicates the total number of cells in the factorial design. For example, a 2 × 2 design will have four cells and a 3 × 3 × 2 design will have 18 cells.

Figure 11.4 illustrates the simplest 2 × 2 factorial design. In Figure 11.4 there are two factors. Type of instruction has two levels, personalized and traditional, and IQ has two levels, high and low. Each of the groups in the four design cells represents a combination of a level of one factor and a level of the other factor. Thus, group 1 is composed of high IQ students receiving personalized instruction (PI), group 2 is composed of high IQ students receiving traditional instruction (TI), group 3 is composed of low IQ students receiving PI, and group 4 is composed of low IQ students receiving TI. To implement this design, high IQ students would be randomly assigned to either group 1 or group 2, and a similar number of low IQ students would be randomly assigned to either group 3 or group 4. This approach should be familiar, since it involves stratified sampling. Also, in case the question crossed your mind, the study shown in Figure 11.4 would not necessarily require four classes; there could be two classes, the personalized class and the traditional class, and each of these two classes could be subdivided to obtain similar numbers of high and low IQ students. In a 2 × 2 design both variables may be manipulated or one group may be a manipulated variable and the other a nonmanipulated variable. The nonmanipulated variable is often referred to as a control variable. In this example, IQ is a nonmanipulated, control variable. Control variables are usually physical or mental characteristics of the participants such as gender, years of experience, or aptitude. When describing and symbolizing such designs, the manipulated variable is traditionally placed first. Thus, a study with two independent variables, type of instruction (three types, manipulated) and gender (male, female), would be symbolized as 3 × 2, not 2 × 3.

The purpose of a factorial design is to determine whether the effects of an independent variable are generalizable across all levels or are specific to particular levels. A factorial design also can demonstrate relationships that a single-variable design cannot. For example, a variable found not to be effective in a single-variable study may be found to interact significantly with another variable. The second example in Figure 11.5 illustrates this possibility.

FIGURE	11.5

Illustration of Interaction and No Interaction in a 2 × 2 Factorial Experiment

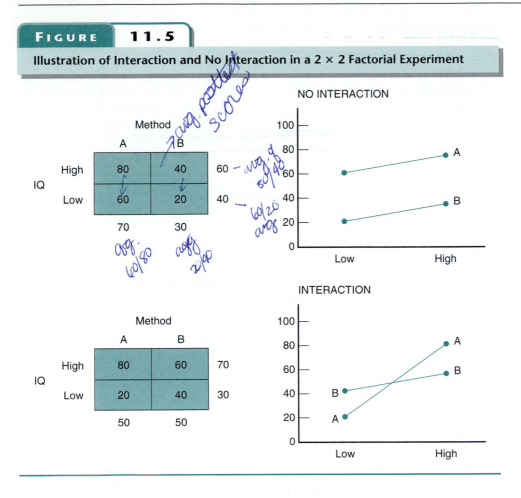

Figure 11.5 represents two possible outcomes for an experiment involving a 2 × 2 factorial design. The number in each box, or cell, represents the average posttest score of that group. Thus, the high IQ students under method A had an average posttest score of 80 and the low IQ students under method B had an average score of 20. The row and column numbers outside of the boxes represent average scores across boxes, or cells. Thus, in the top example, the average score for high IQ students was 60 (found by averaging the scores for all high IQ participants regardless of treatment; 80 + 40 = 120; 120/2 = 60), and for low IQ students the average score was 40. The average score for students under method A was 70 (found by averaging the scores of all the participants under method A regardless of IQ level; 80 + 60 = 140; 140/2 = 70), and for students under method B, 30. By examining the cell averages, we see that method A was better than method B for high IQ students (80 versus 40), and method A was also better for low IQ students (60 versus 20). Thus, method A was better, regardless of IQ level; there was no interaction between method and IQ. The high IQ students in each method outperformed the low IQ students in each method (no big surprise), and the students in method A outperformed the students in method B at each IQ level. The graph to the right of the results illustrates the lack of interaction.

In the bottom example of Figure 11.5, which method was better, A or B? The answer, as is frequently the case, is, "It depends!" On what? On which IQ level we are talking about. For high IQ students, method A was better (80 versus 60), for low IQ students, method B was better (20 versus 40). Even though high IQ students did better than low IQ students regardless of method, how well they did depended on which method they were in. It cannot be said that either method was generally better, because which method was better depended on which IQ level one focuses. Now suppose the study had not used a factorial design but had simply compared two groups of participants, one group receiving method A and one group receiving method B. High and low IQ students were not separated as in the factorial design. What would the researcher have concluded? The researcher would have concluded that method A and method B were equally effective, since the overall average score for both methods A and B was 50! Using a factorial design, however, it was determined that an interaction existed between the variables such that each of the methods are differentially effective, depending on the IQ level of the participants. The crossed lines in the graph to the right of the results illustrate an interaction effect.

There are many possible factorial designs depending upon the nature and the number of independent variables. Theoretically, a researcher could simultaneously investigate 10 factors in a $2 \times 2 \times 2 \times 2 \times 2 \times 2 \times 2 \times 2 \times 2 \times 2$ design. In reality, however, more than three factors are rarely used because each additional factor increases the number of participants needed to fill the cells. Four cells are easier to fill than 10 cells. A 2×2 design with 20 participants per cell (a relatively small number) requires at least 80 participants ($2 \times 2 = 4 \times 20 = 80$). It is easy to see that as the number of cells increases, things quickly get out of hand, and the results of studies with small sample sizes in each cell require extra cautious interpretations. Moreover, when too many factors are included, resulting interactions become difficult, if not impossible, to interpret. Interpretation of a two-way interaction, such as the one illustrated in Figure 11.5 is relatively straightforward. But how, for example, would you interpret a five-way interaction between teaching method, IQ, gender, aptitude, and anxiety? Not only is it difficult to graph five-way interactions, they also tend to be uninterpretable! When used reasonably, factorial designs are very effective for testing research hypotheses that cannot be tested with a single-variable design.

SINGLE-SUBJECT EXPERIMENTAL DESIGNS

As you would probably guess, single-subject experimental designs (also referred to as single-case experimental designs) are designs that can be applied when the sample size is one or when a number of individuals are considered as one group. These designs are typically used to study the behavior change an individual exhibits as a result of some treatment. In single-subject designs, each participant serves as his or her own control, similar to a time-series design. Basically, the participant is exposed to a nontreatment and a treatment phase and performance is measured during each phase. The nontreatment condition is symbolized as A and the treatment condition is symbolized as B. For example, if we (1) observed and recorded a student's out-of-seat behavior on five occasions, (2) applied a behavior modification procedure and observed behavior on five more occasions, and (3) stopped the behavior modification procedure and observed behavior five more times, our design would be symbolized as A–B–A. Although single-subject designs have their roots in clinical psychology and psychiatry, they are useful in many educational settings, particularly those involving studies of students with disabilities.

SINGLE-SUBJECT VERSUS GROUP DESIGNS

As single-subject designs have become progressively refined and capable of dealing with threats to validity, they are increasingly viewed as acceptable substitutes for traditional group designs in a number of situations. Most traditional experimental research studies use group designs. This is mainly because the desired results are intended to be generalized to other groups. As an example, if we were investigating the comparative effectiveness of two approaches to teaching reading, we would be interested in which approach generally produces better reading achievement, since schools usually seek strategies that are beneficial for groups of students, not individual students. Thus, group comparison designs are widely used. A single-subject design would not be very practical for such a research study, since it focuses on single students and requires multiple measurements over the course of the study. Remember the earlier example of 15 separate observations, 5 for each phase. It would be highly impractical to administer a reading achievement test 15 times to the same students.

There are, however, some research questions for which traditional group designs are not appropriate. First, group comparison designs are sometimes opposed on ethical or philosophical grounds because such designs include a control group that does not receive the experimental treatment. Withholding students with a demonstrated need from a potentially beneficial program may be opposed or prohibited, as in the case with certain federally funded programs. If the treatment is potentially effective, it may raise objections when eligible participants are denied it. Second, group comparison designs are not possible in many cases because of the size of the population of interest. There may simply not be enough potential participants to permit the formulation of two equivalent groups. If, for example, the treatment is aimed at improving the social skills of profoundly emotionally disturbed children, the number of such children available in any one locale is probably too small to conduct comparative research. A single-subject design is clearly preferable to the formulation of two more-or-less equivalent treatment groups composed of five children each. Further, single-subject designs are most frequently applied in clinical settings where the primary emphasis is on therapeutic impact, not contribution to a research base. In such settings, the overriding objective is the identification of intervention strategies that will change the behavior of a specific individual, who might, for example be engaging in self-abusive or aggressive behavior.

EXTERNAL VALIDITY

A major criticism of single-subject research studies is that they suffer from low external validity; results cannot be generalized to a population of interest. Although this criticism is basically true, it is also true that the results of a study using a group design cannot be directly generalized to any individual within the group. Thus, group designs and single-subject designs each have their own generalizability problems. If your aim is to improve the functioning of an individual, a group design is not going to be appropriate.

Nonetheless, we usually are interested in generalizing the results of our research to persons other than those directly involved in the study. For single-subject designs, the key to generalizability is replication. If a researcher applies the same treatment using the same single-subject design individually to a number of participants and gets essentially the same results in every case (or even in most cases), confidence in the generalizability of the findings is increased. Different students respond similarly to the treatment. The more diverse the replications are (i.e., different kinds of participants, different behaviors, different settings), the more generalizable the results are.

One important generalizability problem associated with many single-subject designs is the effect of the baseline condition on the subsequent effects of the treatment condition. We can never be sure that the treatment effects are the same as they would have been if the treatment phase had come before the baseline phase. This problem parallels the pretest-treatment interaction problem associated with a number of the group designs.

INTERNAL VALIDITY

If proper controls are exercised in connection with the application of a single-subject design, the internal validity of the resulting study may be quite good.

Repeated and Reliable Measurement

In a time-series design, pretest performance is measured a number of times prior to implementation of the treatment. In single-subject designs similar multiple measures of pretest performance are referred to as baseline measures. By obtaining baseline measures over a period of time, sources of invalidity such as maturation are controlled in the same way that they are for the time-series design. However, unlike the time-series design, the single-subject design measures performance at various points in time while the treatment is being applied. This added dimension greatly reduces the potential threat to validity from history, a threat to internal validity in time-series design.

One very real threat to the internal validity of most single-subject designs is instrumentation, the unreliability or inconsistency of measuring instruments. Because repeated measurement is a characteristic of all single-subject designs, it is especially important that measurements of participants' performance be as consistent as possible. Every effort should be made to obtain observer reliability by clearly defining and measuring the dependent variable. Since single-subject designs often rely on some type of observed behavior as the dependent variable, it is critical that the observation conditions (e.g., location, time of day) be standardized. If a single observer makes all the observations, intraobserver reliability should be obtained. If more than one observer makes observations, interobserver reliability should be obtained. Measurement consistency is especially crucial when moving from phase to phase. If a change in measurement procedures occurs at the same time a new phase is begun, the result can be invalid assessment of the treatment effect.

Relatedly, the nature and conditions of the treatment should be specified in sufficient detail to permit replication. For example, an A–B–A–B design has a baseline phase, a treatment phase, a return to baseline conditions (withdrawal of the treatment), and a second treatment phase. If effects at each phase are to be validly assessed, the treatment must have the same procedures each time it is introduced. Also, since the key to the generalizability of single-subject designs is replication, it is clearly a necessity for the treatment to be sufficiently standardized so that other researchers can apply it as it was originally applied.

Baseline Stability

The length of the baseline and treatment phases can influence the internal validity of single-subject designs. A key question is, "How many measurements of behavior should be taken before treatment is introduced?" There is no single answer to this question. The purpose of the baseline measurements is to provide a description of the target behavior as it naturally occurs before the treatment is applied. The baseline serves as the comparison for determining the effectiveness of the treatment. If most behaviors were very stable, there would be no problem with the baseline phase. But human behavior is variable, often very variable. For example, if a student's disruptive behavior were being measured, we would not expect the student to exhibit exactly the same number of disruptive acts in each observation period. The student would likely be more disruptive at some times than at others. Fortunately, such fluctuations usually fall within some consistent range, permitting the researcher to establish a pattern or range of student baseline performance. We might observe, for example, that the child normally exhibits 5 to 10 disruptive behaviors during a 30-minute period. These figures then become our basis of comparison for assessing the effectiveness of the treatment. If during the treatment phase the number of disruptive behaviors ranges from, say, 0 to 3, or steadily decreases until it reaches 0, and if the number of disruptive behaviors increases when treatment is withdrawn, the effectiveness of the treatment is demonstrated.

The existence of a trend can affect the number of baseline data points needed. If the baseline behavior is observed to be getting progressively worse, fewer measurements are required to establish the baseline pattern. If, on the other hand, the baseline behavior is getting progressively better, there is no point in introducing the treatment until, or unless, the behavior stabilizes. Three data points are usually considered the minimum number of measurements necessary to establish baseline stability, but as noted, more than three are often required. Normally, the length of the treatment phase and the number of measurements taken during the treatment phase should parallel the length and measurements of the baseline phase. If baseline stability is established after 10 observation periods, then the treatment phase should include 10 observation periods.

The Single Variable Rule

An important principle of single-subject research is that only one variable at a time should be manipulated. In other words, as we move from phase to phase only one variable should be added or withdrawn at any phase. Sometimes an attempt is made to simultaneously manipulate two variables in order to assess their interactive effects. This is not sound practice in single-subject designs because it prevents us from assessing adequately the effects of either variable.

TYPES OF SINGLE-SUBJECT DESIGNS

Single-subject designs are classified into three major categories: A–B–A withdrawal, multiple-baseline, and alternating treatments designs. A–B–A designs involve alternating phases of baseline (A) and treatment (B). Multiple-baseline designs entail the systematic addition of behaviors, participants, or settings for intervention. They are utilized mainly for cases in which a baseline cannot be recovered once treatment is introduced, and for cases in which treatment cannot or should not be withdrawn once it is applied. Alternating treatment designs involves the relatively rapid alternating of treatments for a single subject. Its purpose is to assess the relative effectiveness of two (or more) treatment conditions. This section describes these basic designs and some common variations.

A–B–A Withdrawal Designs

There are a number of variations of the basic A–B–A withdrawal design, the least complex of which is the A–B design. Although this design is an improvement over the simple case-study approach, its internal validity is suspect. When this design is used, baseline measurements (*O*) are repeatedly made until stability is established. Then the treatment (*X*) is introduced and an appropriate number of measurements (*O*) are made during treatment implementation. If behavior improves during the treatment phase, the effectiveness of the treatment is allegedly demonstrated. The specific number of measurements involved in each phase will vary from experiment to experiment. We could symbolize this design as follows:

$$O \quad O \quad O \quad O \mid X \quad O \quad X \quad O \quad X \quad O \quad X \quad O$$

baseline phase   treatment phase
A   B

The problem with this design is that we don't know if behavior improved because of the treatment or because of some other nontreatment reason. It is possible that the observed behavior change occurred as a result of some other, unknown variable or that the behavior would have improved naturally without the treatment.

The A–B–A Design. By simply adding a second baseline phase to the A–B design we get a much improved design, the A–B–A design. If the behavior is better during the treatment phase than during either baseline phase, the effectiveness of the treatment has been demonstrated. Symbolically, we can represent this design in the following way:

$$O \quad O \quad O \quad O \quad X \quad O \quad X \quad O \quad X \quad O \quad X \quad O \quad O \quad O \quad O$$

baseline   treatment   baseline
phase   phase   phase
A   B   A

During the initial baseline phase we might observe on-task behaviors during five observation sessions. We might then introduce tangible reinforcement in the form of small toys for on-task behaviors and observe on-task behaviors during five observation periods in the treatment phase. Lastly, we might stop the tangible reinforcement and observe on-task behaviors during an additional five sessions. If on-task behavior was greater during the treatment phase, we would conclude that the tangible reinforcement was the probable cause.

FIGURE 11.6

Percentage of Attending Behavior of a Subject During Successive Observation Periods in a Study Utilizing an A–B–A Design

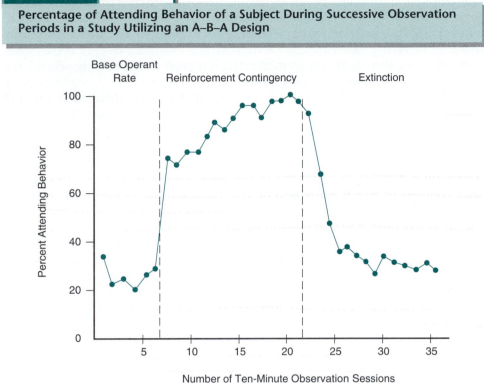

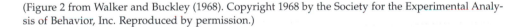

(Figure 2 from Walker and Buckley (1968). Copyright 1968 by the Society for the Experimental Analysis of Behavior, Inc. Reproduced by permission.)

The impact of positive reinforcement on the attending behavior of an easily distracted 9-year-old boy was studied using the A–B–A design.[5] A reinforcement program was developed for the student. Prior to actual data collection, observer training was conducted until interrater reliability was .90 or above for five randomly selected attending behavior observations of 10 minutes each. Figure 11.6 shows the three stages of the design: baseline, treatment, and baseline. Each dot represents a data collection point. The reinforcement program established for the student improves his attending behaviors a great deal compared to the initial baseline. When the treatment was removed, attending behavior decreased, demonstrating the effectiveness of the reinforcement program.

It should be noted that there is some terminology confusion in the literature concerning A–B–A designs. A–B–A withdrawal designs are frequently referred to as reversal designs, which they are not, since treatment is generally withdrawn following baseline assessment, not reversed. You should be alert to this distinction.

The internal validity of the A–B–A design is superior to that of the A–B design. With the A–B design it is possible that behaviors improved without treat-

[5]Walker, H. M. & Buckley, N. K. (1968). The use of positive reinforcement in conditioning attending behavior. *Journal of Applied Behavior Analysis, 1,* 245–250.

ment intervention. It is very unlikely, however, that behavior would coinciden-tally improve during the treatment phase and coincidentally deteriorate during the subsequent baseline phase, as is the case in A–B–A designs. The major prob-lem with this design is an ethical one, since the experiment ends with the partic-ipant not receiving the treatment. Of course if the treatment has not been shown to be effective, there is no problem. But if it has been found to be beneficial, the desirability of removing it is questionable.

A variation of the A–B–A design that eliminates this problem is the B–A–B design, which involves a treatment phase (B), a withdrawal phase (A), and a re-turn to treatment phase (B). Although this design provides an experiment that ends with the participant receiving treatment, the lack of an initial baseline phase makes it very difficult to assess the effectiveness of the treatment. Some studies have involved a short baseline phase prior to application of the B–A–B design, but this strategy only approximates a better solution, which is application of an A–B–A–B design.

The A-B-A-B Design. The A–B–A–B design is the A–B–A design with the ad-dition of a second treatment phase. Not only does this design overcome ethical objections to the A–B–A design, it also greatly strengthens the research conclu-sions by demonstrating the effects of the treatment twice. If treatment effects are essentially the same during both treatment phases, the possibility that the effects are a result of extraneous variables, is greatly reduced. The A–B–A–B design can be symbolized as:

$$O \ O \ O \ O \ X \ O \ X \ O \ X \ O \ X \ O \ O \ O \ O \ O \ X \ O \ X \ O \ X \ O \ X \ O$$

baseline phase A	treatment phase B	baseline phase A	treatment phase B

When application of this design is feasible, it provides very convincing evi-dence of treatment effectiveness.

Figure 11.7 shows a hypothetical example of the A–B–A–B design. The figure shows the summarized results of five days of observations in each of the four de-sign phases. Baseline A_1 shows the student's average talking out behavior for a five day period. Treatment B_1 shows the effect of a reinforcement program de-signed to diminish talking out behavior. The figure shows that talking out be-havior diminished greatly with the treatment. Baseline A_2 shows that removal of the treatment led to increased talking out behavior. The reintroduction of treat-ment B_2 again led to diminished talking out behavior. These patterns strongly suggest the efficacy of the treatment.

Multiple-Baseline Designs

Multiple-baseline designs are used when it is not possible to withdraw a treat-ment and have performance return to baseline. They are also used when a treat-ment can be withdrawn but the effects of the treatment "carry over" so that a re-turn to baseline conditions is difficult or impossible. The effects of many treatments do not disappear when a treatment is removed (see Figure 11.3, pat-tern C). In many cases it is highly desirable for treatment effects to sustain. Rein-forcement techniques, for example, are designed to produce improved behavior that will be maintained when external reinforcements are withdrawn.

Talking Out Behavior During Four 5-day Observations of a Student: Baseline 1, Treatment 1 (Reinforcement Program), Baseline 2 (No Treatment), and Treatment 2 (Reinforcement Program)

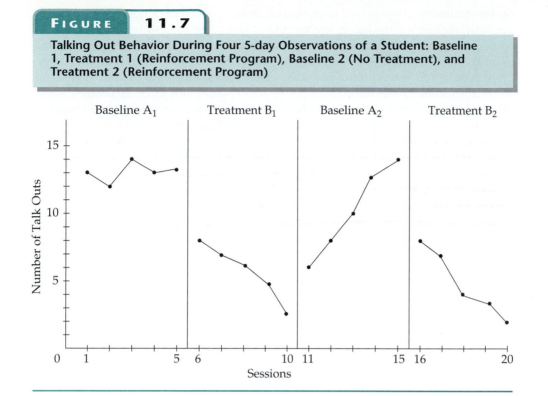

The three basic types of multiple-baseline designs are across behaviors, across participants, and across settings designs. With a multiple-baseline design, instead of collecting baseline data on one specific behavior, data are collected on (1) several behaviors for one participant, (2) one behavior for several participants, or (3) one behavior and one participant in several settings. Then, over a period of time, the treatment is systematically applied to each behavior (or participant, or setting) one at a time until all behaviors (or participants, or settings) are exposed to the treatment. The "multiple" part of a multiple-baseline designs refers to the study of more than one behavior, participant, or setting. For example, a study might seek to sequentially change three different behaviors using the multiple-baseline design. If measured performance improves only after a treatment is introduced, then that treatment is judged to be effective. There are, of course, variations that can be applied. We might, for example, collect data on one target behavior for several participants in several settings. In this case, performance for the group of participants in each setting would be summed or averaged, and results would be presented for the group as well as for each individual.

The multiple-baseline design can be symbolized as:

behavior 1   *O   O   OXOXOXOXOXOXOXOXOXOXOXOXO*
behavior 2   *O   O   O   O   O   OXOXOXOXOXOXOXOXOXO*
behavior 3   *O   O   O   O   O   O   O   O   OXOXOXOXOXOXO*

In this example, a treatment was applied to three different behaviors, behavior 1 first, then behavior 2, and then behavior 3 until all three behaviors were under treatment. If measured performance improved for each behavior only after the treatment was introduced, the treatment would be judged to be effective. We could symbolize examination of different participants or settings in the same manner. In all cases, the more behaviors, participants, or settings involved, the more convincing the evidence is for the effectiveness of the treatment. What constitutes a sufficient minimum number of replications, however, is another issue. While some investigators believe that four or more are necessary, three replications are generally accepted to be an adequate minimum.

When applying treatments across behaviors, it is important that the behaviors be independent of one another. If we apply treatment to behavior 1, behaviors 2 and 3 should remain at baseline levels. If the other behaviors change when behavior 1 is treated, the design is not valid for assessing treatment effectiveness. When applying treatment across participants, they should be as similar as possible (matched on key variables such as age and gender), and the experimental setting should be as identical as possible for each participant. When applying treatment across settings, it is preferable that the settings be natural, not artificial. We might, for example, systematically apply a treatment (e.g., tangible reinforcement) to successive class periods. Or we might apply the treatment first in a clinical setting, then at school, and then at home. Sometimes it is necessary, due to the nature of the target behavior, to evaluate the treatment in a contrived, or simulation, setting. The target behavior may be an important one, but one that does not often occur naturally. For example, if we are teaching a child who is mentally challenged how to behave in various emergency situations (e.g., fires, injuries, intruders) simulated settings may be the only feasible approach.

Figure 11.8 shows a study using a hypothetical multiple-baseline design. The treatment, a program for improving social awareness, was applied to three behaviors: (1) social behaviors, (2) seeking help, and (3) handling criticism. Figure 11.8 shows that performance increased for each of the three behaviors after each treatment, thus indicating that the treatment was effective.

Although multiple-baseline designs are generally used when there is a problem with returning to baseline conditions, they can be used very effectively for situations in which baseline conditions are recoverable. We could, for example, target talking-out behavior, out-of-seat behavior, and aggressive behavior, which over time could return to baseline conditions. If we applied an A–B–A design within a multiple-baseline framework, the result could be symbolized as:

talking-out behavior	A–B–A–A–A
out-of-seat behavior	A–A–B–A–A
aggressive behavior	A–A–A–B–A

OR

talking-out behavior	O O OXOXOXO O O O O O O O O O
out-of-seat behavior	O O O O O OXOXOXO O O O O O
aggressive behavior	O O O O O O O O OXOXOXO O O O

Such a design would combine the best features of the A–B–A and the multiple-baseline design and would provide convincing evidence regarding treatment effects. In essence it would represent three replications of an A–B–A experiment. Whenever baseline is recoverable and there are no carryover effects, any of the A–B–A designs can be applied within a multiple-baseline framework.

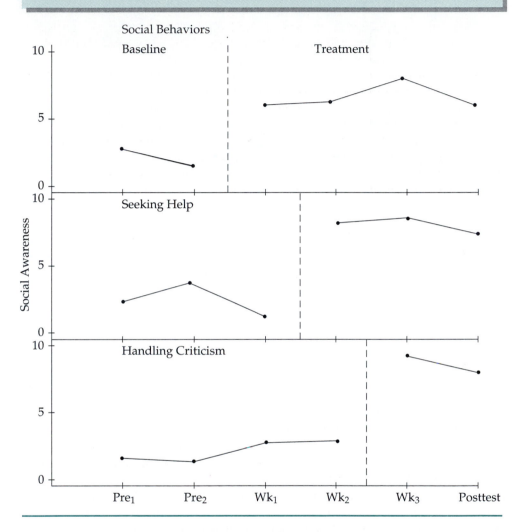

FIGURE 11.8

Multiple-Baseline Analysis of Social Awareness Training on a Student's Social Behaviors, Seeking Help, and Handling Criticism

Alternating Treatments Design

The alternating treatments design is useful in assessing the relative effectiveness of two (or more) treatments, in a single-subject context. Although the alternating treatments design has many names (multiple schedule design, multielement baseline design, multielement manipulation design, and simultaneous treatment design), there is some consensus that "alternating treatments" most accurately describes the nature of the design. The name of the design describes what it involves; namely, the relatively rapid alternation of treatments for a single subject. The qualifier *relatively* is attached to *rapid* because alternation does not necessarily occur within fixed intervals of time. If a child with behavior problems saw a therapist who used an alternating treatment design every Tuesday, the design would require that on some Tuesdays the child would receive one treatment (e.g.,

FIGURE 11.9

Hypothetical Example of an Alternating Treatments Design Comparing Treatments T_1 and T_2

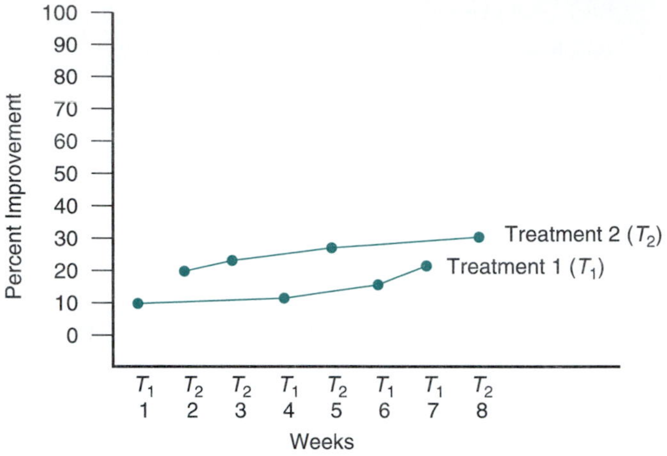

(Figure 8-1, p. 254, from Barlow and Hersen (1992). Copyright 1992 by Allyn & Bacon. Reproduced by permission.)

verbal reinforcement), and on other Tuesdays another treatment (e.g., tangible reinforcement). The treatments (call them as T_1 and T_2) would not be alternated in a regular, ordered pattern (T_1–T_2–T_1–T_2). Rather, to avoid potential validity threats, the treatments would be alternated on a random basis, e.g., T_1–T_2–T_2–T_1–T_2–T_1–T_1–T_2. Figure 11.9 illustrates this random application of two treatments. In this example, treatment T_2 appears to be more effective for this participant than T_1, since the data points are consistently higher for treatment T_2 than for T_1. To determine whether T_2 would be more effective for other participants would require replication.

This design has several pluses that make it attractive to investigators. First, no withdrawal is necessary; thus, if one treatment is found to be more effective, it may be continued. Second, no baseline phase is necessary, because we are usually attempting to determine which treatment is more effective, not whether a treatment is better than no treatment. Another major advantage is that a number of treatments can be studied more quickly and efficiently than with other designs. However, one potential problem with this design is multiple-treatment interference—that is, carryover effects from one treatment to the other.

DATA ANALYSIS AND INTERPRETATION

Data analysis in single-subject research typically is based on visual inspection and analysis of a graphic presentations of results. First, an evaluation is made concerning the adequacy of the design. Second, assuming a sufficiently valid design, an assessment of treatment effectiveness is made. The primary criterion of effectiveness is typically clinical significance, not statistical significance. Clinical effects that are small may not be large enough to make a sufficient difference in the behavior of a participant. As an example, suppose the participant is an 8-year-old male who exhibits dangerous, aggressive behavior toward other children. A treatment that produced a 5% reduction in such behavior may be statistically significant, but it is clearly not clinically significant. There are a number of statistical analyses available to the single-subject researcher, including t and F tests (to be discussed in chapter 13). Whether statistical tests should be used in single-subject research is currently debated. To date, they have not been widely used in single-subject.

REPLICATION

Replication is a vital part of all research and especially for single-subject research, since initial findings are generally based on one or a few participants. The more results are replicated, the more confidence we have in the procedures that produced those results. This is true for all types of research. Replication also serves to establish the generalizability of findings by providing data about the participants' behaviors, and settings to which results are applicable. There are three basic types of replication of single-subject experiments: direct, systematic, and clinical. Direct replication refers to replication by the same investigator, with the same or different participants, in a specific setting (e.g., a classroom). Generalizability is promoted when replication is done with other participants who share the same problem, matched closely on relevant variables. When replication is done on a number of participants with the same problem, location, or time, the process is referred to as simultaneous replication. Systematic replication refers to replication that follows direct replication, and which involves different investigators, behaviors, or settings. Over an extended period of time, techniques are identified that are consistently effective in a variety of situations. We know, for example, that teacher attention can be a powerful factor in behavior change. At some point, enough data is amassed to permit the third stage of replication, clinical replication. Clinical replication involves the development of treatment packages, composed of two or more interventions that have been found to be effective individually, designed for persons with complex behavior disorders. Individuals with autism, for example, exhibit a number of characteristics, including apparent sensory deficit, mutism, and self-injurious behavior. Clinical replication would utilize research on each of these individually to develop a total program to apply to individuals with autism. Regardless of the type, replication is critically important in establishing the generalizability of single-subject research.

The following pages present an example of experimental research. See if you can figure out which experimental design was used. *Hint:* Students were randomly assigned to one of three treatment groups. Also, don't be concerned because you don't understand the statistics; focus on the problem, the procedures, and the conclusions.

Effects of Word Processing on Sixth Graders' Holistic Writing and Revisions

GAIL F. GREJDA
Clarion University of Pennsylvania

MICHAEL J. HANNAFIN
Florida State University

ABSTRACT   The purpose of this study was to examine the effects of word processing on overall writing quality and revision patterns of sixth graders. Participants included 66 students who were randomly assigned to one of three revision treatments: paper and pencil, word processing, and a combination of the two techniques. Training in word processing was provided, and instruction was subsequently given during the 3-week study. The students were given a standard composition to revise and were also required to write and revise an original composition. Significant differences were found for both mechanical and organizational revisions in favor of the word-processing group. In addition, word-processing students tended to correct more first-draft errors and to make fewer new errors than their counterparts did. Although a similar pattern was found, no significant differences were discovered for holistic writing quality.

Interest in the potential of word processors to improve writing has grown substantially during the past decade. Various authorities have lauded the capability to increase writer productivity (Zaharias, 1983), to reduce the tediousness of recopying written work (Bean, 1983; Daiute, 1983; Moran, 1983, to increase the frequency of revising (Bridwell, Sirc, & Brooke, 1985; Daiute, 1986), and to improve both attitudes toward writing (Rodriguez, 1985) and the writing process (McKenzie, 1984; Olds, 1982). Some researchers have argued that word processors alter both individuals' writing styles and the methods used to teach writing (Bertram, Michaels, & Watson-Geges, 1985).

Yet, research findings on the effects of word processing have proved inconsistent (Fitzgerald, 1987). Some researchers have reported positive effects on writing (Daiute, 1985), whereas others have reported mixed effects (Wheeler, 1985). Although word processing seems to increase the frequency of revision, the revisions are often surface level and do little to improve the overall quality of composition (Collier, 1983; Hawisher, 1987). In some cases, word processing has actually hampered different aspects of writing (Grejda & Hannafin, in press; Perl, 1978).

However, comparatively little has been demonstrated conclusively. Attempts to study word processing have been confounded by both typing requirements and limited word-processing proficiency. Inadequate definition has also plagued word-processing research. Many studies have isolated only mechanical attributes of revision, such as punctuation, requiring only proofreading rather than sophisticated revision skills (Collier, 1983; Dalton & Hannafin, 1987). Other research has focused only on global writing measures, with little attribution possible for observed changes in writing quality (Boone, 1985; Woodruff, Bereiter, & Scardamalia, 1981-82). Both mechanical and holistic aspects of writing are important, but they are rarely considered concurrently (cf. Humes, 1983).

Although comparatively few studies have focused on young writers, the results have been encouraging. Daiute (1986) reported that junior high school students using word processors were more likely to expand their compositions, as well as to identify and correct existing errors, than were paper-and-pencil students. Likewise, word-processing students were more likely than paper-and-pencil students were to revise their language-experience stories (Barber, 1984; Bradley, 1982). Boone (1985) reported that the compositions of fourth, fifth, and sixth graders became increasingly sophisticated through revisions focusing on both mechanics and higher level organizations. In contrast, despite improving students' attitudes, word processing has failed to improve overall compositions based upon holistic ratings of writing quality (Woodruff, Bereiter, & Scardamalia, 1981-82).

The purpose of this study was to examine the effects of word processing on the holistic writing quality and revision patterns of sixth graders. We predicted that word processing would improve both the accuracy of revisions as well as the overall holistic quality of student writing.

Address correspondence to Gail F. Grejda, Education Department, 110 Stevens Hall, Clarion University of Pennsylvania, Clarion, PA 16214.

Grejda, G. F., & Hannafin, M. J. (1992). Effects of word processing on sixth graders' holistic writing and revisions. *The Journal of Educational Research, 85,* 144–149. Reprinted with the permission of the Helen Dwight Reid Educational Foundation. Published by Heldref Publications, 1319 Eighteenth St., N. W., Washington, DC 20036-1802, Copyright © 1992.

January/February 1992 [Vol. 85(No. 3)]

Methods

Subjects

The subjects included 66 sixth graders (23 girls and 43 boys), and 3 classroom teachers. The students were enrolled in a school in a rural university community. Overall language achievement of the participating students, based upon the Language Scale of the Stanford Achievement Test, was at the 79th percentile.

Preliminary Training

Prior to the study, the sixth-grade teachers and the students in word-processing groups received 1 hour of word-processing training during each of 5 days. The *Bank Street Writer* was used because of its widespread availability and popularity among elementary school teachers. The training included entering text, deleting and inserting characters, capitalizing letters, moving the cursor, centering, indenting, making corrections, moving and returning blocks of text, erasing and unerasing, saving, retrieving, and printing. In addition, the purpose and design of the study, as well as procedural information and materials required, were presented.

Revision Instruction

An hour of daily instruction on mechanical and organizational revisions was provided for 10 days of the 3-week study. The instruction reviewed previously taught revision rules commonly found in sixth-grade language books and focused on errors typical of those in the compositions of young writers.

The first 5 days included instruction on five mechanical error categories: capitalization, commas, punctuation, possessive nouns, and sentence structure. Daily lessons included rules for the error category under consideration, pertinent examples of each rule, and a paragraph containing numerous violations of the rules that were subsequently identified and revised by the students. During the next 5 days, the subjects focused on revising the following organizational errors, phrasing the main idea, adding relevant detail sentences, deleting irrelevant sentences, sequencing or ordering sentences, and, finally, applying the rhetorical devices vital to paragraph unity and coherence.

Original Writing Sample

All the students were allotted 60 min to write an original composition on a given topic. The task was to describe a planned trip itinerary to Canada, a topic based on a recently completed unit of study. The writing sample was obtained to provide a unique composition for each student, and it was subsequently used to identify and to make needed revisions in individual writing. All the students used paper and pencil to create the initial compositions.

Standard Composition

A standard composition was developed to determine each student's ability to identify and revise typical mechanical and organizational errors. The writing yielded a common metric from which revision comparisons could be made across students. The composition contained 57 mechanical errors and eight organizational writing errors. The errors, violations of rules found in typical sixth-grade language books, required the application of rules stressed during the daily lessons.

Instructional Groups

The students were assigned to one of three groups, depending on how revisions were made: exclusively with computer word processing (C-C); exclusively with paper and pencil (P-P); or a combination of the two techniques (C-P). All the treatment groups received identical revision instruction.

In the C-C group, the students used word-processing software during all phases of the study. That gorup examined the influence of continuous access to word processing on student editing, revising, and writing quality. The students in the P-P treatment group used paper and pencil to make all revisions on both compositions throughout the 10 days of instruction. That group approximated writing without the aid of the word processor. In the C-P treatment, the students used a word processor to revise the 10 daily lessons and paper and pencil to revise the compositions. That method examined the potential transfer of word-processing skills to non-computer writing and approximated the circumstances encountered when word processors were provided for some, but not all, of a student's writing needs.

Design and Data Analysis

In this study we used a one-way design, featuring three word-processing groups: pencil-pencil (P-P), computer-computer (C-C), and computer-pencil (C-P). Individual scores on the Stanford Achievement Test–Language Scale were used as a covariate in the analysis to adjust for potential prestudy writing differences. In addition, because of the relatively high prior achievement in the sample (only 4 students scored below the 50th percentile on the language scale) and the high correlation between writing and general language, the use of the standardized test scores as a covariate in the analysis permitted greater precision in isolating true treatment effects. The highly significant effect for the covariate, paired with the nonsignificant preliminary test for homogeneity of slopes, further supported the analysis.

A one-way multivariate analysis of covariance (MANCOVA), with the four composition subscale scores and the holistic writing rating, was run to test for treatment group effects. Analysis of covariance (ANCOVA) proce-

Journal of Educational Research

dures were subsequently executed for each measure: a priori contrasts were constructed to test for differences between the C-C group and each of the other word-processing groups. The remaining scores were used to provide descriptive data related to revision strategies.

Procedures

Regularly assigned sixth-grade classroom teachers were presented an overview of the purpose and design of the study, procedural information, and required materials. The students were randomly assigned to one of the three treatment groups. The students and teachers in both word-processing groups (C-C and C-P) were then given word-processing training.

The students in each group were allotted 60 min to write their original composition. All students wrote the preliminary composition with pencil and paper. The compositions of students in the C-C group were subsequently entered electronically by a typist, because those students were required to revise the writing via word processing.

Next, instruction on revising mechanical and organizational writing error categories was provided. Each lesson included rules for the error category under consideration, pertinent examples of each rule, and a paragraph containing violations of the rules to be identified and revised by the students. After discussing the rules and examples of applications, the students revised the given paragraph, using their designated writing instrument. Upon completion, the students were given an errorless copy of the paragraph and were instructed to correct any existing errors. On subsequent days the subjects followed the same format, each day focusing on another of the mechanical and organizational error categories. During the study, the first author scheduled regular conferences with the classroom teachers to ensure compliance with current instruction topics as well as to preview upcoming lessons. In addition, the first author randomly rotated among the classes to ensure that planned activities were implemented as scheduled.

After the 10 daily lessons were completed, the students revised both the standard composition and the original composition. On the standard composition, students were allotted 60 min to revise mechanical errors in capitalization, punctuation, commas, possessive nouns, sentence structure, and organizational errors, including rephrasing the main idea, adding relevant detail sentences, deleting irrelevant sentences, sequencing sentences, and applying rhetorical devices vital to paragraph unity and coherence. None of the mechanical or organizational errors were cued in any way. The score for each measure was a percentage of the number of correct revisions to the total possible errors (57 mechanical, 8 organizational) on the standard composition.

The students were also provided 60 min to revise the mechanical and organizational errors on their original composition. The number of possible errors varied in each student's composition, so percentage correction scores were derived to account for differences in the number of mechanical and organizational errors. The score was a percentage of the correct revisions versus the total number of initial mechanical and organizational errors on the students' original composition.

Each original composition was then evaluated holistically for overall writing quality based on the procedures developed by Myers (1980) and Potkewitz (1984). Three trained composition instructors, experienced in both process writing and holistic scoring, served as raters; none of them were participants in the study. Each composition was evaluated "blind" by at least two of the raters by comparing the works to a rubric consisting of six competency levels ranging from lowest (1) to highest (6). If the two ratings were within one point of one another, the ratings were summed to yield a total rating score. If discrepancies of greater than one point were found, the third evaluator rated the composition independently, and the most discrepant rating of the three was discarded. Interrater agreement, based upon the percentage of rating pairs identical or within one point of one another, was .91. Discrepancies of more than one point in the initial ratings occurred on only 6 of the 66 compositions.

The students inadvertently introduced additional errors in their revisions, so new errors in the final compositions were also tallied. New errors, mechanical as well as organizational, were computed beyond those provided in the standard composition or generated by the students in the original composition. The errors were tallied according to the same criteria established for mistakes in the standard and original compositions.

Finally, revisions on both the standard and original compositions were classified to examine the nature of editorial revisions made by different writing groups. The instructors tallied word insertions and deletions, sentence insertions and deletions, sentences moved, sentence fragments and run-on sentences inserted, and sentence fragments or run-on sentences corrected.

All compositions were typed, printed, coded, and randomized to prevent rater bias. In addition, that step allowed the students to work with comparably "clean" copies, and equalized the time spent revising versus recopying: To isolate specific revision skills without the confounding of either excessive typing or manual recopying, we provided the students with typed versions of their work.

Results

The means for each of the subscales, adjusted for the influence of the covariate, are contained in Table 1. The one-way MANCOVA revealed a significant difference among word-processing groups, $F(2, 62) = 9.28$, $p < .001$. ANCOVA results, shown in Table 2, revealed a sig-

January/February 1992 [Vol. 85(No. 3)]

Table 1.—Adjusted Percentage Means for Composition Subscales

Source	C-C	C-P	P-P
Standard composition			
Mechanical revisions	74.86	68.59	68.23
Organizational revisions	81.14	58.82	66.18
Original composition			
Mechanical revisions	57.32	42.91	45.00
Organizational revisions	63.64	48.55	42.73

Table 2.—ANCOVA Source Data for Composition Subscales

Source	df	M	F	$p<$
Standard composition				
Mechanical revisions				
Covariate (prior achievement)	1	7,915.55	76.11	.0001
Writing group	2	459.58	4.42	.016
Error	62	104.00		
Organizational revisions				
Covariate (prior achievement)	1	8,463.83	13.62	.0001
Writing group	2	3,353.83	5.40	.007
Error	62	621.48		
Original composition				
Mechanical revisions				
Covariate (prior achievement)	1	5,156.74	6.27	.015
Writing group	2	1,590.89	1.93	nsd
Error	62	822.93		
Organizational revisions				
Covariate (prior achievement)	1	5,027.33	7.69	.007
Writing group	2	2,818.37	4.31	.018
Error	62	653.86		

nificant difference among treatment groups for all scales except for the mechanical revisions on the original composition. A priori contrasts for each significant difference indicated that the C-C students corrected a higher percentage of mechanical and organizational errors than the C-P or P-P groups did, on both the standard and original compositions (min. $p < .05$ in each case). No differences were found between the C-P and P-P groups for any of the subscales. In addition, although not statistically significant, the performance pattern for the mechanical revisions on original compositions was similar to the other subscales, with the C-C group performing best.

A profile of revision errors is shown in Table 3. The C-C word-processing group made fewer new mechanical and organizational errors than the other groups on both the standard and the original compositions. The C-C students also made fewer new errors on their own compositions. Paper-and-pencil and mixed-writing groups cor-

rected a comparable percentage of organizational errors on both compositions.

Revision patterns, summarized in Table 4, suggest different strategies among the three groups. On the original composition, word-processing students inserted more words and sentences, moved more sentences, and corrected more sentence fragments or run-on sentences than did students in the remaining groups. On the standard composition, word-processing students were more likely to insert words and move sentences, but less likely to delete words, than their counterparts.

Students in all groups revised the standard composition more effectively than their original compositions; that was true for both mechanical and organizational revisions. Comparatively few new mechanical and organization errors were made by the word-processing students, whereas new errors were substantially more common for the other writing groups.

Although adjusted means for holistic ratings fell in the predicted direction, there were only marginal differences in

Table 3.—Frequency of New Errors Introduced During Final Revision

Revision type	C-C	C-P	P-P
Original			
Mechanical	12	20	39
Organizational	2	45	56
Standard			
Mechanical	0	7	12
Organizational	5	38	43

Table 4.—Revision Types for Original and Standard Compositions

Revision activity	C-C	C-P	P-P
Original composition			
Words inserted	167	52	31
Words deleted	13	9	17
Sentences inserted	121	47	64
Sentences deleted	9	14	3
Sentences moved	27	3	0
Sentence fragments/run-on sentences inserted	2	19	13
Sentence fragments/run-on sentences corrected	26	12	18
Standard composition			
Words inserted	9	0	0
Words deleted	0	15	23
Sentences inserted	0	1	0
Sentences deleted	59	43	38
Sentences moved	31	3	0
Sentence fragments/run-on sentences inserted	0	4	5
Sentence fragments/run-on sentences corrected	37	29	23

Journal of Educational Research

overall writing quality, $F(2, 62) = 2.31$, $p > .107$. Computer word-processing students (6.36) and the mixed-treatment group (6.27) were marginally higher than the paper-and-pencil group (5.00).

Discussion

Several findings warrant further discussion. Consistent with much research on revising (Bridwell, Sirc, & Brooke, 1985; Daiute, 1986), word-processing students performed consistently better than other students did. Those students were more successful in revising existing as well as original writing, and they made more revisions to their work. In the present study, face evidence for improving editing via word processing is strong.

Yet, consistent with other researchers (Collier, 1983; Hawisher, 1987), overall quality did not improve significantly. Though word-processing groups performed marginally better than the paper-and-pencil group did, reliable differences were not detected. Despite strong evidence that mechanical and organizational revisions improved significantly, holistic writing quality was only marginally affected. Overall quality improvements may require substantially more time to develop (Riel, 1984). Word processing may, in the absence of concerted efforts to offset the tendency, inadvertently direct proportionately more attention to structural than holistic aspects of writing. Structural skills are important and yield the most visible features of composition, but they do not, by themselves, ensure improvement in the holistic quality of compositions (Flower & Hayes, 1981).

Editing is a necessary, but not sufficient, skill for effective writing (cf. Hodges, 1982; Sommers, 1980). The conceptual aspects of holistic writing, although not diminished in our study by word processing, require more than simple mechanical and even organizational changes in written products (Hairston, 1986; Humes, 1983; Kintsch & van Dijk, 1978). Yet, word processors seem to bias students toward mechanical editing. A spelling or capitalization error is substantially more apparent than an error of logic, argumentation, or internal inconsistency. Process-writing advocates promote recursive methods in the teaching of writing—methods designed to promote writer-level problem solving in their expression. Though such goals are likely attainable and supportable through well-constructed writing-via-word-processing efforts, they are less likely to be supported directly in typical word-processing software. Mechanical improvements may be necessary to overall quality, but they are clearly insufficient when emphasized exclusively.

Contrary to the findings of some researchers (Bartlett, 1982), more revisions were made and a higher proportion of initial errors were detected on the standard composition than on the original composition. That finding is not surprising because the standard composition was essentially an editing task. On the other hand, the students were more likely to embellish their own compositions by inserting words and sentences. In this study, in which we used both types of composition, different revision patterns clearly emerged for student- versus instructor-generated compositions.

In contrast to the findings of others, the students in this study focused principally on in-text revisions, and they made few new additions during revisions. Daiute (1986) noted that word-processing students appended words to their text rather than making corrections within the text. In this study, however, word-processing students made both mechanical and organizational revisions throughout the text. They also corrected more first-draft errors and made fewer new errors than did students in the other treatment groups. The emphasis on identifying and revising in-text errors rather than on adding new text during the instructional phase of the study might account for that difference.

Various authorities have expressed concern that providing writing instruction exclusively via word processors may ultimately interfere with conventional writing (Keifer & Smith, 1983). The rationale has been that students develop writing strategies that are dependent upon technological capabilities of limited accessibility. The combined word-processing and paper-and-pencil group was designed to test the transfer of revision skills developed via word processing to traditional writing tools. Consistent with previous research (Grejda & Hannafin, in press), intermittent word processing neither improved nor impeded transfer to paper-and-pencil formats.

Several other aspects of the present study are noteworthy. The initial training provided to both students and teachers, paired with control of supporting instruction, permitted increased precision in localizing those effects reasonably attributable to word processing. The short-term effects of word processing appear most pronounced for structural revisions; the long-term effects on both structural and holistic aspects remain unproved. Likewise, examining revision skills on both standard and student-generated compositions allowed us to focus on both specific editing and the constructive aspects of process writing.

Considerable work is needed to refine both research methods and instructional practices. Keyboarding, although not a major issue in our study, remains a concern. Young students can be trained nominally, but few of them actually develop proficiency. Daiute (1983) suggested that sustained word-processing training, for as much as 1 year, may be needed before sufficient technical proficiency is acquired to improve writing. In addition, the potential antagonism between the structural versus holistic approaches to word processing is troublesome. Methods designed to optimize both are needed, but the present findings suggest that one often benefits at the expense of the other.

January/February 1992 [Vol. 85(No. 3)]

From a research perspective, we have not generated clear-cut answers but, rather, clarifications regarding the relevant questions and needed methods of study. Neither writing nor the tools available to improve writing are likely to be advanced appreciably through studies that simplify complex processes artificially or control everyday factors unrealistically. From an academic perspective, educators must temper the enthusiasm for technologies and tools of such high-face validity with the sobering reality that a word processor "does not a writer make."

REFERENCES

Barber, B. (1984). Creating Bytes of language. *Language Arts, 59,* 472–475.

Bartlett, E. J. (1982). Learning to revise. In M. Nystrand (Ed.), *What writers know* (pp. 345–363). New York: Academic Press.

Bean, H. C. (1983). Computerized word processing as an aid to revision. *College Composition and Communication, 34,* 146–148.

Bertram, B., Michaels, S., & Watson-Geges, K. (1985). How computers can change the writing process. *Language Arts, 2,* 143–149.

Boone, R. A. (1985). *The revision processes of elementary school students who write using a word processing computer program.* Unpublished doctoral dissertation. University of Oregon, Eugene, OR.

Bradley, V. (1982). Improving students' writing with microcomputers. *Language Arts, 59,* 732–743.

Bridwell, L., Sirc, G., & Brooke, R. (1985). Revising and computing: Case studies of student writers. In S. W. Fredman (Ed.), *The acquisition of written language: Response and revision* (pp. 172–194). Norwood, NJ: Ablex.

Collier, R. M. (1983). The word processor and revison strategies. *College Composition and Communication, 34,* 149–155.

Daiute, C. (1983). The computer as stylus and audience. *College Composition and Communication, 34,* 134–145.

Daiute, C. (1985). *Writing and computers.* Reading, MA: Addison-Wesley.

Daiute, C. (1986). Physical and cognitive factors in revising: Insights from studies with computers. *Research in the Teaching of English, 20,* 141–159.

Dalton, D., & Hannafin, M. J. (1987). The effects of word processing on written composition. *Journal of Educational Research, 80,* 338–342.

Fitzgerald, J. (1987). Research on revision in writing. *Review of Educational Research, 57(4),* 481–506.

Flower, L., & Hayes, J. (1981). A cognitive process theory of writing. *College Composition and Communication, 32,* 365–387.

Grejda, G. F., & Hannafin, M. J. (in press). The influence of word processing on the revisions of fifth graders. *Computers in the Schools.*

Hairston, M. (1986). *Different products, different processes: A theory about writing. College Composition and Communication, 37,* 12.

Hawisher, G. (1987). The effects of word processing on the revision strategies of college freshmen. *Research in the Teaching of English, 21,* 145–159.

Hodges, K. (1982). A history of revision: Theory versus practice. In R. Sudol (Ed.), *Revising: New essays for teachers of writing* (pp. 24–42). Urbana, IL: National Council of Teachers of English.

Humes, A. (1983). Research on the composing process. *Review of Educational Research, 53,* 201–216.

Keifer, K., & Smith, C. (1983). Textual analysis with computers: Tests of Bell Laboratories' computer software. *Research in the Teaching of English, 17,* 201–214.

Kintsch, W., & van Dijk, T. (1978). Toward a model of text comprehension and production. *Psychological Review, 85,* 363–394.

McKenzie, J. (1984). Accordion writing: Expository composition with the word processor. *English Journal, 73,* 56–58.

Moran, C. (1983). Word processing and the teaching of writing. *English Journal, 72,* 113–115.

Myers, M. (1980). *A procedure for writing assessment and holistic scoring.* Urbana, IL: National Council of Teachers of English.

Olds, H. (1982). Word processing: How will it shape the student as writer? *Classroom Computer News, 3,* 24–26.

Perl, S. (1979). The composing process of unskilled college writers. *Research in the Teaching of English, 13,* 317–336.

Potkewitz, R. (1984). *The effect of writing instruction on the written language proficiency of fifth and sixth grade pupils in remedial reading programs.* Unpublished doctoral dissertation.

Riel, M. M. (1984). *The computer chronicles newswire: A functional learning environment for acquiring skills.* Paper developed for Laboratory of Comparative Human Cognition, San Diego, CA.

Rodrigues, D. (1985). Computers and basic writers. *College Composition and Communication, 36,* 336–339.

Sommers, N. (1980). Revision strategies of student writers and experienced adult writers. *College Composition and Communication, 31,* 378–388.

Wheeler, F. (1985). "Can word processing help the writing process?" *Learning, 3,* 54–62.

Woodruff, E., Bereiter, C., & Scardamalia, M. (1981–82). On the road to computer-assisted composition. *Journal of Educational Technology Systems, 10,* 133–148.

Zaharias, J. (1983). Microcomputers in the language arts classroom: Promises and pitfalls. *Language Arts, 60,* 990–995.

Summary/Chapter 11

Experimental Research: Definition and Purpose

manipulates
≥ 1 ind. V
controls other
observes the effect on
≥ 1 dep V

1. In an experimental study, the researcher manipulates at least one independent variable, controls other relevant variables, and observes the effect on one or more dependent variables.

2. The independent variable, also called the experimental variable, the cause, or the treatment, is that process or activity believed to make a difference in performance. The dependent variable, also called the criterion variable, effect, or posttest, is the outcome of the study, the measure of the change or difference resulting from manipulation of the independent variable.

3. Well conducted, experimental studies produce the soundest evidence concerning hypothesized cause–effect relationships.

THE EXPERIMENTAL PROCESS

4. The steps in an experimental study are basically the same as for other types of research: selection and definition of a problem, selection of participants and measuring instruments, selection of a design, execution of procedures, analysis of data, and formulation of conclusions.

5. An experimental study is guided by at least one hypothesis that states an expected causal relationship between two treatment variables.

6. In an experimental study, the researcher forms or selects the groups, decides what treatments each group receives, controls extraneous variables, and observes or measures the effect on the groups at the end of the study.

7. The experimental group typically receives a new, or novel, treatment, while the control group either receives a different treatment or is treated as usual.

8. The two groups that are to receive different treatments are equated on all other variables that might be related to performance on the dependent variable.

9. After the groups have been exposed to the treatment for some period, the researcher administers the dependent variable and then determines whether there is a significant difference between the groups.

MANIPULATION AND CONTROL

10. Direct manipulation by the researcher of at least one independent variable is the one single characteristic that differentiates experimental research from other types of research.

11. The three different forms of the independent variable are presence versus absence (A versus no A), presence in varying degrees (a lot of A versus a little A), and presence of one kind versus presence of another kind (A versus B).
A vs no A
A vs B
alot A vs little A

12. Control refers to efforts to remove the influence of any variable (other than the independent variable) that might affect performance on the dependent variable.

13. Two different kinds of variables need to be controlled, participant variables, on which participants in the different groups might differ, and environmental variables, which might cause unwanted differences between groups.

Threats to Experimental Validity — *Internal & External*

14. Any uncontrolled extraneous variables that affect performance on the dependent variable are threats to the validity of an experiment. An experiment is valid if results obtained are due only to the manipulated independent variable, and if they are generalizable to situations outside of the experimental setting.

15. Internal validity is concerned with ensuring that observed differences on the dependent variable are a direct result of manipulation of the independent variable, not some other variable. External validity is concerned with ensuring that results are generalizable to

groups and environments outside of the experimental setting.

16. The researcher must strive for a balance between control and realism, but if a choice is involved, the researcher should err on the side of control.

Pretest-treatment Interaction

THREATS TO INTERNAL VALIDITY

↗ post-test sensitizing

istory

17. History refers to the occurrence of an event that is not part of the experimental treatment but that may affect performance on the dependent variable.

aturation

18. Maturation refers to physical or mental changes that may occur within the participants over a period of time. These changes may affect the participants' performance on the measure of the dependent variable.

multiple-treat interference

* sting*

19. Testing refers to improved scores on a posttest resulting from participants having taken a pretest.

✓ selection-treatment interact

nstrument

20. Instrumentation refers to unreliability, or lack of consistency, in measuring instruments that may result in invalid assessment of performance.

specificity

atistical Regression

21. Statistical regression usually occurs when participants are selected on the basis of their extreme scores and refers to the tendency of participants who score highest on a pretest to score lower on a posttest, and of those who score lowest on a pretest to score higher on a posttest.

ifferential Selection

22. Differential selection usually occurs when already-formed groups are used and refers to the fact that the groups may be different before the study begins, and this initial difference influences posttest differences.

ortality

Experimenter Effects

23. Mortality, or attrition, refers to the fact that participants who drop out of a study may alter the characteristics of the treatment groups.

24. Selection may also interact with factors such as maturation, history, and testing. This means that if already-formed groups are used, one group may profit more (or less) from a treatment or have an initial advantage (or disadvantage) because of maturation, history, or testing factors.

Reactive Arrangements

1. Hawthorne
2. John Henry
3. Novelty

THREATS TO EXTERNAL VALIDITY

25. Threats affecting to whom research results can be generalized are called threats to external validity.

if sample given pretest, population must

26. Pretest–treatment interaction occurs when participants respond or react differently to a treatment because they have been pretested.

27. Posttest sensitization refers to the possibility that treatment effects may be affected by giving a pretest. The pretest may provide information that influences the posttest results.

28. Multiple-treatment interference can occur when the same participants receive more than one treatment in succession and when the carryover effects from an earlier treatment influence a later treatment.

29. Selection–treatment interaction occurs when participants are not randomly selected for treatments. Interaction effects aside, the very fact that participants are not randomly selected from a population severely limits the researcher's ability to generalize since representativeness of the sample is in question.

30. Specificity is a threat to generalizability when the treatment variables are not clearly operationalized, making it unclear to whom the variable generalizes.

31. Generalizability of results may be affected by short-term or long-term events that occur while the study is taking place. This potential threat is referred to as interaction of history and treatment effects.

32. Interaction of time of measurement and treatment effects results from the fact that posttesting may yield different results depending on when it is done.

33. Passive and active researcher bias or expectations can influence participants. Examples of experimenter effects are when the researcher affects participants' behavior or is unintentionally biased when scoring different treatment groups.

34. Reactive arrangements refer to a number of factors associated with participants performing nontypically because they are aware of being in a study. The Hawthorne, John Henry, and novelty effects are examples of reactive arrangements.

35. The placebo effect is sort of the antidote for the Hawthorne and John Henry effects. Its application in educational research is that all groups in an experiment should appear to be treated the same.

Group Experimental Designs

36. The validity of an experiment is a direct function of the degree to which extraneous variables are controlled. Participant variables include organismic variables and intervening variables. Organismic variables are characteristics of the participant, or organism (such as age), which cannot be directly controlled, but which can be controlled for.

37. Intervening variables intervene between the independent variable and the dependent variable (such as anxiety or boredom), which cannot be directly observed or controlled, but which can be controlled for.

CONTROL OF EXTRANEOUS VARIABLES

38. *Randomization* is the best single way to control for extraneous variables. Randomization is effective in creating equivalent, representative groups that are essentially the same on all relevant variables thought of by the researcher, and probably even a few not thought of. Randomly formed groups are a characteristic unique to experimental research; they are a control factor not possible with causal–comparative research.

39. Randomization should be used whenever possible; participants should be randomly selected from a population and be randomly assigned to groups, and treatments should be randomly assigned to groups.

40. Certain environmental variables can be controlled by holding them constant for all groups. Controlling participant variables is critical.

41. *Matching* is a technique for equating groups. The most commonly used approach to matching involves random assignment of pair members, one member to each group.

42. A major problem with such matching is that there are invariably participants who do not

have a match and must be eliminated from the study. One way to combat loss of participants is to match less closely. A related procedure is to rank all of the participants, from highest to lowest, based on their scores on the control variable; each two adjacent scores constitute a pair.

43. Another way of controlling an extraneous variable is to compare groups that are homogeneous with respect to that variable. A similar but more satisfactory approach is to form subgroups representing all levels of the control variable.

44. If the researcher is interested not just in controlling the variable but also in seeing if the independent variable affects the dependent variable differently at different levels of the control variable, the best approach is to build the control variable right into the design.

45. Using participants as their own controls involves exposing the same group to the different treatments, one treatment at a time.

46. The *analysis of covariance* is a statistical method for equating randomly formed groups on one or more variables. It adjusts scores on a dependent variable for initial differences on some other variable related to the dependent variable.

TYPES OF GROUP DESIGNS

47. Selection of a given design dictates such factors as whether there will be a control group, whether participants will be randomly assigned to groups, whether each group will be pretested, and how resulting data will be analyzed.

48. Different designs are appropriate for testing different types of hypotheses and designs vary widely in the degree to which they control the various threats to internal and external validity. From the designs that are appropriate and feasible, you select the one that controls the most sources of internal and external invalidity.

49. There are two major classes of experimental designs, single-variable designs, which involve one independent variable (which is manipulated), and factorial designs, which

involve two or more independent variables (at least one of which is manipulated).

50. Single-variable designs are classified as pre-experimental, true experimental, or quasi-experimental, depending on the control they provide for sources of internal and external invalidity. Pre-experimental designs do not do a very good job of controlling threats to validity and should be avoided. True experimental designs represent a very high degree of control and are always to be preferred. Quasi-experimental designs do not control as well as true experimental designs but do a much better job than the pre-experimental designs.

51. Factorial designs are basically elaborations of true experimental designs and permit investigation of two or more variables, individually and in interaction with each other.

Single Variable

1) **Pre-Experimental Designs**

52. The one-shot case study involves one group which is exposed to a treatment (*X*) and then posttested (*O*). None of the threats to validity that are relevant is controlled.

X O

53. The one-group pretest–posttest design involves one group which is pretested (*O*), exposed to a treatment (*X*), and posttested (*O*). It controls several sources of invalidity not controlled by the one-shot case study, but additional factors are not controlled.

O X O

54. The static-group comparison involves at least two groups; one receives a new, or unusual, treatment and both groups are posttested. Since participants are not randomly assigned to groups, and since there is no pretest data, it is difficult to determine just how equivalent the treatment groups are.

X₂ O

2) **True Experimental Designs**

55. True experimental designs control for nearly all sources of internal and external invalidity. True experimental designs have one characteristic in common that none of the other designs has: random assignment of participants to groups. Ideally, participants should be randomly selected and randomly assigned to treatments.

56. All the true designs have a control group.

57. The pretest–posttest control group design involves at least two groups, both of which are

$R\ O X_1 O$
$R\ O X_2 O$
$R\ O X_3 O$

formed by random assignment; both groups are administered a pretest of the dependent variable, one group receives a new, or unusual, treatment, and both groups are posttested. The combination of random assignment and the presence of a pretest and a control group serve to control for all sources of internal invalidity.

58. The only definite weakness with this design is a possible interaction between the pretest and the treatment that may make the results generalizable only to other pretested groups. A variation of this design involves random assignment of members of matched pairs to the groups to more closely control extraneous variables.

$R X_2 O$
$R X, O$
$R X_3 O$

59. The posttest-only control group design is the same as the pretest–posttest control group design, except there is no pretest. Participants are randomly assigned to groups, exposed to the independent variable, and posttested to determine the effectiveness of the treatment. The combination of random assignment and the presence of a control group serve to control for all sources of invalidity except mortality, which is not controlled because of the absence of pretest data. A variation of this design is random assignment of matched pairs.

60. The Solomon four-group design involves random assignment of participants to one of four groups. Two of the groups are pretested and two are not; one of the pretested groups and one of the unpretested groups receive the experimental treatment. All four groups are posttested. This design controls all threats to internal validity.

$R\ X, O$
$R\ X_2 O$
$R O X_3 O$
$R O X_4 O$

61. The best way to analyze data resulting from the Solomon four-group design is to use a 2×2 factorial analysis of variance. This procedure indicates whether there is an interaction between the treatment and the pretest.

3) **Quasi-Experimental Designs**

62. When it is not possible to randomly assign participants to groups, quasi-experimental designs are available to the researcher. They provide adequate control of sources of invalidity.

63. The nonequivalent control group design looks very much like the pretest–posttest

$O X_1 O$
$O X_2 O$

control group design, except that the non-equivalent control group design does not involve random assignment. The lack of random assignment raises the possibility of interactions between selection and variables such as maturation, history, and testing. Reactive effects are minimized.

64. In this design, every effort should be made to use groups that are as equivalent as possible. If differences between the groups on any major extraneous variable are identified, analysis of covariance can be used to statistically equate the groups.

65. In the time-series design, one group is repeatedly pretested, exposed to a treatment, and then repeatedly posttested. If a group scores essentially the same on a number of pretests and then significantly improves following a treatment, the researcher has more confidence in the effectiveness of the treatment than if just one pretest and one posttest are administered. History is a problem, as is pretest-treatment interaction.

OOOOXOOOO

66. Determining the effectiveness of the treatment in the time-series design basically involves analysis of the pattern of the test scores. A variation of the time-series design, which is referred to as the multiple time-series design, involves the addition of a control group to the basic design. This variation eliminates all threats to internal invalidity.

67. In a counterbalanced design, all groups receive all treatments but in a different order. The number of groups should equal the number of treatments. This design is usually employed when intact groups must be used and when administration of a pretest is not possible. A weakness of this design is potential multiple-treatment interference.

$X_1 O X_2 O X_3 O$
$X_2 O X_3 O X_1 O$
$X_3 O X_1 O X_2 O$

Factorial Designs

68. Factorial designs involve two or more independent variables, at least one of which is manipulated by the researcher. They permit investigation of two or more variables, individually and in interaction with each other. The term *factorial* indicates that the design has several factors, each with two or more levels. The 2×2 is the simplest factorial design.

69. The purpose of a factorial design is to determine whether an interaction between the independent variables exists. If one value of the independent variable is more effective regardless of level of the control variable, there is no interaction. If an interaction exists between the variables, different values of the independent variable are differentially effective depending upon the level of the control variable. Rarely are more than three factors in a factorial design.

Single-Subject Experimental Designs

70. Single-subject experimental designs are commonly referred to as single-case experimental designs. They can be applied when the sample size is one and are typically used to study the behavior change an individual exhibits as a result of some intervention, or treatment.

71. Basically, the participant is alternately exposed to a nontreatment and a treatment condition, or phase, and performance is repeatedly measured during each phase. The nontreatment condition is symbolized as A and the treatment condition is symbolized as B.

72. At the very least, single-subject designs are considered to be valuable complements to group designs. There are two limitations of traditional group designs: (1) they frequently opposed on ethical or philosophical grounds since by definition such designs involve a control group that does not receive the experimental treatment and (2) application of a group comparison design is not possible in many cases because of the small sample sizes. Single-subject designs are most frequently applied in clinical settings where the primary emphasis is on therapeutic, not statistical, outcomes.

didn't cover in class

EXTERNAL VALIDITY

73. Results of single-subject research cannot be generalized to the population of interest as they can with group design research. For single-subject designs, the key to generaliz-

ability is replication. A main threat to these designs is the possible effect of the baseline condition on the subsequent effects of the treatment condition.

74. Single-subject designs require repeated and reliable measurements or observations. Pretest performance is measured or observed a number of times prior to implementation of the treatment to obtain a stable baseline. Performance is also obtained at various points while the treatment is being applied. Since repeated data collection is a fundamental characteristic of all single-subject designs, it is especially important that measurement or observation of performance be standardized. Intraobserver and interobserver reliability should be estimated.

75. Also, the nature and conditions of the treatment should be specified in sufficient detail to permit replication. If its effects are to be validly assessed, the treatment must involve the same procedures each time it is introduced.

76. The purpose of the baseline measurements is to provide a description of the target behavior as it naturally occurs prior to the treatment. The baseline serves as the basis of comparison for assessing the effectiveness of the treatment. The establishment of a baseline pattern is referred to as baseline stability.

77. Normally, the length of the treatment phase and the number of measurements taken during it should parallel the length and measurements of the baseline phase.

78. An important principle of single-subject research is that only one variable at a time should be manipulated.

TYPES OF SINGLE-SUBJECT DESIGNS

79. When the A–B design is used, baseline measurements are repeatedly made until stability is established, treatment is then introduced and multiple measurements are made during treatment. If behavior improves during the treatment phase, the effectiveness of the treatment is allegedly demonstrated. This design is open to many internal and external validity threats.

80. By simply adding a second baseline phase to the A–B design we obtain a much improved design, the A–B–A design. The internal validity of the A–B–A design is superior to that of the A–B design. It is unlikely that behavior would coincidentally improve during the treatment phase and coincidentally deteriorate during the subsequent baseline phase. A problem with this design is the ethical concern that the experiment ends with the treatment being removed.

81. The B–A–B design involves a treatment phase (B), a withdrawal phase (A), and a return to treatment phase (B). Although the B–A–B design does yield an experiment that ends with the participant receiving treatment, the lack of an initial baseline phase makes it difficult to assess the effectiveness of treatment.

82. The A–B–A–B design is basically the A–B–A design with the addition of a second treatment phase. This design overcomes the ethical objection to the A–B–A design and greatly strengthens the conclusions of the study by demonstrating the effects of the treatment twice. When application of the A–B–A–B design is feasible, it provides very convincing evidence of treatment effectiveness. The second treatment phase can be extended beyond the termination of the actual study to examine stability of treatment.

83. Multiple-baseline designs are used when the treatment is such that it is not possible to withdraw or return it to baseline or when it would not be ethical to withdraw it or reverse it. They are also used when treatment can be withdrawn, but the effects of the treatment "carry over" into other phases of the study.

84. There are three basic types of multiple-baseline designs: across behaviors, across participants, and across settings designs.

85. In a multiple-baseline design, data are collected on several behaviors for one participant, one behavior for several participants, or one behavior and one participant in several settings. Systematically, over a period of time, the treatment is applied to each behavior (or participant, or setting) one at a time until all behaviors (or participants, or set-

tings) are under treatment. If performance improves in each case only after a treatment is introduced, then the treatment is judged to be effective.

86. When applying a treatment across behaviors, it is important that the behaviors treated be independent of each other. When applying treatment across participants, they and the setting should be as similar as possible. When applying treatment across settings, it is preferable that the settings be natural, although this is not always possible.

87. Whenever baseline is recoverable and there are no carryover effects, any of the A–B–A designs can be applied within a multiple-baseline framework.

88. The alternating treatments design represents highly valid approach to assessing the relative effectiveness of two (or more) treatments, within a single-participant context. The alternating treatments design involves the relatively rapid alternation of treatments for a single participant. To avoid potential validity threats such as ordering effects, treatments are alternated on a random basis (e.g., T_1–T_2–T_2–T_1–T_2–T_1–T_1–T_2.

89. This design has several pluses which make it attractive to investigators. First, no withdrawal is necessary. Second, no baseline phase is necessary. Third, a number of treatments can be studied more quickly and efficiently than with other designs. One potential problem with this design is multiple-treatment interference (carryover effects from one treatment to the other).

not covered

DATA ANALYSIS AND INTERPRETATION

90. Data analysis in single-subject research usually involves visual and graphical analysis. Given the small sample size, the primary criterion is the clinical significance of the results, rather than the statistical significance. Effects that are small, but statistically significant, may not be large enough to make a sufficient difference in the behavior of a participant. Statistical analyses may supplement visual and graphical analysis.

91. In all the designs discussed, the key to sound data evaluation is judgment. The use of statistical analyses does not remove this responsibility from the researcher.

not covered

REPLICATION

92. The more results are replicated, the more confidence that can be placed in the procedures that produced those results. Also, replication serves to delimit the generalizability of findings.

93. There are three types of replication. Direct replication refers to replication by the same investigator, with the same participant or with different participants, in a specific setting (e.g., a classroom). Systematic replication refers to replication that follows direct replication, and that involves different investigators, behaviors, or settings. Clinical replication involves the development of a treatment package, composed of two or more interventions that have been found to be effective individually, designed for persons with complex behavior disorders.

Task 6 *Performance Criteria* ■

The description of participants should describe the population from which the sample was selected (allegedly, of course!), including its size and major characteristics.

The description of the instrument(s) should describe the purpose of the instrument (what it is intended to measure), and available validity and reliability coefficients.

The description of the design should indicate why it was selected, potential threats to validity associated with the design, and aspects of the study that are believed to have minimized their potential effects. A figure should be included illustrating how the selected design was applied in the study. For example, you might say: Since random assignment of participants to groups was possible, and since administration of a pretest was not advisable due to the reactive nature of the dependent variable (attitudes toward school), the posttest-only control group design was selected for this study (see Figure 1).

FIGURE 1

Experimental Design

GROUP	ASSIGNMENT	N	TREATMENT	POSTTEST
I	Random	25	Daily Homework	So-so Attitude Scale
II	Random	25	No Homework	So-so Attitude Scale

The description of procedures should describe in detail all steps that were executed in conducting the study. The description should include: (1) the manner in which the sample was selected and the groups formed; (2) how and when pretest data were collected (if applicable); (3) the ways in which the groups were different (the independent variable, or treatment); (4) aspects of the study that were the same or similar for all groups; and (5) how and when posttest data were collected. (Note: If the dependent variable was measured with a test, you should name the specific test or tests administered. If a test was administered strictly for selection-of-participants purposes, that is, not as a pretest of the dependent variable, it too should be described.)

The following pages present an example that illustrates the performance called for by Task 6. (See Task 6 example.) Again, the task was prepared by the same student who developed previous task examples, and you should therefore be able to see how Task 6 builds on previous tasks. Note especially how Task 3, the research plan, has been refined and expanded. Keep in mind that Tasks 3, 4, and 5 will not appear in your final research report; Task 6 will. Therefore, all of the important points in those previous tasks should be included in Task 6.

Additional examples for this and subsequent tasks are included in the *Student Guide* that accompanies this text.

1

Effect of Interactive Multimedia on the Achievement
of 10th-Grade Biology Students

Method

Participants

The sample for this study was selected from the total population of 213 10th-grade students at an upper-middle class
all-girls Catholic high school in Miami, Florida. The population was 90% Hispanic, mainly of Cuban-American descent,
9% Caucasian non-Hispanic, and 1% African-American. Sixty
students were randomly selected (using a table of random
numbers) and randomly assigned to two groups of 30 each.

Instrument

The biology test of the National Proficiency Survey Series
(NPSS) was used as the measuring instrument. The test was
designed to measure individual student performance in biology at the high school level but the publishers also recommended it as an evaluation of instructional programs. Content validity is good; items were selected from a large
item bank provided by classroom teachers and curriculum experts. High school instructional materials and a national
curriculum survey were extensively reviewed before objectives were written. The test objectives and those of the
biology classes in the study were highly correlated. Although the standard error of measurement is not given for
the biology test, the range of KR-20s for the entire battery is from .82 to .91 with a median of .86. This is satisfactory because the purpose of the test was to evaluate
instructional programs not to make decisions concerning individuals. Catholic-school students were included in the
battery norming which procedures were carried out in April

2

and May of 1988 using 22,616 students in grades 9-12 from 45 high schools in 20 states.

Experimental Design

The design used in this study was the posttest-only control group design (see Figure 1). This design was selected because it provides control for most sources of invalidity and random assignment to groups was possible. A pretest was not necessary since the final science grades from June 1993 were available to check initial group equivalence and to help control mortality, a potential threat to internal validity with this design. Mortality, however, was not a problem, as no students dropped from either group.

Group	Assignment	n	Treatment	Posttest
1	Random	30	IMM instruction	NPSS:B[a]
2	Random	30	Traditional instruction	NPSS:B

[a]National Proficiency Survey Series: Biology

Figure 1. Experimental design.

Procedure

Prior to the beginning of the 1993-94 school year, before classes were scheduled, 60 of the 213 10th-grade students were randomly selected and randomly assigned to two groups of 30 each, the average biology class size; each group became a biology class. One of the classes was randomly chosen to receive IMM instruction. The same teacher taught both classes.

The study was designed to last eight months beginning on the first day of class. The control group was taught using traditional methods of lecturing and open class discussions. The students worked in pairs for laboratory

3

investigations which included the use of microscopes. The teacher's role was one of information disseminator.

The experimental classroom had 15 workstations for student use, each one consisting of a laser disc player, a video recorder, a 27-inch monitor, and a Macintosh computer with a 40 MB hard drive, 10 MB RAM and a CD-ROM drive. The teacher's workstation incorporated a Macintosh computer with CD-ROM drive, a videodisc player and a 27-inch monitor. The workstations were networked to the school library so students had access to online services such as Prodigy and Infotrac as well as to the card catalog. Two laser printers were available through the network for the students' use.

In the experimental class the teacher used a videodisc correlated to the textbook. When barcodes provided in the text were scanned a section of the videodisc was activated and appeared on the monitor. The section might be a motion picture demonstrating a process or a still picture offering more detail than the text. The role of the teacher in the experimental group was that of facilitator and guide. After the teacher had introduced a new topic, the students worked in pairs at the workstations investigating topics connected to the main idea presented in the lesson. Videodiscs, CD-ROM's and online services were all available as sources of information. The students used HyperStudio to prepare multimedia reports, which they presented to the class.

Throughout the study the same subject matter was covered and the two classes used the same text. Although the students of the experimental group paired up at the workstations, the other group worked in pairs during lab time thus equalizing any effect from cooperative learning. The classes

4

could not meet at the same time, as they were taught by the same teacher, so they met during second and third periods. First period was not chosen, as the school sometimes has a special schedule that interferes with first period. Both classes had the same homework reading assignments, which were reviewed in class the following school day. Academic objectives were the same for each class and all tests measuring achievement were identical.

   During the first week of May, the biology test of the NPSS was administered to both classes to compare their achievement in biology.

PART SEVEN

Data Analysis and Interpretation Or . . . The Word Is *Statistics*, not *Sadistics*

Statistics is a set of procedures for describing, synthesizing, analyzing, and interpreting quantitative data. For example, 1,000 scores can be represented by a single number. Application of the appropriate statistic helps you to decide if the difference between groups is big enough to represent a true difference, rather than a chance difference.

Choice of appropriate statistical techniques is determined to a great extent by your research design, hypothesis, and the kind of data that will be collected. The statistical procedures and techniques of the study should be identified and described in detail in the research plan. Analysis of the data is as important as any other component of the research process. Regardless of how well the study is conducted, inappropriate analyses can lead to inappropriate research conclusions. However, the complexity of the analysis is not necessarily an indication of its "goodness"; often, a simple statistic is more appropriate than a more complicated one.

There are many statistical approaches available to a researcher. This part will describe and explain those commonly used in educational research. The focus is upon your ability to apply and interpret these statistics, not your ability to describe their theoretical rationale and mathematical derivation. To calculate the statistics in this part you only need to know how to add, subtract, multiply, and divide. That is all. No matter how gross or complex a formula is, it can be turned into an arithmetic problem when applied to your data. The arithmetic problems involve only addition, subtraction, multiplication, and division; the formulas tell you how often, and in what order, to perform those operations.

Now, you might be thinking, "H-m-m-m, what about square roots?" Although it is true that many of the statistical formulas involve square roots, you do not have to know how to find the square root of anything, since virtually all calculators have a square root button.

Even if you haven't had a math course since junior high school, you will be able to calculate statistics. In fact, you are encouraged to use a calculator! Trust us. You are going to be pleasantly surprised to see just how easy statistics is.

The goal of Part Seven is for you to be able to select, apply, and correctly interpret analyses appropriate for a given study. After you have read Part Seven, you should be able to perform the following task.

TASK 7

Based on Tasks 2 through 6, which you have already completed, write the results section of a research report. Specifically:

1. Generate data for each of the participants in your study.
2. Summarize and describe data using descriptive statistics.
3. Statistically analyze data using inferential statistics.
4. Interpret the results in terms of your original research hypothesis.
5. Present the results of your data analyses in a summary table.

If STATPAK, the microcomputer program that accompanies this text, is available to you, use it to check your work. (See Performance Criteria, p. 525.)

CHAPTER 12

"Looks bad, right? (p. 455)."

Descriptive Statistics

![] OBJECTIVES

OBJECTIVES

After reading chapter 12, you should be able to:

1. List the steps involved in scoring standardized and self-developed tests.
2. Describe the process of coding data, and give three examples of variables that would require coding.
3. List the steps involved in constructing a frequency polygon.
4. Define or describe three measures of central tendency.
5. Define or describe three measures of variability.
6. List four characteristics of normal distributions.
7. List two characteristics of positively skewed distributions and negatively skewed distributions.
8. Define or describe two measures of relationship.
9. Define or describe four measures of relative position.
10. Generate a column of numbers, and, using those numbers or "scores," give the formula and compute the following (show your work): mean, standard deviation, z scores, and Pearson r (divide the column in half and make two columns of five scores each).

If STATPAK, the microcomputer program that accompanies this text, is available to you, use it to check your work.[1] Isn't this fun?

PREPARING DATA FOR ANALYSIS

A research study usually produces a mass of raw data such as the responses of participants to an achievement, ability, interest, or attitude test. Collected data must be accurately scored and systematically organized to facilitate data analysis.

SCORING PROCEDURES

All instruments administered should be scored accurately and consistently; each participant's test should be scored using the same procedures and criteria. When a standardized instrument is used, the scoring process is greatly facilitated. The test manual usually spells out the steps to be followed in scoring each test, and a scoring key is usually provided. If the manual is followed conscientiously and each test is scored carefully, errors are minimized. It is usually a good idea to recheck all, or at least some, of the tests (say 25% or every third test).

Scoring self-developed instruments is more complex, especially if open-ended items are involved. There is no manual to follow, and the researcher has to develop and refine a scoring procedure. Steps for scoring each item and for arriving at a total score must be delineated and carefully followed. If other than

---

[1] A helpful tutorial on CD-ROM (for windows only) is: Bonfadini, J. (1999). Educational Research CD-ROM Tutorial. Upper Saddle River, NJ: Prentice Hall.

objective-type items (such as multiple-choice questions) are to be scored, it is advisable to have at least one other person independently score some or all of the tests as a reliability check. Planned scoring procedures should be tried out by administering the instrument to some individuals from the same or a similar population as the one from which research participants will be selected for the actual study. In this way, problems with the instrument or its scoring can be identified and corrected prior to the start of the study. The procedure ultimately used to score study data should be described in detail in the final research report.

If your test questions can be responded to on a standard, machine-scorable answer sheet, you can save yourself a lot of time and increase the accuracy of the scoring process. If tests are to be machine scored, answer sheets should be checked carefully for stray pencil marks and a percentage of them should be scored by hand just to make sure that the key is correct and that the machine is scoring properly. The fact that your tests are being scored by a machine does not relieve you of the responsibility of carefully checking your data before and after processing.

TABULATION AND CODING PROCEDURES

After instruments have been scored, the results are transferred to summary data sheets and/or entered into a computer. Tabulation involves organizing the data. Recording the scores in a systematic manner facilitates examination and analysis of the data. If analysis consists of a comparison of the posttest scores of two or more groups, data would generally be placed in columns, one for each group, with the data arranged in ascending or descending order. If pretest scores are involved, similar, additional columns are formed. If analyses involve subgroup comparisons, scores should be tabulated separately for each subgroup. For example, in a study investigating the interaction between two types of mathematics instruction and two levels of aptitude (a 2×2 factorial design), four subgroups are involved, as shown in Table 12.1. This is the common method of dealing with quantitative data. If the data to be analyzed are categorical, tabulation usually involves counting responses. For example, a superintendent might be interested in comparing the attitude toward unions of elementary and secondary teachers. Thus, for a question such as, "Would you join a union if given the opportunity?" the superintendent would tally the number of "yes," "no," and "undecided" responses separately for elementary and secondary teachers.

When a number of different kinds of data are collected from each participant, such as demographic information and several test scores, both the variable names and the actual data are frequently coded. The variable "pretest reading comprehension scores," for example, may be coded as PRC, and gender of participants may be recorded as "M" or "F" or "1" or "2." Use of a computer for tabulating data and doing data analysis is recommended in general, but particularly if complex or multiple analyses are to be performed, or if a large number of participants are involved. In these cases, coding of the data is especially important. The major advantage of using a computer to organize and analyze data is the capacity to rearrange data by subgroups and extract information without reentering all the data.

The first step in coding data is to give each participant an ID number. If there are 50 participants, for example, number them from 01 to 50. As this example illustrates, if the highest value for a variable is two digits (e.g., 50), then all represented values must be two digits. Thus, the first participant is 01, not 1. Similarly, achievement scores that range from, 75 to 132 are coded 075 to 132. The next step is to make decisions as to how nonnumerical, or categorical, data will be coded. Nominal or categorical data include variables such as gender, group membership, and college level (e.g., sophomore). Thus, if the study involves 50 participants, two groups of 25, then group membership may be coded "1" or "2" or "experimental" or "control." Categorical data also occur in survey instruments on which participants choose from a small number of alternatives representing a wider range of values. For example, teachers might be asked the following question:

How many hours of classroom time do you spend per week in nonteaching activities?
(a) 0–5   (b) 6–10   (c) 11–15   (d) 16–20

Responses might be coded (a) = 1, (b) = 2, (c) = 3, and (d) = 4.

TABLE 12.1

Hypothetical Results of a Study Based on a 2 × 2 Factorial Design

	METHOD A	METHOD B
	68	55
	72	60
	76	65
	78	70
	80	72
	84	74
	84	74
High Aptitude	85	75
	86	75
	86	76
	88	76
	90	76
	91	78
	92	82
	96	87

	METHOD A	METHOD B
	50	60
	58	66
	60	67
	62	68
	64	69
	64	69
	65	70
Low Aptitude	65	70
	66	71
	67	71
	70	72
	72	75
	72	76
	75	77
	78	79

> **Spreadsheets**
>
> An electronic spreadsheet is a grid with an unlimited number of cells that can hold numerical information. The cells form rows and columns. For use with questionnaire data, it will be necessary to format your spreadsheet so that each column corresponds to an item on your questionnaire and each row represents a respondent.
>
> After you have entered each respondent's responses into the spreadsheet, you can use formulas and other commands to total the data and/or copy it from the spreadsheet into a word processing or statistical program. The data can be sorted according to any category you set. It can also be graphed in a number of ways, giving you a visual representation of your data. Some spreadsheets, such as Excel and Lotus 1-2-3, also give the user the option of completing advanced statistical analyses of the data.
>
> Many people are more familiar with electronic spreadsheet programs than with statistical programs, so they prefer to enter their data first onto a spreadsheet and then import it into a statistical program like SPSS or SAS for advanced statistical analysis. However, this is just a matter of personal taste.

Once the data have been prepared for analysis, the choice of statistical procedures to be applied is determined not only by the research hypothesis and design, but also by the type of measurement scale (categorical, ordinal, interval, ratio) represented by the data.

USING A COMPUTER

Generally the computer is a logical choice for data analysis. However, a good guideline for beginning researchers is not to use the computer to perform an analysis that they have never done themselves by hand, or at least studied extensively. For example, after you have performed several analyses of variance on various sets of data you will have the experience to understand the information produced by a computer analysis. In addition, instructions for preparing data for computer processing will make sense to you, and you will know what the resulting output should look like.

Some people feel the same way about using computers as they do about statistics—not good! As with statistics, however, it is a lot easier than it might seem. Rapid technological advances, and the development of "user friendly" equipment and programs, have made it possible for researchers to perform a wide variety of analyses. In many cases, using the computer can be as simple as selecting from a list of available statistics (a menu) and typing in your data as directed. One of the most popular statistical packages, commonly used in many colleges and universities, is some version of the Statistical Package for the Social Sciences (SPSS). The good news concerning SPSS usage is that no mathematical or programming background is required. The bad news is that it may take a while to master the program. For an easy start, however, STATPAK, the data analysis program that accompanies this text, was designed specifically for use with the text. It is easy to use and performs all of the statistics that are computed in chapters 12 and 13.

TYPES OF DESCRIPTIVE STATISTICS

The first step in data analysis is to describe, or summarize, the data using descriptive statistics. In some studies, particularly survey ones, the entire data analysis procedure may consist solely of calculating and interpreting descriptive statistics. Descriptive statistics permit the researcher to meaningfully describe many pieces of data with a few indices. If such indices are calculated for a sample drawn from a population, the resulting values are referred to as *statistics*; if they are calculated for an entire population, they are referred to as *parameters*. Most of the statistics used in educational research are based on data collected from well-defined samples, so most analyses deal with statistics, not parameters. Recall that statistics are quantitative indices describing performance of a sample or samples, while parameters are quantitative indices describing the performance of a population.

The major types of descriptive statistics are measures of central tendency, measures of variability, measures of relative position, and measures of relationship. Measures of central tendency are used to determine the typical or average score of a group of scores. Measures of variability indicate how spread out a group of scores are. Measures of relative position describe a participant's performance compared to the performance of all other participants. Measures of relationship indicate the degree to which two sets of scores are related (remember correlation?). Before actually calculating any of these measures, it is often useful to present the data in graphic form.

GRAPHING DATA

As discussed, data are usually recorded on summary sheets or in computers in columns placed in ascending order. Data in this form are easily graphed, permitting the researcher to see what the distribution of scores looks like. The shape of the distribution may not be self-evident, especially if a large number of scores are involved, and, as we shall see later, the shape of the distribution may influence our choice of certain descriptive statistics.

The most common method of graphing data is to construct a frequency polygon. The first step in constructing a frequency polygon is to list all scores and to tabulate how many participants received each score. If 85 tenth-grade students were administered an achievement test, the results might be as shown in Table 12.2.

Once the scores are tallied, the steps are as follows:

1. Place all the scores on a horizontal axis, at equal intervals, from lowest score to highest.
2. Place the frequencies of scores at equal intervals on the vertical axis, starting with zero.
3. For each score, find the point where the score intersects with its frequency of occurrence and make a dot.
4. Connect all the dots with straight lines.

TABLE	12.2

Frequency Distribution Based on 85 Hypothetical Achievement Test Scores

SCORE	FREQUENCY OF SCORE
78	1
79	4
80	5
81	7
82	7
83	9
84	9
85	12
86	10
87	7
88	6
89	3
90	4
91	1
	Total: 85 students

From Figure 12.1 we can see that most of the 10th graders scored at or near 85, with progressively fewer students achieving higher or lower scores. In other words, the scores appear to form a relatively normal or bell-shaped distribution, a concept to be discussed a little later. This knowledge would be helpful in selecting an appropriate measure of central tendency.

FIGURE	12.1

Frequency Polygon and Pie Chart Based on 85 Hypothetical Achievement Test Scores

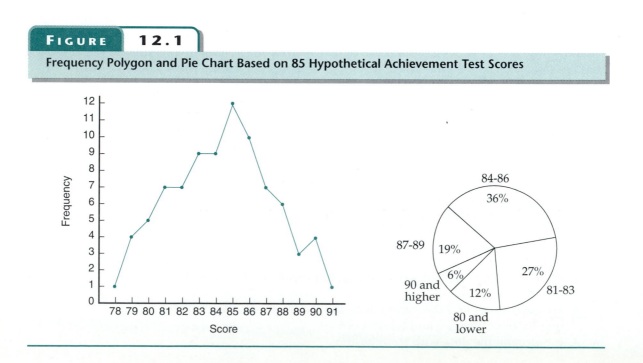

There are many types of other data-graphing approaches such as bar graphs, pie graphs, scatterplots (see Figure 9.1), boxplots, and stem-and-leaf charts.[2] Examining a picture of your data can give some clues about which statistics are appropriate analyses.

MEASURES OF CENTRAL TENDENCY

Measures of central tendency provide a convenient way of describing a set of data with a single number. The number resulting from computation of a measure of central tendency represents the average or typical score attained by a group of participants. The three most frequently encountered indices of central tendency are the mode, the median, and the mean. Each of these indices is used with a different scale of measurement: the mode is appropriate for describing nominal data, the median for describing ordinal data, and the mean for describing interval or ratio data. Most measurement in educational research uses an interval scale, so the mean is the most frequently used measure of central tendency.

The Mode

The mode is the score that is attained by more participants than any other score. The data presented in Figure 12.1, for example, shows that the group mode is 85, since more participants (12) achieved that score than any other. The mode is not established through calculation; it is determined by looking at a set of scores or at a graph of scores and seeing which score occurs most frequently. There are several problems associated with the mode, and it is therefore of limited value and seldom used. For one thing, a set of scores may have two (or more) modes, in which case they are referred to as bimodal. Another problem with the mode is that it is an unstable measure of central tendency; equal-sized samples randomly selected from the same accessible population are likely to have different modes. However, when nominal data are being analyzed, the mode is the only appropriate measure of central tendency.

The Median

The median is that point, after scores are organized from low to high or high to low, above and below which are 50% of the scores. In other words, the median is the midpoint (like the median strip on a highway). If there are an odd number of scores, the median is the middle score (assuming the scores are arranged in order). For example, for the scores 75, 80, 82, 83, 87, the median is 82, because it is the middle score. If there is an even number of scores, the median is the point halfway between the two middle scores. For example, for the scores 21, 23, 24, 25, 26, 30, the median is 24.5; for the scores 50, 52, 55, 57, 59, 61, the median is 56. Thus, the median is not necessarily the same as one of the scores. There is no calculation for the median except finding the midpoint when there are an even number of scores.

The median does not take into account each and every score; it focuses on the middle scores. Two quite different sets of scores may have the same median. For

[2]Wallgren, A., Wallgren, B., Persson, R., Jorner, U., & Haaland, J. (1996). *Graphing statistics and data.* Thousand Oaks, CA: Sage Publications

example, for the scores 60, 62, 65, 67, 72, the median is 65; for the scores 30, 55, 65, 72, 89, the median is also 65. As we shall see shortly, this apparent lack of precision can be advantageous at times.

The median is the appropriate measure of central tendency when the data represent an ordinal scale. For certain distributions, the median may be the most appropriate measure of central tendency even though the data represent an interval or ratio scale. Although the median appears to be a rather simple index to determine, it cannot always be arrived at by simply looking at the scores; it does not always neatly fall between two different scores. For example, determining the median for the scores 80, 82, 84, 84, 84, 88 would require application of a relatively complex formula.

The Mean

The mean is the arithmetic average of the scores and is the most frequently used measure of central tendency. It is calculated by adding up all of the scores and dividing that total by the number of scores. In general, the mean is the preferred measure of central tendency. It is appropriate when the data represent either interval or ratio scores and is more precise than the median and the mode, because if equal-sized samples are randomly selected from the same population, the means of those samples will be more similar to each other than either the medians or the modes. By the very nature of the way in which it is computed, the mean takes into account, or is based on, each and every participant's score. Because all scores count, the mean can be affected by extreme scores. Thus, in certain cases, the median may actually give a more accurate estimate of the typical score.

When there are one or more extreme scores, the mean will not be the most accurate representation of the performance of the total group but it will be the best index of typical performance. As an example, suppose you had the following IQ scores: 96, 96, 97, 99, 100, 101, 102, 104, 195. For these scores, the three measures of central tendency are:

mode = 96 (most frequent score)
median = 100 (middle score)
mean = 110 (arithmetic average)

In this case, the median clearly best represents the typical score. The mode is too low, and the mean is higher than all of the scores except one. The mean is "pulled up" in the direction of the 195 score, whereas the median essentially ignores it. The different pictures presented by the different measures are part of the reason for the phrase "lying with statistics." And in fact, by selecting one index of central tendency over another, you may present a particular point of view in a stronger light. In a labor–versus–management union dispute over salary, for example, each side will calculate different estimates of typical employee salaries, based on which index of central tendency is used. Let us say that the following are typical of employee salaries in a union company: $12,000, $13,000, $13,000, $15,000, $16,000, $18,000, $45,000. For these salaries, the measures of central tendency are:

mode = $13,000 (most frequent score)
median = $15,000 (middle salary)
mean = $18,857 (arithmetic average)

Both labor and management could overstate their case, labor by using the mode and management by using the mean. The mean is higher than every salary except one, $45,000, which in all likelihood would be the salary of a company manager. Thus, in this case, the most appropriate, and most accurate, index of typical salary would be the median. In research, we are not interested in "making cases," but in describing the data in the most accurate way. For the majority of sets of data the mean is the appropriate measure of central tendency.

MEASURES OF VARIABILITY

Although measures of central tendency are useful statistics for describing a set of data, they are not sufficient. Two sets of data that are very different can have identical means or medians. As an example, consider the following sets of data:

set A:	79	79	79	80	81	81	81
set B:	50	60	70	80	90	100	110

The mean of both sets of scores is 80 and the median of both is 80, but set A is very different from set B. In set A the scores are all very close together and are clustered around the mean. In set B the scores are much more spread out; in other words, there is much more variation or variability in set B. Thus, there is a need for a measure that indicates how spread out the scores are, that is, how much variability there is. A number of descriptive statistics serve this purpose, and they are referred to as measures of variability. The three most frequently encountered are the range, the quartile deviation, and the standard deviation. Although the standard deviation is by far the most often used, the range is the only appropriate measure of variability for nominal data, and the quartile deviation is the appropriate index of variability for ordinal data. As with measures of central tendency, measures of variability appropriate for nominal and ordinal data may be used with interval or ratio data, even though the standard deviation is generally the preferred index for such data.

The Range

The range is simply the difference between the highest and the lowest score once the scores are arranged in order and is determined by subtraction. As an example, the range for the scores 79, 79, 79, 80, 81, 81, 81, is 2, while the range for the scores 50, 60, 70, 80, 90, 100, 110 is 60. Thus, if the range is small the scores are close together, whereas if the range is large the scores are more spread out. Like the mode, the range is not a very stable measure of variability, and its chief advantage is that it gives a quick, rough estimate of variability.

The Quartile Deviation

In "research talk" the quartile deviation is half of the difference between the upper quartile and the lower quartile in a distribution. In English, the upper quartile is the 75th percentile, that point below which are 75% of the scores. Correspondingly, the lower quartile is the 25th percentile, that point below which are 25% of the scores. By subtracting the lower quartile from the upper quartile and then dividing the result by two, we get a measure of variability. If the quartile deviation is small the scores are close together, whereas if the quartile deviation is large the scores are more spread out. The quartile deviation is a more stable measure of variability than the range and is appropriate whenever the median is appropriate. Calculation of the quartile deviation involves a process very similar to that used to calculate the median, which just happens to be the second quartile or the 50th percentile.

Variance

Variance indicates the amount of spread among test scores. If the variance is small, the scores are close together; if the variance is large, the scores are more spread out. The square root of the variance is called the *standard deviation*. Like variance, a small standard deviation indicates that scores are close together and a large standard deviation indicates that the scores are more spread out.

Calculation of the variance is quite simple. For example, five students took a test and received scores of 35, 25, 30, 40, and 30. The mean of these scores is— what? Right, 32. The difference of each student's score from the mean is 0.

$$35 - 32 = 3$$
$$25 - 32 = -7$$
$$30 - 32 = -2$$
$$40 - 32 = 8$$
$$30 - 32 = -2 \quad \text{(Notice that the sum of the differences is: 0. That's why we have to square the differences in the next step.)}$$

Squaring each difference gives $9 + 49 + 4 + 64 + 2 = 130$. Dividing the squared differences by the number of scores gives us $130/5 = 26$. This is called the variance of the scores. Variance is seldom used itself, but is used to obtain the standard deviation. The standard deviation is the square root of the variance (26). Get your calculator out. The square root of 26 is 5.1, and this is the standard deviation of the five scores.

The Standard Deviation

The standard deviation is used when the data are interval or ratio, and is by far the most frequently used index of variability. Like the mean, its central tendency counterpart, the standard deviation is the most stable measure of variability and includes every score in its calculation. In fact, the first step in calculating the standard deviation is to find out how far away each score is from the mean by subtracting the mean from each score. If you know the mean and the standard deviation of a set of scores you have a pretty good picture of what the distribution looks like. If the distribution of scores is relatively normal or bell-shaped (about which we will have more to say shortly), then the mean plus 3 standard deviations and the mean minus 3 standard deviations encompass more than 99% of the scores. In other words, each score distribution has its own mean and its own standard deviation that are calculated based on the scores. Once the mean and standard deviation are computed, 3 times the standard deviation added to the mean, and 3 times the standard deviation subtracted from the mean, will include just about all the scores. The number 3 is a constant. In other words, for any normal distribution of scores, the standard deviation multiplied by 3 and then added to the mean and subtracted from the mean will include almost all the scores in the distribution. The symbol for the mean is $\overline{X}$ and the standard deviation is usually abbreviated as *SD*. Thus, the above described concept can be expressed as follows: $\overline{X} \pm 3\ SD = 99+\%$ of the scores.

As an example, suppose that the mean of a set of scores $(\overline{X})$ is calculated to be 80 and the standard deviation (*SD*) to be 1. In this case the mean plus 3 standard deviations, $\overline{X} + 3\ SD$, is equal to $80 + 3(1) = 80 + 3 = 83$. The mean minus 3 standard deviations, $\overline{X} - 3\ SD$, is equal to $80 - 3(1) = 80 - 3 = 77$. Thus, almost all the scores fall between 83 and 77. This makes sense because, as we mentioned before, a small standard deviation (in this case $SD = 1$) indicates that the scores are close together, not very spread out.

As another example, suppose that a different set of scores had a mean $(\overline{X})$ calculated to be 80, but this time the standard deviation (*SD*) is calculated to be 4. In this case the mean plus three standard deviations, $\overline{X} + 3\ SD$, is equal to $80 + 3(4) = 80 + 12 = 92$. In case you still do not see,

$$80 + 1\ SD = 80 + 4 = 84$$
$$80 + 2\ SD = 80 + 4 + 4 = 88$$
$$80 + 3\ SD = 80 + 4 + 4 + 4 = 92$$

Or, to explain it another way, 80 plus 1 $SD = 80 + 4 = 84$, plus another $SD = 84 + 4 = 88$, plus one more (the third) $SD = 88 + 4 = 92$. Now, the mean minus three standard deviations, $\overline{X} - 3\ SD$, is equal to $80 - 3(4) = 80 - 12 = 68$. In other words,

$$80 - 1\ SD = 80 - 4 = 76$$
$$80 - 2\ SD = 80 - 4 - 4 = 72$$
$$80 - 3\ SD = 80 - 4 - 4 - 4 = 68$$

Or, to explain it another way, 80 minus 1 $SD = 80 - 4 = 76$, minus another $SD = 76 - 4 = 72$, minus one more (the third) $SD = 72 - 4 = 68$. Thus, almost all the scores fall between 68 and 92. This makes sense because a larger standard deviation (in this case $SD = 4$) indicates that the scores are more spread out. Clearly, if you know the mean and standard deviation of a set of scores you have a pretty good idea of what the scores look like. You know the mean score and you know how spread out or variable the scores are. Together you can describe a set of data quite well.

THE NORMAL CURVE

The plus and minus 3 concept is valid only when the scores are normally distributed—that is, form a normal, or bell-shaped score distribution. Many, many variables, such as height, weight, IQ scores, and achievement scores yield a normal curve if a sufficient number of participants are measured.

If a variable is normally distributed, that is, forms a normal curve, then several things are true:

1. Fifty percent of the scores are above the mean and 50% are below the mean.
2. The mean, the median, and the mode are the same value.
3. Most scores are near the mean and the farther from the mean a score is, the fewer the number of participants who attained that score.
4. The same number, or percentage, of scores is between the mean and plus one standard deviation $(\overline{X} + 1\ SD)$ as is between the mean and minus

one standard deviation ($\overline{X} - 1\ SD$), and similarly for $\overline{X} \pm 2\ SD$ and $\overline{X} \pm 3\ SD$ (See Figure 12.2).

In Figure 12.2, the symbol σ (the Greek letter sigma) is used to represent the standard deviation, that is, $1\ σ = 1\ SD$, and the mean ($\overline{X}$) is designated as 0 (zero). The symbol σ is used to indicate that the curve represents a population, whereas *SD* generally indicates that the curve represents the scores of a sample. Since most research is done with samples, we will mainly use *SD* in the following discussion. The vertical lines at each of the *SD* (σ) points delineate a certain percentage of the total area under the curve. As Figure 12.2 indicates, if a set of scores forms a normal distribution, the $\overline{X} + 1\ SD$ includes 34.13% of the scores and the $\overline{X} - 1\ SD$ includes 34.13% of the scores. Each succeeding standard deviation encompasses a constant percentage of the cases. $\overline{X} \pm 2.58\ SD$ includes 99% of the cases, so we see that $\overline{X} \pm 3\ SD$ includes almost all the scores, as pointed out previously.

Below the row of *SD*s is a row of percentages. As you move from left to right, from point to point, the cumulative percentage of scores that fall below each point is indicated. Thus, at the point corresponding to $-3\ SD$, we see that only 0.1% of the scores fall below this point. The numerical value corresponding to +1 *SD*, on the other hand, is a figure higher than 84.1% (rounded to 84% on the next row) of the scores. Relatedly, the next row, percentile equivalents, also involves cumulative percentages. The figure 20 in this row, for example, indicates that 20% of the scores fall below this point. We will discuss percentiles and the remaining rows further as we proceed through this chapter, but let's look at one more row now. Near the bottom of Figure 12.2, under Wechsler Scales, is a row labeled Deviation IQs. This row indicates that the mean IQ for the Wechsler Scale is 100 and the standard deviation is 15 (115 is in the column corresponding to +1 *SD*) and since the mean is 100, 115 represents $\overline{X} + 1\ SD = 100 + 15 = 115$. An IQ of 145 represents a score 3 *SD*s above the mean (average) IQ. If your IQ is in this neighborhood, you are certainly a candidate for Mensa! An IQ of 145 corresponds to a percentile of 99.9. On the other side of the curve we see that an IQ of 85 corresponds to a score one standard deviation below the mean ($\overline{X} - 1\ SD = 100 - 15 = 85$) and to the 16th percentile. Note that the mean always corresponds to the 50th percentile. In other words, the average score is always that point above which are 50% of the cases and below which are 50% of the cases. Thus, if scores are normally distributed the following statements are true:

$$\overline{X} \pm 1.0\ SD = \text{approximately 68\% of the scores}$$
$$\overline{X} \pm 2.0\ SD = \text{approximately 95\% of the scores}$$
$$\text{(1.96 } SD \text{ is exactly 95\%)}$$
$$\overline{X} \pm 2.5\ SD = \text{approximately 99\% of the scores}$$
$$\text{(2.58 } SD \text{ is exactly 99\%)}$$
$$\overline{X} \pm 3.0\ SD = \text{approximately 99.9\% of the scores}$$

And similarly, the following are always true:

$$\overline{X} - 3.0\ SD = \text{approximately the 0.1 percentile}$$
$$\overline{X} - 2.0\ SD = \text{approximately the 2nd percentile}$$
$$\overline{X} - 1.0\ SD = \text{approximately the 16th percentile}$$
$$\overline{X} = \text{the 50th percentile}$$
$$\overline{X} + 1.0\ SD = \text{approximately the 84th percentile}$$
$$\overline{X} + 2.0\ SD = \text{approximately the 98th percentile}$$
$$\overline{X} + 3.0\ SD = \text{approximately the 99th+ percentile}$$

FIGURE 12.2

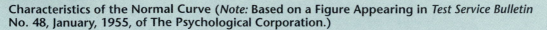

Characteristics of the Normal Curve (*Note:* Based on a Figure Appearing in *Test Service Bulletin No. 48*, January, 1955, of The Psychological Corporation.)

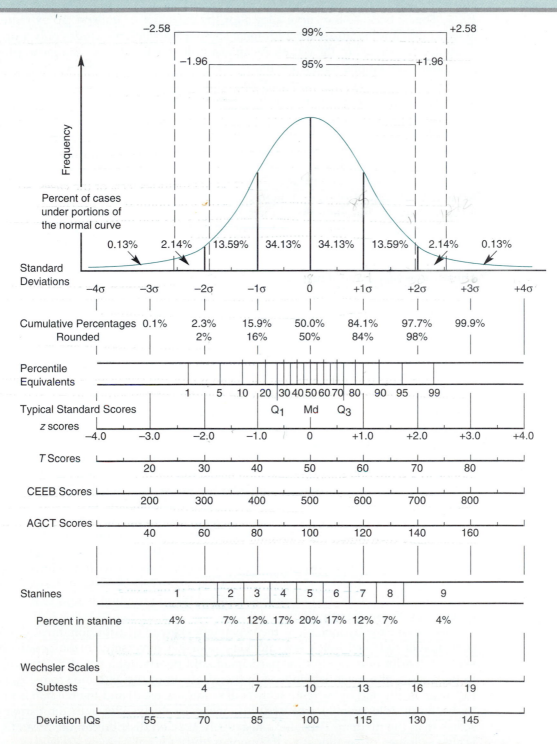

Note. This chart cannot be used to equate scores on one test to scores on another test. For example, both 600 on the CEEB and 120 on the AGCT are one standard deviation above their respective means, but they do not represent "equal" standings because the scores were obtained from different groups.

You might have noticed that the ends of the curve never touch the baseline and that there is no definite number of standard deviations that corresponds to 100%. This is because the curve allows for the existence of unexpected extremes at either end and because each additional standard deviation includes only a tiny fraction of a percent of the scores. As an example, for the IQ test, the mean plus 5 standard deviations would be $100 + 5(15) = 100 + 75 = 175$. Surely 5 SDs would include everyone. Wrong! A very small number of persons have scored near 200, which corresponds to $+6.67$ SDs. Thus, while ± 3 SDs includes just about everyone, the exact number of standard deviations required to include every score varies from variable to variable.

As mentioned earlier, many variables form a normal distribution, including physical measures, such as height and weight, and psychological measures, such as intelligence and aptitude. In fact, most variables measured in education form normal distributions if enough participants are tested. Note however, that a variable that is normally distributed in a population may not be normally distributed in smaller samples from the population. Depending on the size and nature of a particular sample, the assumption of a normal curve may or may not be valid. Since research studies deal with a finite number of participants, and often a not very large number, research data only more or less approximate a normal curve. Correspondingly, all of the equivalencies (standard deviation, percentage of cases, and percentile) are also only approximations. This is an important point because most statistics used in educational research are based on the assumption that the variable is normally distributed. If this assumption is badly violated in a given sample, then certain statistics should not be used. In general, however, the fact that most variables are normally distributed allows us to quickly determine many useful pieces of information concerning a set of data.

Skewed Distributions

When a distribution is not normal, it is said to be skewed. A normal distribution is symmetrical and the values of the mean, the median, and the mode are the same. A distribution that is skewed is not symmetrical, and the values of the mean, the median, and the mode are different. In a symmetrical distribution, there are approximately the same number of extreme scores (very high and very low) at each end of the distribution. In a skewed distribution there are more extreme scores at one end than the other. If the extreme scores are at the lower end of the distribution, the distribution is said to be negatively skewed. If the extreme scores are at the higher end of the distribution, the distribution is said to be positively skewed (see Figure 12.3).

As we can see by looking at the negatively skewed distribution, most of the participants did well but a few did very poorly. Conversely, in the positively skewed distribution, most of the participants did poorly but a few did very well. In both cases, the mean is "pulled" in the direction of the extreme scores. Since the mean is affected by extreme scores (all scores are used) and the median is not (only the middle score(s) are used), the mean is always closer to the extreme scores than the median. Thus, for a negatively skewed distribution the mean ($\overline{X}$) is always lower, or smaller, than the median (md); for a positively skewed distribution the mean is always higher or greater than the median. Since the mode is not affected by extreme scores, no "always" statements can be made concerning its relationship to the mean and the median in a skewed distribution. Usually,

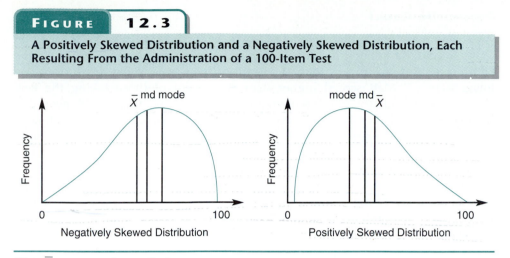

FIGURE **12.3**

A Positively Skewed Distribution and a Negatively Skewed Distribution, Each Resulting From the Administration of a 100-Item Test

Negatively Skewed Distribution   Positively Skewed Distribution

(*Note.* $\overline{X}$ = mean; md = median)

however, as Figure 12.3 indicates, in a negatively skewed distribution the mean and the median are lower, or smaller, than the mode, whereas in a positively skewed distribution the mean and the median are higher, or greater, than the mode.

To summarize:

negatively skewed: mean < median < mode
positively skewed: mean > median > mode

Because the relationship between the mean and the median is a constant, the skewness of a distribution can be determined without constructing a frequency polygon. If the mean is less than the median, the distribution is negatively skewed; if the mean and the median are the same, or very close, the distribution is symmetrical; if the mean is greater than the median, the distribution is positively skewed. The farther apart the mean and the median are, the more skewed is the distribution. If the distribution is very skewed, then the assumption of normality required for many statistics is violated.

MEASURES OF RELATIVE POSITION

Measures of relative position indicate where a score is in relation to all other scores in the distribution. In other words, measures of relative position permit you to express how well an individual has performed as compared to all other individuals in the sample who have been measured on the same variable. In chapter 5 this was called *norm-referenced measurement*. A major advantage of such measures is that they make it possible to compare the performance of an individual on two or more different tests. For example, if Angelica's score in reading is 40 and her score in math is 35, it does not follow that she did better in reading; 40 may have been the lowest score on the reading test and 35 the highest score on the math test! Measures of relative position express different scores on a common scale. The two most frequently used measures of relative position are percentile ranks and standard scores.

Percentile Ranks

A percentile rank indicates the percentage of scores that fall at or below a given score. If Matt Mathphobia's score of 65 corresponds to a percentile rank of 80 (the 80th percentile), this means that 80 percent of the scores in the distribution are lower than 65. Matt scored higher than 80 percent of those taking the test. Conversely, if Dudley Veridull scored at the 7th percentile, this would mean that Dudley only did better than, or received a higher score than, 7% of the test takers.

Percentiles are appropriate for data representing an ordinal scale, although they are mainly computed for interval data. The median of a set of scores corresponds to the 50th percentile, which makes sense because the median is the middle point and therefore the point below which are 50% of the scores. Although percentile ranks are not used very often in research studies, they are frequently used in the public schools to report test results of students in a form that is understandable by most audiences.

Standard Scores

Figure 12.2 depicts a number of standard scores. Basically, a standard score is a derived score that expresses how far a given raw score is from some reference point, typically the mean, in terms of standard deviation units. A standard score is a measure of relative position that is appropriate when the test data represent an interval or ratio scale of measurement. The most commonly reported and used standard scores are z scores, T scores (or Z scores), and stanines. Standard scores allow scores from different tests to be compared on a common scale and, unlike percentiles, permit valid mathematical operations such as averages to be computed. Averaging nonstandard scores on a series of tests in order to obtain an overall average score is like averaging apples and oranges and getting an "orapple." Such tests are likely to vary in level of difficulty and variability of scores. By converting test scores to standard scores, however, we can average them and arrive at a valid final index of average performance.

The normal curve equivalencies indicated in Figure 12.2 for the various standard scores are accurate only to the degree to which the distribution is normal. Further, standard scores can be compared only if all the derived scores are based on the raw scores (number correct) of the same group. For example, a CEEB (College Entrance Examination Board) score of 700 is not equivalent to a Wechsler IQ of 130 because the tests were normed on different groups. If a set of raw scores is normally distributed, then so are the standard score equivalents. But, as noted, all distributions are not normal. For example, height is normally distributed, but the measured heights of the girls in a seventh-grade gym class may not be. There is a procedure for transforming raw scores that ensures that the distribution of standard scores will be normal. Raw scores thus transformed are referred to as *normalized* scores. All resulting standard scores are normally distributed and the normal curve equivalencies are accurate.

z Scores. A z score is the most basic standard score. It expresses how far a score is from the mean in terms of standard deviation units. A score that is exactly "on" the mean corresponds to a z score of 0. A score that is exactly 1 standard deviation above the mean corresponds to a z score of $+1.00$ and a z score that is exactly 2 standard deviations below the mean corresponds to a z score of -2.00. Get it?

As Figure 12.2 indicates, if a set of scores is transformed into a set of z scores (each score is expressed as a z score), the new distribution has a mean of 0 and a standard deviation of 1.

The major advantage of z scores is that they allow scores from different tests or subtests to be compared. As an example, suppose Bobby Bonker's mother, a woman who is really on top of things, comes in and asks his teacher, "How is Bobby doing in the basic skills area?" If the teacher tells her that Bobby's reading score was 50 and his math score was 40, she still does not know how well Bobby is doing. In fact, she might get the false impression that he is better in reading, when in fact 50 might be a very low score on the reading test and 40 might be a very good score on the math test. Now suppose Bobby's teacher also tells his mother that the average score (the mean, $\overline{X}$) on the reading test was 60, and the average score on the math test was 30. Aha! Now it looks as if Bobby is better in math than in reading. Further, if the standard deviation (SD) on both tests was 10, Bobby's true status becomes even more evident. Since his score in reading is exactly 1 SD below the mean ($60 - 10 = 50$), his z score is -1.00. On the other hand, his score in math is 1 SD above the mean ($30 + 10 = 40$) and his z score is $+1.00$. As shown, z scores can be translated into percentiles to show that Bobby is clearly better in math than in reading.[3]

	RAW SCORE	$\overline{X}$	**SD**	**z**	**PERCENTILE**
Reading	50	60	10	-1.00	16th
Math	40	30	10	$+1.00$	84th

We can use Figure 12.2 to estimate percentile equivalents for given z scores, but this becomes more difficult for z scores that fall between the values given in Figure 12.2, for example, z scores of .63 or -1.78. A better approach is to use Table A.3 in the Appendix. For each z between -3.00 and $+3.00$ in the column labeled Area, Table A.3 gives the proportion of cases that are included up to that point. In other words, for any value of z, the area created to the left of the line on the curve represents the proportion of cases that falls below that z score. Thus, for z = .00 (the mean score), we go down the z columns until we come to .00 and we see that the corresponding area to the left is .5000, representing 50% of the cases and the 50th percentile. For Bobby, we simply go down the z columns until we come to -1.00 (his z score for reading), and we see that the corresponding area under the curve is .1587. By multiplying by 100 and rounding, we see that Bobby's reading score corresponds to approximately the 16th percentile (16% of the cases fall below $z = -1.00$). Similarly, for his math score of $+1.00$, the area is .8413, or approximately the 84th percentile.

Of course there are lots of other fun things we can do with Table A.3. If we want to know the proportion of cases in the area to the right of a given z score, for example, we simply subtract the left area value from 1.00, since the total area under the curve equals all, or 1.00 (100% of the cases). So, if we want to know the percentage of students who did better than Bobby on the reading test, we sub-

[3]This analysis is based on the assumption that the same groups took the test and that the tests were normally distributed.

tract .1587 from 1.00 and we get .8413, or approximately 84%. Similarly, if we want to know the percentage of scores for any test that falls between $z = -1.00$ and $z = +1.00$, we subtract .1587 from .8413 and we get .6826, or approximately 68%. In other words, approximately 68% (68.26% to be exact) of the scores fall between $z = -1.00$ and $z = +1.00$ (as indicated by Figure 12.2, 34.13% + 34.13% = 68.26%). Thus, we can find the percentage of cases that falls between any two z scores by subtracting their Table A.3 area values.

Also by subtraction, we can find the percentage of cases that falls between the mean ($z = .00$, area = .5000) and any other z score. A-a-and, we can also reverse the process to find, for example, the z score that corresponds to a given percentile. To become a member of Mensa, for example, you have to have an IQ at or higher than the 98th percentile. The closest area value in Table A.3 that reflects 98th percentile is .9803, which corresponds to $z = 2.06$. In other words, your IQ has to be approximately two standard deviations ($+2\,\sigma$) above average, which corresponds to an IQ of 130 (see Figure 12.2).

Of course, as mentioned previously and as Table A.3 indicates, scores are not always exactly 1 *SD* (or 2 *SD* or 3 *SD*) above or below the mean. Usually we have to apply the following formula to convert a raw score to a z score.

$$z = \frac{X - \overline{X}}{SD}, \text{ where } X \text{ is the raw score}$$

The only problem with z scores is that they involve negative numbers and decimals. It would be pretty hard to explain to Mrs. Bonker that her son was a -1.00. How do you tell a mother her son is a negative?! A simple solution is to transform z scores into T (or Z) scores. As Figure 12.2 indicates, z scores are actually the building blocks for a number of standard scores. Other standard scores represent transformations of z scores that communicate the same information in a more generally understandable form by eliminating negatives and/or decimals.

T Scores. A T score is nothing more than a z score expressed in a different form. To transform a z score to a T score, you simply multiply the z score by 10 and add 50. In other words, $T = 10z + 50$. Thus, a z score of 0 (the mean score) becomes a T score of 50 [$T = 10(0) + 50 = 0 + 50 = 50$]. A z score of $+1.00$ becomes a T score of 60 [$T = 10(1.00) + 50 = 10 + 50 = 60$], and a z score of -1.00 becomes a T score of 40 [$T = 10(-1.00) + 50 = -10 + 50 = 40$]. Thus, when scores are transformed to T scores, the new distribution has a mean of 50 and a standard deviation of 10 (see Figure 12.2). It would clearly be much easier to communicate to Mrs. Bonker that Bobby is a 40 in reading and a 60 in math and that the average score is 50 than to tell her that he is a $+1.00$ and a -1.00 and the average score is .00.

If the raw score distribution is normal, then so is the z score distribution and the T score distribution. If, on the other hand, the original distribution is not normal (such as when a small sample group is involved), then neither are the z and T score distributions. In such cases the distribution resulting from the $10z + 50$ transformation is more accurately referred to as a Z distribution. However, even with a set of raw scores that are not normally distributed, we can produce a set of normalized Z scores. In either case, we can use the normal curve equivalencies to convert such scores into corresponding percentiles, or vice versa. As Figure 12.2 indicates, for example, a T of 50 = a percentile of 50%. Similarly, a T of 30 corresponds to a percentile of 2 and a T of 60 corresponds to the 84th percentile. The same is true for the other standard score transformations illustrated in Figure 12.2. The CEEB distribution is formed by multiplying T scores by 10 to eliminate decimals; it is calculated directly using CEEB = $100z + 500$. The AGCT (Army General Classification Test) distribution is formed by multiplying T scores by 2, and is formed directly using AGCT = $20z + 100$. In both cases, given values can be converted to percentiles (and vice versa) using normal curve equivalencies. Thus, a CEEB score of 400 corresponds to the 16th percentile and the 98th percentile corresponds to an AGCT score of 140.

Stanines. Stanines are standard scores that divide a distribution into nine parts. Stanine (short for "standard nine") equivalencies are derived using the formula $2z + 5$ and rounding resulting values to the nearest whole number. Stanines 2 through 8 each represent $\frac{1}{2}$ SD of the distribution; stanines 1 and 9 include the remainder. In other words, stanine 5 includes $\frac{1}{2}$ SD around the mean ($\overline{X}$); that is, it equals $\overline{X} \pm \frac{1}{4}$ SD. Stanine 6 goes from $+ \frac{1}{4}$ SD to $+ \frac{3}{4}$ SD ($\frac{1}{4}$ $SD + \frac{1}{2}$ $SD = \frac{3}{4}$ SD), and so forth. Stanine 1 includes any score that is less than $-1\frac{3}{4}$ SD (-1.75 SD) below the mean, and stanine 9 includes any score that is greater than $+1\frac{3}{4}$ SD ($+1.75$ SD) above the mean. As Figure 12.2 indicates (see the row of figures directly beneath the stanines), stanine 5 includes 20% of the scores, stanines 4 and 6 each contain 17%, stanines 3 and 7 each contain 12%, 2 and 8 each contain 7%, and 1 and 9 each contain 4% of the scores (percentages approximate). Thus, if a student was at the 7th stanine her percentile would be approximately $4 + 7 + 12 + 17 + 20 + 17 + 12 = 89$ percentile.

Like percentiles, stanines are frequently reported in norms tables for standardized tests. They are very popular with school systems because they are so easy to understand and to explain to others. Although they are not as exact as other standard scores, they are useful for a variety of purposes. They are frequently used as a basis for grouping and are also used as a criterion for selecting students for special programs. A remediation program, for example, may select students who scored in the first and second stanine on a standardized reading test.

Use Figure 12.2 and Appendix A.3 to answer the following questions.

1. What percentile corresponds to a z score of $+2.00$?
2. What z score corresponds to a percentile of $-.20$?
3. Approximately what percentile corresponds to a stanine of 3?
4. What range of z scores encompasses 95% of the area in a normal curve?
5. What is the relationship of the mean, median, and mode in the normal distribution?

MEASURES OF RELATIONSHIP

Correlational research, the examination of the relationships between variables, was discussed in detail in chapter 9. You will recall that correlational research involves collecting data in order to determine whether, and to what degree, a relationship exists between two or more quantifiable variables—not a causal relationship, just a relationship. Degree of relationship is expressed as a correlation coefficient, which is computed using two sets of scores from a single group of participants. The correlation coefficient provides an estimate of just how related two variables are. If two variables are highly related, a correlation coefficient near +1.00 (or −1.00) will be obtained; if two variables are not related, a coefficient near .00 will be obtained. There are a number of different methods of computing a correlation coefficient; which one is appropriate depends on the scale of measurement represented by the data. The two most frequently used correlational analyses are the rank difference correlation coefficient, usually referred to as the Spearman rho, and the product moment correlation coefficient, usually referred to as the Pearson r. See Table 9.2 for other correlational approaches, including the phi coefficient, biserial, and intraclass correlations, among others.

The Spearman Rho

The Spearman rho coefficient is used to correlate data that are ranked. The Spearman rho is thus appropriate when the data represent an ordinal scale (although it may be used with interval data) and is used when the median and quartile deviation are used. If only one of the variables to be correlated is ranked the other variable to be correlated must also be expressed in terms of ranks. Thus, if intelligence were to be correlated with class rank, students' intelligence scores would have to be translated into ranks. If more than one participant receives the same score, then the corresponding ranks are averaged. So, for example, if two participants have the same, highest score, they are each assigned the average of rank 1 and rank 2, namely rank 1.5, and the next highest score is assigned rank 3. Similarly, the 24th and 25th highest scores, if identical, would each be assigned the rank 24.5. Like most other correlation coefficients, the Spearman rho produces a coefficient somewhere between −1.00 and +1.00. If, for example, a group of participants achieves identical ranks on both variables, the coefficient will be +1.00.

The Pearson r

The Pearson r correlation coefficient is the most appropriate measure when the variables to be correlated are either interval or ratio. Like the mean and the standard deviation, the Pearson r takes into account each and every score in both distributions; it is also the most stable measure of correlation. Because most educational measures represent interval scales, the Pearson r is usually the most used coefficient for determining relationship. An assumption associated with the application of the Pearson r is that the relationship between the variables being correlated is a linear one. If this is not the case, the Pearson r will not yield a valid indication of relationship. If there is any question concerning the linearity of the relationship, the two sets of data should be plotted as previously shown in Figure 9.1.

CALCULATION FOR INTERVAL DATA

Since most educational data are represented in interval scales, we will calculate the measure of central tendency, variability, relationship, and relative position appropriate for interval data. There are several alternate formulas available for computing each of these measures; in each case, however, we will use the easiest, raw score formula. At first glance some of the formulas may look scary but they are really easy. The only reason they look hard is because they involve symbols with which you may be unfamiliar. As promised, however, each formula transforms "magically" into an arithmetic problem; all you have to do is substitute the correct numbers for the correct symbols.

For those of you who have not done any arithmetic problems lately and would like a little review of the basics, worksheets and step-by-step answer keys are provided in Appendix C. Appendix C is taken from *Statistics with a Sense of Humor: A Humorous Workbook and Guide to Study Skills*, which also includes worksheets and step-by-step answer keys for all of the statistics to be discussed in this text. If you enjoy the review and would like to obtain a copy of the complete workbook, write to Fred Pyrczak, Publisher, P.O. Box 39731, Los Angeles, CA 90039.

> Following the various calculations, the corresponding STATPAK printout is presented. Because of differences in "rounding off" strategies, the text values may not exactly match the STATPAK values. Similarly, for any analysis you might check using STATPAK, your result may not match exactly.

SYMBOLS

Before we start calculating, let's get acquainted with a few basic statistical symbols. First, X (without a bar) is usually used to symbolize a score. If you see a column of numbers, and at the top of that column is an X, you know that the column represents a set of scores. If there are two sets of scores they may be labeled X_1 and X_2 or X and Y, it does not matter which.

Another symbol used frequently is the Greek letter Σ, which is used to indicate addition. Σ means "the sum of," or "add them all up." Thus ΣX means "add up all the Xs" and ΣY means "add up all the Ys." Isn't this easy? Now, if any symbol has a bar over it, such as $\bar{X}$, that indicates the mean, or arithmetic average, of the scores. Thus $\bar{X}$ refers to the mean of the X scores and $\bar{Y}$ refers to the mean of the Y scores.

A capital N refers to the number of participants; $N = 20$ means that there are 20 participants (N is for number; makes sense, doesn't it?). If one analysis involves several groups, the number of participants in each group is indicated with a lowercase letter n and a subscript indicating the group. If there are three groups, and the first group has 15 participants, the second group has 18, and the third group has 20, this is symbolized as $n_1 = 15$, $n_2 = 18$, and $n_3 = 20$. The total number of participants is represented with a capital $N = 53$ ($15 + 18 + 20 = 53$).

Finally, you must get straight the difference between ΣX^2 and $(\Sigma X)^2$; they do not mean the same thing. Different formulas may include one or the other or both, and it is very important to interpret each correctly, since a formula tells you what to do, and you must do exactly what it tells you. Now let us look at ΣX^2. What does it tell you? The Σ tells you that you are supposed to add something up. What you are supposed to add up are X^2s. What do you suppose X^2 means? Right. It means the square of the score; if $X = 4$, then $X^2 = 4 \times 4 = 16$. Thus, ΣX^2 says to square each score and then add up all the squares. Now let us look at $(\Sigma X)^2$. Since whatever is in the parentheses is always done first, the first thing we do is ΣX. You already know that means, "add up all the scores." And then what? Right. After you add the scores, you square the total. As an example:

X	X^2	
1	1	
2	4	$\Sigma X^2 = 55$
3	9	
4	16	$(\Sigma X)^2 = 225$
5	25	
$\Sigma X = 15$	$\Sigma X^2 = 55$	

As you can see, there is a big difference between ΣX^2 and $(\Sigma X)^2$, so watch out! To summarize, symbols commonly used in statistical formulas are as follows:

X = a score
Σ = the sum of; add them up
ΣX = the sum of all the scores
$\overline{X}$ = the mean, or arithmetic average, of the scores
N = total number of participants
n = number of particpants in a particular group
ΣX^2 = the sum of the squares; square each score and add up all the squares
$(\Sigma X)^2$ = the square of the sum; add up the scores and square the sum, or total

If you approach each statistic in an orderly fashion, it makes your statistical life easier. A suggested procedure is to:

1. Make the columns required by the formula (e.g., X, X^2, as just shown) and find the sum of each column.
2. Label the sum of each column; in the previous example, the label for the sum of the X column = ΣX, and the label for the sum of the X^2 column = ΣX^2.
3. Write the formula.
4. Write the arithmetic equivalent of the formula (e.g., $(\Sigma X) = (15)^2$).
5. Solve the arithmetic problem (e.g., $(15)^2 = 225$).

THE MEAN

We have already calculated means, but we will review here as the basis for making other calculations. Although sample sizes of 5 are hardly ever considered to be acceptable, we will use this number of participants so that you can concentrate on how the calculation is being done and will not get lost in the numbers. For the same reason we will also use small numbers. Now, assume we have the following scores for some old friends of ours and we want to compute the mean, or arithmetic average.

	X	
Iggie	1	Remember that a column
Hermie	2	labeled X means "here
Fifi	3	come the scores!"
Teenie	4	
Tiny	5	

The formula for the mean is $\overline{X} = \dfrac{\Sigma X}{N}$

You are now looking at a statistic. Looks bad, right? Now let us first see what it really says. It reads "the mean ($\overline{X}$) is equal to the sum of the scores (ΣX) divided by the number of participants (N)." So, in order to find $\overline{X}$ we need ΣX and N.

X
1
2
3
4
5
$\Sigma X = 15$

Clearly, $\Sigma X = 1 + 2 + 3 + 4 + 5 = 15$
$N = 5$ (there are 5 participants, right?)

Now we have everything we need to find the mean and all we have to do is substitute the correct number for each symbol.

$$\overline{X} = \frac{\Sigma X}{N} = \frac{15}{5} = 3$$

Now what do we have? Right! An arithmetic problem. And hardly a difficult one! More like an elementary school arithmetic problem. And all we did was to substitute each symbol with the appropriate number. Thus,

$$\overline{X} = \frac{\Sigma X}{N} = \frac{15}{5} = 3 \ (3.00)$$

and the mean is equal to 3.00. If you look at the scores you can see that 3 is clearly the average score. Traditionally, statistical results are given with two decimal places, so our "official" answer is 3.00.

Was that hard? Cer-tain-ly not! And guess what—you just learned how to do a statistic! Are they all going to be that easy? Of course!

THE STANDARD DEVIATION

Earlier we explained the fact that the standard deviation is the square root of the variance, which is based on the distance of each score from the mean. To calculate the standard deviation (SD), however, we do not have to calculate variance scores; we can use a raw score formula that gives us the same answer with less grief. Now, before you look at the formula, remember that no matter how bad it looks, it is going to turn into an easy arithmetic problem. Ready?

$$SD = \sqrt{\frac{SS}{N-1}} \text{ where } SS = \Sigma X^2 - \frac{(\Sigma X)^2}{N}$$

or

$$SD = \sqrt{\frac{\Sigma X^2 - \frac{(\Sigma X)^2}{N}}{N-1}}$$

In other words, the SD is equal to the square root of the sum of squares (SS) divided by $N - 1$.

If the standard deviation of a population is being calculated, the formula is exactly the same, except we divide sum of squares by N, instead of $N - 1$. The reason is that a sample standard deviation is considered to be a biased estimate of the population standard deviation. When we select a sample, especially a small sample, the probability is that participants will come from the middle of the distribution and that extreme scores will not be represented. Thus, the range of sample scores will be smaller than the population range, as will be the sample standard deviation. As the sample size increases, so do the chances of getting extreme scores; thus, the smaller the sample, the more important it is to correct for the downward bias. By dividing by $N - 1$ instead of N, we make the denominator (bottom part!) smaller, and thus $\dfrac{SS}{N - 1}$ is larger, closer to the population SD than $\dfrac{SS}{N}$. For example, if $SS = 18$ and $N = 10$, then

$$\frac{SS}{N - 1} = \frac{18}{9} = 2.00 \qquad \frac{SS}{N} = \frac{18}{10} = 1.80$$

Now just relax and look at each piece of the formula; you already know what each piece means. Starting with the easy one, N refers to what? Right—the number of participants. How about (ΣX)? Right—the sum of the scores. And $(\Sigma X)^2$? Right—the square of the sum of the scores. That leaves ΣX^2, which means the sum of what? . . . Fantastic. The sum of the squares. Okay, let us use the same scores we used to calculate the mean. The first thing we need to do is to square each score and then add those squares up—while we are at it we can also go ahead and add up all the scores.

	X	X^2	
Iggie	1	1	
Hermie	2	4	$\Sigma X = 15$
Fifi	3	9	$\Sigma X^2 = 55$
Teenie	4	16	$N = 5$
Tiny	5	25	$N - 1 = 4$
	$\Sigma X = 15$	$\Sigma X^2 = 55$	

Does the formula ask for anything else? No. We are in business. Substituting each symbol with its numerical equivalent we get:

$$SS = \Sigma X^2 - \frac{(\Sigma X)^2}{N} = 55 - \frac{(15)^2}{5}$$

Now what do we have? A statistic? No! An arithmetic problem? Yes! A hard arithmetic problem? No! It is harder than 15/5 but it is not hard. If we just do what the formula tells us to do, we will have no problem at all. First, we need to square 15:

$$SS = \Sigma X^2 - \frac{(\Sigma X)^2}{N} = 55 - \frac{(15)^2}{5} = 55 - \frac{225}{5}$$

So far so good? Next, we divide 225 by 5: which equals 45. It is looking a lot better; now it really is an easy arithmetic problem. The next step is to subtract 45 from 55, and we get a sum of squares (SS) equal to 10.00

Mere child's play. Think you can figure out how to get the *SD*? Terrific! Now that we have *SS*, we simply substitute it into the *SD* formula as follows:

$$SD = \sqrt{\frac{SS}{N-1}} = \sqrt{\frac{10}{4}} = \sqrt{2.5}$$

To find the square root of 2.5, simply enter 2.5 into your calculator and hit the square root button ($\sqrt{}$); the square root of 2.5 is 1.58. Substituting in our square root we have:

$$SD = \sqrt{2.5} = 1.58$$

and the standard deviation is 1.58. If we had calculated the standard deviation for the IQ distribution shown in Figure 12.2, what would we have gotten? Right—15. Now you know how to do two useful descriptive statistics. Were they hard? No! The STATPAK printout for this example follows.

```
================================================================================

            STANDARD DEVIATION FOR SAMPLES AND POPULATIONS

================================================================================

     STATISTIC                                                    VALUE
--------------------------------------------------------------------------------

     NO. OF SCORES (N)                                              5

     SUM OF SCORES (ΣX)                                          15.00

     MEAN (X̄)                                                     3.00

     SUM OF SQUARED SCORES (ΣX²)                                 55.00

     SUM OF SQUARES (SS)                                         10.00

     STANDARD DEVIATION FOR A POPULATION                          1.41

     STANDARD DEVIATION FOR A SAMPLE                              1.58

================================================================================
```

STANDARD SCORES

Your brain has earned a rest, and the formula for a *z* score is a piece of cake:

$$z = \frac{X - \bar{X}}{SD}$$

To convert scores to *z* scores we simply apply that formula to each score. We have already computed the mean and the standard deviation for the following scores:

	X	
Iggie	1	
Hermie	2	$\bar{X} = 3$
Fifi	3	
Teenie	4	$SD = 1.58$
Tiny	5	

Let's find Iggie's z score. Get out your calculator.

$$\text{Iggie} \quad z = \frac{X - \overline{X}}{SD} = \frac{1 - 3}{1.58} = \frac{-2}{1.58} = -1.26$$

This tells us that Iggie's standard score was 1.26 standard deviations below average. In case you have forgotten, if the signs are the same (two positives or two negatives), the answer in a multiplication or division problem is a positive number; if the signs are different, the answer is a negative number, as in Iggie's case. For the rest of our friends, the results are:

$$\text{Hermie} \quad z = \frac{X - \overline{X}}{SD} = \frac{-1}{1.58} = -.63$$

$$\text{Fifi} \quad z = \frac{X - \overline{X}}{SD} = \frac{0}{1.58} = .00$$

$$\text{Teenie} \quad z = \frac{X - \overline{X}}{SD} = \frac{1}{1.58} = +.63$$

$$\text{Tiny} \quad z = \frac{X - \overline{X}}{SD} = \frac{2}{1.58} = +1.26$$

Notice that since Fifi's score was the same as the mean score. Her z score is .00, meaning that her score is no distance from the mean (it's on the mean). On the other hand, Iggie's and Hermie's scores were below the mean, so their z scores are negative, whereas Teenie and Tiny scored above the mean and their z scores are positive. If we want to eliminate the negatives, we can convert each z score to a Z score. Remember those? Multiplying each z score by 10 and adding 50 gives $Z = 10z + 50$? If we apply the z score formula we get

$$
\begin{aligned}
\text{Iggie} \quad Z &= 10z + 50 = 10(-1.26) + 50 \\
&= -12.6 + 50 \\
&= 50 - 12.6 \\
&= 37.40
\end{aligned}
$$

$$
\begin{aligned}
\text{Hermie} \quad Z &= 10z + 50 = 10(-.63) + 50 \\
&= -6.3 + 50 \\
&= 50 - 6.3 \\
&= 43.70
\end{aligned}
$$

$$
\begin{aligned}
\text{Fifi} \quad Z &= 10z + 50 = 10(.00) + 50 \\
&= .00 + 50 \\
&= 50 + .00 \\
&= 50.00
\end{aligned}
$$

$$
\begin{aligned}
\text{Teenie} \quad Z &= 10z + 50 = 10(+.63) + 50 \\
&= 6.3 + 50 \\
&= 50 + 6.3 \\
&= 56.30
\end{aligned}
$$

$$
\begin{aligned}
\text{Tiny} \quad Z &= 10z = 50 = 10(+1.26) + 50 \\
&= 12.6 + 50 \\
&= 50 + 12.6 \\
&= 62.60
\end{aligned}
$$

We told you it would be easy! The STATPAK results are shown as follows.

```
=================================================================

             STANDARD SCORES FOR SAMPLES AND POPULATIONS

=================================================================:
    STATISTIC                                                VALUE
-----------------------------------------------------------------

    NO. OF SCORES (N)                                          5

    MEAN (X̄)                                                 3.00

    STANDARD DEVIATION FOR A POPULATION                       1.41

    STANDARD DEVIATION FOR A SAMPLE                           1.58

-----------------------------------------------------------------

                      z  A N D   T - S C O R E S

                   RAW          POPULATION            SAMPLE
                  SCORE     z-SCORE T-SCORE  z-SCORE T-SCORE

-----------------------------------------------------------------

       ITEM NO:  1    1.00      -1.41   35.86   -1.26   37.35
       ITEM NO:  2    2.00      -0.71   42.93   -0.63   43.68
       ITEM NO:  3    3.00       0.00   50.00    0.00   50.00
       ITEM NO:  4    4.00       0.71   57.07    0.63   56.32
       ITEM NO:  5    5.00       1.41   64.14    1.26   62.65

=================================================================
```

THE PEARSON *r*

Now that your brain is rested, you are ready for the Pearson *r*. The formula for the Pearson *r* *looks* very, very complicated, but it is not (have we lied to you so far?). It looks tough because it has a lot of pieces, but each piece is quite simple to calculate. To calculate correlations including a Pearson *r* we need two sets of scores. Let us assume we have the following sets of scores for two variables for our old friends:

	X	Y
Iggie	1	2
Hermie	2	3
Fifi	3	4
Teenie	4	3
Tiny	5	5

The question is, "Are these two variables related?" Positively? Negatively? Not at all?

In order to answer those questions we apply the formula for the Pearson *r* to the data. Here goes!

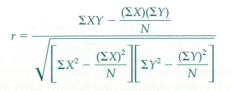

$$r = \frac{\Sigma XY - \dfrac{(\Sigma X)(\Sigma Y)}{N}}{\sqrt{\left[\Sigma X^2 - \dfrac{(\Sigma X)^2}{N}\right]\left[\Sigma Y^2 - \dfrac{(\Sigma Y)^2}{N}\right]}}$$

Now, if you look at each piece you will see that you already know how to calculate all of them except one. You should have no problem with ΣX, ΣY, ΣX^2, or ΣY^2. And even though there are 10 scores there are only 5 participants, so $N = 5$. What is left? The only new symbol in the formula is ΣXY. What could that mean? Well, you know that it is the sum of something, namely the XYs, whatever they are. An XY is just what you would guess it is—the product of an X score and its corresponding Y score. Thus, Iggie's XY score is $1 \times 2 = 2$, and Teenie's XY score is $4 \times 3 = 12$. Okay, let us get all the pieces we need:

	X	Y	X^2	Y^2	XY
Iggie	1	2	1	4	2
Hermie	2	3	4	9	6
Fifi	3	4	9	16	12
Teenie	4	3	16	9	12
Tiny	5	5	25	25	25
	15	17	55	63	57
	ΣX	ΣY	ΣX^2	ΣY^2	ΣXY

Now guess what we are going to do. Right! We are going to turn that horrible-looking statistic into a horrible-looking arithmetic problem! Just kidding. Of course it will really be an easy arithmetic problem if we do it one step at a time.

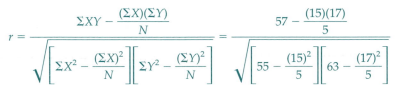

$$r = \frac{\Sigma XY - \dfrac{(\Sigma X)(\Sigma Y)}{N}}{\sqrt{\left[\Sigma X^2 - \dfrac{(\Sigma X)^2}{N}\right]\left[\Sigma Y^2 - \dfrac{(\Sigma Y)^2}{N}\right]}} = \frac{57 - \dfrac{(15)(17)}{5}}{\sqrt{\left[55 - \dfrac{(15)^2}{5}\right]\left[63 - \dfrac{(17)^2}{5}\right]}}$$

It still doesn't look good, but you have to admit it looks better! Let's start with the numerator (for you nonmathematical types, the top part). The first thing the formula tells you to do is multiply 15 by 17:

$$= \frac{57 - \dfrac{255}{5}}{\sqrt{\left[55 - \dfrac{(15)^2}{5}\right]\left[63 - \dfrac{(17)^2}{5}\right]}}$$

The next step is to divide 255 by 5:

$$= \frac{57 - 51}{\sqrt{\left[55 - \dfrac{(15)^2}{5}\right]\left[63 - \dfrac{(17)^2}{5}\right]}}$$

The next step is a real snap. All you have to do is subtract 51 from 57:

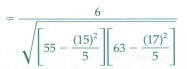

$$= \frac{6}{\sqrt{\left[55 - \dfrac{(15)^2}{5}\right]\left[63 - \dfrac{(17)^2}{5}\right]}}$$

So much for the numerator. Was that hard? NO! *Au contraire*, it was very easy. Right? Right. Now for the denominator (the bottom part). If you think hard, you will realize that you have seen part of the denominator before. Hint: It was not in connection with the mean. Let us go through it step by step anyway just in case you did not really understand what we were doing the last time we did it. The first thing the formula says to do is to square 15:

$$= \frac{6}{\sqrt{\left[55 - \frac{225}{5}\right]\left[63 - \frac{(17)^2}{5}\right]}}$$

Now we divide 225 by 5:

$$= \frac{6}{\sqrt{\left[55 - 45\right]\left[63 - \frac{(17)^2}{5}\right]}}$$

Did you get that? All we did was divide 225 by 5 and we got 45. Can you figure out the next step? Good. We subtract 45 from 55:

$$= \frac{6}{\sqrt{\left[10\right]\left[63 - \frac{(17)^2}{5}\right]}}$$

It is looking a lot better, isn't it? Okay, now we need to square 17; $17 \times 17 = 289$.

$$= \frac{6}{\sqrt{\left[10\right]\left[63 - \frac{289}{5}\right]}}$$

Next, we divide 289 by 5 (Sorry, life doesn't always come out even):

$$= \frac{6}{\sqrt{[10][63 - 57.8]}}$$

We are getting there. Now we subtract 57.8 from 63. Do not let the decimals scare you:

$$\frac{6}{\sqrt{[10][63 - 57.8]}} = \frac{6}{\sqrt{[10][5.2]}}$$

Can you figure out what to do next? If you find this difficult, hang in there, we're almost finished. If you find this easy, also hang in there. Next, we multiply 10 by 5.2:

$$\frac{6}{\sqrt{[10][5.2]}} = \frac{6}{\sqrt{52}}$$

Next, we find the square root of 52:

$$\frac{6}{\sqrt{52}} = \frac{6}{7.2}$$

Almost done. All we have to do is divide 6 by 7.2:

$$\frac{6}{7.2} = .83$$

Fanfare! Ta-ta-ta-ta! We are through. In case you got lost in the action, .83 is the correlation coefficient, the Pearson *r*. In other words, *r* = +.83. The STATPAK printout follows.

```
============================================================================

                    PEARSON'S PRODUCT MOMENT CORRELATION

============================================================================
     STATISTIC                                                    VALUE
----------------------------------------------------------------------------

     N                                                                 5
     ΣX                                                            15.00
     ΣY                                                            17.00
     ΣX²                                                           55.00
     ΣY²                                                           63.00
     MEAN OF 'X' SCORES                                             3.00
     MEAN OF 'Y' SCORES                                             3.40
     ΣXY                                                           57.00
     PEARSON'S r                                                    0.83
     df                                                                3
============================================================================
```

Is .83 good? Does it represent a true relationship? Is .83 significantly different from .00? If you recall the related discussion in chapter 9, you know that a correlation coefficient of .83 indicates a high positive relationship between the variables. To determine whether .83 represents a true relationship we need a table that indicates how large our correlation needs to be in order to be significant, that is, different from zero, given the number of participants we have and the level of significance at which we are working (see Table A.2 in the Appendix). The number of participants affects the degrees of freedom, which for the Pearson *r* are always computed by the formula $N - 2$. Thus, for our example, degrees of freedom $(df) = N - 2 = 5 - 2 = 3$. If we select $\alpha = .05$ as our level of significance, we are now ready to use Table A.2. Degrees of freedom and level of significance are among the coming attractions of chapter 13.

Look at Table A.2 and find the column labeled *df* and run your left index finger down the column until you hit 3, the *df* associated with our Pearson *r*; keep your left finger right there for the time being. Now run your right index finger across the top of the table until you come to .05, the significance level we have selected. Now, run your left finger straight across the table and your right finger straight down the table until they meet. If you follow directions well, you should have ended up at .8783, which rounds off to .88. Now we compare our coefficient to the table value. Is .83 greater than or equal to .88? No. Therefore, our coefficient does not indicate a true relationship between variables *X* and *Y*. Even though the correlation looks big, it is not big enough given that we only have five participants. We are not absolutely positive that there is no relationship (remember measurement error), but the odds are against it. Note that if we had had just one more participant ($N = 6$) our *df* would have been 4 ($N - 2 = 6 - 2 = 4$) and

Table A.2 would have indicated a significant relationship (.83 is greater than .81). Note, too, that the same table would have been used if *r* had been a negative number, −.83. The table does not know or care whether the *r* is positive or negative. It only tells you how large *r* must be in order to indicate a true relationship, that is, a relationship significantly different from .00.

Do not forget, however, that even if a correlation coefficient is statistically significant it does not imply a causal relationship, nor does it necessarily mean that the coefficient has any practical significance. Whether the coefficient is useful depends on the use to which it will be put; a coefficient to be used in a prediction study needs to be much higher than a coefficient to be used in a relationship study.

POSTSCRIPT

Almost always in a research study, descriptive statistics such as the mean and standard deviation are computed separately for each group in the study. A correlation coefficient is usually only computed in a correlational study (unless it is used to compute the reliability of an instrument used in a causal–comparative or experimental study). Standard scores are rarely used in research studies. However, in order to test our hypothesis we almost always need more than descriptive statistics; we need the application of one or more inferential statistics to test hypotheses and determine the significance of results.

Summary/Chapter 12

Preparing Data for Analysis

1. All instruments administered should be scored accurately and consistently, using the same procedures and criteria.
2. When a standardized instrument is used the test manual usually spells out the steps to be followed in scoring and a scoring key is often provided.
3. Scoring self-developed instruments is more complex, especially if open-ended items are involved. Steps for scoring each item and for arriving at a total score must be delineated and carefully followed. If open-ended items are to be scored, have at least one other person score the tests as a reliability check. Tentative scoring procedures should always be tried out beforehand by administering the instrument to individuals similar to but not part of the study participants.
4. After instruments have been scored, the results are transferred to summary data sheets or, more commonly, to a computer program. If planned analyses involve subgroup comparisons, scores should be tabulated for each subgroup.
5. The more complex the data are, the more useful computer recordkeeping and analysis can be.
6. Computers can facilitate data analysis and should be used when possible. However, a good guideline is that you should not use the computer to perform an analysis that you have never done yourself by hand, or at least studied extensively.

Types of Descriptive Statistics

7. The first step in data analysis is to describe, or summarize, the data using descriptive statistics, which permit the researcher to meaningfully describe many, many scores with a small number of indices.
8. The values calculated for a sample drawn from a population are referred to as statistics. The values calculated for an entire population are referred to as parameters.

GRAPHING DATA

9. The shape of the distribution may not be self-evident, especially if a large number of scores are involved. The most common method of graphing research data is to construct a frequency polygon. Other methods include the boxplot, pie chart, and the stem-and-leaf chart.

MEASURES OF CENTRAL TENDENCY

10. Measures of central tendency are a convenient way of describing a set of data with a single number.

11. The number resulting from computation of a measure of central tendency represents the average or typical score attained by a group of participants. Each index of central tendency is appropriate for a different scale of measurement; the mode is appropriate for nominal data, the median for ordinal data, and the mean for interval or ratio data.

12. The mode is the score that is attained by more participants than any other score. It is determined by looking at a set of scores or at a graph of scores and seeing which score occurs most frequently. A set of scores may have two (or more) modes. When nominal data are involved, however, the mode is the only appropriate measure of central tendency.

Mode

13. The median is that point in a distribution above and below which are 50% of the scores; in other words, the median is the midpoint. The median does not take into account each and every score; it ignores, for example, extremely high scores and extremely low scores.

Median

14. The mean is the arithmetic average of the scores and is the most frequently used measure of central tendency. The mean takes into account, or includes, each and every score in its computation. It is a more precise, stable index than both the median and the mode, except in situations in which there are extreme scores, making the median the best index of typical performance.

Mean

MEASURES OF VARIABILITY

15. Two sets of data that are very different can have identical means or medians, thus creat-

ing a need for a measure that indicates how spread out the scores are—how much variability there is.

16. Although the standard deviation is used with interval and ratio data and is the most commonly used measure of variation, the range is the only appropriate measure of variability for nominal data, and the quartile deviation is the appropriate index of variability for ordinal data.

17. The range is simply the difference between the highest and lowest score in a distribution and is determined by subtraction. It is not a very stable measure of variability, but its chief advantage is that it gives a quick, rough estimate of variability.

Range

18. The quartile deviation is one half of the difference between the upper quartile (the 75th percentile) and lower quartile (the 25th percentile) in a distribution. The quartile deviation is a more stable measure of variability than the range and is appropriate whenever the median is appropriate.

Quartile Dev.

19. Like the mean, the standard deviation is the most stable measure of variability and takes into account each and every score. If you know the mean and the standard deviation of a set of scores, you have a pretty good picture of what the distribution looks like.

Stand. Dev.

20. If the score distribution is relatively normal, then the mean plus 3 standard deviations and the mean minus 3 standard deviations encompasses just about all the scores, more than 99% of them.

THE NORMAL CURVE

21. Many variables do yield a normal, bell-shaped curve if a sufficient number of participants are measured.

22. If a variable is normally distributed, then several things are true. First, 50% of the scores are above the mean and 50% of the scores are below the mean. Second, the mean, the median, and the mode are the same. Third, most scores are near the mean and the further from the mean a score is, the fewer the number of participants who attained that score. Fourth, the same number, or percentage, of scores is between the mean and plus one standard deviation $(X + 1\ SD)$ as is between the mean and minus one stan-

dard deviation $(\overline{X} - 1\ SD)$, and similarly for $\overline{X} \pm 2\ SD$ and $\overline{X} \pm 3\ SD$.

23. If scores are normally distributed, the following are true statements:

% Rank

$\overline{X} \pm 1.0\ SD$ = approximately 68% of the scores
$\overline{X} \pm 2.0\ SD$ = approximately 95% of the scores
      (1.96 *SD* is exactly 95%)
$\overline{X} \pm 2.5\ SD$ = approximately 99% of the scores
      (2.58 *SD* is exactly 99%)
$\overline{X} \pm 3.0\ SD$ = approximately 99+% of the scores

And similarly, the following are always true:

Standard Score —
z score

$\overline{X} - 3.0\ SD$ = approximately the 0.1 percentile
$\overline{X} - 2.0\ SD$ = approximately the 2nd percentile
$\overline{X} - 1.0\ SD$ = approximately the 16th percentile
        X = the 50th percentile
$X + 1.0\ SD$ = approximately the 84th percentile
$\overline{X} + 2.0\ SD$ = approximately the 98th percentile
$\overline{X} + 3.0\ SD$ = approximately the 99th+ percentile

24. Since research studies deal with a finite number of participants, and often a not very large number, research data only more or less approximate a normal curve.

Stanines

Skewed Distributions

25. When a distribution is not normal, it is said to be skewed, and the values of the mean, the median, and the mode are different.
26. In a skewed distribution, there are more extreme scores at one end than the other. If the extreme scores are at the lower end of the distribution, the distribution is said to be negatively skewed; if the extreme scores are at the upper, or higher, end of the distribution, the distribution is said to be positively skewed. In both cases, the mean is "pulled" in the direction of the extreme scores.
27. For a negatively skewed distribution the mean $(\overline{X})$ is always lower, or smaller, than the median (md); for a positively skewed distribution the mean is always higher, or greater, than the median.

Spearman Rho

Measures of Relative Position

28. Measures of relative position indicate where a score is in relation to all other scores in the distribution. They make it possible to com-

pare the performance of an individual on two or more different tests.

29. A percentile rank indicates the percentage of scores that fall at or below a given score. Percentiles are appropriate for data representing an ordinal scale, although they are frequently computed for interval data. The median of a set of scores corresponds to the 50th percentile.
30. A standard score is a measure of relative position that is appropriate when the data represent an interval or ratio scale. A z score expresses how far a score is from the mean in terms of standard deviation units. If a set of scores is transformed into a set of z scores, the new distribution has a mean of 0 and a standard deviation of 1. The z score allows scores from different tests to be compared.
31. A table of normal curve areas corresponding to various z scores can be used to determine the proportion (and percentage) of cases that falls below a given z score, above a given z score, and between any two z scores.
32. A problem with z scores is that they can involve negative numbers and decimals. A simple solution is to transform z scores into Z scores by multiplying the z score by 10 and adding 50.
33. Stanines are standard scores that divide a distribution into nine parts.

Measures of Relationship

34. Degree of relationship is expressed as a correlation coefficient, which is computed from two sets of scores from a single group of participants. If two variables are highly related, a correlation coefficient near +1.00 (or −1.00) will be obtained; if two variables are not related, a coefficient near .00 will be obtained.
35. The Spearman rho is the appropriate measure of correlation when the variables are expressed as ranks instead of scores. It is appropriate when the data represent an ordinal scale (although it may be used with interval data) and is used when the median and quartile deviation are used.
36. The Spearman rho is interpreted in the same way as the Pearson r and produces a coefficient somewhere between −1.00 and +1.00. If more than one participant receives the

same score, then their corresponding ranks are averaged.

37. The Pearson r is the most appropriate measure of correlation when the sets of data to be correlated represent either interval or ratio scales, as most educational measures do. An assumption associated with the application of the Pearson r is that the relationship between the variables being correlated is a linear one.

Pearson r

Calculation for Interval Data

SYMBOLS

38. Symbols commonly used in statistical formulas are as follows:

X	=	any score
Σ	=	the sum of; add them up
ΣX	=	the sum of all the scores
$\overline{X}$	=	the mean, or arithmetic average, of the scores
N	=	total number of subjects
n	=	number of subjects in a particular group
ΣX^2	=	the sum of the squares; square each score and add up all the squares

$(\Sigma X)^2$ = the square of the sum; add up the scores and square the sum, or total

THE MEAN

39. The formula for the mean is $\overline{X} = \dfrac{\Sigma X}{N}$

40. The formula for the standard deviation is

$$SD = \sqrt{\dfrac{SS}{N-1}} \text{ where } SS = \Sigma X^2 - \dfrac{(\Sigma X)^2}{N}$$

41. The formula for a z score is $z = \dfrac{X - \overline{X}}{SD}$

The formula for a Z score is $Z = 10z + 50$.

THE PEARSON r

42. The formula for the Pearson r is

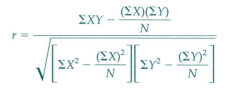

$$r = \dfrac{\Sigma XY - \dfrac{(\Sigma X)(\Sigma Y)}{N}}{\sqrt{\left[\Sigma X^2 - \dfrac{(\Sigma X)^2}{N}\right]\left[\Sigma Y^2 - \dfrac{(\Sigma Y)^2}{N}\right]}}$$

43. The formula for degrees of freedom for the Pearson r is $N - 2$.

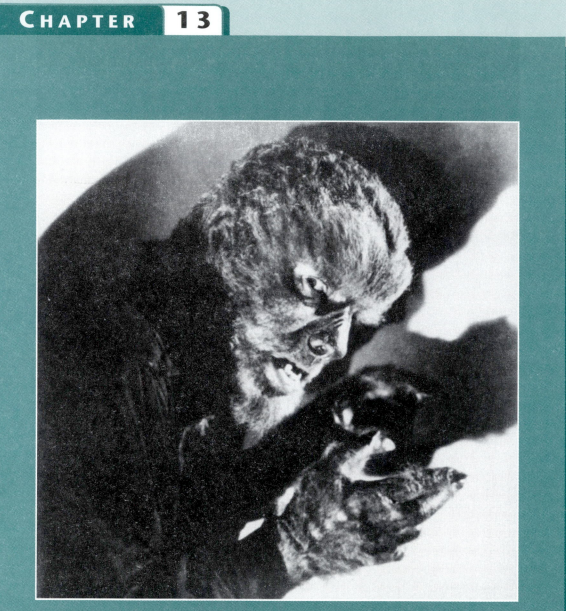

"Does it look bad? Is it? What will it turn into? (p. 485)."

Inferential Statistics

▄▄▄ OBJECTIVES

After reading chapter 13, you should be able to:

1. Explain the concept of standard error.
2. Describe how sample size affects standard error.
3. Describe the null hypothesis.
4. State the purpose of a test of significance.
5. Describe Type I and Type II errors.
6. Describe the concept of significance level (probability level).
7. Describe one-tailed and two-tailed tests.
8. Explain the difference between parametric tests and nonparametric tests.
9. State the purpose, and explain the strategy, of the *t* test.
10. Describe independent and nonindependent samples.
11. State the purpose and appropriate use of the *t* test for independent samples.
12. State the purpose and appropriate use of the *t* test for nonindependent samples.
13. Describe one major problem associated with analyzing gain or difference scores.
14. State the purpose of the simple analysis of variance.
15. State the purpose of multiple comparison procedures.
16. State the purpose of a factorial analysis of variance.
17. State the purpose of analysis of covariance.
18. State two uses of multiple regression.
19. State the purpose of chi square.
20. Generate three columns of five one-digit numbers ("scores"), compute each of the following statistics (give the formula and show your work), state whether each result is statistically significant at $\alpha = .05$, and interpret each result:
    a. *t* test for independent samples
    b. *t* test for nonindependent samples
    c. simple analysis of variance for three groups
    d. the Scheffé test
    e. chi square (Sum the numbers in each column and treat them as if they were the total number of people responding yes, no, and undecided, respectively, in a survey.)

If STATPAK, the microcomputer program that accompanies this text, is available to you, use it to check your work.

CONCEPTS UNDERLYING INFERENTIAL STATISTICS

Inferential statistics deal with, of all things, inferences. Inferences about what? Inferences about populations based on the results of samples. Inferential statistics allow researchers to generalize to a population of individuals based on information obtained from a limited number of research participants. Most educational research studies deal with samples from larger populations. Recall that the appropriateness of the various sampling techniques discussed in chapter 4 is based on their effectiveness in producing representative samples of the populations from which they are drawn. The more representative a sample is, the more generalizable its results will be to the population from which the sample was selected. Results that are representative only of that particular sample are of very limited research use. Consequently, random samples are preferred.

Inferential statistics are concerned with determining whether results obtained from a sample or samples are the same as would have been obtained for the entire population. As mentioned in chapter 12, sample values, such as the mean, are referred to as statistics. The corresponding values in the population are referred to as parameters. Thus, if a mean is based on a sample, it is a statistic; if it is based on an entire population, it is a parameter. Inferential statistics are used to make inferences about parameters, based on the statistics from a sample. If a difference between means is found for two groups at the end of a study, the question of interest is whether a similar difference exists in the population from which the samples were selected. That is, can the results of the study be generalized to the larger population? It could be that no real difference exists in the population and that the difference found for the samples was a chance one (remember sampling error?).

And now we get to the heart of inferential statistics, the concept of "how likely is it?" If your study indicates a difference between two sample means (say $X_1 = 35$ and $X_2 = 43$), how likely is it that this difference is a real one in the population? What kind of process can you use to determine whether the difference between X_1 and X_2 is a real, significant one rather than one attributable to sampling error? It is important to understand that using samples to make inferences about populations produces only probability statements about the populations. The degree to which the results of a sample can be generalized to a population is expressed in terms of probabilities; analyses do not "prove" results are true or false. There are many concepts underlying the application of inferential statistics that must be discussed prior to describing and illustrating types of inferential statistics.

STANDARD ERROR

Inferences about populations are based on information from samples. However, the chances of any sample being exactly identical to its population are virtually nil. Even when random samples are used, we cannot expect that the sample characteristics will be exactly the same as those of the population. For example, if we randomly select a number of samples from the same population and compute the mean for each, it is very likely that the means will be somewhat different from each other and that none of the means will be identical to the population mean. This expected random, or chance, variation among the means is referred to as *sampling error*. Recall that in chapter 4 we discussed the fact that, unlike sampling bias, sampling error is not the researcher's fault. Sampling error just happens, and is as inevitable as taxes and educational research courses! Thus, if a difference is found between two sample means, the important question is whether the difference is a true or significant one or is just the result of sampling error.

A useful characteristic of sampling errors is that they are normally distributed. As discussed in chapter 12, sampling errors vary in size (small errors versus large errors), and these errors tend to form a normal, bell-shaped curve. Thus, if a large number of samples of the same size are randomly selected from a population, we know that all the samples will not be the same, but that the means of all these samples should form a normal distribution around the population mean.

Further, the mean of all these sample means will yield a good estimate of the population mean.[1] Most of the sample means will be close to the population mean, and the number of means that are considerably different from the population mean will decrease as the size of the difference increases. In other words, very few means will be much higher or much lower than the population mean. An example may help to clarify this concept.

Let us suppose that we do not know what the population mean IQ is for the deviation IQs of the Stanford-Binet, Form L.M (although we do know from Figure 12.2). To determine the population mean, suppose we randomly select 100 samples of the same size from the possible Stanford-Binet scores (the population of scores). We might get the following 100 means:

64	82	87	94	98	100	104	108	114	121
67	83	88	95	98	101	104	109	115	122
68	83	88	96	98	101	105	109	116	123
70	84	89	96	98	101	105	110	116	124
71	84	90	96	98	102	105	110	117	125
72	84	90	97	99	102	106	111	117	127
74	84	91	97	99	102	106	111	118	130
75	85	92	97	99	103	107	112	119	131
75	86	93	97	100	103	107	112	119	136
78	86	94	97	100	103	108	113	120	142

If we compute the mean of these sample means, we get $10,038/100 = 100.38$, which is a darn good estimate of the population mean, which we know is 100. Further, if you check the scores, you will discover that 71% of the scores fall between 84 and 116, and 96% of the scores fall between 68 and 132. Since we know that the standard deviation is 16 (from Figure 12.2), our distribution approximates a normal curve quite well. The percentage of cases falling within each successive standard deviation is very close to the percentage characteristic of a normal curve (71% as compared to 68%, and 96% as compared to 95%). The concept illustrated by this example is a comforting one. It tells us, in essence, that most of the sample means we obtain will be close to the population mean and only a few will be very far away. In other words, once in a while, just by chance, we will get a sample that is quite different from the population, but not very often.

As with any normal distribution, a distribution of sample means has not only its own mean (the mean of the means) but also its own standard deviation (the difference of each sample mean from the mean of the means). The standard deviation of the sample means is usually called the standard error of the mean. The word *error* indicates that the various sample means making up the distribution contain some error in their estimate of the population mean. The standard error of the mean (SE_x) tells us by how much we would expect our sample means to differ if we used other samples from the same population. According to the normal curve percentages (Figure 12.2), we can say that approximately 68% of the sample means will fall between plus and minus one standard error of the mean (remember, the standard error of the mean is a standard deviation), 95% will fall between plus and minus two standard errors, and 99+% will fall between plus and minus three standard errors. In other words, if the mean is 60, and the

---

[1]To find the mean of the sample means, you simply add up all the sample means and divide by the number of means, as long as the size of each sample is the same.

standard error of the mean is 10, we can expect 68% of the sample means to be between 50 and 70 [60 ± 10]; 95% of the sample means to fall between 40 and 80 [60 ± 2 (10)]; and 99% of the sample means to fall between 30 and 90 [60 ± 3(10)]. Thus, in this example it is very likely that a sample mean might be 65, but a sample mean of 98 is highly unlikely, since ±3 standard errors (99%) falls between 30 and 90. Thus, given a number of large, randomly selected samples we can estimate quite well population parameters by computing the mean and standard deviation of the sample means. The smaller the standard error, the more accurate are the sample means as estimators of the population mean.

However, it is not necessary to select a large number of samples from a population to estimate the standard error. There is a formula for estimating the standard error of the mean from the standard deviation of a single sample. The formula is:

$$SE_{\overline{X}} = \frac{SD}{\sqrt{N-1}}$$

where

$SE_{\overline{X}}$ is the standard error of the mean

SD is the standard deviation for a sample

N is the sample size

Thus, if the SD of a sample is 12 and the sample size is 100,

$$SE_{\overline{X}} = \frac{12}{\sqrt{100-1}} = \frac{12}{\sqrt{99}} = \frac{12}{9.95} = 1.21$$

Using this estimate of the $SE_{\overline{X}}$, the sample mean, $\overline{X}$, and the normal curve, we can estimate probable limits within which the population mean falls. These limits are referred to as confidence limits. Thus, if a sample X is 80 and the SE is 1.00, the population mean falls between 79 and 81 ($X ± 1\ SE_{\overline{X}}$) approximately 68% of the time, the population mean falls between 78 and 82 ($X ± 2\ SE_{\overline{X}}$) approximately 95% of the time, and the population mean falls between 77 and 83 ($\overline{X} ± 3\ SE_{\overline{X}}$) approximately 99+% of the time. In other words, the probability of the population mean being less than 78 or greater than 82 is only 5/100, or 5% (± 2 SD) and the probability of the population mean being less than 77 or higher than 83 is only 1/100, or 1% (± 3 SD). Note that as our degree of confidence increases, the limits get farther apart. This makes sense because we are 100% confident that the population mean is somewhere between our sample mean plus infinity and minus infinity!

You have probably realized by now that the smaller the standard error of the mean, the better, since a smaller standard error indicates less sampling error. The major factor affecting the standard error of the mean is sample size. As the size of the sample increases, the standard error of the mean decreases. This makes sense because if we used the whole population there would be no sampling error at all. A large sample is more likely to represent a population than a small sample. This discussion should help you to understand why samples should be as large as possible; smaller samples include more error than larger samples. Another factor affecting the standard error of the mean is the size of the population standard deviation. If it is large, members of the population are very spread out on the variable of interest, and sample means will also be very spread out. Although researchers have no control over the size of the population standard deviation, they can control sample size to some extent. Thus, researchers should make every effort to acquire as many participants as possible so that inferences about the population of interest will be as error-free as possible.

This discussion has been in reference to the standard error of a mean. However, estimates of standard error can also be computed for other statistics such as measures of variability, relationship, and relative position. Further, an estimate of standard error can also be calculated for the difference between two or more means. Thus, at the conclusion of an experimental study we may have data on two sample means, the experimental and the control groups. In order to determine whether the difference between those two means represents a true population difference, we need an estimate of the standard error of the difference between the two means. Differences between two sample means are normally distributed around the mean difference in the population. Most differences will be close to the true difference and a few will be way off. In order to determine whether a difference found between sample means probably represents a true difference or a chance difference, tests of significance are applied to the data. Tests of significance allow us to determine whether there is a significant or real difference between the means, not one due to chance sampling error. Many tests of significance are based on an estimate of standard error and they typically test a null hypothesis.

THE NULL HYPOTHESIS

Hypothesis testing is a process of decision making about the results of a study. If the experimental group's mean is 35 and the control group's mean is 27, the researcher has to decide whether the difference between the two means represents a real, significant difference in the treatments or simply sampling error. When we talk about the difference between two sample means being a true or real difference we mean that the difference was caused by the treatment (the independent variable), and not by chance. In other words, an observed difference is either caused by the treatment, as stated in the research hypothesis, or is the result of chance, random sampling error. The chance explanation for the difference is called the null hypothesis. The null hypothesis states that there is no true difference or relationship between parameters in the populations, and that any difference or relationship found for the samples is the result of sampling error. A null hypothesis might state:

> There is no significant difference between the mean reading comprehension of first-grade students who receive whole language reading instruction and first-grade students who receive basal reading instruction.

This hypothesis says that there really is not any difference between the two methods, and if you find one in your study, it is not a true difference, but a chance difference resulting from sampling error.

The null hypothesis for a study is usually (although not necessarily) different from the research hypothesis. The research hypothesis typically states that one method is expected to be more effective than another, while the null hypothesis states that there is no difference between the methods. Why have both? Good question! It is difficult to explain simply, but essentially the reason is that rejection of a null hypothesis is more conclusive support for a positive research hypothesis. In other words, if the results of your study support your research hypothesis, you only have one piece of evidence based on one sample in one situation. If you reject a null hypothesis, your case is stronger. As an analogy, suppose you hypothesize that all research textbooks contain a chapter on sampling. If you examine a research textbook and it does contain a sampling chapter, you have not proven your hypothesis, since you have found only one piece of evidence to support your hypothesis. There may always be a research book somewhere that does not contain a chapter on sampling. If, on the other hand, the textbook you examine does not contain a chapter on sampling, your hypothesis is disproven. We can never prove our hypothesis, only disprove it. Thus, one book is enough to disprove your hypothesis, but 1,000 books are not enough to prove it. The null hypothesis is needed because hypothesis testing is a process of disproving or rejecting, and the null hypothesis is best suited for this purpose.

In a research study, the test of significance selected to determine whether a difference between means is a true difference provides a test of the null hypothesis. As a result, the null hypothesis is either rejected as being probably false, or not rejected as being probably true. Notice the word *probably.* We never know with total certainty that we are making the correct decision; what we can do is estimate the probability of our being wrong. After we make the decision to reject or not reject the null hypothesis, we make an inference back to our research hypothesis. If, for example, our research hypothesis states that A is better than B, and if we reject the null hypothesis (that there is no difference between A and B), and if the mean for A is greater than the mean for B, then we conclude that our research hypothesis was supported—not proven! If we do not reject the null hypothesis (A is not different from B), then we conclude that our research hypothesis was not supported.

In order to test a null hypothesis we need a test of significance and we need to select a probability level that indicates how much risk we are willing to take that the decision we make is wrong.

TESTS OF SIGNIFICANCE

At the end of an experimental research study the researcher typically has two or more group means. These means are very likely to be at least a little different. The researcher must then decide whether the means are significantly different—different enough to conclude that they represent a true difference. In other words, the researcher must decide whether to reject the null hypothesis. The researcher does not make this decision based on a best guess. Instead, the researcher selects and applies an appropriate test of significance. A test of significance helps us to decide whether we can reject the null hypothesis and infer that the difference is significantly greater than that of chance. If the difference is too large to be attributed to chance, we reject the null hypothesis because there is a real difference between A and B. If not, we do not reject it because there is not a difference between A and B.

The test of significance is usually carried out using a preselected probability level that serves as a criterion to determine whether we reject or fail to reject the null hypothesis. The usual preselected probability level is either 5 out of 100 or 1 out of 100 chances that the observed difference did not occur by chance. If the probability of the difference between two means is likely to occur less than 5 times in 100 (or 1 time in 100), it is very unlikely to have occurred by chance, sampling error. Thus, there is a high (but not perfect) probability that the difference between the means did not occur by chance. Thus, the most likely explanation for the difference is that the two treatments were differentially effective. That is, there was a real difference between the means. Obviously, if we can say we would expect such a difference by chance only 1 time in 100 times, we are more confident in our decision than if we say we would expect such a chance difference 5 times in 100. How confident we are depends on the level of significance, or probability level, at which we perform our test of significance.

A number of different statistical tests of significance can be applied in different research studies. Factors such as the scale of measurement represented by the data (e.g., nominal or ordinal), method of participant selection, number of groups being compared, and number of independent variables determine which test of significance should be used in a given study. Shortly, we will discuss and calculate several frequently used tests of significance—the *t* test, analysis of variance, and chi square.

DECISION MAKING: LEVELS OF SIGNIFICANCE AND TYPE I AND TYPE II ERRORS

Based on a test of significance the researcher will either reject or not reject the null hypothesis as a probable explanation for results. In other words, the researcher will make the decision that the difference between the means is, or is not, too large to attribute to chance. As noted, because we are dealing with probability, not certainty, the researcher never knows for sure whether he or she is correct. There are four possibilities that can occur when testing the null hypothesis. If the null hypothesis is really true (there is no difference), and the researcher agrees that it is true (does not reject it), the researcher has made a correct decision. Similarly, if the null hypothesis is false (there really is a difference), and the researcher rejects it (says there is a difference), the researcher also makes the correct decision. But what if the null hypothesis is true, (there really is no difference), and the researcher rejects it and says there is a difference? The researcher makes an incorrect decision. Similarly, if the null hypothesis is false, (there really is a significant difference between the means), but the researcher concludes that the null hypothesis is true and does not reject it, the researcher also makes an incorrect decision. In other words, the four possibilities are:

1. The null hypothesis is true (A = B), and the researcher concludes that it is true. Correct!
2. The null hypothesis is false (A ≠ B), and the researcher concludes that it is false. Correct!
3. The null hypothesis is true (A = B), and the researcher concludes that it is false. Oops!
4. The null hypothesis is false (A ≠ B) and the researcher concludes that it is true. Ooops!

The two wrong decisions (Oops and Ooops) have "official" names. If the researcher rejects a null hypothesis that is really true (number 3), the researcher makes a Type I error. If the researcher fails to reject a null hypothesis that is really false (number 4), the researcher makes a Type II error. Figure 13.1 illustrates the four possible outcomes of decision making.

When the researcher makes the decision to reject or not reject the null hypothesis, she or he does so with a given probability of being correct. This proba-

FIGURE	13.1

The Four Possible Outcomes of Decision Making Concerning Rejection of the Null Hypothesis

		The true status of the null hypothesis. It is really	
		True (should not be rejected)	False (should be rejected)
The researcher's decision. The researcher concludes that the null hypothesis is	True (does not reject)	Correct Decision	Type II Error
	False (rejects)	Type I Error	Correct Decision

bility is referred to as the significance level, or probability level, of the test of significance. If the decision is made to reject the null hypothesis, the means are concluded to be significantly different—too different to be the result of chance error. If the null hypothesis is not rejected, the means are determined to be not significantly different, and the difference is attributed to sampling error. The level of significance, or probability level, selected determines how large the difference between the means must be in order to be declared significantly different. As noted, the most commonly used probability level (*alpha*, symbolized as α) is the $\alpha = .05$ level. Some studies use $\alpha = .01$, and occasionally an exploratory study will use $\alpha = .10$.

The probability level selected determines the probability of committing a Type I error, that is, of rejecting a null hypothesis that is really true. Thus, if you select $\alpha = .05$, you have a 5% probability of making a Type I error, whereas if you select $\alpha = .01$, you have only a 1% probability of committing a Type I error. The less chance of being wrong you are willing to take, the greater must be the difference between the means. As an example, examine the six possible outcomes presented here and decide whether you think the means are significantly different. The means are the final performances on a 100-item test for two groups of 20 subjects each:

GROUP MEAN A		GROUP MEAN B	
1.	70.0	1.	70.4
2.	70.0	2.	71.0
3.	70.0	3.	72.0
4.	70.0	4.	75.0
5.	70.0	5.	80.0
6.	70.0	6.	90.0

How about outcome 1? Is 70.0 likely to be significantly different from 70.4? Probably not; such a difference could easily occur by chance. How about outcome

2, 70.0 versus 71.0 (a difference of 1.0)? Probably not significantly different. How about outcome 6, 70.0 versus 90.0 (a difference of 20.0)? That difference probably is significant. How about 5, 70.0 versus 80.0? Probably a significant difference. How about 4, 70.0 versus 75.0? H-m-m-m. Is a 5-point difference a big enough difference for significance? It's a tough call. In general, large differences probably indicate a true difference, while small differences do not. Where is that magic point? When does a difference stop being too small and become "big enough" to be significant? The answer to these questions depends on the probability or significance level at which we perform our selected test of significance. The smaller our probability level, the larger the difference must be. In this example, if we were working at $\alpha = .05$, then a difference of 5 (say, 70.0 versus 75.0) might be significant. If, on the other hand, we were working at $\alpha = .01$ (a smaller chance of being wrong), a difference of at least 10 might be needed to reach significance. Got the idea?

Thus, if you are working at $\alpha = .05$, and as a result of your test of significance you reject the null hypothesis, you are saying that there is a real difference between the means. You are saying, in essence, that you do not believe the null hypothesis (no difference) is true because the chances are only 5 out of 100 (.05) that a difference as large (or larger) as the one you have found would occur solely by chance. In other words, there is a 95% chance that the difference resulted from the independent variable, not chance or random error. Similarly, if you are working at $\alpha = .01$ and reject the null hypothesis, you are saying that a difference as large as the one you have found would be expected to occur by chance only once for every 100 studies—highly unlikely to occur by chance. In essence, we are saying that any differences between ± 2 SD will be considered as chance differences at the .05 level and any differences between ± 3 SD will be considered as chance differences at the .01 level. Thus, real or significant differences fall outside of ± 2 SD (.05) or ± 3 SD (.01). Figure 13.2 illustrates the regions of significance and nonsignificance on the normal curve.

So why not set α at .000000001 and hardly ever be wrong? Good question; glad you asked it. If you select α to be very, very small, you definitely decrease your chances of committing a Type I error; you will hardly ever reject a true null hypothesis. But, guess what happens to your chances of committing a Type II error? Right. As you decrease the probability of committing a Type I error, you increase the probability of committing a Type II error, that is, of not rejecting a null hypothesis when you should (another catch 22!). For example, you might conduct a study for which a mean difference of 9.5 represents a true difference. If you set α at .0001, however, you might require a mean difference of 20.0 to reach significance. If the difference actually found was 11.0, you would not reject the null hypothesis (11.0 is less than 20.0), although there really is a difference (11.0 is greater than 9.5). How do you decide which level to work at, and when do you decide?

The choice of a probability level, α, is made prior to execution of the study. The researcher considers the relative seriousness of committing a Type I versus a Type II error and selects α accordingly. In other words, the researcher compares the consequences of making the two possible wrong decisions. As an example, suppose you are a teacher and one day your principal comes up to you and says: "I understand you have research training and I want you to do a study for me. I'm considering implementing the Whoopee-Do Reading method in the school next year. This program is very costly, and if implemented, we will have to spend a great deal of money on materials and inservice training. I don't want to do that

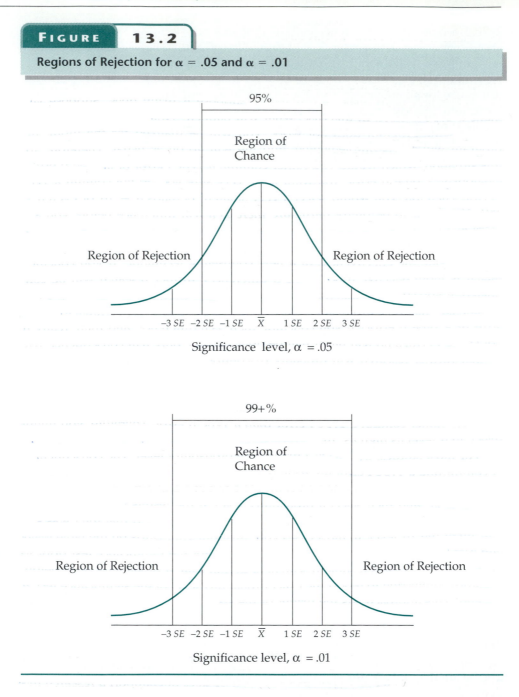

FIGURE 13.2

Regions of Rejection for α = .05 and α = .01

Significance level, α = .05

Significance level, α = .01

unless it really works. I want you to conduct a pilot study this year with several groups and then tell me if the Whoopee-Do program really results in better reading achievement. You have my complete support in setting up the groups the way you want to and in implementing the study."

In this case, which would be more serious, a Type I error or a Type II error? Suppose you conclude that the groups are significantly different, that the Whoopee-Do program really works. But suppose it really does not. Suppose you make a Type I error. In this case, the principal is going to be very upset if a big investment is made based on your decision and at the end of a year's period there is no difference in achievement. On the other hand, suppose you conclude that the groups are not significantly different, that the Whoopee-Do program does not really make a difference. Suppose it really does. Suppose you make a Type II error. In this case, what will happen? Nothing. You will tell the principal the program does not work, you will be thanked for the input, the program will not be implemented, and life will go on as usual. Therefore, for this situation, which would you rather commit, a Type I error or a Type II error? Obviously, a Type II error. You want to be very sure you do not commit a Type I error. Therefore you would select a very small α, perhaps $\alpha = .01$ or even $\alpha = .001$. You want to be pretty darn sure there is a real difference before you say there is.

As another example, suppose you are going to conduct an exploratory study to investigate the effectiveness of a new counseling technique. If you conclude that it is more effective (does make a difference), further research will be conducted. If you conclude that it does not make a difference, the new technique will be labeled "not very promising." Now, which would be more serious, a Type I error or a Type II error? If you conclude there is a difference, and there really is not (Type I error), no real harm will be done and the only real consequence will be that further research will probably disconfirm your finding. If, on the other hand, you conclude that the technique makes no difference, and it really does (Type II error), a technique may be prematurely abandoned; with a little refinement, this new technique might make a real difference. In this case, you would probably rather commit a Type I error than a Type II error. Therefore, you might select an α level as high as .10.

For most studies, $\alpha = .05$ is a reasonable probability level. The consequences of committing a Type I error are usually not too serious. However, a no-no in selecting a probability level is to first compute a test of significance to see "how significant it is" and then select a probability level. If the results just happen to be significant at $\alpha = .01$, you do not say, "Oh goodie!" and report that the t was significant at the .01 level. In most cases you must put your cards on the table *before* you play the game, by stating a probability level for the significance test prior to data analysis. However, some researchers do not state a probability level before the study, preferring to report the exact probability level of the significance test at the end. This approach lets the reader of the study judge whether the results are "significant" for their purpose or use. It is recommended that you stick to stating your α value at the start of your study.

A common misconception is the notion that if you reject a null hypothesis you have "proven" your research hypothesis. However, as stated, rejection or lack of rejection of a null hypothesis supports or does not support a research hypothesis. It does not prove it. If you reject a null hypothesis and conclude that the groups are really different, it does not necessarily mean that they are different for the reason you hypothesized. They may be different for some other reason. On the other hand, if you fail to reject the null hypothesis, it does not necessarily mean that your research hypothesis is wrong. The study, for example, may not have represented a fair test of your hypothesis. To use a former example, if you were investigating cooperative learning and the cooperative learning group and the control group each received its respective treatment for one day only, you probably would not find any differences between the groups. This would not mean that cooperative learning is not effective. If your study were conducted over a 6-month period, it might very well make a difference.

TWO-TAILED AND ONE-TAILED TESTS

Tests of significance are almost always two-tailed. The null hypothesis states that there is no difference between the groups (A = B), and a two-tailed test allows for the possibility that a difference may occur in either direction: either group mean may be higher than the other (A > B or B > A). A one-tailed test assumes that a difference can only occur in one direction. The null hypothesis states that one group is not better than another, and the one-tailed test assumes that if a difference occurs it will be in favor of that particular group (A > B). Remember that a "tail" represents the region of rejection. As an example, suppose a research hypothesis were:

> Kindergarten children who receive a mid-morning snack exhibit better behavior during the hour before lunch than kindergarten students who do not receive a mid-morning snack.

For this research hypothesis the null hypothesis would state:

> There is no difference between the behavior during the hour before lunch of kindergarten students who receive a mid-morning snack and kindergarten students who do not receive a mid-morning snack.

A two-tailed test of significance would allow for the possibility that either the group that received a snack or the group that did not might exhibit better behavior. For a one-tailed test, the null hypothesis might state:

> Kindergarten children who receive a mid-morning snack do not exhibit better behavior during the hour before lunch than kindergarten children who do not receive a mid-morning snack.

In this case, the assumption would be that if a difference were found between the groups it would be in favor of the group that received the snack. In other words, the researcher would consider it highly unlikely that not receiving a snack could result in better behavior than receiving one (although it could if they were fed super sugar-coated chocolate twinkos!).

Tests of significance are almost always two-tailed. To select a one-tailed test of significance, the researcher has to be pretty darn sure that a difference will only occur in one direction, and this is not very often the case. When appropriate, a one-tailed test has one major advantage. The score difference required for significance is smaller than for a two-tailed test. In other words, it is "easier" to obtain a significant difference. It is difficult to explain simply why this is so, but it has to do with α. Suppose you are computing a test of significance at $\alpha = .05$. If your test is two-tailed, you are allowing for the possibility of a positive t or a negative t; in other words, you are allowing that the mean of the first group may be higher than the mean of the second group ($\overline{X}_1 - \overline{X}_2$ = a positive number), or that the mean of the second group may be higher than the mean of the first group ($\overline{X}_1 - \overline{X}_2$ = a negative number). Thus, our significance level, say .05, has to be di-

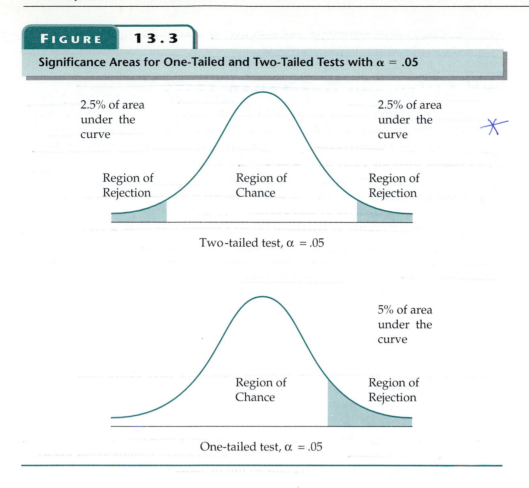

FIGURE **13.3**

Significance Areas for One-Tailed and Two-Tailed Tests with α = .05

2.5% of area under the curve

2.5% of area under the curve

Region of Rejection

Region of Chance

Region of Rejection

Two-tailed test, α = .05

5% of area under the curve

Region of Chance

Region of Rejection

One-tailed test, α = .05

vided into two halves (.025 and .025) to cover both possible outcomes ($\overline{X}_1 - \overline{X}_2$ is positive and $\overline{X}_1 - \overline{X}_2$ is negative). For a one-tailed test, the entire significance level, say .05, is concentrated on only one side of the normal curve. Since .025 is a smaller probability of committing a Type I error than .05, a larger *t* value is required. This explanation applies to any α value and to other tests of significance besides the *t* test. This is definitely not the most scientific explanation of two-tailed and one-tailed tests, but it should give you some conceptual understanding. The darkened areas of Figure 13.3 compare the significance areas of a one- and two-tailed test at α = .05.

DEGREES OF FREEDOM

After you have determined whether your significance test will be two-tailed or one-tailed, selected a probability level, and computed a test of significance, you must consult the appropriate table in order to determine the significance of your results. (Most statistical computer programs provide information about the significance of the results computed in their output.) As you no doubt recall from our discussion of the significance of a correlation coefficient in chapter 9, the appropriate table is usually entered at the intersection of your probability level and your degrees of freedom (*df*). Degrees of freedom are dependent upon the number of participants and the number of groups. Recall that for the correlation coefficient, r, the appropriate degrees of freedom were determined by the formula $N - 2$ (number of participants minus 2.) An illustration may help explain the concept of degrees of freedom. Suppose I ask you to name any five numbers. You agree and say "1, 2, 3, 4, 5." In this case N is equal to 5—you had 5 choices or 5 degrees of freedom to select the numbers. Now suppose I tell you to name 5 numbers and you say "1, 2, 3, 4, . . . ," and I say, "Wait! The mean of the five numbers you choose must be 4." Now you have no choice—your last number must be 10 because $1 + 2 + 3 + 4 + 10 = 20$ and 20 divided by $5 = 4$. You lost one degree of freedom because of the restriction (lack of freedom) that the mean must be 4. In other words, instead of having $N = 5$ degrees of freedom, you only had $N = 4$ $(5 - 1)$ degrees of freedom. Got the idea?

Each test of significance has its own formula for determining degrees of freedom. For the correlation coefficient, r, the formula is $N - 2$. The number 2 is a constant, requiring that degrees of freedom for r are always determined by subtracting 2 from N, the number of participants. Each of the inferential statistics we are about to discuss also has its own formula for degrees of freedom.

TESTS OF SIGNIFICANCE: TYPES

Different tests of significance are appropriate for different types of data. It is important that the researcher select the appropriate test for his or her study, since an incorrect test can lead to incorrect conclusions. The first decision in selecting an appropriate test of significance is whether a parametric or nonparametric test must be selected. Parametric tests are usually more powerful and are generally to be preferred. "More powerful" in this case means more likely to reject a null hypothesis that is false. In other words, the researcher is less likely to commit a Type II error—less likely to not reject a null hypothesis that should be rejected.

Parametric tests, however, require that certain assumptions be met in order for them to be valid. One of the major assumptions underlying use of parametric tests is that the variable measured is normally distributed in the population (or at least that the form of the distribution is known). Since many variables studied in education are normally distributed, this assumption is often met. A second major assumption is that the data represent an interval or ratio scale of measurement. Again, since most measures used in education are or are assumed to be interval data, this assumption is usually met. In fact, this is one major advantage of using an interval scale—it permits the use of a parametric test. A third assumption is that the selection of participants is independent. In other words, that selection of one subject in no way affects selection of any other participant. Recall that random sampling is sampling in which every member of the population has an equal and independent chance to be selected for the sample. Thus, if randomization is used in participant selection, the assumption of independence is met. Another assumption is that the variances of the population comparison groups are equal (or at least that the ratio of the variances is known). Remember, the variance of a group of scores is nothing more than the standard deviation squared.

With the exception of independence, some violation of one or more of these assumptions usually does not make too much difference in the statistical significance of the results. However, if one or more assumptions are greatly violated, such as if the distribution is extremely skewed, parametric statistics should not be used. In such cases, a nonparametric test should be used. Nonparametric tests make no assumptions about the shape of the distribution. They are usually used when the data represent an ordinal or nominal scale, when a parametric assumption has been greatly violated, or when the nature of the distribution is not known.

If the data represent an interval or ratio scale, a parametric test should be used unless one of the assumptions is greatly violated. As mentioned before, parametric tests are more powerful. A nonparametric test is more difficult than a parametric test to reject a null hypothesis at a given level of significance. A nonparametric test usually takes a larger sample size to reach the same level of significance as a parametric test. Another advantage of parametric statistics is that they permit tests of a number of hypotheses that cannot be tested with a nonparametric test, since there are a number of parametric statistics that have no counterpart among nonparametric statistics. Parametric statistics seem to be relatively hardy (i.e., they do their job even with moderate assumption violation), so they are usually selected for analysis of research data.

Statistical Software Programs

You can enter your data directly into a statistical software program rather than importing the data from a spreadsheet program. Statistical programs such as SPSS are actually databases containing rows and columns that can be filled with numerical information. These programs are superior to spreadsheet programs in that the analysis can enter variable labels that correspond to people's responses (e.g., 1 = strongly disagree, 2 = disagree, 3 = agree, 4 = strongly agree). These labels are printed in the computer output, making it easier to interpret than spreadsheet output, which just contains numbers without any referents.

Statistical programs also give you a full set of statistical tests so that you can tell if differences or relationships you detect in your data are significant. They also contain tools to check statistical assumptions. These programs provide descriptive statistics; explore data; perform cross tabulations and measures of association, t tests, ANOVAs, regression analyses, and more. They are absolutely essential in the analysis of questionnaire and other research data. They are also fairly easy to learn, as the latest versions allow the researcher to simply "point and click" at various options, without having to write complicated syntax commands.

In following sections we examine both parametric and nonparametric statistics. Of course, we are not going to discuss each and every statistical test available to the researcher. A number of useful, commonly used statistics will be described, and a smaller number of frequently used statistics will be calculated.

THE t TEST

The t test is used to determine whether two means are significantly different at a selected probability level. In determining significance, the t test makes adjustments for the fact that the distribution of scores for small samples becomes increasingly different from the normal distribution as sample sizes become increasingly smaller. For example, distributions for smaller samples tend to be higher at the mean and at the two ends of the distribution. Because of this, the t values required to reject a null hypothesis are higher for small samples. As the size of the samples becomes larger, the score distribution approaches normality. Table A.4 in the appendix shows the values needed to reject the null hypothesis for different sample sizes (indicated by the degrees of freedom column on the extreme left). As the number of participants increases (df), the value needed to reject the null hypothesis becomes smaller. As already discussed, Table A.4 also shows that as the probability or significance level becomes smaller (.10, .05, .01, .001), it takes a larger value to reject the null hypothesis.

The strategy of the t test is to compare the actual mean difference observed ($\bar{X}_1 - \bar{X}_2$) to the difference expected by chance. The t test involves forming the ratio of these two values. In other words, the numerator for a t test is the difference between the sample means $\bar{X}_1$ and $\bar{X}_2$, and the denominator is the chance difference that would be expected if the null hypothesis were true. Thus, the denominator is the standard error of the difference between the means. The denominator, or error term, is a function of both sample size and group variance. Smaller sample sizes and greater variation within groups are associated with greater random differences between groups. To explain it one more way, even if the null hypothesis is true, you do not expect two sample means to be identical; there is going to be some chance variation. The t test determines whether the observed difference is sufficiently larger than a difference that would be expected solely by chance. After the numerator is divided by the denominator, the resulting t value is compared to the appropriate t table value (depending on the probability level and the degrees of freedom). If the t value is equal to or greater than the table value, then the null hypothesis is rejected. There are two different types of t tests, the t test for independent samples and the t test for nonindependent samples.

Calculating the *t* Test for Independent Samples

Independent samples are two samples that are randomly formed without any type of matching. The members of one sample are not related to members of the other sample in any systematic way, other than that they are selected from the same population. If two groups are randomly formed, the expectation is that at the beginning of a study they are essentially the same with respect to performance on the dependent variable. Therefore, if they are also essentially the same at the end of the study (their means are close), the null hypothesis is probably true. If, on the other hand, their means are not close at the end of the study, the null hypothesis is probably false and should be rejected. The key word is *essentially*. We do not expect the means to be identical at the end of the study—they are bound to be somewhat different. The question of interest, of course, is whether they are significantly different. The t test for independent samples is used to determine whether there is probably a significant difference between the means of two independent samples.

Suppose we have the following sets of posttest scores for two randomly formed groups. (Recognize that samples of five participants in each group are not considered acceptable, but will be used here for simplicity and clarity.)

GROUP 1 POSTTEST SCORES	GROUP 2 POSTTEST SCORES
3	2
4	3
5	3
6	3
7	4

Are these two sets of scores significantly different? They are different, but are they *significantly* different? The appropriate test of significance to answer this question is the *t* test for independent samples. The formula is

$$t = \frac{\bar{X}_1 - \bar{X}_2}{}$$

What does SS stand for?

Does it look bad? Is it? What will it turn into? (The answers are: Yes. No. An arithmetic problem.) If you look at the formula you will see that you are already familiar with each of the pieces. The numerator is simply the difference between the two means $\bar{X}_1$ and $\bar{X}_2$. Each of the *n*s refers to the number of participants in each group; thus, $n_1 = 5$ and $n_2 = 5$. What about the *SS*s? How do we find them? Right! We calculate each *SS* in the same way as we did for the standard deviation. Remember? Okay, lets find each piece. Thus:

$$SS_1 = \Sigma X_1^2 - \frac{(\Sigma X_1)^2}{n_1} \text{ and } SS_2 = \Sigma X_2^2 - \frac{(\Sigma X_2)^2}{n_2}$$

First, let's calculate means, sums, and sums of squares, and let's label the scores for group 1 as X_1 and the scores for group 2 as X_2:

X_1	X_1^2	X_2	X_2^2
3	9	2	4
4	16	3	9
5	25	3	9
6	36	3	9
7	49	4	16
$\Sigma X_1 = 25$	$\Sigma X_1^2 = 135$	$\Sigma X_2 = 15$	$\Sigma X_2^2 = 47$

$$\bar{X}_1 = \frac{25}{5} = 5 \qquad \bar{X}_2 = \frac{15}{5} = 3$$

Next, we need the *SS*s:

$$SS_1 = \Sigma X_1^2 - \frac{(\Sigma X_1)^2}{n_1} \qquad SS_2 = \Sigma X_2^2 - \frac{(\Sigma X_2)^2}{n_2}$$

$$= 135 - \frac{(25)^2}{5} \qquad = 47 - \frac{(15)^2}{5}$$

$$= 135 - 125 \qquad = 47 - 45$$

$$= 10 \qquad = 2$$

SS — Sum of Squares

Statistical significance

Now we have everything we need, and all we have to do is substitute the correct number for each symbol in the formula:

$$t = \cfrac{\bar{X}_1 - \bar{X}_2}{\sqrt{\left(\dfrac{10 + 2}{5 + 5 - 2}\right)\left(\dfrac{1}{5} + \dfrac{1}{5}\right)}} = \cfrac{5 - 3}{\sqrt{\left(\dfrac{10 + 2}{5 + 5 - 2}\right)\left(\dfrac{1}{5} + \dfrac{1}{5}\right)}}$$

Now, if we just do what the formula tells us to do we will have no problem at all. The first thing it says to do is to subtract 3 from 5:

$$= \cfrac{2}{\sqrt{\left(\dfrac{10 + 2}{5 + 5 - 2}\right)\left(\dfrac{1}{5} + \dfrac{1}{5}\right)}}$$

So far, so good. Now let's compute $10 + 2$ and $5 + 5 - 2$, and then add $\frac{1}{5} + \frac{1}{5}$. (Same number on the bottom, so just add the top: $1 + 1$.) What do we have? Right:

$$= \cfrac{2}{\sqrt{\left(\dfrac{12}{8}\right)\left(\dfrac{2}{5}\right)}}$$

Before we go any further, this would be a good time to convert those fractions to decimals. To convert a fraction to a decimal you simply divide the numerator by the denominator. If you are using a calculator, you enter the top number (e.g., 12) first, hit the ÷ key, and then enter the bottom number (e.g., 8). Thus, $12/8 = 1.5$ and $2/5 = .4$.

Substituting the decimals for the fractions we have:

$$t = \cfrac{2}{\sqrt{\left(\dfrac{12}{8}\right)\left(\dfrac{2}{5}\right)}} = \frac{2}{\sqrt{(1.5)\,(.4)}}$$

Since the parentheses indicate multiplication, we next multiply 1.5 by .4, and get:

$$t = \frac{2}{\sqrt{(1.5)\,(.4)}} = \frac{2}{\sqrt{.60}}$$

Now we have to find the square root of .60 (get your calculator out). It's .774. Substituting .774 for the square root and dividing, gives us:

$$t = \frac{2}{\sqrt{.60}} = \frac{2}{.774} = 2.58$$

Therefore, $t = 2.58$.

Assuming we selected $\alpha = .05$, the only thing we need before we go to the t table is the appropriate degrees of freedom. For the t test for independent samples, the formula for degrees of freedom is $n_1 + n_2 - 2$. For our example, $df = n_1 + n_2 - 2 = 5 + 5 - 2 = 8$. Therefore, $t = 2.58$, $\alpha = .05$, $df = 8$. (STATPAK printout follows).

```
================================================================================
                        t-TEST FOR INDEPENDENT SAMPLES
================================================================================
```

STATISTIC	VALUE
NO. OF SCORES IN GROUP ONE	5
SUM OF SCORES IN GROUP ONE	25.00
MEAN OF GROUP ONE	5.00
SUM OF SQUARED SCORES IN GROUP ONE	135.00
SS OF GROUP ONE	10.00
NO. OF SCORES IN GROUP TWO	5
SUM OF SCORES IN GROUP TWO	15.00
MEAN OF GROUP TWO	3.00
SUM OF SQUARED SCORES IN GROUP TWO	47.00
SS OF GROUP TWO	2.00
t-VALUE	2.58
DEGREES OF FREEDOM (df)	8

```
================================================================================
```

Now go to Table A.4 in the Appendix. The p values in the table are the probabilities associated with various α levels. In our case, we are really asking the following question: Given $\alpha = .05$, and $df = 8$, what is the probability of getting $t \geq 2.58$ if there really is no difference? Okay, now run the index finger of your right hand across the probability row at the top of the table until you get to .05. Now run the index finger of your left hand down the degrees of freedom column until you get to 8. Now move your right index finger down the column and your left index finger across; they intersect at 2.306. The value 2.306, or 2.31, is the t value required for rejection of the null hypothesis with $\alpha = .05$ and $df = 8$. Is our t value 2.58 greater than 2.31? Yes, and therefore we reject the null hypothesis. Are the means different? Yes. Are they significantly different? Yes. Was that hard? Of course not. Congratulations! It is useful for beginning researchers to look up p values a few times, but after that, rely on statistical packages to automatically provide the p values.

Note that the table value, 2.306 or 2.31, was the value required to reject the null hypothesis given α equal to .05. If, instead of $t = 2.58$, we got $t = 2.31$, then our probability of committing a Type I error would be exactly .05. But, since our value, $t = 2.58$, was greater than the table value, 2.31, our probability of committing a Type I error is less; $p < .05$. In other words, we got more than we needed, so our chances of being wrong are less.

Suppose our t value were 2.29. What would we conclude? We would conclude that there is no significant difference between the groups, because 2.29 is less than 2.31. We could express this conclusion by stating that $p > .05$; in other words, because our t value is less than that required for $\alpha = .05$, our probability of committing a Type I error is greater. Usually, however, if results are not significant, the abbreviation N.S. is used to represent *not* significant. How about if we concluded that our *t* was *almost* significant or "approached" significance? Boooo! A *t* test is not *almost* significant or *really* significant; it is or it is not significant. Period! You will *not* see research reports that says, "The rats almost made it," or "Gosh, that really approached significance!"

What if we selected $\alpha = .01$? Table A.4 indicates that 3.355, or 3.36, is the *t* value required for rejection of the null hypothesis with $\alpha = .01$ and $df = 8$. Is our value 2.58 > 3.36? No, and therefore we would not reject the null hypothesis at the .01 level. Are the means different? Yes. Are they significantly different? For $\alpha = .05$, the answer is yes, but for $\alpha = .01$, the answer is no. Thus, we see that the smaller the risk we are willing to take of committing a Type I error, the larger our *t* value has to be.

What if our *t* value had been −2.58? (Table A.4 has no negative values.) We would have done exactly what we did; we would have looked up 2.58. The only thing that determines whether the *t* is positive or negative is the order of the means; the denominator is always positive. In our example we had a mean difference of 5 − 3, or 2. If we had reversed the means, we would have had 3 − 5, or −2. As long as we know which mean goes with which group, the order is unimportant. The only thing that matters is the size of the difference. So, if you do not like negative numbers, put the larger mean first. Remember, the table is two-tailed; it is prepared to deal with a difference in favor of either group. Direction does make a difference in one-tailed tests.

Are we having fun yet?

Calculating the *t* Test for Nonindependent Samples

The *t* test for nonindependent samples is used to compare groups that are formed by some type of matching or to compare a single group's performance on a pre- and posttest or on two different treatments. When samples are not independent, the members of one group are systematically related to the members of a second group (especially if it is the same group at two different times). If samples are nonindependent, scores on the dependent variable are expected to be correlated with each other, and a special *t* test for correlated, or nonindependent, means is used. When samples are nonindependent, the error term of the *t* test tends to be smaller, and therefore, there is a higher probability that the null hypothesis will be rejected. Thus, the *t* test for nonindependent samples is used to determine whether there is probably a significant difference between the means of two matched, or nonindependent, samples or between the means for one sample at two different times.

Assume we have the following sets of scores for two matched groups (or pretest and posttest scores for a single group).

X_1	X_2
2	4
3	5
4	4
5	7
6	10

Are these two sets of scores significantly different? They are different, but are they significantly different? The appropriate test of significance to use in order to answer this question is the t test for nonindependent samples. The formula is:

$$t = \frac{\overline{D}}{\sqrt{\dfrac{\Sigma D^2 - \dfrac{(\Sigma D)^2}{N}}{N(N-1)}}}$$

(handwritten annotations: $\overline{D}$ — difference(D), $X_2 - X_1$)

Except for the Ds, the formula should look very familiar. If the Ds were Xs, you would know exactly what to do. Whatever Ds are, we are going to find their mean, $\overline{D}$, add up their squares, ΣD^2, and square their sum $(\Sigma D)^2$. What do you suppose D could possibly stand for? Right! D stands for difference. The difference between what? Yes, D is the difference between the matched pairs of scores. Thus, each D equals $X_2 - X_1$. For our data, the first pair of scores is 2 and 4 and $D = +2$. Find the Ds for each pair of scores. While you're at it, you might as well get the squares, the sums, and the mean. The mean of the Ds is found the same way as any other mean, by adding up the Ds and dividing by the number of Ds:

X_1	X_2	D	D^2
2	4	+2	4
3	5	+2	4
4	4	0	0
5	7	+2	4
6	10	+4	16
		$\Sigma D = 10$	$\Sigma D^2 = 28$

$$\overline{D} = \frac{\Sigma D}{N} = \frac{10}{5} = 2$$

Now we have everything we need, and all we have to do is substitute the numbers for the corresponding symbols in the formula.

$$t = \frac{\overline{D}}{\sqrt{\dfrac{\Sigma D^2 - \dfrac{(\Sigma D)^2}{N}}{N(N-1)}}} = \frac{2}{\sqrt{\dfrac{28 - \dfrac{(10)^2}{5}}{5(5-1)}}}$$

We have another easy arithmetic problem. Now that you are a pro at this, we can solve this arithmetic problem rather quickly.

$$t = \frac{2}{\sqrt{\dfrac{28 - \dfrac{(10)^2}{5}}{5(5-1)}}}$$

$$= \frac{2}{\sqrt{\dfrac{28 - \dfrac{100}{5}}{5(5-1)}}}$$

$10^2 = 100$

$100/5 = 20$

$28 - 20 = 8$

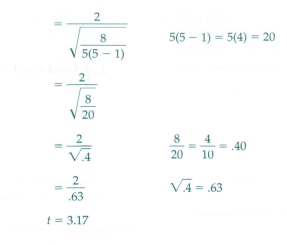

$$= \frac{2}{\sqrt{\dfrac{8}{5(5-1)}}} \qquad 5(5-1) = 5(4) = 20$$

$$= \frac{2}{\sqrt{\dfrac{8}{20}}}$$

$$= \frac{2}{\sqrt{.4}} \qquad \frac{8}{20} = \frac{4}{10} = .40$$

$$= \frac{2}{.63} \qquad \sqrt{.4} = .63$$

$$t = 3.17$$

Thus, $t = 3.17$. Assuming $\alpha = .05$, the only thing we need before we go to the t table is the appropriate degrees of freedom. For the t test for nonindependent samples, the formula for degrees of freedom is $N - 1$, where N is the number of *pairs* minus 1. For our example, $N - 1 = 5 - 1 = 4$. Therefore, $t = 3.17$, $\alpha = .05$, $df = 4$ (STATPAK printout follows).

```
======================================================================
                 t-TEST FOR NONINDEPENDENT SAMPLES
======================================================================
   STATISTIC                                          VALUE
----------------------------------------------------------------------

   NO. OF PAIRS OF SCORES                                5

   SUM OF "D"                                         10.00

   MEAN OF D'S                                         2.00

              2
   SUM OF "D "                                        28.00

   t-VALUE                                             3.17

   DEGREES OF FREEDOM (df)                                4

======================================================================
```

Now go to Table A.4 again. Notice that the t table does not know whether our t is for independent or nonindependent samples. For $\alpha = .05$ and $df = 4$, the table value for t required for rejection of the null hypothesis is 2.776, or 2.78. Is our value $3.17 > 2.78$? Yes, and therefore we reject the null hypothesis. Are the groups different? Yes. Are they significantly different? Yes. We're really rolling now.

Analysis of Gain or Difference Scores

Many researchers think that a viable way to analyze data from two groups who are pretested, treated, and posttested is to (1) subtract each participant's pretest score from his or her posttest score (resulting in a gain, or difference, score), (2) compute the mean gain or difference for each group, and (3) calculate a *t* value for the difference between the two average mean differences. There are two main problems with this approach. First, every participant does not have the same opportunity to gain. A participant who scores very low on a pretest has a large opportunity to gain, but a participant who scores very high has only a small opportunity to improve (referred to as the ceiling effect). Who has improved, or gained, more—a participant who goes from 20 to 70 (a gain of 50) or a participant who goes from 85 to 100 (a gain of only 15 but perhaps a perfect score)? Second, gain or difference scores are less reliable than analysis of posttest scores alone.

The appropriate analysis for two pretest–posttest groups depends on the performance of the two groups on the pretest. For example, if both groups are essentially the same on the pretest, neither group has been previously exposed to its treatment, then posttest scores are best compared using a *t* test. If, on the other hand, there is a difference between the groups on the pretest, the preferred approach is the analysis of covariance. Recall that analysis of covariance adjusts posttest scores for initial differences on some variable (in this case the pretest) related to performance on the dependent variable. To determine whether analysis of covariance is necessary, calculate a *t* test on the two pretest means. If there is a significant difference between the two pretest means use the analysis of covariance. If not, a simple *t* test can be computed on the posttest means.

SIMPLE ANALYSIS OF VARIANCE

Simple, or one-way, analysis of variance (ANOVA) is used to determine whether there is a significant difference between two or more means at a selected probability level. Thus, for a study involving three groups, ANOVA is the appropriate analysis technique. Like two posttest means in the *t* test, three (or more) posttest means in ANOVA are unlikely to be identical, so the key question is whether the differences among the means represent true, significant differences or chance differences due to sampling error. To answer this question ANOVA is used and an *F* ratio is computed. You may be wondering why you cannot just compute a bunch of *t* tests, one for each pair of means. Aside from some statistical problems concerning resulting distortion of your probability level, it is more convenient to perform one ANOVA than to perform several *t* tests. For example, to analyze four means, six separate *t* tests would be required ($\bar{X}_1 - \bar{X}_2$, $\bar{X}_1 - \bar{X}_3$, $\bar{X}_1 - \bar{X}_4$, $\bar{X}_2 - \bar{X}_3$, $\bar{X}_2 - \bar{X}_4$, $\bar{X}_3 - \bar{X}_4$). ANOVA is much more efficient and keeps the error rate under control.

The concept underlying ANOVA is that the total variation, or variance, of scores can be divided into two sources—treatment variance (variance between groups, caused by the treatment groups) and error variance (variance within groups). A ratio is formed, (the *F* ratio) with treatment variance as the numerator (variance between groups) and error variance in the denominator (variance within groups). It is assumed that randomly formed groups of participants are chosen and are essentially the same at the beginning of a study on a measure of the dependent variable. At the end of the study, we determine whether the variance between groups differs from the error variance by more than what would be expected by chance. In other words, if the treatment variance is sufficiently larger than the error variance, a significant *F* ratio results; the null hypothesis is rejected, and it is concluded that the treatment had a significant effect on the dependent variable. If, on the other hand, the treatment variance and error variance do not differ by more than what would be expected by chance, the resulting *F* ratio is not significant and the null hypothesis is not rejected. The greater the difference, the larger the F ratio. To determine whether the F ratio is significant, consult an F table. Find the place corresponding to the selected probability level and the appropriate degrees of freedom. The degrees of freedom for the F ratio are a function of the number of groups and the number of participants.

Suppose we have the following set of posttest scores for three randomly selected groups.

X_1	X_2	X_3
1	2	4
2	3	4
2	4	4
2	5	5
3	6	7

We ask the inevitable question: Are these sets of data significantly different? The appropriate test of significance to answer this question is the simple, or one-way, analysis of variance (ANOVA). Recall that the total variation, or variance, is a combination of between (treatment) variance and within (error) variance. In other words:

total sum of squares = between sum of squares + within sum of squares, or
$$SS_{total} = SS_{between} + SS_{within}$$

In order to compute an ANOVA we need each term, *but*, since C = A + B, or $C(SS_{total}) = A(SS_{between}) + B(SS_{within})$, we only have to compute any two terms and we can easily get the third. Since we only have to calculate two, we might as well do the two easiest, SS_{total} and $SS_{between}$. Once we have these we can get SS_{within} by subtraction; SS_{within} will equal $SS_{total} - SS_{between}$ (B = C − A). The formula for SS_{total} is as follows:

$$SS_{total} = \Sigma X^2 - \frac{(\Sigma X)^2}{N}$$

How easy can you get? First, we need ΣX^2. You know how to get that; all we have to do is square *every* score in all three groups and add up the squares. For the second term, all we have to do is add up *all* the scores ($X_1 + X_2 + X_3$), square the total, and divide by N ($n_1 + n_2 + n_3$). Note that if an X or N refers to a particular group it is subscripted (X_1, X_2, X_3 and n_1, n_2, n_3). If an X or N is not subscripted, it refers to the total for all the groups.

Now let's look at the formula for $SS_{between}$:

$$SS_{between} = \frac{(\Sigma X_1)^2}{n_1} + \frac{(\Sigma X_2)^2}{n_2} + \frac{(\Sigma X_3)^2}{n_3} - \frac{(\Sigma X)^2}{N}$$

This formula has more pieces, but each piece is easy. For the first three terms all we have to do is add up all the scores in each group, square the total for each group, and divide by the number of scores in each group. We will have calculated the fourth term, $(\Sigma X)^2/N$, when we figure out SS_{total}. So, what do we need? We need the sum of scores for each group and the total of all the scores, and the sum of all the squares. That should be easy; let's do it:

X_1	X_1^2	X_2	X_2^2	X_3	X_3^2
1	1	2	4	4	16
2	4	3	9	4	16
2	4	4	16	4	16
2	4	5	25	5	25
3	9	6	36	7	49
10	22	20	90	24	122
ΣX_1	ΣX_1^2	ΣX_2	ΣX_2^2	ΣX_3	ΣX_3^2

$$\Sigma X = \Sigma X_1 + \Sigma X_2 + \Sigma X_3 = 10 + 20 + 24 = 54$$
$$\Sigma X^2 = \Sigma X_1^2 + \Sigma X_2^2 + \Sigma X_3^2 = 22 + 90 + 122 = 234$$
$$N = n_1 + n_2 + n_3 = 5 + 5 + 5 = 15$$

Now we are ready. First let us do SS_{total}.

$$SS_{total} = \Sigma X^2 - \frac{(\Sigma X)^2}{N}$$
$$= 234 - \frac{(54)^2}{15}$$
$$= 234 - \frac{2916}{15} \qquad (54^2 = 2916)$$
$$= 234 - 194.4 \qquad (2916 \div 15 = 194.4)$$
$$= 39.6$$

That was easy. Now let us do $SS_{between}$.[2]

$$SS_{between} = \frac{(\Sigma X_1)^2}{n_1} + \frac{(\Sigma X_2)^2}{n_2} + \frac{(\Sigma X_3)^2}{n_3} - \frac{(\Sigma X)^2}{N}$$

(We already computed the last term, remember?)
$10^2 = 100$
$20^2 = 400$
$24^2 = 576$

$$= \frac{(10)^2}{5} + \frac{(20)^2}{5} + \frac{(24)^2}{5} - 194.4$$

$\frac{100}{5} = 20$

$$= \frac{100}{5} + \frac{400}{5} + \frac{576}{5} - 194.4$$

$\frac{400}{5} = 80$

$$= 20 + 80 + 115.2 - 194.4$$
$$= 215.2 - 194.4$$

$\frac{576}{5} = 115.2$

$$= 20.8$$

$20 + 80 + 115.2 = 215.2$

---

[2]For more than three groups, the ANOVA procedure is exactly the same except that $SS_{between}$ has one extra term for each additional group. For example, for four groups

$$SS_{between} = \frac{(\Sigma X_1)^2}{n_1} + \frac{(\Sigma X_2)^2}{n_2} + \frac{(\Sigma X_3)^2}{n_3} + \frac{(\Sigma X_4)^2}{n_4} - \frac{(\Sigma X)^2}{N}$$

Now how are we going to get SS_{within}? Right. We subtract $SS_{between}$ from SS_{total}:

$$SS_{within} = SS_{total} - SS_{between}$$
$$= 39.6 - 20.8$$
$$= 18.8$$

Now we have everything we need to begin! Seriously, we have all the pieces, but we are not quite there yet. Let us fill in a summary table with what we have and you will see what is missing:

SOURCE OF VARIATION	SUM OF SQUARES	df	MEAN SQUARE	F
Between	20.8	$(K - 1)$		
Within	18.8	$(N - K)$		
Total	39.6	$(N - 1)$		

The first thing you probably noticed is that each term has its own formula for degrees of freedom. The formula for the between term is $K - 1$, where K is the number of treatment groups; thus, the degrees of freedom are $K - 1 = 3 - 1 = 2$. The formula for the within term is $N - K$, where N is the total sample size and K is still the number of treatment groups; thus, degrees of freedom for the within term $N - K = 15 - 3 = 12$. We do not need them, but for the total term, $df = N - 1 = 15 - 1 = 14$. Now what about mean squares? Mean squares are found by dividing each sum of squares by its appropriate degrees of freedom. Here we represent mean squares as MS, using the subscript B for between and W for within. Thus, we have the equation:

$$\text{mean square} = \frac{\text{sum of squares}}{\text{degrees of freedom}}$$

or,

$$MS = \frac{SS}{df}$$

For between, MS_B, we get:

$$MS_B = \frac{SS_B}{df}$$
$$= \frac{20.8}{2}$$
$$= 10.40$$

For within, MS_W, we get:

$$MS_W = \frac{SS_W}{df}$$
$$= \frac{18.8}{12}$$
$$= 1.57$$

Now all we need is our F ratio. The F ratio is a ratio of MS_B and MS_W:

$$F = \frac{MS_B}{MS_W}$$

Therefore, for our example:

$$F = \frac{MS_B}{MS_W}$$

$$= \frac{10.40}{1.57}$$

$$= 6.62$$

Filling in the rest of our summary table we have:

Source of Variation	Sum of Squares	df	Mean Square	F
Between	20.8	$(K - 1) = 2$	10.40	6.62
Within	18.8	$(N - K) = 12$	1.57	
Total	39.6	$(N - 1) = 14$		

Note that we simply divided across ($20.8 \div 2 = 10.40$ and $18.8 \div 12 = 1.57$) and then down ($10.40 \div 1.57 = 6.62$). Thus, $F = 6.62$ with 2 and 12 degrees of freedom.

Assuming $\alpha = .05$, we are now ready to go to our F table, Table A.5 in the Appendix. Across the top of Table A.5 the row labeled n_1 refers to the degrees of freedom for the between term, in our case 2. Find it? Down the extreme left-hand side of the table, in the column labeled n_2, are the degrees of freedom for the within term, in our case 12. Find it? Good. Now, where these two values intersect (go down the 2 column and across the 12 row) we find 3.88, the value of F required for statistical significance (required in order to reject the null hypothesis) if $\alpha = .05$. The question is whether our F value, 6.62, is greater than 3.88. Obviously it is. Therefore, we reject the null hypothesis and conclude that there is a significant difference among the three group means. Note that because two separate degrees of freedom, 2 and 12, are involved, a separate table is required for each α level. Thus the .05 α table is on one page and the .01 α table another. (STATPAK printout follows.)

WHEW!! That was long, but you made it, didn't you?

MULTIPLE COMPARISONS

If the F ratio is determined to be nonsignificant, the party is over. But what if it is significant? What do you really know if the F ratio is rejected? All you know is that there is at least one significant difference somewhere among the means, but you do not know where that difference is. You do not know which means are significantly different from which other means. It might be, for example, that three of the four means tested are equal, but all are greater than a fourth mean;

```
==============================================================================
                    SIMPLE ANALYSIS OF VARIANCE (A N O V A)
==============================================================================
     STATISTIC              VALUE
------------------------------------------------------------------------------
```

STATISTIC		VALUE
N_1	=	5
ΣX_1	=	10.00
$\overline{X}_1$	=	2.00
ΣX_1^2	=	22.00
N_2	=	5
ΣX_2	=	20.00
$\overline{X}_2$	=	4.00
ΣX_2^2	=	90.00
N_3	=	5
ΣX_3	=	24.00
$\overline{X}_3$	=	4.80
ΣX_3^2	=	122.00

SOURCE OF VARIATION	SUM OF SQUARES	df		MEAN SQUARE	F RATIO
BETWEEN	20.80	(K − 1)	2	10.40	6.64
WITHIN	18.80	(N − K)	12	1.57	
TOTAL	39.60	(N − 1)	14		

$\overline{X}_1 = \overline{X}_2 = \overline{X}_3$ and each is greater than $\overline{X}_4$. Or it might be that $\overline{X}_1 = \overline{X}_2$, and $\overline{X}_3 = \overline{X}_4$, but $\overline{X}_1$ and $\overline{X}_2$ are each greater than $\overline{X}_3$ and $\overline{X}_4$. Or it might be that $\overline{X}_1$ is greater than $\overline{X}_2$, $\overline{X}_3$, and $\overline{X}_4$.

When the F ratio is significant and more than two means are involved, multiple comparison procedures are used to determine which means are significantly different from which other means. Several different multiple comparison techniques are available to the researcher. In essence, they involve calculation of a special form of the t test. This special t adjusts for the fact that many tests are being executed. When many significance tests are performed, the probability level, α, tends to increase, because doing a large number of significance tests makes it more likely to obtain significant differences. Thus, the chance of finding a significant difference is increased, but so is the chance of committing a Type I error. The comparisons of the means to be made should generally be decided upon before the study is conducted, not after, and should be based on research hypotheses. Such comparisons are called *a priori* (before the fact) or planned comparisons. Often, however, it is not possible to state a priori tests. In these cases we can use *a posteriori* (after the fact) or post hoc comparisons. In either case, multiple comparisons should not be a "fishing expedition" in which the researcher looks for any difference she or he can find.

Of the many multiple comparison techniques available, the Scheffé test is one of the most widely used. It is an a posteriori test. The Scheffé test is appropriate for making any and all possible comparisons involving a set of means. The calculations for this approach are quite simple, and sample sizes do not have to be equal, as is the case with some multiple comparison techniques. The Scheffé test is very conservative, which is good news and bad news. The good news is that the probability of committing a Type I error for any comparison of means is the least likely. The bad news is that it is entirely possible, given the comparisons selected for investigation, to find no significant differences even though the F for the analysis of variance was significant. In general, however, the flexibility of the Scheffé test and its ease of application make it useful for a wide variety of situations. Other common multiple comparison tests are Tukey's HSD test and Duncan's multiple range test. Here we focus on the Scheffé test.

Calculation of Scheffé Multiple Comparisons

We will use the results of the preceding ANOVA example to examine multiple comparisons. In the ANOVA example the only thing the F ratio told us was that there was at least one significant difference somewhere among the three means. In order to find out where, we will apply the Scheffé test. The Scheffé test involves calculation of an F ratio for each mean comparison of interest. As you study the following formula, you will notice that we already have almost all of the information we need to apply the Scheffé test:

$$F = \frac{(\bar{X}_1 - \bar{X}_2)^2}{MS_W \left(\dfrac{1}{n_1} + \dfrac{1}{n_2}\right)(K - 1)} \text{ with } df = (K - 1), (N - K)$$

Where in the world do we get MS_W? Correct! MS_W is the MS_W from the analysis of variance, which is 1.57 (see the STATPAK Simple Analysis of Variance above). The degrees of freedom are also from the ANOVA, 2 and 12. Of course this formula is for the comparison of $\bar{X}_1$ and $\bar{X}_2$. To compare any other two means we simply change the Xs and the ns. So before we can apply the Scheffé test, we have to calculate the mean for each group.

Looking back at our ANOVA example, the sums for each group were 10, 20, and 24, respectively, and the three $\bar{X}$s are: 2.00, 4.00, and 4.80. Applying the Scheffé test to $\bar{X}_1$ and $\bar{X}_2$ we get:

$$F = \frac{(\bar{X}_1 - \bar{X}_2)^2}{MS_W\left(\dfrac{1}{n_1} + \dfrac{1}{n_2}\right)(K-1)} = \frac{(2.00 - 4.00)^2}{1.57\left(\dfrac{1}{5} + \dfrac{1}{5}\right)2}$$

$$= \frac{(-2.00)^2}{1.57\left(\dfrac{2}{5}\right)2}$$

$$= \frac{4}{1.57(.4)2}$$

$$= \frac{4}{1.57(.8)}$$

$$= \frac{4}{1.256}$$

$$= 3.18$$

Since the value of F required for significance is 3.88 if $\alpha = .05$ and $df = 2$ and 12, and since $3.18 < 3.88$, we conclude that there is no significant difference between $\bar{X}_1$ and $\bar{X}_2$. Calculate the Scheffé test for $\bar{X}_1$ and $\bar{X}_3$ and for $\bar{X}_2$ and $\bar{X}_3$ yourself and determine whether there are significant differences between the two sets of means. You should get the following results.

```
===============================================================
SCHEFFÉ   TESTS
---------------------------------------------------------------
GROUP ONE VS GROUP TWO              3.18           fail to reject

GROUP ONE VS GROUP THREE            6.24           reject

GROUP TWO VS GROUP THREE            0.51           fail to reject
===============================================================
```

The Scheffé test can also be used to compare combinations of means. Suppose, for example, that group 1 was a control group and we wanted to compare the mean of group 1 to the mean of groups 2 and 3 combined. First we would have to combine the means for groups 2 and 3 as follows:

$$\bar{X}_{2+3} = \frac{n_2\bar{X}_2 + n_3\bar{X}_3}{n_2 + n_3} = \frac{5(4.00) + 5(4.80)}{5 + 5}$$

$$= \frac{20.00 + 24.00}{10}$$

$$= \frac{44.00}{10}$$

$$= 4.40$$

Of course, since $n_2 = n_3$, we could have simply replaced n_3 with n_2 and averaged the means as follows:

$$\overline{X}_{2+3} = \frac{n_2\overline{X}_2 + n_2\overline{X}_3}{n_2 + n_2}$$

$$\overline{X}_{2+3} = \frac{n_2(\overline{X}_2 + \overline{X}_3)}{n_2(1 + 1)}$$

$$\overline{X}_{2+3} = \frac{\overline{X}_2 + \overline{X}_3}{2} = \frac{4.00 + 4.80}{2} = \frac{8.80}{2} = 4.40$$

Next, we calculate the F ratio using $\overline{X}_1 = 2.00$ and the combined mean $\overline{X}_{2+3}$ = 4.40:

$$F = \frac{(\overline{X}_1 - \overline{X}_{2+3})^2}{MS_W\left(\dfrac{1}{n_1} + \dfrac{1}{n_2 + n_3}\right)(K - 1)} = \frac{(2.00 - 4.40)^2}{1.57\left(\dfrac{1}{5} + \dfrac{1}{10}\right)2}$$

$$= \frac{(-2.4)^2}{1.57(.2 + .1)2}$$

$$= \frac{5.76}{1.57(.3)2}$$

$$= \frac{5.76}{.94}$$

$$= 6.13$$

Since 6.13 > 3.88, we would conclude that there is a significant difference between $\overline{X}_1$ and $\overline{X}_{2+3}$. In other words, the experimental groups performed significantly better than the control group.

FACTORIAL ANALYSIS OF VARIANCE

If a research study uses a factorial design to investigate two or more independent variables and the interactions between them, the appropriate statistical analysis is a factorial, or multifactor, analysis of variance. The factorial analysis provides a separate F ratio for each independent variable and for each interaction. For example, analysis of the 2 × 2 factorial presented in Figure 13.4 would yield three F ratios—one for the independent variable (Method), one for the control independent variable (IQ), and one for the interaction between Method and IQ. For the No Interaction example in Figure 13.4, the F for Method would probably be significant because method A appears to be significantly more effective than method B (70 versus 30). The F for IQ would also probably be significant because high IQ participants appear to have performed significantly better than low IQ participants (60 versus 40). The F for the interaction between Method and IQ would not be significant because method A is more effective than method B for both IQ groups (80 > 40 and 60 > 20).

On the other hand, for the Interaction example, the F for Method would not be significant because, overall, method A is equally as effective as method B (50 for A and 50 for B). The F for IQ would probably be significant because high IQ participants have performed significantly better than low IQ participants (70 versus 30). The F for the interaction between Method and IQ, however, would probably be significant because the methods appear to be differentially effective,

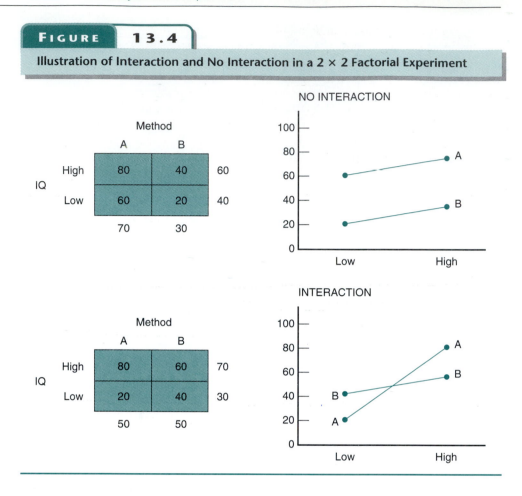

FIGURE 13.4

Illustration of Interaction and No Interaction in a 2 × 2 Factorial Experiment

depending on the IQ level. That is, method A is better for high IQ participants (80 versus 60) and method B is better for low IQ participants (20 versus 40). Another way of looking at it is to see that for the No Interaction example (80 + 20) = (60 + 40); for the Interaction example (80 + 40) ≠ (20 + 60).

A factorial analysis of variance is not as difficult to calculate as you may think. If no more than two variables are involved, and if you have access to a calculator, it can be performed without too much difficulty. Most statistics texts outline the procedure to be followed. If more than two variables are involved, it is usually better to use a computer if possible.

ANALYSIS OF COVARIANCE

Analysis of covariance (ANCOVA) is used in two major ways, as a technique for controlling extraneous variables and as a means of increasing power. ANCOVA is a form of ANOVA and is a statistical, rather than an experimental, method that can be used to equate groups on one or more variables. Use of ANCOVA is essentially equivalent to matching groups on the variable or variables to be controlled. Essentially, ANCOVA adjusts posttest scores for initial differences on a variable and compares the adjusted scores; groups are equalized with respect to the control variable and then compared. It's sort of like handicapping in bowling;

in an attempt to equalize teams, high scorers are given little or no handicap, low scorers are given big handicaps, and so forth. Any variable that is correlated with the dependent variable can be controlled for using covariance. Examples of variables commonly controlled using ANCOVA are pretest performance, IQ, readiness, and aptitude. By using covariance we are attempting to reduce variation in posttest scores that is attributable to another, nontreatment, variable. Ideally, we would like all posttest variance to be attributable to the treatment conditions.

Analysis of covariance is a control technique used in both causal–comparative studies in which already formed, but not necessarily equal, groups are involved and in experimental studies in which either existing groups or randomly formed groups are involved. Remember, randomization does not guarantee that groups will be equated on all variables. Unfortunately, the situation for which ANCOVA is least appropriate is the situation for which it is most often used. Use of AN-COVA assumes that participants have been randomly assigned to treatment groups. Thus, it is best used in true experimental designs. If existing, or intact, groups are not randomly selected but are assigned to treatment groups randomly, ANCOVA may still be used, but results must be interpreted with caution. If covariance is used with existing groups and nonmanipulated independent variables, as in causal–comparative studies, the results are likely to be misleading at best. There are other assumptions associated with the use of analysis of covariance. Violation of these assumptions is not as serious, however, if participants have been randomly assigned to treatment groups.

A second, not previously discussed, function of ANCOVA is that it increases the power of a statistical test by reducing within-group (error) variance. *Power* refers to the statistical ability to reject a false null hypothesis; that is, to make a correct decision to reject the null hypothesis. Although increasing sample size also increases power, the researcher is often limited to samples of a given size because of financial and practical reasons. Because ANCOVA can reduce random sampling error by "equating" different groups, it increases the power of the significance test. The power-increasing function of ANCOVA is directly related to the degree of randomization involved in formation of the groups. The results of ANCOVA are least likely to be valid when groups have not been randomly selected and assigned. As pointed out before, application of the analysis of covariance technique is quite a complex, lengthy procedure and is hardly ever hand calculated. Almost all researchers use computer programs for reasons of accuracy and sanity!

MULTIPLE REGRESSION

As discussed in Part Six, a combination of variables usually results in a more accurate prediction than any single variable. A prediction equation that includes more than one predictor is referred to as a multiple regression equation. A multiple regression equation uses variables that are known to individually predict (correlate with) the criterion to make a more accurate prediction. Thus, for example, we might use high school GPA, Scholastic Assessment Test (SAT) scores, and rank in graduating class to predict college GPA at the end of the first semester of college. Use of multiple regression is increasing, primarily because of its versatility and precision. It can be used with data representing any scale of measurement and can be used to analyze the results of experimental and causal–comparative, as well as correlational, studies. Further, it determines not only whether variables are related, but also the degree to which they are related.

To see how multiple regression works, we will use the example of college GPA. The first step in multiple regression is to identify the variable that best predicts the criterion, that is, the variable most highly correlated with it. Since past performance is generally the best predictor of future performance, high school GPA would probably be the best predictor for college GPA. The next step is to identify a second variable that will most improve the prediction. Usually this is a variable that is related to the criterion (college GPA), but uncorrelated with other predictors. In our case, the question would be, "Do we get a more accurate prediction using high school GPA and SAT scores or using high school GPA and rank in graduating class?" The results of multiple regression would give us the answer to that question and would also tell us by how much the prediction was improved. In our case, the answer might be high school GPA and SAT scores. That would leave rank in graduating class as the last variable, and the results of multiple regression would tell us by how much our prediction would be improved if we included it. Since our three predictors would most probably all be correlated with each other to some degree, as well as to the criterion, it might be that rank in graduating class adds very little to the accuracy of a prediction based on high school GPA and SAT scores. A study involving more than three variables works exactly the same way; at each step it is determined which variable adds the most to the prediction and how much it adds. (See pages 333–334 for another example of multiple regression).

The sign, positive or negative, of the relationship between a predictor and the criterion has nothing to do with how good a predictor it is. Recall that $r = -1.00$ represents a relationship just as strong as $r = +1.00$; the only difference indicated is the nature of the relationship. It should also be noted that the number of predictor variables is related to the sample size; the larger the number of variables, the larger the sample size needs to be. Large sample sizes increase the probability that the prediction equation will generalize to groups beyond those involved in creating the initial equation.

With increasing frequency, multiple regression is being used as an alternative to the various analysis of variance techniques. When this is the case, the dependent variable, or posttest scores, becomes the criterion variable, and the predictors include group membership (e.g., experimental versus control) and any other appropriate variables, such as pretest scores. The results indicate not only whether group membership is significantly related to posttest performance, but also the magnitude of the relationship. For analyses such as these, the researcher typically specifies the order in which variables are to be checked. For analysis of covariance, with pretest scores as the covariate, for example, the researcher specifies that pretest scores be entered into the equation first; it can then be determined whether group membership significantly improves the equation.

CHI SQUARE

Chi square, symbolized as χ^2, is a nonparametric test of significance appropriate when the data are in the form of frequency counts or percentages and proportions that can be converted to frequencies. Two or more mutually exclusive categories are required. Thus, chi square is appropriate when the data are a nominal scale and the categories are either true (e.g., male vs. female) or artificial (e.g., tall vs. short). A chi square test compares the proportions actually observed in a study to the proportions expected, to see if they are significantly different. Expected proportions are usually the frequencies that would be expected if the groups were equal, although occasionally they also may be based on past data. The chi square value increases as the difference between observed and expected frequencies increases. Whether the chi square is significant is determined by consulting a chi square table.

One-Dimensional Chi Square

The chi square can be used to compare frequencies occurring in different categories or groups. As an example, suppose you stopped 90 shoppers in a supermarket and asked them to taste three unlabeled different brands of peanut butter (X, Y, Z) and to tell you which one tasted best. Suppose that 40 of the 90 shoppers chose brand X, 30 chose brand Y, and 20 chose brand Z. If the null hypothesis were true—if there was no difference in taste among the three brands—we would expect an equal number of shoppers to select each brand—30, 30, and 30. We can present our data in what is called a contingency table as shown below:

#that chose Brand X ←

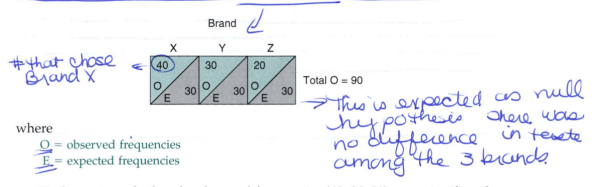

Brand ✓

→ *This is expected as null hypothesis there was no difference in taste among the 3 brands.*

where

   O = observed frequencies
   E = expected frequencies

To determine whether the observed frequencies (40, 30, 20) were significantly different from the expected frequencies (30, 30, 30), a chi square test could be carried out. If the chi square were significant, the null hypothesis would be rejected, and it would be concluded that the brands do taste different.

As another example, you might wish to investigate whether college sophomores prefer to study alone or with others. Tabulation, based on a random sample of 100 sophomores, might reveal that 45 prefer to study alone, and 55 prefer to study with others. The null hypothesis of no preference would suggest a 50–50 split. The corresponding contingency table would look as follows:

Study Preference

Alone	Others	
45	55	
O / 50	O / 50	Total O = 100
/ E	/ E	

In order to determine whether the groups were significantly different, you would compare the observed frequencies (45, 55) with the expected frequencies (50, 50) using a chi square test of significance.

Two-Dimensional Chi Square

The chi square may also be used when frequencies are categorized along more than one dimension, sort of a factorial chi square. In the study sequence example, you might select a stratified sample, comprising 50 males and 50 females. Responses could then be classified by study preference and by gender, a two-way classification that would allow us to see whether study preference is related to gender. The corresponding contingency table would be set up as follows:

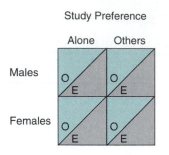

Although 2 × 2 applications are quite common, contingency tables may be based on any number of categories, for example, 2 × 3, 3 × 3, 2 × 4, and so forth. When a two-way classification is used, calculation of expected frequencies is a little more complex, but is not difficult.

Calculating Chi Square

A one-dimensional chi square (χ^2) is the easiest statistic of all. In our peanut butter example, we asked 90 people to indicate which brand they thought tasted best; 40 picked brand X, 30 picked brand Y, and 20 picked brand Z. If there were no difference among the brands we would expect the same number of people to choose each brand, 30 (90 ÷ 3 = 30). Therefore, we have the following table:

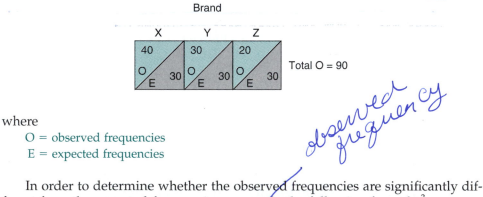

where

O = observed frequencies
E = expected frequencies

In order to determine whether the observed frequencies are significantly different from the expected frequencies, we apply the following formula:[3]

$$\chi^2 = \sum \left[\frac{(fo - fe)^2}{fe} \right]$$

Now that is some sum sign! However, all this formula says is that for each cell (X, Y, and Z) we subtract the expected frequency (fe) from the observed frequency (fo), square the difference (fo − fe), and then divide by the expected frequency, fe.

---

[3]Often, in writing chi square formulas, fo (observed frequency) and fe (expected frequency) are used instead of O and E.

The big Σ says that after we do all that for each term we add up the resulting values. Thus, substituting our table values into the formula we get:

X		Y		Z
fo fe		fo fe		fo fe
$\chi^2 = \dfrac{(40-30)^2}{30}$	$+$	$\dfrac{(30-30)^2}{30}$	$+$	$\dfrac{(20-30)^2}{30}$
fe		fe		fe
$= \dfrac{(10)^2}{30}$	$+$	$\dfrac{(0)^2}{30}$	$+$	$\dfrac{(-10)^2}{30}$
$= \dfrac{100}{30}$	$+$	0	$+$	$\dfrac{100}{30}$
$= 3.333$	$+$	0	$+$	3.333
$= 6.67$				

Thus, $\chi^2 = 6.67$. The degrees of freedom for a one-dimensional chi square are determined by the formula $(C - 1)$, where C equals the number of columns, in our case 3. Thus, $df = 3 - 1 = 2$. Therefore, we have $\chi^2 = 6.67$, $\alpha = .05$, $df = 2$. (STATPAK printout follows).

```
=================================================================================
              C E L L   C H I - S Q U A R E    V A L U E S

   ROW 1 COL 1 "O"=    40.000 "E"=    30.000 CHI-SQUARE      3.333
   ROW 1 COL 2 "O"=    30.000 "E"=    30.000 CHI-SQUARE      0.000
   ROW 1 COL 3 "O"=    20.000 "E"=    30.000 CHI-SQUARE      3.333

   C H I - S Q U A R E  =      6.667

   THERE WAS  1 ROW AND THERE WERE  3 COLUMNS IN THE CONTINGENCY TABLE.

   DEGREES OF FREEDOM = (C - 1) = ( 3  - 1) =   2

=================================================================================
```

To determine whether the differences between observed and expected frequencies are significant, we compare our chi square value to the appropriate value in Table A.6 in the Appendix. Run the index finger of your right hand across the top until you find $\alpha = .05$. Now run the index finger of your left hand down the extreme left-hand column and find $df = 2$. Run your left hand across and your right hand down and they will intersect at 5.991, or 5.99. Is our value of $6.67 > 5.99$? Yes. Therefore, we reject the null hypothesis. There is a significant difference between observed and expected proportions; the brands of peanut butter compared do taste different! Suppose we selected $\alpha = .01$. The chi square value required for significance would be 9.210, or 9.21. Is our value of $6.67 > 9.21$? No. Therefore, we would not reject the null hypothesis and we would conclude that there is no significant difference between observed and expected proportions; the three brands of peanut butter taste the same. Thus, once again you can see that selection of an α level is important; different conclusions may very well be drawn with different α levels.

Now let's look at our study preference example. We asked 100 college sophomores whether they preferred to study alone or with others; 45 said alone and 55 said with others. Under a null hypothesis of no preference we would expect a 50–50 split. Therefore, we have the following table:

Study Preference

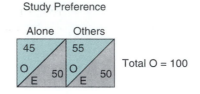

Total O = 100

Applying the chi square formula we get:

$$\chi^2 = \frac{(45-50)^2}{50} + \frac{(55-50)^2}{50}$$

$$= \frac{(-5)^2}{50} + \frac{(5)^2}{50}$$

$$= \frac{25}{50} + \frac{25}{50}$$

$$= .50 + .50$$

$$\chi^2 = 1.00$$

Since degrees of freedom are $C - 1$, we have $2 - 1$, or 1. Thus, $\chi^2 = 1.00$, $\alpha = .05$, $df = 1$ (STATPAK printout below).

```
=================================================================================
            CELL   CHI - SQUARE    VALUES

ROW 1 COL 1 "O"=    45.000 "E"=    50.000 CHI-SQUARE        0.500
ROW 1 COL 2 "O"=    55.000 "E"=    50.000 CHI-SQUARE        0.500

CHI - SQUARE   =        1.000

THERE WAS  1 ROW AND THERE WERE   2 COLUMNS IN THE CONTINGENCY TABLE.

DEGREES OF FREEDOM = (C - 1) = ( 2  - 1) =  1

=================================================================================
```

Table A.6 indicates that for $\alpha = .05$ and $df = 1$, the required value is 3.841, or 3.84. Is our value of $1.00 > 3.84$? No. Therefore, we do not reject the null hypothesis. There is not a significant difference between observed and expected proportions; sophomores do not prefer to study alone or with others.

Now suppose we wanted to know if study preference is related to the gender of the students. Our 2×2 contingency table might look as follows:

Study Preference

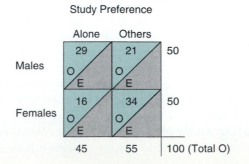

To find the expected frequency for a particular cell, or category, we multiply the corresponding row total by the corresponding column total and divide by the overall total. This isn't as bad as it sounds, honest. So, for males who prefer to study alone, the observed frequency is 29. To find the expected frequency, we multiply the total for the male row (50) by the total for the alone column (45) and divide by the overall total (100):

$$\text{males} - \text{alone} = \frac{50 \times 45}{100} = \frac{2250}{100} = 22.5$$

Similarly, for the other cells, we get:

$$\text{males} - \text{others} = \frac{50 \times 55}{100} = \frac{2750}{100} = 27.5$$

$$\text{females} - \text{alone} = \frac{50 \times 45}{100} = \frac{2250}{100} = 22.5$$

$$\text{females} - \text{others} = \frac{50 \times 55}{100} = \frac{2750}{100} = 27.5$$

Now we can fill in the expected frequencies in our table and it looks as follows:

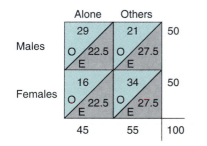

Chi square is calculated in the same way as for the other examples except now we have four terms:

$$\chi^2 = \frac{(29 - 22.5)^2}{22.5} + \frac{(21 - 27.5)^2}{27.5} + \frac{(16 - 22.5)^2}{22.5} + \frac{(34 - 27.5)^2}{27.5}$$

$$= \frac{(6.5)^2}{22.5} + \frac{(-6.5)^2}{27.5} + \frac{(-6.5)^2}{22.5} + \frac{(6.5)^2}{27.5}$$

$$= \frac{42.25}{22.5} + \frac{42.25}{27.5} + \frac{42.25}{22.5} + \frac{42.25}{27.5}$$

$$= 1.88 \quad + \quad 1.54 \quad + \quad 1.88 \quad + \quad 1.54$$

$$\chi^2 = 6.84$$

The degrees of freedom for a two-dimensional chi square are determined by the following formula:

$$df = (R - 1)(C - 1)$$

where
   R = the number of rows in the contingency table
   C = the number of columns in the contingency table

Since we have two rows and two columns,

$$df = (R - 1)(C - 1) = (2 - 1)(2 - 1) = 1 \times 1 = 1$$

Therefore, we have $\chi^2 = 6.84$, $\alpha = .05$, $df = 1$ (See the STATPAK printout). The table value for $\alpha = .05$ and $df = 1$ is 3.841, or 3.84. Is our value of $6.84 > 3.84$? Yes. Therefore, we conclude that gender is related to study preference. For larger contingency tables (e.g., a 3×2), expected frequencies and chi square are calculated in the same way. The only difference is that the number of terms increases; for a 3×2, for example, the number of terms is 6 ($3 \times 2 = 6$).

---

2 X 2 CONTINGENCY TABLE

O = 29.000 E = 22.500 $\overset{2}{X}$ = 1.878	O = 21.000 E = 27.500 $\overset{2}{X}$ = 1.536	50.000
O = 16.000 E = 22.500 $\overset{2}{X}$ = 1.878	O = 34.000 E = 27.500 $\overset{2}{X}$ = 1.536	50.000
45.000	55.000	100.000

PRESS ANY KEY TO CONTINUE:

```
=================================================================
            C E L L   C H I - S Q U A R E   V A L U E S

   ROW 1 COL 1 "O"=    29.000 "E"=    22.500 CHI-SQUARE    1.878
   ROW 1 COL 2 "O"=    21.000 "E"=    27.500 CHI-SQUARE    1.536
   ROW 2 COL 1 "O"=    16.000 "E"=    22.500 CHI-SQUARE    1.878
   ROW 2 COL 2 "O"=    34.000 "E"=    27.500 CHI-SQUARE    1.536

   C H I - S Q U A R E  =      6.828

   THERE WERE 2 ROWS AND 2 COLUMNS IN THE CONTINGENCY TABLE.

   DEGREES OF FREEDOM = (R - 1)(C - 1) = (2 - 1)(2 - 1) =  1
=================================================================
```

There are many parametric and nonparametric statistical methods; too many to describe in detail here. Figure 13.5 provides an overview of some of the more commonly used parametric and nonparametric statistical tests. The figure is best used by first identifying the levels of measurement your study is dealing with. Then examine the purpose statements that fit your levels of measurement and select the one that comes closest to the purpose of your significance test. This should narrow your selection. Other information in Figure 13.5 will help in carrying out your significance test. If you have not used or been exposed to the selected test, you should find out more about your test before using it.

FIGURE 13.5

Descriptions of Commonly Used Parametric and Nonparametric Significance Tests

NAME OF TEST	TEST STATISTIC	df	PARAMETRIC (P) NONPARAMETRIC (NP)	PURPOSE	VAR 1 INDEPENDENT	VAR 2 DEPENDENT
t test for independent samples	t	$n_1 + n_2 - 2$	P	test difference between means of two independent groups	nominal	interval or ratio
t test for dependent samples	t	$N - 1$	P	test difference between means of two dependent groups	nominal	interval or ratio
analysis of variance	F	$SS_B = \text{groups} - 1$; $SS_W = \text{participants} - \text{groups} - 1$	P	test the difference among three or more independent groups	nominal	interval or ratio
Pearson product correlation	r	$N - 2$	P	test whether a correlation is different from zero (a relationshipship exists)	interval or ratio	interval or ratio
chi square test	χ^2	$\text{rows} - 1$ times $\text{column} - 1$	NP	test the difference in proportions in two or more groups	nominal	nominal
median test	χ^2	$\text{rows} - 1$ times $\text{columns} - 1$	NP	test the difference of the medians of two independent groups	nominal	ordinal
Mann–Whitney U test	U	$N - 1$	NP	test the difference in the ranks of two independent groups	nominal	ordinal
Wilcoxon signed rank test	Z	$N - 2$	NP	test the difference in the ranks of two related groups	nominal	ordinal
Kruskal–Wallis test	H	$\text{groups} - 1$	NP	test the difference in the ranks of three or more independent groups	nominal	ordinal
Freidman test	X	$\text{groups} - 1$	NP	test the difference in the ranks of three or more dependent groups	nominal	ordinal
Spearman's rho	ρ	$N - 2$	NP	test whether a correlation is different from zero	ordinal	ordinal

Summary/Chapter 13

Concepts Underlying Inferential Statistics — *Purpose of I.S.*

1. Inferential statistics deal with inferences about populations based on the behavior of samples. Inferential statistics are concerned with determining how likely it is that results based on a sample or samples are the same results that would have been obtained for the entire population.

2. Values calculated from samples, such as the mean, are referred to as statistics. The corresponding population values are referred to as parameters.

3. The question that guides inferential statistics is whether expected differences are real, significant ones or only the result of sampling errors.

4. Inferences concerning populations provide only probability statements; the researcher is never perfectly certain when he or she makes an inference about a population.

Standard Error

5. Expected, chance variation among the means is referred to as sampling error. Sampling errors are normally distributed.

6. If a sufficiently large number of equal-sized large samples are randomly selected from a population, all samples will not have the same mean on the variable measured, but the means of those samples will be normally distributed around the population mean. The mean of all the sample means will yield a good estimate of the population mean.

7. A distribution of sample means not only has its own mean but also its own standard deviation. The standard deviation of the sample means (the standard deviation of sampling errors) is usually referred to as the standard error of the mean ($SE_{\bar{X}}$).

8. In a normal curve, approximately 68% of the sample means will fall between plus and minus one standard error of the mean, 95% will fall between plus and minus two standard errors, and 99+% will fall between plus and minus three standard errors.

9. In most cases, we do not know the mean or standard deviation of the population, so we estimate the standard error by dividing the standard deviation of the sample by the square root of the sample size minus one.

10. The smaller the standard error of the mean, the less sampling error. As the size of the sample increases, the standard error of the mean decreases. The researcher should make every effort to acquire as large a sample as possible.

11. A standard error can also be calculated for other measures of central tendency as well as measures of variability, relationship, and relative position. Further, a standard error can also be determined for the difference between means.

The Null Hypothesis

12. When we talk about the real or significant difference between two sample means, we mean that the difference was caused by the treatment (the independent variable), and not by chance.

13. The null hypothesis says that there is no true difference or relationship between parameters in the populations and that any differences or relationship found for the samples is the result of sampling error.

14. Rejection of a null hypothesis provides more conclusive support for a positive research hypothesis. The test of significance selected to determine whether a difference between means is a true difference provides a test of the null hypothesis. The null hypothesis is either rejected, as being probably false, or not rejected, being probably true.

15. In order to test a null hypothesis we need a statistical test of significance, and we need to select a probability level which indicates how much risk we are willing to take that the decision we make is wrong. After we make the decision to reject or not reject the null hypothesis, we make an inference back to our research hypothesis.

TESTS OF SIGNIFICANCE

16. A test of significance helps us to decide whether we can reject the null hypothesis and infer that the difference is a true one, not a chance one resulting from sampling error. A test of significance is made at a preselected probability level that allows us to state that we have rejected the null hypothesis because we would expect to find a difference as large as we have found by chance only 5 times out of every 100 studies, or only 1 time in every 100 studies, for example.

17. There are a number of different tests of significance. Factors such as the scale of measurement represented by the data, method of participant selection, the number of groups, and the number of independent variables determine which test of significance should be selected for a given experiment.

DECISION MAKING: LEVELS OF SIGNIFICANCE AND TYPE I AND TYPE II ERRORS

18. There are four possibilities that can result from testing the null hypothesis. If the null hypothesis is really true, and the researcher agrees that it is true (does not reject it), the researcher makes the correct decision. Similarly, if the null hypothesis is false, and the researcher rejects it (says there is a difference), the researcher also makes the correct decision. But if the null hypothesis is true, there really is no difference, and the researcher rejects it and says there is a difference, the researcher makes an incorrect decision referred to as a Type I error. Similarly, if the null hypothesis is false, there really is a significant difference between the means, but the researcher concludes that the null hypothesis is true and does not reject it, the researcher also makes an incorrect decision referred to as a Type II error.

19. When the researcher makes the decision to reject the null hypothesis, she or he does so with a given probability of being incorrect. This probability of being incorrect is referred to as the significance level, or probability level, of the test of significance.

20. If the decision is made to reject the null hypothesis, the means are concluded to be significantly different, too different to be the result of chance error. If the null hypothesis is not rejected, the means are determined to be not significantly different. The selected level of significance or probability selected determines how large the difference between the means must be in order to be declared significantly different. The most commonly used probability levels (symbolized as α) are the .05 and the .01 levels.

21. The probability level selected determines the probability of committing a Type I error, that is, of rejecting a null hypothesis that is really true. The smaller the probability level is, the larger the mean difference must be in order to be a significant difference.

22. As the probability of committing a Type I error decreases, the probability of committing a Type II error, that is, of not rejecting a null hypothesis when you should, increases.

23. The choice of a probability level, α, should be made prior to execution of the study. Rejection of a null hypothesis, or lack of rejection, only supports or does not support a research hypothesis; it does not "prove" it.

TWO-TAILED AND ONE-TAILED TESTS

24. Tests of significance are usually two-tailed. The null hypothesis states that there is no difference between groups (A = B) and a two-tailed test allows for the possibility that a difference may occur in either direction. That is, either group mean may be higher than the other (A > B or B > A).

25. A one-tailed test assumes that a difference can only occur in one direction; the null hypothesis states that one group is not better than another. The one-tailed test assumes that if a difference occurs it will be in favor of that particular group (A > B). To select a one-tailed test of significance the researcher has to be quite sure that a difference can only occur in one direction.

26. If there is strong evidence for a one-tailed test, the level of the test of significance required for significance is smaller. In other

words, it is "easier" to find a significant difference.

DEGREES OF FREEDOM

27. Inferential statistics are dependent on degrees of freedom to test hypotheses. Each test of significance has its own formula for determining degrees of freedom. Degrees of freedom are a function of such factors as the number of subjects and the number of groups. The intersection of the probability level and the degrees of freedom, *df*, determine the level needed to reject the null hypothesis.

Tests of Significance: Types

28. Different tests of significance are appropriate for different sets of data. The first decision in selecting an appropriate test of significance is whether a parametric test may be used or whether a nonparametric test must be selected.

29. Parametric tests are more powerful and are generally to be preferred. "More powerful" means more likely to reject a null hypothesis that is false; in other words, the researcher is less likely to commit a Type II error (not rejecting a null hypothesis that should be rejected).

30. Parametric tests require that certain assumptions be met in order for them to be valid. One of the major assumptions underlying use of parametric tests is that the variable measured is normally distributed in the population. A second major assumption is that the data represent an interval or ratio scale of measurement. A third assumption is that participants are randomly selected for the study. Another assumption is that the variances of the population comparison groups are equal (or at least that the ratio of the variances is known).

31. With the exception of independence, some violation of one or more of these assumptions usually does not make too much difference in the decision made concerning the statistical significance of the results.

32. If one or more of the parametric assumptions are greatly violated, a nonparametric test should be used. Nonparametric tests make no assumptions about the shape of the distribution. Nonparametric tests are used when the data represent an ordinal or nominal scale, when a parametric assumption has been greatly violated, or when the nature of the distribution is not known. If the data represent an interval or ratio scale, a parametric test should be used unless another of the assumptions is greatly violated.

THE *T* TEST

33. The *t* test is used to determine whether two means are significantly different at a selected probability level. For a given sample size, the *t* indicates how often a difference as large or larger ($\bar{X}_1 - \bar{X}_2$) would be found when there is no true population difference.

34. The *t* test makes adjustments for the fact that the distribution of scores for small samples becomes increasingly different from a normal distribution as sample sizes become increasingly smaller.

35. For a given significance level, the values of *t* required to reject a null hypothesis are progressively higher as sample sizes become smaller; as the sample size becomes larger the *t* value required to reject the null hypothesis becomes smaller.

36. The *t* test compares the observed mean difference ($\bar{X}_1 - \bar{X}_2$) to the difference expected by chance. The *t* test forms a ratio of these two values. The numerator for a *t* test is the difference between the sample means $\bar{X}_1$ and $\bar{X}_2$ and the denominator is the chance difference that would be expected if the null hypothesis were true—the standard error of the difference between the means.

37. The *t* ratio determines whether the observed difference is sufficiently larger than a difference that would be expected by chance. After the numerator is divided by the denominator, the resulting *t* value is compared to the appropriate *t* table value (depending on the probability level and the degrees of freedom); if the calculated *t* value is equal to or greater than the table value, then the null hypothesis is rejected.

38. There are two different types of *t* tests, the *t* test for independent samples and the *t* test for nonindependent samples. Independent samples are samples that are randomly formed. If two groups are randomly formed, the expectation is that they are essentially the same at the beginning of a study with respect to performance on the dependent variable. Therefore, if they are essentially the same at the end of the study, the null hypothesis is probably true; if they are different at the end of the study, the null hypothesis is probably false; that is, the treatment probably makes a difference.

39. Nonindependent samples are samples formed by some type of matching, or a single sample being pre- and posttested. When samples are not independent, the members of one group are systematically related to the members of a second group, especially if it is the same group at two different times. If samples are nonindependent, scores on the dependent variable are expected to be correlated and a special *t* for correlated, or nonindependent, means must be used.

40. There are a number of problems associated with the use of gain or difference scores. The major one is lack of equal opportunity to grow. Every subject does not have the same room to gain. If two groups are essentially the same on a pretest, their posttest scores can be directly compared using a *t* test. If a *t* test between the groups shows a difference on the pretests, the preferred posttest analysis is analysis of covariance.

SIMPLE ANALYSIS OF VARIANCE

41. Simple, or one-way, analysis of variance (ANOVA) is used to determine whether there is a significant difference between two or more means at a selected probability level.

42. In ANOVA, the total variation, or variance, of scores is attributed to two sources—variance between groups (variance caused by the treatment) and variance within groups (error variance). As with the *t* test, a ratio is formed (the *F* ratio) with group differences as the numerator (variance between groups) and an error term as the denominator (variance within groups). We determine whether the between groups (treatment) variance differs from the within groups (error) variance by more than what would be expected by chance.

43. The degrees of freedom for the *F* ratio are a function of the number of groups and the number of subjects.

MULTIPLE COMPARISONS

44. Multiple comparison procedures are used following ANOVA to determine which means are significantly different from which other means. A special *t* test that adjusts for the fact that many tests are being executed is used because when many tests are performed, the probability level, tends to increase, thus increasing the likelihood of finding a spurious significant result.

45. The mean comparisons to be examined should be decided upon before, not after, the study is conducted. Of the many multiple comparison techniques available, a commonly used one is the Scheffé test, which is a very conservative test. The calculations for the Scheffé test are quite simple and sample sizes do not have to be equal.

FACTORIAL ANALYSIS OF VARIANCE

46. If a research study is based on a factorial design and investigates two or more independent variables and the interactions between them, the appropriate statistical analysis is a factorial, or multifactor, analysis of variance. This analysis yields a separate *F* ratio for each independent variable and one for each interaction.

ANALYSIS OF COVARIANCE (ANCOVA)

47. Analysis of covariance (ANCOVA) is used as a technique for controlling extraneous variables and as a means of increasing power, the statistical ability to reject a false null hy-

pothesis. ANCOVA increases the power of a statistical test by reducing within-group (error) variance.

48. ANCOVA is a form of ANOVA and is a method that can be used to equate groups on one or more variables. Essentially, AN-COVA adjusts posttest scores for initial differences on some variable (such as pretest performance or IQ) and compares adjusted scores.

49. ANCOVA is based on the assumption that subjects have been randomly assigned to treatment groups. It is therefore best used in conjunction with true experimental designs. If existing, or intact, groups are involved but treatments are assigned to groups randomly, ANCOVA may still be used but results must be interpreted with due caution.

MULTIPLE REGRESSION

50. A multiple regression equation uses variables that are known to individually predict (correlate with) the criterion to make a more accurate prediction about a criterion variable.

51. Use of multiple regression is increasing, primarily because of its versatility and precision. It can be used with data representing any scale of measurement, and can be used to analyze the results of experimental and causal–comparative, as well as correlational, studies. It determines not only whether variables are related, but also the degree to which they are related.

52. The first step in multiple regression is to identify the variable that best predicts (is most highly correlated with) the criterion. Variables are added to the multiple regression equation based on their likelihood to be correlated with the criterion but not highly correlated with the other predictor variables.

53. With increasing frequency, multiple regression is being used as an alternative to the various analysis of variance techniques. When this is the case, the dependent vari-

able, or posttest scores, becomes the criterion variable, and the predictors include group membership (e.g., experimental versus control) and any other appropriate variables, such as pretest scores.

CHI SQUARE

54. Chi square, symbolized as χ^2, is a nonparametric test of significance appropriate when the data are in the form of frequency counts occurring in two or more mutually exclusive categories. Chi square is appropriate when the data represent a nominal scale, and the categories may be true categories (e.g., male versus female) or artificial categories (e.g., tall versus short).

55. Expected frequencies are usually the frequencies that would be expected if the groups were equal.

56. One-dimensional chi square is used to compare frequencies occurring in different categories so that the chi square is comparing groups with respect to the frequency of occurrence of different events. Data are presented in a contingency table.

57. Two-dimensional chi square is used when frequencies are categorized along more than one dimension, sort of a factorial chi square. Although 2 × 2 applications are quite common, contingency tables may be based on any number of categories, such as 2 × 3, 3 × 3, or 2 × 4.

58. Each inferential statistic described determines significance in the same general way. A significance level is selected (usually .05 or .01). The degrees of freedom are determined. A chart or computer program indicates the value that corresponds to the intersection of the significance level and the degrees of freedom in the appropriate reference table. The value is compared to the results of the study. If the value of the study results exceeds the reference table value, the null hypothesis is rejected. If not, it is not rejected.

MANOVA
perpensity

CHAPTER 14

"When travelling, your data should be given a royal escort to protect its journey (p. 519)."

Postanalysis Considerations

VERIFICATION AND STORAGE OF DATA

After you have completed all the statistical analyses necessary to describe your data and test your hypothesis, you do not say, "Thank goodness, I'm done!" and happily throw away all your data and your worksheets. Whether you do your analyses by hand, calculator, or computer, all data should be thoroughly checked and stored in an organized manner.

VERIFICATION AND DATA CLEANING

Verification involves double-checking the data, cleaning and organizing it, and evaluating the research conclusion. Double-checking data may seem a bit excessive, but conclusions are only valid to the degree that data are accurate. Remember the motto GIGO—garbage in . . . garbage out. Thus, the original data should be rechecked, preferably in total but at least for a high percentage of it. If raw data were coded into a smaller number of categories, the coded data should be compared to the initial uncoded data to make sure

coding was done properly. If data are kept in a computer, they should be printed out and examined. Considering that a study is worthless if inaccurate data are analyzed, and considering all the effort that has been expended to this point of the study, time involved in rechecking data is time well spent. It is better for you to find any errors than for your advisor or a reader to find them.

When analyses are done by hand or with a calculator, both the accuracy of computations and the reasonableness of the results should be checked. Usually, if the data have been entered correctly into a computer (always check this), the results of the computer analysis will be accurate. This is an advantage of computers. You noticed that in the previous chapters we applied each statistic step by step. This was probably helpful to some readers and annoying to others. Math superstar types seem to derive great satisfaction from doing several steps in a row "in their heads" and listing the results instead of separately recording the result of each step. This may save time in the short run, but not necessarily in the long run. If you end up with a result that just does not look right, it is a lot easier to spot an error if every step is in front of you. Computer analyses rarely show each step in the analysis process, only the final result. This is a disadvantage of computer usage, especially if the researcher is not familiar with the analysis being used.

A very frustrated student once came to one of the authors, quite upset and with a very sad tale about being up all night, rechecking his work over and over and over, and still getting a negative sum of squares in his ANOVA. He was at the point where he could easily have been convinced that the square of a number can be negative! An inspection of his work revealed very quickly that the problem was not in his execution of the ANOVA, but in the numbers he was using to do the ANOVA. Early in the game he had added ΣX_1, ΣX_2, and ΣX_3 and obtained a number much, much larger than their actual sum. From that point on, he was doomed. The moral of the story is that if you have checked an analysis or a set of figures several times and they still seem incorrect, do not check them 50 more times. Look elsewhere! For example, make sure you are using the correct formula or make sure you have used the correct numbers. The anecdote also illustrates that the research results should make sense. If your scores range from 20 to 94 and you get a standard deviation of 1.20 you have probably made a mistake somewhere, because 1.20 is not a reasonable value with such a large range. Similarly, if your means are 24.20 and 26.10 and you get a t ratio of 44.82, you had better recheck your data and analysis.

When analyses are done by computer, output must be checked very carefully. Some people are under the mistaken impression that if a result was produced by a computer, it is automatically correct. "The results must be right, the computer did them!" Wrong! Computers may not make mistakes but people do, and people input the data and select analyses for the computer. Computer analyses are generally accurate, *if the data are properly entered* into the computer. However, one way to check for accurate entry of data is to examine the reasonableness of the results. Don't succumb to a "blind faith" view of the computer. Also, don't be one of those persons who uses the computer to perform analyses they do not understand themselves. Computer usage has almost been made too easy. A person with little or no knowledge of analysis of covariance, for example, can, by following directions, have a computer perform the analysis. However, such a person could not possibly know the nuances of interpretation and whether the results make sense. You may now be beginning to understand the wisdom of our prior advice to never use the computer to apply a statistic that you have not previously done by hand. Also, although you can usually be pretty safe in assuming that the computer will accurately execute each analysis, it is a good idea to spot check. The computer only does what it has been programmed to do and programming errors do occur. Thus, if the computer gives you six F ratios, calculate at least one yourself. If it agrees with the one the computer produced, the rest are most probably also correct.

STORAGE

When you are convinced that your work is accurate, data should be labeled, organized, and filed in a safe place. You never know when you might need your data again. Sometimes an additional analysis is desired either by the original researcher, an advisor, or another researcher who wishes to analyze the data using a different statistical technique. Also, it is not unusual to reuse data from one study in a later study. Therefore, all of the data should be carefully labeled with as many identification labels as possible, labels such as the dates of the study, the nature of each treatment group, and whether data are pretest data, posttest data, or data for a control variable. Find a safe place and guard it very carefully. When travelling, your data should be given a royal escort to protect its journey. If you use a computer, keep one set of data in your computer or hard drive, but also keep a labeled, back-up floppy disk in case your computer or hard drive crashes.

INTERPRETATION OF RESEARCH RESULTS

The product of a test of significance is a number, a value that is statistically significant or not statistically significant. What the number actually means requires interpretation by the researcher. The results of statistical analyses need to be interpreted in terms of the purpose of the study, the original research hypothesis, and with respect to other studies that have been conducted in the same area of research.

HYPOTHESIZED RESULTS

You must discuss whether the results support the research hypothesis and why they do or do not. Are the results in agreement with other findings? Why or why not? Minimally, this means that you will state, for example, that hypotheses one and two were supported, and that hypothesis three was not. The supported hypotheses are relatively simple to deal with; unsupported hypotheses require some explanation regarding possible reasons. There may have been validity or reliable problems in your study, for example. Similarly, if your results are not in agreement with other research findings, possible reasons for the discrepancy should be discussed. There may have been validity problems in your study, or you may have discovered a relationship previously not uncovered.

Remember, if you reject a null hypothesis (there is a difference), your research hypothesis may be supported but it is not proven. One study does not prove anything except that in this one instance the research hypothesis was supported (and the null hypothesis was rejected). A supported research hypothesis does not necessarily mean that your treatment would "work" with different populations, different materials, and different dependent variables. As an example, if token reinforcement is found to be effective in improving the behavior of first graders, this does not mean that token reinforcement will necessarily be effective in reducing referrals to the principal at the high school level. In other words, do not overgeneralize your results.

If you do not reject the null hypothesis (there is no difference), so that your research hypothesis (there is a difference) is not supported, do not feel badly and apologize for your results. A common reaction of some researchers in this situation is to be very disappointed; after all, "I didn't find a significant difference." In the first place, failure to reject a null hypothesis does not necessarily mean that your research hypothesis is false. But more importantly, even if significance is not attained, it is just as important to know what does not work as what does. The researcher's task is to carry out a well-designed, well-analyzed study. It is the researcher's responsibility to provide a fair and valid examination of the study hypotheses. It is not the researcher's task to reject the null hypothesis or to produce statistically significant results. If every researcher knew what the results of his or her study would be before doing the study, there would be no need to carry it out.

Of course if there were some problems with your study, you should describe them in detail. For example, if your study encountered high participant mortality or if intact groups instead of randomly selected ones were compared, this should be reported. There are many problems or threats to validity that can arise in a study that are not the researcher's fault. These should be reported when describing your research results. But do not rationalize. If your study was well planned and well conducted, and no unforeseen mishaps occurred, do not try to come up with some reason why your study did not "come out right." It may very well have "come out right"; remember, the null hypothesis might be true for this particular study.

Unhypothesized Results

Results that are not hypothesized but appear during a study should be interpreted with great care. Often, during a study, an apparent relationship will be noticed that was not hypothesized. For example, you might notice that the experimental group appears to require fewer examples than the control group to learn new math concepts—an unhypothesized relationship. In such a circumstance, do not change your original hypothesis to conform to this new apparent finding, and don't add the unhypothesized finding as a new hypothesis. Hypothesis should be formulated a priori—before the study—based on deductions from theory and/or experience. A true test of a hypothesis comes from its ability to explain and predict what *will* happen, not *what is* happening. You can collect and analyze data on these unforeseen relationships and present your results as such—but don't change or add to your original hypotheses. These unexpected findings may then form the basis for a later study, conducted by yourself or another investigator, specifically designed to test a hypothesis related to your findings. Do not fall into the trap, however, of searching frantically for something that might be significant if your study does not appear to be going as hypothesized. Fishing expeditions in experimental studies are just as bad as fishing expeditions in correlational studies.

Statistical and Methodological Issues

Inferential statistics are based on making inferences about a population based on a sample. To make valid inferences and legitimate conclusions about a population, two factors must apply. In order to make valid inferences about the target population, the sample must be representative and the assumptions of the statistical test must be met. When randomization is not possible, as is often the case in educational research, researchers choose their samples by matching or selecting intact groups. The lack of randomized samples can introduce bias into a study and limit its usefulness. Analogously, the statistical procedures used to analyze data have assumptions that underlie the statistics. For example, most parametric statistics assume an underlying normal distribution and that each participant's scores are independent of any other participant's scores. If these assumptions are not met, bias enters into the statistics used, weakening research generalizations.

A number of methodological practices can lead to invalid or inaccurate research results. Three such practices are ignoring measurement error, low statistical power, and performing multiple comparisons. Most statistical models assume error-free measurement, particularly of the independent variables. However, as discussed in chapter 5, measurements are seldom error-free. Large amounts of measurement error hamper the ability to find statistically significant research results. Recall that in parametric significance tests, the denominator in the significance test is a measure of error. Thus, the larger the denominator, the larger the numerator must be to attain significance.

Statistical power is the probability of avoiding a Type II error (i.e., the probability of rejecting the null hypothesis when it should be rejected). If an analysis has little statistical power, the researcher is likely to overlook or miss the outcome he or she desired to discover. The analysis did not have enough power to detect a significant difference that would have been evident if the statistical power had been greater. The power of a significance test depends on three interrelated factors: (1) the sample size, (2) the significance level selected and the directionality of the significance test, and (3) the effect size, which indicates degree of the departure from the null hypothesis. The greater the departure from the null hypothesis, the greater the effect size. As the sample size, significance level, and effect size increase, so does the power of the significance test. For example, power increases automatically with an increase in sample size. Thus, virtually any difference can be made significant if the sample is large enough. However, it is difficult to interpret the practical meaning of small but significant results obtained primarily by using a very large sample.

The higher the level of significance at which the null hypothesis will be rejected, the more powerful the test. Increasing the significance level—say, from .05 to .10—increases power by making it easier to reject the null hypothesis. Further, if a one-tailed test is justified, it will increase the power to reject the null hypothesis when it should be rejected (reducing the Type II error). However, although the researcher is likely to know the significance level of the study and its sample size, he or she is not likely to know the effect size. Without all three pieces of information, the power of the statistical test cannot be determined. There are three strategies that can be used to estimate the effect size.[1] First, the effect sizes of studies of the same phenomenon can be found and used as guidelines for the likely effect size in the proposed study. Second, a cut-off score below which an effect size is judged unimportant may be used to estimate effect size. For example, a researcher might decide that if a new treatment did not have an effect size of .40 or higher, it would not be worth pursuing. Thus, an effect size of .40 would be chosen. Third, conventional, generally agreed upon definitions of small, medium, and large effect sizes can be chosen. For example, for *t* tests, an effect size of .20 is considered small, .50 is considered medium, and .80 is considered high. Given a desired effect size (say .50) and a significance level (say .05), one can enter a table that shows that to attain an effect size of .50 for a *t* test at significance level .05, a total of 30 participants in each group are needed in the study.

Normally, a researcher would examine the power of his or her study before beginning the study in order to determine whether the power will be sufficient. If the examination shows that the power is insufficient, the researcher can revise the study to increase power, usually by increasing the sample size or significance level.

---

[1]Cohen, J. and Cohen, P. (1975). *Applied multiple regressions/correlation analysis for the behavioral sciences.* Hillsdale, N.J.: Lawrence Erlbaum Associates.

Another statistical issue is the use of multiple comparison techniques such as the Scheffé to test the significance of a large number of means. This practice can lead to erroneous interpretations. Simply put, the more significance tests one carries out in a study, the more likely that false rejections of the null hypotheses (Type I errors) will occur. Suppose, for example, that a researcher did 100 significance tests at the .05 level. Suppose also that there really were no significant differences among all the 100 tests. However, given the .05 level, how many of the tests are likely to be significant? How about at least 5? Remember, we deal in probabilities, not certainties, and at the .05 level we leave 5% for error. In simple terms, a large number of multiple comparisons enhances the likelihood of Type I errors.

STATISTICAL VERSUS PRACTICAL SIGNIFICANCE

The difference between statistical significance and practical significance is often unclear to those who deal with statistical results. The fact that results are statistically significant does not automatically mean that they are of any educational value (i.e., that they have practical significance). Statistical significance only means that your results would be likely to occur by chance a certain percentage of the time, say 5%. This means that the observed statistical relationship or difference is probably a real one, but not necessarily an important one. Significance in the statistical sense is, as noted in the previous section, largely a function of sample size, significance level, and a valid research design. For example, very large samples can result in statistically significant relationships or differences, but they may have no real practical use to anybody. As the sample size increases, the error term (denominator) tends to decrease, and thus increases the r or t ratio so that very large samples with very small correlations or mean differences may become significant. A mean difference of two points might be statistically significant but is probably not worth the effort of revising a curriculum.

Thus, in a way, the smaller sample sizes typically used in educational research studies actually have a redeeming feature. Given that smaller sample sizes mean less power, and given that a greater mean difference is probably required for rejection of the null hypothesis, typical education sample sizes are probably more practically significant than if much larger samples were involved. Of course, lack of statistical power due to small sample sizes may keep us from finding some important relationships. In any event, you should always take care in interpreting results. The fact that method A is significantly more effective than method B statistically does not mean that the whole world should immediately adopt method A! Always consider the practical significance of statistically significant differences.

Another concern in interpreting the results of research is the difference between research precision and research accuracy. Precision refers to how narrowly an estimate is specified. Accuracy refers to how close an estimate is to the true value. Estimates can be precise but not accurate. Often, a computer user or a zealous calculator user will report data to the sixth or tenth decimal place; 25.046093 or 7.28403749. This is misused and not useful precision. What is really important is the accuracy of the calculated estimates, not the number of digits used to state it. Accuracy is more important in interpreting research outcomes than precision.

In sum, a number of considerations go into interpreting the results of research, including methodological and statistical factors, as well as concerns over the difference between statistical and practical significance.

REPLICATION OF RESULTS

Perhaps the strongest support for a research hypothesis comes from replication of results. Replication means doing the study again. The second (third, etc.) study may be a repetition of the original study, using the same or different subjects, or it may represent an alternative approach to testing the same hypothesis. Repeating the study with the same participants is feasible only in certain types of research, such as single-subject designs. Repeating the study with different participants in the same or different settings increases the generalizability of the findings.

The need for replication is especially great when an unusual or new relationship is found, or when the results have practical significance so that the treatment investigated might really make a difference. Interpretation and discussion of a replicated finding will invariably be less tentative than a first-time-ever finding, and rightly so. The significance of a relationship may also be enhanced if it is replicated in a more natural setting. A highly controlled study, for example, might find that method A is more effective than method B in a laboratory-like environment. Interpretation and discussion of the results in terms of practical significance and implications for classroom practice would have to be stated with due caution. If the same results could then be obtained in a classroom situation, however, the researcher could be less tentative concerning their generalizability.

Summary/Chapter 14

Verification and Storage of Data

1. Whether you do your analyses by hand, calculator, or computer, all data should be thoroughly checked and stored in an organized manner.
2. Verification involves double-checking the data and evaluating the research results. Coded data should be compared with uncoded data to make sure all data were coded properly.
3. When analyses are done by hand, or with a calculator, both the accuracy of the computations and the reasonableness of the results need to be checked. When analyses are done by computer, the key concern is inputting the data correctly.
4. All of the data should be carefully labeled with as many identification labels as possible —labels such as the dates of the study, the nature of each treatment group, and whether data are pretest data, posttest data, or data for a control variable. If data are stored in a computer or hard disk, make a backup disk to protect from computer crashes.

Interpretation of Research Results

5. The results of statistical analyses need to be interpreted in terms of the purpose of the study and the original research hypothesis, and with respect to other studies that have been conducted in the same area of research.
6. The researcher must discuss both whether the results support the research hypothesis and why or why not, and whether the results are in agreement with other findings and why or why not.
7. A supported research hypothesis does not necessarily mean that your treatment would "work" with different populations, different materials, and different dependent variables.
8. Failure to reject a null hypothesis does not necessarily mean that your research hypothesis is false, but even if it is, it is just as important to know what does not work as what does work.
9. Unhypothesized results should be interpreted with great care and should be kept and analyzed separately from the hypotheses stated before the start of the study.

10. Unhypothesized findings may form the basis for a later study.
11. Statistical and methodological issues influence the interpretation of research results. Statistical requirements such as random selection and normal distributions influence interpretation if not met. Methodological factors such as ignoring measurement error, performing multiple comparisons, and using small samples can lead to inaccurate or invalid research results.
12. Statistical power is the probability of avoiding a Type II error; that is, the ability to reject the null hypothesis when it should be rejected. Four factors influence power: sample size, significance level, direction of the significance test, and the effect size. Tables exist that indicate how many participants are required to attain a given power level, given the significance level and desired effect size.
13. The fact that results are statistically significant does not automatically mean that they are of any educational value. With very large samples a very small mean difference may yield a significant t. A mean difference of two points might be statistically significant but probably not worth the effort of revising a curriculum.
14. Replication means that the study is done again. The need for replication is especially great when an unusual or new relationship is found in a study, or when the results have practical significance.

Task 7 *Performance Criteria* ◻

The data that you generate (scores you make up for each participant) should make sense. If your dependent variable is IQ, for example, do not generate scores for your participants like 2, 11, and 15; generate scores like 84, 110, and 120. Got it? Unlike a real study, you can make your study turn out any way you want!

Depending on the scale of measurement represented by your data, select and compute the appropriate descriptive statistics.

Depending on the scale of measurement represented by your data, your research hypothesis, and your research design, select and compute the appropriate test of significance. Determine the statistical significance of your results for a selected probability level. Present your results in a summary statement and in a summary table, and relate how the significance or nonsignificance of your results supports or does not support your original research hypothesis. For example, you might say:

> Computation of a *t* test for independent samples ($\alpha = .05$) indicated that the group that received weekly reviews retained significantly more than the group that received daily reviews (see Table 1). Therefore, the original hypothesis that "ninth-grade algebra students who receive a weekly review will retain significantly more algebraic concepts than ninth-grade algebra students who receive a daily review" was supported. *Note:* Task 7 should look like the results section of a research report. Although your actual calculations should not be part of Task 7, they should be attached to it.

On the following pages, an example is presented that illustrates the performance called for by Task 7 (see Task 7 example). Note that the scores are based on the administration of the test described in Task 5. Note, also, that the student calculated effect size (ES) as described in chapter 8.

Additional examples for this and subsequent tasks are included in the *Student Guide* that accompanies this text.

TABLE 1

Means, Standard Deviations, and *t* for the Daily-Review and Weekly-Review Groups on the Delayed Retention Test

	REVIEW GROUP		*t*
	DAILY	**WEEKLY**	
M	44.82	52.68	2.56*
SD	5.12	6.00	

Note: Maximum score = 65.

*$df = 38$, $p < .05$.

1

Effect of Interactive Multimedia on the Achievement of
10th-Grade Biology Students

Results

Prior to the beginning of the study, after the 60 students were randomly selected and assigned to experimental and control groups, final science grades from the previous school year were obtained from school records in order to check initial group equivalence. Examination of the means and a t test for independent samples ($\alpha = .05$) indicated essentially no difference between the groups (see Table 1). A t test for independent samples was used because the groups were randomly formed and the data were interval.

Table 1

Means, Standard Deviation and t Tests for the Experimental and Control Groups

	Group		
Score	IMM instruction[a]	Traditional instruction[a]	t
Prior Grades			
M	87.47	87.63	−0.08*
SD	8.19	8.05	
Posttest NPSS:B			
M	32.27	26.70	4.22**
SD	4.45	5.69	

Note. Maximum score for prior grades = 100. Maximum score for posttest = 40.

[a]n = 30.

*p > .05. **p < .05.

2

At the completion of the eight-month study, during the first week in May, scores on the NPSS:B were compared, also using a $\underline{t}$ test for independent samples. As Table 1 indicates, scores of the experimental and control groups were significantly different. In fact, the experimental group scored approximately one standard deviation higher than the control group ($\underline{ES}$ = .98). Therefore, the original hypothesis that "10th-grade biology students whose teachers use IMM as part of their instructional technique will exhibit significantly higher achievement than 10th-grade biology students whose teachers do not use IMM" was supported.

PRIOR GRADES

	EXPERIMENTAL			CONTROL	
S	X_1	X_1^2		X_2	X_2^2
1	72	5184		71	5041
2	74	5476		75	5625
3	76	5776		75	5625
4	76	5776		77	5929
5	77	5929		78	6084
6	78	6084		78	6084
7	78	6084		79	6241
8	79	6241		80	6400
9	80	6400		81	6561
10	84	7056		83	6889
11	85	7225		85	7225
12	87	7569		88	7744
13	87	7569		88	7744
14	88	7744		89	7921
15	89	7921		89	7921
16	89	7921		89	7921
17	90	8100		90	8100
18	91	8281		91	8281
19	92	8464		92	8464
20	93	8649		92	8464
21	93	8649		93	8649
22	93	8649		94	8836
23	94	8836		94	8836
24	95	9025		95	9025
25	95	9025		96	9216
26	97	9409		96	9216
27	97	9409		97	9409
28	98	9604		97	9409
29	98	9604		98	9604
30	99	9801		99	9801
	2624	231,460		2629	232,265
	ΣX_1	ΣX_1^2		ΣX_2	ΣX_2^2

$$\overline{X}_1 = \frac{\Sigma X_1}{n_1} = \frac{2624}{30} = 87.47$$

$$\overline{X}_2 = \frac{\Sigma X_2}{n_2} = \frac{2629}{30} = 87.63$$

$$SD_1 = \sqrt{\frac{SS_1}{n_1 - 1}} \qquad\qquad SD_2 = \sqrt{\frac{SS_2}{n_2 - 1}}$$

$$SS_1 = \sum x_1^2 - \frac{\left(\sum x_1\right)^2}{n_1} \qquad SS_2 = \sum x_2^2 - \frac{\left(\sum x_2\right)^2}{n_2}$$

$$= 231,460 - \frac{(2624)^2}{30} \qquad\qquad = 232,265 - \frac{(2629)^2}{30}$$

$$= 231,460 - \frac{6885376}{30} \qquad\qquad = 232,265 - \frac{6911641}{30}$$

$$= 231,460 - 229,512.53 \qquad\qquad = 232,265 - 230388.03$$

$$SS_1 = 1947.47 \qquad\qquad SS_2 = 1876.97$$

$$SD_1 = \sqrt{\frac{1947.47}{29}} \qquad\qquad SD_2 = \sqrt{\frac{1876.97}{29}}$$

$$= \sqrt{67.154} \qquad\qquad = \sqrt{64.72}$$

$$SD_1 = 8.19 \qquad\qquad SD_2 = 8.05$$

$$t = \frac{\bar{x}_1 - \bar{x}_2}{\sqrt{\left(\frac{SS_1 + SS_2}{n_1 + n_2 - 2}\right)\left(\frac{1}{n_1} + \frac{1}{n_2}\right)}} \quad = \frac{87.47 - 87.63}{\sqrt{\left(\frac{1947.47 + 1876.97}{30 + 30 - 2}\right)\left(\frac{1}{30} + \frac{1}{30}\right)}}$$

$$= \frac{-0.16}{\sqrt{\left(\frac{3824.44}{58}\right)\left(\frac{1}{15}\right)}}$$

Note: the t table does not have $df = 58$. To be conservative I used $df = 40$. For $df = 40$ the table value is 2.021

$$= \frac{-0.16}{\sqrt{(65.9386)(.0667)}}$$

$$= \frac{-0.16}{\sqrt{4.398}}$$

$$= \frac{-0.16}{2.097}$$

$$t = -.08 \qquad df = 58 \qquad p < .05$$

POSTTEST   NATIONAL PROFICIENCY SURVEY SERIES: BIOLOGY

EXPERIMENTAL   CONTROL

S	X_1	X_1^2	X_2	X_2^2
1	20	400	15	225
2	24	576	16	256
3	26	676	18	324
4	27	729	20	400
5	28	784	21	441
6	29	841	22	484
7	29	841	22	484
8	29	841	23	529
9	30	900	24	576
10	31	961	24	576
11	31	961	25	625
12	31	961	25	625
13	32	1024	25	625
14	32	1024	26	676
15	33	1089	26	676
16	33	1089	27	729
17	33	1089	27	729
18	34	1156	28	784
19	34	1156	29	841
20	35	1225	29	841
21	35	1225	30	900
22	35	1225	30	900
23	36	1296	31	961
24	36	1296	31	961
25	36	1296	32	1024
26	37	1369	33	1089
27	37	1369	34	1156
28	38	1444	35	1225
29	38	1444	36	1296
30	39	1521	37	1369
	968	31808	801	22327
	ΣX_1	ΣX_1^2	ΣX_2	ΣX_2^2

$$\overline{X}_1 = \frac{\Sigma x_1}{n_1} = \frac{968}{30} = 32.27$$

$$\overline{X}_2 = \frac{\Sigma x_2}{n_2} = \frac{801}{30} = 26.70$$

$$SD_1 = \sqrt{\frac{SS_1}{n_1 - 1}} \qquad\qquad SD_2 = \sqrt{\frac{SS_2}{n_2 - 1}}$$

$$SS_1 = \sum x_1^2 - \frac{(\sum x_1)^2}{n_1} \qquad SS_2 = \sum x_2^2 - \frac{(\sum x_2)^2}{n_2}$$

$$= 31808 - \frac{(968)^2}{30} \qquad\qquad = 22327 - \frac{(801)^2}{30}$$

$$= 31808 - \frac{937024}{30} \qquad\qquad = 22327 - \frac{641601}{30}$$

$$= 31808 - 31234.13 \qquad\qquad = 22327 - 21386.70$$

$$SS_1 = 573.87 \qquad\qquad SS_2 = 940.30$$

$$SD_1 = \sqrt{\frac{573.87}{29}} \qquad\qquad SD_2 = \sqrt{\frac{940.30}{29}}$$

$$= \sqrt{19.789} \qquad\qquad = \sqrt{32.424}$$

$$SD_1 = 4.45 \qquad\qquad SD_2 = 5.69$$

$$t = \frac{\bar{x}_1 - \bar{x}_2}{\sqrt{\left(\frac{SS_1 + SS_2}{n_1 + n_2 - 2}\right)\left(\frac{1}{n_1} + \frac{1}{n_2}\right)}} = \frac{32.27 - 26.70}{\sqrt{\left(\frac{573.87 + 940.30}{30 + 30 - 2}\right)\left(\frac{1}{30} + \frac{1}{30}\right)}}$$

$$= \frac{5.57}{\sqrt{\left(\frac{1514.17}{58}\right)\left(\frac{1}{15}\right)}}$$

$$= \frac{5.57}{\sqrt{(26.1064)(.0667)}}$$

$$= \frac{5.57}{\sqrt{1.7404}}$$

$$= \frac{5.57}{1.3192}$$

$$t = 4.22 \qquad df = 58 \qquad p < .05$$

```
                       STATPAK PRINTOUTS
                         Prior Grades
                     Descriptive Statistics


                      EXPERIMENTAL GROUP
==============================================================

         STANDARD DEVIATION FOR SAMPLES AND POPULATIONS
==============================================================

    STATISTIC                                        VALUE
--------------------------------------------------------------

    NO. OF SCORES (N)                                 30

    SUM OF SCORES (ΣX)                              2624.00

    MEAN (X̄)                                          87.47

    SUM OF SQUARED SCORES (ΣX²)                    231460.00

    SUM OF SQUARES (SS)                             1947.47

    STANDARD DEVIATION FOR A POPULATION               8.06

    STANDARD DEVIATION FOR A SAMPLE                   8.19

==============================================================

                        CONTROL GROUP
==============================================================

         STANDARD DEVIATION FOR SAMPLES AND POPULATIONS
==============================================================

    STATISTIC                                        VALUE
--------------------------------------------------------------

    NO. OF SCORES (N)                                 30

    SUM OF SCORES (ΣX)                              2629.00

    MEAN (X̄)                                          87.63

    SUM OF SQUARED SCORES (ΣX²)                    232265.00

    SUM OF SQUARES (SS)                             1876.97

    STANDARD DEVIATION FOR A POPULATION               7.91

    STANDARD DEVIATION FOR A SAMPLE                   8.05

==============================================================
```

```
                    STATPAK PRINTOUTS
                       Prior Grades
                   Inferential Statistic


=================================================================

               t-TEST FOR INDEPENDENT SAMPLES

=================================================================
   STATISTIC                                      VALUE
-----------------------------------------------------------------

   NO. OF SCORES IN GROUP ONE                       30

   SUM OF SCORES IN GROUP ONE                   2624.00

   MEAN OF GROUP ONE                              87.47

   SUM OF SQUARED SCORES IN GROUP ONE         231460.00

   SS OF GROUP ONE                              1947.47

   NO. OF SCORES IN GROUP TWO                       30

   SUM OF SCORES IN GROUP TWO                   2629.00

   MEAN OF GROUP TWO                              87.63

   SUM OF SQUARED SCORES IN GROUP TWO         232265.00

   SS OF GROUP TWO                              1876.97

   t-VALUE                                        -0.08

   DEGREES OF FREEDOM (df)                          58

=================================================================
```

STATPAK PRINTOUTS
NPSS:B Scores
Descriptive Statistics

EXPERIMENTAL GROUP

===

STANDARD DEVIATION FOR SAMPLES AND POPULATIONS

===

STATISTIC	VALUE
NO. OF SCORES (N)	30
SUM OF SCORES (ΣX)	968.00
MEAN ($\bar{X}$)	32.27
SUM OF SQUARED SCORES (ΣX^2)	31808.00
SUM OF SQUARES (SS)	573.87
STANDARD DEVIATION FOR A POPULATION	4.37
STANDARD DEVIATION FOR A SAMPLE	4.45

===

CONTROL GROUP

===

STANDARD DEVIATION FOR SAMPLES AND POPULATIONS

===

STATISTIC	VALUE
NO. OF SCORES (N)	30
SUM OF SCORES (ΣX)	801.00
MEAN ($\bar{X}$)	26.70
SUM OF SQUARED SCORES (ΣX^2)	22327.00
SUM OF SQUARES (SS)	940.30
STANDARD DEVIATION FOR A POPULATION	5.60
STANDARD DEVIATION FOR A SAMPLE	5.69

===

STATPAK PRINTOUTS

NPSS:B Scores

Inferential Statistic

==

t-TEST FOR INDEPENDENT SAMPLES

==

STATISTIC	VALUE
NO. OF SCORES IN GROUP ONE	30
SUM OF SCORES IN GROUP ONE	968.00
MEAN OF GROUP ONE	32.27
SUM OF SQUARED SCORES IN GROUP ONE	31808.00
SS OF GROUP ONE	573.87
NO. OF SCORES IN GROUP TWO	30
SUM OF SCORES IN GROUP TWO	801.00
MEAN OF GROUP TWO	26.70
SUM OF SQUARED SCORES IN GROUP TWO	22327.00
SS OF GROUP TWO	940.30
t-VALUE	4.22
DEGREES OF FREEDOM (df)	58

==

PART EIGHT

Research Reports

There are a variety of reasons for which people conduct research. The motivation for doing a research project may be no more than that such a project is a degree requirement, or it may come from a strong desire to contribute to educational theory or practice. Whatever the reason for their execution, most research studies culminate with the production of a research report.

A number of manuals are available that describe various formats and styles for writing research reports, although several elements are common to most reports regardless of the format followed. Virtually all research reports, for example, contain a statement of the problem or topic studied, a description of procedures used, and a presentation of results. Unlike a research proposal that focuses on what will be done, a research report describes what has happened in the study and what results were obtained. All research reports strive to communicate as clearly as possible the purpose, procedures, and findings of the study.

You have already written many of the components of a research report through your work in Parts Two through Seven. In Part Eight you will integrate all your previous efforts to produce a complete report. The goal of Part Eight is for you, having conducted a study, to be able to produce a complete report. After you have read Part Eight, you should be able to perform the following task.

TASK 8

Based on Tasks 2, 6, and 7, prepare a research report that follows the general format for a thesis or dissertation. (See Performance Criteria, p. 552.)

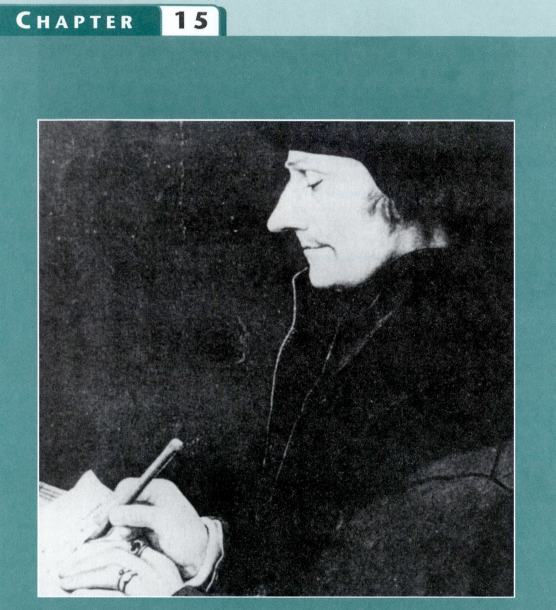

"The research report should . . . reflect scholarship (p. 540)."

Preparation of a Research Report

After reading chapter 15, you should be able to:

1. Identify and briefly describe the major sections of a research report.

2. List general rules for writing and preparing a research report.

GENERAL GUIDELINES

If this chapter were written even a few years ago, it would have focused almost exclusively on writing quantitative research reports. However, in recent years the number of qualitative research reports has grown steadily. As noted in prior chapters, there are some important differences between the purpose and conduct of these two research approaches. In this chapter we emphasize the general issues and practices associated with writing a research report. It is important that you understand that although qualitative and quantitative research reports require that similar areas be addressed, the contents of the areas may differ, given the differences between qualitative and quantitative research emphases. For example, all research reports contain a section describing the topic or problem studied, the review of literature, the description of procedures, and the description of results. However, as seen in earlier chapters, qualitative and quantitative studies address these areas, but in somewhat different ways and emphases. You are encouraged to examine and compare the research reports provided at the end of chapters 7, 8, 9, 10, and 11 to see their differences. Further, when you are actually writing your report, you should look through journals pertinent to your study to view the sections, level of detail, and types of results commonly reported. This is the best way to determine the appropriate format for your report.

While you are conducting your study, you can profitably use spare time to begin revising or refining the introduction and methods sections of your report. After all the data are analyzed you are ready to write the final sections of the report. The major guideline of all stages of writing the report is to make an outline. The chances of your report being presented in an organized, logical manner are greatly increased if the sequence is thought through before anything is actually written. Formulation of an outline greatly facilitates the "thinking through" process. To review briefly, developing an outline involves identification and ordering of major topics followed by differentiation of each major heading into logical subheadings. The time spent in working on an outline is well worth it, because it is much easier to reorganize an outline that is not quite right than to reorganize a document written in paragraph form. Of course this does not mean that your first report draft will be your last. Two or three revisions of each section might be needed. Remember, writing inevitably sparks issues or activities that must be rethought. Each time you read a section you will see ways to improve its organization or clarity. Also, other persons who review your report for you will see areas in need of rethinking or rewording that you have not noticed.

GENERAL RULES FOR WRITING

Probably the foremost rule of research report writing is that the writer should try to relate aspects of the study in a manner that accurately reflects what was done and what was found. Although the style of reporting may vary between quantitative and qualitative studies, the focus of both should be on providing accurate description for the reader. For example, in quantitative reports personal pronouns such as "I" and "we" are usually avoided; the passive voice should be used. In qualitative reports, the tone is often personal and in the voice of the participants. Such stylistic differences do not alter the need for accurate reporting.

Word Processing

Throughout the research process, you will find that your word processing program is one of your most useful tools. A word processing program has many functions beyond enabling you to write down and save your thoughts in a format that can continually be revised and expanded.

Current word processing programs are capable of producing highly professional documents that can be printed in color as well as black and white. Among other features, you can design your own graphics and diagrams, construct complex tables and charts, insert pictures, sort data in alphabetical or numerical order, design outlines, and paste data from other software programs, such as spreadsheets, databases, and statistical programs. In addition, word processing programs have functions that allow you to check your grammar, spelling, sentence complexity, and reading grade level at which you are writing. Most word processing programs also contain thesauruses which inform you of a variety of appropriate terms that you can use in your writing. Before beginning the research process, it is advisable that you become familiar with at least one word processing program.

The research report should be written in a clear, simple, straightforward style and reflect scholarship. You do not have to be boring, just concise. In other words, convey what you wish to convey, do it in an efficient way, avoiding jargon, and use simple language. For example, instead of saying "the population comprised all students who matriculated for the fall semester at Egghead University," it would be better to say "the population was all students enrolled for the fall semester at Egghead University." Obviously the report should reflect scholarship and contain correct spelling, grammatical construction, and punctuation. Your computer will probably have a spelling and grammar checker. Use it, but don't misuse it—it will not catch wrong words spelled write (or is that right?). Even if you don't have a computer, you do have access to a dictionary. It is also a good idea to have someone you know, someone who is perhaps stronger in these areas, review your manuscript and indicate errors.

Although different style manuals emphasize different rules of writing, several rules are common to most manuals. Use of abbreviations and contractions, for instance, is generally discouraged. For example, do not write "the American Psychological Assn." Write "the American Psychological Association." Also, words like shouldn't, isn't, and won't should be avoided. Exceptions to the abbreviation rule include commonly used and understood abbreviations (such as IQ and GPA) and abbreviations defined by the researcher to promote clarity, simplify presentation, or reduce repetition. If the same sequence of words is going to be used repeatedly, the researcher will often define an abbreviation in parentheses the first time the sequence is used and thereafter use only the abbreviation. Authors of cited references are usually referred to by last name only in the main body of the report: first names, initials, and titles are not given. Instead of saying "Professor Dudley Q. McStrudle (1995) concluded . . ." you normally would say "McStrudle (1995) concluded . . ." These guidelines hold only for the main body of the report. Tables, figures, footnotes, and references may include abbreviations; footnotes and references usually give at least the author's initials. Another convention followed by most style manuals is with respect to numbers. If the first word of a sentence is a number ("Six schools were contacted . . ."), or if the number is nine or less ("a total of five lists . . ."), numbers are expressed as words. Otherwise, numbers are generally expressed as Arabic numerals ("a total of 500 questionnaires was sent").

The final report should be proofread carefully at least twice. Reading the report silently to yourself will usually be sufficient to identify major errors. If you have a willing listener, however, reading the manuscript out loud often helps you to identify grammatical or constructional errors. Sometimes sentences do not make nearly as much sense when you hear them as when you write them; also, your listener will frequently be helpful in bringing to your attention sections that are unclear. Reading the report backwards, last sentence first, will also help you to identify poorly constructed or unclear sentences. The process of preparing a research report is greatly facilitated by computer word processing, which commonly provides features such as automatic page numbering and heading centering; the ability to rearrange words, sentences, and paragraphs; and spelling checkers.

FORMAT AND STYLE

Format refers to the general pattern of organization and arrangement of the report. The number and types of headings and subheadings to be included in the report are determined by the format used. Style refers to the rules of spelling, capitalization, punctuation, and word processing followed in preparing the report. Although formats may vary in terms of specific headings included, research reports generally follow a format that parallels the steps involved in conducting a study. For example, one format might call for a discussion section and another format might require a summary, conclusions, and recommendations section (or both), but all formats require a section in which the results of the study are discussed and interpreted. All research reports also include a condensed description of the study, whether it be a summary of a dissertation or an abstract of a journal article.

Style Manual Helps

Besides consulting the most recent manual of style for the paper and bibliographic format that you are following, several Web sites provide current, up-to-date information on the appropriate formats. Some useful Web sites for this purpose are:

http://www.gasou.edu/psychweb.tipsheet/apacrib.htm
http://www.apa.org/journals/faq.html
gopher://gopher.uiuc.edu/11/Libraries/writers/I
http://www.uwsp.edu/acad/psych/apa4.htm#intro
http://www.uwm.edu/people/pcsmith/userguide.htm

The last Web site listed above contains an actual research paper with hyperlinks to additional information about the elements of APA style.

Most colleges, universities, and professional journals either have developed their own, required style manual or have selected one that must be followed. Check with your advisor about the style used in your institution. Do this before beginning writing, since rearranging a format after the fact is a tedious, time-consuming process. One such manual, which is increasingly being required as a guide for theses and dissertations, is the *Publication Manual of the American Psychological Association.* If you are not bound by any particular format and style system, the APA manual is recommended. In addition to acquiring and studying a copy of the selected manual, it is also very helpful to study several reports that have been written following the same manual. For example, look at existing dissertations (especially those directed by your advisor) to get an idea of format and what is expected. To the degree possible (e.g., with respect to tables, figures, references, and student examples of tasks), this text reflects APA guidelines, as does the following discussion. Figure 15.1 illustrates some of the basic APA guidelines using a page from the Task 8 example that appears at the end of this chapter.

SECTIONS OF THESES AND DISSERTATIONS

Although specifics will vary considerably, most research reports prepared for a degree requirement follow the same general format. Table 15.1 presents an outline of the typical contents of such a report. As Table 15.1 indicates, theses and dissertations include a set of fairly standard preliminary pages, components that directly parallel the research process, and supplementary information, which is included in appendices. The contents of a qualitative study would be similar to a quantitative one, except that in the Method section the qualitative report would emphasize the description and selection of the research site, the sampling approach, and the process of data collection.

PRELIMINARY PAGES

The preliminary pages set the stage for the report to follow and indicate where in the report each component, table, and figure can be found. The title page should

FIGURE **15.1**

Some APA Guidelines for Preparing Your Paper

9

Results

 Prior to the beginning of the study, after the 60
students were randomly selected and assigned to experimental
and control groups, final science grades from the previous
school year were obtained from school records in order to
check initial group equivalence. Examination of the means and
a t test for independent samples (α = .05) indicated
essentially no difference between the groups (see Table 1). A
t test for independent samples was used because the groups
were randomly formed and the data were interval.

Table 1
Means, Standard Deviation and t Tests for the Experimental and
Control Groups

Score	Group		t
	IMM instruction[a]	Traditional instruction[a]	
Prior Grades			
M	87.47	87.63	0.08*
SD	8.19	8.05	
Posttest NPSS:B			
M	32.27	26.70	4.22 **
SD	4.45	5.69	

Note. Maximum score for prior grades = 100. Maximum score for
posttest = 40.
[a]n = 30.
*p > .05. **p < .05.

1. Page numbers go in the top right-hand corner, flush with the right margin and between the top of the page and the first line.

2. First level headings are centered, written in upper and lower case, and NOT underlined.

3. All text should be double spaced.

4. All statistical values should be underlined (e.g., p < .05).

5. Margins should always be uniform all around (1 inch is the minimum).

indicate the major focus of the study. Recall when you reviewed the literature made initial decisions about the relevance of a source based on its title. A good title should communicate what the study is about. When a title is well constructed, it is fairly easy to determine the nature of the topic. When it is vaguely worded it is often difficult to determine the topic without going into the body of the report. After you write your title, apply the communication test: Would you know what the study was about if you read the title in an index? Ask a friend or colleague to describe what he or she understands from your title.

TABLE	15.1
Common Components of a Research Report Submitted for a Degree Requirement	

PRELIMINARY PAGES
  Title page
  Acknowledgments page
  Table of Contents
  List of Tables and Figures
  Abstract
MAIN BODY OF THE REPORT
  Introduction
    Statement of the Problem
    Review of Related Literature
    Statement of the Hypothesis
    Significance of the Study
  Method
    Participants
    Instruments
    Design
    Procedure
  Results
  Discussion (Conclusions and Recommendations)
  References (Bibliography)
APPENDIXES

Most theses and dissertations include an acknowledgments page. This page permits the writer to express appreciation to persons who have contributed significantly to the completion of the report. Notice the word *significant*. Everyone who had anything to do with the study or the report cannot (and should not!) be mentioned. It is acceptable to thank your major professor for his or her guidance and assistance; it is not acceptable to thank your third-grade teacher for giving you confidence in your ability. (Remember the Academy Awards!)

The table of contents is basically an outline of your report that indicates on which page each major section (or chapter) and subsection begins. The list of tables and figures, which is presented on a separate page, gives the number and title of each table and figure and the page on which it can be found. Many colleges and universities require an abstract, while others require a summary, but the current trend is in favor of abstracts. The content of abstracts and summaries is identical, only the positioning differs: an abstract precedes the main body of the report and a summary follows the Discussion section. Abstracts are often required to be no more than a given number of words, usually between 100 and 500. Many institutions require abstracts to be no more than 350 words, which is the maximum allowed by Dissertation Abstracts International, a repository of dissertation abstracts. Most APA journals require abstracts that are between 100 and 150 words. Since the abstract of a report is often the only part read, it should briefly describe the most important aspects of the study, including the topic investigated, the type of participants and instruments involved, the data collection procedures, and the major results and conclusions. For example, a 100-word abstract for a study investigating the effect of a writing-oriented curriculum on the reading comprehension of fourth-grade students might read as follows:

> The purpose of this study was to determine the effectiveness of a curriculum that emphasized writing with respect to the reading comprehension of fourth-grade students reading at least one level below grade level. Using a posttest-only control group design and the *t* test for independent samples, it was found that after 8 months the students ($n = 20$) who participated in a curriculum that emphasized writing achieved significantly higher scores on the reading comprehension subtest of the Stanford Achievement Test, Primary Level 3 (grades 3.5–4.9) than the students ($n = 20$) who did not [$t (38) = 4.83, p < .05$]. It was concluded that the curriculum emphasizing writing was more effective in promoting reading comprehension.

THE MAIN BODY

The body of the report contains information about the topic studied, literature reviewed, hypotheses (if any) posited, participants, instruments, procedures, results, and discussion. The introduction section includes a description of the research problem or topic, a review of related literature, a statement of hypotheses or issues, and a definition of uncommon or important terms. A well-written statement of a problem or topic generally indicates the variables examined in the study. The statement of the problem or topic should be accompanied by a presentation of its background, including a justification for the study in terms of its significance; that is, why should anyone care about this study?

The review of related literature indicates what is known about your problem or topic. Its function is to educate the reader about the area being studied. The review of related literature is not a series of abstracts or annotations, but rather an analysis and an integration of the relationships and differences among relevant studies and reports. The review should flow in such a way that the least-related references are discussed first, and the most-related references are discussed last, just prior to the statement of the hypothesis. The review should conclude with a brief summary of the literature and its implications.

A good hypothesis clearly states the expected relationship (or difference) between the variables and defines those variables in operational, measurable terms. The hypothesis (or hypotheses) logically follows the review of related literature and it is based on the implications of previous research. A well-developed hypothesis is testable, that is, can be confirmed or disconfirmed. The qualitative researcher is unlikely to state hypotheses as focused as those of a quantitative researcher, but the qualitative researcher may have some hunches about what the study may show. The introduction section also includes operational definitions of terms used in the study that do not have a commonly agreed meaning.

METHOD

The method section includes a description of participants, instruments, design, procedure, assumptions, and limitations. A qualitative study may also include a detailed description of the site studied and the nature and length of interactions with the participants. The description of participants includes information about how they were selected and, mainly for quantitative researchers, the population they represent. A description of the sample should indicate its size and major characteristics such as age, grade level, ability level, and socioeconomic status. A good description of the sample enables the readers of the report to determine how similar study participants are to participants they are concerned with.

Data collection procedures should be described fully, be they tests, questionnaires, interviews, or observations. The description should indicate the purpose of the procedure, its application, and its validity and reliability. If a procedure has been developed by the researcher, the description needs to be more detailed and should also state the manner in which it was developed, its pretesting, revisions, steps involved in scoring, and guidelines for interpretation. A copy of the instrument, accompanying scoring keys, and other pertinent data related to a newly developed test are generally placed in the appendix of the thesis or dissertation.

The description of the design is especially important in an experimental study. In other types of research the description of the design may be combined with procedure. In an experimental study, the description of the basic design (or variation of a basic design) applied in the study should include a rationale for selection and a discussion of sources of invalidity associated with the design, and why they may have been minimized in the study being reported.

The procedure section should describe the steps followed in conducting the study, in chronological order and in sufficient detail to permit the study to be replicated by another researcher. It should be clear exactly how participants were assigned to groups treatments or the conditions under which qualitative participants were observed or interviewed. In essence, a step by step description of what went on during the study should be provided. In many cases, qualitative researchers will have more complex and detailed procedural descriptions than quantitative researchers.

The results section describes the statistical techniques or the inferential interpretations that were applied to the data and the results of these analyses. For each hypothesis, the statistical test of significance selected and applied to the data is described, followed by a statement indicating whether the hypothesis was supported or not supported. Tables present numerical data in rows and columns and usually include descriptive statistics, such as means and standard deviations, and the results of tests of significance, such as t and F ratios. Good tables and figures are uncluttered and self-explanatory; it is better to use two tables (or figures) than one that is crowded. They should stand alone, that is, be interpretable without the aid of related textual material. Tables and figures follow their related textual discussion and are referred to by number, not name or location. In other words, the text should say "see Table 1," not "see the table with the means" or "see the table on the next page." Examine the variety of tables and figures throughout this text to get a perspective on how data can be presented.

Qualitative research reporting tends to be based mainly on descriptions and quotations that support or illustrate the study results. Charts and diagrams showing the relationships among identified topics, categories, and patterns are also useful in presenting the results of a study. The logic and description of the interpretations linked to qualitative charts and diagrams is an important aspect of qualitative research reporting.

All research reports have a section that discusses and interprets the results, draws conclusions and implications, and makes recommendations. Interpretation of results may be presented in a separate section titled "Discussion," or it may be included in the same section as the other analysis of results items. What this section (or sections) is called is unimportant; what is important is how well it is constructed. Each result should be discussed in terms of its relation to the topic studied and in terms of its agreement or disagreement with previous results obtained by other researchers.

Two common errors are to confuse results and conclusions and to overgeneralize results. A result is the outcome of a test of significance or a qualitative analysis. The corresponding conclusion is that the original hypothesis or topic was or was not supported by the data. In qualitative reports, the conclusion may simply be a summarizing description of what was observed. Overgeneralization refers to the statement of conclusions that are not warranted by the results. For example, if a group of first graders receiving personalized instruction were found to achieve significantly higher on a test of reading comprehension than a group receiving traditional instruction, it would be an overgeneralization to conclude that personalized instruction is a superior method of instruction for elementary students. Similarly, if a qualitative study about teacher burnout consisted of four interviewees, it would be an overgeneralization to infer that all teachers felt the same about burnout.

The report should also discuss the theoretical and practical implications of the findings and make recommendations for future research or future action. In this portion of the report the researcher is permitted more freedom in expressing opinions that are not necessarily direct outcomes of data analysis. The researcher is free to discuss any possible revisions or additions to existing theory and to encourage studies designed to test hypotheses suggested by the results. The researcher may also discuss implications of the findings for educational practice and suggest studies designed to replicate the study in other settings, with other participants, and in other curricular areas, in order to increase the generalizability of the findings. The researcher may also suggest next-step studies designed to investigate another dimension of the problem investigated. For example, a study finding type of feedback to be a factor in retention might suggest that amount of feedback may also be a factor and recommend further research in that area.

The references, or bibliography, section of the report lists all the sources, alphabetically by authors' last names, that were directly used in writing the report. Every source cited in the paper must be included in the references, and every entry listed in the references must appear in the paper; in other words, the sources in the paper and the sources in the references must correspond exactly. If APA style is being used, secondary sources are not included in the references. Citations for secondary sources should indicate the primary source from which they were taken; the primary source should be included in the references. For example, you might say: "Nerdfais (cited in Snurd, 1995) found that yellow chalk . . . ." The Snurd source would be listed in the references. Note that no year would be given for the Nerdfais study. For thesis and dissertation studies, if sources were consulted that were not directly cited in the main body of the report, these may be included in an appendix. The style manual being followed will determine the form that each reference must take. If the style manual to be used is known while the review of related literature is being conducted, the researcher can save time by writing each reference in the proper form initially. Table 15.2 shows APA formats for most common references in theses or dissertations.

Appendixes are usually necessary in thesis and dissertation reports to provide information and data pertinent to the study that either are not important enough to be included in the main body of the report or are too lengthy. Appendixes contain such entries as materials especially developed for the study (for example, tests, questionnaires, and cover letters), raw data, and data analysis sheets.

TABLE 15.2

APA Reference Formats

The following are examples of many of the types of references you may need to include in your research paper. These examples follow the APA style guidelines set forth in the fourth edition of the *Publication Manual of the American Psychological Association.*

PERSONAL COMMUNICATION

S. W. Metzger (personal communication, November 5, 1998).

BOOK

Bandura, A. J. (1977). *Social learning theory.* Englewood Cliffs, NJ: Prentice Hall.

BOOK, EDITED

Robinson, D. N. (Ed.). (1992). *Social discourse and moral judgment.* San Diego, CA: Academic Press.

BOOK, CHAPTER

O'Neil, J. M., & Egan, J. (1992). Men's and women's gender role journeys: Metaphor for healing, transition, and transformation. In B. R. Wainrib (Ed.), *Gender issues across the life cycle* (pp. 107–123). New York: Springer.

BOOK, TRANSLATION

Laplace, P. S. (1951). *A philosophical essay on probabilities* (F. W. Truscott & F. L. Emory, Trans.). New York: Dover. (Original work published 1814).

BOOK REVIEW

Baumeister, R. F. (1993). Exposing the self-knowledge myth [Review of the book *The self-knower: A hero under control*]. *Contemporary Psychology, 38,* 466–467.

JOURNAL ARTICLE

Klimoski, R., & Palmer, S. (1993). The ADA and the hiring process in organizations. *Consulting Psychology Journal: Practice and Research, 45* (2), 10–36.

TABLE 15.2

(continued)

NEWSPAPER ARTICLE

Shwartz, J. (1993, September 30). Obesity affects economic, social status. *The Washington Post,* pp. A1, A4.

ABSTRACT

Nakazato, K., Shimonaka, Y., & Homma, A. (1992). Cognitive functions of centenarians: The Tokyo Metropolitan Centenarian Study. *Japanese Journal of Developmental Psychology, 3,* 9–16. (From PsycSCAN: *Neuropsychology,* 1993, 2, Abstract No. 604)

ERIC REFERENCE

Mead, J. V. (1992). *Looking at old photographs: Investigating the teacher tales that novice teachers bring with them* (Report No. NCRTL-RR-92-4). East Lansing, MI: National Center for Research on Teacher Learning. (ERIC Document Reproduction Service No. ED 346 082)

DISSERTATION (UNPUBLISHED)

Wilfley, D. E. (1989). *Interpersonal analyses of bulimia: Normal-weight and obese.* Unpublished doctoral dissertation, University of Missouri, Columbia.

UNPUBLISHED PAPER

Stinson, C., Milbrath, C., Reidbord, S., & Bucci, W. (1992). *Thematic segmentation of psychotherapy transcripts for convergent analyses.* Unpublished manuscript.

(All examples from *Publication Manual of the American Psychological Association* (4th ed.). Washington, DC: American Psychological Association, pp. 194–215.)

If you need to reference an electronic source, such as an on-line periodical or a paper posted on the World Wide Web, the *Publication Manual of the American Psychological Association* also contains useful guidelines for referencing electronic sources.

Summary/Chapter 15

General Guidelines

1. A major facilitator for writing a research report is making an outline. Development of an outline involves identification and ordering of major topics, followed by differentiation of each major heading into logical subheadings.
2. A research report is written in the past tense.

General Rules for Writing

3. Probably the foremost rule of research report writing is to relate aspects of the study in a manner that accurately reflects what was done and what was found.
4. Although quantitative and qualitative research approaches differ in many ways, both cover similar topics in their research reports. However, while the general topics are similar, the emphases within the topics vary, depending on which of the two approaches is being reported.
5. The research report should be written in a clear, simple, straightforward style and correct spelling, grammar, and punctuation are expected. Most computers have the capability to check spelling and grammar.
6. Authors of cited references are usually referred to by last name only in the main body of the report.
7. If the first word of a sentence is a number, or if the number is nine or less, numbers are usually expressed as words. Otherwise, numbers are generally expressed as Arabic numerals.
8. Carefully proofread the final report.

Format and Style

9. Most research reports consistently follow a selected system for format and style. Format refers to the general pattern of organization and arrangement of the report. Style refers to the rules of spelling, capitalization, punctuation, and typing followed in preparing the report.
10. Many colleges and universities either have developed their own format or require use

of a published style manual. It is also very helpful to study several reports that have been written following the same manual.

Sections of Theses and Dissertations

11. The title page usually includes the title of the report, the author's name, the degree requirement being fulfilled, the name and location of the college or university awarding the degree, the date of submission of the report, and signatures of approving committee members. The title should describe the purpose of the study as clearly as possible.
12. The acknowledgments page allows the writer to express appreciation to persons who have contributed significantly to the completion of the report.
13. The table of contents is basically an outline of your report that indicates on which page each major section (or chapter) and subsection begins. The list of tables and figures, which is presented on a separate page, gives the number and title of each table and figure and the page on which it can be found.
14. Most colleges and universities require an abstract or summary of the study. The number of pages for each will be specified; they usually range from 100 to 500 words. The abstract should describe the most important aspects of the study, including the problem investigated, the type of participants and instruments, the design, the procedures, the major results, and the major conclusions.
15. The introduction section is the first section of the main body of the report and includes a well-written description of the problem, a review of related literature, a statement of the hypothesis, and definition of terms.
16. The review of related literature describes and analyzes what has already been done related to your problem.
17. A good hypothesis in a quantitative study states as clearly and concisely as possible the expected relationship (or difference) between two variables, and defines those variables in operational, measurable terms.

18. The introduction also includes operational definition of terms used in the study that do not have a commonly known meaning.
19. The method section includes a description of participants, instruments, design, procedure, assumptions, and limitations.
20. The description of participants in a quantitative study includes a definition and description of the population from which the sample was selected and may describe the method used in selecting the participants. The description of participants in a qualitative study will include description of the way participants were selected, why they were selected, and a detailed description of the context in which they function.
21. The description of each instrument should relate the function of the instrument in the study (for example, selection of participants or a measure of the dependent variable), what the instrument is intended to measure, and data related to validity and reliability.
22. The procedure section should describe each step followed in conducting the study, in chronological order, in sufficient detail to permit the study to be replicated by another researcher.
23. The results section describes the statistical techniques or qualitative interpretation that were applied to the data and the results of the analyses. Information about the process applied during data analysis should be provided.
24. Tables and figures are used to present findings in summary or graph form and add clarity to the presentation. Good tables and figures are uncluttered and self-explanatory; it is better to use two tables (or figures) than one that is crowded. Tables and figures follow their related textual discussion and are referred to by number, not name or location.
25. Each research finding or result should be discussed in terms of its agreement or disagreement with previous results obtained by other researchers in other studies or hypotheses stated at the start of the study.
26. Overgeneralization refers to the statement of conclusions that are not warranted by the results and should be avoided.
27. The researcher should discuss the theoretical and practical implications of the findings and make recommendations for future research or future action.
28. The reference or bibliography section of the report lists all the sources, alphabetically by authors' last names, that were directly used in writing the report. Every source cited in the paper must be included in the references, and every entry listed in the references must appear in the paper.
29. The required style manual will guide the format of various types of references.
30. Appendixes include information and data pertinent to the study that either are not important enough to be included in the main body of the report or are too lengthy—for example, tests, questionnaires, and cover letters, raw data, and data analysis sheets.

◻ **Task 8** *Performance Criteria*

Your research report should include all the components presented in Table 15.1, with the possible exceptions of an acknowledgments page and appendixes. Development of Task 8 basically involves combining Tasks 2, 6, and 7, writing a discussion section, and preparing the appropriate preliminary pages (including an abstract) and references. In other words, you have already written most of Task 8.

On the following pages, an example is presented that illustrates the performance called for by Task 8 (see Task 8 example). This example represents the synthesis of the previously presented tasks related to the effects of interactive multimedia on biology achievement. To the degree possible with a student paper, this example follows the guidelines of the *Publication Manual of the American Psychological Association.*

Additional examples for this and other tasks are included in the *Student Guide* that accompanies this text.

Effect of Interactive Multimedia on the Achievement
of 10th-Grade Biology Students
Sara Jane Calderin
Florida International University

Submitted in partial fulfillment of
the requirements for EDF 5481
April, 1994

Table of Contents

i

List of Tables and Figures

Table   Page

1. Means, Standard Deviation,

   and t Tests for the Experimental

   and Control Groups   8

Figure

1. Experimental Design   5

ii

Abstract

The purpose of this study was to investigate the effect of interactive multimedia on the achievement of 10th-grade biology students. Using a posttest-only control group design and a t test for independent samples, it was found that after approximately 8 months the students (n = 30) who were instructed using interactive multimedia achieved significantly higher scores on the biology test of the National Proficiency Survey Series than did the students (n = 30) whose instruction did not include interactive multimedia, t (58) = 4.22, p < .05. It was concluded that the interactive multimedia instruction was effective in raising the achievement level of the participating students.

iii

1

Introduction

One of the major concerns of educators and parents alike is the decline in student achievement. An area of particular concern is science education, where the higher-level thinking skills and problem solving techniques so necessary for success in our technological society need to be developed (Smith & Westhoff, 1992).

Research is constantly providing new proven methods for educators to use, and technology has developed many kinds of tools ideally suited to the classroom. One such tool is interactive multimedia (IMM). IMM provides teachers with an extensive amount of data in a number of different formats including text, sound, and video. This makes it possible to appeal to all the different learning styles of the students and to offer a variety of material for students to analyze (Howson & Davis, 1992).

When teachers use IMM, students become highly motivated, which results in improved class attendance and more completed assignments (O'Connor, 1993). In addition, students also become actively involved in their own learning, encouraging comprehension rather than mere memorization of facts (Kneedler, 1993; Reeves, 1992).

Statement of the Problem

The purpose of this study was to investigate the effect of IMM on the achievement of 10th-grade biology students. IMM was defined as "a computerized database that allows users to access information in multiple forms, including text, graphics, video and audio" (Reeves, 1992, p. 47).

2

<u>Review of Related Literature</u>

Due to modern technology, such as video tapes and video discs, students receive more information from visual sources than they do from the written word (Helms & Helms, 1992), and yet in school the majority of information is still transmitted through textbooks. While textbooks cover a wide range of topics superficially, IMM can provide in-depth information on essential topics in a format that students find interesting (Kneedler, 1993). Smith and Westhoff (1992) note that when student interest is sparked, curiosity levels are increased and students are motivated to ask questions. The interactive nature of multimedia allows students to seek out their own answers, and by so doing they become owners of the concept involved. Ownership translates into comprehension (Howson & Davis, 1992).

Many science concepts are learned through observation of experiments. By using IMM, students can participate in a variety of experiments which are either too expensive, too lengthy or too dangerous to carry out in the school laboratory (Howson & Davis, 1992; Leonard, 1989; Louie, Sweat, Gresham & Smith, 1991). While observing experiments students can discuss what is happening and ask questions. At the touch of a button teachers are able to replay any part of the proceedings, and they also have random access to related information which can be used to illustrate completely the answer to the question (Howson & Davis, 1992). By answering students' questions in this detailed way, the content becomes more relevant to the needs of the students (Smith & Westhoff, 1992). When knowledge is relevant students are able to use it to solve problems and in so doing develop higher-level thinking skills (Helms & Helms, 1992; Sherwood, Kinzer, Bransford, & Franks, 1987).

3

A major challenge of science education is to provide students with large amounts of information that will encourage them to be analytical (Howson & Davis, 1992; Sherwood et al. 1987). IMM offers electronic access to extensive information allowing students to organize, evaluate and use it in the solution of problems (Smith & Wilson, 1993). When information is introduced as an aid to problem solving it becomes a tool with which to solve other problems, rather than a series of solitary, disconnected facts (Sherwood et al. 1987).

Although critics complain that IMM is entertainment and students do not learn from it (Corcoran, 1989), research has shown that student learning does improve when IMM is used in the classroom (Sherwood et al. 1987; Sherwood & Others, 1990). A 1987 study by Sherwood et al., for example, showed that seventh- and eighth-grade science students receiving instruction enhanced with IMM had better retention of that information, and O'Connor (1993) found that the use of IMM in high school mathematics and science increased the focus on students' problem solving and critical thinking skills.

Statement of the Hypothesis

The quality and quantity of software available for science classes has dramatically improved during the past decade. Although some research has been carried out on the effects of IMM on student achievement in science, due to promising updates in the technology involved, further study is warranted. Therefore, it was hypothesized that 10th-grade biology students whose teachers use IMM as part of their instructional technique will exhibit significantly higher achievement than 10th-grade biology students whose teachers do not use IMM.

4

Method

Participants

The sample for this study was selected from the total population of 213 tenth-grade students at an upper middle class all girls Catholic high school in Miami, Florida. The population was 90% Hispanic, mainly of Cuban-American descent. Sixty students were randomly selected (using a table of random numbers) and randomly assigned to two groups of 30 each.

Instrument

The biology test of the National Proficiency Survey Series (NPSS) was used as the measuring instrument. The test was designed to measure individual student performance in biology at the high school level but the publishers also recommended it as an evaluation of instructional programs. Content validity is good; items were selected from a large item bank provided by classroom teachers and curriculum experts. High school instructional materials and a national curriculum survey were extensively reviewed before objectives were written. The test objectives and those of the biology classes in the study were highly correlated. Although the standard error of measurement is not given for the biology test, the range of KR-20s for the entire battery is from .82 to .91 with a median of .86. This is satisfactory since the purpose of the test was to evaluate instructional programs not to make decisions concerning individuals. Catholic school students were included in the battery norming procedures which were carried out in April and May of 1988 using 22,616 students in grades 9-12 from 45 high schools in 20 states.

Experimental Design

The design used in this study was the posttest-only control group design (see Figure 1). This design was selected

5

because it provides control for most sources of invalidity and random assignment to groups was possible. A pretest was not necessary since the final science grades from June 1993 were available to check initial group equivalence and to help control mortality, a potential threat to internal validity with this design. Mortality, however, was not a problem as no students dropped from either group.

Group	Assignment	n	Treatment	Posttest
1	Random	30	IMM instruction	NPSS:B[a]
2	Random	30	Traditional instruction	NPSS:B

[a]National Proficiency Survey Series: Biology

Figure 1. Experimental design.

Procedure

Prior to the beginning of the 1993-94 school year, before classes were scheduled, 60 of the 213 tenth-grade students were randomly selected and randomly assigned to two groups of 30 each, the average biology class size; each group became a biology class. One of the classes was randomly chosen to receive IMM instruction. The same teacher taught both classes.

The study was designed to last eight months beginning on the first day of class. The control group was taught using traditional methods of lecturing and open class discussions. The students worked in pairs for laboratory investigations

6

which included the use of microscopes. The teacher's role was one of information disseminator.

The experimental classroom had 15 workstations for student use, each one consisting of a laserdisc player, a video recorder, a 27 inch monitor, and a Macintosh computer with a 40 MB hard drive, 10 MB RAM and a CD-ROM drive. The teacher's workstation incorporated a Macintosh computer with CD-ROM drive, a videodisc player and a 27 inch monitor. The workstations were networked to the school library so students had access to online services such as Prodigy and Infotrac as well as to the card catalogue. Two laser printers were available through the network for the students' use.

In the experimental class the teacher used a videodisc correlated to the textbook. When barcodes provided in the text were scanned, a section of the videodisc was activated and appeared on the monitor. The section might be a motion picture demonstrating a process or a still picture offering more detail than the text. The role of the teacher in the experimental group was that of facilitator and guide. After the teacher had introduced a new topic, the students worked in pairs at the workstations investigating topics connected to the main idea presented in the lesson. Videodiscs, CD-ROMs and online services were all available as sources of information. The students used HyperStudio to prepare multimedia reports which they presented to the class.

Throughout the study the same subject matter was covered and the two classes used the same text. Although the students of the experimental group paired up at the workstations, the other group worked in pairs during lab time thus equalizing any effect from cooperative learning. The classes could not meet at the same time as they were taught

7

by the same teacher, so they met during second and third periods. First period was not chosen as the school sometimes has a special schedule which interferes with first period. Both classes had the same homework reading assignments which were reviewed in class the following school day. Academic objectives were the same for each class and all tests measuring achievement were identical.

During the first week of May, the biology test of the NPSS was administered to both classes to compare their achievement in biology.

8

Results

Prior to the beginning of the study, after the 60 students were randomly selected and assigned to experimental and control groups, final science grades from the previous school year were obtained from school records in order to check initial group equivalence. Examination of the means and a t test for independent samples (α = .05) indicated essentially no difference between the groups (see Table 1). A t test for independent samples was used because the groups were randomly formed and the data were interval.

Table 1

Means, Standard Deviation and t Tests for the Experimental and Control Groups

	Group		
Score	IMM instruction[a]	Traditional instruction[a]	t
Prior Grades			
M	87.47	87.63	−0.08*
SD	8.19	8.05	
Posttest NPSS:B			
M	32.27	26.70	4.22**
SD	4.45	5.69	

Note. Maximum score for prior grades = 100. Maximum score for posttest = 40.

[a] n = 30.

*p > .05. **p < .05.

9

At the completion of the eight-month study, during the first week in May, scores on the NPSS:B were compared, also using a t test for independent samples. As Table 1 indicates, scores of the experimental and control groups were significantly different. In fact, the experimental group scored approximately one standard deviation higher than the control group (ES=.98). Therefore, the original hypothesis that "10th-grade biology students whose teachers use IMM as part of their instructional technique will exhibit significantly higher achievement than 10th-grade biology students whose teachers do not use IMM" was supported.

10

Discussion

The results of this study support the original hypothesis: 10th-grade biology students whose teachers used IMM as part of their instructional technique did exhibit significantly higher achievement than 10th-grade biology students whose teachers did not use IMM. The IMM students' scores were 5.57 (13.93%) points higher than those of the other group. Also, it was informally observed that the IMM instructed students were eager to discover information on their own and to carry on the learning process outside scheduled class hours.

Results cannot be generalized to all classrooms because the study took place in an all-girls Catholic high school with the majority of the students having an Hispanic background. However, the results were consistent with research on IMM in general, and in particular with the findings of Sherwood et. al. (1987) and O'Connor (1993) concerning the improvement of student achievement.

IMM appears to be a viable educational tool with applications in a variety of subject areas and with both cognitive and psychological benefits for students. While further research is needed, especially using other software and in other subject areas, the suggested benefits to students' learning offered by IMM warrant that teachers should be cognizant of this instructional method. In this technological age it is important that education takes advantage of available tools which increase student motivation and improve academic achievement.

11

References

Corcoran, E. (1989, July). Show and tell: Hypermedia turns
    information into a multisensory event. Scientific
    American, 261, 72, 74.

Helms, C. W., & Helms, D. R. (1992, June). Multimedia in
    education (Report No. IR-016-090). Proceedings of the
    25th Summer Conference of the Association of Small
    Computer Users in Education. North Myrtle Beach, SC.
    (ERIC Document Reproduction Service No. ED 357 732)

Howson, B.A., & Davis, H. (1992). Enhancing comprehension
    with videodiscs. Media and Methods, 28(3), 12-14.

Kneedler, P. E. (1993). California adopts multimedia science
    program. Technological Horizons in Education Journal,
    20(7), 73-76.

Lehmann, I.J. (1990). Review of National Proficiency Survey
    Series. In J. J. Kramer & J. C. Conoley (Eds.), The
    eleventh mental measurements yearbook (pp. 595-599).
    Lincoln: University of Nebraska, Buros Institute of
    Mental Measurement.

Leonard, W. H. (1989). A comparison of student reaction to
    biology instruction by interactive videodisc or
    conventional laboratory. Journal of Research in Science
    Teaching, 26, 95-104.

Louie, R., Sweat, S., Gresham, R., & Smith, L. (1991).
    Interactive video: Disseminating vital science and math
    information. Media and Methods, 27(5), 22-23.

O'Connor, J. E. (1993, April). Evaluating the effects of
    collaborative efforts to improve mathematics and
    science curricula (Report No. TM-019-862). Paper
    presented at the Annual Meeting of the American

12

Educational Research Association, Atlanta, GA. (ERIC
Document Reproduction Service No. ED 357 083)

Reeves, T. C. (1992). Evaluating interactive multimedia.
<u>Educational Technology, 32</u> (5), 47-52.

Sherwood, R. D., Kinzer, C. K., Bransford, J. D., & Franks,
J. J. (1987). Some benefits of creating macro-contexts
for science instruction: Initial findings. <u>Journal of
Research in Science Teaching,</u> 24, 417-435.

Sherwood, R. D., & Others. (1990, April). <u>An evaluative study
of level one videodisc based chemistry program</u> (Report
No. SE-051-513). Paper presented at a Poster Session at
the 63rd Annual Meeting of the National Association for
Research in Science Teaching, Atlanta, GA. (ERIC
Document Reproduction Service No. ED 320 772)

Smith, E. E., & Westhoff, G. M. (1992). The Taliesin project:
Multidisciplinary education and multimedia. <u>Educational
Technology, 32,</u> 15-23.

Smith, M. K., & Wilson, C. (1993, March). <u>Integration of
student learning strategies via technology</u> (Report No.
IR-016-035). Proceedings of the Fourth Annual
Conference of Technology and Teacher Education. San
Diego, CA. (ERIC Document Reproduction Service No: ED
355 937)

PART NINE

Research Critiques

Anyone who reads a newspaper, listens to the radio, or watches television is a consumer of research. We are constantly bombarded with the latest research findings concerning the relationship between diet and heart disease, the wrinkle-reducing powers of face creams, and the positive effects of aspirin, to name a few. Many people uncritically accept and act on such findings because they are presented by someone in a white lab coat or because they are labeled "research." Very few people question the procedures utilized or the generalizability of the findings from such research. As a professional, you are required to possess critical evaluation skills. In addition to being critical of data transmitted by the media, you have a responsibility to be informed concerning the latest findings in your professional area and to be able to differentiate "good" from "poor" research. Normally a researcher critically evaluates all aspects of a study and does not consider poorly executed research. Decisions made based on the basis of poor research are likely to be bad or ineffective ones. Research results that contain one or more serious flaws are frequently published. Competent evaluation of a research study requires knowledge of each of the components of the research process. Your work in previous chapters has given you that knowledge.

The goal of Part Nine is for you to be able to analyze and evaluate research reports. After you have read Part Nine, you should be able to perform the following task.

TASK 9

Given a reprint of a research report and an evaluation form, evaluate the components of the report. (See Performance Criteria, p. 580.)

"Normally a researcher critically evaluates all aspects of a study and does not consider poorly executed research (p. 569)."

Evaluation of a Research Report

▆ OBJECTIVES

After reading chapter 16, you should be able to:

1. List, for each of the major sections and subsections of a research report, at least three questions that should be asked in determining its adequacy.
2. List, for each of the following types of research, at least three questions that should be asked in determining the adequacy of a study representing that type:

Qualitative research
Historical research
Descriptive research
Correlational research
Causal–comparative research
Experimental research

GENERAL EVALUATION CRITERIA

The fact that a study is completed or even published does not necessarily mean that it is a good study or that it is reported adequately. The most common flaw in studies is lack of validity and reliability information about data-gathering procedures such as tests, observations, questionnaires, and interviews. Other common flaws include weaknesses in the research design, inappropriate or biased selection of participants, failure to state limitations in the research, and a general lack of description about the study. These common problems in studies reinforce the importance of being a competent consumer of research reports; they also highlight common pitfalls to be avoided in your own research.

At your current level of expertise you may not be able to evaluate every component of every study. For example, you would not be able to determine whether the appropriate degrees of freedom were used in the calculation of an analysis of covariance. There are, however, a number of basic errors or weak-

nesses that you should be able to detect in research studies. You should, for example, be able to identify the sources of invalidity associated with a study based on a one-group pretest–posttest design. You should also be able to detect obvious indications of experimenter bias that may have affected qualitative or quantitative research results. For example, a statement in a research report that "the purpose of this study was to prove . . ." should alert you to a probable bias effect.

As you read a research report—either as a consumer of research keeping up with the latest findings in your professional area or as a producer of research reviewing literature related to a defined problem—you should ask yourself questions about the adequacy of a study and its components. The answers to some of these questions are more critical than the answers to others. An inadequate title is not a critical flaw; an inadequate research plan is. Some questions are difficult to answer if the study is not directly in your area of expertise. If your area of specialization is reading, for example, you are probably not in a position to judge the adequacy of a review of literature related to anxiety effects on learning. And, admittedly, the answers to some questions are more subjective than objective. Whether a good design was used is pretty clear and objective; most quantitative researchers would agree that the randomized posttest-only control group design is a good design. Whether the most appropriate design was used, given the problem under study, often involves a degree of subjective judgment. For example, the need for inclusion of a pretest might be a debatable point, depending on the study and its design. However, despite the lack of complete agreement in some areas, evaluation of a research report is a worthwhile and important activity. Major problems and shortcomings are usually readily identifiable, and by considering a number of questions you can formulate an overall impression of the quality of the study. This chapter lists evaluative questions about research strategies and areas for your consideration. This list is by no means exhaustive and, as you read it, you may very well think of additional questions to ask. You will also note that not every criterion equally applies to both quantitative and qualitative research studies.

Introduction

Problem

Is there a statement of the problem or a qualitative topic of study? Does the problem or topic indicate a particular focus of study?

Is the problem "researchable"? That is, can it be investigated through the collection and analysis of data?

Is background information on the problem presented?

Is the educational significance of the problem discussed?

Does the quantitative problem statement indicate the variables of interest and the specific relationship between those variables that were investigated?

Does the qualitative problem statement provide a general indication of the research topic or issue?

When necessary, are variables directly or operationally defined?

Does the researcher have the knowledge and skill to carry out the proposed research?

Review of Related Literature

Is the review comprehensive?

Are all cited references relevant to the problem under investigation?

Are most of the sources primary (i.e., are there only a few or no secondary sources)?

Have the references been analyzed and critiqued, and the results of various studies compared and contrasted (i. e., is the review more than a series of abstracts or annotations)?

Is the relevancy of each reference explained?

Is the review well organized? Does it logically flow in such a way that the references least related to the problem are discussed first and the most-related references are discussed last? Does it educate the reader about the problem or topic?

Does the review conclude with a summary and interpretation of the literature and its implications for the problem investigated?

Do the implications discussed form an empirical or theoretical rationale for the hypotheses that follow?

Are references cited completely and accurately?

Hypotheses

Are specific questions to be answered listed or specific hypotheses to be tested stated?

Does each hypothesis state an expected relationship or difference?

If necessary, are variables directly or operationally defined?

Is each hypothesis testable?

METHOD

Participants

Are the size and major characteristics of the population studied described?

Are the accessible and target populations described?

If a sample was selected, is the method of selecting the sample clearly described?

Does the method of sample selection suggest any limitations or biases in the sample? For example, is stratified sampling used to obtain sample subgroups?

Are the size and major characteristics of the sample described?

Does the sample size meet the suggested guideline for minimum sample size appropriate for quantitative analyses?

Instruments

Do instruments and their administration meet guidelines for protecting participants? Have needed permissions been obtained?

Is the rationale given for the selection of the instruments (or measurements) used?

Is each instrument described in terms of purpose, content, validity, and reliability?

Are the instruments appropriate for measuring the intended variables?

Does the researcher have the needed skills or experience to construct or administer an instrument?

Is evidence presented to indicate that the instruments are appropriate for the intended sample? For example, is the reading level of an instrument suitable for sample participants?

If appropriate, are subtest reliabilities given?

If an instrument was developed specifically for the study, are the procedures involved in its development and validation described?

If an instrument was developed specifically for the study, are administration, scoring or tabulating, and interpretation procedures fully described?

Is the correct type of instrument used for data collection (e.g., using a norm-referenced instrument when a criterion-referenced one is more suitable)?

Design and Procedure

Are the design and procedures appropriate for examining the research question or testing the hypotheses of the study?

Are the procedures described in sufficient detail to permit them to be replicated by another researcher?

Do procedures logically relate to each other?

Are instruments and procedures applied correctly?

If a pilot study was conducted, are its execution and results described, as well as its effect on the subsequent study?

Are control procedures described?

Did the researcher discuss or account for any potentially confounding variables that he or she was unable to control?

Is the application of the qualitative method chosen described in detail?

Is the context of the qualitative study described in detail?

RESULTS

Are appropriate descriptive statistics presented?

Was the probability level, α, at which the results of the tests of significance were evaluated, specified in advance of the data analyses? Was every hypothesis tested?

If parametric tests were used, is there evidence that the researcher avoided violating the required assumptions for parametric tests?

Are the described tests of significance appropriate, given the hypotheses and design of the study?

Was the inductive logic used to produce results in a qualitative study made explicit?

Are the tests of significance interpreted using the appropriate degrees of freedom?

Are the results clearly presented?

Are the tables and figures (if any) well organized and easy to understand?

Are the data in each table and figure described in the text?

DISCUSSION (CONCLUSIONS AND RECOMMENDATIONS)

Is each result discussed in terms of the original hypothesis or topic to which it relates?

Is each result discussed in terms of its agreement or disagreement with previous results obtained by other researchers in other studies?

Are generalizations consistent with the results?

Are the possible effects of uncontrolled variables on the results discussed?

Are theoretical and practical implications of the findings discussed?

Are recommendations for future action made?

Are the suggestions for future action based on practical significance or on statistical significance only (i.e., has the author avoided confusing practical and statistical significance)?

ABSTRACT OR SUMMARY

Is the problem restated?

Are the number and type of participants and instruments described?

Is the design used identified?

Are procedures described?

Are the major results and conclusions restated?

TYPE-SPECIFIC EVALUATION CRITERIA

In addition to general criteria that can be applied to almost any study, there are additional questions that should be asked, depending on the type of research represented by the study. In other words, there are concerns that are specific to historical studies, and likewise to qualitative, descriptive, correlational, causal–comparative, and experimental studies.

QUALITATIVE RESEARCH

Does the topic to be studied describe a general sense of the study focus?

Is the purposive sampling procedure described and related to the study focus?

Is each data collection strategy described?

Is the role the researcher assumed stated (e.g., observer, participant observer, interviewer)?

Is the research site and the researcher's entry into it described?

Were the data collection strategies used appropriately, given the purpose of the study?

Were strategies used to strengthen the validity and reliability of the data (e.g., triangulation)?

Is there a description of how any unexpected ethical issues were handled?

Were strategies that were used to minimize observer bias and observer effect described?

Are the researcher's reactions and notes differentiated from descriptive field notes?

Are data coding strategies described and examples of coded data given?

Did the researcher specify the inductive logic applied to the data to produce results?

Are conclusions supported by data (e.g., using direct quotes to illustrate points)?

HISTORICAL RESEARCH

Were the sources of data related to the problem mostly primary?

Was each piece of data subjected to external criticism?

Was each piece of data subjected to internal criticism?

Does the researcher examine the possibility of personal bias in the study analysis and conclusion?

Are causal inferences or conclusions warranted given the data studied?

Is the report of the study an integrated, synthesized, chronological presentation of the results?

DESCRIPTIVE RESEARCH

Questionnaire Studies

Are questionnaire validation procedures described?

Was the questionnaire pretested?

Are pilot study procedures and results described?

Are directions to questionnaire respondents clear?

Does each item in the questionnaire relate to one of the objectives of the study?

Does each questionnaire item deal with a single concept?

When necessary, is a point of reference given for questionnaire items?

Are leading questions avoided in the questionnaire?

Are there sufficient alternatives for each questionnaire item?

Does the cover letter explain the purpose and importance of the study and give the potential responder a good reason for cooperating?

If appropriate, is confidentiality or anonymity of responses assured in the cover letter?

What is the percentage of returns, and how does it affect the study results?

Are follow-up activities to increase returns described?

If the response rate was low, was any attempt made to determine any major differences between responders and nonresponders?

Are data analyzed in groups or clusters rather than a series of many single-variable analyses?

Interview Studies

Were the interview procedures pretested?

Are pilot study procedures and results described?

Does each item in the interview guide relate to a specific objective of the study?

When necessary, is a point of reference given in the guide for interview items?

Are leading questions avoided in the interview guide?

Is the language and complexity of the questions appropriate for the participants?

Does the interview guide indicate the type and amount of prompting and probing that was permitted?

Are the qualifications and special training of the interviewers described?

Is the method used to record responses described?

Did the researcher use the most reliable, unbiased method of recording responses that could have been used?

Did the researcher specify how the responses to semistructured and unstructured items were quantified and analyzed?

Observation Studies

Are observational variables defined?

How were observers trained?

Did different observers work and score independently?

Were observers required to observe only one behavior at a time?

Was a coded recording instrument used?

Are the qualifications and special training of the observers described?

Was the level of inter-observer reliability obtained from at least two independent raters, and is the result reported?

Is the level of inter-observer reliability sufficiently high?

Were efforts made to overcome observer bias and observer effect?

Was observation of participants the most appropriate approach for data collection (as opposed to use of some unobtrusive measure)?

Was a description of how the observational data were analyzed provided?

CORRELATIONAL RESEARCH

Relationship Studies

Were variables carefully selected? That is, was a shotgun approach avoided?

Is the rationale for variable selection described?

Are conclusions and recommendations based on values of correlation coefficients corrected for attenuation or restriction in range?

Do the conclusions avoid suggesting causal relationships between the variables investigated?

Prediction Studies

Is a rationale given for selection of predictor variables?

Is the criterion variable well defined?

Was the resulting prediction equation validated with at least one other group?

CAUSAL–COMPARATIVE RESEARCH

Are the characteristics or experiences that differentiate the groups (the independent variable) clearly defined or described?

Are critical extraneous variables identified?

Were any control procedures applied to equate the groups on extraneous variables?

Are causal relationships found discussed with due caution?

Are plausible alternative hypotheses discussed?

EXPERIMENTAL RESEARCH

Was an appropriate experimental design selected?

Is a rationale for design selection given?

Are sources of invalidity associated with the design identified and discussed?

Is the method of group formation described?

Was the experimental group formed in the same way as the control group?

Were groups randomly formed and the use of existing groups avoided?

Were treatments randomly assigned to groups?

Were critical extraneous variables identified?

Were any control procedures applied to equate groups on extraneous variables?

Were possible reactive arrangements (e.g., the Hawthorne effect) controlled for?

Were tables clear and pertinent to the research results?

Were the results generalized to the appropriate group?

Summary/Chapter 16

General Evaluation Criteria

1. Even a beginning researcher should be able to detect basic errors or weaknesses in a research study.
2. You should be able to detect obvious indications of experimenter bias that may have affected the results.
3. As you read a research report—either as a consumer of research keeping up with the latest findings in your professional area or as a producer of research reviewing literature related to a defined problem—you should ask yourself questions concerning the adequacy of execution of the various components.
4. The answers to some of these questions are more critical than the answers to others.
5. Major problems and shortcomings are usu-

ally readily identifiable, and by mentally responding to a number of questions one formulates an overall impression concerning the validity of the study.

INTRODUCTION

6. Problem   See page 572.
7. Review of Related Literature   See page 572.
8. Hypotheses   See page 573.

METHOD

9. Participants   See page 573.
10. Instruments   See page 573.
11. Design and Procedure   See page 574.

RESULTS

12. See page 574.

DISCUSSION (CONCLUSIONS AND RECOMMENDATIONS)

13. See page 574.

ABSTRACT OR SUMMARY

14. See page 575.

Type-Specific Evaluation Criteria

15. In addition to general criteria which can be applied to almost any study, there are additional questions which should be asked depending upon the type of research represented by the study.

QUALITATIVE RESEARCH

16. See page 575.

HISTORICAL RESEARCH

17. See page 576.

DESCRIPTIVE RESEARCH

18. Questionnaire Studies   See page 576.
19. Interview Studies   See page 576.
20. Observation Studies   See page 577.

CORRELATIONAL RESEARCH

21. Relationship Studies   See page 577.
22. Prediction Studies   See page 577.

CAUSAL–COMPARATIVE RESEARCH

23. See page 577.

EXPERIMENTAL RESEARCH

24. See page 578.

◻ **Task 9** *Performance Criteria*

The evaluation form will list a series of questions about an article to which you must indicate a yes or no response. For example, you might be asked if there is a statement of hypotheses. If the answer is yes, you must indicate where the asked-for component is located in the study. For example, you might indicate a statement of a hypothesis on page 32, paragraph 3, lines 2–6. In addition, if the study is experimental you will be asked to identify and diagram the experimental design that was applied.

On the following pages a research report is reprinted (see Task 9 example). Following the report, a form is provided for you to use in evaluating the report. In answering the questions, use the following code:

Y = Yes
N = No
NA = Question is not applicable (e.g., a pilot study was not done)
?/X = Cannot tell from information given, or, given your current level of expertise, you are not in a position to make a judgment

Effects of Using an Instructional Game on Motivation and Performance

JAMES. D. KLEIN
ERIC FREITAG
Arizona State University

ABSTRACT **Although many educators theorize that instructional games are effective for providing students with motivating practice, research on instructional gaming is inconclusive. The purpose of this study was to determine the effect on motivation and performance of using an instructional game. The effect of using a supplemental reading on motivation and performance was also examined. We randomly assigned 75 undergraduates to one of two treatments after they had attended a lecture on the information-processing model of learning. The subjects in one treatment group used an instructional board game to practice the material presented in the lecture, while those in the other group practiced using a traditional worksheet. Results indicated that using the instructional game significantly affected the four motivational components of attention, relevance, confidence, and satisfaction. The instructional game did not influence performance. The results also suggested that the subjects who reported completion of a supplemental reading had significantly better performance and confidence than did the subjects who reported that they had not completed the reading. Implications for the design of practice are discussed.**

Providing students with an opportunity to practice newly acquired skills and knowledge is an important component in designing an instructional strategy. Although many instructional design theories include recommendations for designing practice activities, Salisbury, Richards, and Klein (1986) have emphasized that most of the theories fail to address how to design practice that is motivational.

Some educators have theorized that instructional games are effective for providing motivating practice of newly acquired skills and information. They have argued that instructional games are motivational because they generate enthusiasm, excitement, and enjoyment, and because they require students to be actively involved in learning (Coleman, 1968; Ernest, 1986; Rakes & Kutzman, 1982; Wesson, Wilson, & Mandlebaum, 1988). Other scholars have theorized that instructional games decrease student motivation. Those authors have suggested that the motivational aspects of instructional games are limited to those who win, and that losing an instructional game produces a failure syndrome and reduces self-esteem (Allington & Strange, 1977; Andrews & Thorpe, 1977).

Whereas theorists have argued about the motivational aspects of instructional games, researchers have investigated the effect of using games on student motivation. Some researchers have reported that the use of instructional gaming increases student interests, satisfaction, and continuing motivation (DeVries & Edwards, 1973; Sleet, 1985; Straus, 1986). In addition, investigators have reported that instructional games influence school attendance. Allen and Main (1976) found that including instructional gaming in a mathematics curriculum helped to reduce the rate of absenteeism of students in inner-city schools. Studies by Raia (1966) and Boseman and Schellenberger (1974) indicated that including games in a college business course has a positive affect on course attendance but not on expressed interest and satisfaction. Others have reported that playing a game does not influence student satisfaction or attitude toward school (DeVries & Slavin, 1978).

In addition to the possible motivational benefits of games, many educators have theorized that games are effective for increasing student performance. They have argued that instructional games make practice more effective because students become active participants in the learning process (Ernest, 1986; Rakes & Kutzman, 1982; Wesson et al., 1988). Others have suggested that games foster incorrect responding and inefficiently use instructional time; also, the rate of practice in a game cannot compare with that of a flashcard drill or reading a connected text (Allington & Strange, 1977; Andrews & Thorpe, 1977).

Researchers have attempted to answer whether instructional games are an effective method for learning. Some

Address correspondence to James D. Klein, Learning and Instruction, College of Education, Arizona State University, Tempe, AZ 85287-0611.

Journal of Educational Research

investigators have reported that instructional games are effective for assisting students to acquire, practice, and transfer mathematical concepts and problem-solving abilities (Bright, 1980; Bright, Harvey, & Wheeler, 1979; DeVries & Slavin, 1978; Dienes, 1962; Rogers & Miller, 1984). Others have reported that using an instructional game to practice mathematics skills assists slow learners but not more able students (Friedlander, 1977). Research on the use of instructional games in college business courses has produced inconclusive or nonsignificant findings in many studies (Boseman & Schellenberger, 1974; Greenlaw & Wyman, 1973; Raia, 1966), whereas instructional games have positively influenced learning in actual business training settings (Jacobs & Baum, 1987; Pierfy, 1977). Even advocates of instructional gaming are unsure whether games teach intellectual content and skills (Boocock, 1968).

There are several explanations for the inconsistent findings from research concerning the effect of instructional games on motivation and learning. A few authors (Reiser & Gerlach, 1977; Remus, 1981; Stone, 1982) have suggested that much of the research on instructional gaming has been conducted using flawed experimental designs and methods. Another explanation is that many studies on instructional gaming have not investigated the integration of games in an instructional system. Gaming advocates have suggested that games should be used with other instructional methods such as lecture and textbooks (Clayton & Rosenbloom, 1968). A third explanation is that researchers examining the effect of instructional gaming on motivation have not adequately defined and operationalized the variable of motivation. After an extensive review of instructional gaming, Wolfe (1985) indicated, "No rigorous research has examined a game's motivational power, [or] what types of students are motivated by games" (p. 279).

Our purpose in this article is to describe the results of a study conducted to determine the effects on student motivation and performance of using an instructional game as practice. Because the study was designed to integrate the game into an instructional system, we also attempted to determine how using a supplemental reading affects student motivation and performance. Motivation was defined using the ARCS model of motivation (Keller, 1987a). The model suggests that motivation in an instructional setting consists of four conditions: attention, relevance, confidence, and satisfaction. According to Keller (1987a), all four conditions must be met for students to become and remain motivated. We hypothesized that students using an instructional game to practice newly acquired information would indicate that the method enhanced their attention, relevance, confidence, and satisfaction. We also believed that students who reported that they had completed a supplemental reading would perform better on a posttest than would those who reported that they did not complete the reading.

Method

Subjects

Our subjects were 75 undergraduate education majors enrolled in a required course in educational psychology at a large southwestern university. Although students in this class were required to participate in one research study during the semester, participation in this particular study was not mandatory.

Materials

Materials used in this study were an instructional game and a worksheet (both designed to provide practice of information and concepts presented in a lecture), the textbook *Essentials of Learning for Instruction* by Gagne & Driscoll (1988), the Instructional Materials Motivation Scale (Keller, 1987b), and a measure of performance.

The term *game* has various meanings, and several characteristics are important to understand the construct of game. In general, most games include a model or representation of reality, a set of rules that describe how to proceed, a specified outcome, and a group of players who act individually or collectively as a team (Atkinson, 1977; Coleman, 1968; Fletcher, 1971; Shubik, 1975, 1989). Games usually require active participation by players and can include elements of competition and cooperation (Orbach, 1979; Shubik, 1989). Games used for instructional purposes should be based on specific educational objectives and provide immediate feedback to participants (Atkinson, 1977; Jacobs & Baum, 1987; Orbach, 1979).

The instructional game used in this study included the elements listed above. We developed the game to provide students with practice on objectives from a unit on the information-processing model of learning. The instructional game consisted of a board that graphically represented the information-processing model, a direction card that explained the rules of the game, and a set of 25 game cards. Each game card had a practice question about the information-processing model of learning on the front and feedback with knowledge of correct results on the back. The rules were developed to encourage cooperation, competition, and active participation. The rules specified that team members should discuss each question among themselves before providing an answer. Teams were also told that they would be playing against another team.

We also developed the worksheet to provide subjects with practice on the information-processing model of learning. The worksheet was four pages in length and included the same 25 questions that appeared on the game cards. After subjects completed a set of five questions, the worksheet instructed subjects to turn to the last page for feedback.

May/June 1991 [Vol. 84(No. 5)]

We used the Instructional Materials Motivation Scale (IMMS) developed by Keller (1987b), to measure student perception of the motivational characteristics of the instructional materials. The IMMS includes four subscales to measure the degree to which subjects believe that a set of instructional materials address the motivational components of attention, relevance, confidence, and satisfaction. Keller reported that Cronbach's alpha reliability of the instrument is .89 for attention, .81 for relevance, .90 for confidence, .92 for satisfaction, and .96 for overall motivation.

A 15-item constructed response posttest was used to measure student performance. We developed the items on this posttest to determine subject mastery of the information-processing model. The Kuder-Richardson internal consistency reliability of this measure was .77.

Procedures

All of the subjects attended a 50-min lecture on the information-processing model of learning and were told afterward to read chapter 2 in the textbook, *Essentials of Learning for Instruction*, by Gagne & Driscoll (1988). Two days later, the subjects were randomly assigned to one of two treatment groups. The subjects in both groups were given 30 min to practice the information presented in the lecture and assigned reading by using either the instructional game or the worksheet.

One group of subjects used the instructional game to practice the information-processing model. Those subjects were randomly placed in groups of 8 to 10 and formed into two teams of players. Each group received the game materials described above, and the experimenter read the game rules aloud. Subjects in this group played the game for 30 min. The other group of subjects used the worksheet to practice the same items. The latter group worked individually for 30 min to complete the worksheet. The subjects were told to review incorrect items if time permitted.

Upon completion of the practice activity, all the subjects completed the Instructional Materials Motivation Scale and then took the posttest. The subjects also were asked if they had attended the lecture on the information-processing model and if they had completed the assigned

reading from the textbook. Completion of the activities took approximately 15 min.

Results

Motivation

We used a multivariate analysis of variance (MANOVA) to test for an overall difference between groups on the motivation scales. Stevens (1986) indicated that MANOVA should be used when several dependent variables are correlated and share a common conceptual meaning. An alpha level of .05 was set for the MANOVA tests. The analyses were followed by univariate analyses on each of the four IMMS subscales. To account for the possibility of inflated statistical error, we set the alpha at .0125 for the univariate analyses, using the Bonferroni method (Stevens, 1986). To determine the size of the treatment effect for each variable, we calculated effect-size estimates expressed as a function of the overall standard deviation (Cohen, 1969).

Results indicated that using the instructional game to practice information had a significant effect on motivation. A significant MANOVA effect, $F(4, 64) = 6.57$, $p < .001$, was found for the treatment on the motivation measures. Univariate analyses revealed that subjects who played the game rated this method of practice as motivational in the four areas of attention, $F(1, 67) = 21.91$, $p < .001$; relevance, $F(1, 67) = 15.05$, $p < .001$; confidence, $F(1, 67) = 16.80$, $p < .001$; and satisfaction, $F(1, 67) = 24.71$, $p < .001$. Effect-size estimates for each motivation variable were .61 for attention, .91 for relevance, 1.01 for confidence, and 1.23 for satisfaction. Cohen (1969) indicated that an effect size of .80 should be considered large for most statistical tests in psychological research. Table 1 includes a summary of means and standard deviations on each motivation subscale for the game and the nongame groups.

Results also suggested that subject self-report about completion of the reading assignment was significantly related to motivation. A significant MANOVA effect $F(4, 64) = 2.94$, $p < .05$, was found for this variable on the motivation measures. Follow-up univariate analyses revealed that the motivational area of considence was sig-

Table 1.—Means and Standard Deviations on Attention (A), Relevance (R), Confidence (C), Satisfaction (S), and Performance (P) Measures, by Treatment Group

Group	A	R	C	S	P
Game	4.22	3.71	4.06	3.88	10.49
($n = 37$)	(0.58)	(0.58)	(0.57)	(0.86)	(3.20)
Nongame	3.77	3.13	3.31	2.72	9.39
($n = 38$)	(0.89)	(0.69)	(0.90)	(1.02)	(3.60)

Note. Maximum scores = 5.00 for A, R, C, S and 15.00 for P.

Journal of Educational Research

nificantly related to completion of reading assignment, $F(1, 67) = 6.52$, $p < .0125$. Attention, relevance, and satisfaction were not significantly related to self-reported completion of reading assignment. In addition, a test of the interaction between self-reported completion of reading assignment and the treatment was not statistically significant, $F(4, 64) = 0.97$, $p > .05$.

Performance

We measured performance using a 15-item constructed response posttest. Analysis of variance (ANOVA) was used to test for differences between groups on the performance measure. An alpha level of .05 was set for all statistical tests.

Analysis of the posttest data revealed that self-reported completion of assigned reading was significantly related to performance, $F(2, 71) = 14.87$, $p < .001$. Subjects who indicated that they had read the assigned text ($n = 40$) performed significantly better on the posttest than those who indicated that they did not complete the reading ($n = 35$). The mean performance score of subjects who reported reading the text was 11.25 ($SD = 3.07$), whereas the mean performance score for those who reported that they did not read the text was 8.45 ($SD = 3.22$).

No statistically significant difference was found on the performance measure when the treatment groups were compared. The mean performance score for subjects using the game was 10.49 ($SD = 3.20$), and the mean performance score for those in the nongame group was 9.39 ($SD = 3.61$). In addition, a test of the interaction between the treatment and self-reported completion of reading assignment was not statistically significant, $F(2, 71) = 0.14$, $p > .05$.

Discussion

The major purpose of this study was to determine the effect of using an instructional game on student motivation and performance. The results of the study suggest that using an instructional game as a method of delivering practice did enhance the motivation of students in the four areas of attention, relevance, confidence, and satisfaction. However, the results show that using the instructional game to practice information did not contribute to enhanced performance when compared with a traditional method of practice. There are several possible explanations for the results found in this study.

In keeping with established ideas of the characteristics of a game, we used a game board that provided students with a visual representation of the information-processing model of learning and required players to be active participants. Keller (1987a) indicated that visual representations and active participation are two strategies that can increase student attention in an instructional setting.

Furthermore, use of the game may have contributed to the results found for attention, because of a novelty effect. Some researchers have reported that student motivation and interest fluctuate and decrease as the novelty effect of a game wears off (Dill, 1961; Greenlaw & Wyman, 1973), whereas others have reported that interest tends to persist over time in gaming settings (Dill & Doppelt, 1963). Although novelty may be a reason for increased attention in this study, instructional designers who are concerned with providing motivating practice to students should consider that explanation as positive. Motivation and attention can be increased when variability and novelty are used in the classroom (Brophy, 1987; Keller, 1983).

The results found in this study for the motivational factor of relevance are consistent with the theories proposed by gaming advocates. Both Abt (1968) and Rogers and Miller (1984) argued that students will not question the relevance of educational content when it is presented via an instructional game. In addition, instruction can be made relevant to students by designing materials that are responsive to their needs (Keller, 1983). Orbach (1979) indicated that games are excellent methods to motivate students with a high need for achievement, because a game can include an element of competition. Orbach (1979) also theorized that games can motivate students with a high need for affiliation when the game requires interaction among individuals and teams. The instructional game used in this study included a moderate level of competition and required students to interact cooperatively through the team approach.

The instructional game used in this study also provided circumstances for student-directed learning. As a motivational strategy, researchers have linked student-centered learning with increased confidence (Keller & Dodge, 1982). The finding that the game increased student confidence is consistent with theorists who have suggested that games can influence student efficacy (Abt, 1968) and with researchers who reported that students rate the task of gaming as less difficult than other instructional techniques (DeVries & Edwards, 1973).

The positive finding for satisfaction is also consistent with theory and research. Some scholars have indicated that instructional games contribute to motivation because they provide intrinsic reward and enjoyment (Coleman, 1968; Ernest, 1986; Rakes & Kutzman, 1982). Researchers have reported that instructional games lead to increases in student satisfaction (DeVries & Edwards, 1973; Strauss, 1986). The results of this study support theorists and researchers who have suggested that students enjoy the gaming approach in instruction.

Although our results did suggest that the instructional game had an effect on student motivation, the game used in this study did not have a significant impact on student performance. However, subjects who reported completing an assigned reading performed significantly better

May/June 1991 [Vol. 84(No. 5)]

and had more confidence about their performance than those who reported that they did not complete the reading. The results may have occurred because of the nature of the reading. Even though all the students were provided with necessary concepts and information in a lecture, the textbook, *Essentials of Learning for Instruction* (Gagne & Driscoll, 1988), provided readers with practice and feedback in addition to supplementing the lecture. The additional practice and feedback more than likely influenced both the performance and confidence of those who completed the assigned reading.

The findings of this study have some implications for the design of practice. Although many instructional design theorists have indicated that students should be provided with an opportunity to practice newly acquired skills and knowledge, most fail to address how to design practice that is motivational (Salisbury, Richards, & Klein, 1985). The results of this study suggest that instructional designers can provide students with a motivating practice alternative that is as effective as more traditional methods of practice by including a game into instruction. Although using the game to practice did not have an effect on immediate performance in this short-term study, motivating practice alternatives can possibly influence long-term performance because of increased student contact with materials that they find motivational. Future research should investigate the impact of gaming on long-term performance.

The current study also suggests that instructional designers should include reading assignments that provide additional practice in their instruction. The use of those types of readings will not only increase student performance, but also will lead to increases in student confidence about that performance.

As in our study, future research should integrate instructional games into a system to determine if the method has an impact on educational outcomes. Besides using a game as practice, research could be conducted to examine the effect of using a game to present other instructional events, such as stimulating recall of prior knowledge or as a review of learning. Researchers of instructional gaming should continue to investigate the effect of using a game on student motivation and should be specific in their operational definition of motivation. Implementation of our suggestions will assist us in determining how to design practice that is both effective and motivational.

REFERENCES

Abt, C. C. (1968). Games for learning. In S. S. Boocock & E. O. Schild (Eds.), *Simulation games in learning* (pp. 65–84). Beverly Hills, CA: Sage.

Allen, L. E., & Main, D. B. (1976). The effect of instructional gaming on absenteeism: The first step. *Journal for Research in Mathematics Education, 7*(2), 113–128.

Allington, R. L., & Strange, M. (1977). The problem with reading games. *The Reading Teacher, 31,* 272–274.

Andrews, M., & Thorpe, H. W. (1977). A critical analysis of instructional games. *Reading Improvement, 14,* 74–76.

Atkinson, F. D. (1977). Designing simulation/gaming activities: A systems approach. *Educational Technology, 17*(2), 38–43.

Boocock, S. S. (1968). From luxury item to learning tool: An overview of the theoretical literature on games. In S. S. Boocock and E. O. Schild (Eds.), *Simulation games in learning* (pp. 53–64). Beverly Hills, CA: Sage.

Boseman, F. G., & Schellenberger, R. E. (1974). Business gaming: An empirical appraisal. *Simulation & Games, 5,* 383–401.

Bright, G. W. (1980). Game moves as they relate to strategy and knowledge. *Journal of Experimental Education, 48,* 204–209.

Bright, G. W., Harvey, J. G., & Wheeler, M. M. (1979). Using games to retrain skills with basic multiplication facts. *Journal for Research in Mathematics Education, 10,* 103–110.

Brophy, J. (1987). Synthesis of research on strategies for motivating students to learn. *Educational Leadership, 45*(2), 40–48.

Clayton, M., & Rosenbloom, R. (1968). Goals and designs. In S. S. Boocock & E. O. Schild (Eds.), *Simulation games in learning* (pp. 85–92). Beverly Hills, CA: Sage.

Cohen, J. (1969). *Statistical power analysis for the behavioral sciences.* New York: Academic Press.

Coleman, J. S. (1968). Social processes and social simulation games. In S. S. Boocock & E. O. Schild (Eds.), *Simulation games in learning* (pp. 29–51). Beverly Hills, CA: Sage.

Dienes, Z. P. (1962). *An experimental study of mathematics learning.* New York: Hutchinson.

DeVries, D. L., & Edwards, K. L. (1973). Learning games and student teams: Their effects on classroom process. *American Educational Research Journal, 10,* 307–318.

DeVries, D. L., & Slavin, R. E. (1978). Teams-games-tournaments (TGT): Review of ten classroom experiments. *Journal of Research and Development in Education, 12,* 28–37.

Dill, W. R. (1961). The educational effects of management games. In W. R. Dill (Ed.), *Proceeding of the Conference on Business Games as Teaching Devices* (pp. 61–72). New Orleans, LA: Tulane University.

Dill, W. R., & Doppelt, N. (1963). The acquisition of experience in a complex management game. *Management Science, 10,* 30–46.

Ernest, P. (1986). Games: A rationale for their use in the teaching of mathematics in school. *Mathematics in School,* 2–5.

Fletcher, J. L. (1971). The effectiveness of simulation games as learning environments. *Simulation and Games, 2,* 259–286.

Friedlander, A. (1977). The Steeplechase. *Mathematics Teaching, 80,* 37–39.

Gagne, R. M., & Driscoll, M. P. (1988). *Essentialsl of learning for instruction* (2nd ed.). Englewood Cliffs, NJ: Prentice Hall.

Greenlaw, P. S., & Wyman, F. P. (1973). The teaching effectiveness of games in collegiate business courses. *Simulation & Games, 4,* 259–294.

Jacobs, R. L., & Baum, M. (1987). Simulation and games in training and development. *Simulation & Games, 18,* 385–394.

Keller, J. M. (1983). Motivational design of instruction. In C. M. Reigeluth (Ed.), *Instructional-design theories and models: An overview of their current status* (pp. 386–434). Hillsdale, NJ: Lawrence Erlbaum.

Keller, J. M. (1987a). Development and use of the ARCS model of instructional design. *Journal of Instructional Development, 10*(3), 2–10.

Keller, J. M. (1987b). *Instructional materials motivation scale (IMMS).* Unpublished manuscript. Florida State University, Tallahassee, FL.

Keller, J.M., & Dodge, B. (1982). *The ARCS model: Motivational strategies for instruction.* Unpublished manuscript. Syracuse University, Syracuse, NY.

Orbach, E. (1979). Simulation games and motivation for learning: A theoretical framework. *Simulation & Games, 10,* 3–40.

Pierfy, D. (1977). Comparative simulation game research: Stumbling blocks and stepping stones. *Simulation & Games, 8,* 255–269.

Raia, A. P. (1966). A study of the educational value of management games. *Journal of Business, 39,* 339–352.

Rakes, T. A., & Kutzman, S. K. (1982). The selection and use of reading games and activities. *Reading Horizons,* 67–70.

Reiser, R. A., & Gerlach, V. S. (1977). Research on simulation games in education: A critical analysis. *Educational Technology, 17*(12), 13–18.

Remus, W. E. (1981). Experimental designs for analyzing data on

Journal of Educational Research

games. *Simulation & Games, 12*, 3–14.

Rogers, P. J., & Miller, J. V. (1984). Playway mathematics: Theory, practice, and some results. *Educational Research, 26*, 200–207.

Salisbury, D. F., Richards, B. F., & Klein, J. D. (1986). Prescriptions for the design of practice activities for learning. *Journal of Instructional Development, 8*(4), 9–19.

Shubik, M. (1975). *The uses and methods of gaming.* New York: Elsevier.

Shubik, M. (1989). Gaming: Theory and practice, past and future. *Simulation & Games, 20*, 184–189.

Sleet, D. A. (1985). Application of a gaming strategy to improve nutrition education. *Simulation & Games, 16*, 63–70.

Stevens, J. (1986). *Applied multivariate statistics for the social sciences.* Hillsdale, NJ: Lawrence Erlbaum.

Stone, E. F. (1982). *Research design issues in studies assessing the effects of management education.* Paper presented at the National Academy of Management Conference, New York.

Straus, R. A. (1986). Simple games for teaching sociological perspectives. *Teaching Sociology, 14*, 119–128.

Wesson, C., Wilson, R., & Mandlebaum, L. H. (1988). Learning games for active student responding. *Teaching Exceptional Children*, 12–14.

Wolfe, J. (1985). The teaching effectiveness of games in collegiate business courses. *Simulation & Games, 16*, 251–288.

EFFECTS OF USING AN INSTRUCTIONAL GAME ON MOTIVATION AND PERFORMANCE

SELF-TEST FOR TASK 9

Y = Yes
N = No
NA = Not applicable
?/X = Can't tell/Don't know

General Evaluation

Introduction

CODE

Problem

Is there a statement of the problem? _____

Is the problem "researchable"? That is, can it be investigated through the collection and analysis of data? _____

Is background information on the problem presented? _____

Is the educational significance of the problem discussed? _____

Does the problem statement indicate the variables of interest and the specific relationship between those variables that was investigated? _____

When necessary, are variables directly or operationally defined? _____

Does the researcher have the knowledge and skill to carry out the proposed research? _____

Review of Related Literature

Is the review comprehensive? _____

Are all cited references relevant to the problem under investigation? _____

Are most of the sources primary (i.e., are there only a few or no secondary sources)? _____

Have the references been critically analyzed and the results of various studies compared and contrasted (i.e., is the review more than a series of abstracts or annotations)? _____

Is the relevancy of each reference explained? _____

Is the review well organized? Does it logically flow in such a way that the references least related to the problem are discussed first and the most-related references are discussed last? _____

Does the review conclude with a brief summary of the literature and its implications for the problem investigated? _____

Do the implications discussed form an empirical or theoretical rationale for the hypotheses that follow? _____

Are references cited completely and accurately? _____

CODE

Hypotheses

Are specific questions to be answered listed or specific hypotheses to be tested stated?   _____

Does each hypothesis state an expected relationship or difference?   _____

If necessary, are variables directly or operationally defined?   _____

Is each hypothesis testable?   _____

Method

Participants

Are the size and major characteristics of the population studied described?   _____

Are the accessible and target populations described?   _____

If a sample was selected, is the method of selecting the sample clearly described?   _____

Does the method of sample selection suggest any limitations or biases in the sample? For example, is stratified sampling used to obtain sample subgroups?   _____

Are the size and major characteristics of the sample described?   _____

Does the sample size meet the suggested guidelines for minimum sample size appropriate for the method of research represented?   _____

Instruments

Do instruments and their administration meet guidelines for protecting participants? Have needed permissions been obtained?   _____

Is a rationale given for the selection of the instruments (or measurements) used?   _____

Is each instrument described in terms of purpose, content, validity, and reliability?   _____

Are the instruments appropriate for measuring the intended variables?   _____

Does the researcher have the needed skills or experience to construct or administer an instrument?   _____

Is evidence presented that indicates that the instruments are appropriate for the intended sample? For example, is the reading level of an instrument suitable for sample participants?   _____

If appropriate, are subtest reliabilities given?   _____

If an instrument was developed specifically for the study, are the procedures involved in its development and validation described?   _____

If an instrument was developed specifically for the study, are administration, scoring or tabulating, and interpretation procedures fully described?   _____

Is the correct type of instrument used for data collection (e.g., using a norm-referenced instrument when a criterion-referenced one is more suitable)?   _____

CODE

Design and Procedure

Is the design appropriate for answering the questions or testing the hypotheses of the study?   _____

Are procedures described in sufficient detail to permit replication by another researcher?   _____

Do procedures logically relate to each other? Are instruments and procedures applied correctly?   _____

If a pilot study was conducted, are its execution and results described, as well as its effect on the subsequent study?   _____

Are control procedures described?

Did the researcher discuss or account for any potentially confounding variables that he or she was unable to control?   _____

Is the application of the qualitative method chosen described in detail?   _____

Is the context of the qualitative study described in detail?   _____

Results

Are appropriate descriptive statistics presented?   _____

Was the probability level, α, at which the results of the tests of significance were evaluated, specified in advance of data analysis?   _____

If parametric tests were used, is there evidence that the researcher avoided violating the required assumptions for parametric tests?   _____

Are the described tests of significance appropriate, given the hypotheses and design of the study?   _____

Was the inductive logic used to produce results in a qualitative study made explicit?   _____

Are the tests of significance interpreted using the appropriate degrees of freedom?   _____

Are the results clearly presented?   _____

Are the tables and figures (if any) well organized and easy to understand?   _____

Are the data in each table and figure described in the text?   _____

Discussion (Conclusions and Recommendations)

Is each result discussed in terms of the original hypothesis or topic to which it relates?   _____

Is each result discussed in terms of its agreement or disagreement with previous results obtained by other researchers in other studies?   _____

Are generalizations consistent with the results?   _____

Are the possible effects of uncontrolled variables on the results discussed?   _____

Are theoretical and practical implications of the findings discussed?   _____

CODE

Are recommendations for future action made?   _____

Are the suggestions for future action based on practical significance or on statistical significance only (i.e., has the author avoided confusing practical and statistical significance)?   _____

Abstract or Summary

Is the problem restated?   _____

Are the number and type of participants and instruments described?   _____

Is the design used identified?   _____

Are procedures described?   _____

Are the major results and conclusions restated?   _____

Type-Specific Evaluation Criteria

Identify and diagram the experimental design used in this study:

Was an appropriate experimental design selected?   _____

Is a rationale for design selection given?   _____

Are sources of invalidity associated with the design identified and discussed?   _____

Is the method of group formation described?   _____

Was the experimental group formed in the same way as the control group?   _____

Were groups randomly formed and the use of existing groups avoided?   _____

Were treatments randomly assigned to groups?   _____

Were critical extraneous variables identified?   _____

Were any control procedures applied to equate groups on extraneous variables?   _____

Were possible reactive arrangements (e.g., the Hawthorne effect) controlled for?   _____

PART TEN

Action Research in the Schools

Until quite recently, educational research was considered to be the main responsibility of university academics and large scale, research-oriented think tanks. The accepted view was that these organizations were most capable of producing rigorous, generalizable, and useful research. Although there was truth to this viewpoint, trends in the past 10 or so years have sparked interest in the advantages of "real world," practically oriented research done by practitioners and focused on their own needs, problems, and concerns. A number of factors have produced this broadened view of where and why research can be conducted.[1] Poor performance by students on national and international tests has been associated in part with weaknesses of teachers and the need for them to improve their practice. New state certification requirements mandated on-going teacher evaluation and demonstrations of personal proficiency. New models of teaching and learning relied heavily on teachers' need to make decisions about the appropriateness of their practice. Many years of research by many researchers provided little practical guidance to school practitioners. In short, an emphasis on teachers' needs to examine and improve their own classroom practice greatly accelerated the rise of teacher-based, in-school, practice-oriented action research activities. This "democratizing" of research is most clearly emerging in schools, where practitioners are conducting in-school studies singly and in groups to inform and enhance their own classroom practices and understanding. They are collecting data about their daily activities, problems, and outcomes for the purpose of improving themselves as teachers and enhancing the attainment of their students.

The goals of Part Ten are to introduce the reasons and strategies of school-based action research and to differentiate action research from other forms of research. After reading Part Ten, you should be able to perform the following task.

TASK 10

Develop a design for an action research study to answer a school-based research question.

---

[1]Kennedy, M. M. (1997). The connection between research and practice. *Educational Researcher, 26,* 7, pp. 4–12.

"In action research, it is the teacher who identifies the research topic . . ., the teacher who collects information to investigate the topic, and the teacher who interprets and judges the research results . . . . The teacher is at the center of action research (p. 593)."

Action Research in the Schools

OBJECTIVES

After reading chapter 17, you should be able to:

1. Describe the purposes of action research.
2. Identify common data collection strategies used to carry out action research in schools.
3. List the main criteria that define good school-based action research.

SCHOOL-BASED ACTION RESEARCH

School-based research carried out by school practitioners has many different names: teacher research, action research, practitioner inquiry, teacher professional development, teacher as researcher, and teacher self-evaluation. We will use the term *action research* to describe teacher-initiated, school-based research. Action research is a type of practitioner research that is used to improve the practitioner's practice; action implies doing or changing something. Practitioner research means that the research is done by practitioners about their own practice. Action research is a process in which individual or several teachers collect evidence and make decisions about their own knowledge, performance, beliefs, and effects in order to understand and improve them. Thus, the main reason for teachers engaging in action research is to learn and improve *their own* teaching activities. Providing opportunities for teachers to conduct action research can lead them to re-examine their practice and alter their taken-for-granted beliefs and understandings. In action research, it is the teacher who identifies the research topic related to his or her practice, the teacher who collects information to investi-

gate the topic, and the teacher who interprets and judges the research results in terms of their meaning for his or her practice. The teacher is at the center of action research.

Four beliefs underlie action research:

1. Teachers should have opportunity to engage in professional growth.
2. Teachers want to improve their practice and need data to do so.
3. Given the opportunity and resources (including time), teachers are able to carry out action research studies that will inform their practice.
4. A justification for action research is that no matter how conclusive research findings are regarding a particular practice or innovation, it may not be applicable to certain classrooms. Thus, it is important for teachers to examine findings in their own context.

Table 17.1 lists a number of reasons why action research is important for teachers to use.

Note that while we focus on the teacher as action researcher, mainly because it is teachers who are most involved in action

TABLE	17.1
Reasons Action Research Is Important for Teachers	

- It is a professional responsibility.
- It focuses professional development and improvement on the classroom or school level, where teachers have their greatest expertise and effect.
- It recognizes that organizational change is usually the result of individuals changing themselves and their personal practices, not of "top-down" mandates.
- It gives teachers a "voice" and control over their own practice.
- It grows from the immediacy and complexity of the classroom, as do teachers' motives and incentives.
- It treats the teacher as a professional and can help improve teacher morale and motivation.
- It encourages collegial interactions and discussions about teaching.

Source: Airasian, P., and Gullickson, A. *Teacher self-evaluation tool kit.* Corwin Press. Copyright 1997 Corwin Press. Reprinted by permission of Corwin Press, Inc.

research, it is important to note that other school personnel (e.g., principals, counselors, aides) also conduct in-school research. Similarly, although we focus on the teacher as action researcher, we recognize that in many cases, groups of teachers join together to conduct action research on issues of common interest. For example, a group of fifth-grade teachers might form a researcher group to examine and improve their hands-on science activities. Alternatively, a single teacher might carry out action research to determine how well homework assignments are helping students to learn. For the most part, the research results produced by action research are limited to a particular school or teacher's classroom.

COMPARISON OF ACTION RESEARCH WITH OTHER FORMS OF RESEARCH

We have seen throughout this text that there are different ways of conducting research studies. However, some processes and procedures are common to all kinds of research, and they define research as *research,* as opposed to *opinions* or ad hoc activities. Good action research shares many of the characteristics of other research approaches. For example, systematic inquiry is a feature of all research. Systematic means ordered and planned, the application of a logical approach to examining a topic or problem. Inquiry implies asking questions for which you do not know the answer. That is the purpose of research. Similarly, good research is informed—that is, it requires the collection and interpretation of data to produce results. Action research includes these characteristics.

Action research also has some characteristics that differentiate it from other forms of research. For example, the purpose of action research is to find problems and to correct them. In most other types of research, the "fix things up" aspect of action research is not present. Further, the "fix things up" aspect is carried out by the teacher researcher, while in other types of research, the researcher rarely becomes involved in undertaking remediation that derives from his or her work. In fact, "fixing things up" is not a part of most research processes, which rely upon not intervening in the object of research during the research activities. Finally, action research is value based. The action researcher's intention is to change a situation so that it is similar to his or her value preference. Most other research approaches try to remain value neutral in planning and carrying out the research.

One commonly misunderstood aspect of action research is the role of teacher reflection. Although reflection is an important aspect of action research, not all forms of reflection are equally useful. For example, reflection that is spurred spontaneously during classroom activities happens so fast that it tends to be momentary, fleeting, intuitive, and tacit. These characteristics of reflection greatly diminish its use in action research. The unexpressed, fleeting, and tacit nature of these spontaneous reflections make it very difficult to use them to guide studies for teacher improvement. A second form of teacher reflection is post hoc reflection, or reflection that takes place out of the immediacy of practice. It is these reflections that teachers have when they are alone in their classrooms or relaxing at home. These reflections permit more concentrated, aware reflections than those occurring while teaching is going on. However, teachers' after-the-fact reflections depend on accurate recall. In addition, after-the-fact reflections occur in a closed system in which the teacher is both the observer and observee. There is no external or alternative perspective in the reflection, opening it to bias, misinterpretation, and lapses in memory. Thus, regardless of whether reflections occur in or after classroom activities, there is nothing to validate or contradict the teachers' reflections and interpretations. This lack of external information is important because teachers' criteria, standards, and interpretations—like those of all of us—are influenced by preexisting biases and experiences. Thus, while reflection is an important aspect of action research, not all types of reflections are useful in the process.

The most useful reflections for action research are those based on formal, tangible evidence about one's practice. The use of formal evidence about practice allows teachers to obtain tangible information that can be used to independently corroborate or validate their own views of practice. For example, it is more useful for a teacher to gather formal information by polling students about the usefulness of homework assignments than to base a decision on a teacher perception obtained from comments of one or two students. Similarly, it is better to have a colleague observe and provide feedback about a teacher's cooperative learning lesson than to have the teacher alone try to capture, recall, and reflect on features of the lesson. The use of formal and tangible data is in keeping with the view of action research as systematic, inquiry based, and data driven. Although research done in a classroom by a teacher or group of teachers may not attain the methodological rigor and generalizability of results from forms of research approaches discussed previously, action research can provide valuable information to teachers about their practice and effects.

STEPS IN ACTION RESEARCH

The steps in action research are similar to those of other types of research. What is different is that the problem or topic studied is identified by a teacher, carried out in the teacher's classroom, and used to improve the teacher's practice. Note that the typical focus on research in a single classroom is similar to the typical qualitative focus on a single context. However, as will be discussed presently, the range of data collection approaches in action research extend beyond the observation and interviewing that predominates in qualitative research studies. There are four steps in action research.

PROBLEM OR TOPIC IDENTIFICATION

A question, topic, or problem derived from a review of a teacher's practice is the first step in action research. Common action research problems or topics arise from questions such as:

Can I make this better by . . .

Would it be better if I . . .

Will doing this improve students understanding of . . .

How do students feel about my . . .

Why does this approach not work with . . .

How can I improve . . .

The problems or topics chosen are ones that interest or concern the teacher and are derived from issues in his or her practice. Two notable aspects of problem or topic identification deserve mention. First, especially for novice teachers, the problem or topic selected should be narrowly stated, unless a group of teachers are working together on a long-term project. Problems or topics should be manageable and feasible in order to fit into teachers' busy schedules. Further, the more focused the problem or topic investigated, the easier it is to adopt or adapt it to one's practice. Examination of broader, more complex problems or topics results in more lengthy action research and more complex implementation of the research findings. For example, it is better to examine a topic such as "how many students participate in my classroom discussions?" than a topic such as "how successful is my general questioning procedure during class discussion?" The latter topic is broad and contains many specific aspects, while the former topic can be examined relatively quickly because it focuses on only one aspect of classroom discussions. Second, while classroom reflections carried out in and after classroom events and observations are not always useful for conducting action research, they are frequently very useful in identifying questions or topics to study using action research.

DATA GATHERING

Given a topic or problem, the next stage is to determine what type or types of data collection procedures are most appropriate for gathering information about the topic or problem. Although some informal or anecdotal data can be collected, it is strongly recommended that more formal, tangible evidence be the main form of data collected. Tangible data in the form of questionnaires, videotapes, or peer observations, rather than solely teacher reflection, help foster a more objective awareness of teacher practice and a basis for comparison with teachers' own pre-research expectations. Action research utilizes all the forms of inquiry that can be used to examine, critique, and understand a researcher's practice. Both quantitative and qualitative approaches are useful, depending on the topic or problem examined. In the qualitative tradition, action research emphases usually focus on posing and answering questions in a particular classroom or school. Generalization is not a major feature of action research. Although methods of action research are not always as rigorous and sophisticated as those of other research methods (although some are), action research is purposeful, systematic, data-based, and evaluative in its conduct. Typical data collection techniques used in action research are shown in Table 17.2.

Because action research is often focused on a single classroom in which students and teachers are continually interacting, data collection should have four important characteristics. First, when students are asked to complete checklists, rating scales, or questionnaires as part of the action research process, they should be allowed to respond anonymously to protect students and to improve the validity of the data gathered. Second, because the teacher is the interpreter of the data collected, it is a good idea for the teacher researcher to build a comparison

TABLE 17.2

Action Research Data Collection Approaches

1. *Teacher self-reflection tools* are designed to be completed by teachers to evaluate their performance in the areas identified on the self-reflection tool. These tools usually are in the form of a checklist, rating scale, or questionnaire.

2. *Media recording and analysis* use media like audio- or videotape to record a sample of teacher performance for subsequent analysis by the teacher, peers, or both. Microteaching is one example of media recording.

3. *Student feedback tools* are similar to the self-reflection tools except that pupils instead of the teacher complete the forms. Teacher-made questionnaires, Minute Surveys, and journals are examples of sources of student feedback.

4. *Teacher portfolios* are prepared by teachers to provide evidence about their beliefs, knowledge, skills, and effectiveness. The process of collecting and analyzing portfolio pieces provides another form of self-evaluation evidence.

5. *Student performance data* include all student products that can be used to help teachers assess their own instructional effectiveness. Test results (teacher-made or standardized), essays, classroom projects, and the like are examples of student performance data.

6. *External or peer observation* involves having a peer or colleague observe, assess, and provide suggestions about an aspect of the teacher's practice such as questioning behavior, lesson organization, or feedback to students.

7. *Journaling* requires the teacher to maintain and reflect on a record of classroom events or activities with the intent of recognizing recurring problems, themes, successes, and needs.

8. *Collegial dialogue, experience sharing, and joint problem solving* all encourage collaboration among teachers to discuss common problems, share procedures and strategies, and compare perceptions. Exposure to the ideas and practices of colleagues is a potent strategy for teacher reflection and change.

Source: Airasian, P., and Gullickson, A. *Teacher self-evaluation tool kit.* Corwin Press, pp. 16–17. Copyright 1997 Corwin Press. Reprinted by permission of Corwin Press, Inc.

into data collection. For example, if a teacher is planning to ask students to complete a checklist about the teacher's fairness in grading, *before administering the checklist* the teacher should write a prediction of what he or she thinks the students will respond in their replies. After the anonymous student responses are collected, the teacher can compare the student results to his or her pre-checklist projection. Large discrepancies between the teacher's prediction and student responses should be a red flag for the teacher to reexamine current practice.

Third, when data collection is carried out using techniques such as video or audio taping or peer observations, teachers should identify the specific aspects of performance that will be examined. A set of criteria that focuses observations and interpretations on a limited number of specific performances provides more relevant information than general, unstructured data collection. For example, if a teacher were videotaping a cooperative learning lesson, or if a peer were observing the teacher teach the lesson, focusing criteria such as "appropriateness of the topic for students," "desired activities explained clearly to students," "all teams visited at least once," and "lesson summarized at end of lesson" will provide more specific feedback to the teacher than unfocused, general feedback. Also, stating criteria helps teachers gather information about their specific concerns and makes it easier to carry out changes in practice. Fourth, no single data collection approach can provide appropriate data for all of a teacher's questions or topics. Different approaches inform different types of questions. For example, questionnaires are useful for providing information about respondents' attitudes and points of view, while observation or videotaping is useful for providing direct information about teachers' actual teaching activities. The data collection method should fit the type of information needed to examine the problem or topic. The concept of triangulation introduced in chapter 7 is useful in action research. Triangulation seeks regularities in data by comparing different participants, settings, and activities to identify recurring results. It examines multiple data sources.

DECISION MAKING

The data collected must be summarized and interpreted in order to help teachers make decisions about their practices. This activity is the same as, though often less complex than, qualitative and quantitative data interpretation procedures. Nonetheless, data must be interpreted and decisions made about how to use the data for teacher understanding or improvement. In most cases the data gathered will not be extensive, especially if the action research topic is narrowly defined, as suggested. Teachers will primarily count quantitative data and summarize qualitative data. Remember, in action research, the teacher is the data interpreter and decision maker.

RESULTING ACTION

As the name suggests, action research is action-oriented. The purpose of action research is to affect teachers' actions, activities, beliefs, and effects; action research is directed toward both understanding and improving practice. Thus, the last step in the action research process is relating the interpreted data and the decisions emanating from the data to plan what steps, if any, need to be taken to alter or improve practice. This is the ultimate aim of action research.

APPLICATIONS OF ACTION RESEARCH

Tables 17.3, 17.4, 17.5, and 17.6 provide examples of action research. Of course, these examples do not exhaust the wide range of approaches that are included under the umbrella of action research. However, they do demonstrate different data collection strategies and different lengths of action research. Each example indicates the data collection strategy or strategies that can be used to carry out the research, a description of the area of practice being researched, and questions and criteria to focus the problem or topic. These examples can also be used as templates to generate research in other areas of practice. Finally, the examples represent different lengths of study. Tables 17. 3 and 17.4 provide relatively quick feedback about particular aspects of the teacher's practice. Note, however, that Table 17.4 also could be used a number of times to provide an indication of teacher improvement. Tables 17.5 and 17.6 provide examples of longer action research studies that might be examined in an ongoing cyclical manner.

TABLE	17.3

Self-Evaluation Strategy: Student Feedback Tool

This student-completed questionnaire can be used to help a teacher assess the environment of the classroom as perceived by the students. If the teacher predicts how students will respond before administering the questionnaire, he or she can compare student perceptions to his or her own perceptions.

This strategy can be used to gather information on many aspects of student perceptions.

Distribute the questionnaire to students and ask them to respond (anonymously) to each question by circling 1 for *seldom*, 2 for *sometimes*, and 3 for *always*.

How We Work Together

Do I praise your good work?	1	2	3
Do I like you?	1	2	3
Do I call on you when you raise your hand?	1	2	3
Do I work with you as much as with other students?	1	2	3
Do I grade your work fairly?	1	2	3
Do I like your work?	1	2	3
Do I explain clearly what I want done?	1	2	3
Do I give you enough time to do your work?	1	2	3
Do I help you when you need help?	1	2	3

When soliciting student feedback, it is extremely important that the students be granted anonymity by not having to sign their names, having a student collect the feedback, and, if possible, having students summarize the results.

Make and record your own projections of what the results will be before asking for student feedback.

Source: Airasian, P., and Gullickson, A. *Teacher self-evaluation tool kit.* Corwin Press, p. 31. Copyright 1997 Corwin Press. Reprinted by permission of Corwin Press, Inc.

TABLE	**17.4**

Self-Evaluation Strategy: Media Recording or External Observation

This self-evaluation strategy focuses on important aspects of a cooperative learning lesson. It can be used by an individual teacher who could videotape and analyze his or her performance. It can be used by having a colleague or administrator sit in on the lesson and observe and record the teacher's performance in light of the selected important aspects listed below. If an observer is used, it would be helpful for that person to have some idea of the focus of the cooperative group lesson.

Observe the teacher's performance during the lesson in terms of the following criteria. Rate each criterion as *excellent, good,* or *needs improvement* by writing an X under the appropriate category. If possible, jot down suggestions or significant observations to point out to the teacher later.

Cooperative Learning Lesson

Activity	*Excellent*	*Good*	*Needs Improvement*
Appropriateness of topic for students			
Materials ready at start of lesson			
Groups preformed or formed efficiently			
Goals and purpose of lesson explained			
Procedures for cooperation explained			
Desired group activities explained			
Smooth transition into group activities			
Teams helped during lesson			
All teams visited at least once			
Lesson ended with summary or directions for continuation			
Other comments on strong and weak points of the lesson:			

Source: Airasian, P., and Gullickson, A. *Teacher self-evaluation tool kit.* Corwin Press, p. 27. Copyright 1997 Corwin Press. Reprinted by permission of Corwin Press, Inc.

VALIDITY ISSUES IN ACTION RESEARCH

Much of action research is teacher determined, teacher conducted, and teacher interpreted. Moreover, the central focus of the research is the teacher's practice. These realities raise important issues about validation. Validation of action research studies is important because it relates to the claims and practices that derive from the study. Validity should be a feature of action research.

Action research validation strategies include both qualitative and quantitative approaches. For example, validity is enhanced if students respond to questionnaires anonymously, if clear and understood criteria focus the data collection, if tangible data are collected, and if some comparison is built into data collection and analysis. All of these quantitatively oriented strategies can be used to examine the validity of action research.

TABLE	**17.5**

Self-Evaluation Strategy: Student Performance Data, Media Recording, External Observation, or Student Feedback Tool

This strategy is aimed at identifying the nature and quality of the feedback teachers provide to students. Feedback may come in different forms for different assignments and subject areas, so this strategy may be usefully employed in more than one subject area or context (e.g., homework, tests, class discussion).

Information to assess teacher feedback may be gathered by reviewing the comments on a set of student papers (reports, tests, drafts, etc.) after they have been graded or reviewed, tape- or video-recording a lesson, asking students for feedback, or having another teacher observe a lesson. In any case, some questions that should guide information gathering and analysis of feedback include the following:

1. How soon do I provide feedback on student papers and ideas?

2. How specific is the feedback? Do I use vague or general words or phrases in my feedback, such as "good," "poor vocabulary," or "Work on this"? Or do I use specific wording in my feedback that informs the student, such as "good combination of adjectives to convey meaning," "The vocabulary you use is stilted and reads like you've just picked obscure words from a thesaurus," or "Try to be sure to use singular verbs with singular subjects and plural verbs with plural subjects"?

3. Do I focus feedback on specific behaviors students can work on?

4. Do I show students how to perform correctly or give them examples of good performance?

5. Do I try to balance negative feedback with positive feedback?

6. Do I try to teach students to judge their own performances? Do I give them practice in doing this?

Once a teacher has a sense of his or her general practices in providing feedback, he or she can begin to consider whether these practices are consistent across various student groups (e.g., males–females, high ability–low ability).

Source: Airasian, P., and Gullickson, A. *Teacher self-evaluation tool kit.* Corwin Press, p. 30. Copyright 1997 Corwin Press. Reprinted by permission of Corwin Press, Inc.

Another form of validation is for action researchers to test their claims of improvements in their practice. Do the changes produce the desired outcomes? Testing such claims may be done in either a quantitative (measuring change) or a qualitative (colleague consensus) format. Action research is often confined to a single classroom or school, with no intent to generalize beyond the classroom or school, so qualitatively oriented validation approaches are useful. One approach is to determine whether other persons who know the classroom or school share the researcher's conclusions and strategies—a form of triangulation. Often action researchers form a validation group from teachers and administrators in their school to offer feedback and advice and to corroborate the research results and interpretations. Thus, validation of action research can involve a mix of self- and peer validation, along with more quantitative strategies such as those already described.

TABLE 17.6

Self-Evaluation Strategy: Teacher Self-Reflection Tool or External Observation

The purpose of this strategy is to provide a simple and quick format to review a lesson that you have taught. All teachers have impressions about the success of a particular class or lesson they have just taught. This part went well, this part was too long, I lost them at this point, and so on. Usually, these self-critiques are lost when we move on to the next class or lesson. It might be helpful to compile information on the strong and weak points of lessons to view over time for patterns and for comparison to student feedback from Minute Surveys or other strategies.

This form could also be completed by a peer who observed the lesson.

Lesson Review

1. What was the single best aspect of this lesson? Why?

2. What was the single most disappointing aspect of this lesson? Why?

3. What is one thing you can do next time to improve this lesson or lessons like it?

Over time, one might look at these lesson reviews to determine whether there are patterns of strengths and weaknesses; whether these patterns are consistent across classes, lessons, or subject areas; and whether improvements made in prior lessons were successful. There is also potential to increase teachers' repertoire of instructional strategies through the implementation of new practices to overcome past problems.

Source: Airasian, P., and Gullickson, A. *Teacher self-evaluation tool kit.* Corwin Press, p. 29. Copyright 1997 Corwin Press. Reprinted by permission of Corwin Press, Inc.

Common pitfalls in validation of action research include:

- Failing to separate descriptions from explanations
- Failing to understand the difference between data and evidence
- Failing to collect tangible data
- Failing to define commonly understood criteria for aspects of practice being investigated
- Presenting raw rather than summarized data
- Failing to differentiate between the action and the action research
- Failing to recognize that validation is part of action research

Summary/Chapter 17

School-Based Action Research

1. Action research is a type of practitioner research that is used to improve the practitioner's practice. The main reason teachers engage in action research is to understand and improve their own teaching activities. The teacher is at the center of action research.

2. Action research is also known as teacher research, practitioner inquiry, teacher professional development, teacher as researcher, and teacher self-evaluation.

3. A number of reasons support action research: it is a professional responsibility, it takes place in classrooms where teachers have their greatest expertise, it gives teachers a "voice" in their practice, it grows from the immediacy and complexity of the classroom, and it encourages collegial interactions.

4. Good action research is characterized by a systematic, problem based, data based, and valid approach. It shares these characteristics with other forms of research.

5. Action research differs from most other forms of research because it aims to find and correct problems of practice, it is designed, conducted, and interpreted by the teacher researcher, and it is value-based rather than value-neutral in approaching a study.

6. Reflection is an important aspect of action research, but the most useful reflections are those that grow out of tangible data collected to inform a study. Reflections in and after classroom activities have limited usefulness in action research, except for forming problems to investigate.

7. Four steps characterize action research: problem or topic identification, data gathering, decision making, and resulting action.

8. Action research problems or topics are ones of interest to teachers' and are derived from issues in their practice. Completing prompts such as "How can I improve . . . ," "How do students feel about my . . . ," and "Can I make this better if I . . . ." Narrowly stated problems or topics are more manageable and alterable than broad, encompassing problems or topics.

9. There is a broad range or quantitatively and qualitatively data collection approaches that are used in action research. Although informal, tacit data are sometimes used in action research, formal, tangible data help foster an objective perspective by the teacher researcher. Generalization beyond a particular classroom or school is not a major concern of most action researcher.

10. Three strategies to improve the validity of data collected are to: allow students to respond anonymously to questionnaires, build a comparison into data collection, and develop criteria to identify and narrow the specific aspects of practice that will be examined.

11. The results of action research are used to plan what steps, if any, need to be taken to alter and improve practice.

12. Validity is an important feature of action research and can encompass both quantitatively and qualitatively oriented approaches. Quantitative aspects of validity include using clear criteria to focus data collection, building a comparison into the study, and examining the effects of practices altered on the basis of the research. Qualitative aspects of validity include the formation of validation groups and the extent to which teachers and administrators in a school concur with the research results and changes in practice.

◻ **Task 10** *Performance Criteria*

You must develop a design for an action research study. You must select one of the prompts on page 596 and use it to state a problem or topic to study. Select and state some aspect of teaching practice such as oral questioning, students' attitudes about your grading, the explanations you give at the start of projects, and so on. After selecting an action research topic to study, state at least five specific criteria that will guide your data collection. See Table 17.4 for examples of criteria. Select at least one method to gather data about the criteria. Explain why you chose the method you did. Explain who will provide the data (e.g., students, peers, yourself). Describe how you will validate the study you have planned.

APPENDIX A

Reference Tables

Table A.1
Ten Thousand Random Numbers

	00–04	05–09	10–14	15–19	20–24	25–29	30–34	35–39	40–44	45–49
00	54463	22662	65905	70639	79365	67382	29085	69831	47058	08186
01	15389	85205	18850	39226	42249	90669	96325	23248	60933	26927
02	85941	40756	82414	02015	13858	78030	16269	65978	01385	15345
03	61149	69440	11268	88218	58925	03638	52862	62733	33451	77455
04	05219	81619	81619	10651	67079	92511	59888	72095	83463	75577
05	41417	98326	87719	92294	46614	50948	64886	20002	97365	30976
06	28357	94070	20652	35774	16249	75019	21145	15217	47286	76305
07	17783	00015	10806	83091	91530	36466	39981	62481	49177	75779
08	40950	84820	29881	85966	62800	70326	84740	62660	77379	90279
09	82995	64157	66164	41180	10089	41757	78258	96488	88629	37231
10	96754	17676	55659	44105	47361	34833	86679	23930	53249	27083
11	34357	88040	53364	71726	45690	66334	60332	22554	90600	71113
12	06318	37403	49927	57715	50423	67372	63116	48888	21505	80182
13	62111	52820	07243	79931	89292	84767	85693	73947	22278	11551
14	47534	09243	67879	00544	23410	12740	02540	54440	32949	13491
15	98614	75993	84460	62846	59844	14922	49730	73443	48167	34770
16	24856	03648	44898	09351	98795	18644	39765	71058	90368	44104
17	96887	12479	80621	66223	86085	78285	02432	53342	42846	94771
18	90801	21472	42815	77408	37390	76766	52615	32141	30268	18106
19	55165	77312	83666	36028	28420	70219	81369	41943	47366	41067
20	75884	12952	84318	95108	72305	64620	91318	89872	45375	85436
21	16777	37116	58550	42958	21460	43910	01175	87894	81378	10620
22	46230	43877	80207	88877	89380	32992	91380	03164	98656	59337
23	42902	66892	46134	01432	94710	23474	20523	60137	60609	13119
24	81007	00333	39693	28039	10154	95425	39220	19774	31782	49037
25	68089	01122	51111	72373	06902	74373	96199	97017	41273	21546
26	20411	67081	89950	16944	93054	87687	96693	87236	77054	33848
27	58212	13160	06468	15718	82627	76999	05999	58680	96739	63700
28	70577	42866	24969	61210	76046	67699	42054	12696	93758	03283
29	94522	74358	71659	62038	79643	79169	44741	05437	39038	13163
30	42626	86819	85651	88678	17401	03252	99547	32404	17918	62880
31	16051	33763	57194	16752	54450	19031	58580	47629	54132	60631
32	08244	27647	33851	44705	94211	46716	11738	55784	95374	72655
33	59497	04392	09419	89964	51211	04894	72882	17805	21896	83864
34	97155	13428	40293	09985	58434	01412	69124	82171	59058	82859
35	98409	66162	95763	47420	20792	61527	20441	39435	11859	41567
36	45476	84882	65109	96597	25930	66790	65706	61203	53634	22557
37	89300	69700	50741	30329	11658	23166	05400	66669	48708	03887
38	50051	95137	91631	66315	91428	12275	24816	68091	71710	33258
39	31753	85178	31310	89642	98364	02306	24617	09609	83942	22716
40	79152	53829	77250	20190	56535	18760	69942	77448	33278	48805
41	44560	38750	83635	56540	64900	42912	13953	79149	18710	68618
42	68328	83378	63369	71381	39564	05615	42451	64559	97501	65747
43	46939	38689	58625	08342	30459	85863	20781	09284	26333	91777
44	83544	86141	15707	96256	23068	13782	08467	89469	93842	55349
45	91621	00881	04900	54224	46177	55309	17852	27491	89415	23466
46	91896	67126	04151	03795	59077	11848	12630	98375	53068	60142
47	55751	62515	22108	80830	02263	29303	37204	96926	30506	09808
48	85156	87689	95493	88842	00664	55017	55539	17771	69448	87530
49	07521	56898	12236	60277	39102	62315	12239	07105	11844	01117

Reprinted by permission from *Statistical Methods* by George W. Snedecor and William G. Cochran, sixth edition © 1967 by Iowa State University Press, p. 543–46.

Table A.1
(continued)

	50–54	55–59	60–64	65–69	70–74	75–79	80–84	85–89	90–94	95–99
00	59391	58030	52098	82718	87024	82848	04190	96574	90464	29065
01	99567	76364	77204	04615	27062	96621	43918	01896	83991	51141
02	10363	97518	51400	25670	98342	61891	27101	37855	06235	33316
03	96859	19558	64432	16706	99612	59798	32803	67708	15297	28612
04	11258	24591	36863	55368	31721	94335	34936	02566	80972	08188
05	95068	88628	35911	14530	33020	80428	33936	31855	34334	64865
06	54463	47237	73800	91017	36239	71824	83671	39892	60518	37092
07	16874	62677	57412	13215	31389	62233	80827	73917	82802	84420
08	92494	63157	76593	91316	03505	72389	96363	52887	01087	66091
09	15669	56689	35682	40844	53256	81872	35213	09840	34471	74441
10	99116	75486	84989	23476	52967	67104	39495	39100	17217	74073
11	15696	10703	65178	90637	63110	17622	53988	71087	84148	11670
12	97720	15369	51269	69620	03388	13699	33423	67453	43269	56720
13	11666	13841	71681	98000	35979	39719	81899	07449	47985	46967
14	71628	73130	78783	75691	41632	09847	61547	18707	85489	69944
15	40501	51089	99943	91843	41995	88931	73631	69361	05375	15417
16	22518	55576	98215	82068	10798	86211	36584	67466	69373	40054
17	75112	30485	62173	02132	14878	92879	22281	16783	86352	00077
18	80327	02671	98191	84342	90813	49268	94551	15496	20168	09271
19	60251	45548	02146	05597	48228	81366	34598	72856	66762	17002
20	57430	82270	10421	00540	43648	75888	66049	21511	47676	33444
21	73528	39559	34434	88586	54086	71693	43132	14414	79949	85193
22	25991	65959	70769	64721	86413	33475	42740	06175	82758	66248
23	78388	16638	09134	59980	63806	48472	39318	35434	24057	74739
24	12477	09965	96657	57994	59439	76330	24596	77515	09577	91871
25	83266	32883	42451	15579	38155	29793	40914	65990	16255	17777
26	76970	80876	10237	39515	79152	74798	39357	09054	73579	92359
27	37074	65198	44785	68624	98336	84481	97610	78735	46703	98265
28	83712	06514	30101	78295	54656	85417	43189	60048	72781	72606
29	20287	56862	69727	94443	64936	08366	27227	05158	50326	59566
30	74261	32592	86538	27041	65172	85532	07571	80609	39285	65340
31	64081	49863	08478	96001	18888	14810	70545	89755	59064	07210
32	05617	75818	47750	67814	29575	10526	66192	44464	27058	40467
33	26793	74951	95466	74307	13330	42664	85515	20632	05497	33625
34	65988	72850	48737	54719	52056	01596	03845	35067	03134	70322
35	27366	42271	44300	73399	21105	03280	73457	43093	05192	48657
36	56760	10909	98147	34736	33863	95256	12731	66598	50771	83665
37	72880	43338	93643	58904	59543	23943	11231	83268	65938	81581
38	77888	38100	03062	58103	47961	83841	25878	23746	55903	44115
39	28440	07819	21580	51459	47971	29882	13990	29226	23608	15873
40	63525	94441	77033	12147	51054	49955	58312	76923	96071	05813
41	47606	93410	16359	89033	89696	47231	64498	31776	05383	39902
42	52669	45030	96279	14709	52372	87832	02735	50803	72744	88208
43	16738	60159	07425	62369	07515	82721	37875	71153	21315	00132
44	59348	11695	45751	15865	74739	05572	32688	20271	65128	14551
45	12900	71775	29845	60774	94924	21810	38636	33717	67598	82521
46	75086	23537	49939	33595	13484	97588	28617	17979	70749	35234
47	99495	51534	29181	09993	38190	42553	68922	52125	91077	40197
48	26075	31671	45386	36583	93459	48599	52022	41330	60651	91321
49	13636	93596	23377	51133	95126	61496	42474	45141	46660	42338

Table A.1
(continued)

	00–04	05–09	10–14	15–19	20–24	25–29	30–34	35–39	40–44	45–49
50	64249	63664	39652	40646	97306	31741	07294	84149	46797	82487
51	26538	44249	04050	48174	65570	44072	40192	51153	11397	58212
52	05845	00512	78630	55328	18116	69296	91705	86224	29503	57071
53	74897	68373	67359	51014	33510	83048	17056	72506	82949	54600
54	20872	54570	35017	88132	25730	22626	86723	91691	13191	77212
55	31432	96156	89177	75541	81355	24480	77243	76690	42507	84362
56	66890	61505	01240	00660	05873	13568	76082	79172	57913	93448
57	41894	57790	79970	33106	86904	48119	52503	24130	72824	21627
58	11303	87118	81471	52936	08555	28420	49416	44448	04269	27029
59	54374	57325	16947	45356	78371	10563	97191	53798	12693	27928
60	64852	34421	61046	90849	13966	39810	42699	21753	76192	10508
61	16309	20384	09491	91588	97720	89846	30376	76970	23063	35894
62	42587	37065	24526	72602	57589	98131	37292	05967	26002	51945
63	40177	98590	97161	41682	84533	67588	62036	49967	01990	72308
64	82309	76128	93965	26743	24141	04838	40254	26065	07938	76236
65	79788	68243	59732	04257	27084	14743	17520	94501	55811	76099
66	40538	79000	89559	25026	42274	23489	34502	75508	06059	86682
67	64016	73598	18609	73150	62463	33102	45205	87440	96767	67042
68	49767	12691	17903	93871	99721	79109	09425	26904	07419	76013
69	76974	55108	29795	08404	82684	00497	51126	79935	57450	55671
70	23854	08480	85983	96025	50117	64610	99425	62291	86943	21541
71	68973	70551	25098	78033	98573	79848	31778	29555	61446	23037
72	36444	93600	65350	14971	25325	00427	52073	64280	18847	24768
73	03003	87800	07391	11594	21196	00781	32550	57158	58887	73041
74	17540	26188	36647	78386	04558	61463	57842	90382	77019	24210
75	38916	55809	47982	41968	69760	79422	80154	91486	19180	15100
76	64288	19843	69122	42502	48508	28820	59933	72998	99942	10515
77	86809	51564	38040	39418	49915	19000	58050	16899	79952	57849
78	99800	99566	14742	05028	30033	94889	55381	23656	75787	59223
79	92345	31890	95712	08279	91794	94068	49337	88674	35355	12267
80	90363	65162	32245	82279	79256	80834	06088	99462	56705	06118
81	64437	32242	48431	04835	39070	59702	31508	60935	22390	52246
82	91714	53662	28373	34333	55791	74758	51144	18827	10704	76803
83	20902	17646	31391	31459	33315	03444	55743	74701	58851	27427
84	12217	86007	70371	52281	14510	76094	96579	54853	78339	20839
85	45177	02863	42307	53571	22532	74921	17735	42201	80540	54721
86	28325	90814	08804	52746	47913	54577	47525	77705	95330	21866
87	29019	28776	56116	54791	64604	08815	46049	71186	34650	14994
88	84979	81353	56219	67062	26146	82567	33122	14124	46240	92973
89	50371	26347	48513	63915	11158	25563	91915	18431	92978	11591
90	53422	06825	69711	67950	64716	18003	49581	45378	99878	61130
91	67453	35651	89316	41620	32048	70225	47597	33137	31443	51445
92	07294	85353	74819	23445	68237	07202	99515	62282	53809	26685
93	79544	00302	45338	16015	66613	88968	14595	63836	77716	79596
94	64144	85442	82060	46471	24162	39500	87351	36637	42833	71875
95	90919	11883	58318	00042	52402	28210	34075	33272	00840	73268
96	06670	57353	86275	92276	77591	46924	60839	55437	03183	13191
97	36634	93976	52062	83678	41256	60948	18685	48992	19462	96062
98	75101	72891	85745	67106	26010	62107	60885	37503	55461	71213
99	05112	71222	72654	51583	05228	62056	57390	42746	39272	96659

Table A.1
(continued)

	50–54	55–59	60–64	65–69	70–74	75–79	80–84	85–89	90–94	95–99
50	32847	31282	03345	89593	69214	70381	78285	20054	91018	16742
51	16916	00041	30236	55023	14253	76582	12092	86533	92426	37655
52	66176	34037	21005	27137	03193	48970	64625	22394	39622	79085
53	46299	13335	12180	16861	38043	59292	62675	63631	37020	78195
54	22847	47839	45385	23289	47526	54098	45683	55849	51575	64689
55	41851	54160	92320	69936	34803	92479	33399	71160	64777	83378
56	28444	59497	91586	95917	68553	28639	06455	34174	11130	91994
57	47520	62378	98855	83174	13088	16561	68559	26679	06238	51254
58	34978	63271	13142	82681	05271	08822	06490	44984	49307	61617
59	37404	80416	69035	92980	49486	74378	75610	74976	70056	15478
60	32400	65482	52099	53676	74648	94148	65095	69597	52771	71551
61	89262	86332	51718	70663	11623	29834	79820	73002	84886	03591
62	86866	09127	98021	03871	27789	58444	44832	36505	40672	30180
63	90814	14833	08759	74645	05046	94056	99094	65091	32663	73040
64	19192	82756	20553	58446	55376	88914	75096	26119	83898	43816
65	77585	52593	56612	95766	10019	29531	73064	20953	53523	58136
66	23757	16364	05096	03192	62386	45389	85332	18877	55710	96459
67	45989	96257	23850	26216	23309	21526	07425	50254	19455	29315
68	92970	94243	07316	41467	64837	52406	25225	51553	31220	14032
69	74346	59596	40088	98176	17896	86900	20249	77753	19099	48885
70	87646	41309	27636	45153	29988	94770	07255	70908	05340	99751
71	50099	71038	45146	06146	55211	99429	43169	66259	99786	59180
72	10127	46900	64984	75348	04115	33624	68774	60013	35515	62556
73	67995	81977	18984	64091	02785	27762	42529	97144	80407	64524
74	26304	80217	84934	82657	69291	35397	98714	35104	08187	48109
75	81994	41070	56642	64091	31229	02595	13513	45148	78722	30144
76	59337	34662	79631	89403	65212	09975	06118	86197	58208	16162
77	51228	10937	62396	81460	47331	91403	95007	06047	16846	64809
78	31089	37995	29577	07828	42272	54016	21950	86192	99046	84864
79	38207	97938	93459	75174	79460	55436	57206	87644	21296	43393
80	88666	31142	09474	89712	63153	62333	42212	06140	42594	43671
81	53365	56134	67582	92557	89520	33452	05134	70628	27612	33738
82	89807	74530	38004	90102	11693	90257	05500	79920	62700	43325
83	18682	81038	85662	90915	91631	22223	91588	80774	07716	12548
84	63571	32579	63942	25371	09234	94592	98475	76884	37635	33608
85	68927	56492	67799	95398	77642	54913	91583	08421	81450	76229
86	56401	63186	39389	88798	31356	89235	97036	32341	33292	73757
87	24333	95603	02359	72942	46287	95382	08452	62862	97869	71775
88	17025	84202	95199	62272	06366	16175	97577	99304	41587	03686
89	02804	08253	52133	20224	68034	50865	57868	22343	55111	03607
90	08298	03879	20995	19850	73090	13191	18963	82244	78479	99121
91	59883	01785	82403	96062	03785	03488	12970	64896	38336	30030
92	46982	06682	62864	91837	74021	89094	39952	64158	79614	78235
93	31121	47266	07661	02051	67599	24471	69843	83696	71402	76287
94	97867	56641	63416	17577	30161	87320	37752	73276	48969	41915
95	57364	86746	08415	14621	49430	22311	15836	72492	49372	44103
96	09559	26263	69511	28064	75999	44540	13337	10918	79846	54809
97	53873	55571	00608	42661	91332	63956	74087	59008	47493	99581
98	35531	19162	86406	05299	77511	24311	57257	22826	77555	05941
99	28229	88629	25695	94932	30721	16197	78742	34974	97528	45447

Table A.2
Values of the Correlation Coefficient for Different Levels of Significance

df	p			
	.10	.05	.01	.001
1	.98769	.99692	.99988	.99999
2	.90000	.95000	.99000	.99900
3	.8054	.8783	.95873	.99116
4	.7293	.8114	.91720	.97406
5	.6694	.7545	.8745	.95074
6	.6215	.7067	.8343	.92493
7	.5822	.6664	.7977	.8982
8	.5494	.6319	.7646	.8721
9	.5214	.6021	.7348	.8471
10	.4973	.5760	.7079	.8233
11	.4762	.5529	.6835	.8010
12	.4575	.5324	.6614	.7800
13	.4409	.5139	.6411	.7603
14	.4259	.4973	.6226	.7420
15	.4124	.4821	.6055	.7246
16	.4000	.4683	.5897	.7084
17	.3887	.4555	.5751	.6932
18	.3783	.4438	.5614	.6787
19	.3687	.4329	.5487	.6652
20	.3598	.4227	.5368	.6524
25	.3233	.3809	.4869	.5974
30	.2960	.3494	.4487	.5541
35	.2746	.3246	.4182	.5189
40	.2573	.3044	.3932	.4896
45	.2428	.2875	.3721	.4648
50	.2306	.2732	.3541	.4433
60	.2108	.2500	.3248	.4078
70	.1954	.2319	.3017	.3799
80	.1829	.2172	.2830	.3568
90	.1726	.2050	.2673	.3375
100	.1638	.1946	.2540	.3211

Table A.2 is taken from Table VII of Fisher and Yates: *Statistical Tables for Biological, Agricultural and Medical Research,* published by Longman Group Ltd., London (previously published by Oliver and Boyd, Edinburgh), and by permission of the authors and publishers.

Table A.3
Standard Normal Curve Areas

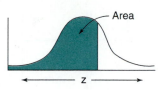

z	Area	z	Area	z	Area	z	Area
−3.00	.0013						
−2.99	.0014	−2.64	.0041	−2.29	.0110	−1.94	.0262
−2.98	.0014	−2.63	.0043	−2.28	.0113	−1.93	.0268
−2.97	.0015	−2.62	.0044	−2.27	.0116	−1.92	.0274
−2.96	.0015	−2.61	.0045	−2.26	.0119	−1.91	.0281
−2.95	.0016	−2.60	.0047	−2.25	.0122	−1.90	.0287
−2.94	.0016	−2.59	.0048	−2.24	.0125	−1.89	.0294
−2.93	.0017	−2.58	.0049	−2.23	.0129	−1.88	.0301
−2.92	.0018	−2.57	.0051	−2.22	.0132	−1.87	.0307
−2.91	.0018	−2.56	.0052	−2.21	.0136	−1.86	.0314
−2.90	.0019	−2.55	.0054	−2.20	.0139	−1.85	.0322
−2.89	.0019	−2.54	.0055	−2.19	.0143	−1.84	.0329
−2.88	.0020	−2.53	.0057	−2.18	.0146	−1.83	.0336
−2.87	.0021	−2.52	.0059	−2.17	.0150	−1.82	.0344
−2.86	.0021	−2.51	.0060	−2.16	.0154	−1.81	.0351
−2.85	.0022	−2.50	.0062	−2.15	.0158	−1.80	.0359
−2.84	.0023	−2.49	.0064	−2.14	.0162	−1.79	.0367
−2.83	.0023	−2.48	.0066	−2.13	.0166	−1.78	.0375
−2.82	.0024	−2.47	.0068	−2.12	.0170	−1.77	.0384
−2.81	.0025	−2.46	.0069	−2.11	.0174	−1.76	.0392
−2.80	.0026	−2.45	.0071	−2.10	.0179	−1.75	.0401
−2.79	.0026	−2.44	.0073	−2.09	.0183	−1.74	.0409
−2.78	.0027	−2.43	.0075	−2.08	.0188	−1.73	.0418
−2.77	.0028	−2.42	.0078	−2.07	.0192	−1.72	.0427
−2.76	.0029	−2.41	.0080	−2.06	.0197	−1.71	.0436
−2.75	.0030	−2.40	.0082	−2.05	.0202	−1.70	.0446
−2.74	.0031	−2.39	.0084	−2.04	.0207	−1.69	.0455
−2.73	.0032	−2.38	.0087	−2.03	.0212	−1.68	.0465
−2.72	.0033	−2.37	.0089	−2.02	.0217	−1.67	.0475
−2.71	.0034	−2.36	.0091	−2.01	.0222	−1.66	.0485
−2.70	.0035	−2.35	.0094	−2.00	.0228	−1.65	.0495
−2.69	.0036	−2.34	.0096	−1.99	.0233	−1.64	.0505
−2.68	.0037	−2.33	.0099	−1.98	.0239	−1.63	.0516
−2.67	.0038	−2.32	.0102	−1.97	.0244	−1.62	.0526
−2.66	.0039	−2.31	.0104	−1.96	.0250	−1.61	.0537
−2.65	.0040	−2.30	.0107	−1.95	.0256	−1.60	.0548

Table A.3
(continued)

z	Area	z	Area	z	Area	z	Area
−1.59	.0559	−1.19	.1170	−0.79	.2148	−0.39	.3483
−1.58	.0571	−1.18	.1190	−0.78	.2177	−0.38	.3520
−1.57	.0582	−1.17	.1210	−0.77	.2206	−0.37	.3557
−1.56	.0594	−1.16	.1230	−0.76	.2236	−0.36	.3594
−1.55	.0606	−1.15	.1251	−0.75	.2266	−0.35	.3632
−1.54	.0618	−1.14	.1271	−0.74	.2296	−0.34	.3669
−1.53	.0630	−1.13	.1292	−0.73	.2327	−0.33	.3707
−1.52	.0643	−1.12	.1314	−0.72	.2358	−0.32	.3745
−1.51	.0655	−1.11	.1335	−0.71	.2389	−0.31	.3783
−1.50	.0668	−1.10	.1357	−0.70	.2420	−0.30	.3821
−1.49	.0681	−1.09	.1379	−0.69	.2451	−0.29	.3859
−1.48	.0694	−1.08	.1401	−0.68	.2483	−0.28	.3897
−1.47	.0708	−1.07	.1423	−0.67	.2514	−0.27	.3936
−1.46	.0721	−1.06	.1446	−0.66	.2546	−0.26	.3974
−1.45	.0735	−1.05	.1469	−0.65	.2578	−0.25	.4013
−1.44	.0749	−1.04	.1492	−0.64	.2611	−0.24	.4052
−1.43	.0764	−1.03	.1515	−0.63	.2643	−0.23	.4090
−1.42	.0778	−1.02	.1539	−0.62	.2676	−0.22	.4129
−1.41	.0793	−1.01	.1562	−0.61	.2709	−0.21	.4168
−1.40	.0808	−1.00	.1587	−0.60	.2743	−0.20	.4207
−1.39	.0823	−0.99	.1611	−0.59	.2776	−0.19	.4247
−1.38	.0838	−0.98	.1635	−0.58	.2810	−0.18	.4286
−1.37	.0853	−0.97	.1660	−0.57	.2843	−0.17	.4325
−1.36	.0869	−0.96	.1685	−0.56	.2877	−0.16	.4364
−1.35	.0885	−0.95	.1711	−0.55	.2912	−0.15	.4404
−1.34	.0901	−0.94	.1736	−0.54	.2946	−0.14	.4443
−1.33	.0918	−0.93	.1762	−0.53	.2981	−0.13	.4483
−1.32	.0934	−0.92	.1788	−0.52	.3015	−0.12	.4522
−1.31	.0951	−0.91	.1814	−0.51	.3050	−0.11	.4562
−1.30	.0968	−0.90	.1841	−0.50	.3085	−0.10	.4602
−1.29	.0985	−0.89	.1867	−0.49	.3121	−0.09	.4641
−1.28	.1003	−0.88	.1894	−0.48	.3156	−0.08	.4681
−1.27	.1020	−0.87	.1922	−0.47	.3192	−0.07	.4721
−1.26	.1038	−0.86	.1949	−0.46	.3228	−0.06	.4761
−1.25	.1056	−0.85	.1977	−0.45	.3264	−0.05	.4801
−1.24	.1075	−0.84	.2005	−0.44	.3300	−0.04	.4840
−1.23	.1093	−0.83	.2033	−0.43	.3336	−0.03	.4880
−1.22	.1112	−0.82	.2061	−0.42	.3372	−0.02	.4920
−1.21	.1131	−0.81	.2090	−0.41	.3409	−0.01	.4960
−1.20	.1151	−0.80	.2119	−0.40	.3446	0.00	.5000

Table A.3
(continued)

z	Area	z	Area	z	Area	z	Area
0.01	.5040	0.41	.6591	0.81	.7910	1.21	.8869
0.02	.5080	0.42	.6628	0.82	.7939	1.22	.8888
0.03	.5120	0.43	.6664	0.83	.7967	1.23	.8907
0.04	.5160	0.44	.6700	0.84	.7995	1.24	.8925
0.05	.5199	0.45	.6736	0.85	.8023	1.25	.8944
0.06	.5239	0.46	.6772	0.86	.8051	1.26	.8962
0.07	.5279	0.47	.6808	0.87	.8078	1.27	.8980
0.08	.5319	0.48	.6844	0.88	.8106	1.28	.8997
0.09	.5359	0.49	.6879	0.89	.8133	1.29	.9015
0.10	.5398	0.50	.6915	0.90	.8159	1.30	.9032
0.11	.5438	0.51	.6950	0.91	.8186	1.31	.9049
0.12	.5478	0.52	.6985	0.92	.8212	1.32	.9066
0.13	.5517	0.53	.7019	0.93	.8238	1.33	.9082
0.14	.5557	0.54	.7054	0.94	.8264	1.34	.9099
0.15	.5596	0.55	.7088	0.95	.8289	1.35	.9115
0.16	.5636	0.56	.7123	0.96	.8315	1.36	.9131
0.17	.5675	0.57	.7157	0.97	.8340	1.37	.9147
0.18	.5714	0.58	.7190	0.98	.8365	1.38	.9162
0.19	.5753	0.59	.7224	0.99	.8389	1.39	.9177
0.20	.5793	0.60	.7257	1.00	.8413	1.40	.9192
0.21	.5832	0.61	.7291	1.01	.8438	1.41	.9207
0.22	.5871	0.62	.7324	1.02	.8461	1.42	.9222
0.23	.5910	0.63	.7357	1.03	.8485	1.43	.9236
0.24	.5948	0.64	.7389	1.04	.8508	1.44	.9251
0.25	.5987	0.65	.7422	1.05	.8531	1.45	.9265
0.26	.6026	0.66	.7454	1.06	.8554	1.46	.9279
0.27	.6064	0.67	.7486	1.07	.8577	1.47	.9292
0.28	.6103	0.68	.7517	1.08	.8599	1.48	.9306
0.29	.6141	0.69	.7549	1.09	.8621	1.49	.9319
0.30	.6179	0.70	.7580	1.10	.8643	1.50	.9332
0.31	.6217	0.71	.7611	1.11	.8665	1.51	.9345
0.32	.6255	0.72	.7642	1.12	.8686	1.52	.9357
0.33	.6293	0.73	.7673	1.13	.8708	1.53	.9370
0.34	.6331	0.74	.7704	1.14	.8729	1.54	.9382
0.35	.6368	0.75	.7734	1.15	.8749	1.55	.9394
0.36	.6406	0.76	.7764	1.16	.8770	1.56	.9406
0.37	.6443	0.77	.7794	1.17	.8790	1.57	.9418
0.38	.6480	0.78	.7823	1.18	.8810	1.58	.9429
0.39	.6517	0.79	.7852	1.19	.8830	1.59	.9441
0.40	.6554	0.80	.7881	1.20	.8849	1.60	.9452

Table A.3
(continued)

z	Area	z	Area	z	Area	z	Area
1.61	.9463	1.96	.9750	2.31	.9896	2.66	.9961
1.62	.9474	1.97	.9756	2.32	.9898	2.67	.9962
1.63	.9484	1.98	.9761	2.33	.9901	2.68	.9963
1.64	.9495	1.99	.9767	2.34	.9904	2.69	.9964
1.65	.9505	2.00	.9772	2.35	.9906	2.70	.9965
1.66	.9515	2.01	.9778	2.36	.9909	2.71	.9966
1.67	.9525	2.02	.9783	2.37	.9911	2.72	.9967
1.68	.9535	2.03	.9788	2.38	.9913	2.73	.9968
1.69	.9545	2.04	.9793	2.39	.9916	2.74	.9969
1.70	.9554	2.05	.9798	2.40	.9918	2.75	.9970
1.71	.9564	2.06	.9803	2.41	.9920	2.76	.9971
1.72	.9573	2.07	.9808	2.42	.9922	2.77	.9972
1.73	.9582	2.08	.9812	2.43	.9925	2.78	.9973
1.74	.9591	2.09	.9817	2.44	.9927	2.79	.9974
1.75	.9599	2.10	.9821	2.45	.9929	2.80	.9974
1.76	.9608	2.11	.9826	2.46	.9931	2.81	.9975
1.77	.9616	2.12	.9830	2.47	.9932	2.82	.9976
1.78	.9625	2.13	.9834	2.48	.9934	2.83	.9977
1.79	.9633	2.14	.9838	2.49	.9936	2.84	.9977
1.80	.9641	2.15	.9842	2.50	.9938	2.85	.9978
1.81	.9649	2.16	.9846	2.51	.9940	2.86	.9979
1.82	.9656	2.17	.9850	2.52	.9941	2.87	.9979
1.83	.9664	2.18	.9854	2.53	.9943	2.88	.9980
1.84	.9671	2.19	.9857	2.54	.9945	2.89	.9981
1.85	.9678	2.20	.9861	2.55	.9946	2.90	.9981
1.86	.9686	2.21	.9864	2.56	.9948	2.91	.9982
1.87	.9693	2.22	.9868	2.57	.9949	2.92	.9982
1.88	.9699	2.23	.9871	2.58	.9951	2.93	.9983
1.89	.9706	2.24	.9875	2.59	.9952	2.94	.9984
1.90	.9713	2.25	.9878	2.60	.9953	2.95	.9984
1.91	.9719	2.26	.9881	2.61	.9955	2.96	.9985
1.92	.9726	2.27	.9884	2.62	.9956	2.97	.9985
1.93	.9732	2.28	.9887	2.63	.9957	2.98	.9986
1.94	.9738	2.29	.9890	2.64	.9959	2.99	.9986
1.95	.9744	2.30	.9893	2.65	.9960	3.00	.9987

Table A.4
Distribution of t

df			p	
	.10	.05	.01	.001
1	6.314	12.706	63.657	636.619
2	2.920	4.303	9.925	31.598
3	2.353	3.182	5.841	12.924
4	2.132	2.776	4.604	8.610
5	2.015	2.571	4.032	6.869
6	1.943	2.447	3.707	5.959
7	1.895	2.365	3.499	5.408
8	1.860	2.306	3.355	5.041
9	1.833	2.262	3.250	4.781
10	1.812	2.228	3.169	4.587
11	1.796	2.201	3.106	4.437
12	1.782	2.179	3.055	4.318
13	1.771	2.160	3.012	4.221
14	1.761	2.145	2.977	4.140
15	1.753	2.131	2.947	4.073
16	1.746	2.120	2.921	4.015
17	1.740	2.110	2.898	3.965
18	1.734	2.101	2.878	3.922
19	1.729	2.093	2.861	3.883
20	1.725	2.086	2.845	3.850
21	1.721	2.080	2.831	3.819
22	1.717	2.074	2.819	3.792
23	1.714	2.069	2.807	3.767
24	1.711	2.064	2.797	3.745
25	1.708	2.060	2.787	3.725
26	1.706	2.056	2.779	3.707
27	1.703	2.052	2.771	3.690
28	1.701	2.048	2.763	3.674
29	1.699	2.045	2.756	3.659
30	1.697	2.042	2.750	3.646
40	1.684	2.021	2.704	3.551
60	1.671	2.000	2.660	3.460
120	1.658	1.980	2.617	3.373
∞	1.645	1.960	2.576	3.291

Table A.4 is taken from Table III of Fisher and Yates: *Statistical Tables for Biological, Agricultural and Medical Research,* published by Longman Group Ltd., London (previously published by Oliver and Boyd, Edinburgh), and by permission of the authors and publishers.

Table A.5
Distribution of F

p = .10

n_2**	n_1* 1	2	3	4	5	6
4	4.54	4.32	4.19	4.11	4.05	4.01
5	4.06	3.78	3.62	3.52	3.45	3.40
6	3.78	3.46	3.29	3.18	3.11	3.05
7	3.59	3.26	3.07	2.96	2.88	2.83
8	3.46	3.11	2.92	2.81	2.73	2.67
9	3.36	3.01	2.81	2.69	2.61	2.55
10	3.28	2.92	2.73	2.61	2.52	2.46
11	3.23	2.86	2.66	2.54	2.45	2.39
12	3.18	2.81	2.61	2.48	2.39	2.33
13	3.14	2.76	2.56	2.43	2.35	2.28
14	3.10	2.73	2.52	2.39	2.31	2.24
15	3.07	2.70	2.49	2.36	2.27	2.21
16	3.05	2.67	2.46	2.33	2.24	2.18
17	3.03	2.64	2.44	2.31	2.22	2.15
18	3.01	2.62	2.42	2.29	2.20	2.13
19	2.99	2.61	2.40	2.27	2.18	2.11
20	2.97	2.59	2.38	2.25	2.16	2.09
21	2.96	2.57	2.36	2.23	2.14	2.08
22	2.95	2.56	2.35	2.22	2.13	2.06
23	2.94	2.55	2.34	2.21	2.11	2.05
24	2.93	2.54	2.33	2.19	2.10	2.04
25	2.92	2.53	2.32	2.18	2.09	2.02
26	2.91	2.52	2.31	2.17	2.08	2.01
27	2.90	2.51	2.30	2.17	2.07	2.00
28	2.89	2.50	2.29	2.16	2.06	2.00
29	2.89	2.50	2.28	2.15	2.06	1.99
30	2.88	2.49	2.28	2.14	2.05	1.98
40	2.84	2.44	2.23	2.09	2.00	1.93
60	2.79	2.39	2.18	2.04	1.95	1.87
120	2.75	2.35	2.13	1.99	1.90	1.82
∞	2.71	2.30	2.08	1.94	1.85	1.77

*n_1 = degrees of freedom for the mean square between
**n_2 = degrees of freedom for the mean square within

Table A.5 is taken from Table V of Fisher and Yates: *Statistical Tables for Biological, Agricultural and Medical Research*, published by Longman Group Ltd., London (previously published by Oliver and Boyd, Edinburgh), and by permission of the authors and publishers.

Table A.5
(continued)

$p = .05$

n_2^{**}	n_1^*					
	1	2	3	4	5	6
4	7.71	6.94	6.59	6.39	6.26	6.16
5	6.61	5.79	5.41	5.19	5.05	4.95
6	5.99	5.14	4.76	4.53	4.39	4.28
7	5.59	4.74	4.35	4.12	3.97	3.87
8	5.32	4.46	4.07	3.84	3.69	3.58
9	5.12	4.26	3.86	3.63	3.48	3.37
10	4.96	4.10	3.71	3.48	3.33	3.22
11	4.84	3.98	3.59	3.36	3.20	3.09
12	4.75	3.88	3.49	3.26	3.11	3.00
13	4.67	3.80	3.41	3.18	3.02	2.92
14	4.60	3.74	3.34	3.11	2.96	2.85
15	4.54	3.68	3.29	3.06	2.90	2.79
16	4.49	3.63	3.24	3.01	2.85	2.74
17	4.45	3.59	3.20	2.96	2.81	2.70
18	4.41	3.55	3.16	2.93	2.77	2.66
19	4.38	3.52	3.13	2.90	2.74	2.63
20	4.35	3.49	3.10	2.87	2.71	2.60
21	4.32	3.47	3.07	2.84	2.68	2.57
22	4.30	3.44	3.05	2.82	2.66	2.55
23	4.28	3.42	3.03	2.80	2.64	2.53
24	4.26	3.40	3.01	2.78	2.62	2.51
25	4.24	3.38	2.99	2.76	2.60	2.49
26	4.22	3.37	2.98	2.74	2.59	2.47
27	4.21	3.35	2.96	2.73	2.57	2.46
28	4.20	3.34	2.95	2.71	2.56	2.44
29	4.18	3.33	2.93	2.70	2.54	2.43
30	4.17	3.32	2.92	2.69	2.53	2.42
40	4.08	3.23	2.84	2.61	2.45	2.34
60	4.00	3.15	2.76	2.52	2.37	2.25
120	3.92	3.07	2.68	2.45	2.29	2.17
∞	3.84	2.99	2.60	2.37	2.21	2.10

$^*n_1$ = degrees of freedom for the mean square between
$^{**}n_2$ = degrees of freedom for the mean square within

Table A.5
(continued)

p = .01

n_2**	n_1*					
	1	2	3	4	5	6
4	21.20	18.00	16.69	15.98	15.52	15.21
5	16.26	13.27	12.06	11.39	10.97	10.67
6	13.74	10.92	9.78	9.15	8.75	8.47
7	12.25	9.55	8.45	7.85	7.46	7.19
8	11.26	8.65	7.59	7.01	6.63	6.37
9	10.56	8.02	6.99	6.42	6.06	5.80
10	10.04	7.56	6.55	5.99	5.64	5.39
11	9.65	7.20	6.22	5.67	5.32	5.07
12	9.33	6.93	5.95	5.41	5.06	4.82
13	9.07	6.70	5.74	5.20	4.86	4.62
14	8.86	6.51	5.56	5.03	4.69	4.46
15	8.68	6.36	5.42	4.89	4.56	4.32
16	8.53	6.23	5.29	4.77	4.44	4.20
17	8.40	6.11	5.18	4.67	4.34	4.10
18	8.28	6.01	5.09	4.58	4.25	4.01
19	8.18	5.93	5.01	4.50	4.17	3.94
20	8.10	5.85	4.94	4.43	4.10	3.87
21	8.02	5.78	4.87	4.37	4.04	3.81
22	7.94	5.72	4.82	4.31	3.99	3.76
23	7.88	5.66	4.76	4.26	3.94	3.71
24	7.82	5.61	4.72	4.22	3.90	3.67
25	7.77	5.57	4.68	4.18	3.86	3.63
26	7.72	5.53	4.64	4.14	3.82	3.59
27	7.68	5.49	4.60	4.11	3.78	3.56
28	7.64	5.45	4.57	4.07	3.75	3.53
29	7.60	5.42	4.54	4.04	3.73	3.50
30	7.56	5.39	4.51	4.02	3.70	3.47
40	7.31	5.18	4.31	3.83	3.51	3.29
60	7.08	4.98	4.13	3.65	3.34	3.12
120	6.85	4.79	3.95	3.48	3.17	2.96
∞	6.64	4.60	3.78	3.32	3.02	2.80

*n_1 = degrees of freedom for the mean square between
**n_2 = degrees of freedom for the mean square within

Table A.5
(continued)

$p = .001$

			n_1*			
n_2**	1	2	3	4	5	6
4	74.14	61.25	56.18	53.44	51.71	50.53
5	47.18	37.12	33.20	31.09	29.75	28.84
6	35.51	27.00	23.70	21.92	20.81	20.03
7	29.25	21.69	18.77	17.19	16.21	15.52
8	25.42	18.49	15.83	14.39	13.49	12.86
9	22.86	16.39	13.90	12.56	11.71	11.13
10	21.04	14.91	12.55	11.28	10.48	9.92
11	19.69	13.81	11.56	10.35	9.58	9.05
12	18.64	12.97	10.80	9.63	8.89	8.38
13	17.81	12.31	10.21	9.07	8.35	7.86
14	17.14	11.78	9.73	8.62	7.92	7.43
15	16.59	11.34	9.34	8.25	7.57	7.09
16	16.12	10.97	9.00	7.94	7.27	6.81
17	15.72	10.66	8.73	7.68	7.02	6.56
18	15.38	10.39	8.49	7.46	6.81	6.35
19	15.08	10.16	8.28	7.26	6.62	6.18
20	14.82	9.95	8.10	7.10	6.46	6.02
21	14.59	9.77	7.94	6.95	6.32	5.88
22	14.38	9.61	7.80	6.81	6.19	5.76
23	14.19	9.47	7.67	6.69	6.08	5.65
24	14.03	9.34	7.55	6.59	5.98	5.55
25	13.88	9.22	7.45	6.49	5.88	5.46
26	13.74	9.12	7.36	6.41	5.80	5.38
27	13.61	9.02	7.27	6.33	5.73	5.31
28	13.50	8.93	7.19	6.25	5.66	5.24
29	13.39	8.85	7.12	6.19	5.59	5.18
30	13.29	8.77	7.05	6.12	5.53	5.12
40	12.61	8.25	6.60	5.70	5.13	4.73
60	11.97	7.76	6.17	5.31	4.76	4.37
120	11.38	7.32	5.79	4.95	4.42	4.04
∞	10.83	6.91	5.42	4.62	4.10	3.74

*n_1 = degrees of freedom for the mean square between
**n_2 = degrees of freedom for the mean square within

Table A.6
Distribution of χ^2

df	.10	.05	.01	.001
1	2.706	3.841	6.635	10.827
2	4.605	5.991	9.210	13.815
3	6.251	7.815	11.345	16.266
4	7.779	9.488	13.277	18.467
5	9.236	11.070	15.086	20.515
6	10.645	12.592	16.812	22.457
7	12.017	14.067	18.475	24.322
8	13.362	15.507	20.090	26.125
9	14.684	16.919	21.666	27.877
10	15.987	18.307	23.209	29.588
11	17.275	19.675	24.725	31.264
12	18.549	21.026	26.217	32.909
13	19.812	22.362	27.688	34.528
14	21.064	23.685	29.141	36.123
15	22.307	24.996	30.578	37.697
16	23.542	26.296	32.000	39.252
17	24.769	27.587	33.409	40.790
18	25.989	28.869	34.805	42.312
19	27.204	30.144	36.191	43.820
20	28.412	31.410	37.566	45.315
21	29.615	32.671	38.932	46.797
22	30.813	33.924	40.289	48.268
23	32.007	35.172	41.638	49.728
24	33.196	36.415	42.980	51.179
25	34.382	37.652	44.314	52.620
26	35.563	38.885	45.642	54.052
27	36.741	40.113	46.963	55.476
28	37.916	41.337	48.278	56.893
29	39.087	42.557	49.588	58.302
30	40.256	43.773	50.892	59.703
32	42.585	46.194	53.486	62.487
34	44.903	48.602	56.061	65.247
36	47.212	50.999	58.619	67.985
38	49.513	53.384	61.162	70.703
40	51.805	55.759	63.691	73.402
42	54.090	58.124	66.206	76.084
44	56.369	60.481	68.710	78.750
46	58.641	62.830	71.201	81.400
48	60.907	65.171	73.683	84.037
50	63.167	67.505	76.154	86.661

Table A.6 is taken from Table IV of Fisher and Yates: *Statistical Tables for Biological, Agricultural and Medical Research,* published by Longman Group Ltd., London (previously published by Oliver and Boyd, Edinburgh), and by permission of the authors and publishers.

Glossary of Research-Related Terms

A-B design A single-subject design in which baseline measurements are repeatedly made until stability is presumably established, treatment is introduced, and an appropriate number of measurements are made during treatment.

A-B-A design A single-subject design in which baseline measurements are repeatedly made until stability is presumably established, treatment is introduced, and an appropriate number of measurements are made, and the treatment phase is followed by a second baseline phase.

A-B-A-B design A single-subject design in which baseline measurements are repeatedly made until stability is presumably established, treatment is introduced, and an appropriate number of measurements are made, and the treatment phase is followed by a second baseline phase, which is followed by a second treatment phase.

abstract A summary of a study, which appears at the beginning of the report and describes the most important aspects of the study, including major results and conclusions.

accessible population Refers to the population from which the researcher can realistically select participants.

accidental sampling *See* convenience sampling.

achievement test An instrument that measures the current status of individuals with respect to proficiency in given areas of knowledge or skill.

action research An approach in which teachers study their own problems or concerns in their own classrooms.

additive designs Refers to variations of the A-B design which involve the addition of another phase or phases in which the experimental treatment is supplemented with another treatment.

alternating treatments design A variation of a multiple-baseline design which involves the relatively rapid alternation of treatments for a single participant.

analysis of covariance A statistical method of equating groups on one or more variables and for increasing the power of a statistical test; adjusts scores on a dependent variable for initial differences on some variable such as pretest performance or IQ.

analytic induction A method of identifying regularities in qualitative data, determining their explanation, and finding other contexts to determine whether the explanations hold up.

applied research Research conducted for the purpose of applying, or testing, theory and evaluating its usefulness in solving problems.

aptitude test A measure of potential used to predict how well someone is likely to perform in a future situation.

artificial categories Categories which are operationally defined by the researcher.

assumption Any important "fact" presumed to be true but not actually verified; assumptions should be described in the procedures section of a research plan or report.

attenuation Refers to the principle that correlation coefficients tend to be lowered because less-than-perfectly reliable measures are used.

basic research Research conducted for the purpose of theory development or refinement.

case study The in-depth investigation of one "unit," e.g., individual, group, institution, organization, program, or document.

category The classification of ideas and concepts in qualitative data analysis.

causal–comparative research Research that attempts to determine the cause, or reason, for existing differences in the behavior or status of groups of individuals; also referred to as ex post facto research.

census survey Descriptive research that attempts to acquire data from each and every member of a population.

changing criterion design A variation of the A-B-A design in which the baseline phase is followed by successive treatment phases, each of which has a more stringent criterion for acceptable behavior level.

chi square A nonparametric test of significance appropriate when the data are in the form of frequency counts; it compares proportions actually observed in a study with proportions expected to see if they are significantly different.

clinical replication Refers to the development and application of a treatment package, composed of two or more interventions which have been found to be effective individually, designed for persons with complex behavior disorders.

cluster sampling Sampling in which intact groups, not individuals, are randomly selected.

coefficient alpha (α) *See* Cronbach's alpha.

common variance The variation in one variable that is attributable to its tendency to vary with another variable.

concurrent validity The degree to which the scores on a test are related to the scores on another, already established test administered at the same time, or to some other valid criterion available at the same time.

constant comparison A qualitative method for identifying similarities and differences by comparing new evidence to prior evidence.

construct validity The degree to which a test measures an intended hypothetical construct, or nonobservable trait, which explains behavior.

contamination The situation that exists when the researcher's familiarity with the participants affects the outcome of the study.

content analysis The systematic, quantitative description of the composition of the object of the study.

content validity The degree to which a test measures an intended content area; it is determined by expert judgment and requires both item validity and sampling validity.

control Efforts on the part of the researcher to remove the influence of any variable other than the independent variable that might affect performance on a dependent variable.

control group The group in a research study that either receives a different treatment than the experimental group or is treated as usual.

control variable A nonmanipulated variable, usually a physical or mental characteristic of the participants (such as IQ).

convenience sampling The process of using as the sample whoever happens to be available, e.g., volunteers. (Also referred to as accidental sampling and haphazard sampling.)

correlational research Research that involves collecting data in order to determine whether, and to what degree, a relationship exists between two or more quantifiable variables.

correlation coefficient A decimal number between .00 and ±1.00 that indicates the degree to which two variables are related.

counterbalanced design A quasi-experimental design in which all groups receive all treatments, each group receives the treatments in a different order, the number of groups equals the number of treatments, and all groups are posttested after each treatment.

credibility A term used in qualitative research to indicate that the topic was accurately identified and described.

criterion In a prediction study, the variable that is predicted.

criterion-related validity Validity which is determined by relating performance on a test to performance on another criterion; includes concurrent and predictive validity.

Cronbach's alpha (α) The general formula for estimating internal consistency based on a determination of how all items on a test relate to all other items and to the total test.

(Also referred to as coefficient alpha and Cronbach's coefficient alpha.)

cross-validation Validation of a prediction equation with at least one group other than the group on which it was based; variables that are no longer found to be related to the criterion measure are removed from the equation.

curvilinear relationship A relationship in which increase in one variable is associated with a corresponding increase in another variable to a point, at which point further increase in the first variable is associated with a corresponding decrease in the other variable (or vice versa).

data saturation A point in qualitative research when so much data are collected that it is very unlikely that additional data will add to what is already collected.

deductive hypothesis A hypothesis derived from theory which provides evidence which supports, expands, or contradicts the theory.

dependent variable The change or difference in behavior that occurs as a result of the independent variable; also referred to as the criterion variable, the effect, the outcome, or the posttest.

descriptive statistics Data analysis techniques enabling the researcher to meaningfully describe many scores with a small number of numerical indices.

developmental studies Studies concerned with behavior variables that differentiate children at different levels of age, growth, or maturation.

diagnostic test A type of achievement test yielding multiple scores for each area of achievement measured that facilitate identification of specific areas of deficiency.

differential selection of participants Refers to the fact that groups may be different before a study even begins, and this initial difference may at least partially account for posttest differences.

direct replication Refers to the replication of a study by the same investigator, with the same participants or with different participants, in a specific setting.

ecological validity The degree to which results can be generalized to environments outside of the experimental setting.

educational research The formal, systematic application of the scientific and disciplined inquiry approach to the study of educational problems.

environmental variable A variable in the setting in which a study is conducted that might cause unwanted differences between groups (e.g., learning materials).

equivalent forms Two tests identical in every way except for the actual items included.

equivalent-forms reliability Indicates score variation that occurs from form to form of a test; also referred to as alternate-forms reliability.

ethnographic research A qualitative approach that studies the cultural patterns and perspectives of participants in their natural setting.

ethnomethodology A qualitative approach that studies how participants make sense of their everyday activities to act in a social way.

evaluation The systematic process of collecting and analyzing data in order to make decisions.

experimental group The group in a research study that typically receives a new, or novel, treatment, a treatment under investigation.

experimental research Research in which at least one independent variable is manipulated, other relevant variables are controlled, and the effect on one or more dependent variables is observed.

experimenter bias A situation in which the researcher's expectations concerning the outcomes of the study actually contribute to producing various outcomes.

ex post facto research *See* causal-comparative research.

external criticism The analysis of data to determine their authenticity.

external validity The degree to which results are generalizable, or applicable, to groups and environments outside of the experimental setting.

factorial analysis of variance The appropriate statistical analysis if a study is based on a factorial design and investigates two (or more independent variables and the interactions between them; yields a separate F ratio for each independent variable and one for each interaction.

factorial design An experimental design that involves two or more dependent variables (at least one of which is manipulated) in order to study the effects of the variables individually and in interaction with each other.

fieldwork A qualitative research strategy that involves spending considerable time in the setting under study, immersing oneself in this setting, and collecting as much relevant information as possible as unobtrusively as possible.

follow-up study A study conducted to determine the status of a group of interest after some period of time.

generosity error The tendency to give an individual the benefit of the doubt whenever there is insufficient knowledge to make an objective judgment.

grounded theory Theory based on data collected in real-world settings which reflect what naturally occurred over an extended period of time.

halo effect The phenomenon whereby initial impressions concerning an individual (positive or negative) affect subsequent measurements.

haphazard sampling *See* convenience sampling.

hardcopy Refers to computer output that is printed out on paper.

hardware Refers to the actual equipment, the computer itself and related accessories such as printers.

Hawthorne effect A type of reactive arrangement resulting from the participants' knowledge that they are involved in an experiment, or their feeling that they are in some way receiving "special" attention.

historical research The systematic collection and evaluation of data related to past occurrences in order to describe causes, effects, or trends of those events which may help to explain present events and anticipate future events.

history Any event which is not part of the experimental treatment but which may affect performance on the dependent variable.

hypothesis A tentative, reasonable, testable explanation for the occurrence of certain behaviors, phenomena, or events.

independent variable An activity or characteristic believed to make a difference with respect to some behavior; also referred to as the experimental variable, the cause, and the treatment.

inductive hypothesis A generalization based on observation.

inferential statistics Data analysis techniques for determining how likely it is that results based on a sample or samples are the same results that would have been obtained for an entire population.

instrumentation Unreliability in measuring instruments that may result in invalid assessment of participants' performance.

interaction Refers to the situation in which different values of the independent variable are differentially effective depending upon the level of the control variable.

interjudge reliability The consistency of two (or more) independent scorers, raters, or observers.

internal criticism The analysis of data to determine their accuracy which takes into consideration the knowledge and competence of the author, the time delay between the occurrence and recording of events, biased motives of the author, and consistency of the data.

internal validity The degree to which observed differences on the dependent variable are a direct result of manipulation of the independent variable, not some other variable.

interval scale A measurement scale that classifies and ranks participants, is based upon predetermined equal intervals, but does not have a true zero point.

intervening variable A variable which intervenes between, or alters the relationship between, an independent variable and a dependent variable, which cannot be directly observed or controlled (e.g., anxiety) but which can be controlled for.

intrajudge reliability The consistency of the scoring, rating, or observing of an individual.

item validity The degree to which test items represent measurement in the intended content area.

John Henry effect The phenomenon whereby if for any reason members of a control group feel threatened or challenged by being in competition with an experimental group, they may outdo themselves and perform way beyond what would normally be expected.

judgment sampling The process of selecting a sample which is *believed* to be representative of a given population. (Also referred to as purposive sampling.)

Likert scale An instrument that asks an individual to respond to a series of statements by indicating whether she or he strongly agrees (SA), agrees (A), is undecided (U), disagrees (D), or strongly disagrees (SD) with each statement.

limitation An aspect of a study which the researcher knows may negatively affect the results or generalizability of the results, but over which he or she has no control.

linear relationship The situation in which an increase (or decrease) in one variable is associated with a corresponding increase (or decrease) in another variable.

logical validity Validity which is determined primarily through judgment; includes content validity.

matching A technique for equating groups on one or more variables, resulting in each member of one group having a direct counterpart in another group.

maturation Physical or mental changes which occur within participants over a period of time and which may affect their performance on a measure of the dependent variable.

mean The arithmetic average of a set of scores.

measures of central tendency Indices representing the average or typical score attained by a group of participants.

measures of variability Indices indicating how spread out the scores are in a distribution.

median That point in a distribution above and below which are 50% of the scores.

menu-driven Refers to computer programs which allow the user to select desired analyses from a list, or menu, of options.

meta-analysis A statistical approach to summarizing the results of many studies which have investigated basically the same problem.

mode The score that is attained by more participants in a group than any other score.

modem A device which permits telephone communication between two computers by converting computer language to audiotones.

mortality Refers to the fact that participants who drop out of a study may share a characteristic such that their absence has a significant effect on the results of the study.

multiple-baseline design A single-subject design in which baseline data are collected on several behaviors for one participant or one behavior for several participants and treatment is applied systematically over a period of time to each behavior (or each participant) one at a time until all behaviors (or participants) are under treatment.

multiple comparisons Procedures used following application of analysis of variance to determine which means are significantly different from which other means.

multiple regression equation A prediction equation using two or more variables that individually predict a criterion to make a more accurate prediction.

multiple time-series design A variation of the time-series design that involves the addition of a control group to the basic design.

multiple-treatment interference Refers to the carry-over effects from an earlier treatment that make it difficult to assess the effectiveness of a later treatment.

naturalistic observation Observation in which the observer purposely controls or manipulates nothing, and in fact works very hard at not affecting the observed situation in any way.

negatively skewed distribution A distribution in which there are more extreme scores at the lower end than at the upper, or higher, end.

nominal scale The lowest level of measurement which classifies persons or objects into two or more categories; a person can only be in one category, and members of a category have a common set of characteristics.

nonequivalent control group design A quasi-experimental design involving at least two groups, both of which are pretested; one group receives the experimental treatment, and both groups are posttested.

nonparametric test A test of significance appropriate when the data represent an ordinal or nominal scale, when a parametric assumption has been greatly violated, or when the nature of the distribution is not known.

nonparticipant observation Observation in which the observer is not directly involved in the situation to be observed, i.e., the observer does not intentionally interact with or affect the object of the observation.

nonprobability sampling The process of selecting a sample using a technique which *does not* permit the researcher to specify the probability, or chance, that each member of a population has of being selected for the sample.

novelty effect A type of reactive arrangement resulting from increased interest, motivation, or participation on the part of participants simply because they are doing something different.

null hypothesis States that there is no relationship (or difference) between variables and that any relationship found will be a chance relationship, the result of sampling error, not a true one.

observational research Descriptive research in which the desired data is obtained not by asking individuals for it but through such means as direct observation.

observer bias The phenomenon whereby an observer does not observe objectively and accurately, thus producing invalid observations.

observer effects The phenomenon whereby persons being observed behave atypically simply because they are being observed, thus producing invalid observations.

one-group pretest-posttest design A pre-experimental design involving one group which is pretested, exposed to a treatment, and posttested.

one-shot case study A pre-experimental design involving one group which is exposed to a treatment and then post-tested.

operational definition One which defines concepts in terms of processes, or operations.

ordinal scale A measurement scale that classifies participants and ranks them in terms of the degree to which they possess a characteristic of interest.

organismic variable A characteristic of a participant, or organism (e.g., sex), which can

not be directly controlled but which can be controlled for.

parameter A numerical index describing the behavior of a population.

parametric test A test of significance appropriate when the data represent an interval or ratio scale of measurement and other assumptions have been met.

participant A person who provided data for a research study.

participant observation Observation in which the observer actually becomes a part of, a participant in, the situation to be observed.

participant variable A variable on which participants in different groups in a study might differ, e.g., intelligence.

pattern The connection of categories in qualitative analysis.

Pearson r A measure of correlation appropriate when the data represent either interval or ratio scales; it takes into account each and every score and produces a coefficient between .00 and ±1.00.

percentile rank A measure of relative position indicating the percentage of scores that fall at or below a given score.

phenomenology The experience of an activity or concept from participants' perspectives

pilot study A small-scale study conducted prior to the conducting of the actual study; the entire study is conducted, every procedure is followed, and the resulting data are analyzed—all according to the research plan.

placebo effect Refers to the discovery in medical research that any "medication" could make participants feel better, even sugar and water.

population The group to which the researcher would like the results of a study to be generalizable.

positively skewed distribution A distribution in which there are more extreme scores at the upper, or higher, end than at the lower end.

posttest-only control group design A true experimental design involving at least two randomly formed groups; one group receives a new, or unusual, treatment and both groups are posttested.

power The ability of a significance test to avoid making a Type II error.

prediction study An attempt to determine which of a number of variables are most highly related to a criterion variable, a complex variable to be predicted.

predictive validity The degree to which a test is able to predict how well an individual will do in a future situation.

predictor In a prediction study, the variable upon which the prediction is based.

pretest-postest control group design A true experimental design which involves at least two randomly formed groups; both groups are pretested, one group receives a new, or unusual treatment, and both groups are posttested.

pretest sensitization *See* testing.

pretest-treatment interaction Refers to the fact that participants may respond or react differently to a treatment because they have been pretested.

primary source Firsthand information such as the testimony of an eyewitness, an original document, a relic, or a description of a study written by the person who conducted it.

probability sampling The process of selecting a sample using a sampling technique which permits the researcher to specify the probability, or chance, that each member of a defined population has of being selected for the sample.

problem statement A statement which indicates the variables of interest to the researcher and the specific relationship between those variables which is to be, or was, investigated.

prospective causal–comparative research A variation of the basic approach to causal–comparative research which involves starting with the causes and investigating effects.

purposive sampling *See* judgment sampling.

qualitative approach The collection of extensive narrative data in order to gain insights into phenomena of interest.

qualitative research The collection of extensive narrative data on many variables over an extended period of time, in a naturalistic setting, in order to gain insights not possible using other types of research.

quantitative research The collection of numerical data in order to explain, predict and/or control phenomena of interest.

quartile deviation One-half of the difference between the upper quartile (the 75th percentile) and the lower quartile (the 25th percentile) in a distribution.

quota sampling The process of selecting a sample based on required, exact numbers, or quotas, of persons of varying characteristics.

random sampling The process of selecting a sample in such a way that all individuals in the defined population have an equal and independent chance of being selected for the sample.

range The difference between the highest and lowest score in a distribution.

rationale equivalence reliability An estimate of internal consistency based on a determination of how all items on a test relate to all other items and to the total test.

ratio scale The highest level of measurement that classifies participants, ranks participants, is based upon predetermined equal intervals, and has a true zero point.

reactive arrangements Threats to the external validity of a study associated with the way in which a study is conducted and the feelings and attitudes of the participants involved.

readiness test A test administered prior to instruction or training in a specific area in order to determine whether and to what degree a student is ready for, or will profit from, instruction.

relationship study An attempt to gain insight into the variables, or factors, that are related to a complex variable such as academic achievement, motivation, and self-concept.

reliability The degree to which a test consistently measures whatever it measures.

replication Refers to when a study is done again; the second study may be a repetition of the original study, using different participants, or it may represent an alternative approach to testing the same hypothesis.

research The formal, systematic application of the scientific and disciplined inquiry approach to the study of problems.

research hypothesis A statement of the expected relationship (or difference) between two variables.

research plan A detailed description of a proposed study designed to investigate a given problem.

response set The tendency of an observer to rate the majority of observees the same regardless of the observees' actual behavior.

retrospective causal–comparative research The basic approach to causal–comparative research which involves starting with effects and investigating causes.

review of literature The systematic identification, location, and analysis of documents containing information related to a research problem.

sample A number of individuals selected from a population for a study, preferably in such a way that they represent the larger group from which they were selected.

sample survey Research in which information about a population is inferred based on the responses of a sample selected from that population.

sampling The process of selecting a number of individuals (a sample) from a population, preferably in such a way that the individuals selected represent the larger group from which they were selected.

sampling bias Systematic sampling error; two major sources of sampling bias are the use of volunteers and the use of available groups.

sampling error Expected, chance variation in variables that occurs when a sample is selected from a population.

sampling validity The degree to which a test samples the total intended content area.

Scheffé test A conservative multiple comparison technique appropriate for making any and all possible comparisons involving a set of means.

secondary source Secondhand information, such as a brief description of a study written by someone other than the person who conducted it.

selection-maturation interaction Refers to the fact that if already-formed groups are used in a study, one group may profit more (or less) from treatment or have an initial advantage (or disadvantage) because of maturation factors; selection may also interact with factors such as history and testing.

selection-treatment interaction Refers to the fact that if nonrepresentative groups are used in a study the results of the study may hold only for the groups involved and may not be representative of the treatment effect in the population.

self-report research Descriptive research in which information is solicited from individuals using, for example, questionnaires or interviews.

semantic differential scale An instrument that asks an individual to give a quantitative rating to the participant of the attitude scale on a number of bipolar adjectives such as good-bad, friendly-unfriendly, positive-negative.

shrinkage Refers to the tendency of a prediction equation to become less accurate when used with a different group, a group other than the one on which the equation was originally formulated.

simple analysis of variance (ANOVA) A parametric test of significance used to determine whether there is significant difference between or among two or more means at a selected probability level.

simulation observation Observation in which the researcher creates the situation to be observed and tells the participant what activities they are to engage in.

simultaneous replication Refers to when replication is done on a number of participants with the same problem, at the same location, at the same time.

single-subject experimental designs Designs applied when the sample size is one; used to study the behavior change which an individual exhibits as a result of some intervention, or treatment.

single-variable designs A class of experimental designs involving only one independent variable (which is manipulated).

single variable rule An important principle of single-subject research which states that only one variable should be manipulated at a time.

skewed distribution A nonsymmetrical distribution in which there are more extreme scores at one end of the distribution than the other.

sociometric study A study that assesses and analyzes the interpersonal relationships within a group of individuals.

software Refers to the programs which give instructions to the computer concerning desired operations.

Solomon four-group design A true experimental design that involves random assignment of participants to one of four groups; two groups are pretested, two are not; one of the pretested groups and one of the unpretested groups receive the experimental treatment, and all four groups are posttested.

Spearman rho A measure of correlation appropriate when the data for at least one of the variables are expressed as ranks; it produces a coefficient between .00 and ±1.00.

specificity of variables Refers to the fact that a given study is conducted with a specific kind of participant, using specific measuring instruments, at a specific time, under a specific set of circumstances, factors that affect the generalizability of the results.

split-half reliability A type of reliability that is based on the internal consistency of a test and is estimated by dividing a test into two equivalent halves and correlating the scores on the two halves.

standard deviation The most stable measure of variability which takes into account each and every score in a distribution.

standard error of the mean The standard deviation of sample means which indicates by how much the sample means can be expected to differ if other samples from the same population are used.

standard error of measurement An estimate of how often one can expect errors of a given size in an individual's test score.

standard score A derived score that expresses how far a given raw score is from some reference point, typically the mean, in terms of standard deviation units.

stanines Standard scores that divide a distribution into nine parts.

static group comparison A pre-experimental design that involves at least two nonrandomly formed groups; one receives a new, or unusual, treatment and both are posttested.

statistic A numerical index describing the behavior of a sample or samples.

statistical regression The tendency of participants who score highest on a pretest to score lower on a posttest, and of participants who score lowest on a pretest to score higher on a posttest.

statistical significance The conclusion that results are unlikely to have occurred by chance; the observed relationship or difference is probably a real one.

stratified sampling The process of selecting a sample in such a way that identified subgroups in the population are represented in the sample in the same proportion that they exist in the population or in equal proportion.

structured interview Interview questions that provide options for participants to select from.

structured item A question and a list of alternative responses from which the responder selects; also referred to as a closed-form item.

survey An attempt to collect data from members of a population in order to determine the current status of that population with respect to one or more variables.

systematic replication Refers to replication which follows direct replication, and which involves different investigators, behaviors, or settings.

systematic sampling Sampling in which individuals are selected from a list by taking every Kth name, where K equals the number of individuals on the list divided by the number of participants desired for the sample.

T score A standard score derived from a z score by multiplying the z score by 10 and adding 50.

t test for independent samples A parametric test of significance used to determine whether there is a significant difference between the means of two independent samples at a selected probability level.

t test for nonindependent samples A parametric test of significance used to determine whether there is a significant difference between the means of two matched, or nonindependent, samples at a selected probability level.

target population Refers to the population to which the researcher would ideally like to generalize results.

terminal A device for communicating with a computer which consists of a display screen and a keyboard.

test A means of measuring the knowledge, skill, feelings, intelligence, or aptitude of an individual or group.

testing A threat to experimental validity which refers to improved scores on a posttest which are a result of participants having taken a pretest. (Also referred to as pretest sensitization.)

test objectivity Refers to a situation in which an individual's score is the same, or essentially the same, regardless of who is doing the scoring.

test of significance A statistical test used to determine whether or not there is a significant difference between or among two or more means at a selected probability level.

test-retest reliability The degree to which scores on a test are consistent, or stable, over time.

time-series design A quasi-experimental design involving one group which is repeatedly pretested, exposed to an experimental treatment, and repeatedly posttested.

triangulation The use of multiple methods, data collection strategies, and/or data sources, in order to get a more complete picture and to cross-check information.

true categories Categories into which persons or objects naturally fall, independently of the research study.

Type I error The rejection by the researcher of a null hypothesis which is actually true.

Type II error The failure of a researcher to reject a null hypothesis which is really false.

unobtrusive measures Inanimate objects (such as school suspension lists) which can be observed in order to obtain desired information.

unstructured item A question giving the responder complete freedom of response.

validity The degree to which a test measures what it is intended to measure; a test is valid for a particular purpose for a particular group.

variable A concept that can assume any one of a range of values, e.g., intelligence, height, aptitude.

z score The most basic standard score that expresses how far a score is from a mean in terms of standard deviation.

Z score *See T score.*

APPENDIX C

Math Review

Reprinted by permission from *Statistics with a Sense of Humor: A Humorous Workbook and Guide to Study Skills* by Fred Pyrczak, Publisher, P.O. Box 39731, Los Angeles, CA 90039

Name: _____ Date: _____

Worksheet 1: MATH REVIEW: ORDER OF OPERATIONS

RIDDLE: Why did the bored man cut a hole in the carpet?

Directions: To find the answer to the riddle, write the answers to the problems on the lines. The letter in the solution section beside the answer to the first problem is the first letter in the answer to the riddle, the letter beside the answer to the second problem is the second letter, and so on.

1. 5 x 10 + 6 x 2 = _____

2. 3 + 4 x 9 = _____

3. (9 + 28) x 6 = _____

4. 159 − 66 x 2 = _____

5. 15 x 14 − 8 x 20 = _____

6. 19 − 5 + 2 x 3 = _____

7. 70 − 5 x 3 x 4 = _____

8. 6 + 8 x 1 x 5 = _____

9. 33/1 + 1 x 3 = _____

10. 8/4 + (6)(0) = _____

11. 169/(12 + 1) = _____

12. (2 + 3 + 4)/3 = _____

13. (2 + 18)/(9 − 5) = _____

14. (1 + 5)(3) + (7)(2) = _____

15. (9 + 9)(10 − 1)(2) = _____

16. (15 − 4)(21/7)(63 − 59) = ____

17. (3)(1)(1) + (6/2)(9) = _____

SOLUTION SECTION:

112(B)	62(T)	39(O)	10(H)	780(Y)	222(S)	3(O)
2(L)	63(A)	27(E)	177(Z)	186(X)	13(O)	5(R)
32(S)	50(E)	4,040(D)	20(T)	46(E)	30(W)	70(F)
132(O)	102(K)	36(F)	324(H)	187(B)	1(J)	48(I)

Write the answer to the riddle here, putting one letter on each line:

___ ___   ___ ___ ___   ___ ___ ___

___ ___ ___ ___ ___   ___ ___ ___ ___

Name: _____   Date: _____

Worksheet 2: MATH REVIEW: NEGATIVES

RIDDLE: What did the owner of the wreck of a car say about the noise it makes?

Directions: To find the answer to the riddle, write the answers to the problems on the lines. The word in the solution section beside the answer to the first problem is the first word in the answer to the riddle, the word beside the answer to the second problem is the second word, and so on.

1. $(-10)(-2)$ = _____   7. $19 + -3$ = _____   13. $(-15)(-33)$ = _____

2. $(-5)(47)$ = _____   8. $-28 + -28$ = _____   14. $(-11)(44)$ = _____

3. $(6)(-16)$ = _____   9. $-88 + 18$ = _____   15. $-2178/33$ = _____

4. $15/-3$ = _____   10. $15 - -15$ = _____   16. $188 + -99$ = _____

5. $-144/12$ = _____   11. $-29 - 14$ = _____   17. $-279 + -188$ = _____

6. $-169/-13$ = _____   12. $-30 - -29$ = _____   18. $-399 - 59$ = _____

SOLUTION SECTION:

-20(GARAGE)	235(TWO)	340(SKY)	20(THERE'S)	-96(ONE)
-235(ONLY)	96(ROAD)	-56(THAT)	-70(DOESN'T)	-1(SORT)
-458(HORN)	-467(THE)	5(IS)	-12(ON)	-5(THING)	13(MY)
-13(USE)	16(CAR)	12(BE)	30(MAKE)	0(FIX)	22(BUS)
495(OF)	-484(NOISE)	56(AN)	-66(AND)	70(TRANSPORTATION)
89(THAT'S)	-43(SOME)	-15(ALWAYS)	-59(HIGHWAY)
-495(MECHANIC)	66(BROKEN)	484(STRANDED)	467(FREEWAY)

Write the answer to the riddle here, putting one word on each line:

_____ _____ _____ _____ _____ _____

_____ _____ _____ _____ _____ _____

_____ _____ _____ _____ _____ _____

Name: _____   Date: _____

Worksheet 3: MATH REVIEW: ROUNDING

RIDDLE: What did the psychologist put on a sign in her office to make her patients pay?

Directions: To find the answer to the riddle, write the answers to the problems on the lines. The word in the solution beside the answer to the first problem is the first word in the answer to the riddle, the word beside the answer to the second problem is the second word, and so on.

Round as usual except when rounding off a number ending in a five (5). If the number immediately preceding a five is odd, round up. If the number immediately preceding a five is even, round down. Another way to state this principle is: "round to the nearest even number all numbers ending in 5." For example, 4.85 rounds to 4.8; 4.75 rounds to 4.8. Notice, however, that 4.851, which ends in a value greater than "5," rounds to 4.9.

1. Round 10.543 to the nearest hundredth: _____

2. Round 8.67 to the nearest tenth: _____

3. Round 8.4 to the nearest whole number: _____

4. Round 9.8452 to the nearest thousandth: _____

5. Round 15.839 to the nearest tenth: _____

6. Round 29.5 to the nearest whole number: _____

7. Round 15.86 to the nearest tenth: _____

8. Round 3.945 to the nearest hundredth: _____

9. Round 8.45 to the nearest tenth: _____

10. Round 10.555555 to the nearest hundredth: _____

SOLUTION SECTION:

29(CRAZY)   15.9(THE)   8.7(THE)   30(PAY)   3.95(AM)   8(AMNESIA)

10.56(ADVANCE)   8.4(IN)   8.5(ONLY)   3.94(PSYCHOLOGIST)   15.8(MUST)

9845(IS)   15.4(BILL)   9.85(HELPS)   9.846(NEVER)   10(LOVING)

9.845(PATIENTS)   9(LIFE)   10.54(ALL)   10.5(COUNSELING) 4(DISTURBED)

Write the answer to the riddle here, putting one word on each line:

_____   _____   _____   _____   _____   _____

_____   _____   _____   _____

Name: _____   Date: _____

Worksheet 4: MATH REVIEW: DECIMALS

RIDDLE: What did the bore do to help the party?

Directions: To find the answer to the riddle, write the answers to the problems on the lines. The letter in the solution section beside the answer to the first problem is the first letter in the answer to the riddle, the letter beside the answer to the second problem is the second letter, and so on.

   If an answer has more than two decimal places, round to two.

1. 0.02 multiplied by 1 = _____

2. 1.1 multiplied by 1.11 = _____

3. 5.999 multiplied by 0 = _____

4. 3.77 multiplied by 4.69 = _____

5. 12.4 divided into 169.38 = _____

6. 15.9 divided by 1 = _____

7. 12.1 plus 99.98 = _____

8. 3.11 plus 8.99 = _____

9. 18.3 subtracted from 25.46 = _____

10. 10.01 minus 8.873 = _____

SOLUTION SECTION:

1.22(E)	0.2(C)	0.14(X)	7.16(M)	71.6(D)	0(W)
6.00(K)	2.11(F)	0.02(H)	112.08(H)		101.19(P)
15.9(T)	1.59(B)	13.66(N)	1.21(J)		17.68(E)
1.366(G)	12.10(O)	0.177(R)	1.14(E)		1.111(S)

Write the answer to the riddle here, putting one letter on each line:

____ ____   ____ ____ ____ ____   ____ ____ ____ ____

Name: _____   Date: _____

Worksheet 5: MATH REVIEW: FRACTIONS AND DECIMALS

RIDDLE: Why should you respect the lily?

Directions: To find the answer to the riddle, write the answers to the problems on the lines. The word in the solution section beside the answer to the first problem is the first word in the answer to the riddle, the word beside the answer to the second problem is the second word, and so on. Express fractions in lowest terms.

1. 1/5 + 3/5 = _____   5. 2/3 x 2/3 = _____

2. 1/5 + 1/10 = _____   6. 2/5 x 4/7 = _____

3. 3/9 − 1/9 = _____   7. 2/9 divided by 1/9 = _____

4. 1 − 7/8 = _____   8. 5 divided into 2/3 = _____

9. What is the decimal equivalent of 1/2? = _____

10. What is the decimal equivalent of 3/4? = _____

11. What is the decimal equivalent of 2 and 2/3? = _____

12. What is the decimal equivalent of 2 and 3/4? = _____

13. What is the decimal equivalent of 2 and 1/10? = _____

14. What fraction corresponds to 0.2? = _____

15. What fraction corresponds to 0.11? = _____

16. What fraction corresponds to 0.555? = _____

SOLUTION SECTION:

4/5(NEVER)   2/5(SEE)   3/10(LOOK)   11/20(IS)   0.5(DAY)

0.55(FLOWERS)   2/3(FLORIST)   4/9(A)   2/9(DOWN)   2.1(LOOK)

1/5(DOWN)   11/100(ON)   2/35(CLEAN)   8/35(LILY)   1/8(ON)

2/81(HOPE)   2(BECAUSE)   2/15(ONE)   0.75(A)   2.67(LILY)

2.75(WILL)   111/200(YOU)   8/8(EASTER)   3 1/3(BEAUTIFUL)

Write the answer to the riddle here, putting one word on each line:

_____ _____ _____ _____ _____ _____ _____ _____

_____ _____ _____ _____ _____ _____ _____ _____

Name: _____   Date: _____

Worksheet 6: MATH REVIEW: ALGEBRAIC MANIPULATIONS

RIDDLE: When do actors and actresses get stage fright?

Directions: To find the answer to the riddle, write "T" for "true" or "F" for "false" on the line to the left of each statement. The word at the end of the first true statement is the first word in the answer to the riddle, the word at the end of the second true statement is the second word, and so on.

All variables are distinct from one another; that is, no variable equals any other variable.

_____ 1. If $A = C/D$, then $C = (A)(D)$ (WHEN)

_____ 2. If $A = C/D$, then $D = C/A$ (THEY)

_____ 3. If $P/B = F$, then $P = F/B$ (GET)

_____ 4. If $X + Y = 10$, then $X = 10 - Y$ (SEE)

_____ 5. If $25 = A + B$, then $A = 25 - B$ (AN)

_____ 6. If $X + 25 = W$, then $X = W + 25$ (CURTAIN)

_____ 7. If $A = C - D$, then $D = C + A$ (APPLAUSE)

_____ 8. If $A - D = F$, then $A = F + D$ (EGG)

_____ 9. If $A = F - G - H$, then $F = A - G - H$ (STAGE)

_____ 10. If $(B)(C) = P$, then $B = P/C$ (OR)

_____ 11. If $Y = (B)(F)$, then $B = F/Y$ (SCRIPT)

_____ 12. If $X = (N)(B)(C)$, then $B = X/(N)(C)$ (A)

_____ 13. If $X + Y = B - C$, then $B = X + (Y)(C)$ (VOICE)

_____ 14 If $(B)(Y) = (X)(C)$, then $C = (B)(Y)/X$ (TOMATO)

Write in the answer to the riddle here, putting one word on each line:

_____ _____ _____ _____ _____ _____

_____ _____

CONCISE KEY

Worksheet 1: 1. 62, 2. 39, 3. 222, 4. 27, 5. 50, 6. 20, 7. 10, 8. 46, 9. 36, 10. 2, 11. 13, 12. 3, 13. 5, 14. 32, 15. 324, 16. 132, 17. 30   The answer to the riddle is: "To see the floor show."

Worksheet 2: 1. 20, 2. –235, 3. –96, 4. –5, 5. –12, 6. 13, 7. 16, 8. –56, 9. –70, 10. 30, 11. –43, 12. –1, 13. 495, 14. –484, 15. –66, 16. 89, 17. –467, 18. –458   The answer to the riddle is: "There's only one thing on my car that doesn't make some sort of noise and that's the horn."

Worksheet 3: 1. 10.54, 2. 8.7, 3. 8, 4. 9.845, 5. 15.8, 6. 30, 7. 15.9, 8. 3.94, 9. 8.4, 10. 10.56   The answer to the riddle is: "All the amnesia patients must pay the psychologist in advance."

Worksheet 4: 1. 0.02, 2. 1.22, 3. 0, 4. 17.68, 5. 13.66, 6. 15.9, 7. 112.08, 8. 12.10, 9. 7.16, 10. 1.14   The answer to the riddle is: "He went home."

Worksheet 5: 1. 4/5, 2. 3/10, 3. 2/9, 4. 1/8, 5. 4/9, 6. 8/35, 7. 2, 8. 2/15, 9. 0.5, 10. 0.75, 11. 2.67, 12. 2.75, 13. 2.1, 14. 1/5, 15. 11/100, 16. 111/200   The answer to the riddle is: "Never look down on a lily because one day a lily will look down on you."

Worksheet 6: 1. T, 2. T, 3. F, 4. T, 5. T, 6. F, 7. F, 8. T, 9. F, 10. T, 11. F, 12. T, 13. F, 14. T   The answer to the riddle is: "When they see an egg or a tomato."

STEP-BY-STEP KEY

WORKSHEET 1:

Order of operations: Do all work inside of parentheses first. Perform multiplication and division before performing addition and subtraction.

1. $5 \times 10 + 6 \times 2$
   $= 50 + 12$
   $= 62$

2. $3 + 4 \times 9$
   $= 3 + 36$
   $= 39$

3. $(9 + 28) \times 6$
   $= 37 \times 6$
   $= 222$

4. $159 - 66 \times 2$
   $= 159 - 132$
   $= 27$

5. $15 \times 14 - 8 \times 20$
   $= 210 - 160$
   $= 50$

6. $19 - 5 + 2 \times 3$
   $= 19 - 5 + 6$
   $= 14 + 6$
   $= 20$

7. $70 - 5 \times 3 \times 4$
   $= 70 - 15 \times 4$
   $= 70 - 60$
   $= 10$

8. $6 + 8 \times 1 \times 5$
   $= 6 + 8 \times 5$
   $= 6 + 40$
   $= 46$

9. $33/1 + 1 \times 3$
   $= 33 + 3$
   $= 36$

10. $8/4 + (6)(0)$
    $= 8/4 + 0$
    $= 2 + 0$
    $= 2$

11. $169/(12 + 1)$
    $= 169/13$
    $= 13$

12. $(2 + 3 + 4)/3$
    $= 9/3$
    $= 3$

13. $(2 + 18)/(9 - 5)$
    $= 20/4$
    $= 5$

14. $(1 + 5)(3) + (7)(2)$
    $= (6)(3) + (7)(2)$
    $= 18 + 14$
    $= 32$

15. $(9 + 9)(10 - 1)(2)$
    $= (18)(9)(2)$
    $= (162)(2)$
    $= 324$

16. $(15 - 4)(21/7)(63 - 59)$
    $= (11)(3)(4)$
    $= (33)(4)$
    $= 132$

17. $(3)(1)(1) + (6/2)(9)$
    $= 3 + (3)(9)$
    $= 3 + 27$
    $= 30$

WORKSHEET 2:

Rules for working with positive and negative numbers:

Multiplication:

When a negative number is multiplied by a positive number, the result is negative. When two negative numbers are multiplied, the result is positive.

1. $(-10)(-2) = 20$,   **2.** $(-5)(47) = -235$,   **3.** $(6)(-16) = -96$

Division:

When two numbers with the same sign are divided, the result is positive. When two numbers with opposite signs are divided, the result is negative.

4. $15/-3 = -5$,   **5.** $-144/12 = -12$,   **6.** $-169/-13 = 13$

Addition:

When numbers all have the same sign, add as usual. When numbers have different signs, first add all positive numbers together, then add all negative numbers together, and then subtract the negative sum from the positive sum.

7. $19 + -3 = 16$,   **8.** $-28 + -28 = -56$,   **9.** $-88 + 18 = -70$

Subtraction:

When subtracting negative numbers, change the sign of the number being subtracted and then add:

10. $15 - -15 = 30$,   **11.** $-29 - 14 = -43$,   **12.** $-30 - -29 = -1$

For items 13 through 18, follow the rules given above.

13. 495,   **14.** -484,   **15.** -66,   **16.** 89,   **17.** -467,   **18.** -458

WORKSHEET 3:

See the directions on Worksheet 3 for rules on rounding numbers that end in five (5).

1. Read 10.543 as 10.5(tenth's)4(hundredth's)3(thousandth's); therefore, to the nearest hundredth, 10.543 rounds to 10.54.
2. Read 8.67 as 8.6(tenth's)7(hundredth's); therefore, to the nearest tenth, 8.67 rounds to 8.7.
3. Read 8.4 as 8(whole number, one's place).4(tenth's); therefore, to the nearest whole number, 8.4 rounds to 8.
4. Read 9.8452 as 9.8(tenth's)4(hundredth's)5(thousandth's)2(ten thousandth's); therefore, to the nearest thousandth, 9.8452 rounds to 9.845.
5. 15.839, to the nearest tenth, rounds to 15.8.
6. Because 29.5 ends in 5, round to the nearest even number, which is 30.

7. 15.86 rounds to 15.9.
8. Because 3.945 ends in 5, round to the nearest even number, which is 3.94. (Notice that the "4" in the hundredth's place is even.)
9. Because 8.45 ends in 5, round to the nearest even number, which is 8.4. (Notice that the "4" in the tenth's place is even.)
10. Beyond the hundredth's place are four 5's. Therefore, at the point at which you are rounding, the number does not end in "5"; it ends in "5555," which is greater than 5. Therefore, 10.555555, to the nearest hundredth, rounds to 10.56.

WORKSHEET 4:

1. When multiplying, the answer has the total number of decimal places as the total number in the two multipliers. Since 0.02×1 has a total of two digits to the right of the decimal places, the answer is 0.02, which also has two digits to the right.
2. 1.1×1.11 has three digits to the right; therefore, the answer is 1.221, which rounds to 1.22.
3. Any number multiplied by zero equals zero.
4. (See explanation for item 1.) $3.77 \times 4.69 = 17.6813$ (four decimal places), which rounds to 17.68.
5. When dividing with a calculator, enter the numbers as shown. When dividing by hand, first move the decimal place in the divisor to the far right. (In this case, change 12.4 to 124.) Then, move the decimal place in 169.38 the same number of places to the right, changing 169.38 to 1693.8. Then divide as usual. The answer is 13.660 = 13.66.
6. (See explanation for item 5. Notice the difference between "divided into" and "divided by." This wording usually is not used in textbooks, but your instructor may use it in lectures.) The answer is 15.9. (Notice that division by one has no effect.)
7. Before adding, line up the decimal places one above the other and then add.

$$
\begin{array}{r}
12.1 \\
+\ 99.98 \\
\hline
112.08
\end{array}
$$

8. (See explanation for item 7.) The answer is 12.10.
9. Before subtracting, line up the decimal places one above the other and then subtract.

$$
\begin{array}{r}
25.46 \\
-\ 18.3 \\
\hline
7.16
\end{array}
$$

10. (See explanation for number 9. Notice the difference between "subtracted from" and "minus.")

$$
\begin{array}{r}
10.01 \\
-\ 8.873 \\
\hline
1.137\text{, which rounds to 1.14}
\end{array}
$$

WORKSHEET 5:

(General note: For most beginning students, it is best to convert fractions to their decimal equivalents as soon as permitted under the rules of mathematics. For example, to convert $\frac{1}{5}$, divide 1 by 5, which yields 0.2. This is desirable since most calculators will not allow you to operate directly on fractions. In addition, it is conventional to report statistics with their decimal equivalents for fractional parts.

Knowledge of fractions is important for understanding the meaning of certain statistics and for understanding their derivations, however.)

1. When adding fractions with a common denominator (same denominator), add the numerators and retain the common denominator. Thus, $\frac{1}{5} + \frac{3}{5} = \frac{4}{5}$.

2. When adding fractions with unlike denominators, first convert so that they both have the same denominator. In this case, by multiplying both the numerator and denominator of $\frac{1}{5}$ by 2, the equivalent fraction of $\frac{2}{10}$ is obtained. Then follow the instructions for item 1. Thus, $\frac{2}{10} + \frac{1}{10} = \frac{3}{10}$.

3. When subtracting fractions with a common denominator, subtract the numerators and retain the common denominator. Thus, $\frac{3}{9} - \frac{1}{9} = \frac{2}{9}$.

4. When subtracting a fraction from a whole number, first convert the whole number to a fractional equivalent with the same denominator. In this case, $1 = \frac{8}{8}$. Thus, $\frac{8}{8} - \frac{7}{8} = \frac{1}{8}$.

5. When multiplying fractions, multiply the numerators, then multiply the denominators. For example, $\frac{2}{3} \times \frac{2}{3} = \frac{4}{9}$.

6. (See the explanation for item number 5.) The answer is $\frac{8}{35}$.

7. To divide one fraction by another, invert the divisor (i.e., $\frac{1}{9}$ becomes $\frac{9}{1}$). Then multiply: $\frac{2}{9} \times \frac{9}{1} = \frac{18}{9}$. To simplify when the numerator is evenly divisible by the denominator, divide the denominator into the numerator: 18 divided by 9 = 2, which is the answer.

8. (See the explanation for item 7.) Note the difference in wording of items 7 and 8. In this case, 5 is the divisor; when inverted, it becomes $\frac{1}{5}$. Thus, $\frac{2}{3} \times \frac{1}{5} = \frac{2}{15}$.

9. To find the decimal equivalent of a fraction, divide the numerator by the denominator. In this case, divide 1 by 2, which yields an answer of 0.5.

10. (See the explanation for item 9.) The answer is 0.75.

11. To find the decimal equivalent of a mixed number (i.e., a whole number plus a fractional part), retain the whole number and convert the fractional part as described in the explanation for item 9. In this case, 2 and $\frac{2}{3}$ becomes 2 and .666, which rounds to 2.67.

12. (See the explanation for item 11.) The answer is 2.75.

13. (See the explanation for item 11.) The answer is 2.1.

14. Note that 0.2 is read as "two tenths." Therefore, it is equivalent to $\frac{2}{10}$. Since both the numerator and denominator are evenly divisible by 2, divide both by 2, which yields $\frac{1}{5}$, which is the answer expressed in lowest terms.

15. Note that 0.11 is read as "eleven one hundredths." Therefore, the answer is expressed as $\frac{11}{100}$.

16. Note that 0.555 is read as "five hundred fifty-five one thousandths." Therefore, it is equivalent to $\frac{555}{1000}$. Since 5 will divide evenly into both the numerator and denominator, simplify by division. This gives an answer of $\frac{111}{200}$.

WORKSHEET 6:

1. If $A = \frac{C}{D}$, then $C = (A)(D)$
   $A = \frac{C}{D}$
   $\frac{C}{D} = A$
   $(\frac{C}{D})(D) = (A)(D)$
   $C = (A)(D)$
   Therefore, the statement is true.

2. If $A = \frac{C}{D}$, then $D = \frac{C}{A}$
   $A = \frac{C}{D}$
   $(A)(D) = (\frac{C}{D})(D)$
   $(A)(D) = C$
   $\frac{(A)(D)}{A} = \frac{C}{A}$
   $D = \frac{C}{A}$
   Therefore, the statement is true.

3. If $\frac{P}{B} = F$, then $P = \frac{F}{B}$
   $\frac{P}{B} = F$
   $(\frac{P}{B})(B) = (F)(B)$
   $P = (F)(B)$
   Therefore, the statement is false.

4. If $X + Y = 10$, then $X = 10 - Y$
   $X + Y = 10$
   $X + Y - Y = 10 - Y$
   $X = 10 - Y$
   Therefore, the statement is true.

5. If $25 = A + B$, then $A = 25 - B$
   $25 = A + B$
   $A + B = 25$
   $A + B - B = 25 - B$
   $A = 25 - B$
   Therefore, the statement is true.

6. If $X + 25 = W$, then $X = W + 25$
   $X + 25 = W$
   $X + 25 - 25 = W - 25$
   $X = W - 25$
   Therefore, the statement is false.

7. If $A = C - D$, then $D = C + A$
   $A = C - D$
   $A + D = C - D + D$
   $A + D = C$
   $A + D - A = C - A$
   $D = C - A$
   Therefore, the statement is false.

8. If $A - D = F$, then $A = F + D$
   $A - D = F$
   $A - D + D = F + D$
   $A = F + D$
   Therefore, the statement is true.

9. If $A = F - G - H$, then
   $\quad F = A - G - H$
   $A = F - G - H$
   $F - G - H = A$
   $F - G - H + G = A + G$
   $F - H = A + G$
   $F - H + H = A + G + H$
   $F = A + G + H$
   Therefore, the statement is false.

10. If $(B)(C) = P$, then $B = \frac{P}{C}$
    $(B)(C) = P$
    $\frac{(B)(C)}{C} = \frac{P}{C}$
    $B = \frac{P}{C}$
    Therefore, the statement is true.

11. If $Y = (B)(F)$, then $B = \frac{F}{Y}$
    $Y = (B)(F)$
    $(B)(F) = Y$
    $\frac{(B)(F)}{F} = \frac{Y}{F}$
    $B = \frac{Y}{F}$
    Therefore, the statement is false.

12. If $X = (N)(B)(C)$, then $B = \frac{X}{(N)(C)}$
    $X = (N)(B)(C)$
    $(N)(B)(C) = X$
    $\frac{(N)(B)(C)}{(N)(C)} = \frac{X}{(N)(C)}$
    $B = \frac{X}{(N)(C)}$
    Therefore, the statement is true.

13. If $X + Y = B - C$, then $B = X + (Y)(C)$
    $X + Y = B - C$
    $B - C = X + Y$
    $B - C + C = X + Y + C$
    $B = X + Y + C$
    Therefore, the statement is false.

14. IF $(B)(Y) = (X)(C)$, then $C = \frac{(B)(Y)}{X}$
    $(B)(Y) = (X)(C)$
    $(X)(C) = (B)(Y)$
    $\frac{(X)(C)}{X} = \frac{(B)(Y)}{X}$
    $C = \frac{(B)(Y)}{X}$
    Therefore, the statement is true.

APPENDIX D

Suggested Responses

SELF-TEST FOR TASK 1-A   PART ONE

Motivational Effects on Test Scores of Elementary Students

The Problem. The purpose of this study was to determine the effect of experimentally manipulated motivational conditions on elementary students' mathematical scores.

The Procedures. Pairs of normal, heterogeneous classes at each grade level (3, 4, 6, 7 and 8) from each of three public schools were randomly chosen to participate; classes were selected for experimental and control conditions by a flip of a coin (i.e., one class of each pair became an experimental group and the other a control group). Form 7 of the Mathematics Concepts subtest of the Iowa Tests of Basic Skills (ITBS) was the measuring instrument. Prior to taking the test, all students were given the instructions from the ITBS test manual. Experimental students were also read a brief motivational script on the importance of doing well. All participating teachers were trained to administer the test, and experimental teachers were given additional training regarding the script (e.g., read it exactly as it is written).

The Method of Analysis. An analysis of variance was run (on test scores) to test the effects of the experimental and normal (control) conditions (as well as several other variables).

The Major Conclusion. Students asked to try especially hard did considerably better than those who were given the usual standardized test instructions only.

SELF-TEST FOR TASK 1-B

Type: Experimental
Reasons: A cause-effect relationship was investigated. The independent variable (cause), type of test instructions (motivational instructions versus usual instructions only), was manipulated. The researchers determined which students received motivational instructions and which students did not. The students' performance on the ITBS Mathematics Concepts subtest (the dependent variable, the effect) was compared.

SELF-TEST FOR TASK 9   PART NINE

Effects of Using an Instructional Game on Motivation and Performance

GENERAL EVALUATION CRITERIA

Introduction

Problem	CODE
A statement?	Y
Paragraph (//)7, sentence (S)1[1]	
Researchable?	Y
Background information?	Y
e.g. //2	
Significance discussed?	Y
e.g., //1	
Variables and relationships discussed?	Y
Definitions?	Y
e.g., //7, S3	

Review of Related Literature	
Comprehensive?	?/X
Appears to be	
References relevant?	Y
Sources primary?	Y
Critical analysis?	Y
e.g., //6	
Well organized?	Y
Summary?	N
Rationale for hypotheses?	N

Hypotheses	
Questions or hypotheses?	Y
//7, S6 & 7	
Expected differences stated?	Y
Variables defined?	Y
Testable?	Y

Method

Subjects	CODE
Population described?	Y&N
Very briefly	
Sample selection method described?	NA
Selection method "good"?	NA

---

[1] //7 refers to paragraph 7 of the introduction section of the article. The introduction section ends where Method begins.

CODE

Avoidance of volunteers?	?/X
Hard to say; see //1, S2	
Sample described?	Y&N
Size, yes; characteristics, no	
Minimum sizes?	Y
$n^1 = 37$; $n^2 = 38$	

Instruments

Rationale for selection?	N
Instrument described?	Y
//6 & 7	
Appropriate?	Y
Evidence that it is appropriate for sample?	N
Validity discussed?	N
Reliability discussed?	Y
//6 & 7	
Subtest reliabilities?	Y
//6	
Procedures for development described?	N
Performance posttest not described	
Administration, scoring, and interpretation procedures described? . . .	N

Design and Procedure

Design appropriate?	Y
Procedures sufficiently detailed?	Y
Pilot study described?	NA
Control procedures described?	Y
e.g., //9	
Confounding variables discussed?	Y
e.g., //10, S2	

Results

Appropriate descriptive statistics?	Y
Table 1	
Probability level specified in advance?	Y
e.g., //1	
Parametric assumptions not violated?	Y
Tests of significance appropriate?	Y or ?/X
Every hypothesis tested?	Y
Appropriate degrees of freedom?	Y or ?/X
Results clearly presented?	Y
Tables and figures well organized?	Y
Data in each table and figure described?	Y

Discussion (Conclusions and Recommendations)

	CODE
Results discussed in terms of hypothesis?	Y
Results discussed in terms of previous research?	Y
e.g., //3	
Generalizations consistent with results?	Y
e.g., //1	
Effects of uncontrolled variables discussed?	Y
e.g., //2	
Implications discussed?	Y
e.g., //7	
Recommendations for action?	Y
e.g., //8	
Suggestions based on practical significance?	Y
Effect sizes were presented under Results, //2, S4 & 5	
Recommendations for research?	Y
e.g., //9	

Abstract (or Summary)

Problem restated?	Y
Subjects and instruments described?	Y&N
Subjects briefly; instruments indirectly	
Design identified?	Y
Not named, but described	
Procedures?	Y
Results and conclusions?	Y

METHOD-SPECIFIC EVALUATION CRITERIA

Design used:

Basically a posttest-only control group design. The independent variable was type of practice.

$$R \quad X_1 0 \quad X_1 = \text{game}$$

$$R \quad X_2 0 \quad X_2 = \text{worksheet}$$

$$0 = \text{Motivation scale performance posttest}$$

Because of the inclusion of a second, unmanipulated independent variable, completion versus noncompletion of reading assignment, the design was a 2×2 factorial design, based on a posttest-only control group design.

Design appropriate?	Y
Design selection rationale?	N
Invalidity discussed?	N
But mortality was not a problem	
Group formation described?	Y
Random assignment	

	CODE
Groups formed in same way?	Y
Groups randomly formed?	Y
Treatments randomly assigned?	?/X
Extraneous variables described?	Y
e.g., //6, S3–5	
Groups equated?	N
Reactive arrangements controlled for?	N
But discussed, under Discussion, //2, S3–6	

AUTHOR INDEX

Airasian, P., 597, 599, 601, 602
Ausubel, D.P., 73–74

Barlow, D.H., 410
Bassler, O.C., 337
Biklen, S.K., 201, 206, 211, 212, 217,
        218, 238, 244, 245
Bogdan, R.C., 201, 206, 211, 212, 217,
        218, 238, 244, 245
Bonfadini, J., 433
Bracht, G.H., 377
Brissie, J.S., 337
Brown, S.M., 28
Buckley, N.K., 405

Campbell, D.T., 372, 373, 377, 387, 388
Cohen, J., 521
Cohen, P., 521
Cook, T.D., 373, 387
Corbin, J., 243
Creswell, J.W., 215, 239, 250

Davis, P.W., 257
Denzin, N., 252
Dey, I., 242, 249, 252, 254

Erickson, F., 201, 203, 208

Flanders, N.A., 297
Florescu, R., 231
Fraser, J., 257
Freitag, E., 581

Gay, L.R., 73
Glass, G.V., 301, 302, 377
Gredler, M.E., 8
Green, K.E., 358
Grejda, G.F., 412
Gretchen, B., 251
Guba, E.G., 251
Guilford, J.P., 184
Gullickson, A., 597, 599, 601, 602

Haaland, J., 439
Hannafin, M.J., 412
Hersen, 410
Hoover–Dempsey, K.V., 337
Huberman, A.M., 210, 244, 252

Jones, J.H., 93
Jorner, U., 439

Kelle, E., 249
Kennedy, M.M., 591
Klein, J.D., 581
Krathwohl, D.R., 241
Krejcie, R.V., 134, 135

Lincoln, Y.S., 252

McGaw, B., 301
McNally, R.T., 231
Madaus, G.F., 8
Marshall, C., 252, 256
Meder, Z., 231
Miles, M.B., 210, 244, 249, 252
Milgram, S., 93

Morgan, D.W., 135

Patton, M.Q., 205
Persson, R., 439

Rossman, G., 256

Scriven, M., 8
Seidman, I.E., 223
Singh, R., 257
Smith, M.L., 301
Snurd, 66, 547
Stanley, J.C., 373, 377, 387, 388
Strauss, A., 243, 246
Stufflebeam, D.L., 8

Von Däniken, E., 17

Walberg, H.J., 28, 30, 302
Walker, H.M., 405
Wallgren, A., 439
Wallgren, B., 439
Weitzman, E.A., 249
Wolcott, H.F., 238, 253

Yin, R.K., 204

Interview study, *continued*
    communication during, 293
    compared to other data collection
        methods, 283
    construction of guide, 292
    and evaluation of research report,
        576–577
    gaining entry for, 220
    guidelines for, 223
    pretesting procedure for, 293
    protocols for, 215
    recording responses, 293
    selecting participants, 220
    threats to quality of, 223–224
    types of, 220–222
Intraclass coefficient, 330
Intrajudge reliability, 175–176
Inverse relationship (negative
    relationship), 323
Iowa Tests of Basic Skills, 154
Item validity, 163

Jargon, avoidance of, 284–285
John Henry effect, 382
Joint problem solving, 597
Journaling, 597
Journal of Applied Measurement, 186
Journal of Consulting Psychology, 186
Journal of Educational Measurement,
    186
Journal of Educational Psychology, 186
Journal of Educational Research, 358n,
    412n, 581
Journal of Personnel Psychology, 186
Journal of Statistics in Education, 60
Journals, professional, 186
Judgment sampling, 138, 139–140

Kaufman-Assessment Battery for
    Children (ABC), 155
Kendall's tau, 330
Key Math Diagnostic Inventory of
    Essential Mathematics Test,
    155
Key words
    in computer search, 62
    in literature search, 46, 48, 50–51
Kruskal-Wallis test, 509
Kuder Occupational Interest Survey,
    158
Kuder Preference Record- Vocational,
    158–159
Kuder-Richardson (K-R) formula, 173,
    174, 176

Labeling, of stored data, 518
Legal restrictions on research, 93–101
Letter, with questionnaire, 286–287,
    288

Level of significance (probability
        level), 326–327, 462, 475–480,
        482, 491–492
Library, 40, 49–51
Library User Information Service
        (LUIS), 47
Likert scale, 158
Linear relationships, 330
LISREL (structural equation
        modeling), 335
Listserve, 39
Literary Digest poll, 136
Literature, education, 41
Literature, in historical research, 226,
        227–228
Literature review. *See* Review of
        literature
Longitudinal studies, 279–280
LUIS (Library User Information
        Service), 47

McCarthy Scales of Children's
        Abilities, 155
Managing, data, 240–241
Manipulation of independent variable,
        13, 14, 369, 370–371
    and single variable rule, 403
Mann-Whitney U test, 509
Matching, 355, 384–385
Materials, in research plan, 105, 107
Maturation, and threat to internal
        validity, 373–374, 376
Mean, 356, 440–441
    calculated for interval data,
        454–455
Measurement
    defined, 153
    repeated and reliable, 402–403
    standard error of, 177–178, 470–473
Measurement scales, 149–150
    interval, 482
    nominal, 483
    ordinal, 483
    ratio, 483
Measures of central tendency, 437,
        439–441
    mean, 356, 440–441, 454–455
    median, 439–440
    mode, 439
Measures of relationship, 437, 451–452
    Pearson r, 329, 330, 452, 459–463
    Spearman rho, 329, 330, 452
Measures of relative position, 437,
        447–451
    percentile ranks, 448
    standard scores, 448–451, 457–459
        stanines, 451
        T scores (Z scores), 448, 450–451
        z scores, 448–450
Measures of variability, 437, 441–443

quartile deviation, 441–442
range, 441
standard deviation, 442–443,
        455–457
Measuring instrument, 145–198. *See
        also* Tests, standardized
    characteristics of, 151–154
    constructs, 147–148
    for correlational study, 322–323
    in evaluation of research report,
        573–574
    reliability of, 169–178, 332
    in research plan, 92, 106–107
    scoring procedures for, 433–434
    selecting from alternative, 187–
        189
    terminology of, 153
    validity of, 161–169, 332
    variables, 148
        categorical, 150–151
        combinations of, 151
        dependent, 151
        independent, 151
        interval, 150
        nominal, 149
        ordinal, 149–150
        quantitative, 150–151
        ratio, 150
Medial test, 509
Median, 439–440
Media recording and analysis, 597,
        600, 601
Memo writing, 214
Mental Measurements Yearbooks
        (MMY's), 154, 179–181, 182,
        187
Meta-analysis, 301–303
Method and design. *See* Causal-
        comparative research (ex
        post facto research);
        Correlational research;
        Descriptive research;
        Experimental research;
        Historical research;
        Qualitative research
Method section
    in evaluation of research report,
        573–574
    of research plan, 106–109
    of research report, 545–547
    in study, 251
Metropolitan Achievement Test, 154
Minnesota Multiphasic Personality
        Inventory, 159–160
MMY (Mental Measurements Yearbooks),
        154, 179–181, 182, 187
Model, for stating hypothesis, 75
Monitoring of observers, 300
Mooney Problem Check List, 159
Mortality (attrition), 375, 376
Multimedia, 46, 51, 57